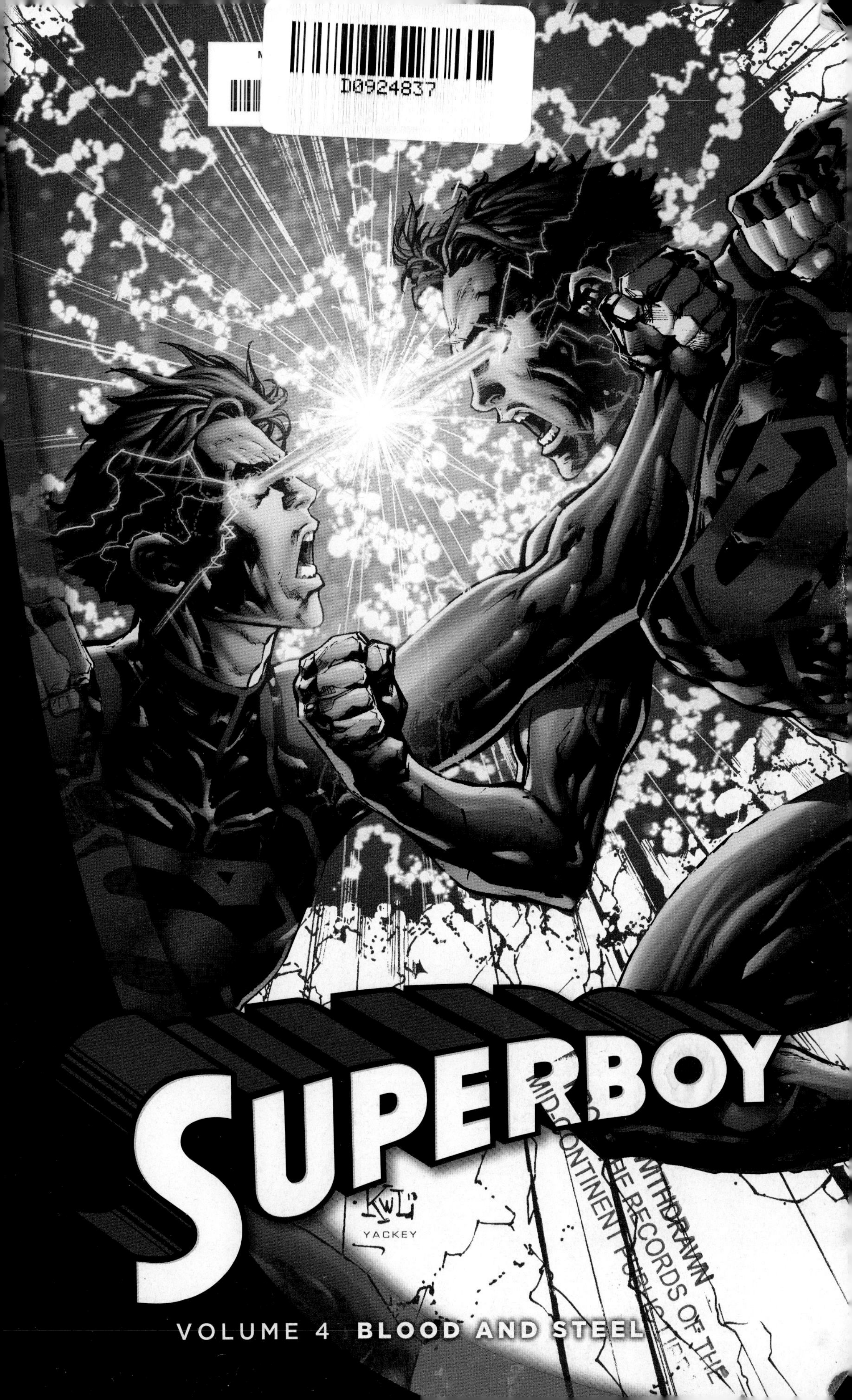
KwLi
YACKEY

SUPERBOY

VOLUME 4 BLOOD AND STEEL

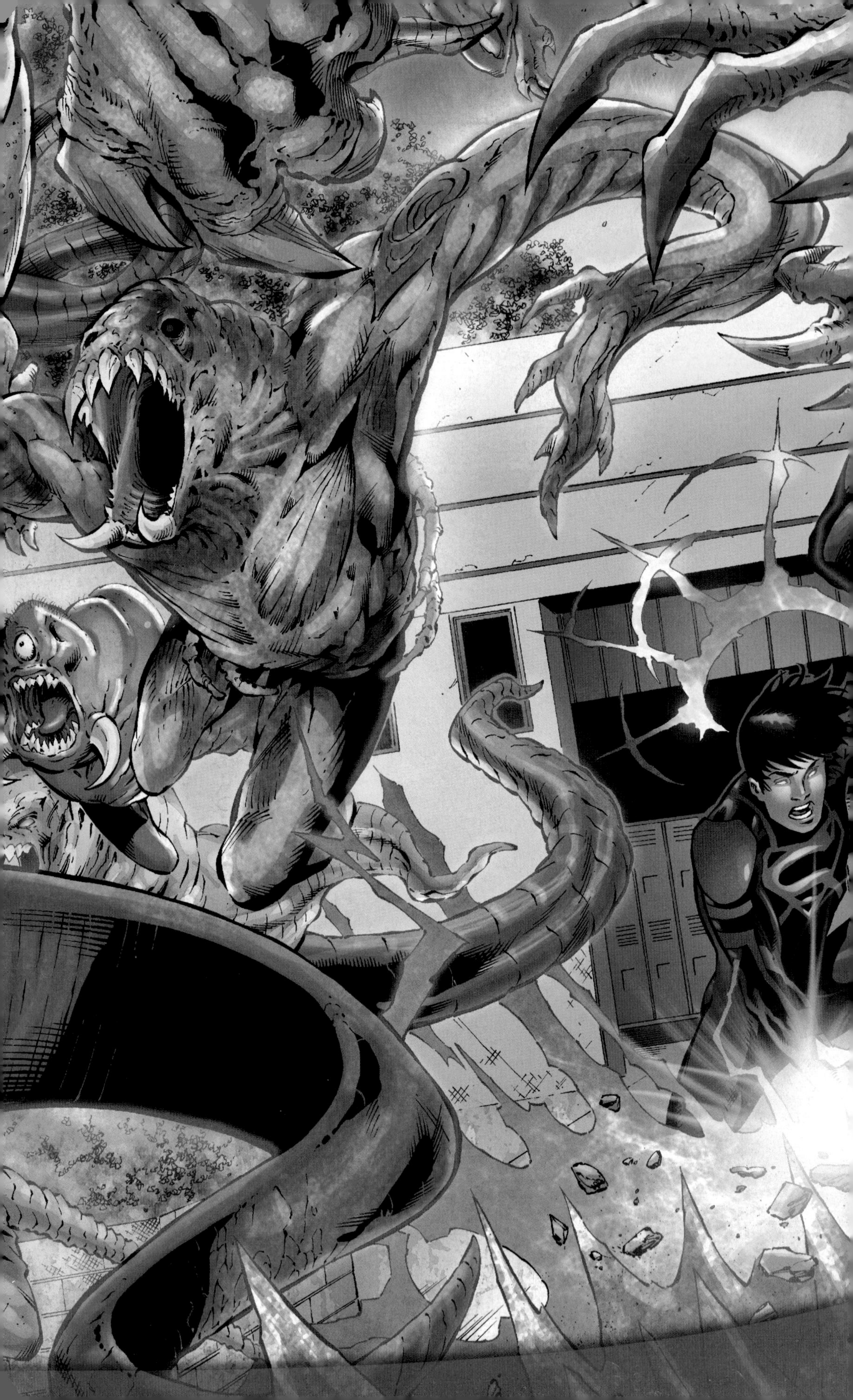

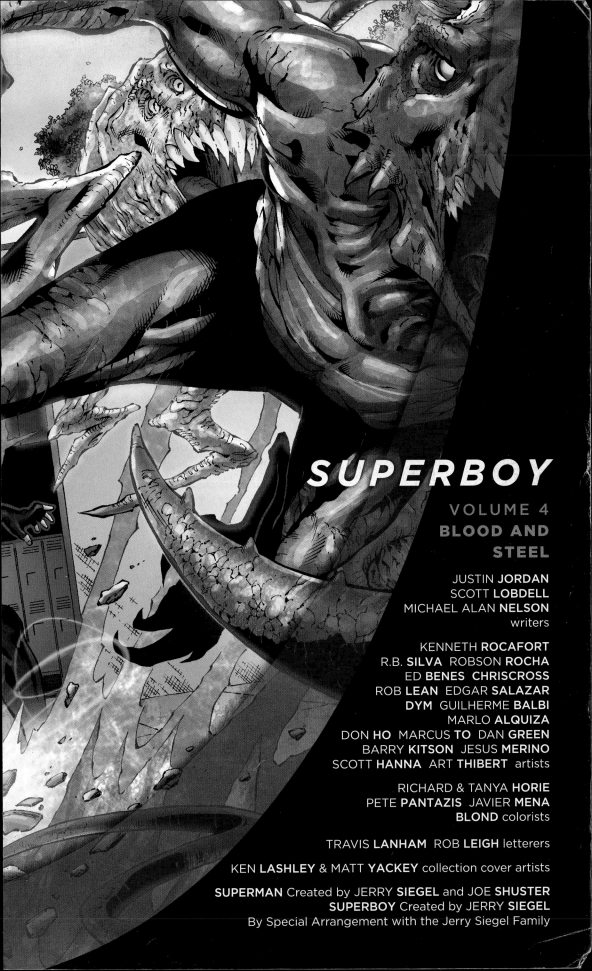

SUPERBOY

VOLUME 4
BLOOD AND
STEEL

JUSTIN **JORDAN**
SCOTT **LOBDELL**
MICHAEL ALAN **NELSON**
writers

KENNETH **ROCAFORT**
R.B. **SILVA** ROBSON **ROCHA**
ED **BENES** **CHRISCROSS**
ROB **LEAN** EDGAR **SALAZAR**
DYM GUILHERME **BALBI**
MARLO **ALQUIZA**
DON **HO** MARCUS **TO** DAN **GREEN**
BARRY **KITSON** JESUS **MERINO**
SCOTT **HANNA** ART **THIBERT** artists

RICHARD & TANYA **HORIE**
PETE **PANTAZIS** JAVIER **MENA**
BLOND colorists

TRAVIS **LANHAM** ROB **LEIGH** letterers

KEN **LASHLEY** & MATT **YACKEY** collection cover artists

SUPERMAN Created by JERRY **SIEGEL** and JOE **SHUSTER**
SUPERBOY Created by JERRY **SIEGEL**
By Special Arrangement with the Jerry Siegel Family

EDDIE BERGANZA MIKE COTTON Editors – Original Series ANTHONY MARQUES RICKEY PURDIN Assistant Editors – Original Series
RACHEL PINNELAS Editor ROBBIN BROSTERMAN Design Director – Books ROBBIE BIEDERMAN Publication Design

BOB HARRAS Senior VP – Editor-in-Chief, DC Comics

DIANE NELSON President DAN DIDIO and JIM LEE Co-Publishers GEOFF JOHNS Chief Creative Officer
JOHN ROOD Executive VP – Sales, Marketing and Business Development AMY GENKINS Senior VP – Business and Legal Affairs
NAIRI GARDINER Senior VP – Finance JEFF BOISON VP – Publishing Planning
MARK CHIARELLO VP – Art Direction and Design JOHN CUNNINGHAM VP – Marketing
TERRI CUNNINGHAM VP – Editorial Administration ALISON GILL Senior VP – Manufacturing and Operations
HANK KANALZ Senior VP – Vertigo and Integrated Publishing JAY KOGAN VP – Business and Legal Affairs, Publishing
JACK MAHAN VP – Business Affairs, Talent NICK NAPOLITANO VP – Manufacturing Administration
SUE POHJA VP – Book Sales COURTNEY SIMMONS Senior VP – Publicity BOB WAYNE Senior VP – Sales

SUPERBOY VOLUME 4: BLOOD AND STEEL

Published by DC Comics. Copyright © 2014 DC Comics. All Rights Reserved.
Originally published in single magazine form in SUPERBOY 20-25, SUPERMAN 25 and TEEN TITANS ANNUAL 2.
Copyright © 2013, 2014 DC Comics. All Rights Reserved. All characters, their distinctive likenesses and related
elements featured in this publication are trademarks of DC Comics. The stories, characters and incidents featured
in this publication are entirely fictional. DC Comics does not read or accept unsolicited ideas, stories or artwork.

DC Comics, 1700 Broadway, New York, NY 10019
A Warner Bros. Entertainment Company.
Printed by RR Donnelley, Salem, VA, USA. 5/30/14. First Printing.

ISBN: 978-1-4012-4685-3

Library of Congress Cataloging-in-Publication Data

Jordan, Justin, author.
Superboy. Volume 4, Blood and Steel / Justin Jordan ; illustrated by RB Silva.
pages cm — (The New 52!)
ISBN 978-1-4012-4685-3 (paperback)
1. Graphic novels. 2. COMICS & GRAPHIC NOVELS / Superheroes. bisacsh I. Silva, R. B., 1985- illustrator.
II. Title. III. Title: Blood and Steel.
PN6728.S87J67 2014
741.5'973—dc23
2014010809

SUSTAINABLE
FORESTRY
INITIATIVE

Certified Chain of Custody
20% Certified Forest Content,
80% Certified Sourcing
www.sfiprogram.org
SFI-01042
APPLIES TO TEXT STOCK ONLY

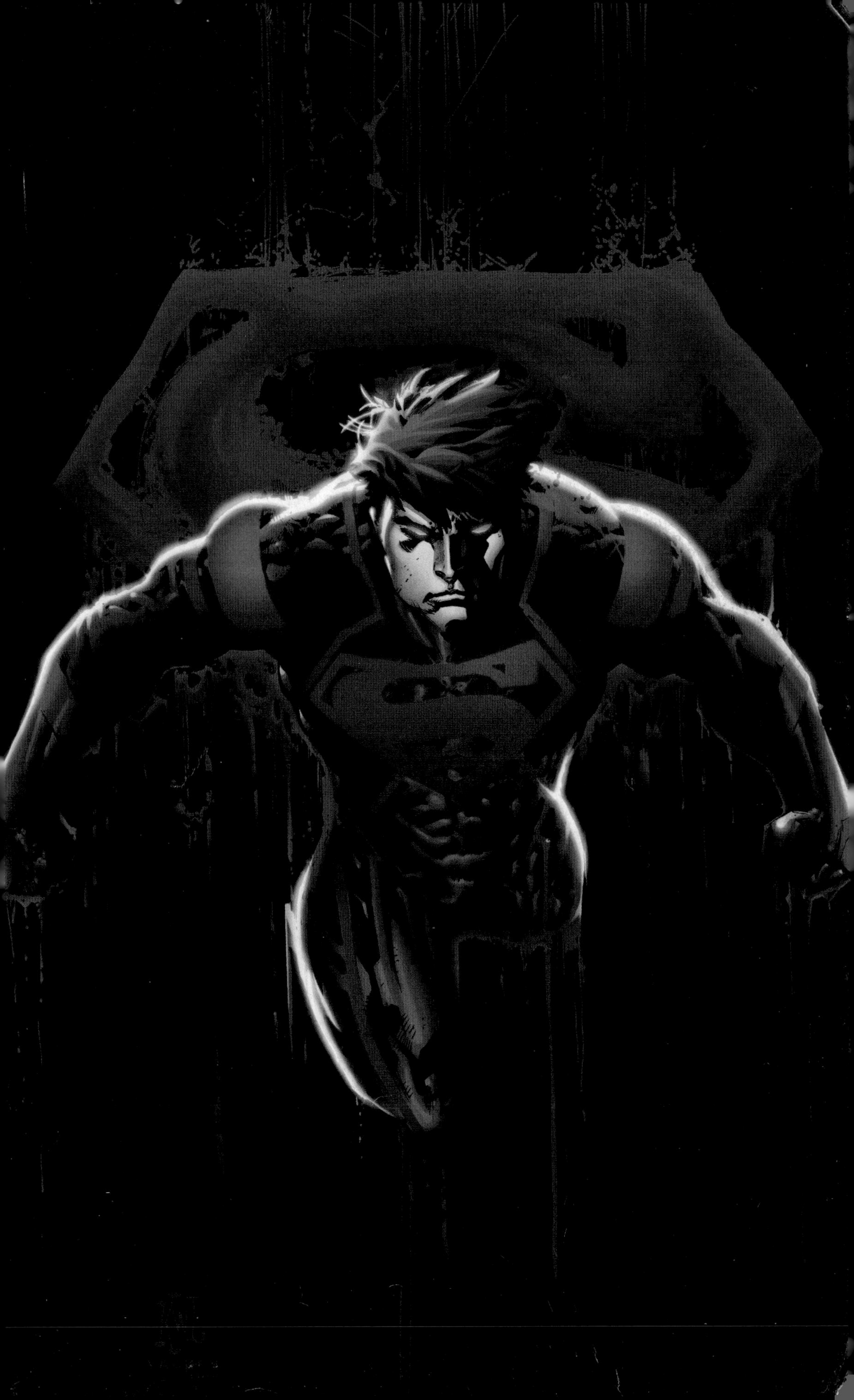

A WRETCHED H.I.V.E.

JUSTIN JORDAN writer CHRISCROSS KENNETH ROCAFORT R.B. SILVA ROB LEAN artists cover art by KEN LASHLEY & MATT YACKEY

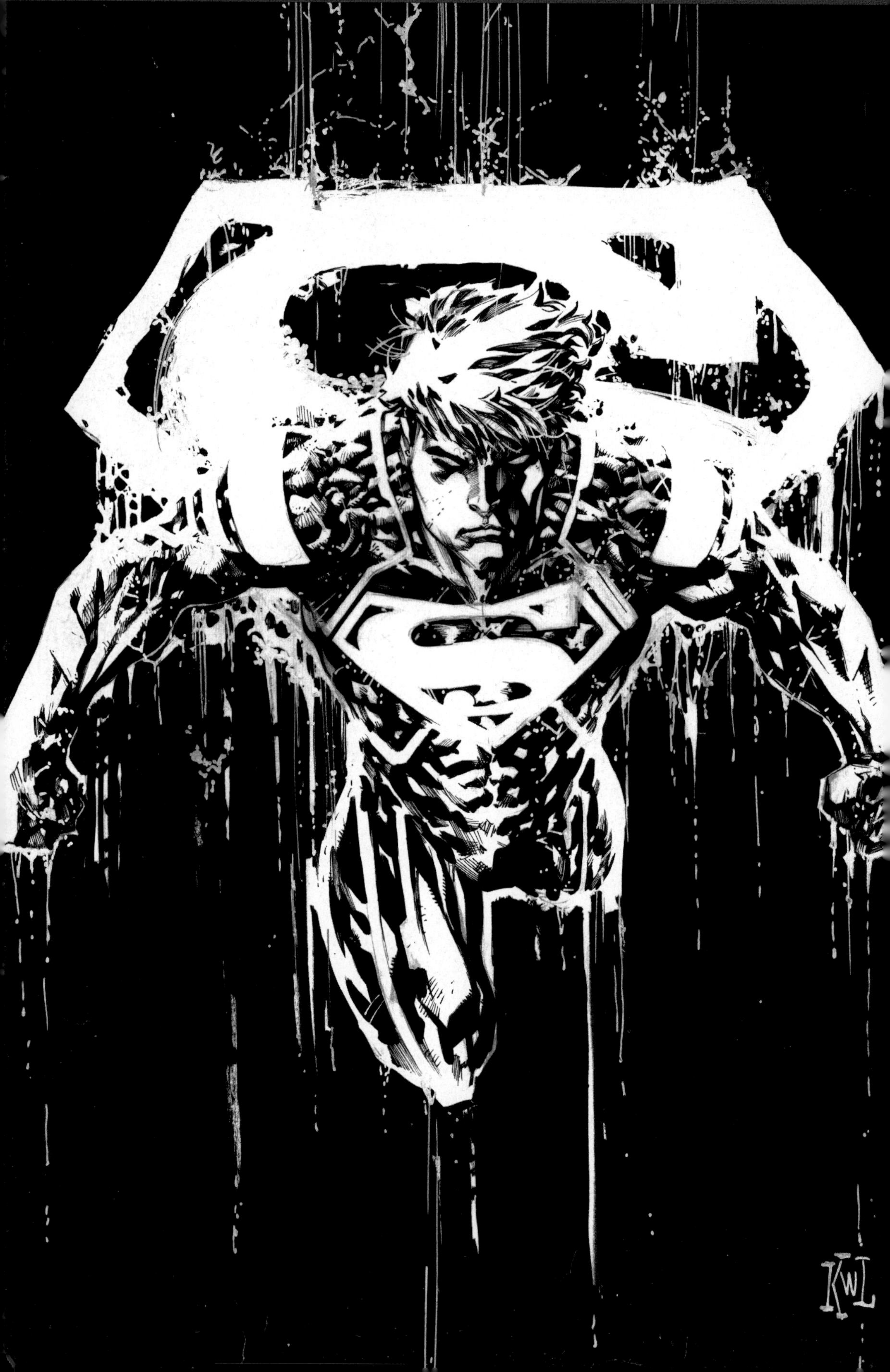

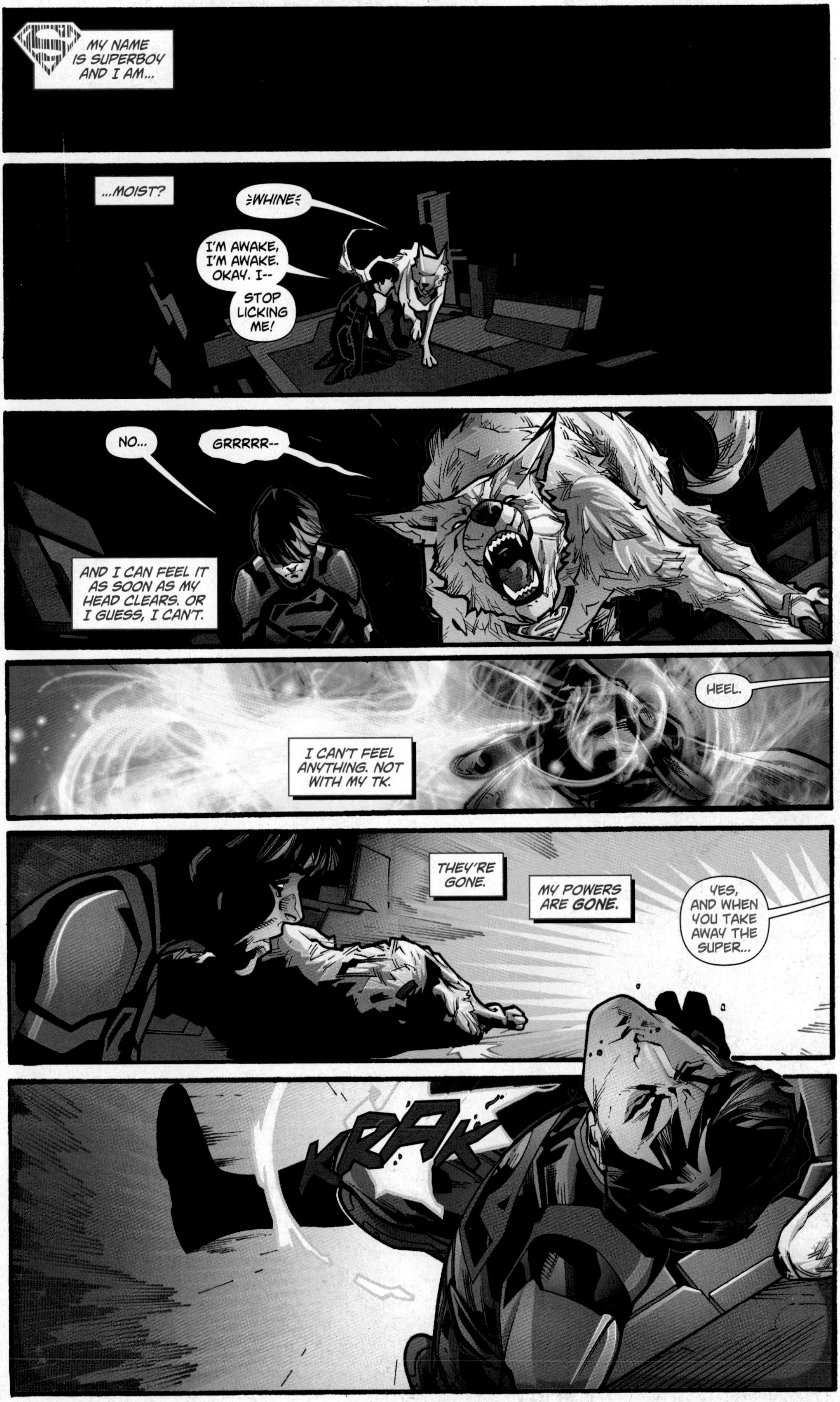
MY NAME IS SUPERBOY AND I AM...
...MOIST?
WHINE
I'M AWAKE, I'M AWAKE. OKAY. I--
STOP LICKING ME!
NO...
GRRRRR--
AND I CAN FEEL IT AS SOON AS MY HEAD CLEARS. OR I GUESS, I CAN'T.
HEEL.
I CAN'T FEEL ANYTHING. NOT WITH MY TK.
THEY'RE GONE.
MY POWERS ARE GONE.
YES, AND WHEN YOU TAKE AWAY THE SUPER...
KRAK

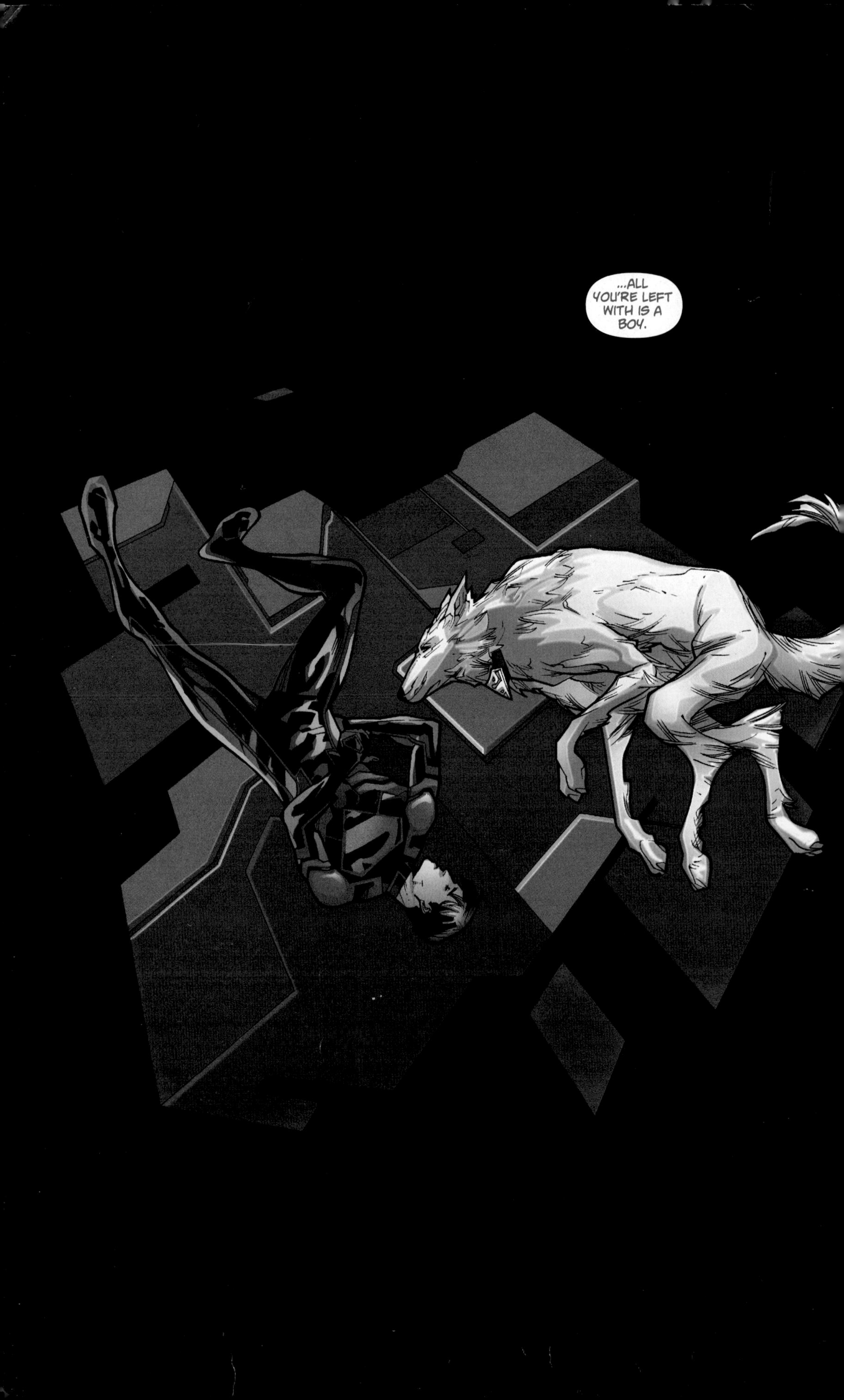
...ALL YOU'RE LEFT WITH IS A BOY.

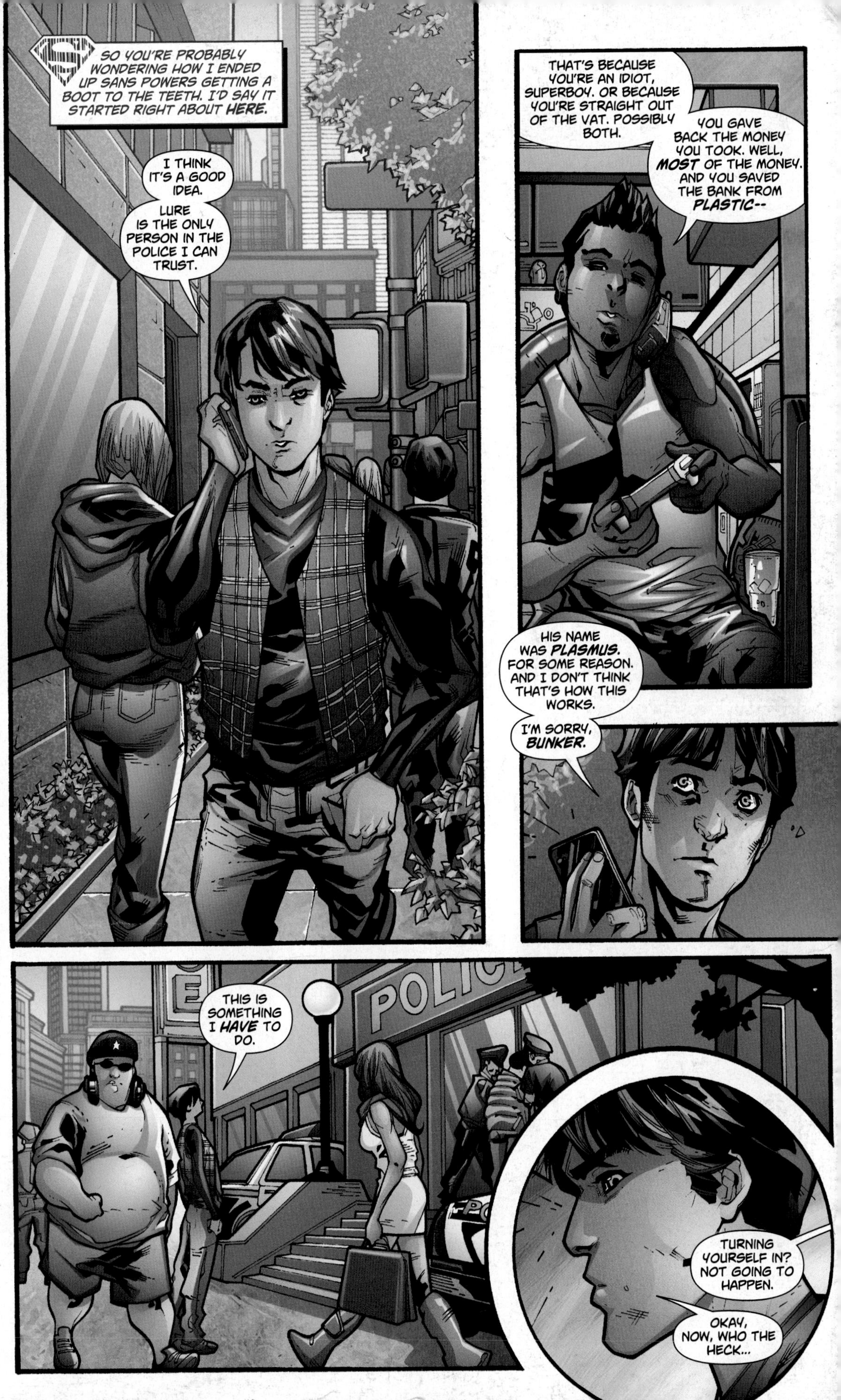
SO YOU'RE PROBABLY WONDERING HOW I ENDED UP SANS POWERS GETTING A BOOT TO THE TEETH. I'D SAY IT STARTED RIGHT ABOUT HERE.
I THINK IT'S A GOOD IDEA.
LURE IS THE ONLY PERSON IN THE POLICE I CAN TRUST.
THAT'S BECAUSE YOU'RE AN IDIOT, SUPERBOY. OR BECAUSE YOU'RE STRAIGHT OUT OF THE VAT. POSSIBLY BOTH.
YOU GAVE BACK THE MONEY YOU TOOK. WELL, MOST OF THE MONEY. AND YOU SAVED THE BANK FROM PLASTIC--
HIS NAME WAS PLASMUS. FOR SOME REASON. AND I DON'T THINK THAT'S HOW THIS WORKS.
I'M SORRY, BUNKER.
THIS IS SOMETHING I HAVE TO DO.
POLICE
TURNING YOURSELF IN? NOT GOING TO HAPPEN.
OKAY, NOW, WHO THE HECK...

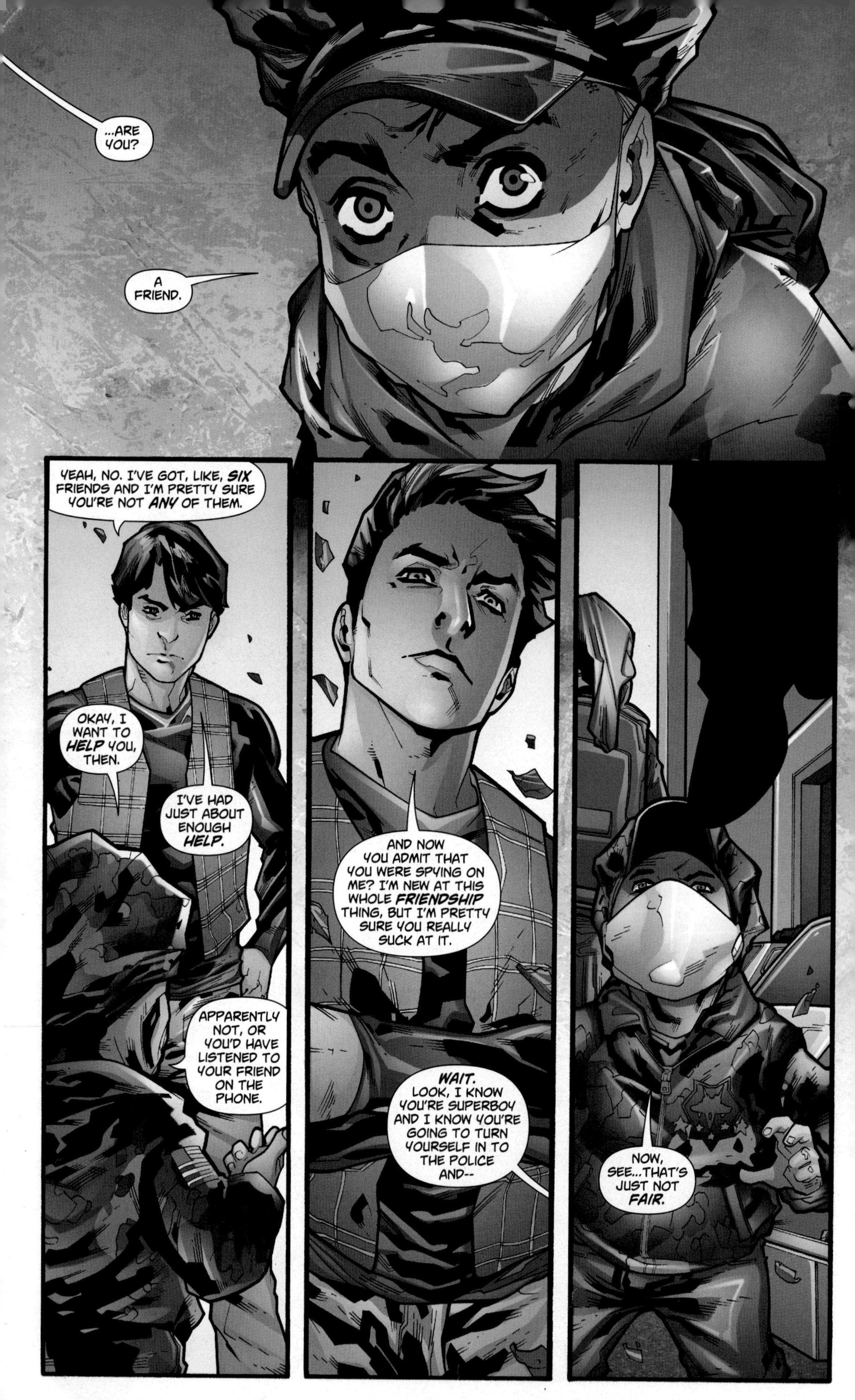
...ARE YOU?
A FRIEND.
YEAH, NO. I'VE GOT, LIKE, SIX FRIENDS AND I'M PRETTY SURE YOU'RE NOT ANY OF THEM.
OKAY, I WANT TO HELP YOU, THEN.
I'VE HAD JUST ABOUT ENOUGH HELP.
APPARENTLY NOT, OR YOU'D HAVE LISTENED TO YOUR FRIEND ON THE PHONE.
AND NOW YOU ADMIT THAT YOU WERE SPYING ON ME? I'M NEW AT THIS WHOLE FRIENDSHIP THING, BUT I'M PRETTY SURE YOU REALLY SUCK AT IT.
WAIT. LOOK, I KNOW YOU'RE SUPERBOY AND I KNOW YOU'RE GOING TO TURN YOURSELF IN TO THE POLICE AND--
NOW, SEE...THAT'S JUST NOT FAIR.

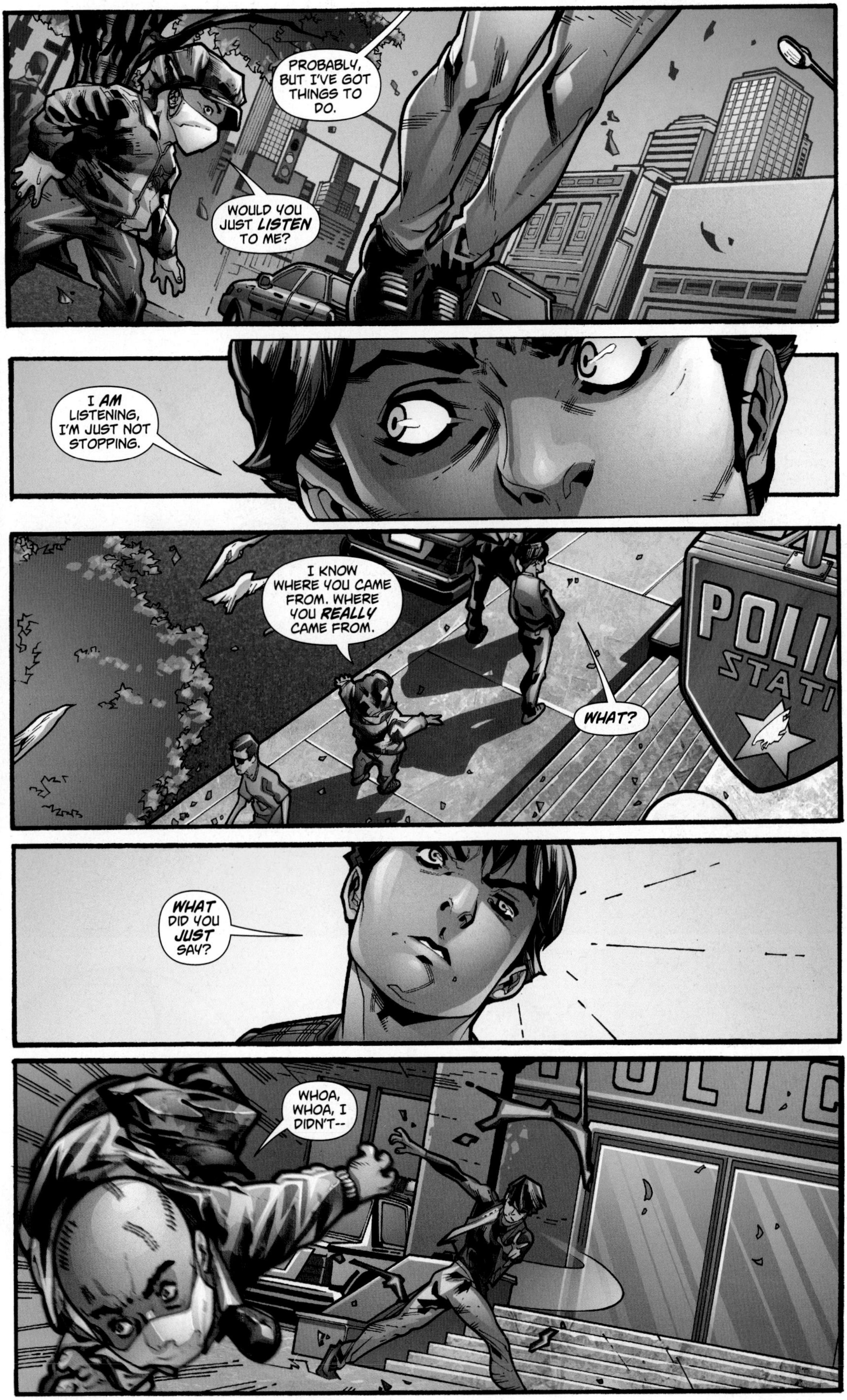
PROBABLY, BUT I'VE GOT THINGS TO DO.
WOULD YOU JUST LISTEN TO ME?
I AM LISTENING, I'M JUST NOT STOPPING.
I KNOW WHERE YOU CAME FROM. WHERE YOU REALLY CAME FROM.
WHAT?
POLI
STATI
WHAT DID YOU JUST SAY?
OLIC
WHOA, WHOA, I DIDN'T--

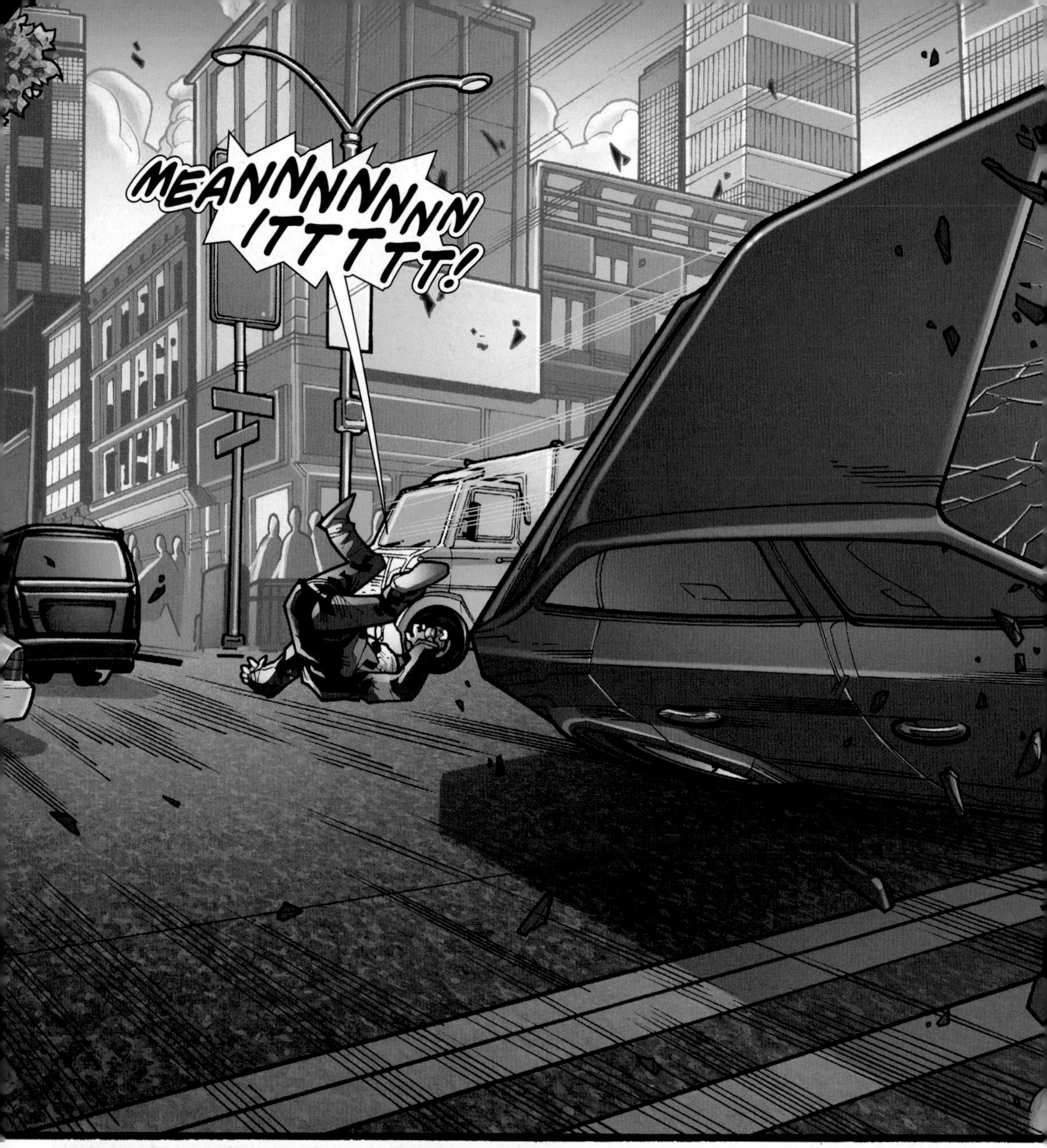
MEANNNNNNN ITTTTTT!

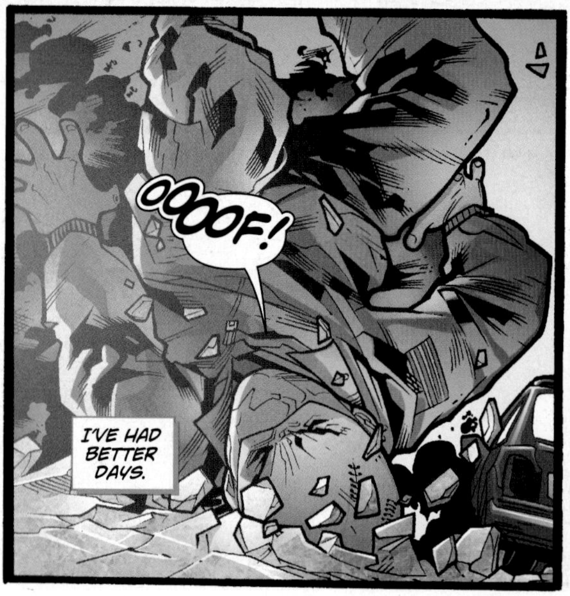
OOOOF!
I'VE HAD BETTER DAYS.

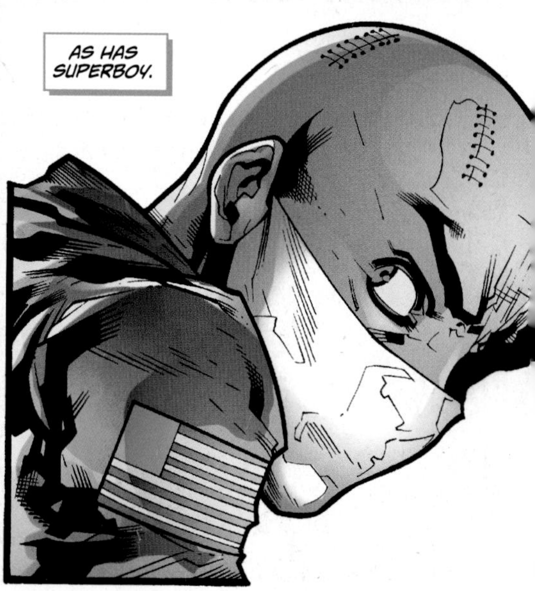
AS HAS SUPERBOY.

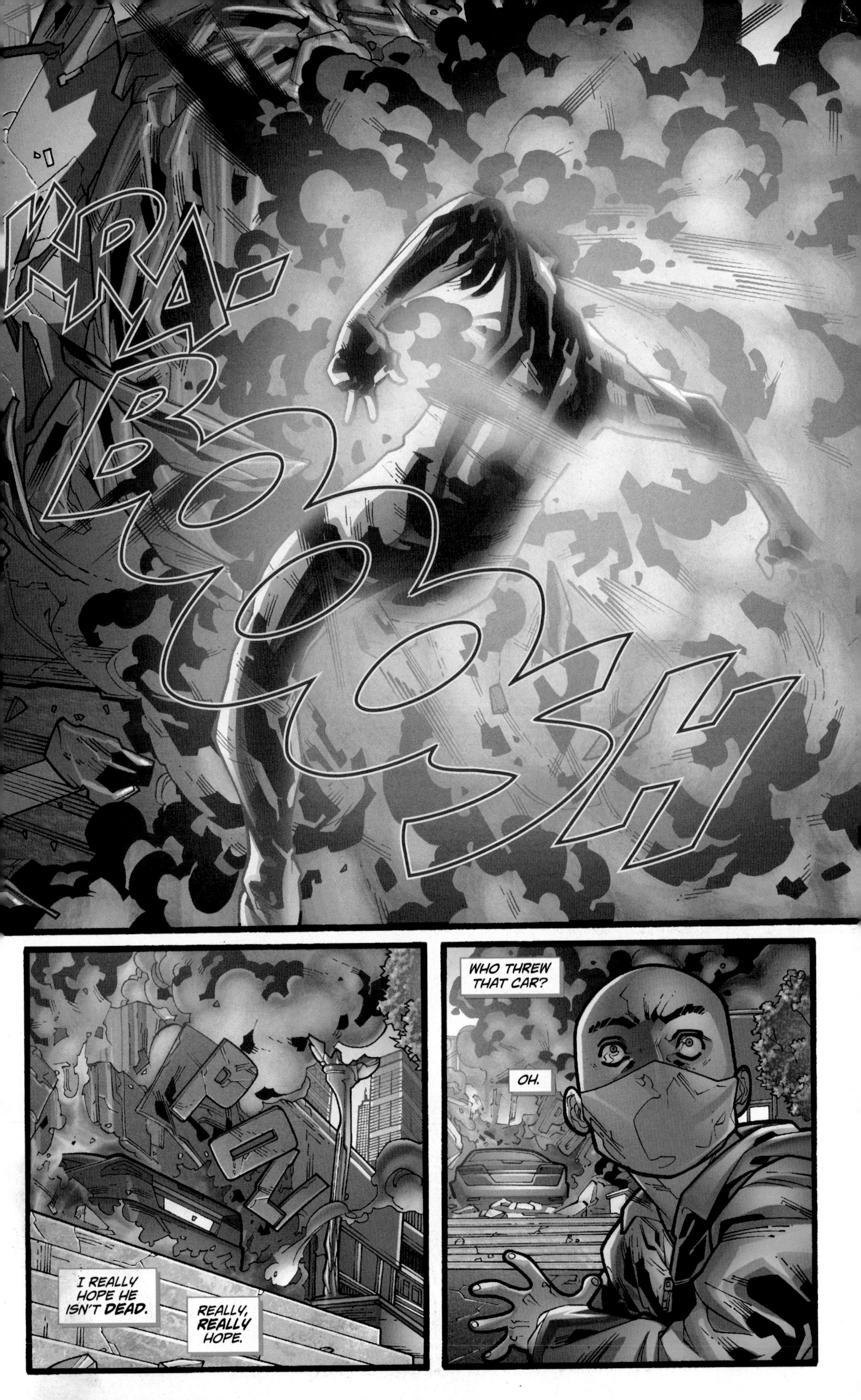
I REALLY HOPE HE ISN'T **DEAD**.
REALLY, **REALLY** HOPE.
WHO THREW THAT CAR?
OH.

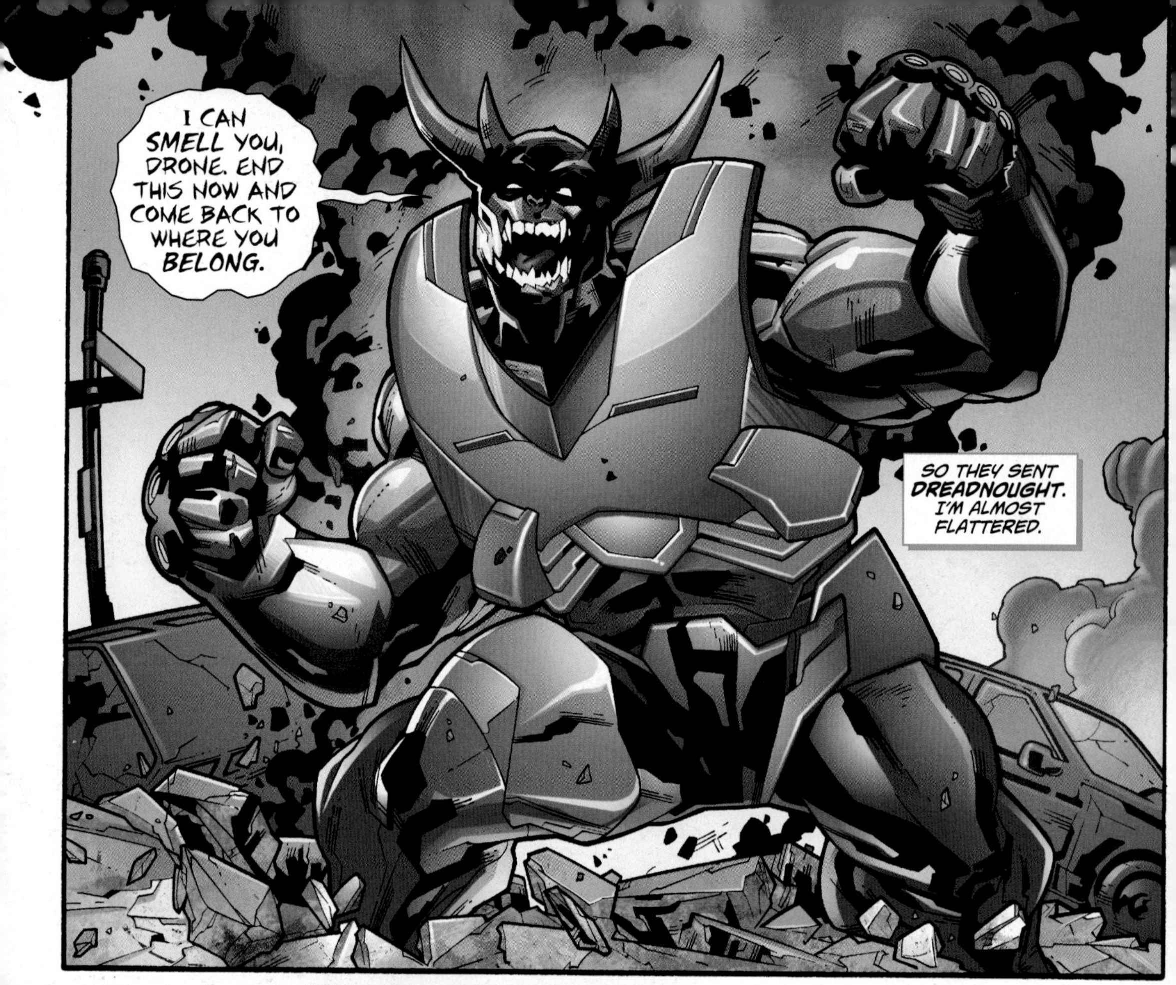
I CAN SMELL YOU, DRONE. END THIS NOW AND COME BACK TO WHERE YOU BELONG.
SO THEY SENT DREADNOUGHT. I'M ALMOST FLATTERED.

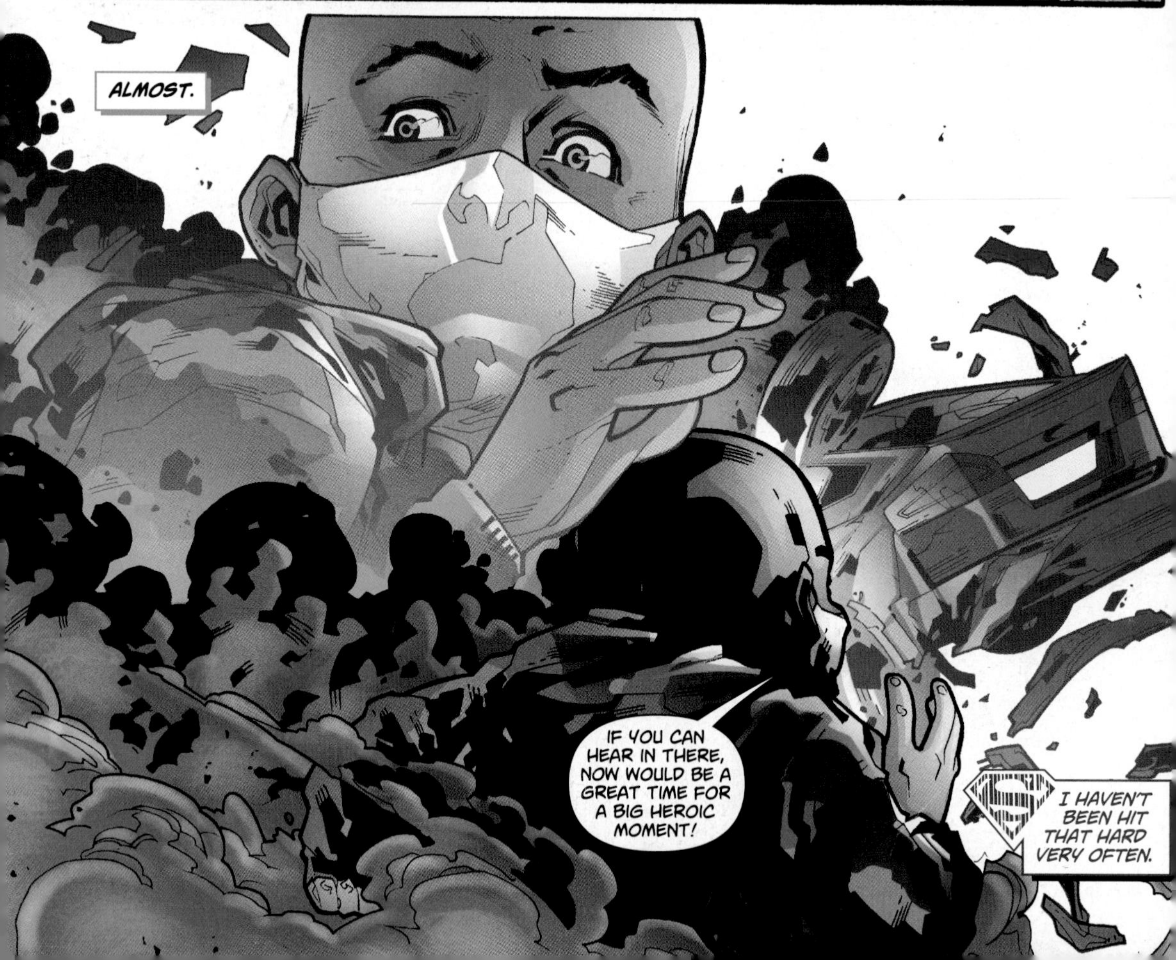
ALMOST.
IF YOU CAN HEAR IN THERE, NOW WOULD BE A GREAT TIME FOR A BIG HEROIC MOMENT!
I HAVEN'T BEEN HIT THAT HARD VERY OFTEN.

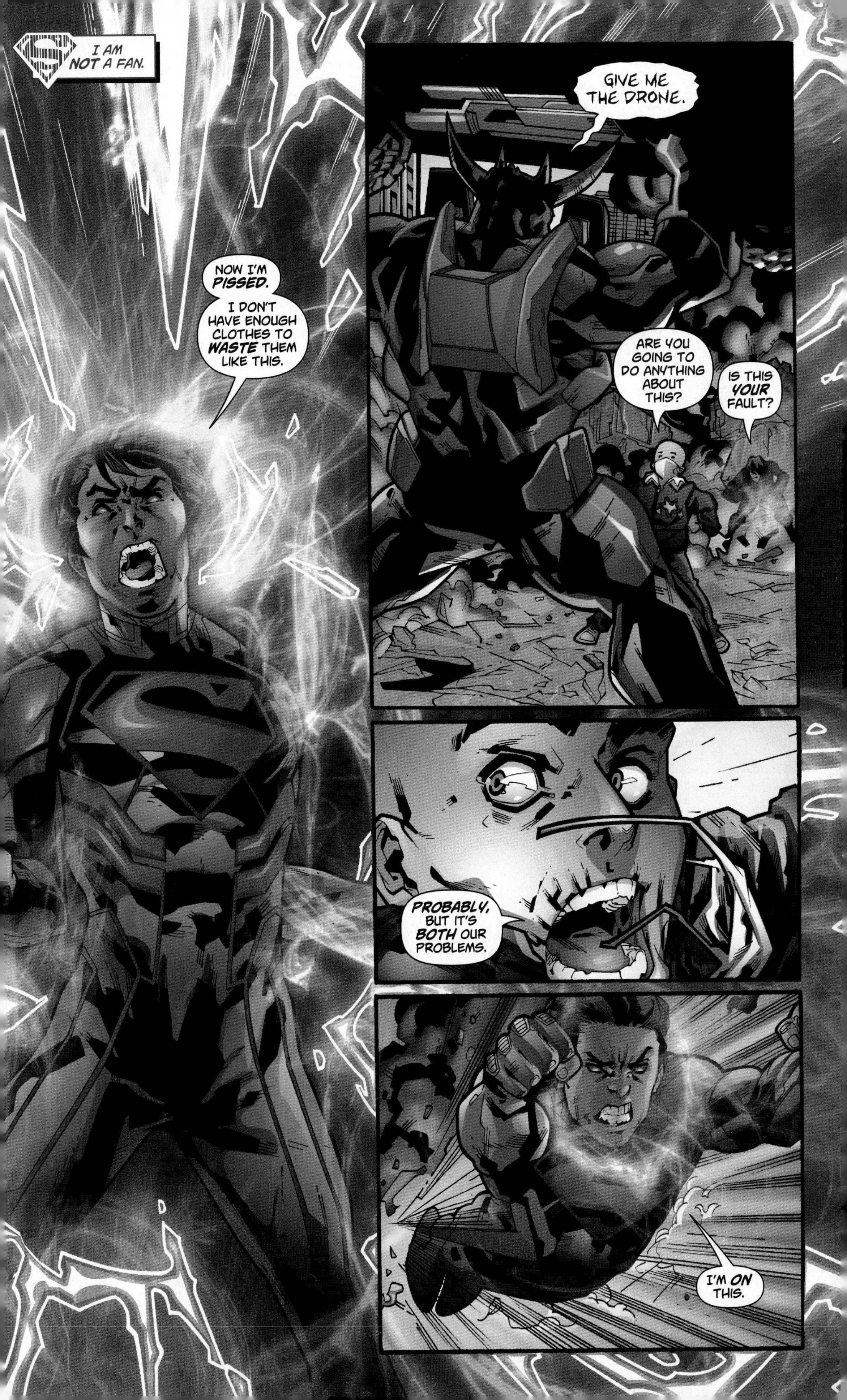
I AM NOT A FAN.
NOW I'M PISSED.
I DON'T HAVE ENOUGH CLOTHES TO WASTE THEM LIKE THIS.
GIVE ME THE DRONE.
ARE YOU GOING TO DO ANYTHING ABOUT THIS?
IS THIS YOUR FAULT?
PROBABLY, BUT IT'S BOTH OUR PROBLEMS.
I'M ON THIS.

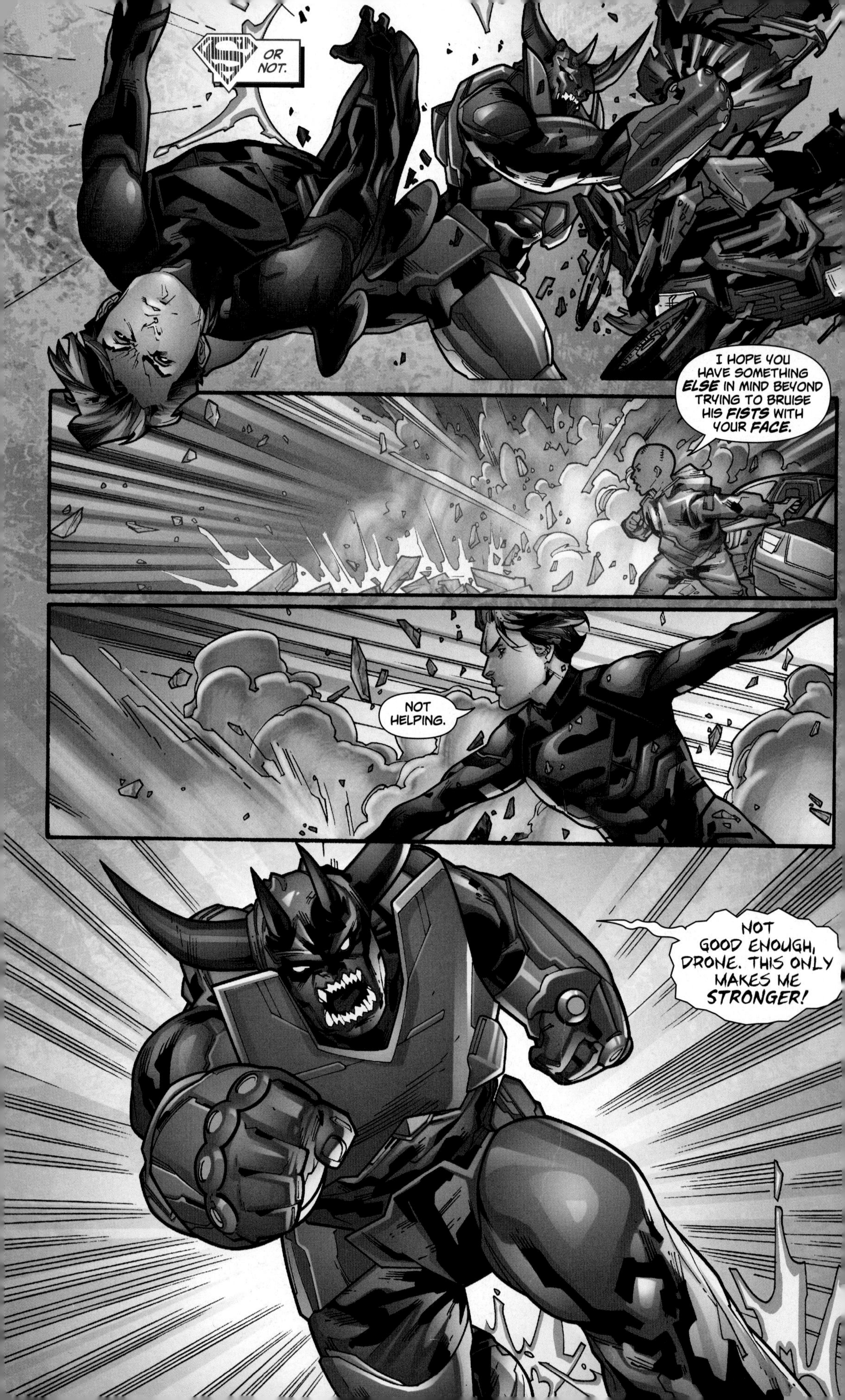
OR NOT.
I HOPE YOU HAVE SOMETHING ELSE IN MIND BEYOND TRYING TO BRUISE HIS FISTS WITH YOUR FACE.
NOT HELPING.
NOT GOOD ENOUGH, DRONE. THIS ONLY MAKES ME STRONGER!

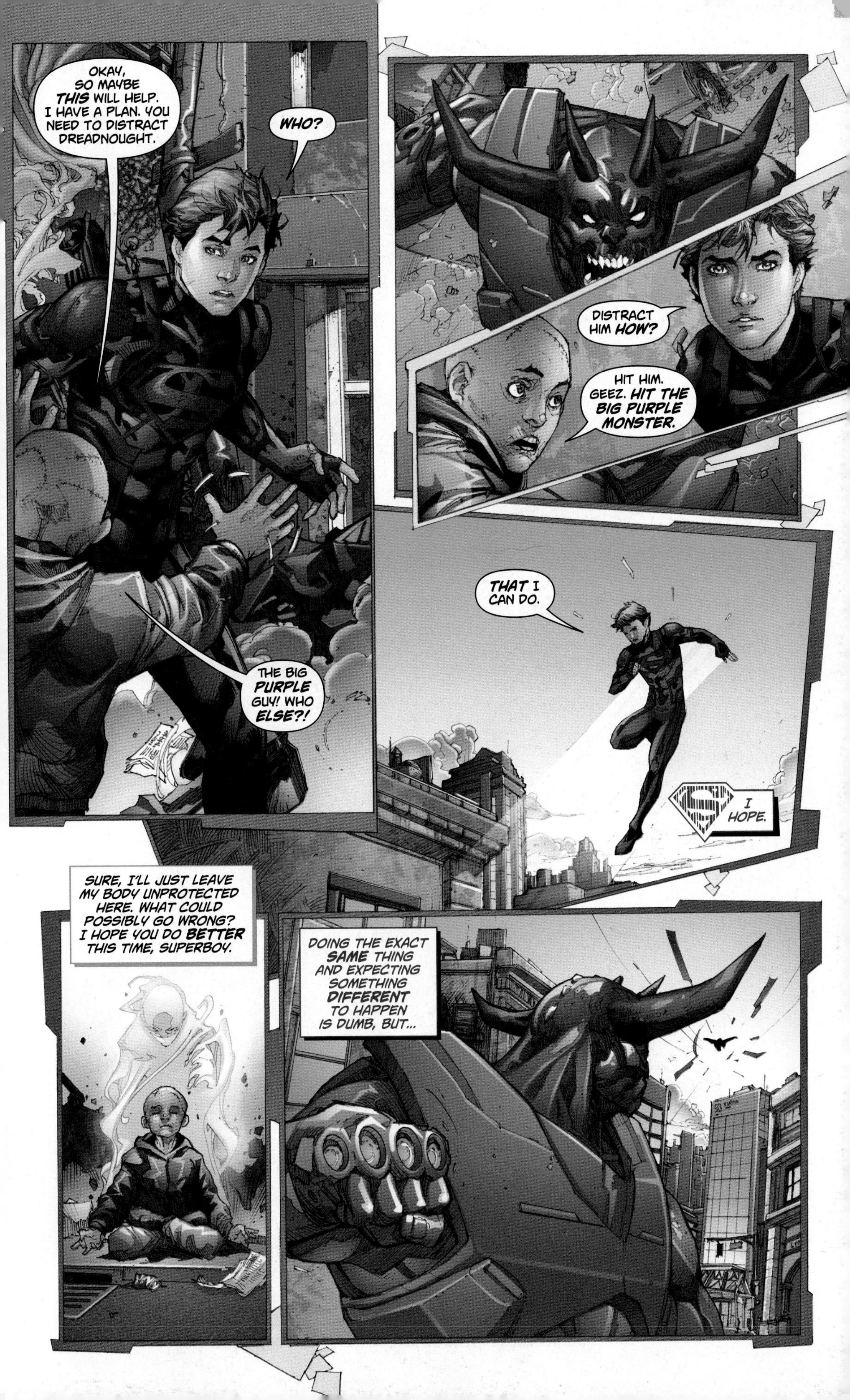
OKAY, SO MAYBE THIS WILL HELP. I HAVE A PLAN. YOU NEED TO DISTRACT DREADNOUGHT.
WHO?
THE BIG PURPLE GUY! WHO ELSE?!
DISTRACT HIM HOW?
HIT HIM. GEEZ. HIT THE BIG PURPLE MONSTER.
THAT I CAN DO.
I HOPE.
SURE, I'LL JUST LEAVE MY BODY UNPROTECTED HERE. WHAT COULD POSSIBLY GO WRONG? I HOPE YOU DO BETTER THIS TIME, SUPERBOY.
DOING THE EXACT SAME THING AND EXPECTING SOMETHING DIFFERENT TO HAPPEN IS DUMB, BUT...

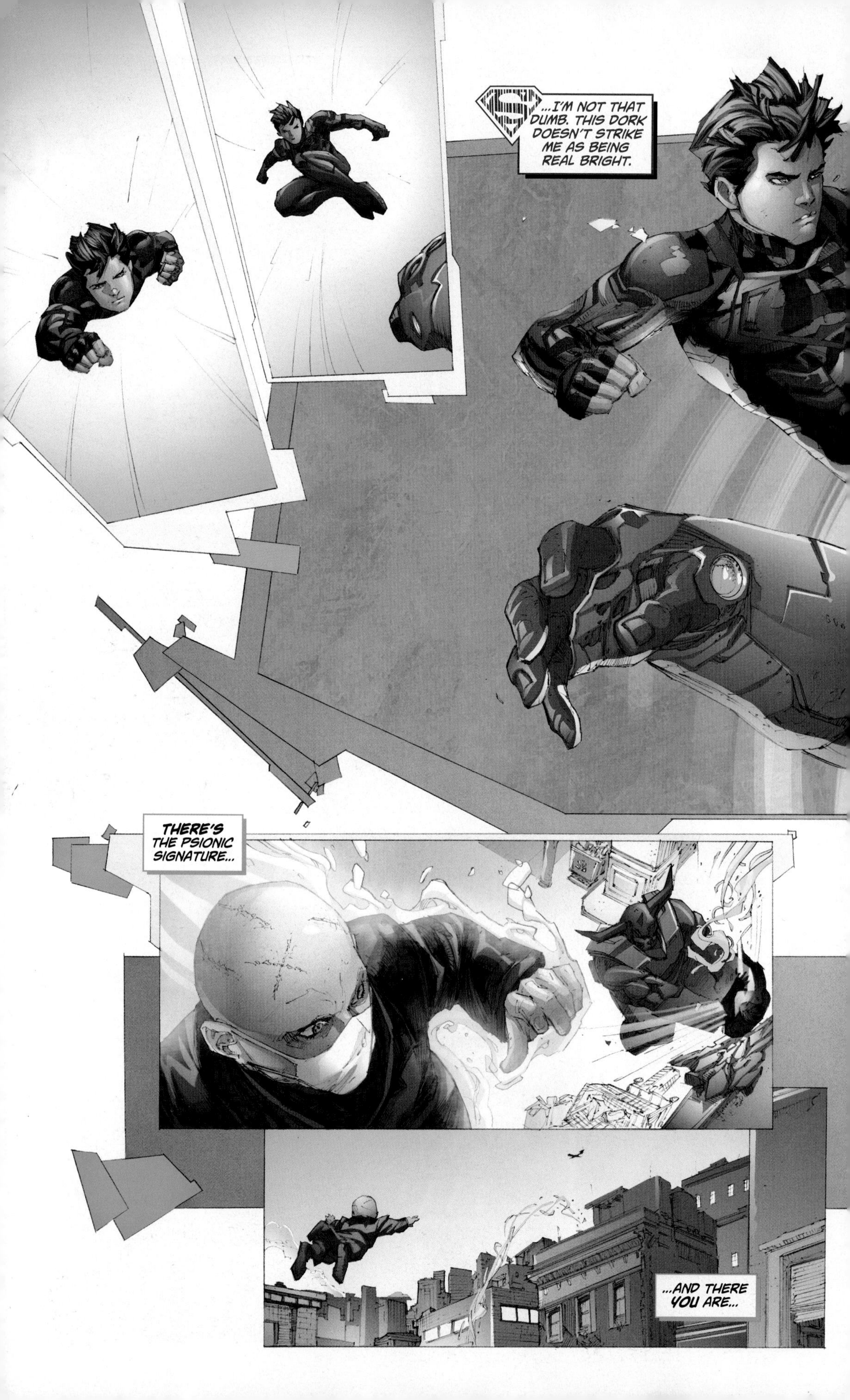
...I'M NOT THAT DUMB. THIS DORK DOESN'T STRIKE ME AS BEING REAL BRIGHT.
THERE'S THE PSIONIC SIGNATURE...
...AND THERE YOU ARE...

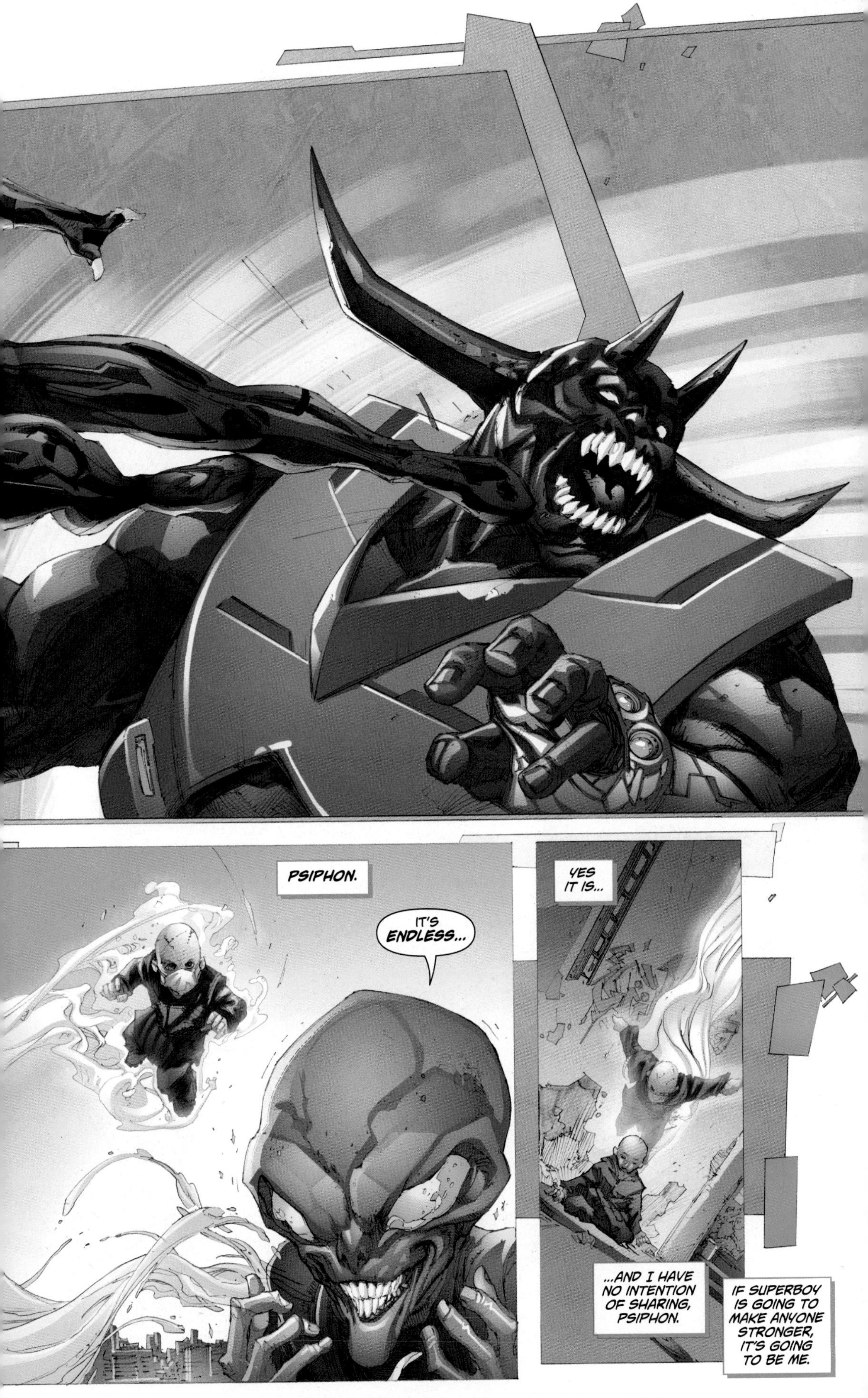
PSIPHON.
IT'S ENDLESS...
YES IT IS...
...AND I HAVE NO INTENTION OF SHARING, PSIPHON.
IF SUPERBOY IS GOING TO MAKE ANYONE STRONGER, IT'S GOING TO BE ME.

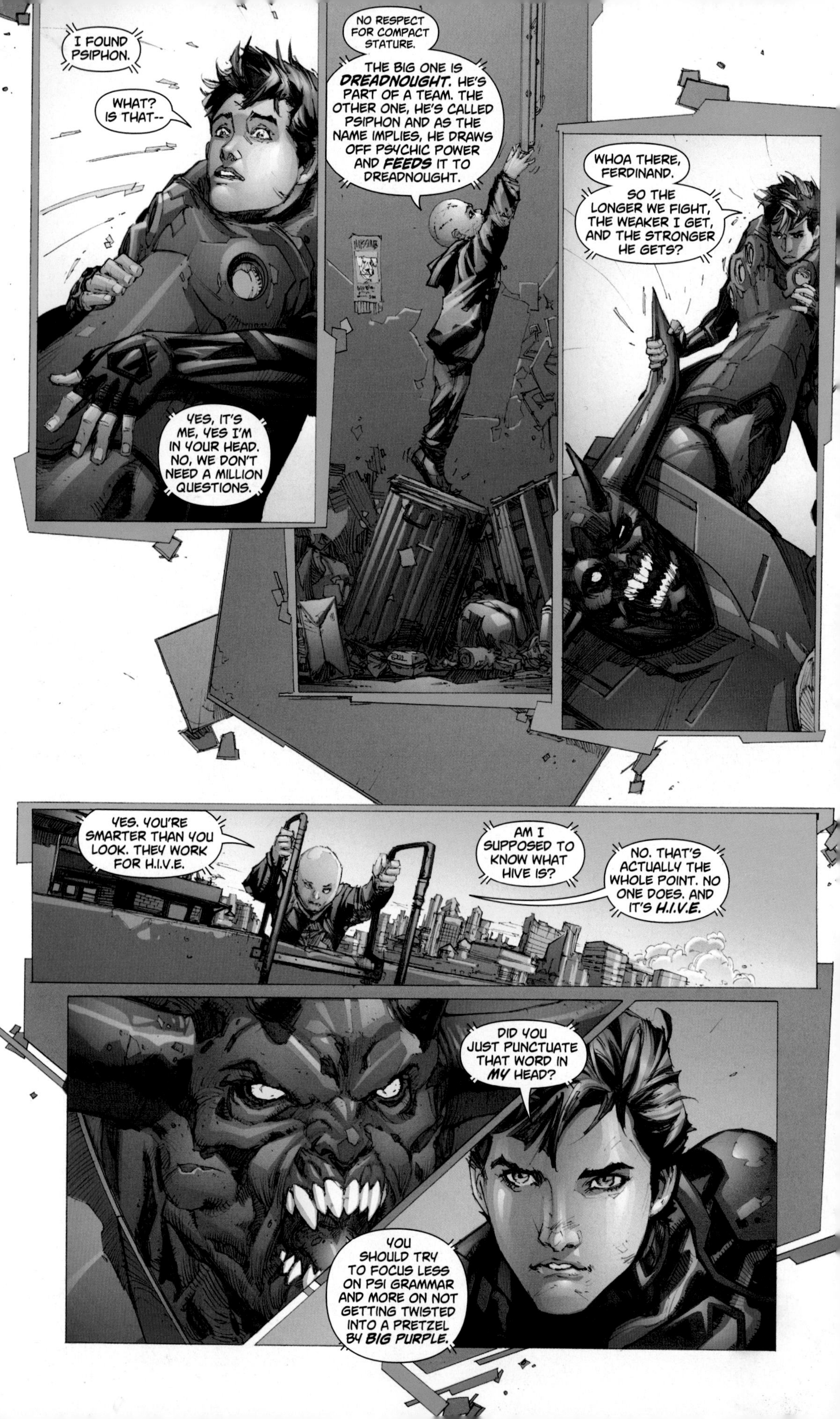
I FOUND PSIPHON.
WHAT? IS THAT--
YES, IT'S ME, YES I'M IN YOUR HEAD. NO, WE DON'T NEED A MILLION QUESTIONS.
NO RESPECT FOR COMPACT STATURE.
THE BIG ONE IS DREADNOUGHT. HE'S PART OF A TEAM. THE OTHER ONE, HE'S CALLED PSIPHON AND AS THE NAME IMPLIES, HE DRAWS OFF PSYCHIC POWER AND FEEDS IT TO DREADNOUGHT.
WHOA THERE, FERDINAND.
SO THE LONGER WE FIGHT, THE WEAKER I GET, AND THE STRONGER HE GETS?
YES. YOU'RE SMARTER THAN YOU LOOK. THEY WORK FOR H.I.V.E.
AM I SUPPOSED TO KNOW WHAT HIVE IS?
NO. THAT'S ACTUALLY THE WHOLE POINT. NO ONE DOES. AND IT'S H.I.V.E.
DID YOU JUST PUNCTUATE THAT WORD IN MY HEAD?
YOU SHOULD TRY TO FOCUS LESS ON PSI GRAMMAR AND MORE ON NOT GETTING TWISTED INTO A PRETZEL BY BIG PURPLE.

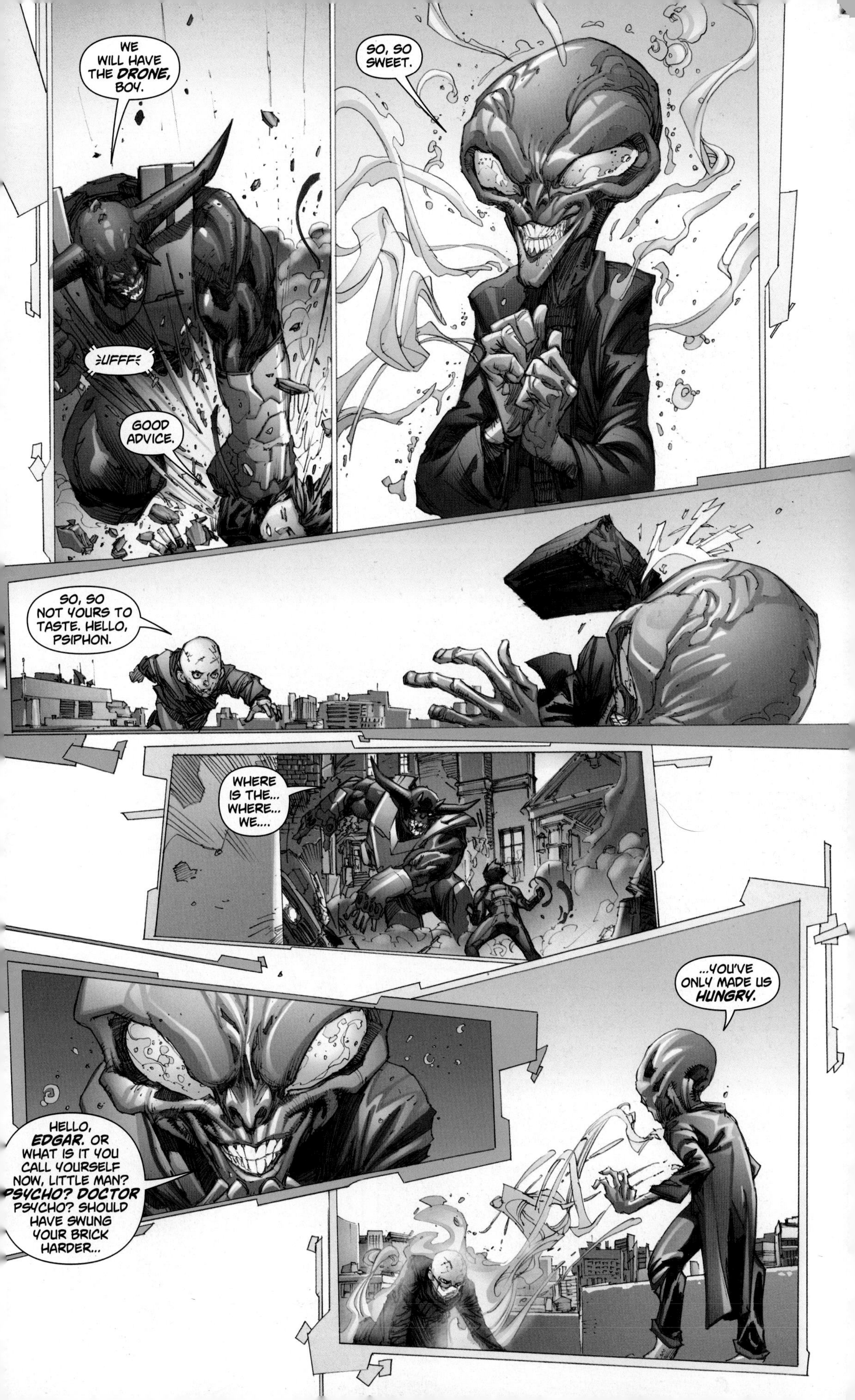
WE WILL HAVE THE DRONE, BOY.
UFFF
GOOD ADVICE.
SO, SO SWEET.
SO, SO NOT YOURS TO TASTE. HELLO, PSIPHON.
WHERE IS THE... WHERE... WE....
...YOU'VE ONLY MADE US HUNGRY.
HELLO, EDGAR. OR WHAT IS IT YOU CALL YOURSELF NOW, LITTLE MAN? PSYCHO? DOCTOR PSYCHO? SHOULD HAVE SWUNG YOUR BRICK HARDER...

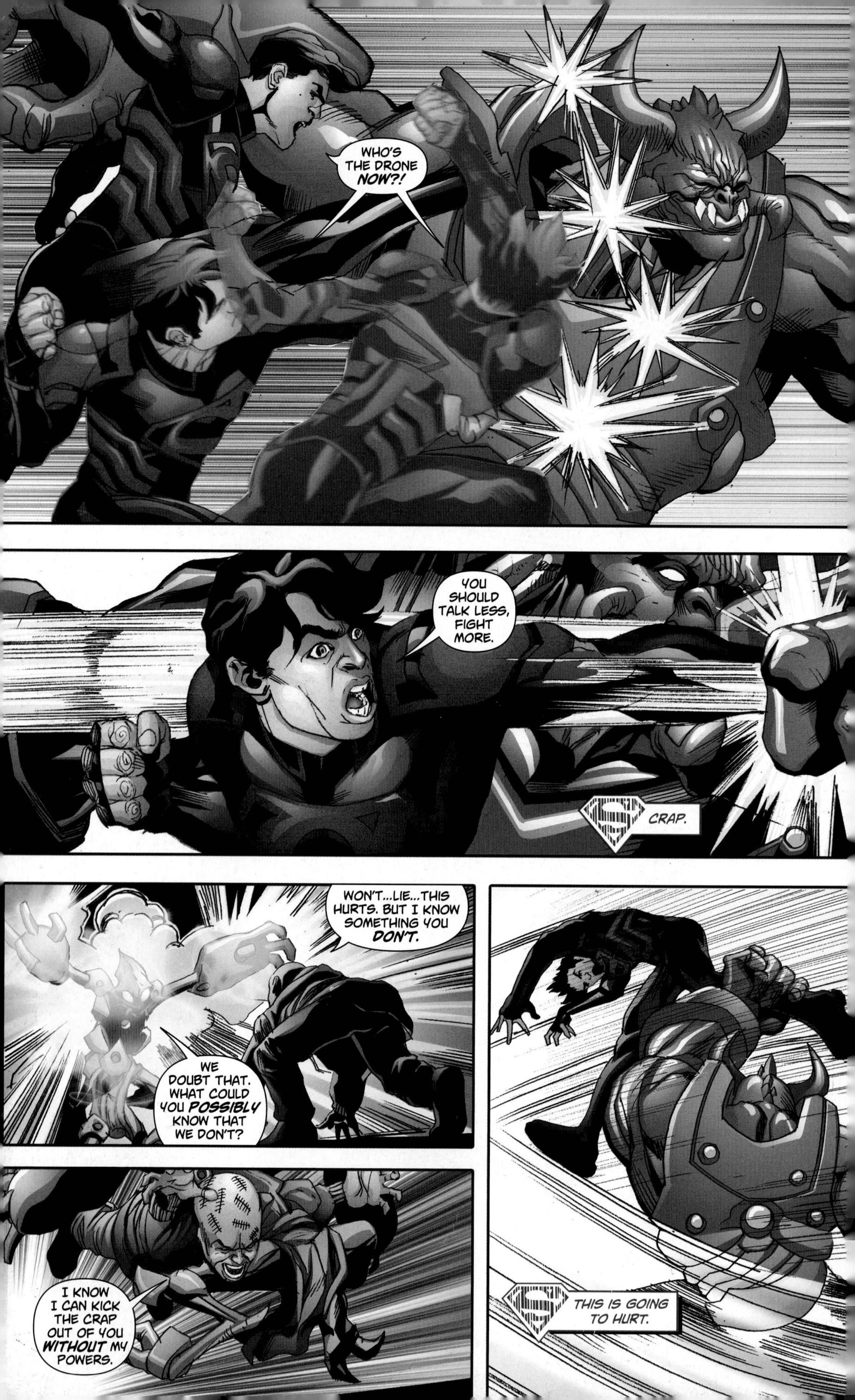
WHO'S THE DRONE NOW?!
YOU SHOULD TALK LESS, FIGHT MORE.
CRAP.
WON'T...LIE...THIS HURTS. BUT I KNOW SOMETHING YOU DON'T.
WE DOUBT THAT. WHAT COULD YOU POSSIBLY KNOW THAT WE DON'T?
I KNOW I CAN KICK THE CRAP OUT OF YOU WITHOUT MY POWERS.
THIS IS GOING TO HURT.

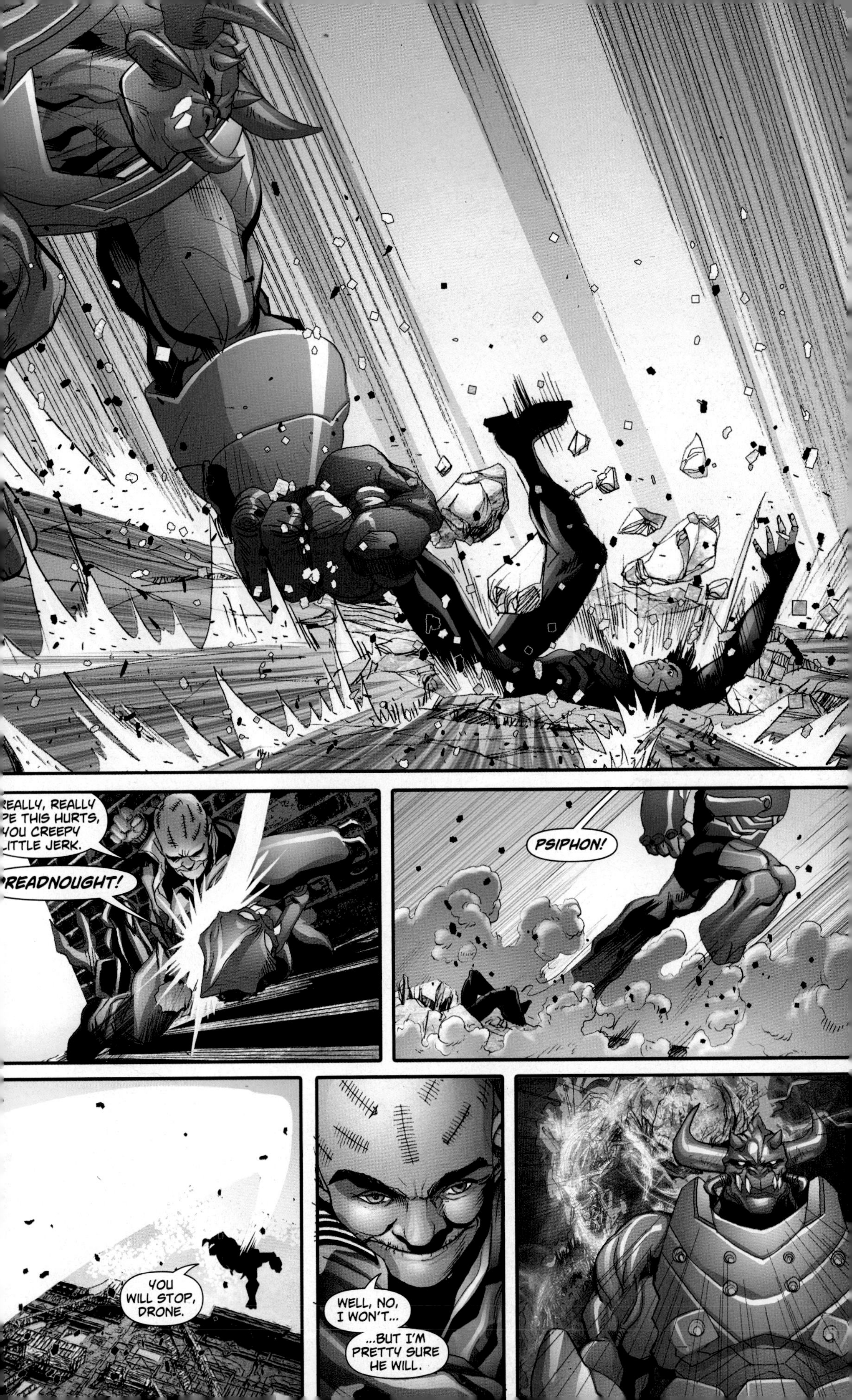
REALLY, REALLY
PE THIS HURTS,
YOU CREEPY
LITTLE JERK.
READNOUGHT!
PSIPHON!
YOU
WILL STOP,
DRONE.
WELL, NO,
I WON'T...
...BUT I'M
PRETTY SURE
HE WILL.

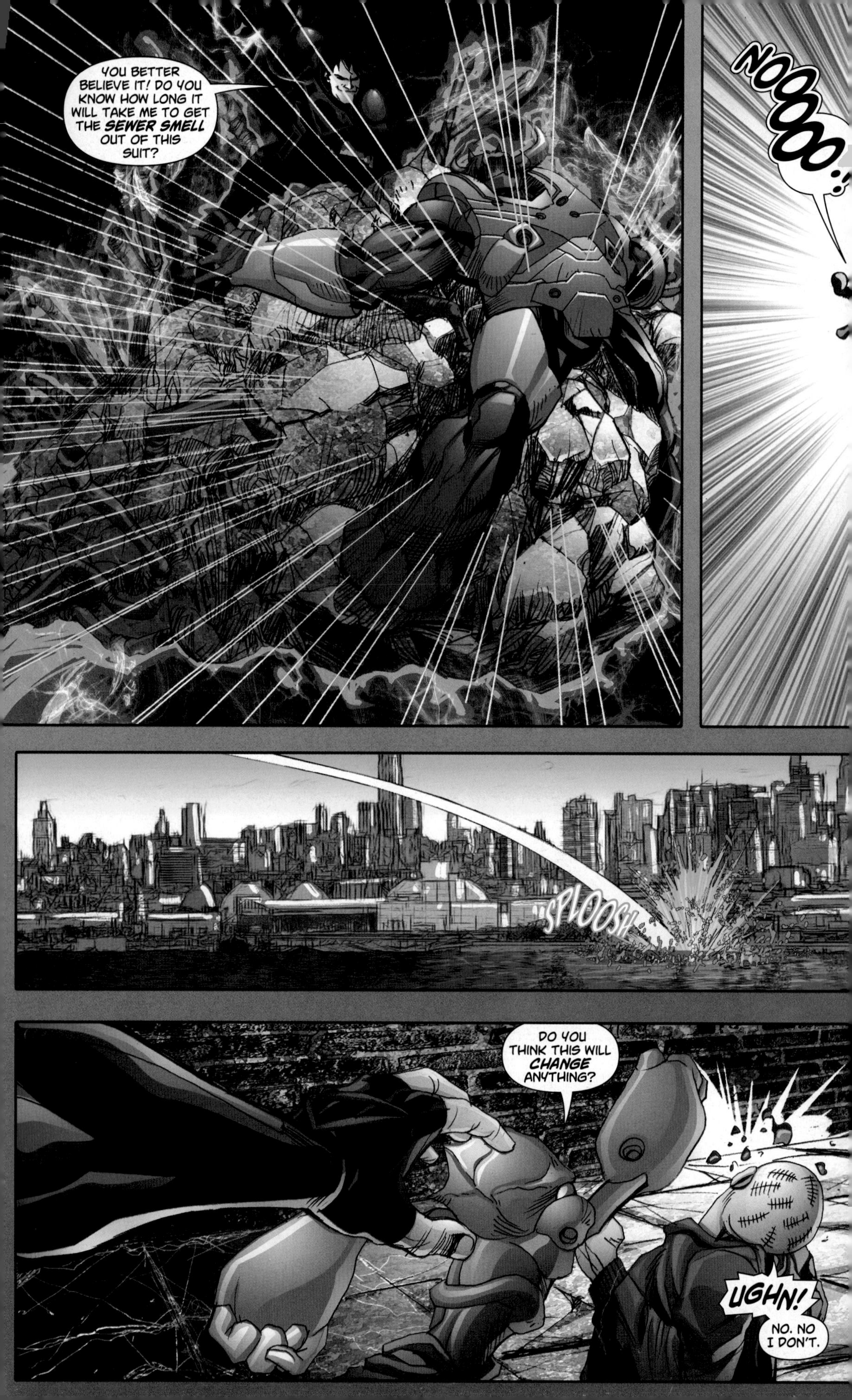
YOU BETTER BELIEVE IT! DO YOU KNOW HOW LONG IT WILL TAKE ME TO GET THE SEWER SMELL OUT OF THIS SUIT?
NOOOOOO..!
SPLOOSH
DO YOU THINK THIS WILL CHANGE ANYTHING?
UGHN!
NO. NO I DON'T.

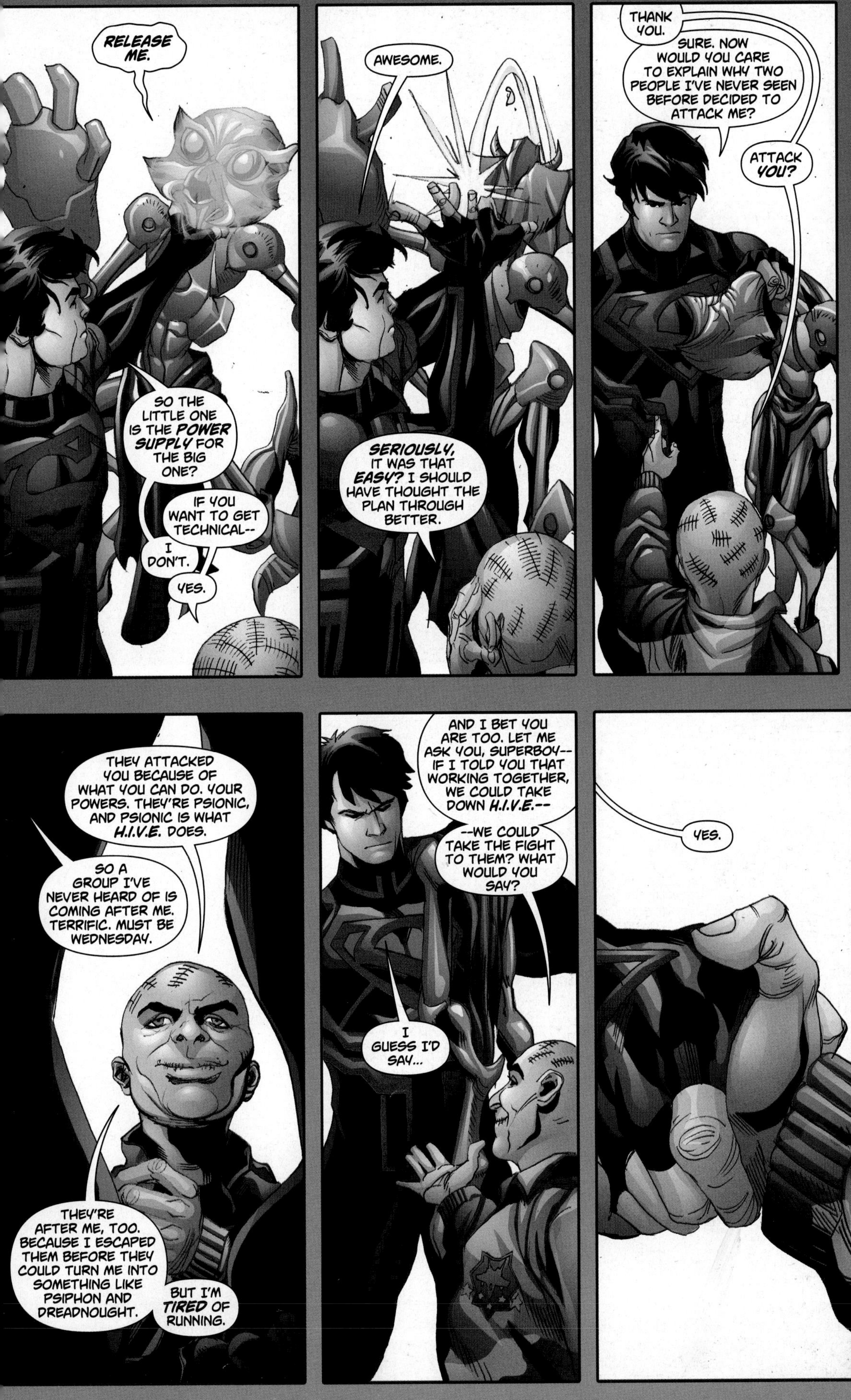
RELEASE ME.
SO THE LITTLE ONE IS THE POWER SUPPLY FOR THE BIG ONE?
IF YOU WANT TO GET TECHNICAL--
I DON'T.
YES.
AWESOME.
SERIOUSLY, IT WAS THAT EASY? I SHOULD HAVE THOUGHT THE PLAN THROUGH BETTER.
THANK YOU.
SURE. NOW WOULD YOU CARE TO EXPLAIN WHY TWO PEOPLE I'VE NEVER SEEN BEFORE DECIDED TO ATTACK ME?
ATTACK YOU?
THEY ATTACKED YOU BECAUSE OF WHAT YOU CAN DO. YOUR POWERS. THEY'RE PSIONIC, AND PSIONIC IS WHAT H.I.V.E. DOES.
SO A GROUP I'VE NEVER HEARD OF IS COMING AFTER ME. TERRIFIC. MUST BE WEDNESDAY.
THEY'RE AFTER ME, TOO. BECAUSE I ESCAPED THEM BEFORE THEY COULD TURN ME INTO SOMETHING LIKE PSIPHON AND DREADNOUGHT.
BUT I'M TIRED OF RUNNING.
AND I BET YOU ARE TOO. LET ME ASK YOU, SUPERBOY-- IF I TOLD YOU THAT WORKING TOGETHER, WE COULD TAKE DOWN H.I.V.E.--
--WE COULD TAKE THE FIGHT TO THEM? WHAT WOULD YOU SAY?
I GUESS I'D SAY...
YES.

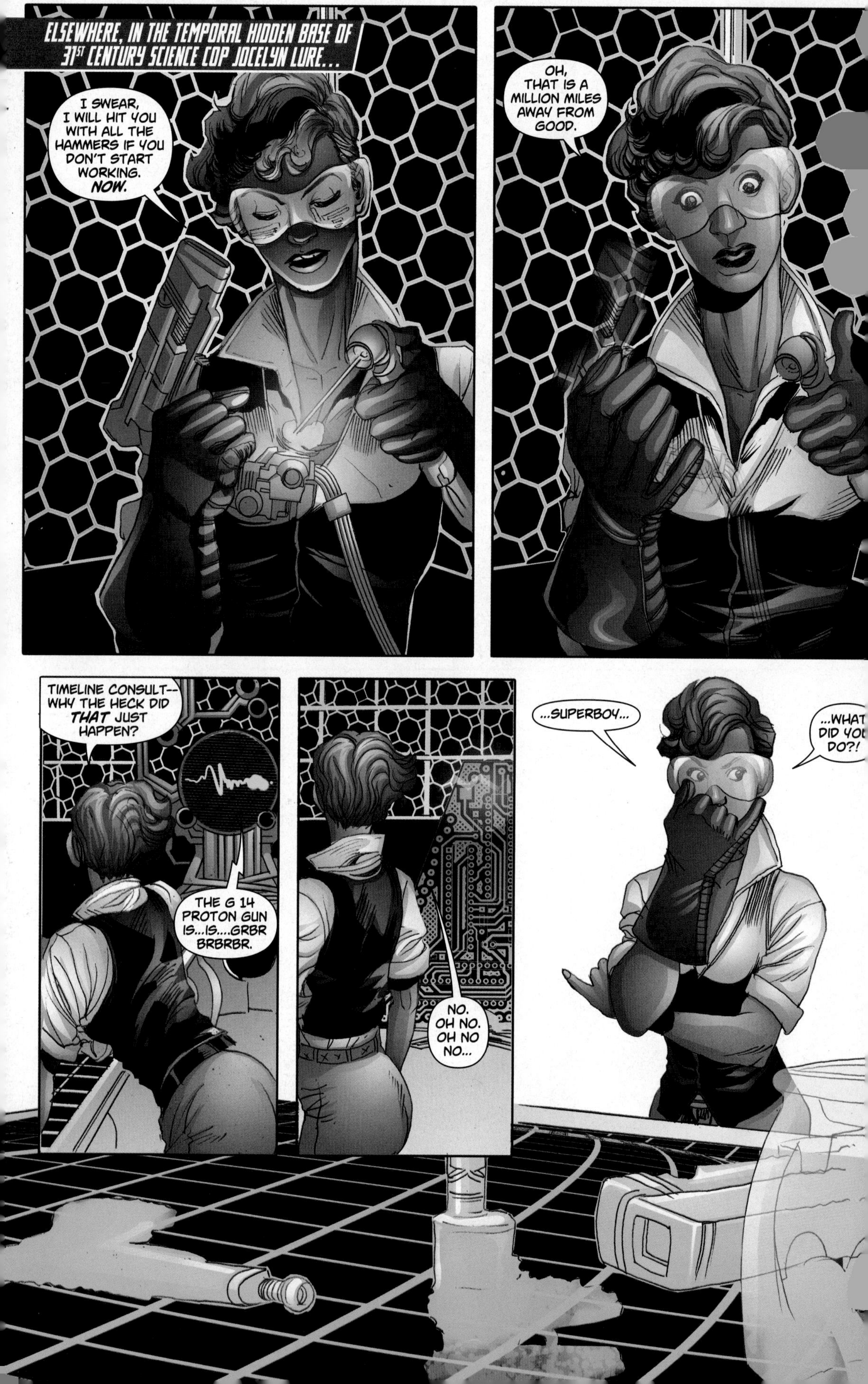
ELSEWHERE, IN THE TEMPORAL HIDDEN BASE OF 31ST CENTURY SCIENCE COP JOCELYN LURE...
I SWEAR, I WILL HIT YOU WITH ALL THE HAMMERS IF YOU DON'T START WORKING. NOW.
OH, THAT IS A MILLION MILES AWAY FROM GOOD.
TIMELINE CONSULT-- WHY THE HECK DID THAT JUST HAPPEN?
THE G 14 PROTON GUN IS...IS....GRBR BRBRBR.
NO. OH NO. OH NO NO...
...SUPERBOY...
...WHAT DID YOU DO?!

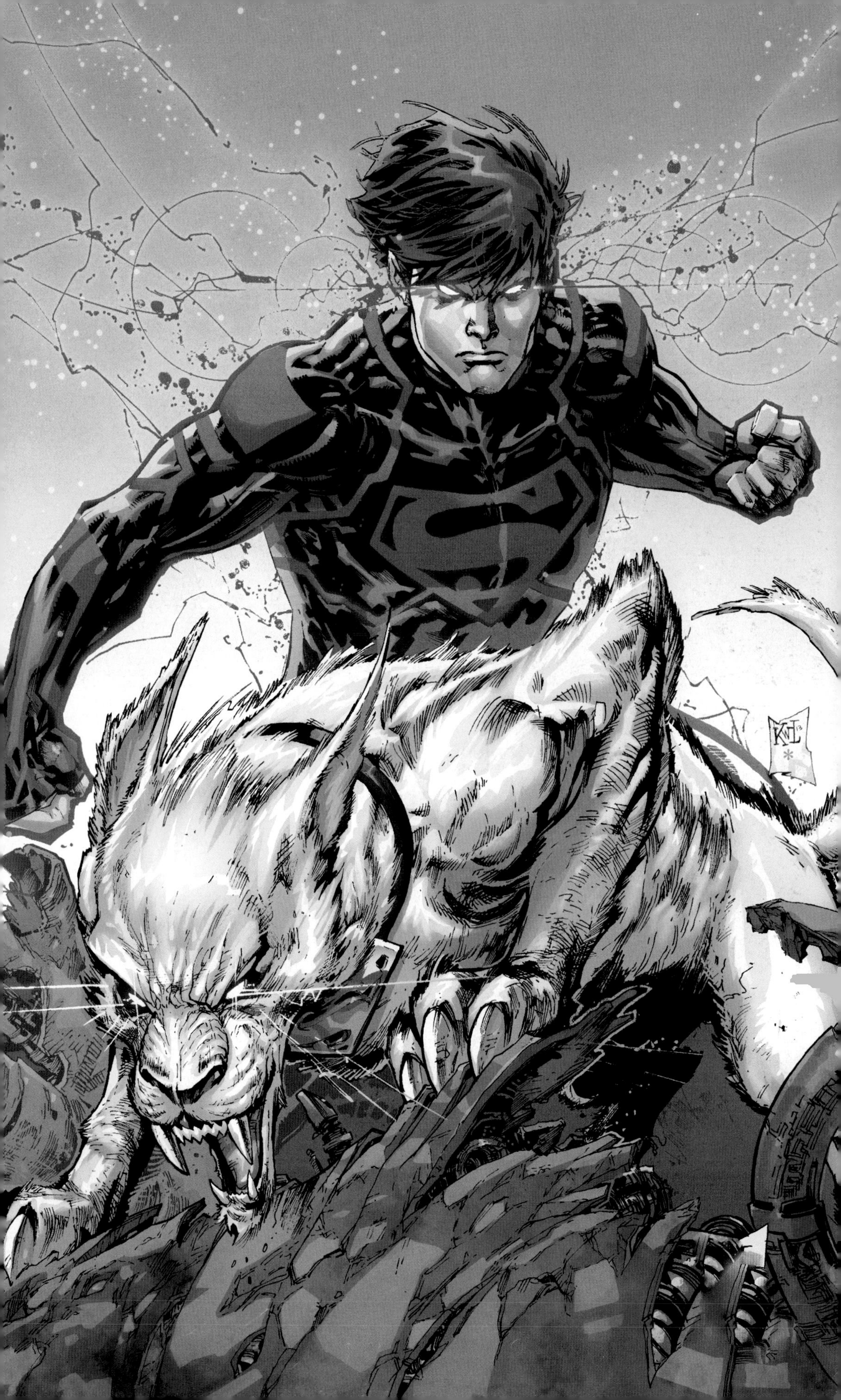

JUSTIN JORDAN writer R.B. SILVA EDGAR SALAZAR pencillers ROB LEAN DYM inkers cover art by KEN LASHLEY & MATT YACKEY

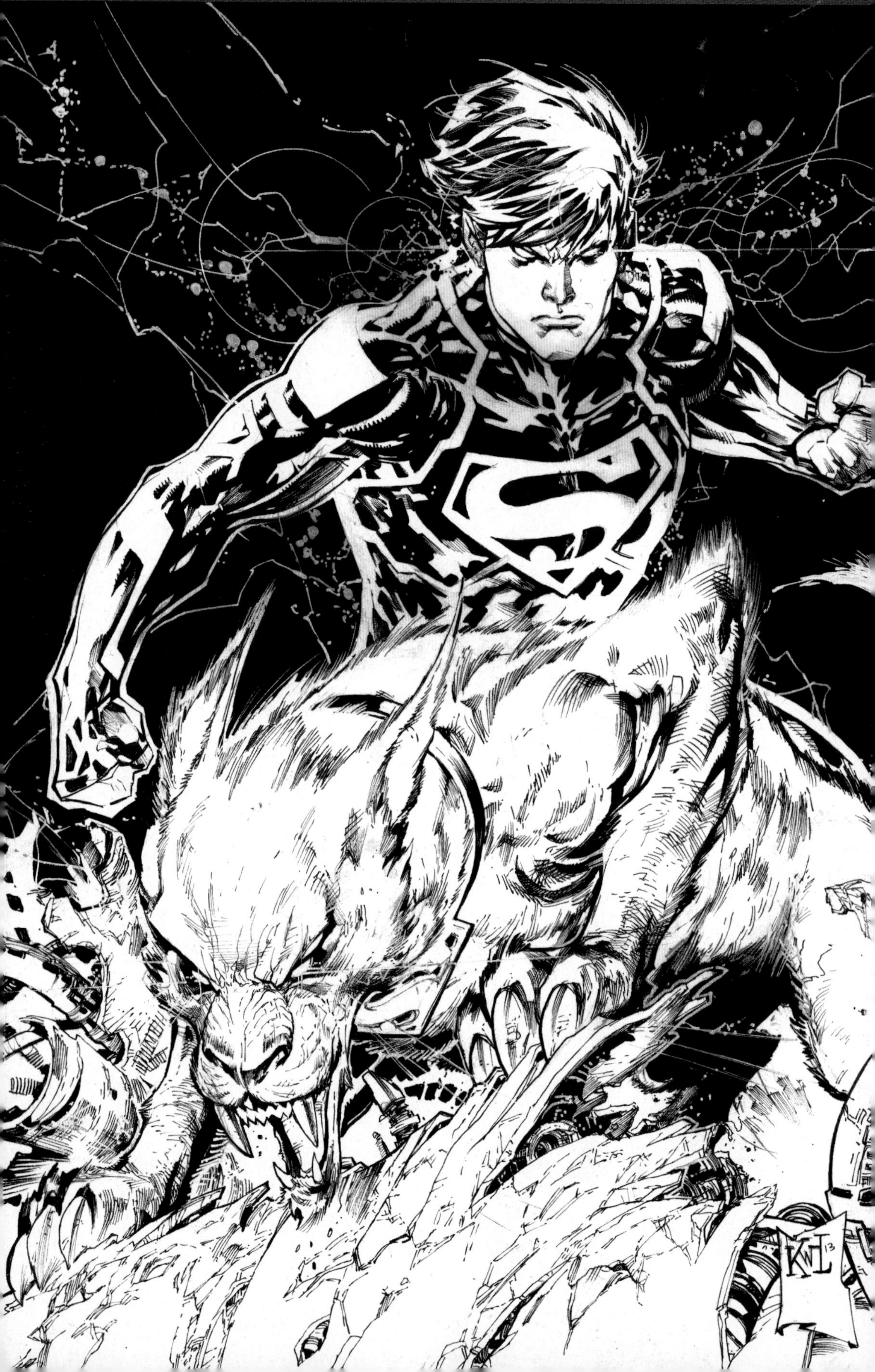

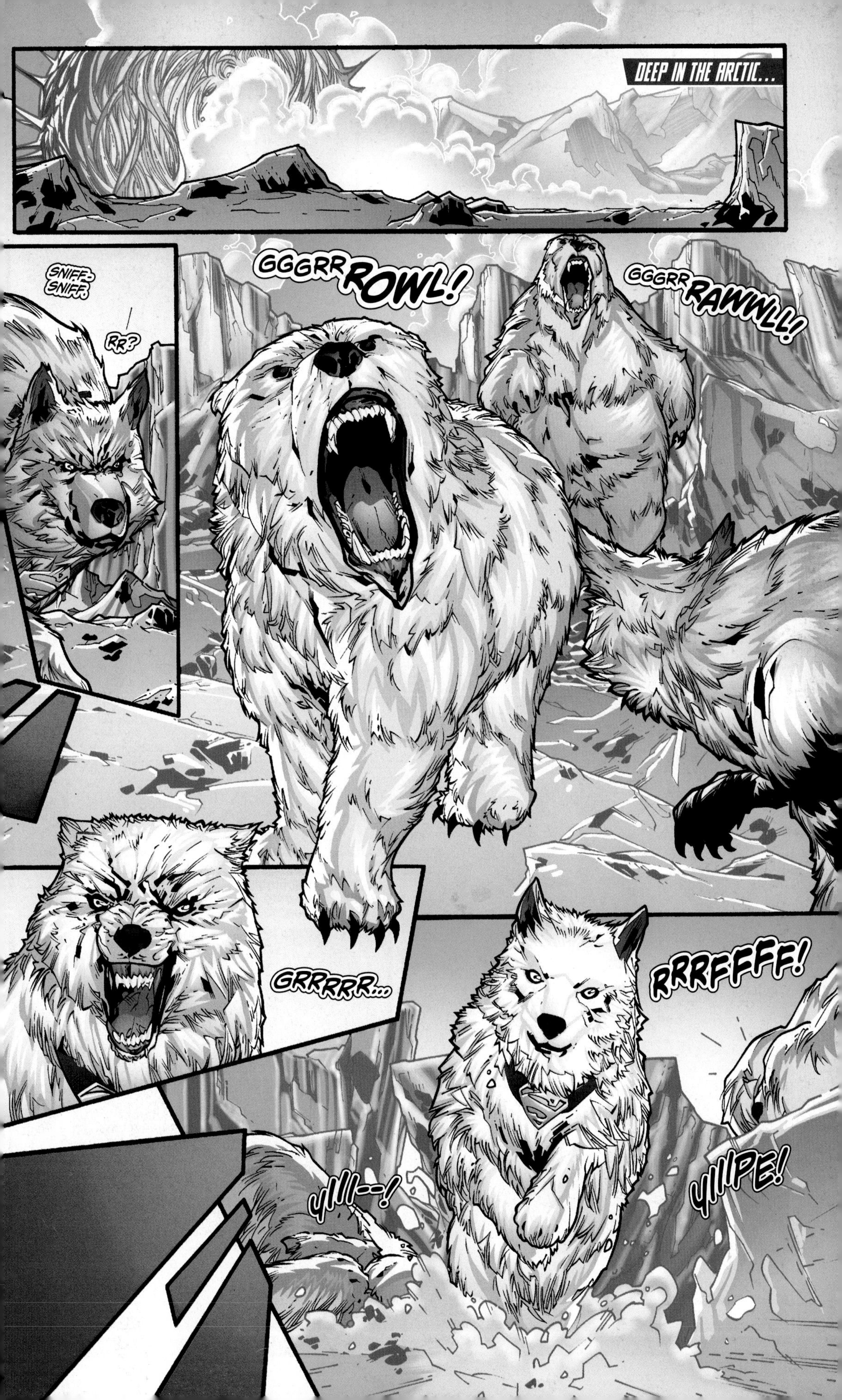
DEEP IN THE ARCTIC...
SNIFF-SNIFF.
RR?
GGGRRROWL!
GGGRRRAWWLL!
GRRRRR...
RRRFFFF!
YIIII--!
YIIIPE!

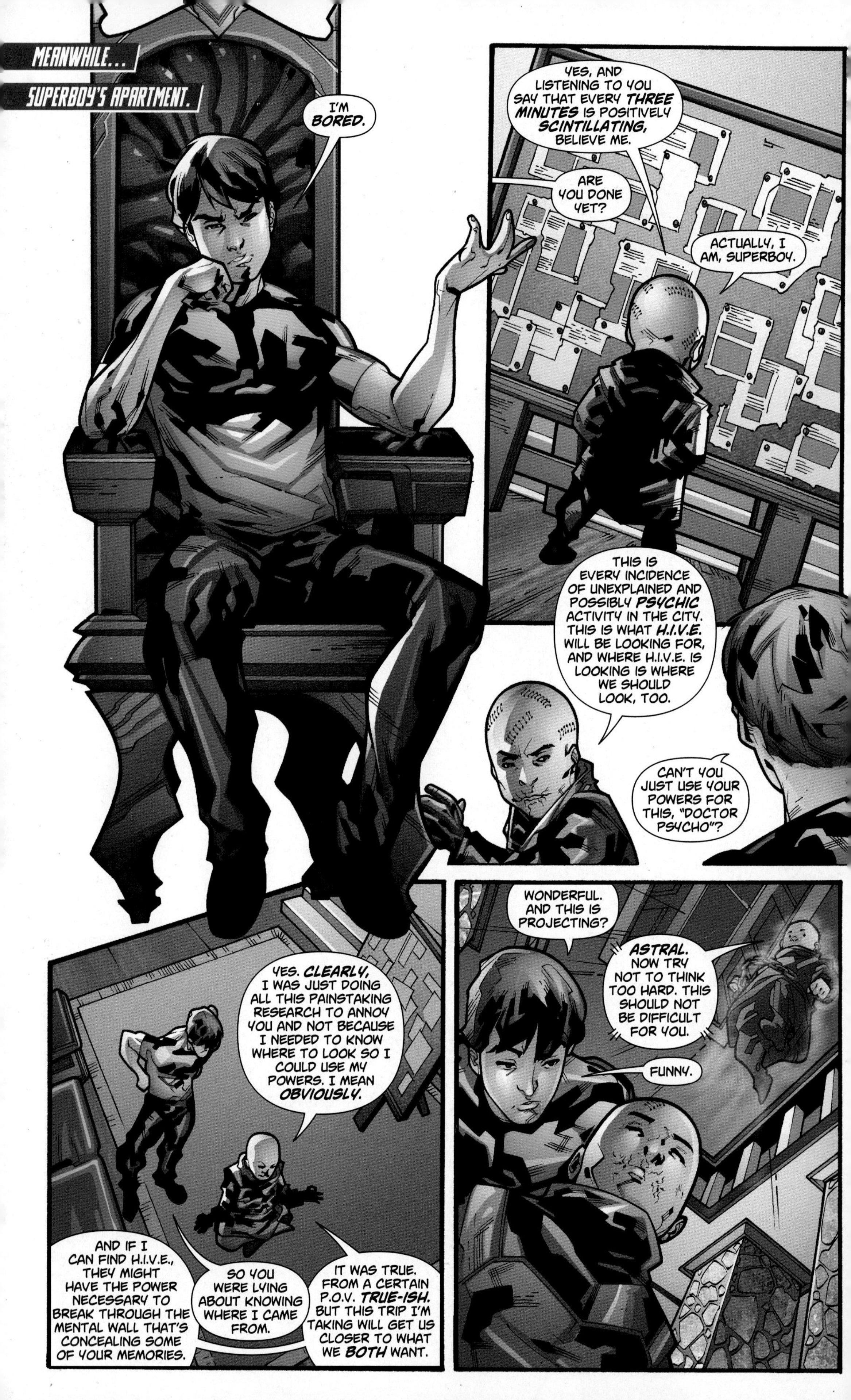
MEANWHILE...
SUPERBOY'S APARTMENT.
I'M BORED.
YES, AND LISTENING TO YOU SAY THAT EVERY THREE MINUTES IS POSITIVELY SCINTILLATING, BELIEVE ME.
ARE YOU DONE YET?
ACTUALLY, I AM, SUPERBOY.
THIS IS EVERY INCIDENCE OF UNEXPLAINED AND POSSIBLY PSYCHIC ACTIVITY IN THE CITY. THIS IS WHAT H.I.V.E. WILL BE LOOKING FOR, AND WHERE H.I.V.E. IS LOOKING IS WHERE WE SHOULD LOOK, TOO.
CAN'T YOU JUST USE YOUR POWERS FOR THIS, "DOCTOR PSYCHO"?
YES. CLEARLY, I WAS JUST DOING ALL THIS PAINSTAKING RESEARCH TO ANNOY YOU AND NOT BECAUSE I NEEDED TO KNOW WHERE TO LOOK SO I COULD USE MY POWERS. I MEAN OBVIOUSLY.
AND IF I CAN FIND H.I.V.E., THEY MIGHT HAVE THE POWER NECESSARY TO BREAK THROUGH THE MENTAL WALL THAT'S CONCEALING SOME OF YOUR MEMORIES.
SO YOU WERE LYING ABOUT KNOWING WHERE I CAME FROM.
IT WAS TRUE. FROM A CERTAIN P.O.V. TRUE-ISH. BUT THIS TRIP I'M TAKING WILL GET US CLOSER TO WHAT WE BOTH WANT.
WONDERFUL. AND THIS IS PROJECTING?
ASTRAL. NOW TRY NOT TO THINK TOO HARD. THIS SHOULD NOT BE DIFFICULT FOR YOU.
FUNNY.

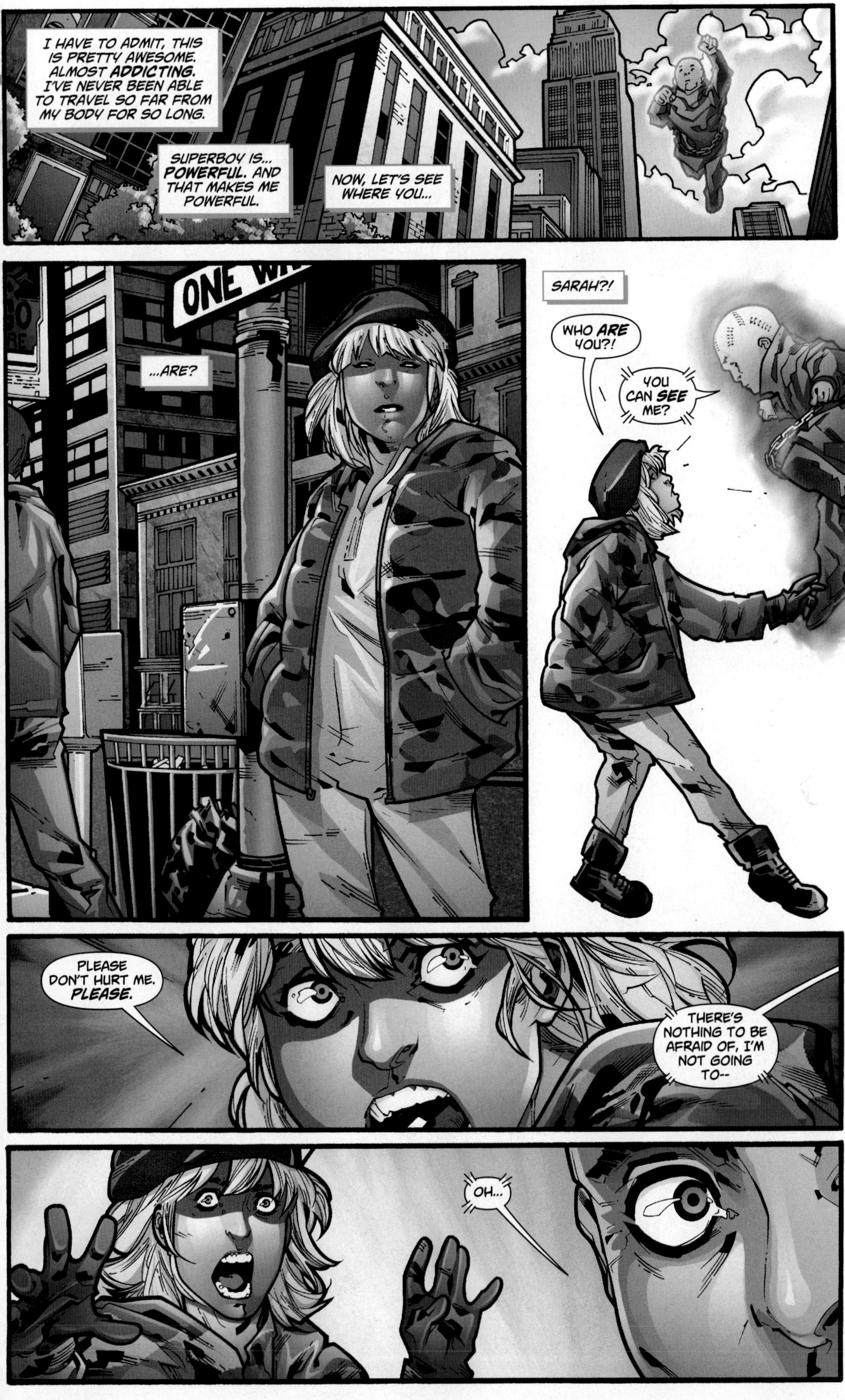
I HAVE TO ADMIT, THIS IS PRETTY AWESOME. ALMOST ADDICTING. I'VE NEVER BEEN ABLE TO TRAVEL SO FAR FROM MY BODY FOR SO LONG.
SUPERBOY IS... POWERFUL. AND THAT MAKES ME POWERFUL.
NOW, LET'S SEE WHERE YOU...
ONE WA
...ARE?
SARAH?!
WHO ARE YOU?!
YOU CAN SEE ME?
PLEASE DON'T HURT ME. PLEASE.
THERE'S NOTHING TO BE AFRAID OF, I'M NOT GOING TO--
OH...

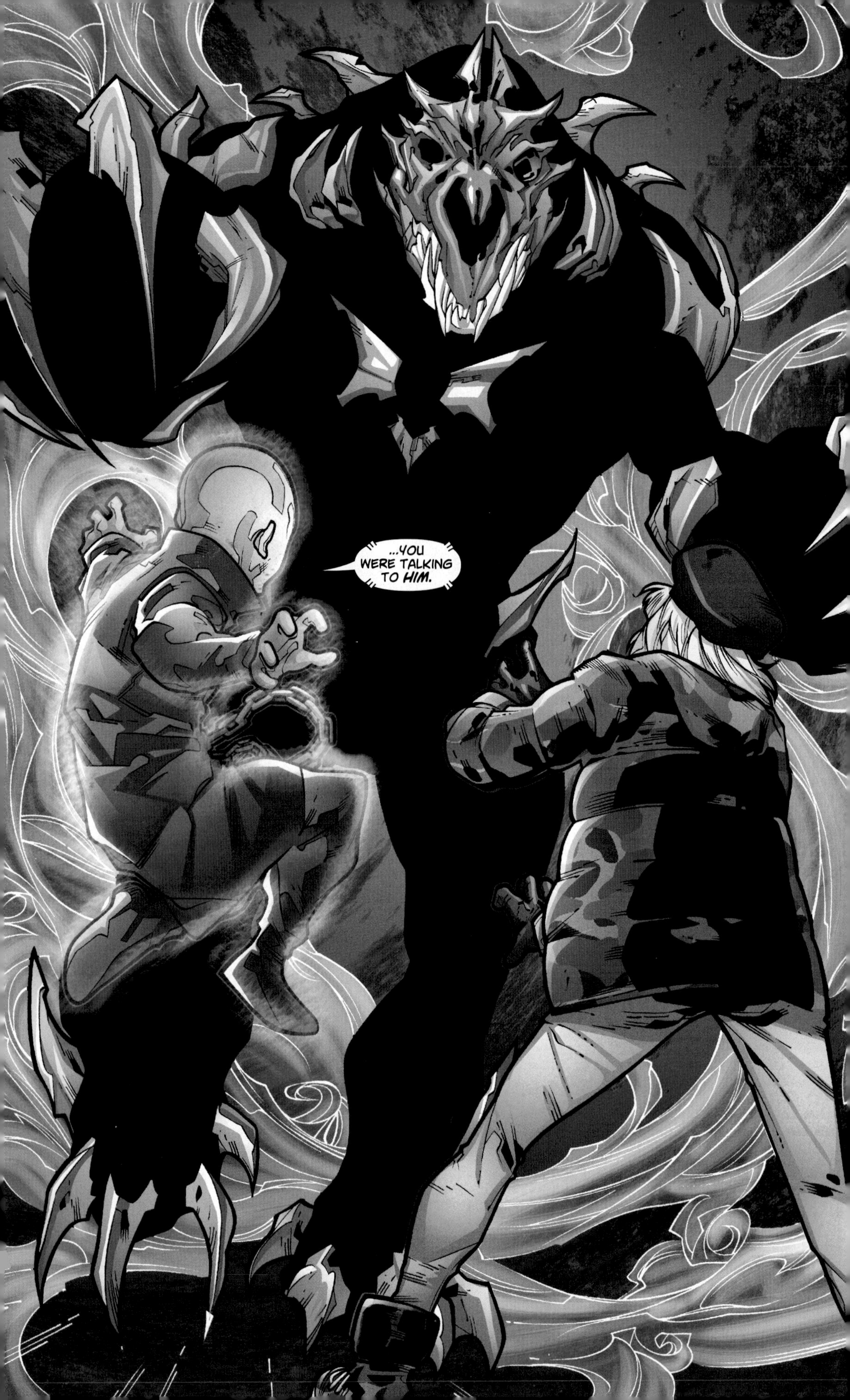
...YOU WERE TALKING TO HIM.

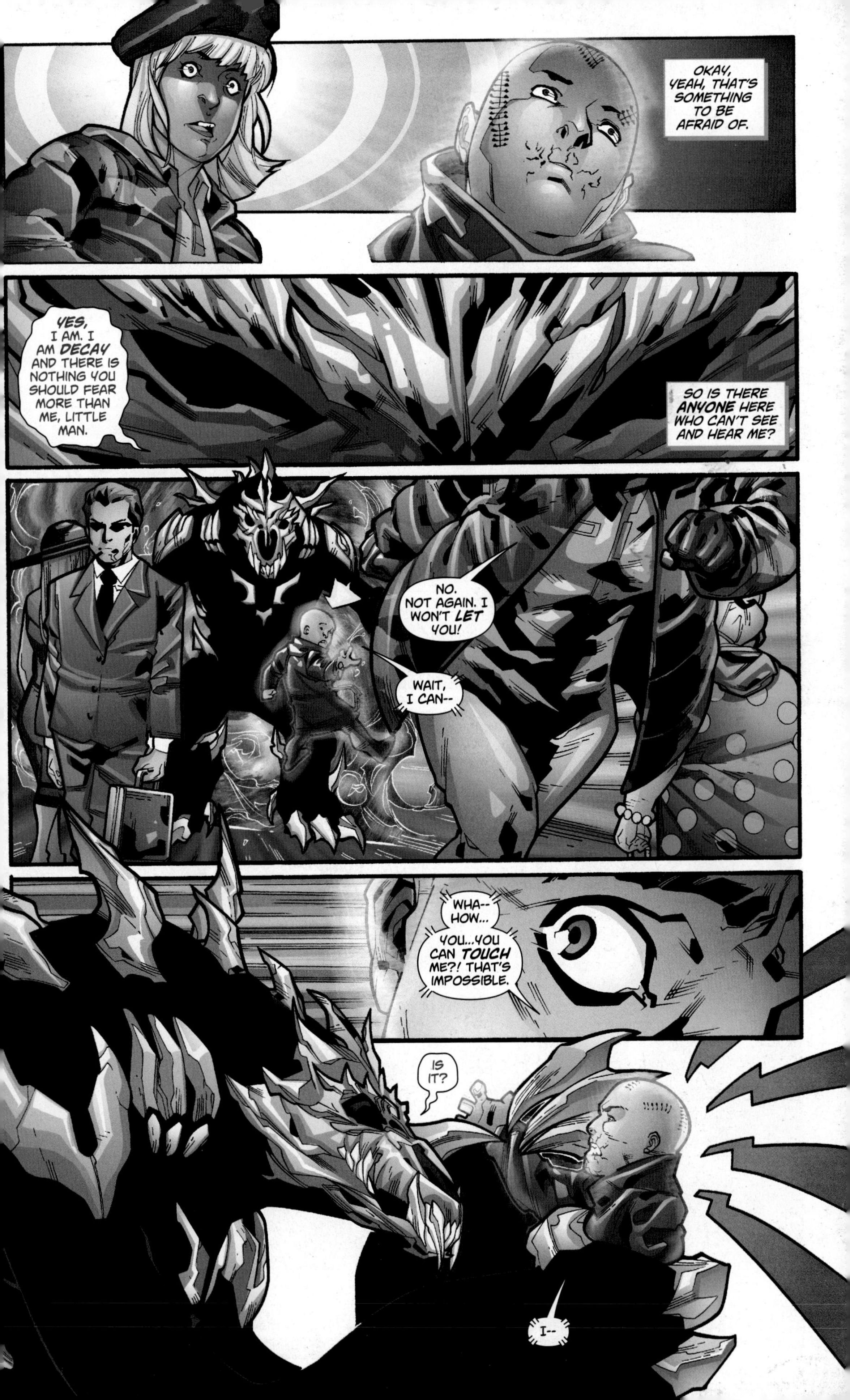
OKAY, YEAH, THAT'S SOMETHING TO BE AFRAID OF.
YES, I AM. I AM DECAY AND THERE IS NOTHING YOU SHOULD FEAR MORE THAN ME, LITTLE MAN.
SO IS THERE ANYONE HERE WHO CAN'T SEE AND HEAR ME?
NO. NOT AGAIN. I WON'T LET YOU!
WAIT, I CAN--
WHA-- HOW...
YOU...YOU CAN TOUCH ME?! THAT'S IMPOSSIBLE.
IS IT?
I--

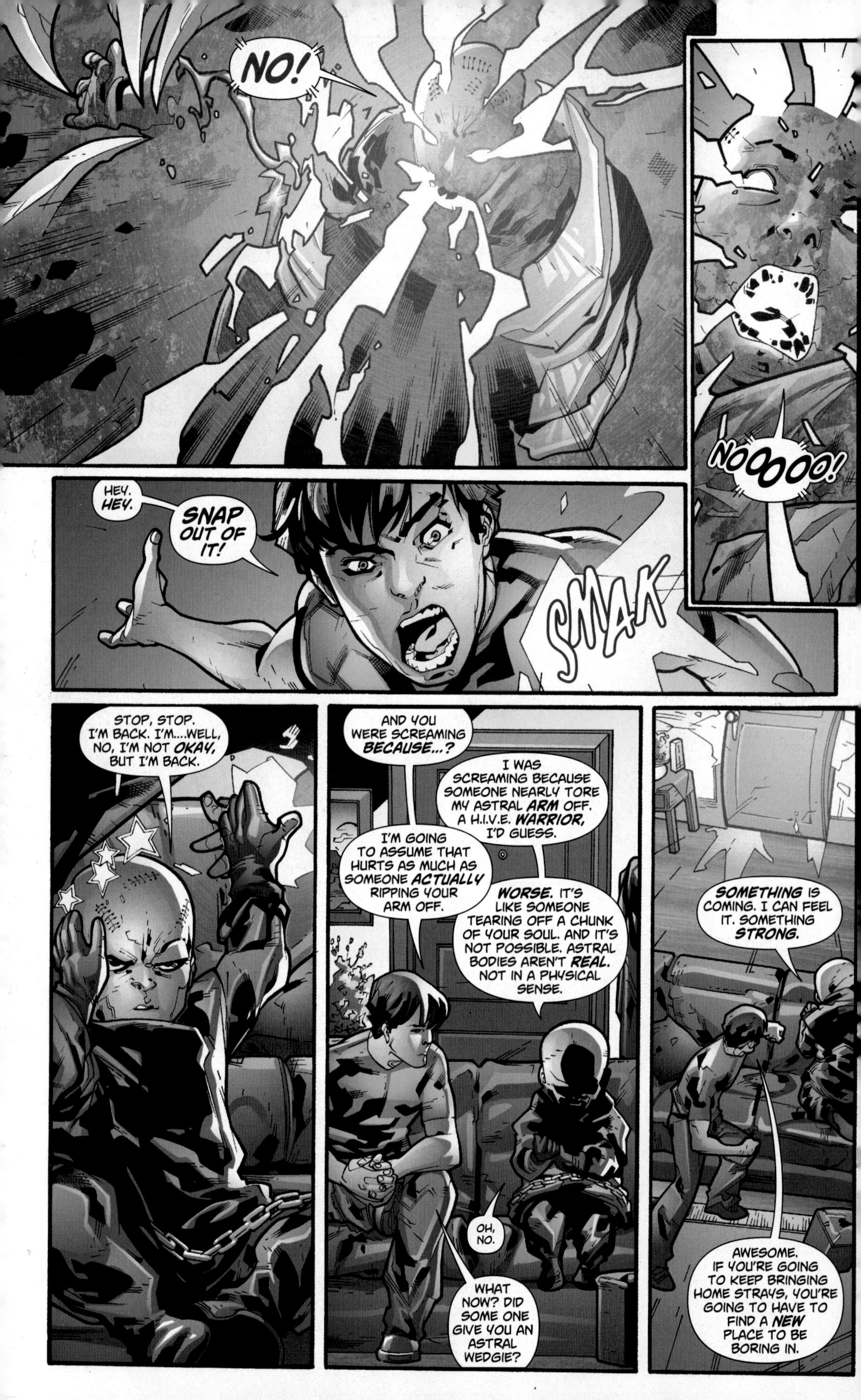
NO!
NOOOOO!
HEY. HEY.
SNAP OUT OF IT!
SMAK
STOP, STOP. I'M BACK. I'M....WELL, NO, I'M NOT OKAY, BUT I'M BACK.
AND YOU WERE SCREAMING BECAUSE...?
I WAS SCREAMING BECAUSE SOMEONE NEARLY TORE MY ASTRAL ARM OFF. A H.I.V.E. WARRIOR, I'D GUESS.
I'M GOING TO ASSUME THAT HURTS AS MUCH AS SOMEONE ACTUALLY RIPPING YOUR ARM OFF.
WORSE. IT'S LIKE SOMEONE TEARING OFF A CHUNK OF YOUR SOUL. AND IT'S NOT POSSIBLE. ASTRAL BODIES AREN'T REAL. NOT IN A PHYSICAL SENSE.
OH, NO.
WHAT NOW? DID SOME ONE GIVE YOU AN ASTRAL WEDGIE?
SOMETHING IS COMING. I CAN FEEL IT. SOMETHING STRONG.
AWESOME. IF YOU'RE GOING TO KEEP BRINGING HOME STRAYS, YOU'RE GOING TO HAVE TO FIND A NEW PLACE TO BE BORING IN.

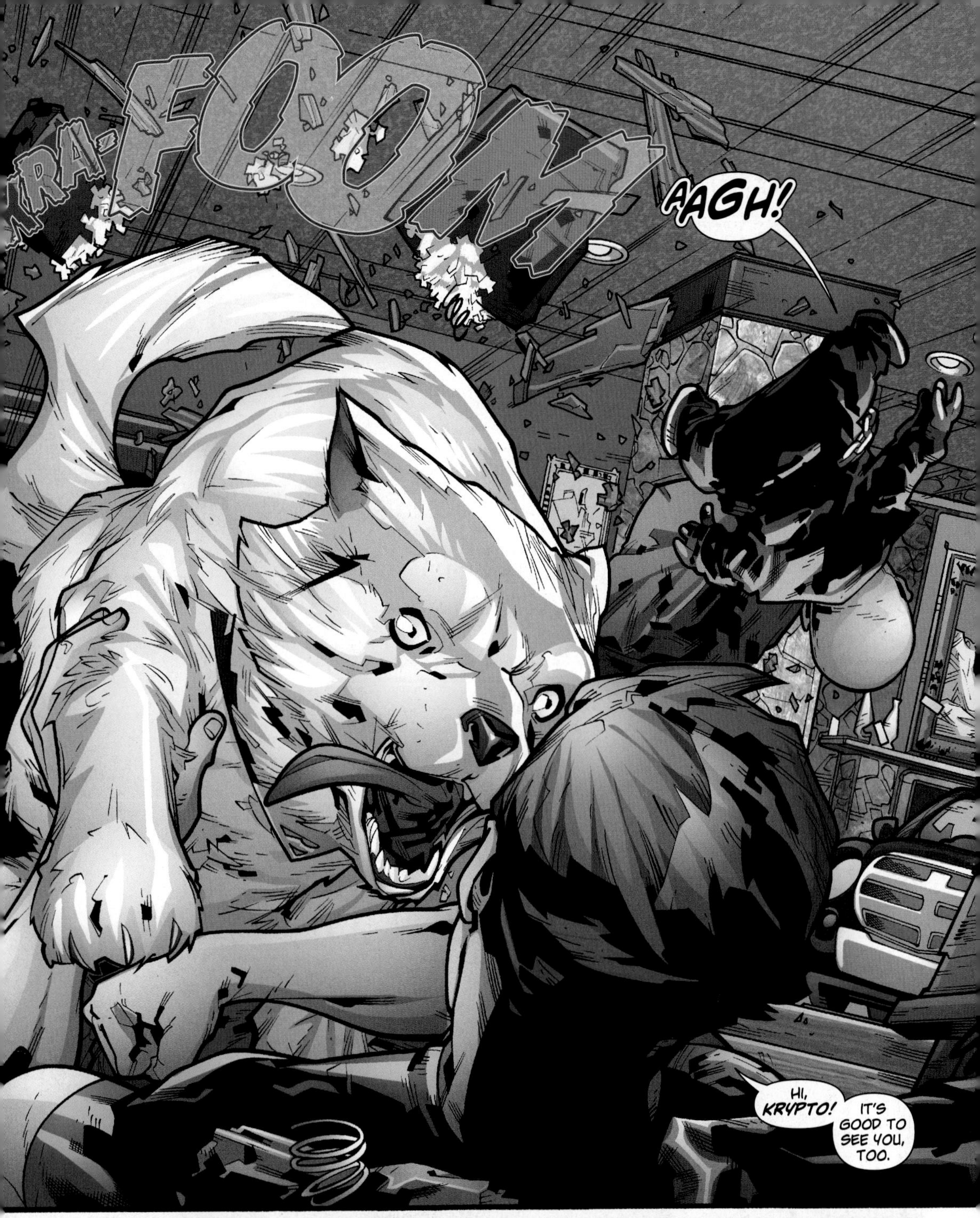
KRA-FOOM
AAGH!
HI, KRYPTO! IT'S GOOD TO SEE YOU, TOO.

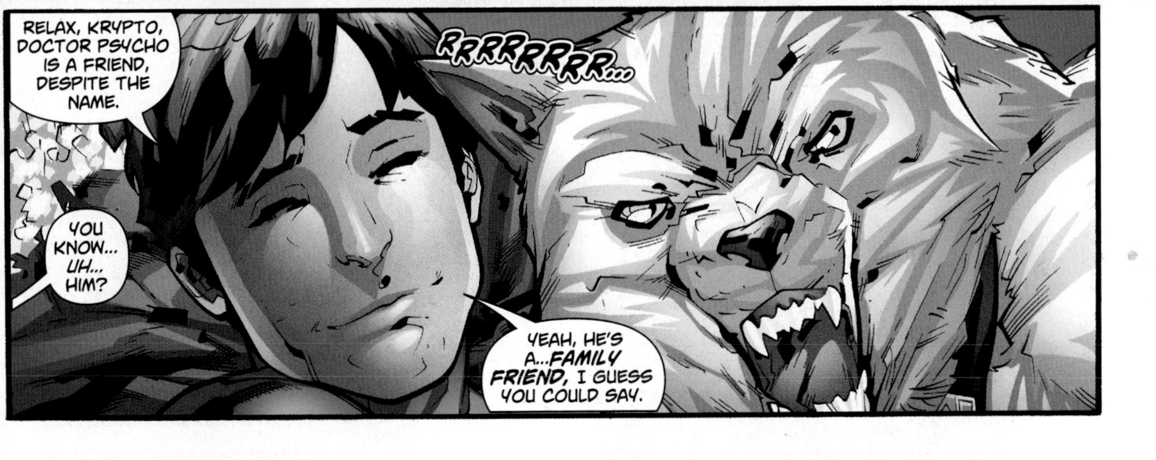
RELAX, KRYPTO, DOCTOR PSYCHO IS A FRIEND, DESPITE THE NAME.
RRRRRRRRR...
YOU KNOW... UH... HIM?
YEAH, HE'S A...FAMILY FRIEND, I GUESS YOU COULD SAY.

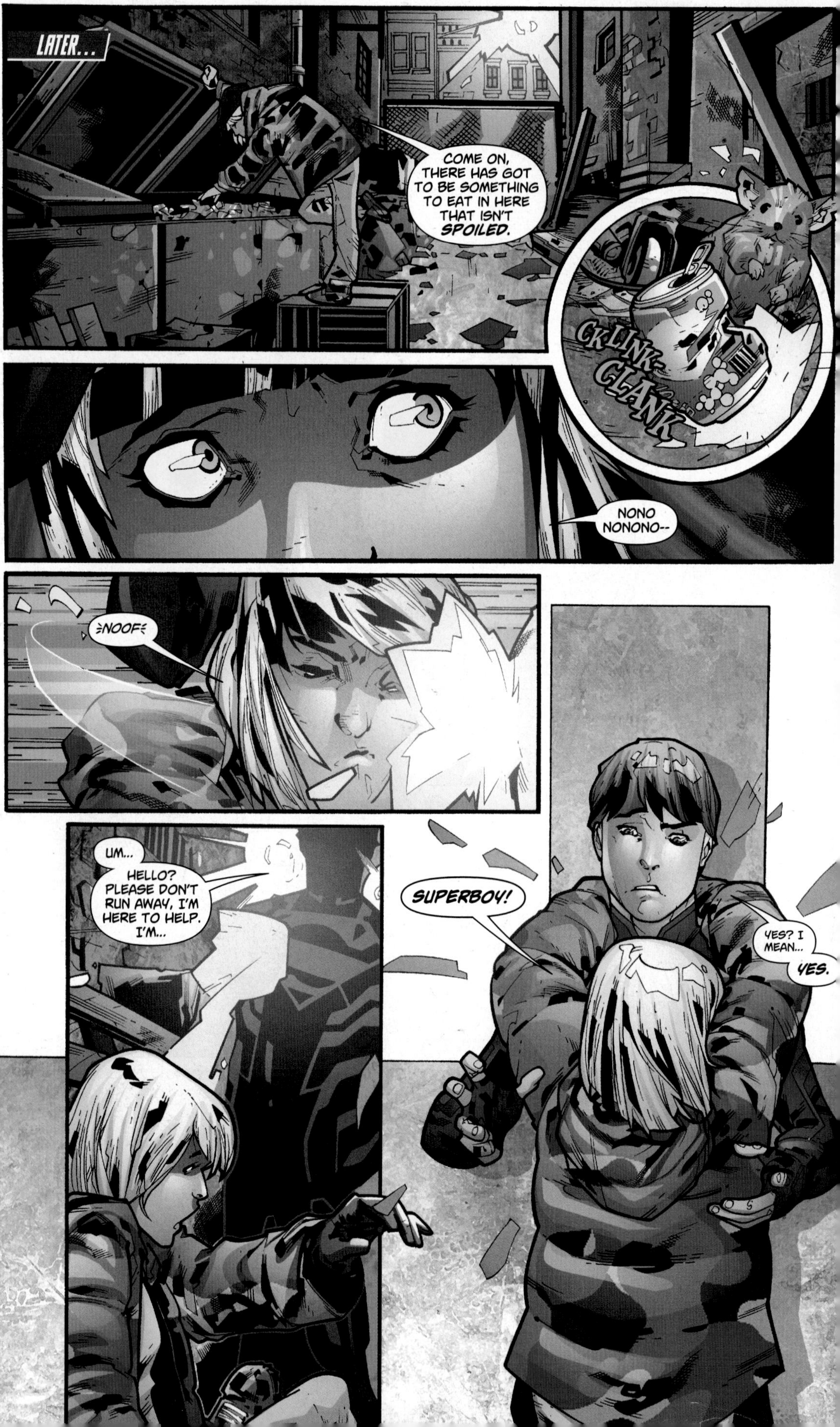
LATER...
COME ON, THERE HAS GOT TO BE SOMETHING TO EAT IN HERE THAT ISN'T SPOILED.
CKLINK-CLANK
NONO NONONO--
NOOF
UM... HELLO? PLEASE DON'T RUN AWAY, I'M HERE TO HELP. I'M...
SUPERBOY!
YES? I MEAN... YES.

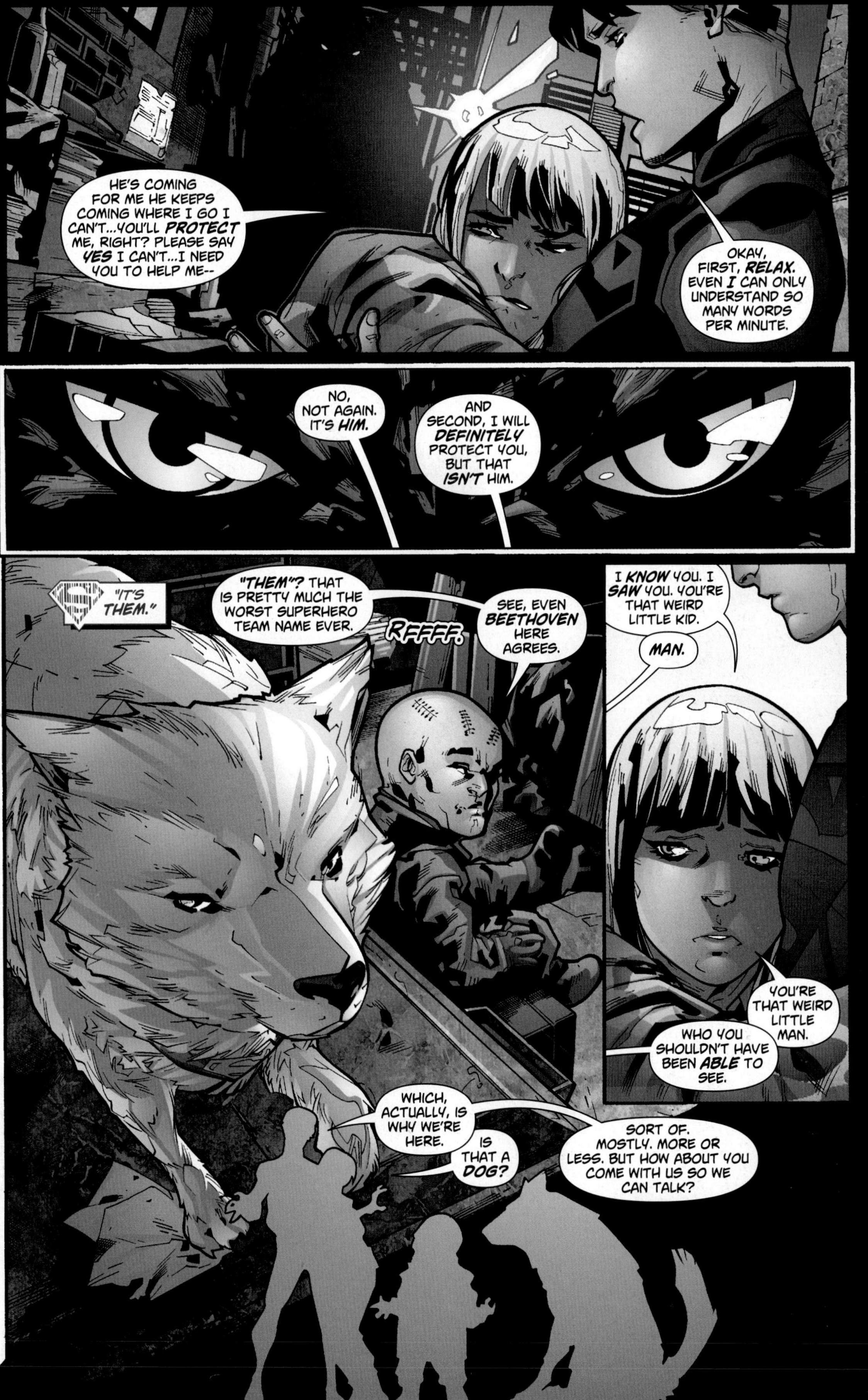

HE'S COMING FOR ME HE KEEPS COMING WHERE I GO I CAN'T...YOU'LL PROTECT ME, RIGHT? PLEASE SAY YES I CAN'T...I NEED YOU TO HELP ME--
OKAY, FIRST, RELAX. EVEN I CAN ONLY UNDERSTAND SO MANY WORDS PER MINUTE.
NO, NOT AGAIN. IT'S HIM.
AND SECOND, I WILL DEFINITELY PROTECT YOU, BUT THAT ISN'T HIM.
"IT'S THEM."
"THEM"? THAT IS PRETTY MUCH THE WORST SUPERHERO TEAM NAME EVER.
RFFFF.
SEE, EVEN BEETHOVEN HERE AGREES.
I KNOW YOU. I SAW YOU. YOU'RE THAT WEIRD LITTLE KID.
MAN.
YOU'RE THAT WEIRD LITTLE MAN.
WHO YOU SHOULDN'T HAVE BEEN ABLE TO SEE.
WHICH, ACTUALLY, IS WHY WE'RE HERE.
IS THAT A DOG?
SORT OF. MOSTLY. MORE OR LESS. BUT HOW ABOUT YOU COME WITH US SO WE CAN TALK?

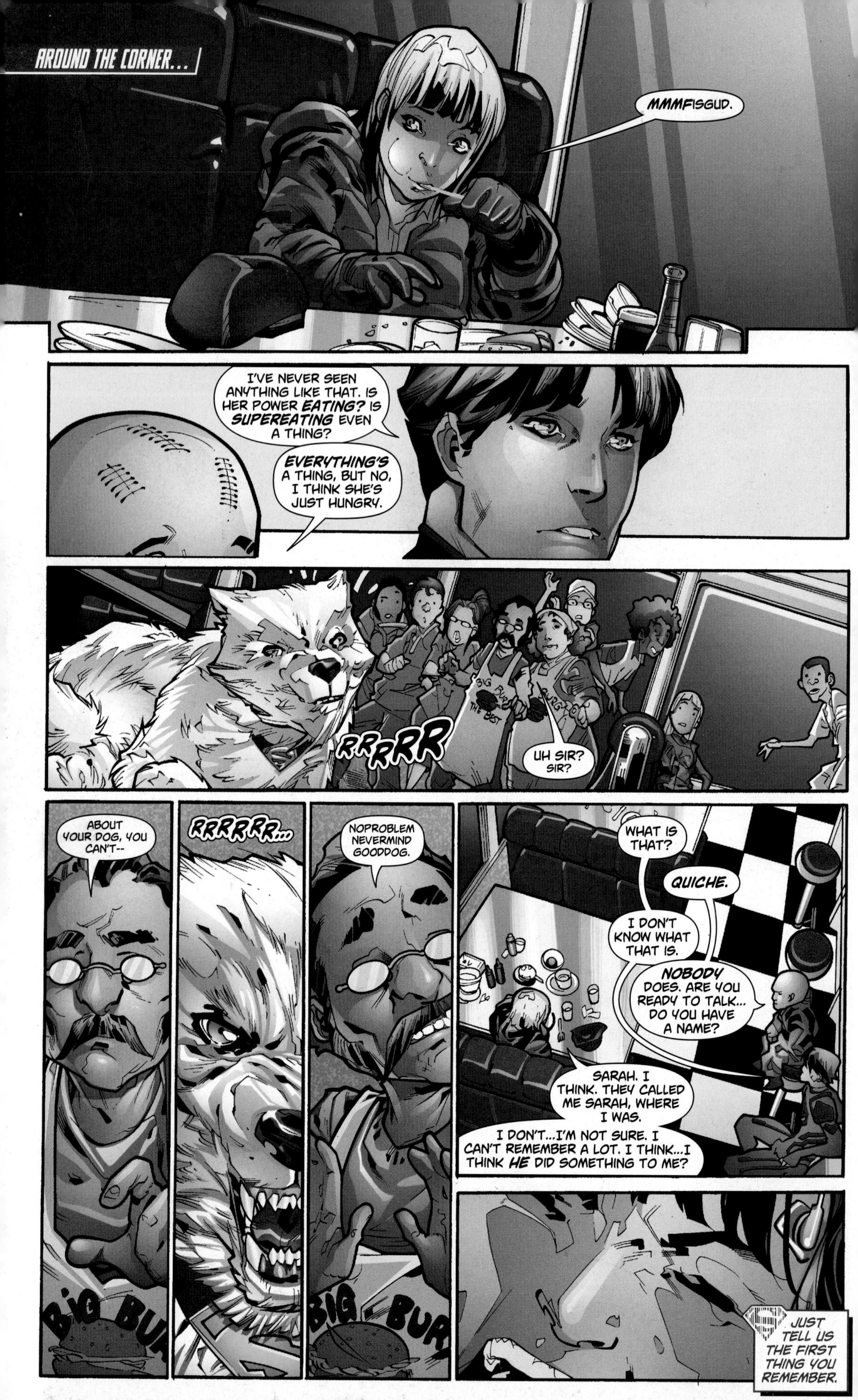
AROUND THE CORNER...
MMMFISGUD.
I'VE NEVER SEEN ANYTHING LIKE THAT. IS HER POWER EATING? IS SUPEREATING EVEN A THING?
EVERYTHING'S A THING, BUT NO, I THINK SHE'S JUST HUNGRY.
BIG BUR THE BEST
BURG
RRRRR
UH SIR? SIR?
ABOUT YOUR DOG, YOU CAN'T--
RRRRRR...
NOPROBLEM NEVERMIND GOODDOG.
WHAT IS THAT?
QUICHE.
I DON'T KNOW WHAT THAT IS.
NOBODY DOES. ARE YOU READY TO TALK... DO YOU HAVE A NAME?
SARAH. I THINK. THEY CALLED ME SARAH, WHERE I WAS.
I DON'T...I'M NOT SURE. I CAN'T REMEMBER A LOT. I THINK...I THINK HE DID SOMETHING TO ME?
BIG BUR
BIG BUR
JUST TELL US THE FIRST THING YOU REMEMBER.

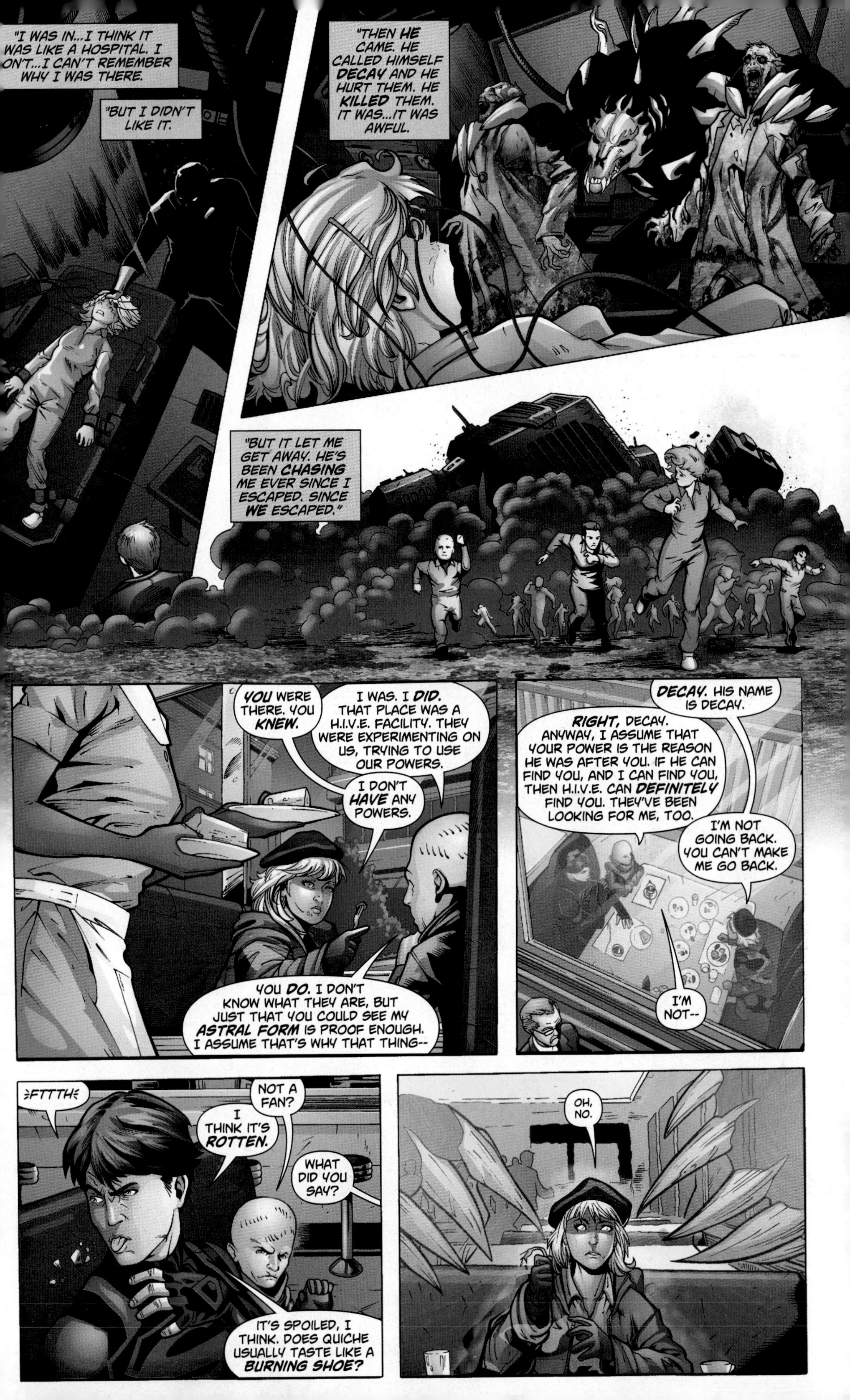
"I WAS IN...I THINK IT WAS LIKE A HOSPITAL. I DON'T...I CAN'T REMEMBER WHY I WAS THERE.
"BUT I DIDN'T LIKE IT.
"THEN HE CAME. HE CALLED HIMSELF DECAY AND HE HURT THEM. HE KILLED THEM. IT WAS...IT WAS AWFUL.
"BUT IT LET ME GET AWAY. HE'S BEEN CHASING ME EVER SINCE I ESCAPED. SINCE WE ESCAPED."
YOU WERE THERE. YOU KNEW.
I WAS. I DID. THAT PLACE WAS A H.I.V.E. FACILITY. THEY WERE EXPERIMENTING ON US, TRYING TO USE OUR POWERS.
I DON'T HAVE ANY POWERS.
YOU DO. I DON'T KNOW WHAT THEY ARE, BUT JUST THAT YOU COULD SEE MY ASTRAL FORM IS PROOF ENOUGH. I ASSUME THAT'S WHY THAT THING--
DECAY. HIS NAME IS DECAY.
RIGHT, DECAY. ANYWAY, I ASSUME THAT YOUR POWER IS THE REASON HE WAS AFTER YOU. IF HE CAN FIND YOU, AND I CAN FIND YOU, THEN H.I.V.E. CAN DEFINITELY FIND YOU. THEY'VE BEEN LOOKING FOR ME, TOO.
I'M NOT GOING BACK. YOU CAN'T MAKE ME GO BACK.
I'M NOT--
FTTTH
NOT A FAN?
I THINK IT'S ROTTEN.
WHAT DID YOU SAY?
IT'S SPOILED, I THINK. DOES QUICHE USUALLY TASTE LIKE A BURNING SHOE?
OH, NO.

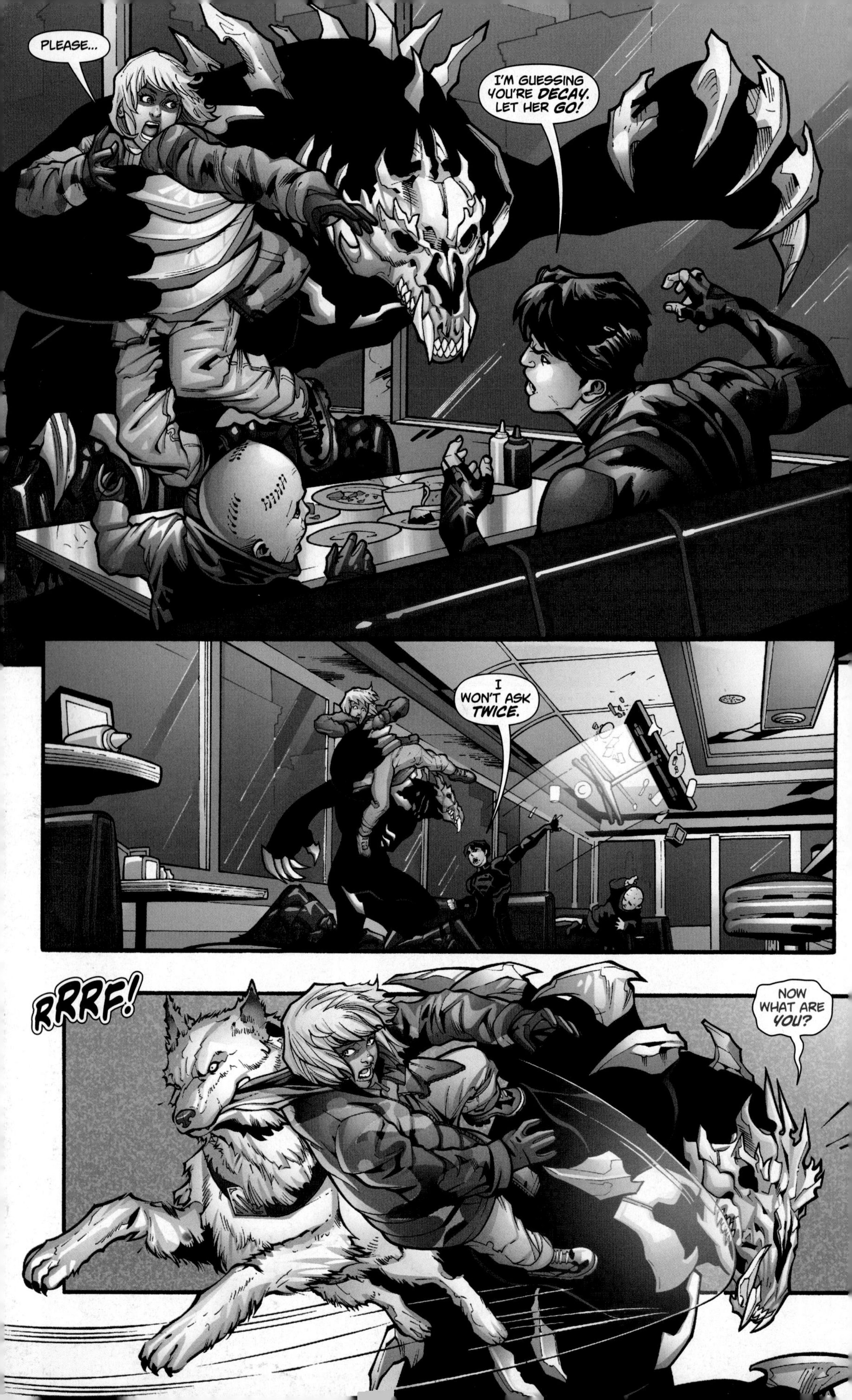
PLEASE...
I'M GUESSING YOU'RE DECAY. LET HER GO!
I WON'T ASK TWICE.
RRRF!
NOW WHAT ARE YOU?

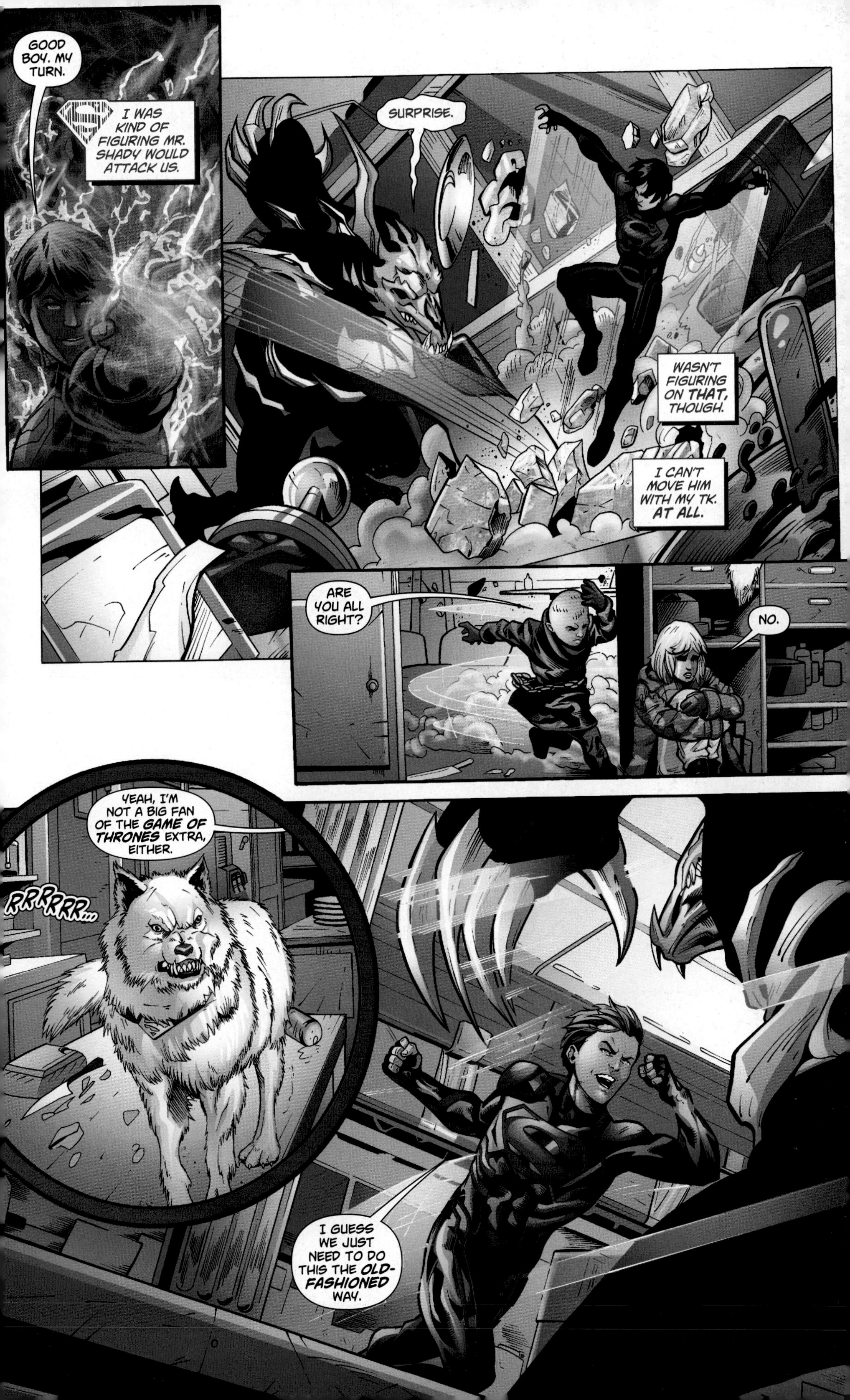
GOOD BOY. MY TURN.
I WAS KIND OF FIGURING MR. SHADY WOULD ATTACK US.
SURPRISE.
WASN'T FIGURING ON THAT, THOUGH.
I CAN'T MOVE HIM WITH MY TK. AT ALL.
ARE YOU ALL RIGHT?
NO.
YEAH, I'M NOT A BIG FAN OF THE GAME OF THRONES EXTRA, EITHER.
RRRRRR...
I GUESS WE JUST NEED TO DO THIS THE OLD-FASHIONED WAY.

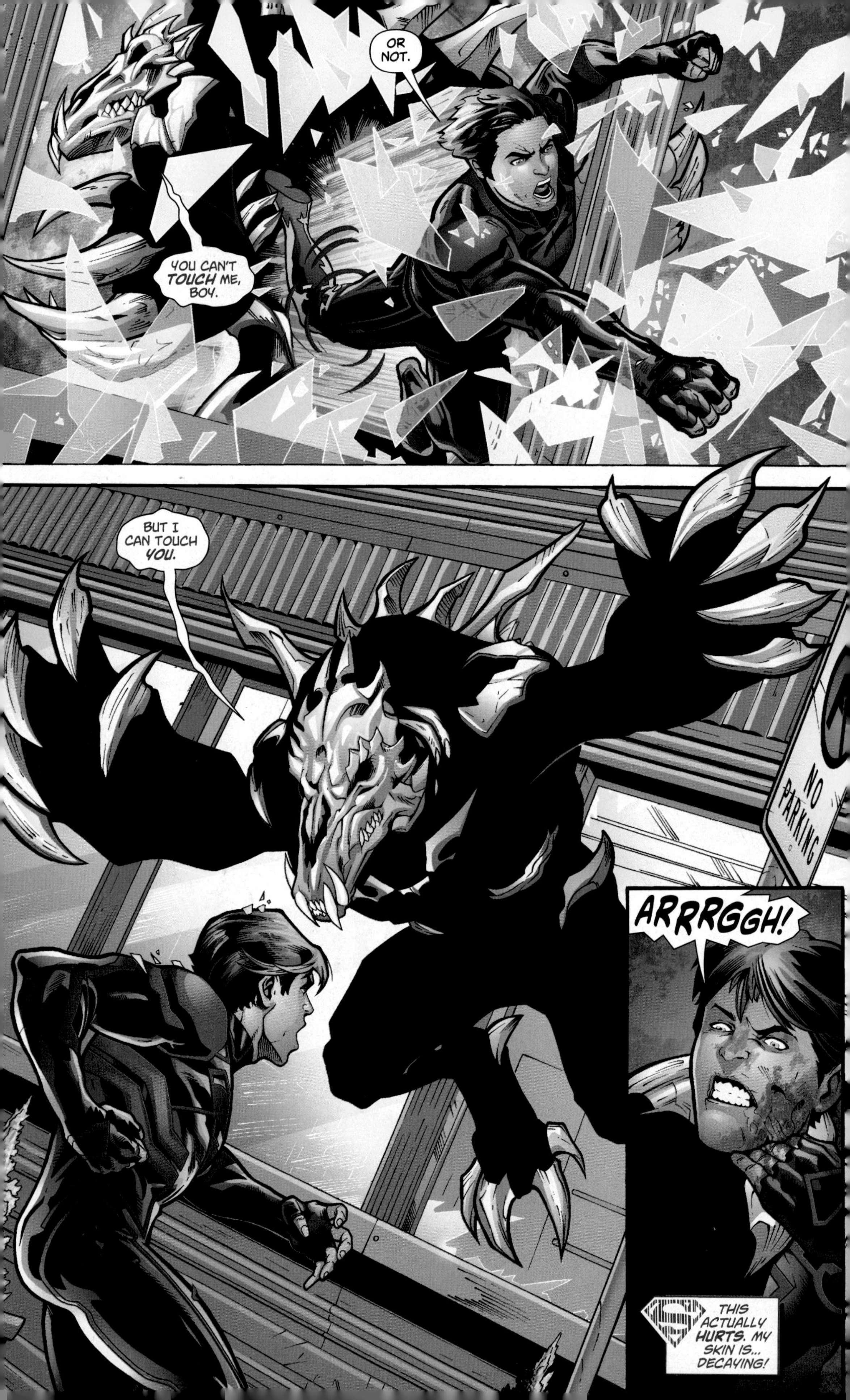
OR NOT.
YOU CAN'T TOUCH ME, BOY.
BUT I CAN TOUCH YOU.
NO PARKING
ARRRGGH!
THIS ACTUALLY HURTS. MY SKIN IS... DECAYING!

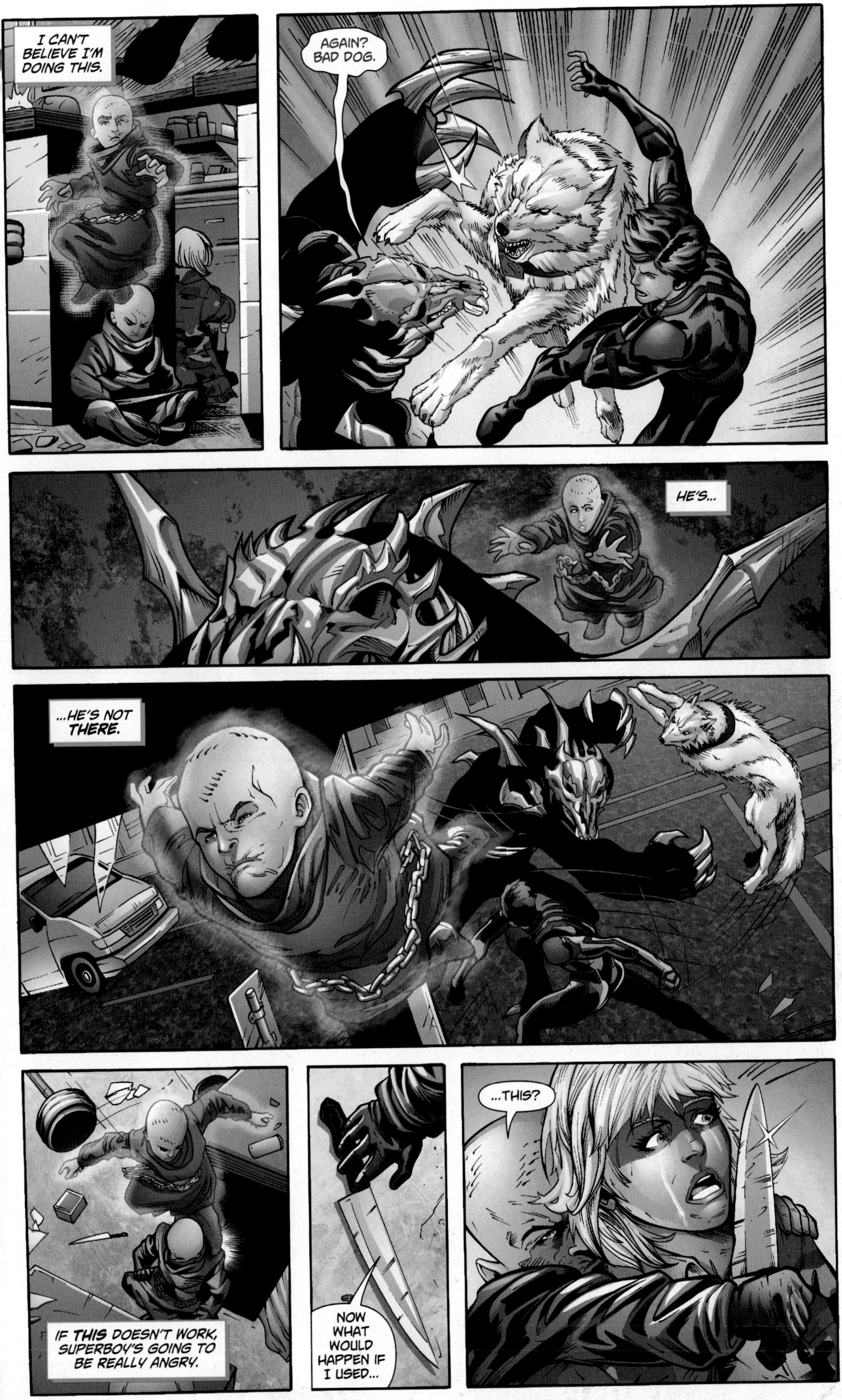

I CAN'T BELIEVE I'M DOING THIS.
AGAIN? BAD DOG.
HE'S...
...HE'S NOT THERE.
IF THIS DOESN'T WORK, SUPERBOY'S GOING TO BE REALLY ANGRY.
NOW WHAT WOULD HAPPEN IF I USED...
...THIS?

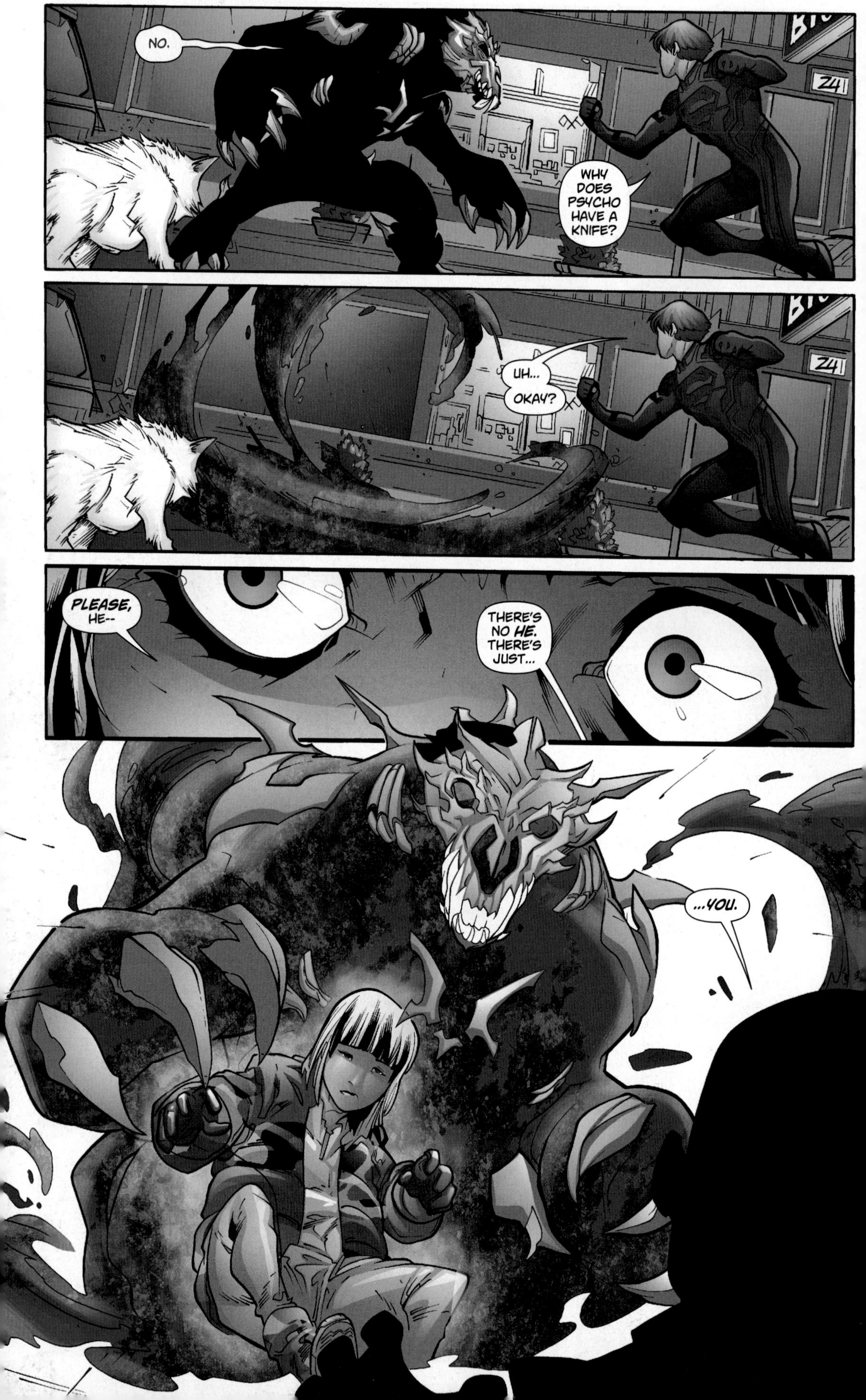
NO.
WHY DOES PSYCHO HAVE A KNIFE?
UH...
OKAY?
PLEASE, HE--
THERE'S NO HE. THERE'S JUST...
...YOU.

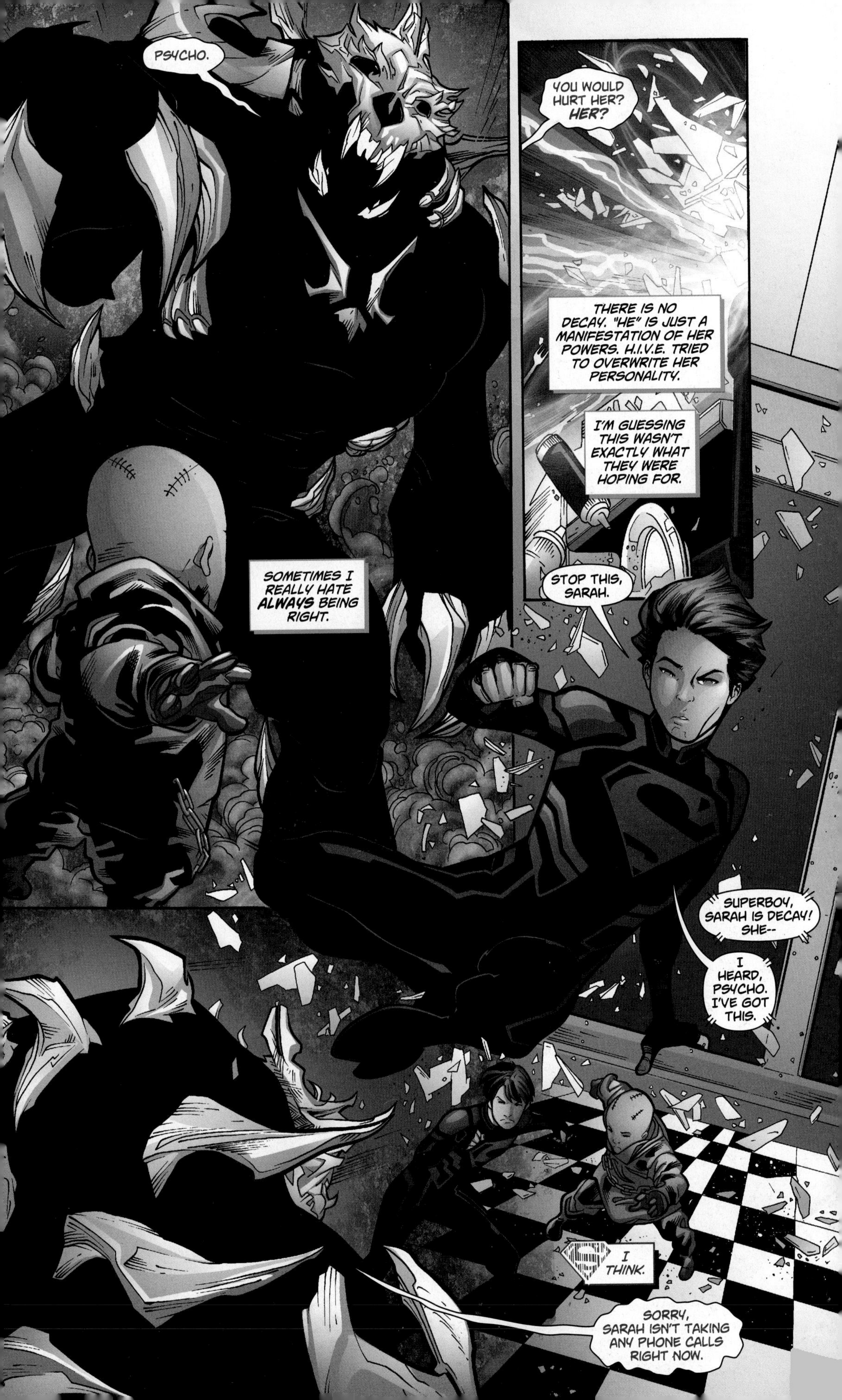
PSYCHO.
YOU WOULD HURT HER? HER?
THERE IS NO DECAY. "HE" IS JUST A MANIFESTATION OF HER POWERS. H.I.V.E. TRIED TO OVERWRITE HER PERSONALITY.
I'M GUESSING THIS WASN'T EXACTLY WHAT THEY WERE HOPING FOR.
SOMETIMES I REALLY HATE ALWAYS BEING RIGHT.
STOP THIS, SARAH.
SUPERBOY, SARAH IS DECAY! SHE--
I HEARD, PSYCHO. I'VE GOT THIS.
I THINK.
SORRY, SARAH ISN'T TAKING ANY PHONE CALLS RIGHT NOW.

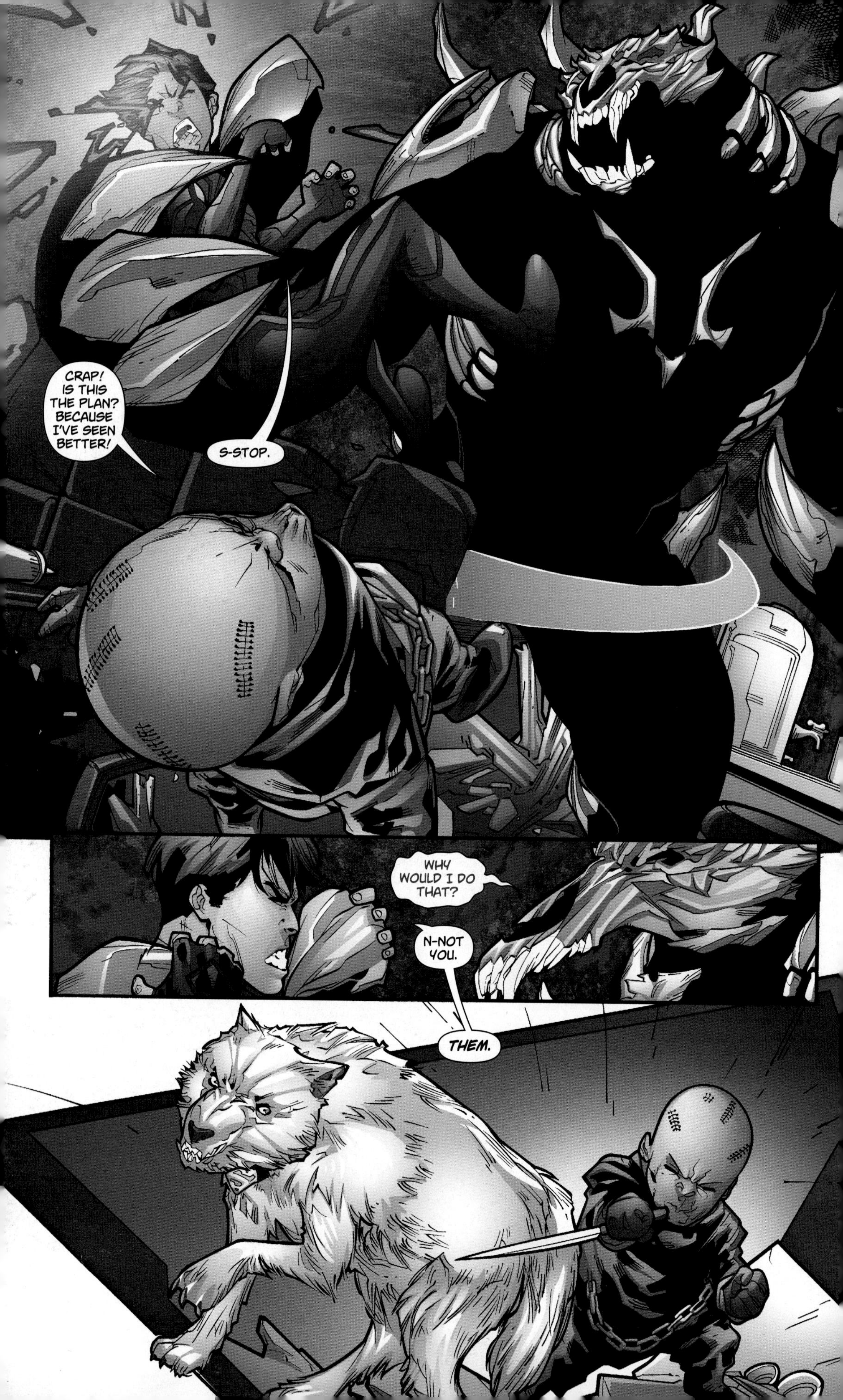
CRAP! IS THIS THE PLAN? BECAUSE I'VE SEEN BETTER!
S-STOP.
WHY WOULD I DO THAT?
N-NOT YOU.
THEM.

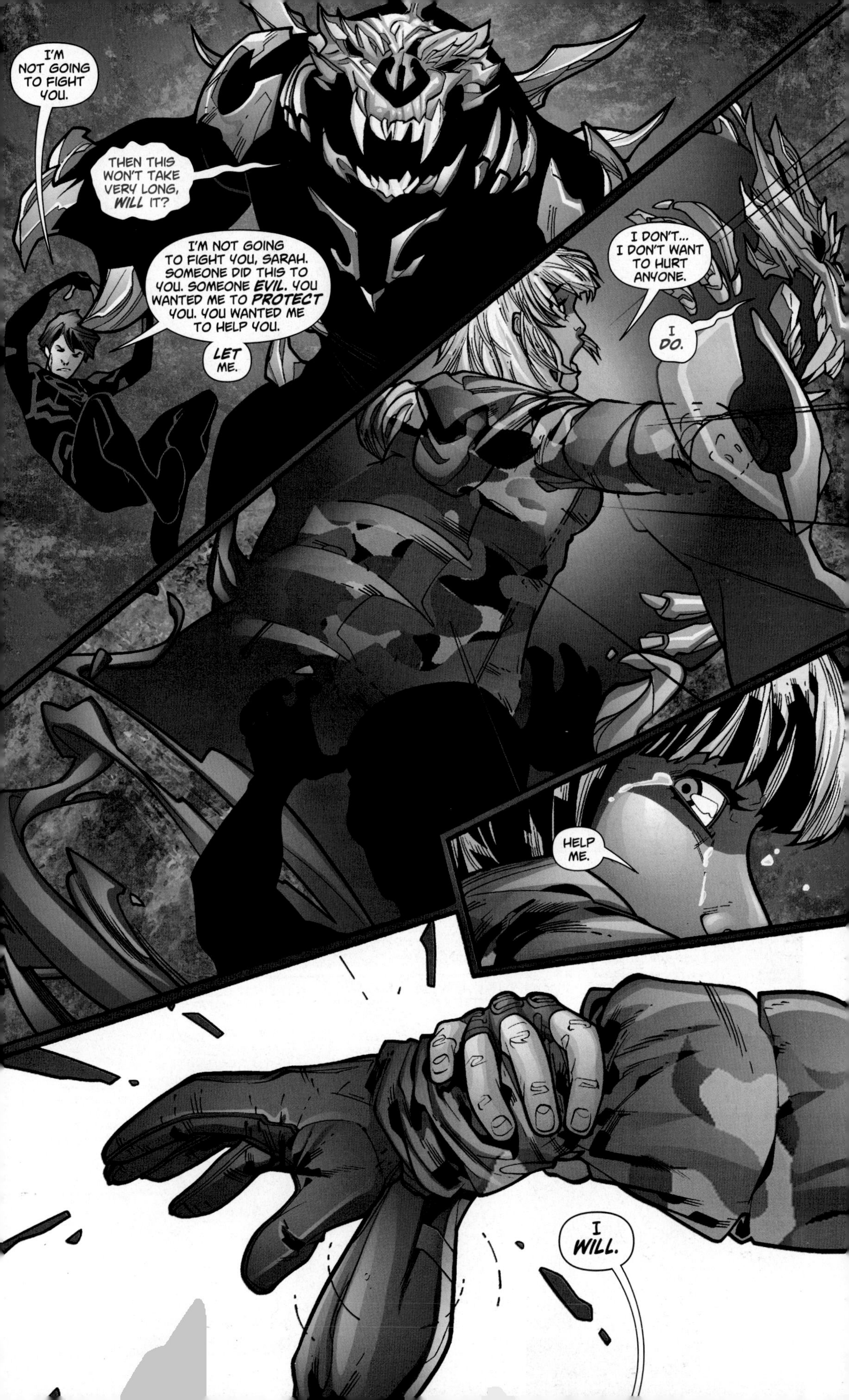
I'M NOT GOING TO FIGHT YOU.
THEN THIS WON'T TAKE VERY LONG, WILL IT?
I'M NOT GOING TO FIGHT YOU, SARAH. SOMEONE DID THIS TO YOU. SOMEONE EVIL. YOU WANTED ME TO PROTECT YOU. YOU WANTED ME TO HELP YOU.
LET ME.
I DON'T... I DON'T WANT TO HURT ANYONE.
I DO.
HELP ME.
I WILL.

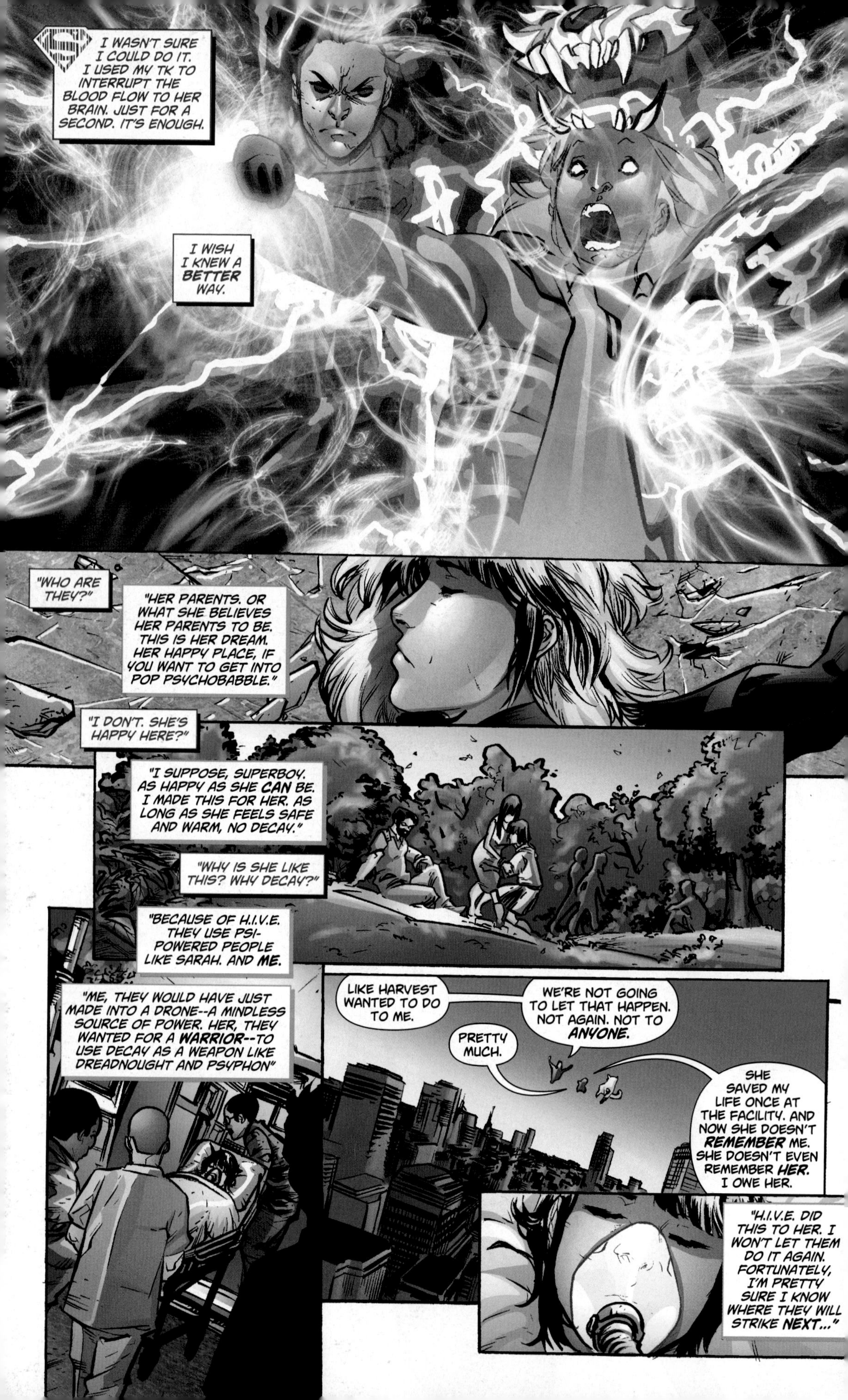

I WASN'T SURE I COULD DO IT. I USED MY TK TO INTERRUPT THE BLOOD FLOW TO HER BRAIN. JUST FOR A SECOND. IT'S ENOUGH.
I WISH I KNEW A BETTER WAY.
"WHO ARE THEY?"
"HER PARENTS. OR WHAT SHE BELIEVES HER PARENTS TO BE. THIS IS HER DREAM. HER HAPPY PLACE, IF YOU WANT TO GET INTO POP PSYCHOBABBLE."
"I DON'T. SHE'S HAPPY HERE?"
"I SUPPOSE, SUPERBOY. AS HAPPY AS SHE CAN BE. I MADE THIS FOR HER. AS LONG AS SHE FEELS SAFE AND WARM, NO DECAY."
"WHY IS SHE LIKE THIS? WHY DECAY?"
"BECAUSE OF H.I.V.E. THEY USE PSI-POWERED PEOPLE LIKE SARAH. AND ME.
"ME, THEY WOULD HAVE JUST MADE INTO A DRONE--A MINDLESS SOURCE OF POWER. HER, THEY WANTED FOR A WARRIOR--TO USE DECAY AS A WEAPON LIKE DREADNOUGHT AND PSYPHON"
LIKE HARVEST WANTED TO DO TO ME.
WE'RE NOT GOING TO LET THAT HAPPEN. NOT AGAIN. NOT TO ANYONE.
PRETTY MUCH.
SHE SAVED MY LIFE ONCE AT THE FACILITY. AND NOW SHE DOESN'T REMEMBER ME. SHE DOESN'T EVEN REMEMBER HER. I OWE HER.
"H.I.V.E. DID THIS TO HER. I WON'T LET THEM DO IT AGAIN. FORTUNATELY, I'M PRETTY SURE I KNOW WHERE THEY WILL STRIKE NEXT..."

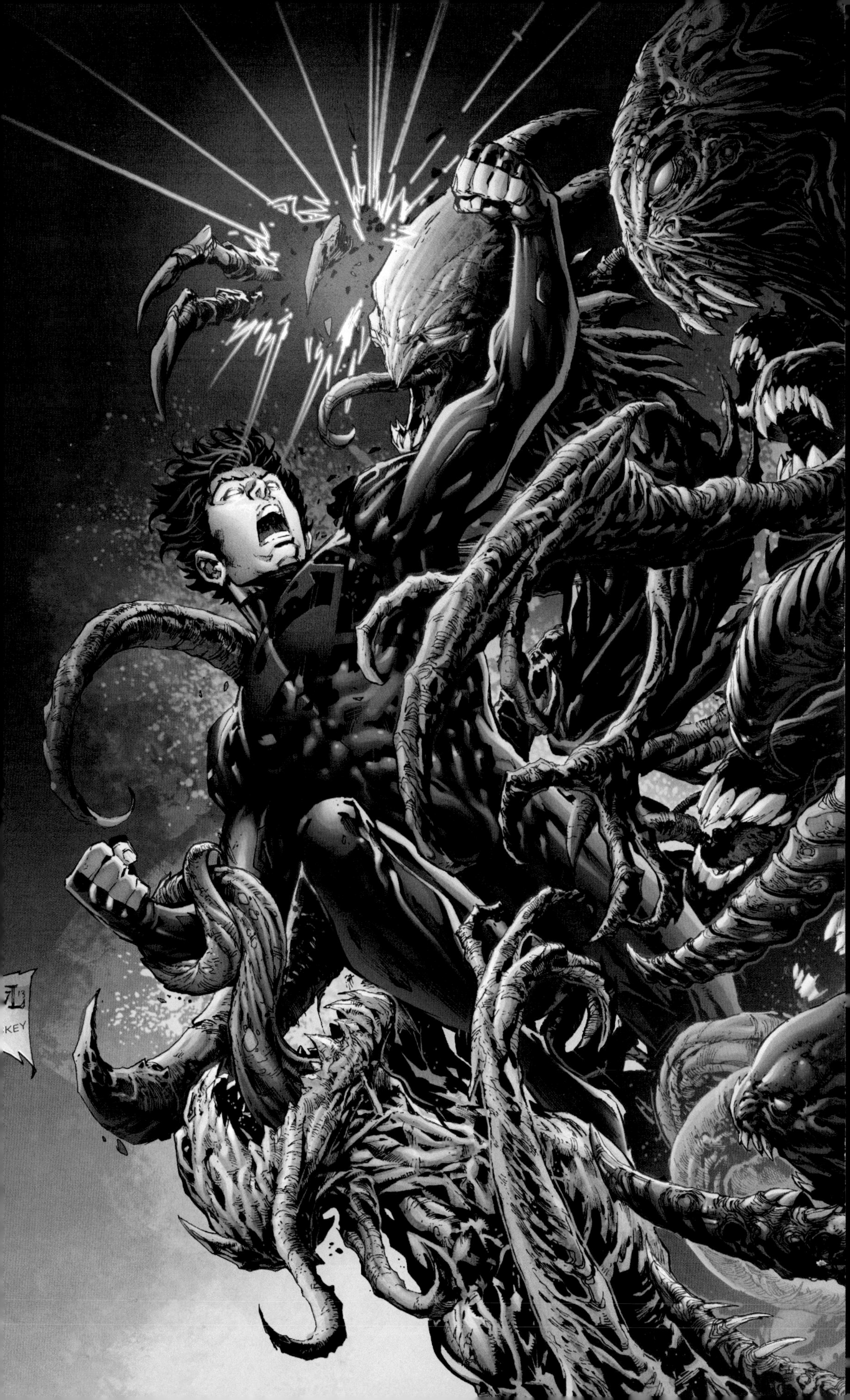

HIGH SCHOOL AND OTHER ASSORTED HORRORS

JUSTIN JORDAN writer **GUILHERME BALBI** penciller **MARLO ALQUIZA DON HO** inkers cover art by **KEN LASHLEY & MATT YACKEY**

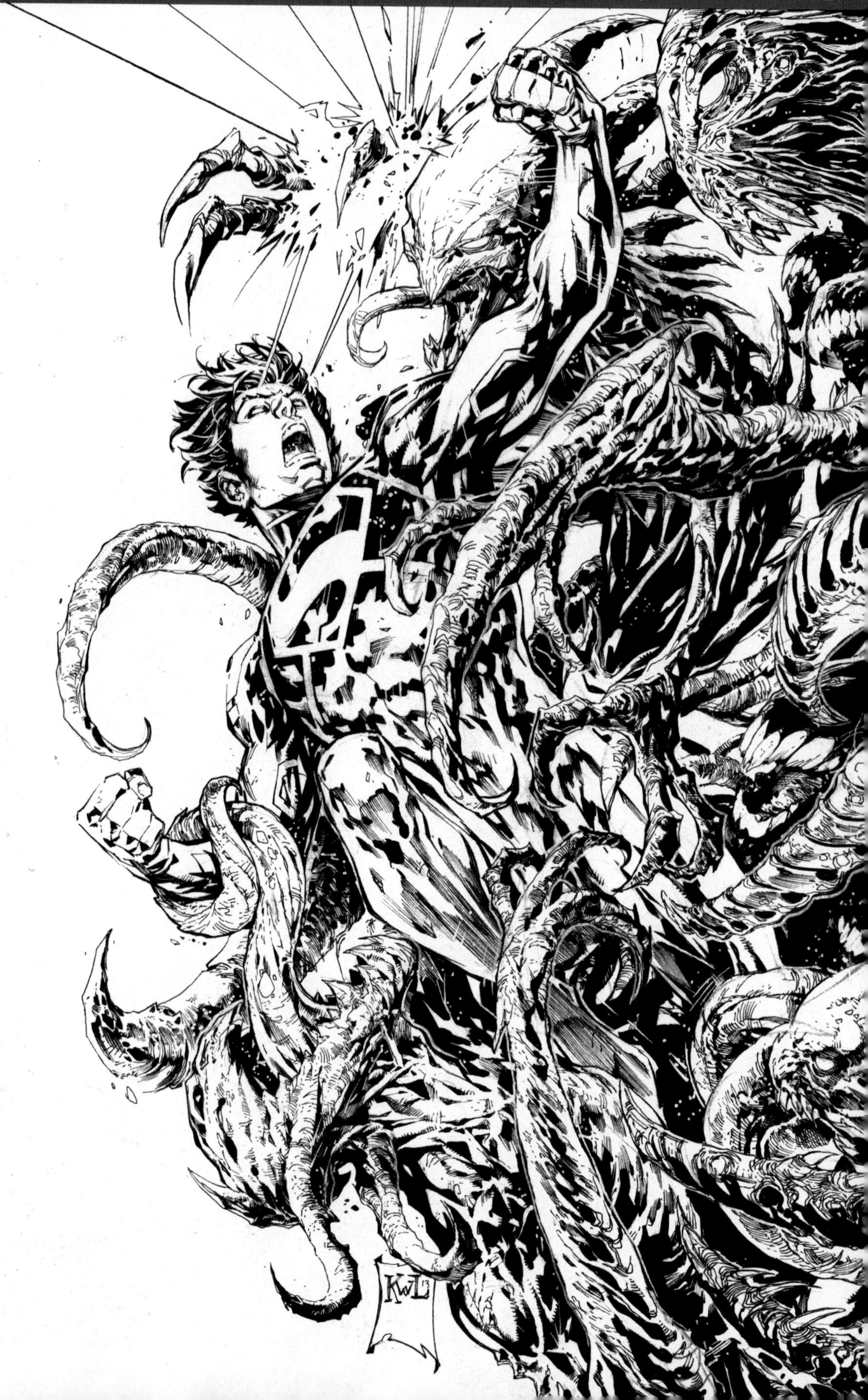

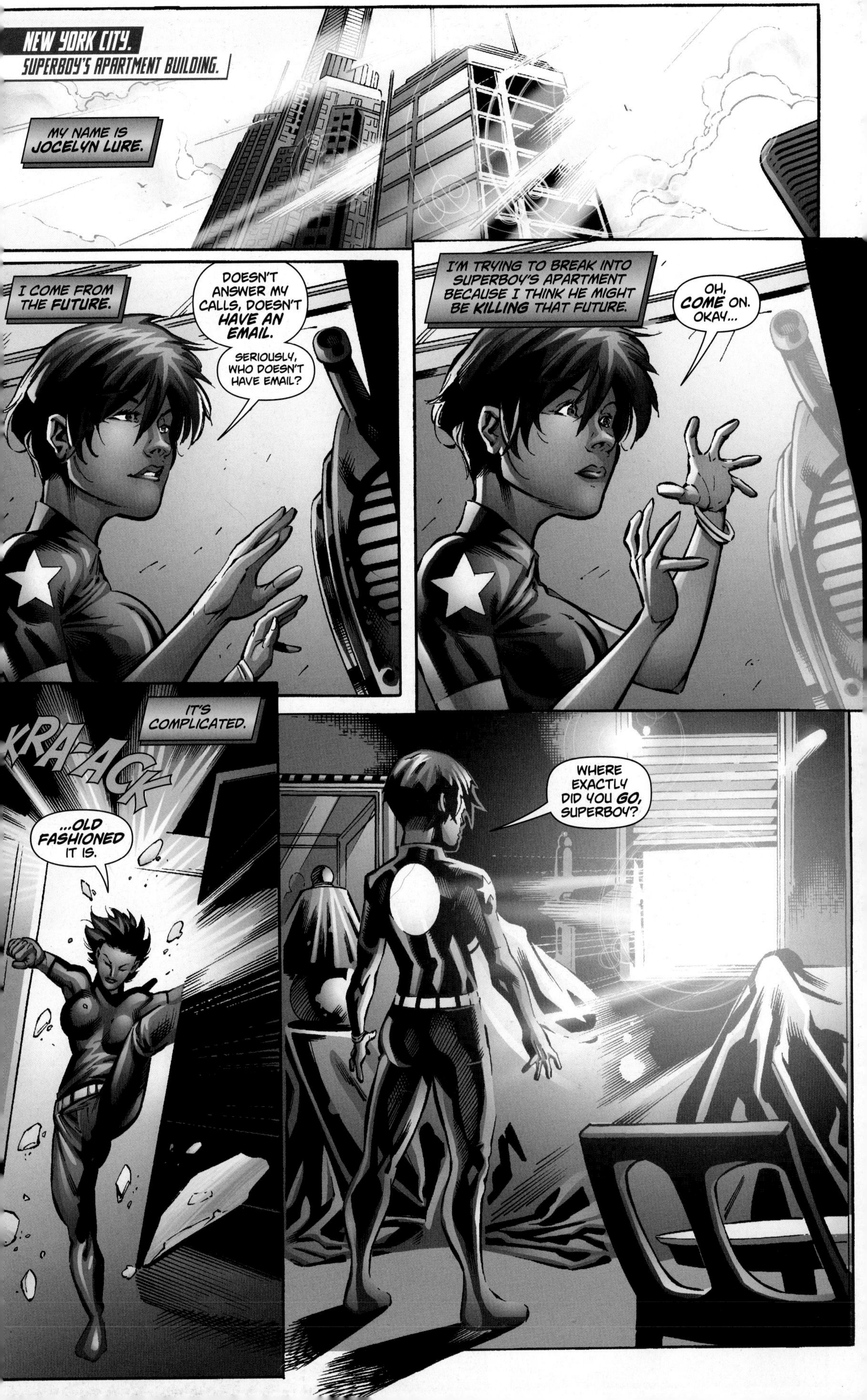
NEW YORK CITY.
SUPERBOY'S APARTMENT BUILDING.
MY NAME IS JOCELYN LURE.
I COME FROM THE FUTURE.
DOESN'T ANSWER MY CALLS, DOESN'T HAVE AN EMAIL.
SERIOUSLY, WHO DOESN'T HAVE EMAIL?
I'M TRYING TO BREAK INTO SUPERBOY'S APARTMENT BECAUSE I THINK HE MIGHT BE KILLING THAT FUTURE.
OH, COME ON. OKAY...
IT'S COMPLICATED.
KRA-ACK
...OLD FASHIONED IT IS.
WHERE EXACTLY DID YOU GO, SUPERBOY?

SO *THIS* IS HIGH SCHOOL.

...

I DON'T LIKE IT.

MCDUFFIE HIGH SCHOOL

YOU HAVEN'T EVEN BEEN *IN* IT. AND STOP TALKING OUT LOUD, SUPERBOY. EVERYONE WILL THINK YOU'RE A...ER... PSYCHO.

SO? WHY WOULD I CARE WHAT PEOPLE I *DON'T KNOW* THINK?

YEAH, YOU REALLY *DON'T* KNOW HOW HIGH SCHOOL WORKS...

ARE YOU HERE, DOCTOR PSYCHO?

I AM. WE'RE IN THE FIELD SHED. KRYPTO ISN'T HAPPY ABOUT IT.

YEAH, I LOVE YOU, TOO, *FURBAG.*

RRRRR...

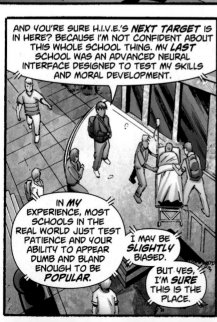

AND YOU'RE SURE H.I.V.E.'S *NEXT TARGET* IS IN HERE? BECAUSE I'M NOT CONFIDENT ABOUT THIS WHOLE SCHOOL THING. MY *LAST* SCHOOL WAS AN ADVANCED NEURAL INTERFACE DESIGNED TO TEST MY SKILLS AND MORAL DEVELOPMENT.

IN *MY* EXPERIENCE, MOST SCHOOLS IN THE REAL WORLD JUST TEST PATIENCE AND YOUR ABILITY TO APPEAR DUMB AND BLAND ENOUGH TO BE *POPULAR.*

I MAY BE *SLIGHTLY* BIASED.

BUT YES, I'M *SURE* THIS IS THE PLACE.

THEY'RE...THEY'RE *EVERYWHERE...*

THESE... WELL--CALL THEM *EPISODES*-- HAVE HAPPENED TO FIVE KIDS. SIX AFTER TODAY'S. AND THEY'RE GETTING *WORSE.* AUTHORITIES ARE BLAMING DRUGS. WHICH THEY CAN'T *FIND.*

BUT I'VE SEEN SOMETHING LIKE THIS BEFORE... BACK *BEFORE* H.I.V.E.

GREAT. WELL, THIS SHOULD BE...

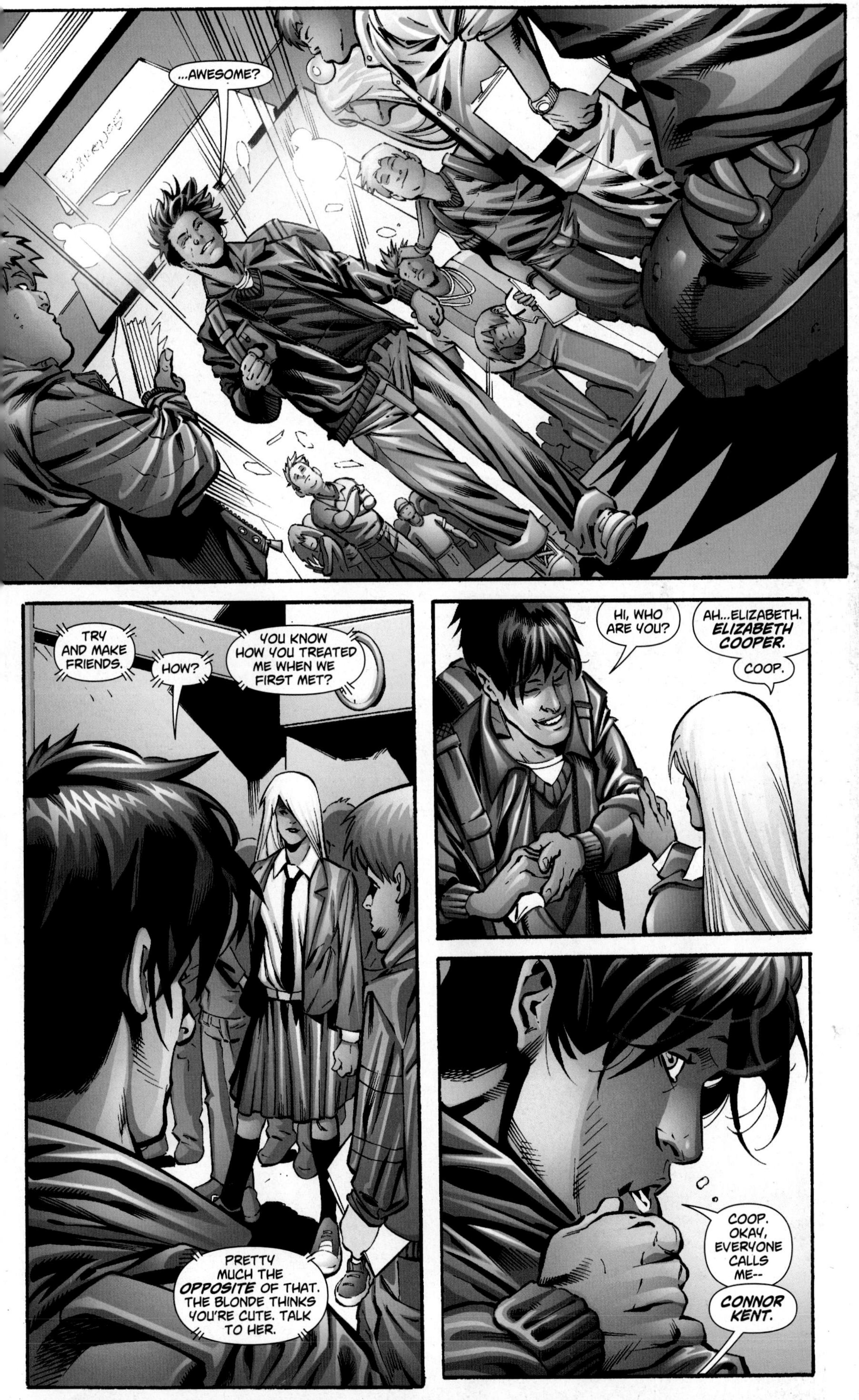

...AWESOME?
TRY AND MAKE FRIENDS.
HOW?
YOU KNOW HOW YOU TREATED ME WHEN WE FIRST MET?
PRETTY MUCH THE OPPOSITE OF THAT. THE BLONDE THINKS YOU'RE CUTE. TALK TO HER.
HI, WHO ARE YOU?
AH...ELIZABETH. ELIZABETH COOPER.
COOP.
COOP. OKAY, EVERYONE CALLS ME--
CONNOR KENT.

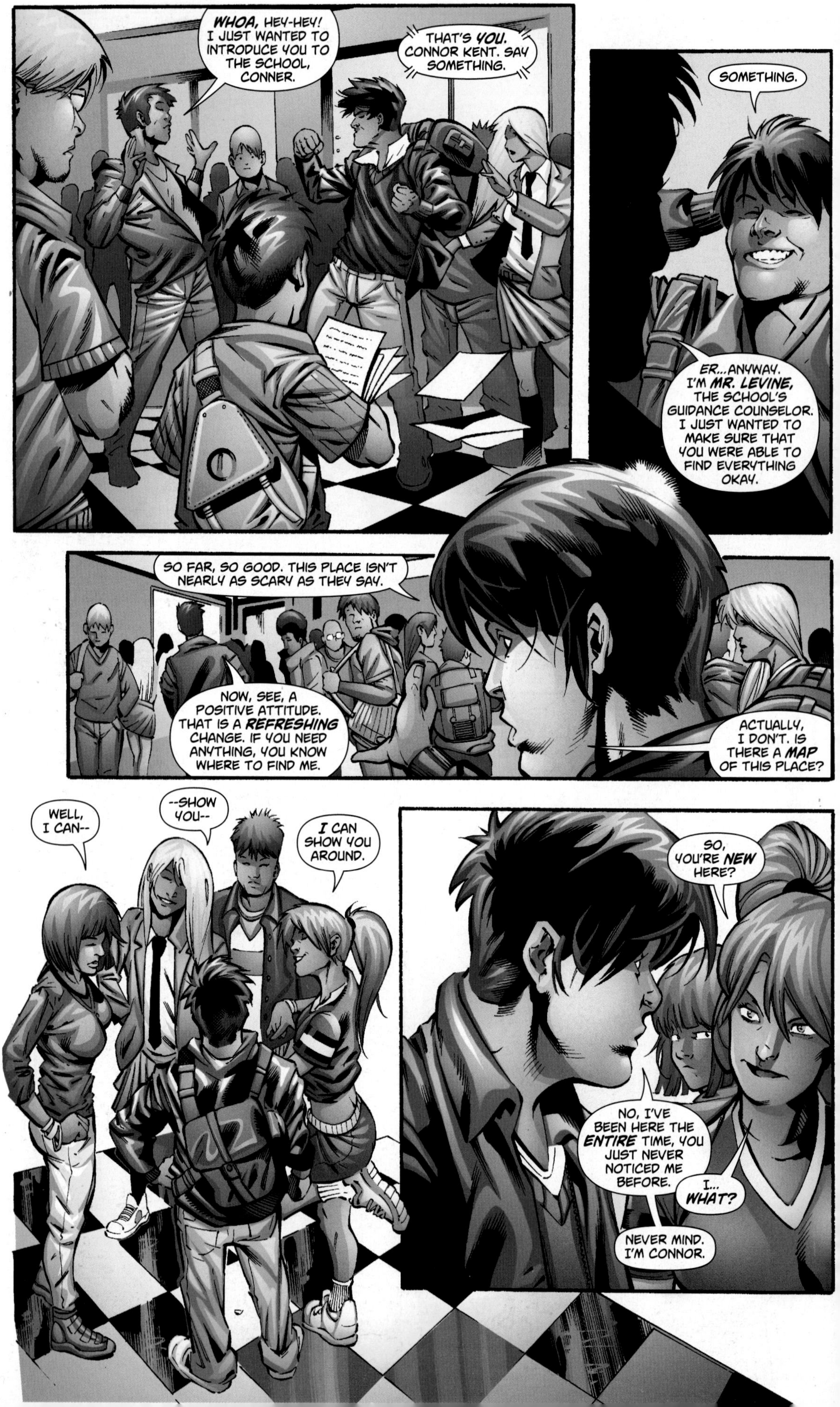
WHOA, HEY-HEY! I JUST WANTED TO INTRODUCE YOU TO THE SCHOOL, CONNER.
THAT'S YOU. CONNOR KENT. SAY SOMETHING.
SOMETHING.
ER...ANYWAY. I'M MR. LEVINE, THE SCHOOL'S GUIDANCE COUNSELOR. I JUST WANTED TO MAKE SURE THAT YOU WERE ABLE TO FIND EVERYTHING OKAY.
SO FAR, SO GOOD. THIS PLACE ISN'T NEARLY AS SCARY AS THEY SAY.
NOW, SEE, A POSITIVE ATTITUDE. THAT IS A REFRESHING CHANGE. IF YOU NEED ANYTHING, YOU KNOW WHERE TO FIND ME.
ACTUALLY, I DON'T. IS THERE A MAP OF THIS PLACE?
WELL, I CAN--
--SHOW YOU--
I CAN SHOW YOU AROUND.
SO, YOU'RE NEW HERE?
NO, I'VE BEEN HERE THE ENTIRE TIME, YOU JUST NEVER NOTICED ME BEFORE.
I... WHAT?
NEVER MIND. I'M CONNOR.

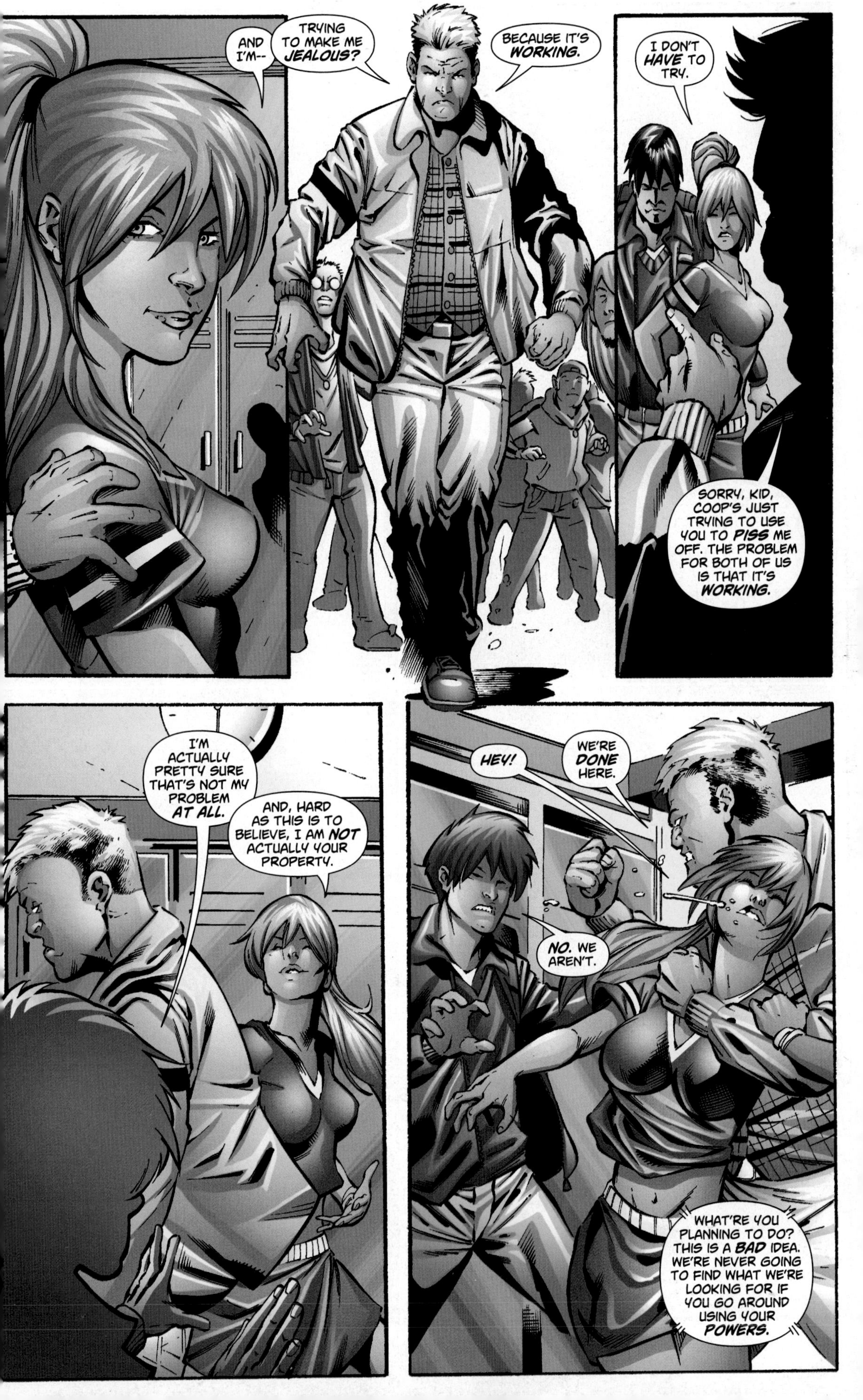
AND I'M--
TRYING TO MAKE ME JEALOUS?
BECAUSE IT'S WORKING.
I DON'T HAVE TO TRY.
SORRY, KID, COOP'S JUST TRYING TO USE YOU TO PISS ME OFF. THE PROBLEM FOR BOTH OF US IS THAT IT'S WORKING.
I'M ACTUALLY PRETTY SURE THAT'S NOT MY PROBLEM AT ALL.
AND, HARD AS THIS IS TO BELIEVE, I AM NOT ACTUALLY YOUR PROPERTY.
HEY!
WE'RE DONE HERE.
NO. WE AREN'T.
WHAT'RE YOU PLANNING TO DO? THIS IS A BAD IDEA. WE'RE NEVER GOING TO FIND WHAT WE'RE LOOKING FOR IF YOU GO AROUND USING YOUR POWERS.

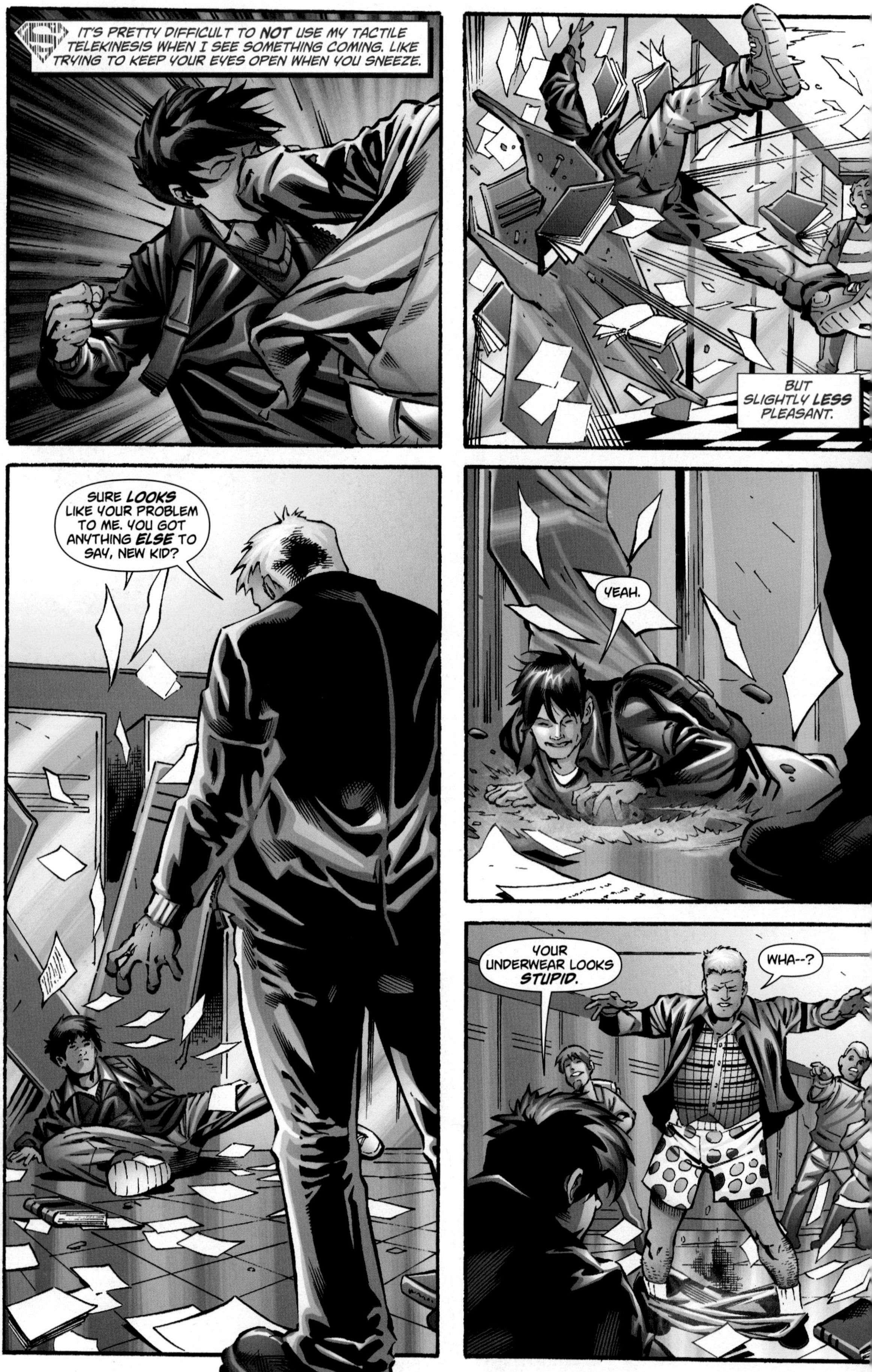
IT'S PRETTY DIFFICULT TO NOT USE MY TACTILE TELEKINESIS WHEN I SEE SOMETHING COMING. LIKE TRYING TO KEEP YOUR EYES OPEN WHEN YOU SNEEZE.
BUT SLIGHTLY LESS PLEASANT.
SURE LOOKS LIKE YOUR PROBLEM TO ME. YOU GOT ANYTHING ELSE TO SAY, NEW KID?
YEAH.
YOUR UNDERWEAR LOOKS STUPID.
WHA--?

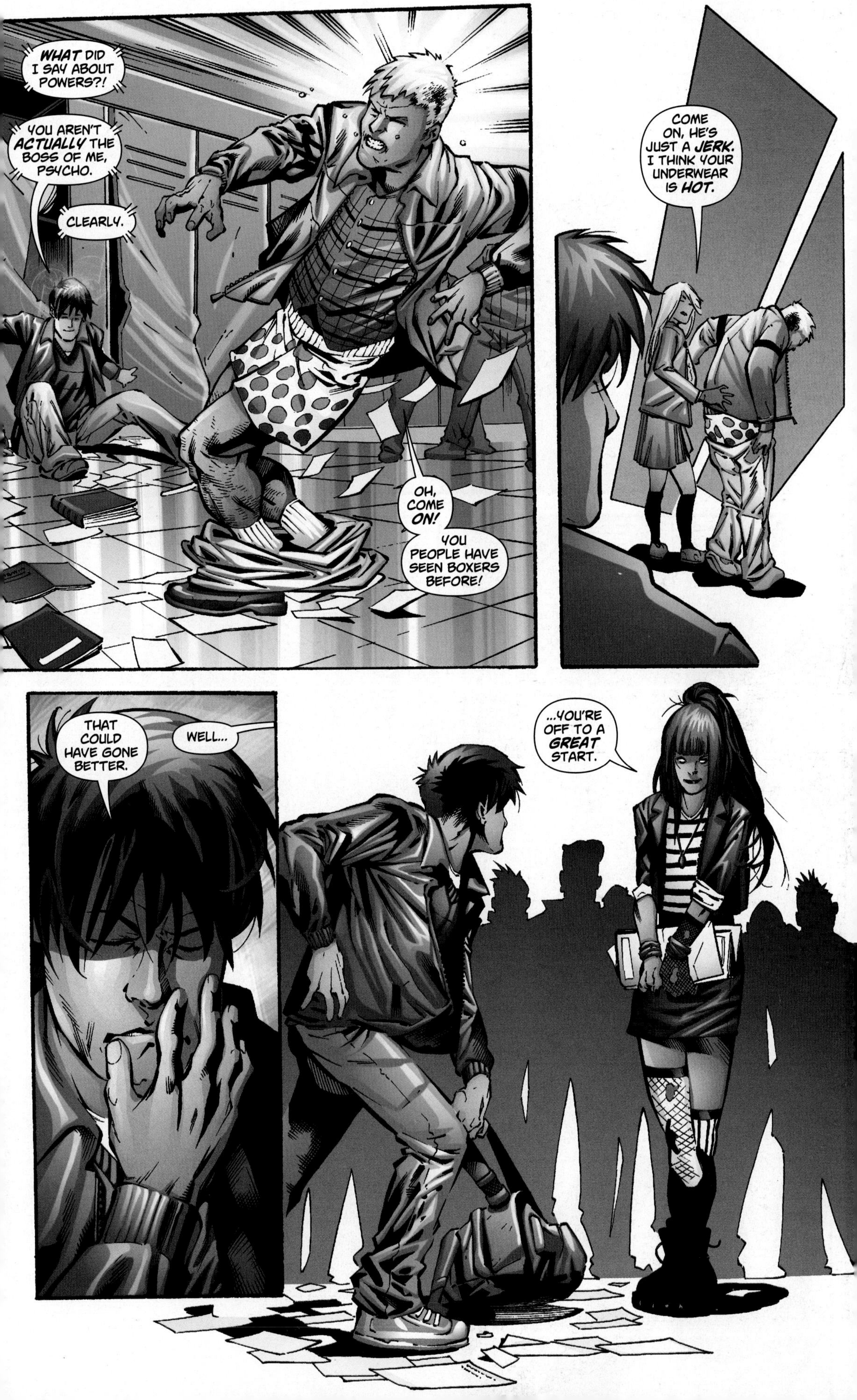
WHAT DID I SAY ABOUT POWERS?!
YOU AREN'T ACTUALLY THE BOSS OF ME, PSYCHO.
CLEARLY.
OH, COME ON!
YOU PEOPLE HAVE SEEN BOXERS BEFORE!
COME ON, HE'S JUST A JERK. I THINK YOUR UNDERWEAR IS HOT.
THAT COULD HAVE GONE BETTER.
WELL...
...YOU'RE OFF TO A GREAT START.

THANKS. I DON'T SUPPOSE YOU'D LIKE TO SHOW ME WHERE STUFF IS? ANYTHING?

I WASN'T GOING TO, WHAT WITH YOU BEING THE HOT NEW GUY, BUT SINCE YOU'VE MANAGED TO GO FROM POTENTIAL *POPULAR* TO SOCIAL *PARIAH* IN ABOUT TEN SECONDS, SURE.

MY NAME IS ELIZA. *ELIZA ELLIS.*

CONNOR KENT, ELIZA "ELIZA" ELLIS.

I'M PRETTY SURE I DON'T LIKE THEM.

NOBODY LIKES THEM, THAT'S WHY THEY'RE POPULAR.

... WHAT?

FIRST TIME AT SCHOOL?

YES.

WAIT, *REALLY?!*

REALLY, REALLY.

HOW DOES THAT HAPPEN?

IT'S *EXTRAORDINARILY* COMPLEX. I NEED A WHOLE *BOOK* TO EXPLAIN IT. MAYBE TWO.

OKAY, THEN WHERE DOES ONE MANAGE TO *NOT* GO TO SCHOOL?

KANSAS.

I'VE NEVER MET ANYONE FROM KANSAS. I WAS ACTUALLY PRETTY MUCH CONVINCED IT WAS AN *ENTIRELY* FICTIONAL STATE.

IT FELT FAIRLY FICTIONAL WHILE I WAS THERE, BUT I WAS HOMESCHOOLED. SO, NO HIGH SCHOOL. NOT REALLY.

YOUR PARENTS ARE SUPER-RELIGIOUS?

I DON'T *HAVE* ANY PARENTS.

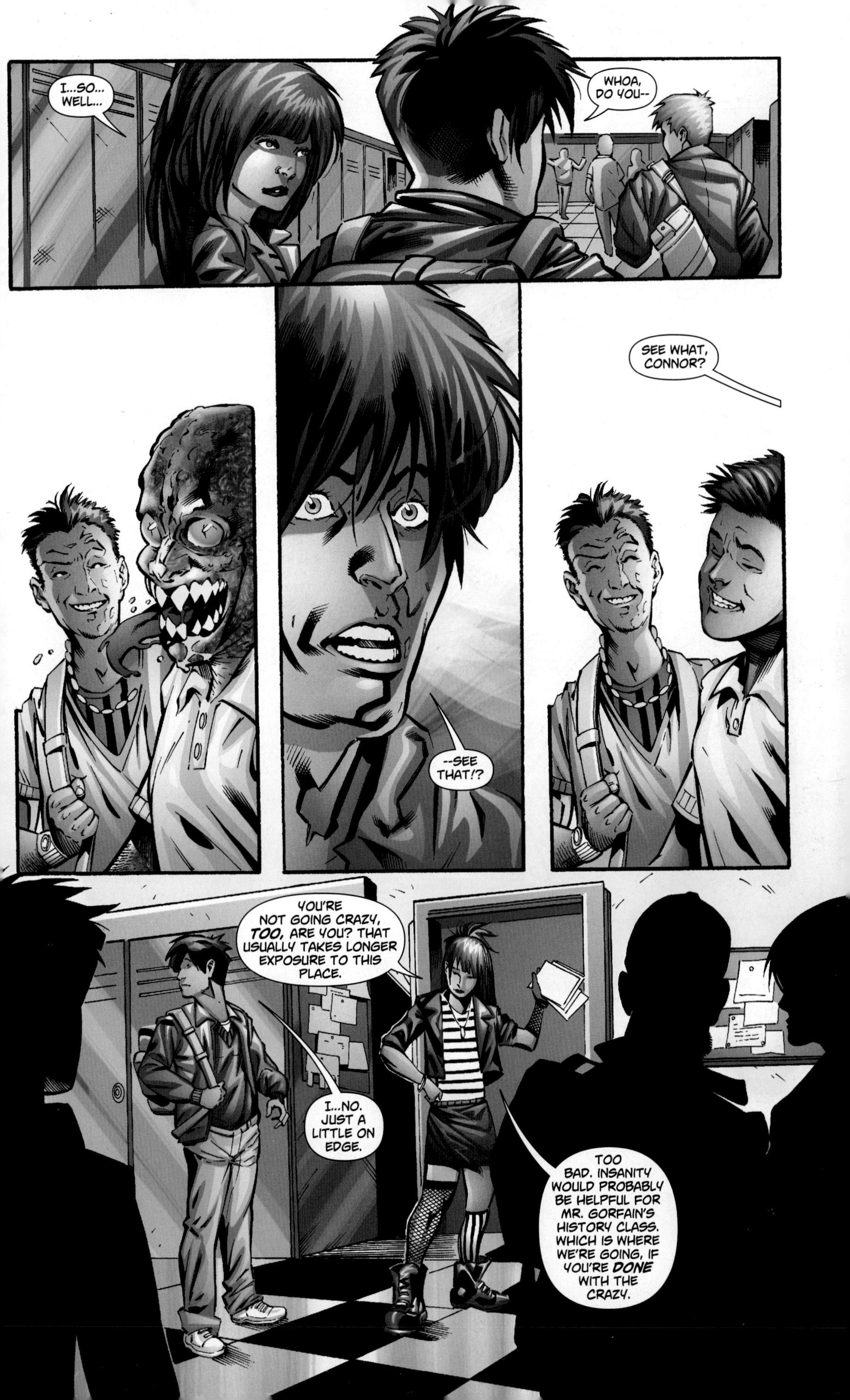
I...SO... WELL...
WHOA, DO YOU--
--SEE THAT!?
SEE WHAT, CONNOR?
YOU'RE NOT GOING CRAZY, TOO, ARE YOU? THAT USUALLY TAKES LONGER EXPOSURE TO THIS PLACE.
I...NO. JUST A LITTLE ON EDGE.
TOO BAD. INSANITY WOULD PROBABLY BE HELPFUL FOR MR. GORFAIN'S HISTORY CLASS. WHICH IS WHERE WE'RE GOING, IF YOU'RE DONE WITH THE CRAZY.

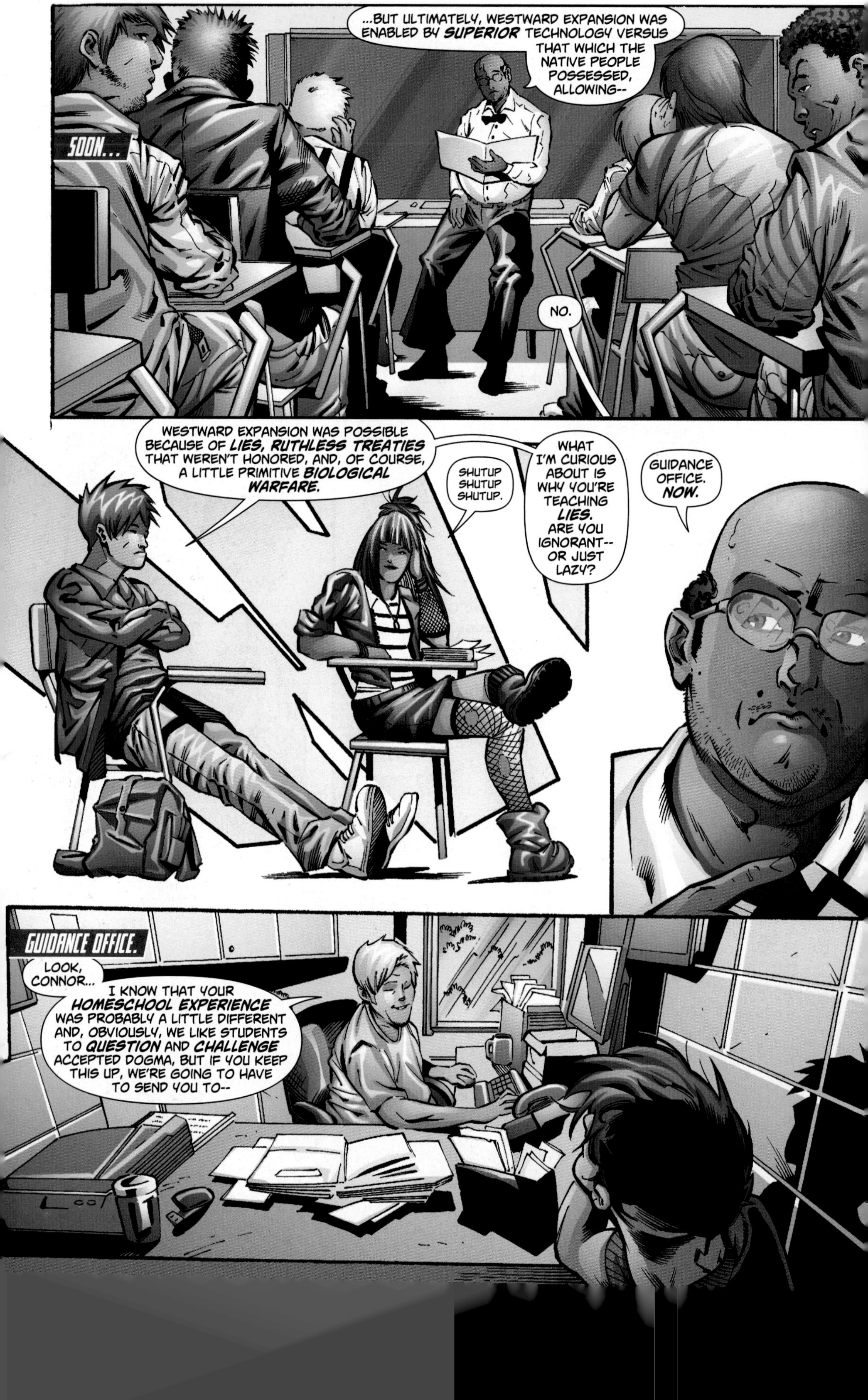
...BUT ULTIMATELY, WESTWARD EXPANSION WAS ENABLED BY SUPERIOR TECHNOLOGY VERSUS THAT WHICH THE NATIVE PEOPLE POSSESSED, ALLOWING--
SOON...
NO.
WESTWARD EXPANSION WAS POSSIBLE BECAUSE OF LIES, RUTHLESS TREATIES THAT WEREN'T HONORED, AND, OF COURSE, A LITTLE PRIMITIVE BIOLOGICAL WARFARE.
SHUTUP SHUTUP SHUTUP.
WHAT I'M CURIOUS ABOUT IS WHY YOU'RE TEACHING LIES. ARE YOU IGNORANT-- OR JUST LAZY?
GUIDANCE OFFICE. NOW.
GUIDANCE OFFICE.
LOOK, CONNOR...
I KNOW THAT YOUR HOMESCHOOL EXPERIENCE WAS PROBABLY A LITTLE DIFFERENT AND, OBVIOUSLY, WE LIKE STUDENTS TO QUESTION AND CHALLENGE ACCEPTED DOGMA, BUT IF YOU KEEP THIS UP, WE'RE GOING TO HAVE TO SEND YOU TO--

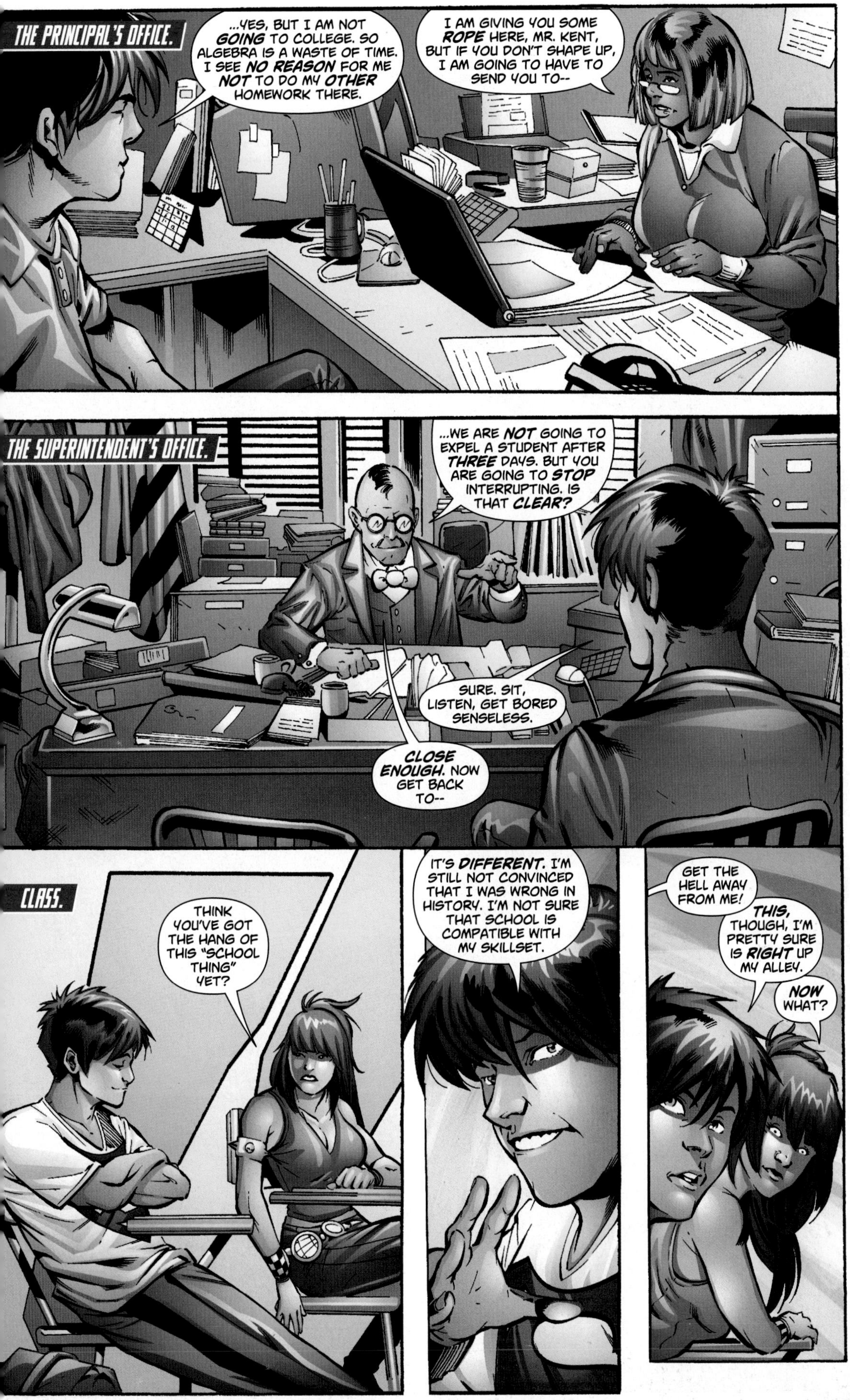
THE PRINCIPAL'S OFFICE.
...YES, BUT I AM NOT GOING TO COLLEGE. SO ALGEBRA IS A WASTE OF TIME. I SEE NO REASON FOR ME NOT TO DO MY OTHER HOMEWORK THERE.
I AM GIVING YOU SOME ROPE HERE, MR. KENT, BUT IF YOU DON'T SHAPE UP, I AM GOING TO HAVE TO SEND YOU TO--
THE SUPERINTENDENT'S OFFICE.
...WE ARE NOT GOING TO EXPEL A STUDENT AFTER THREE DAYS. BUT YOU ARE GOING TO STOP INTERRUPTING. IS THAT CLEAR?
SURE. SIT, LISTEN, GET BORED SENSELESS.
CLOSE ENOUGH. NOW GET BACK TO--
CLASS.
THINK YOU'VE GOT THE HANG OF THIS "SCHOOL THING" YET?
IT'S DIFFERENT. I'M STILL NOT CONVINCED THAT I WAS WRONG IN HISTORY. I'M NOT SURE THAT SCHOOL IS COMPATIBLE WITH MY SKILLSET.
GET THE HELL AWAY FROM ME!
THIS, THOUGH, I'M PRETTY SURE IS RIGHT UP MY ALLEY.
NOW WHAT?

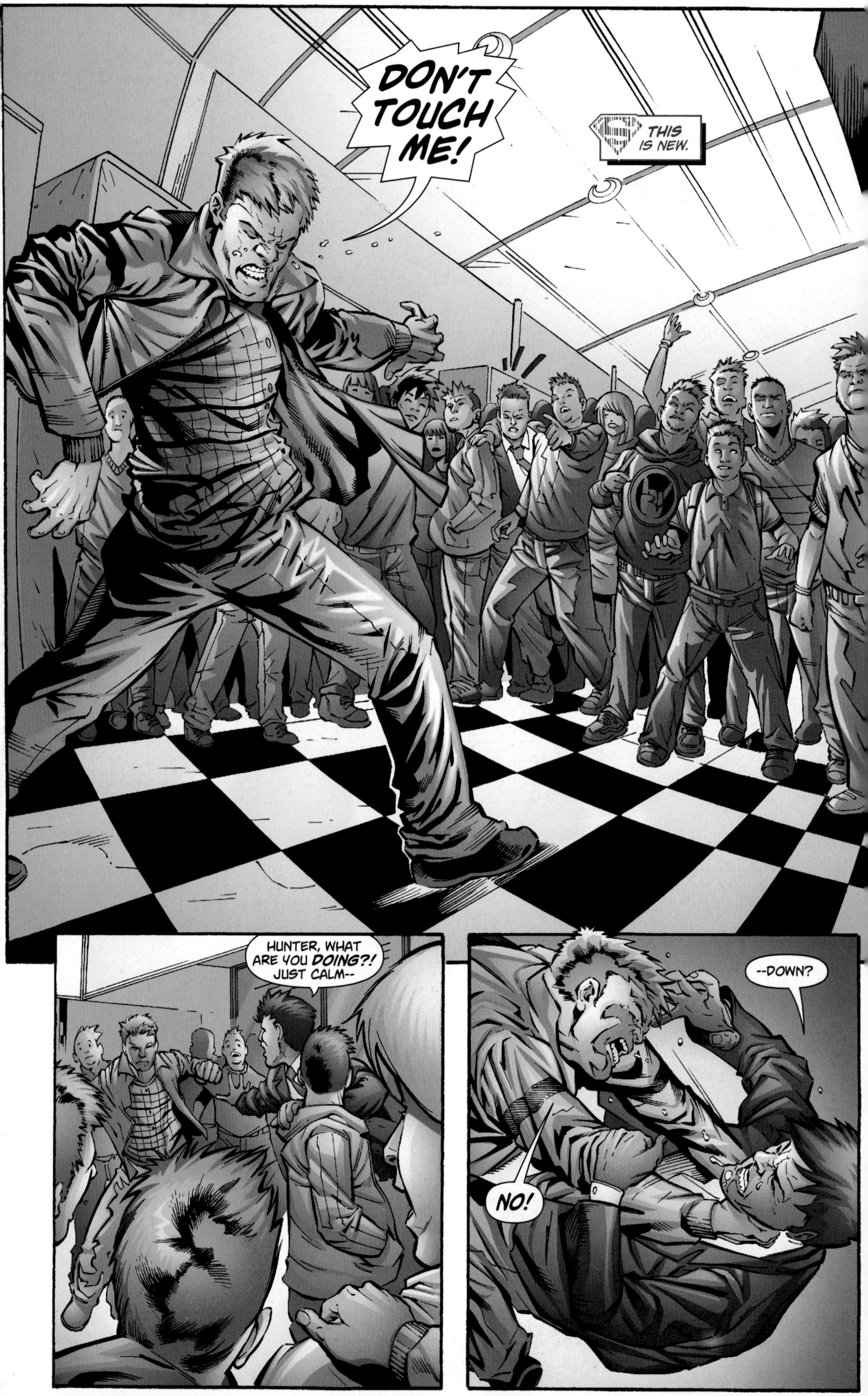
DON'T TOUCH ME!
THIS IS NEW.
HUNTER, WHAT ARE YOU DOING?! JUST CALM--
--DOWN?
NO!

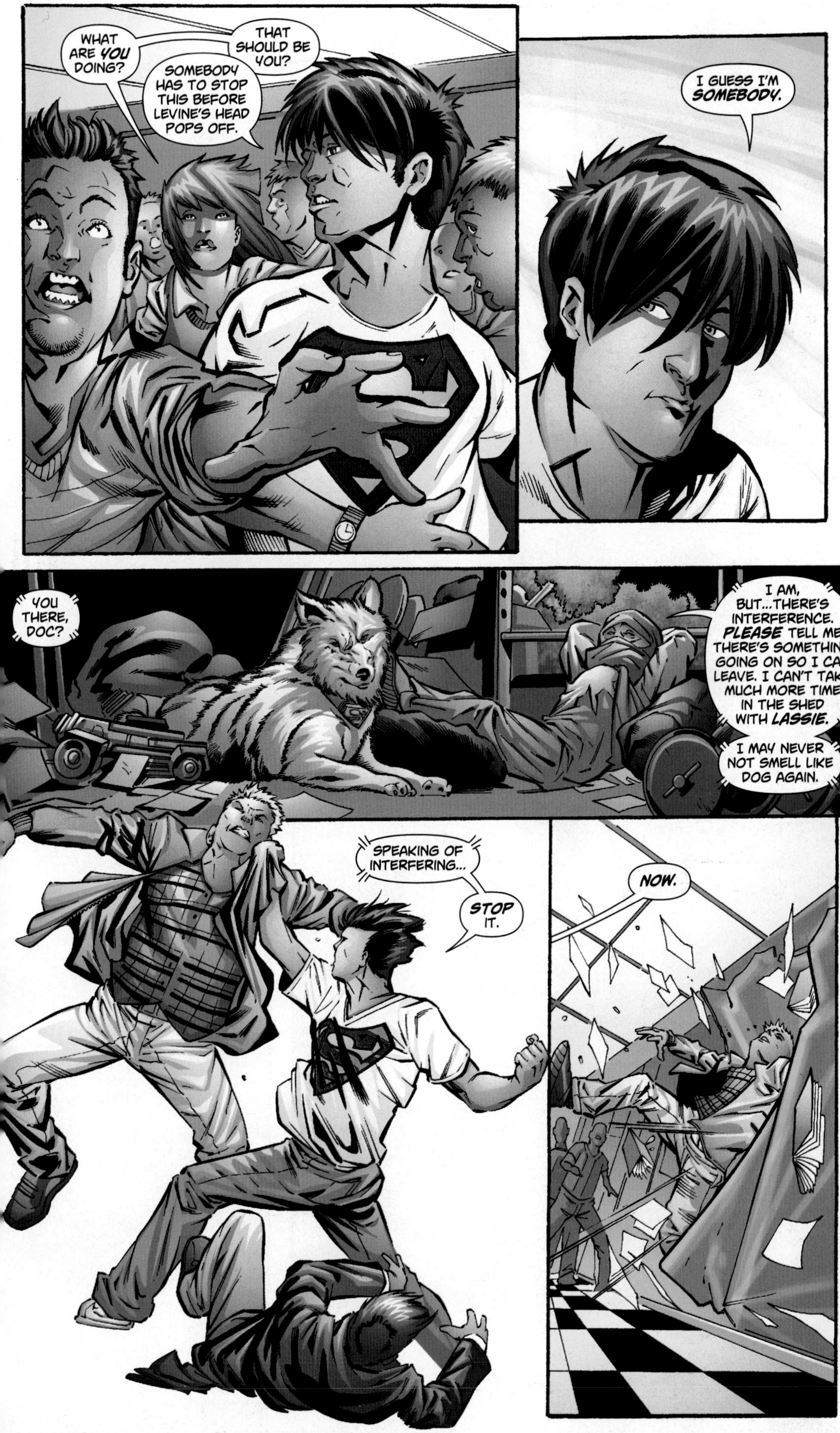
WHAT ARE YOU DOING?
THAT SHOULD BE YOU?
SOMEBODY HAS TO STOP THIS BEFORE LEVINE'S HEAD POPS OFF.
I GUESS I'M SOMEBODY.
YOU THERE, DOC?
I AM, BUT...THERE'S INTERFERENCE. PLEASE TELL ME THERE'S SOMETHING GOING ON SO I CAN LEAVE. I CAN'T TAKE MUCH MORE TIME IN THE SHED WITH LASSIE.
I MAY NEVER NOT SMELL LIKE DOG AGAIN.
SPEAKING OF INTERFERING...
STOP IT.
NOW.

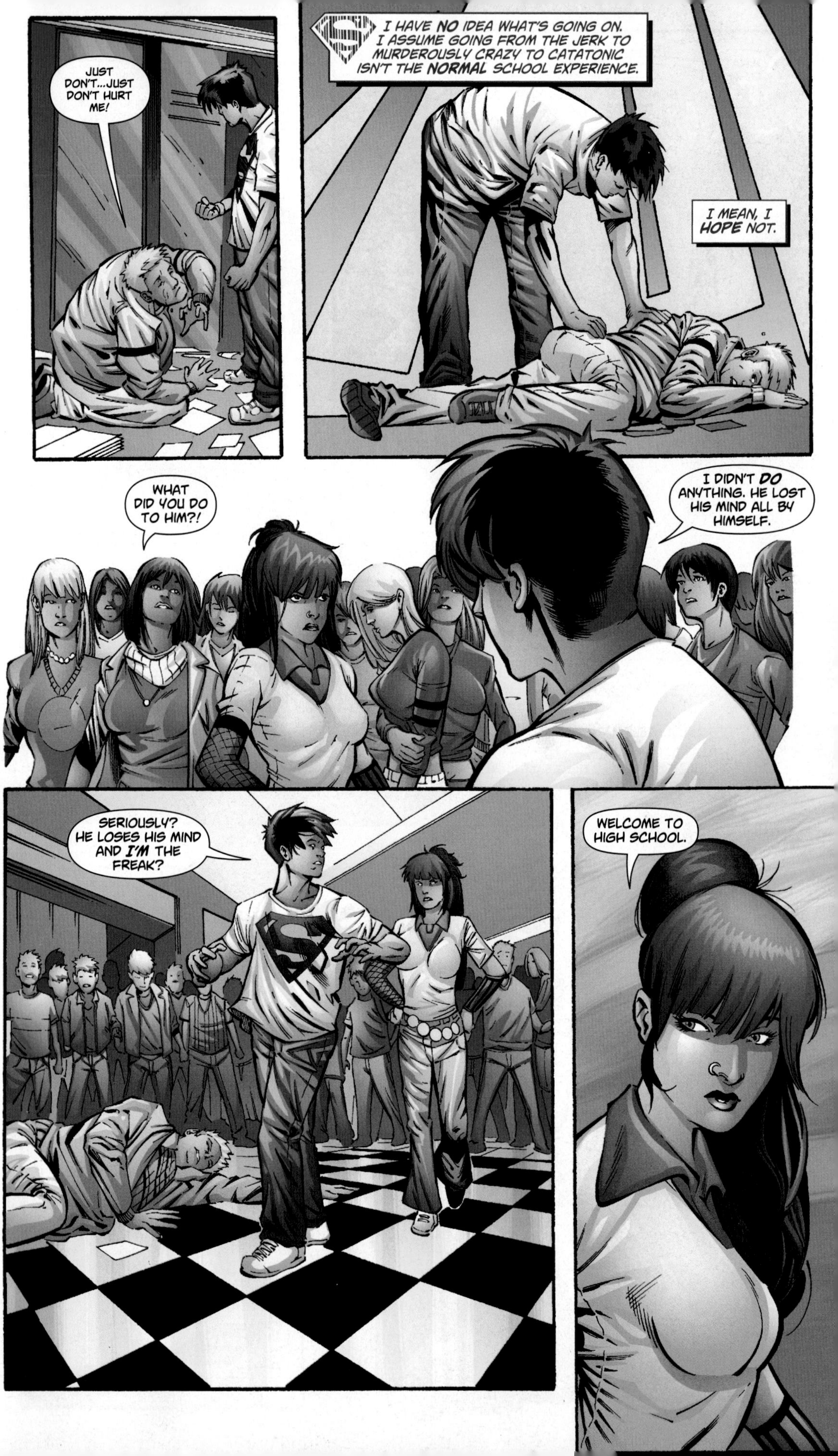
JUST DON'T...JUST DON'T HURT ME!
I HAVE NO IDEA WHAT'S GOING ON. I ASSUME GOING FROM THE JERK TO MURDEROUSLY CRAZY TO CATATONIC ISN'T THE NORMAL SCHOOL EXPERIENCE.
I MEAN, I HOPE NOT.
WHAT DID YOU DO TO HIM?!
I DIDN'T DO ANYTHING. HE LOST HIS MIND ALL BY HIMSELF.
SERIOUSLY? HE LOSES HIS MIND AND I'M THE FREAK?
WELCOME TO HIGH SCHOOL.

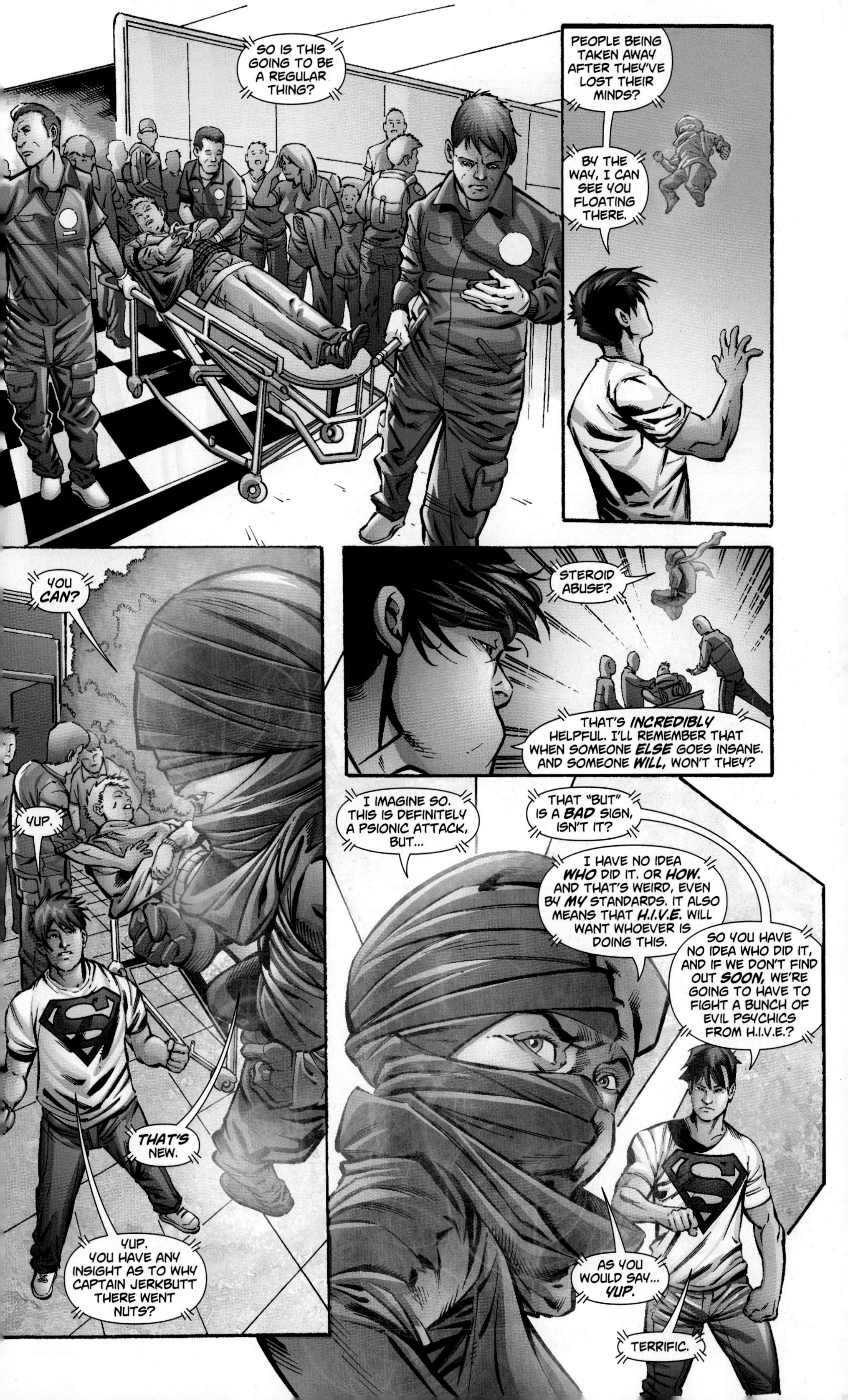
SO IS THIS GOING TO BE A REGULAR THING?
PEOPLE BEING TAKEN AWAY AFTER THEY'VE LOST THEIR MINDS?
BY THE WAY, I CAN SEE YOU FLOATING THERE.
YOU CAN?
YUP.
THAT'S NEW.
YUP. YOU HAVE ANY INSIGHT AS TO WHY CAPTAIN JERKBUTT THERE WENT NUTS?
STEROID ABUSE?
THAT'S INCREDIBLY HELPFUL. I'LL REMEMBER THAT WHEN SOMEONE ELSE GOES INSANE. AND SOMEONE WILL, WON'T THEY?
I IMAGINE SO. THIS IS DEFINITELY A PSIONIC ATTACK, BUT...
THAT "BUT" IS A BAD SIGN, ISN'T IT?
I HAVE NO IDEA WHO DID IT. OR HOW. AND THAT'S WEIRD, EVEN BY MY STANDARDS. IT ALSO MEANS THAT H.I.V.E. WILL WANT WHOEVER IS DOING THIS.
SO YOU HAVE NO IDEA WHO DID IT, AND IF WE DON'T FIND OUT SOON, WE'RE GOING TO HAVE TO FIGHT A BUNCH OF EVIL PSYCHICS FROM H.I.V.E.?
AS YOU WOULD SAY... YUP.
TERRIFIC.

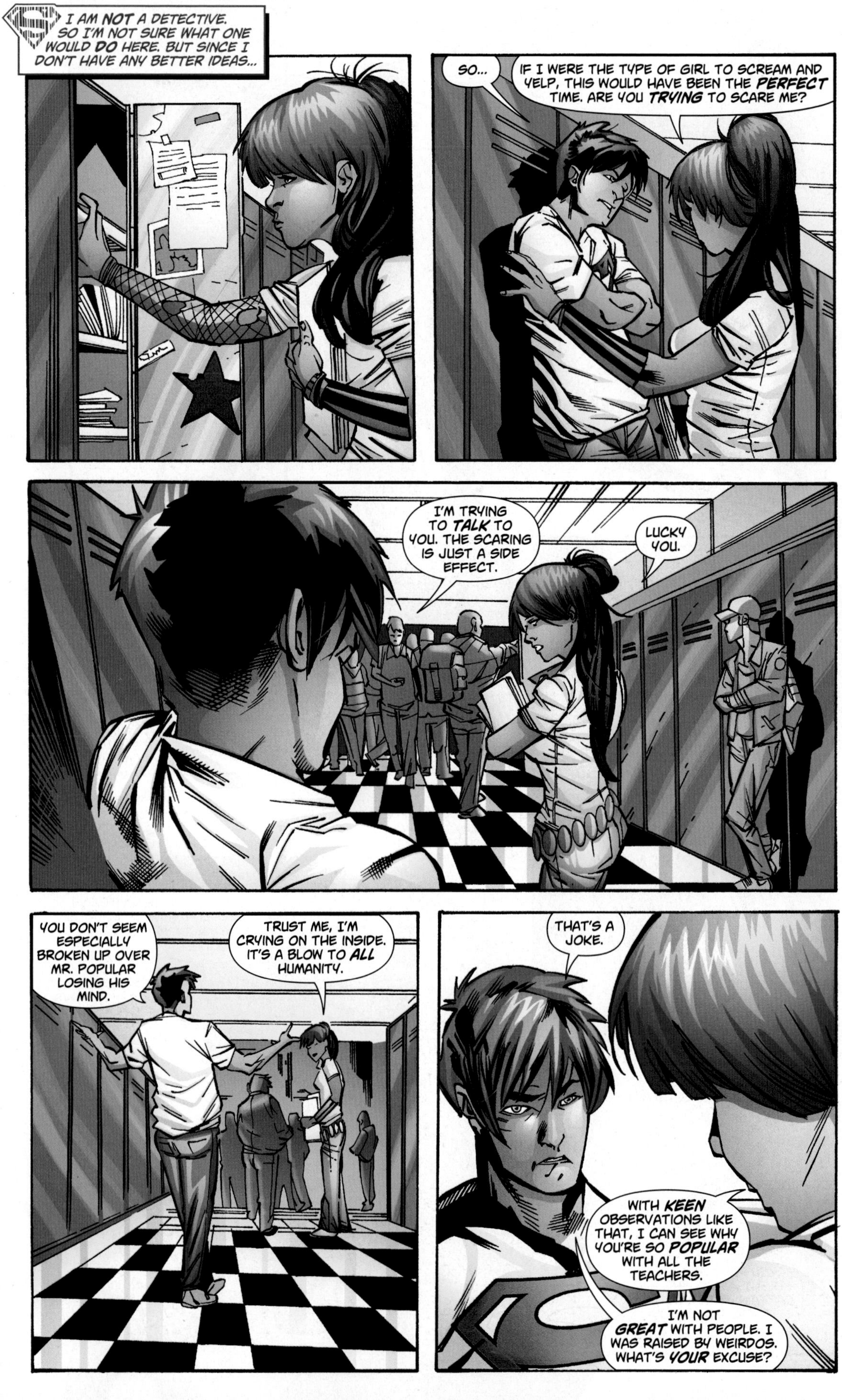

I AM NOT A DETECTIVE. SO I'M NOT SURE WHAT ONE WOULD DO HERE. BUT SINCE I DON'T HAVE ANY BETTER IDEAS...
SO...
IF I WERE THE TYPE OF GIRL TO SCREAM AND YELP, THIS WOULD HAVE BEEN THE PERFECT TIME. ARE YOU TRYING TO SCARE ME?
I'M TRYING TO TALK TO YOU. THE SCARING IS JUST A SIDE EFFECT.
LUCKY YOU.
YOU DON'T SEEM ESPECIALLY BROKEN UP OVER MR. POPULAR LOSING HIS MIND.
TRUST ME, I'M CRYING ON THE INSIDE. IT'S A BLOW TO ALL HUMANITY.
THAT'S A JOKE.
WITH KEEN OBSERVATIONS LIKE THAT, I CAN SEE WHY YOU'RE SO POPULAR WITH ALL THE TEACHERS.
I'M NOT GREAT WITH PEOPLE. I WAS RAISED BY WEIRDOS. WHAT'S YOUR EXCUSE?

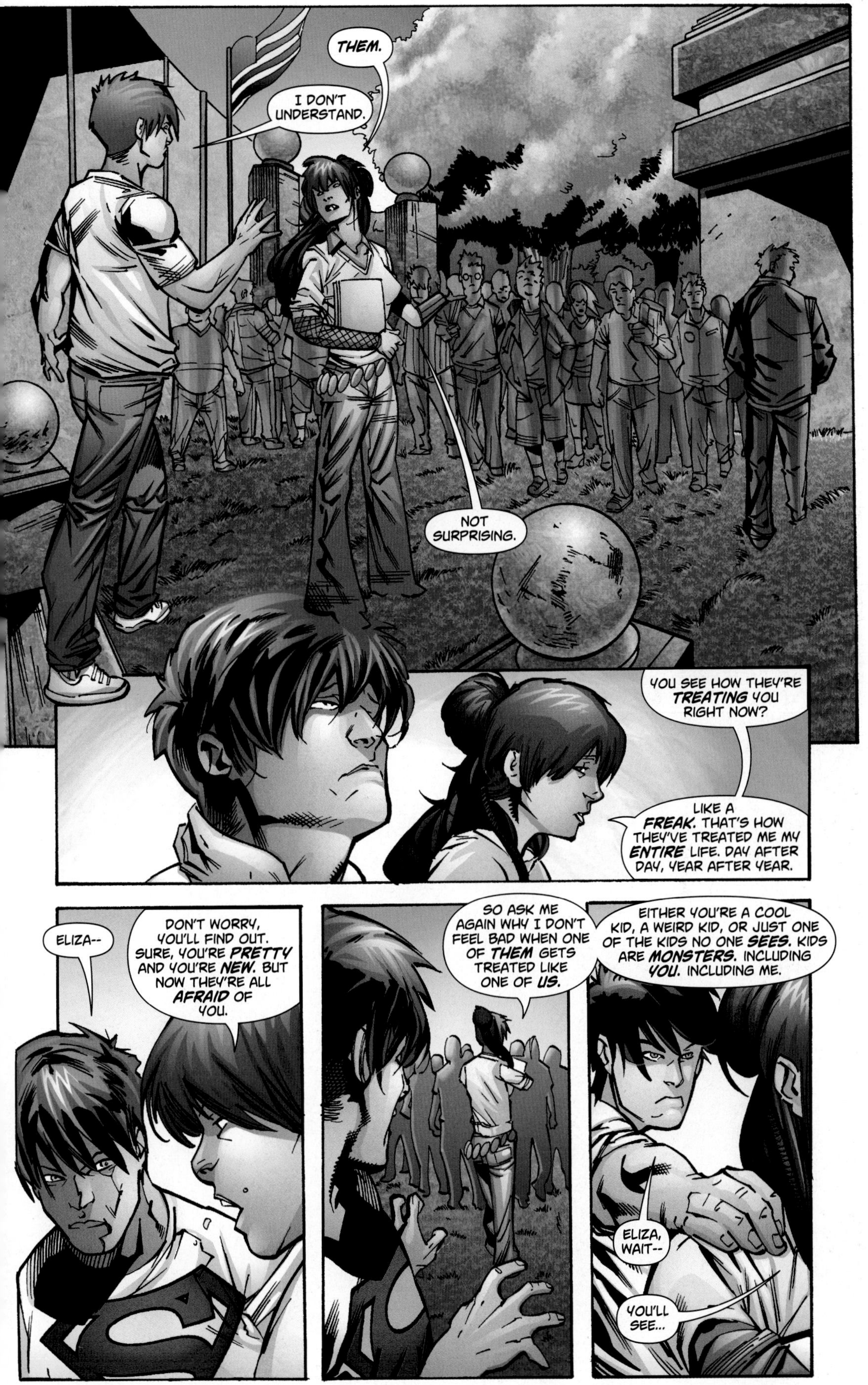
THEM.
I DON'T UNDERSTAND.
NOT SURPRISING.
YOU SEE HOW THEY'RE TREATING YOU RIGHT NOW?
LIKE A FREAK. THAT'S HOW THEY'VE TREATED ME MY ENTIRE LIFE. DAY AFTER DAY, YEAR AFTER YEAR.
ELIZA--
DON'T WORRY, YOU'LL FIND OUT. SURE, YOU'RE PRETTY AND YOU'RE NEW. BUT NOW THEY'RE ALL AFRAID OF YOU.
SO ASK ME AGAIN WHY I DON'T FEEL BAD WHEN ONE OF THEM GETS TREATED LIKE ONE OF US.
EITHER YOU'RE A COOL KID, A WEIRD KID, OR JUST ONE OF THE KIDS NO ONE SEES. KIDS ARE MONSTERS. INCLUDING YOU. INCLUDING ME.
ELIZA, WAIT--
YOU'LL SEE...

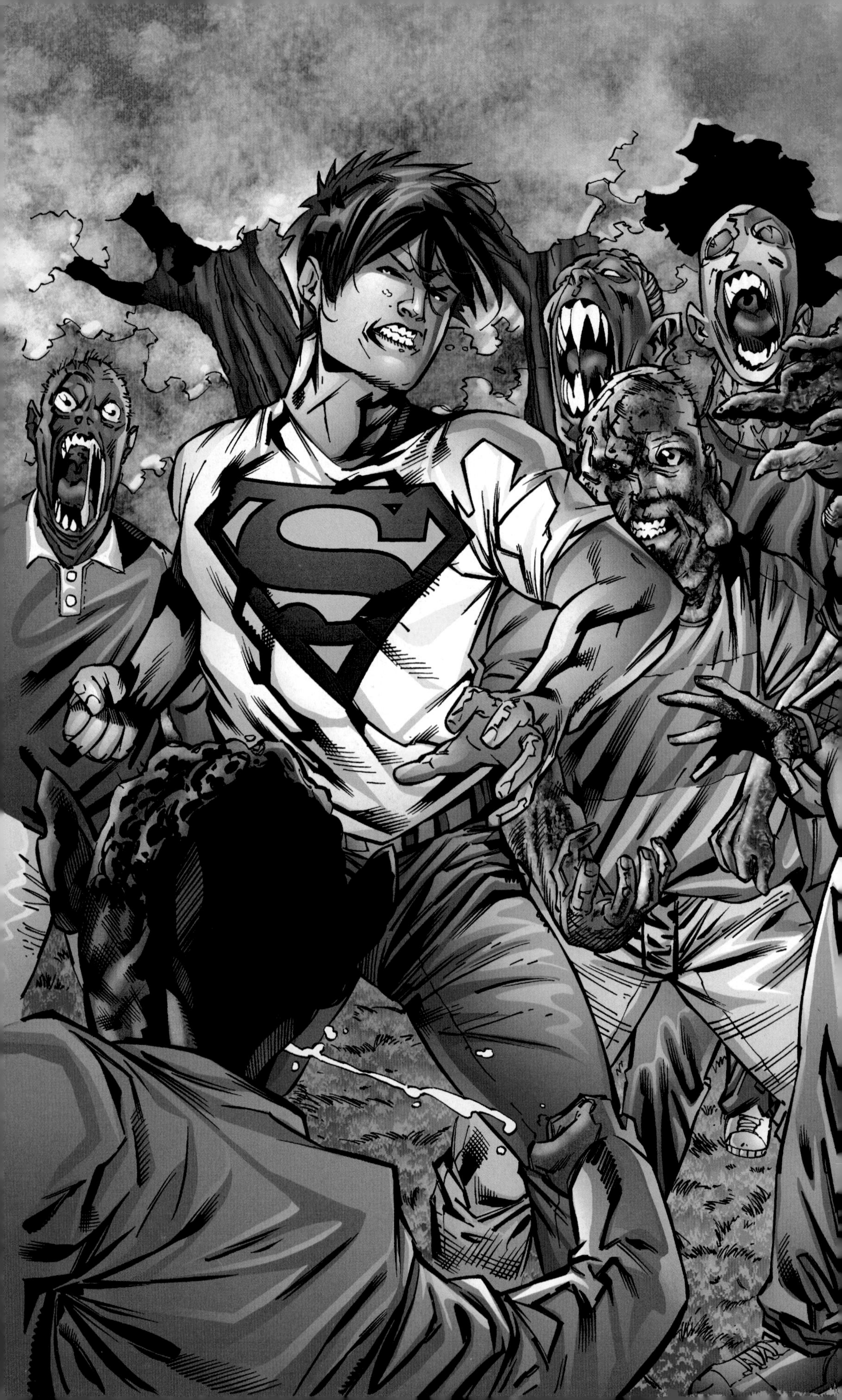

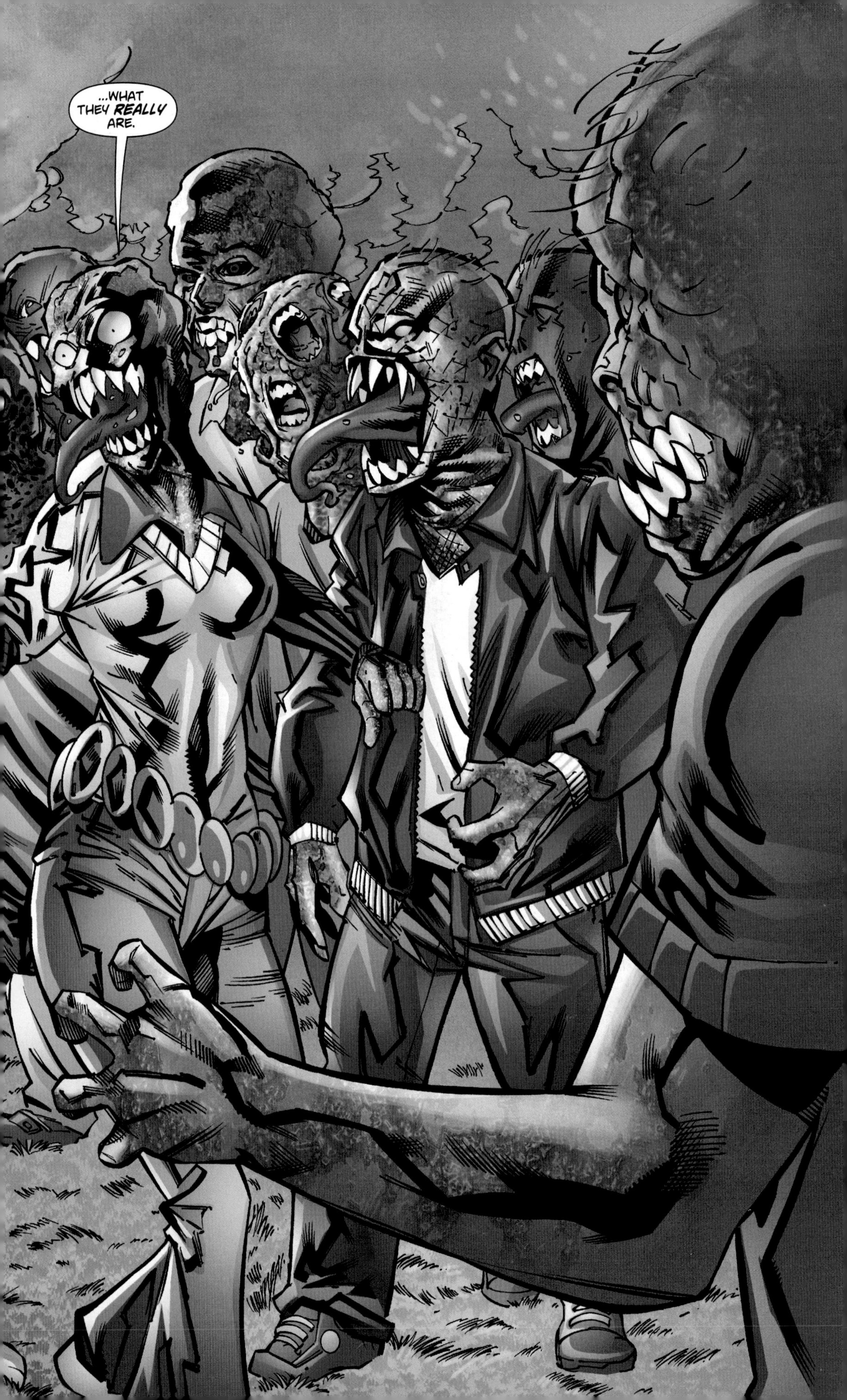
...WHAT THEY REALLY ARE.

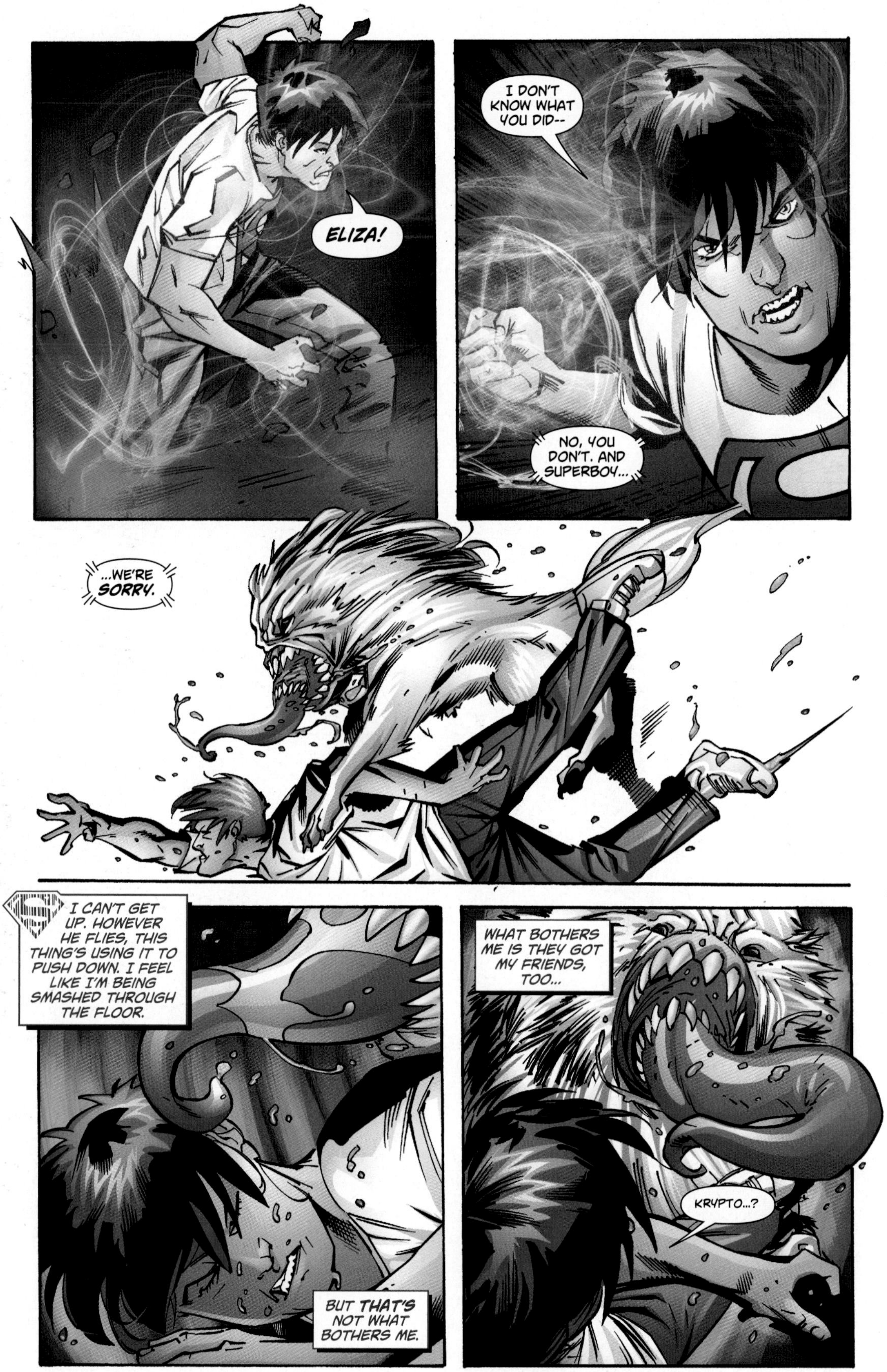
ELIZA!
I DON'T KNOW WHAT YOU DID--
NO, YOU DON'T. AND SUPERBOY...
...WE'RE SORRY.
I CAN'T GET UP. HOWEVER HE FLIES, THIS THING'S USING IT TO PUSH DOWN. I FEEL LIKE I'M BEING SMASHED THROUGH THE FLOOR.
BUT THAT'S NOT WHAT BOTHERS ME.
WHAT BOTHERS ME IS THEY GOT MY FRIENDS, TOO...
KRYPTO...?

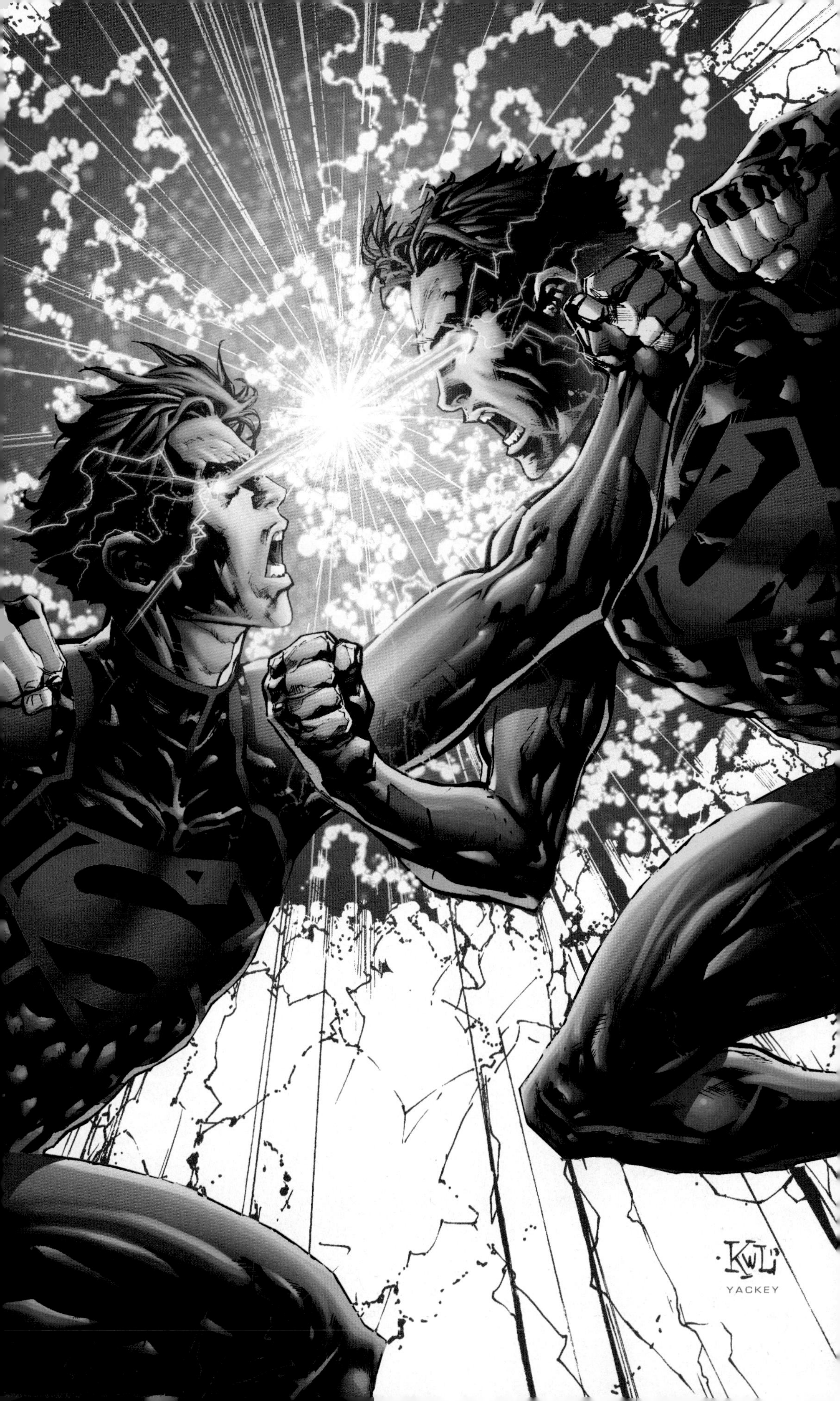
YACKEY

JUSTIN JORDAN writer ROBSON ROCHA MARCUS TO pencillers MARLO ALQUIZA MARCUS TO inkers cover art by KEN LASHLEY & MATT YACKE

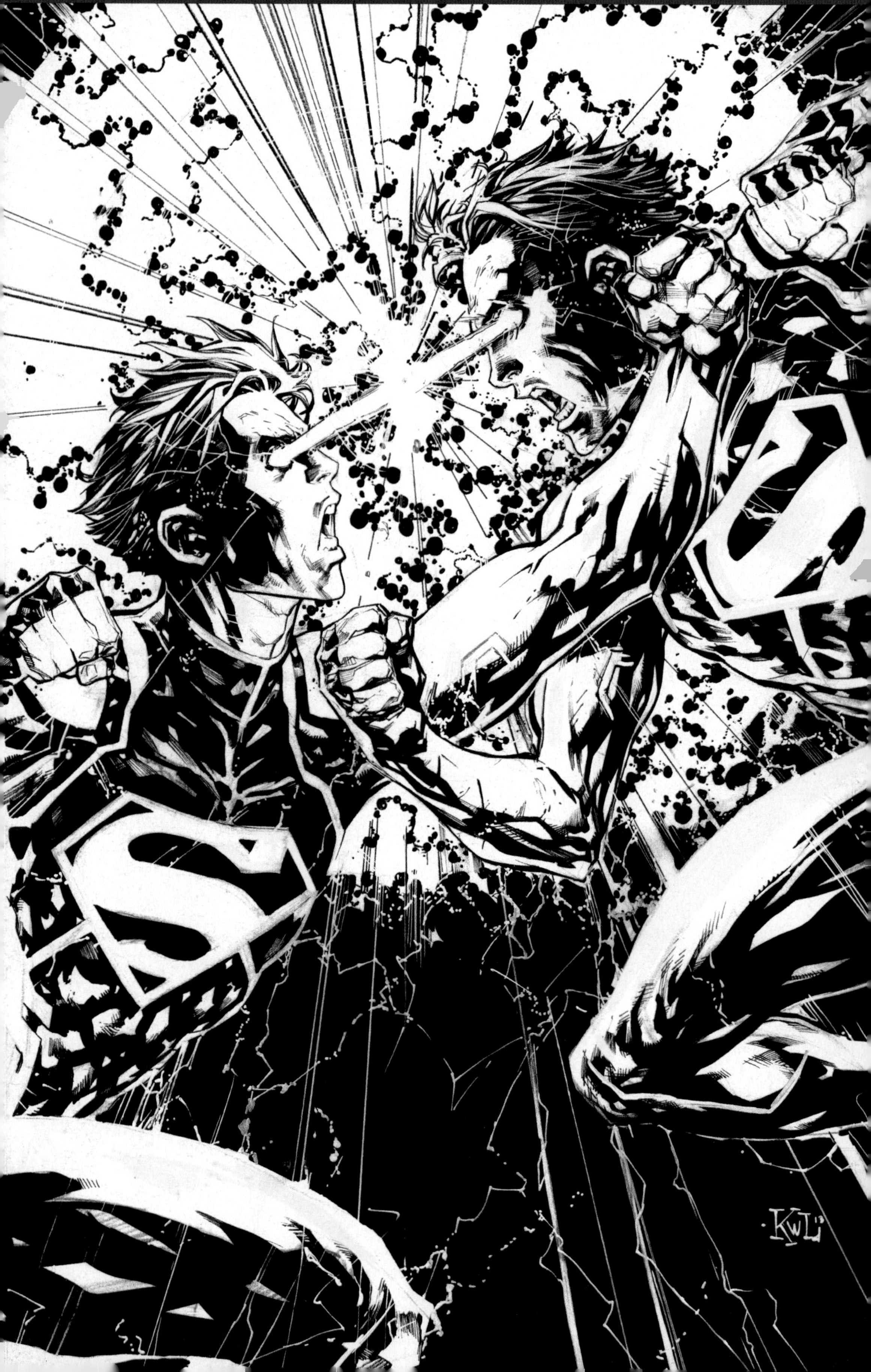

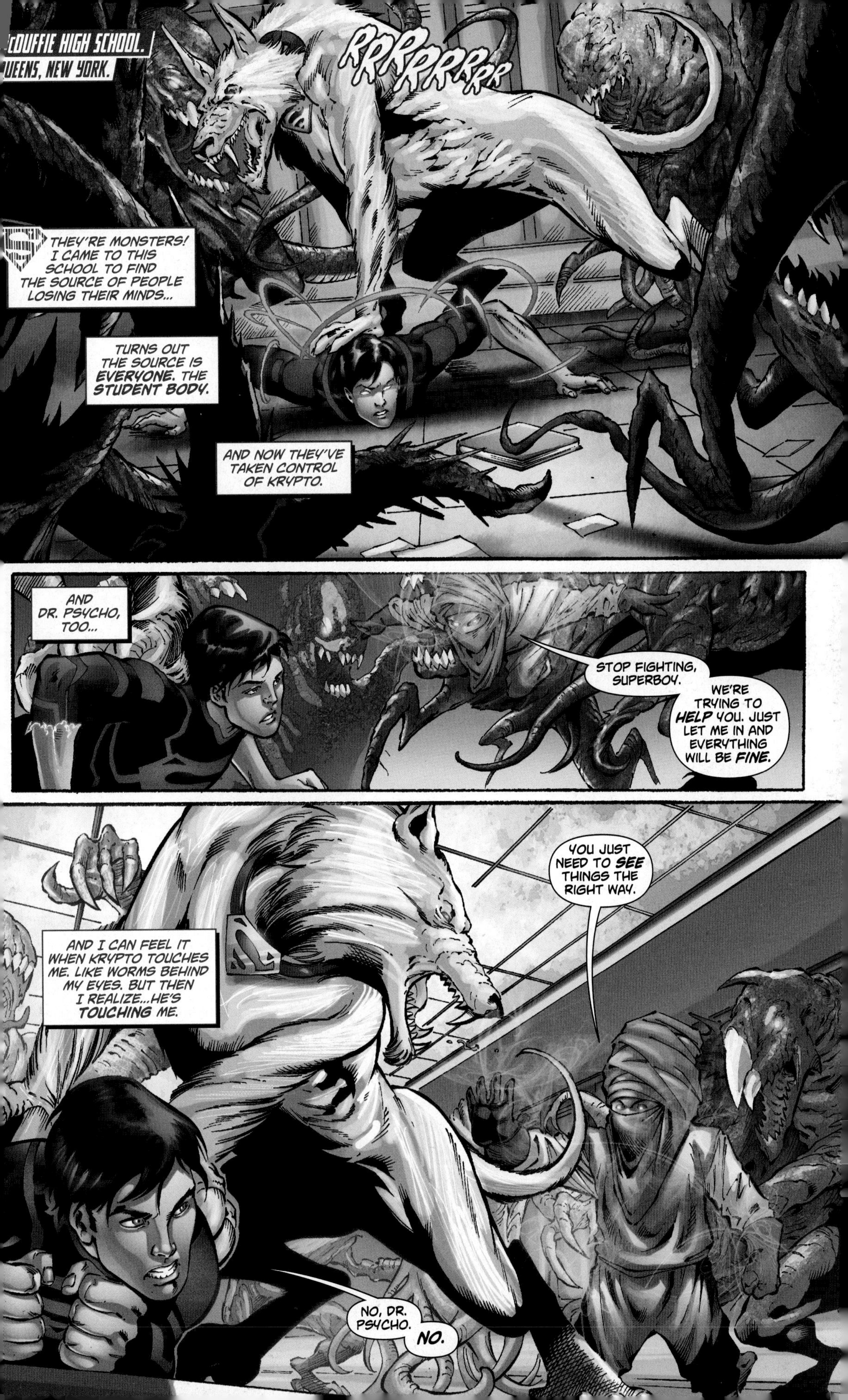

MCCOUFFIE HIGH SCHOOL.
QUEENS, NEW YORK.
RRRRRRRRRR
THEY'RE MONSTERS! I CAME TO THIS SCHOOL TO FIND THE SOURCE OF PEOPLE LOSING THEIR MINDS...
TURNS OUT THE SOURCE IS EVERYONE. THE STUDENT BODY.
AND NOW THEY'VE TAKEN CONTROL OF KRYPTO.
AND DR. PSYCHO, TOO...
STOP FIGHTING, SUPERBOY.
WE'RE TRYING TO HELP YOU. JUST LET ME IN AND EVERYTHING WILL BE FINE.
YOU JUST NEED TO SEE THINGS THE RIGHT WAY.
AND I CAN FEEL IT WHEN KRYPTO TOUCHES ME. LIKE WORMS BEHIND MY EYES. BUT THEN I REALIZE...HE'S TOUCHING ME.
NO, DR. PSYCHO.
NO.

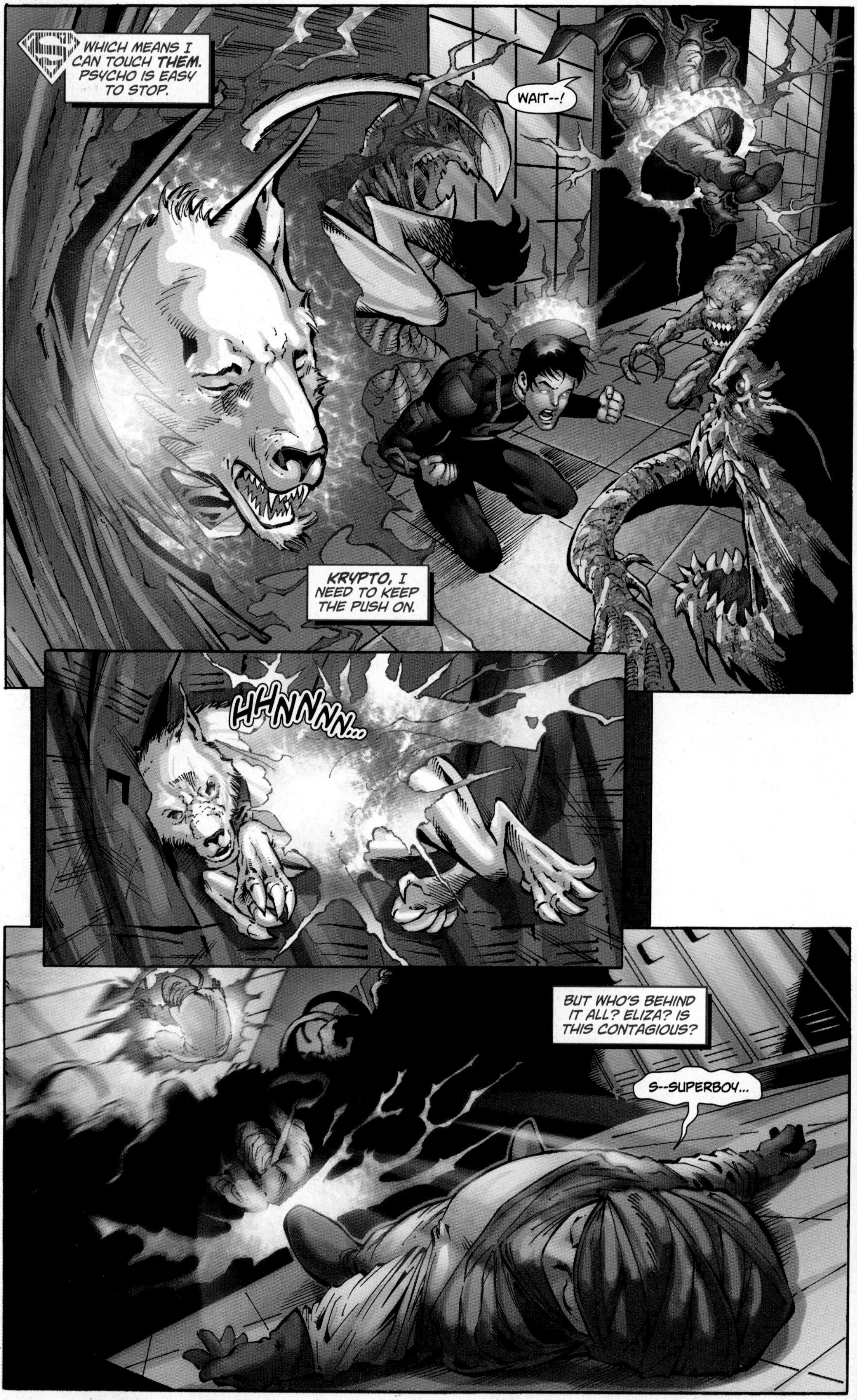
WHICH MEANS I CAN TOUCH **THEM**. PSYCHO IS EASY TO STOP.
WAIT--!
KRYPTO, I NEED TO KEEP THE PUSH ON.
HHNNNN...
BUT WHO'S BEHIND IT ALL? ELIZA? IS THIS CONTAGIOUS?
S--SUPERBOY...

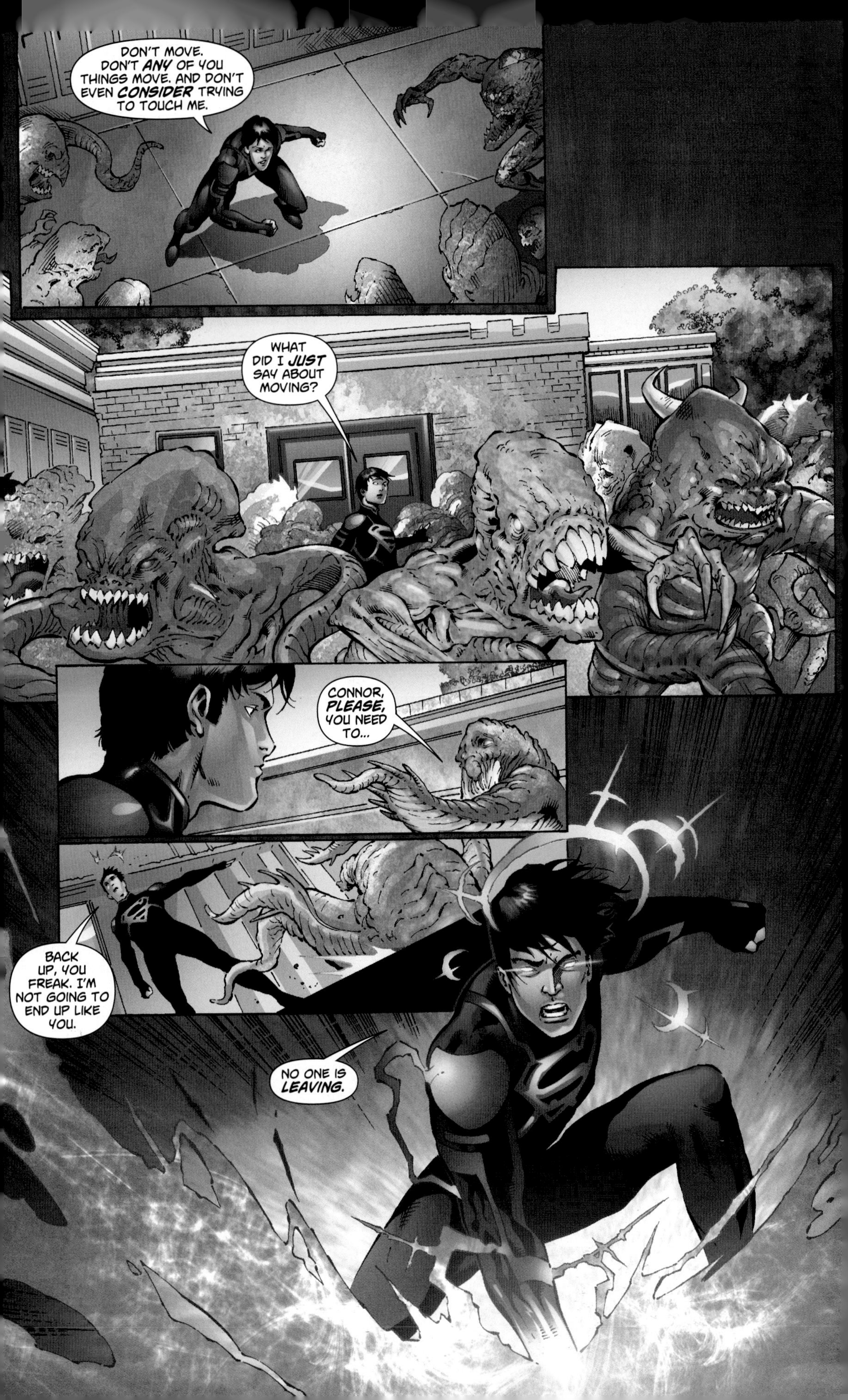
DON'T MOVE. DON'T ANY OF YOU THINGS MOVE. AND DON'T EVEN CONSIDER TRYING TO TOUCH ME.
WHAT DID I JUST SAY ABOUT MOVING?
CONNOR, PLEASE, YOU NEED TO...
BACK UP, YOU FREAK. I'M NOT GOING TO END UP LIKE YOU.
NO ONE IS LEAVING.

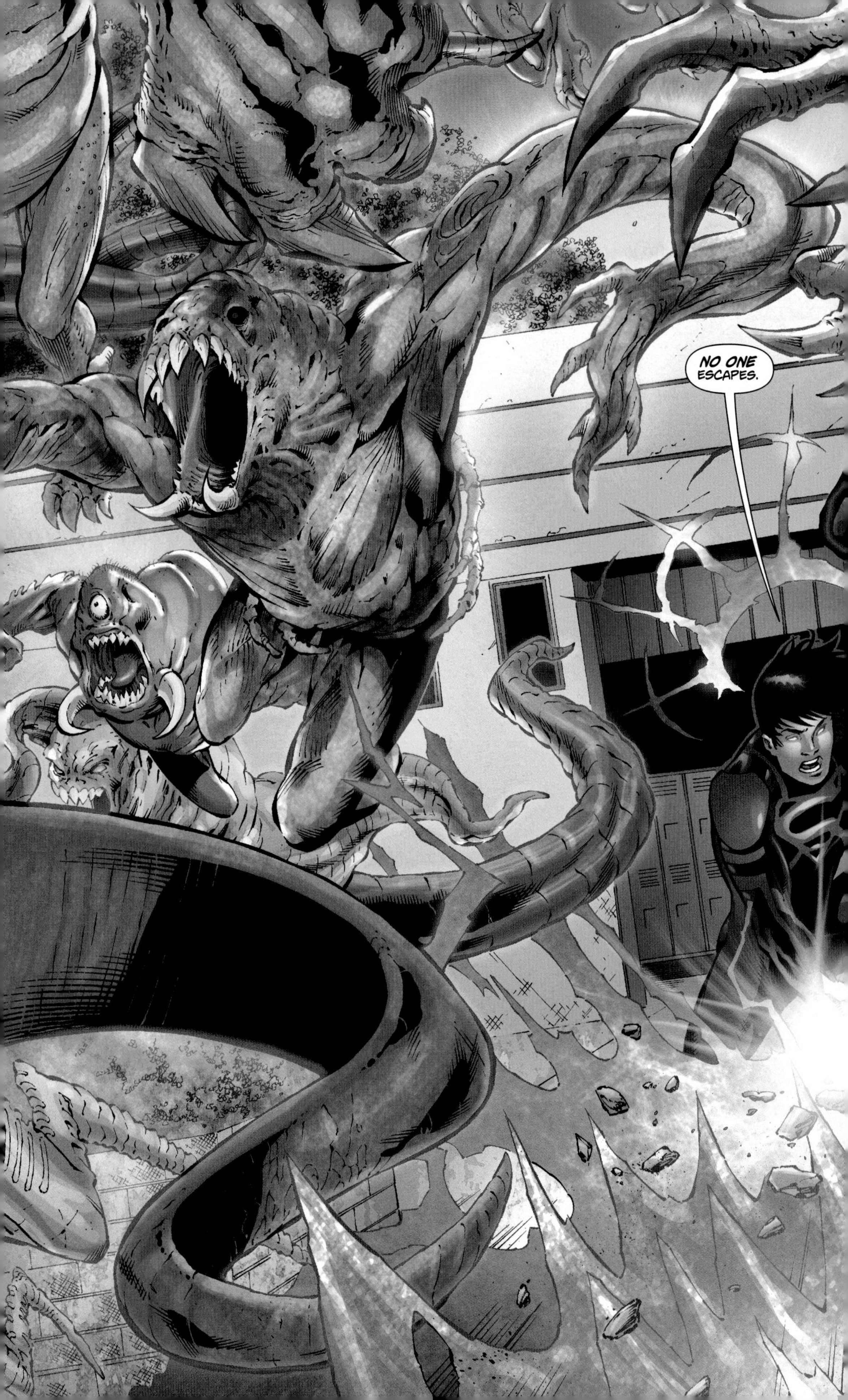
NO ONE ESCAPES.

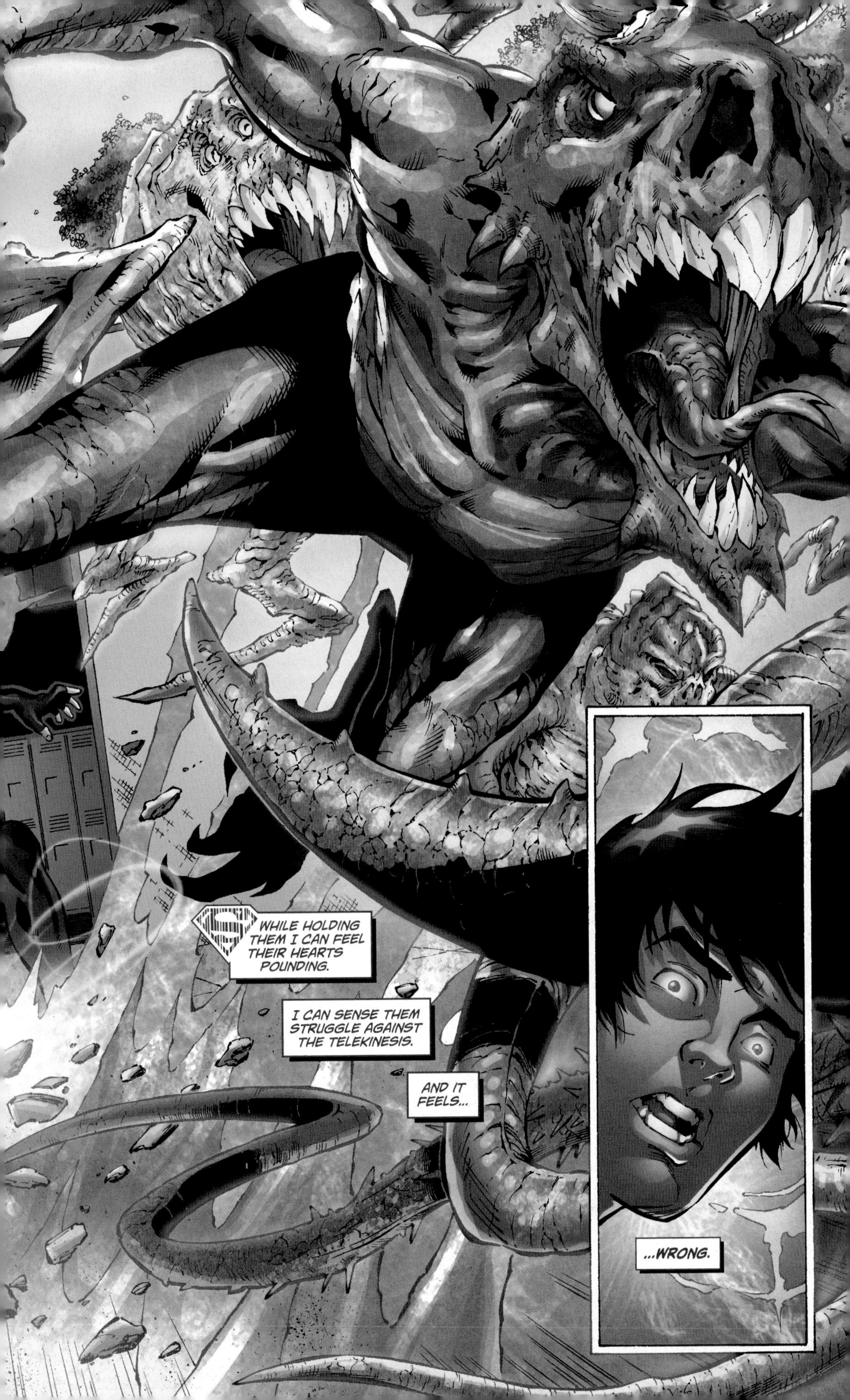
WHILE HOLDING THEM I CAN FEEL THEIR HEARTS POUNDING.
I CAN SENSE THEM STRUGGLE AGAINST THE TELEKINESIS.
AND IT FEELS...
...WRONG.

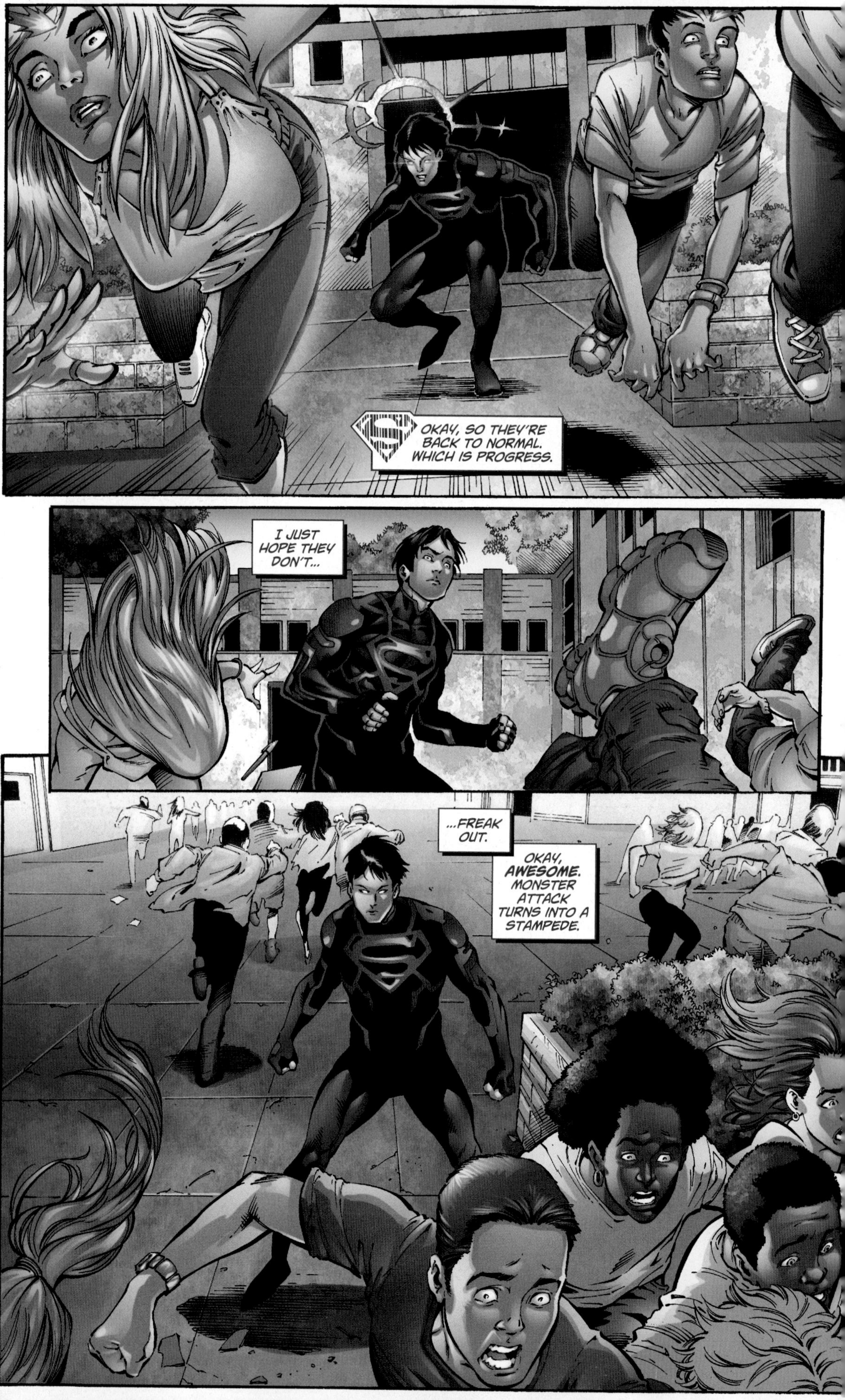
OKAY, SO THEY'RE BACK TO NORMAL. WHICH IS PROGRESS.
I JUST HOPE THEY DON'T...
...FREAK OUT.
OKAY, **AWESOME.** MONSTER ATTACK TURNS INTO A STAMPEDE.

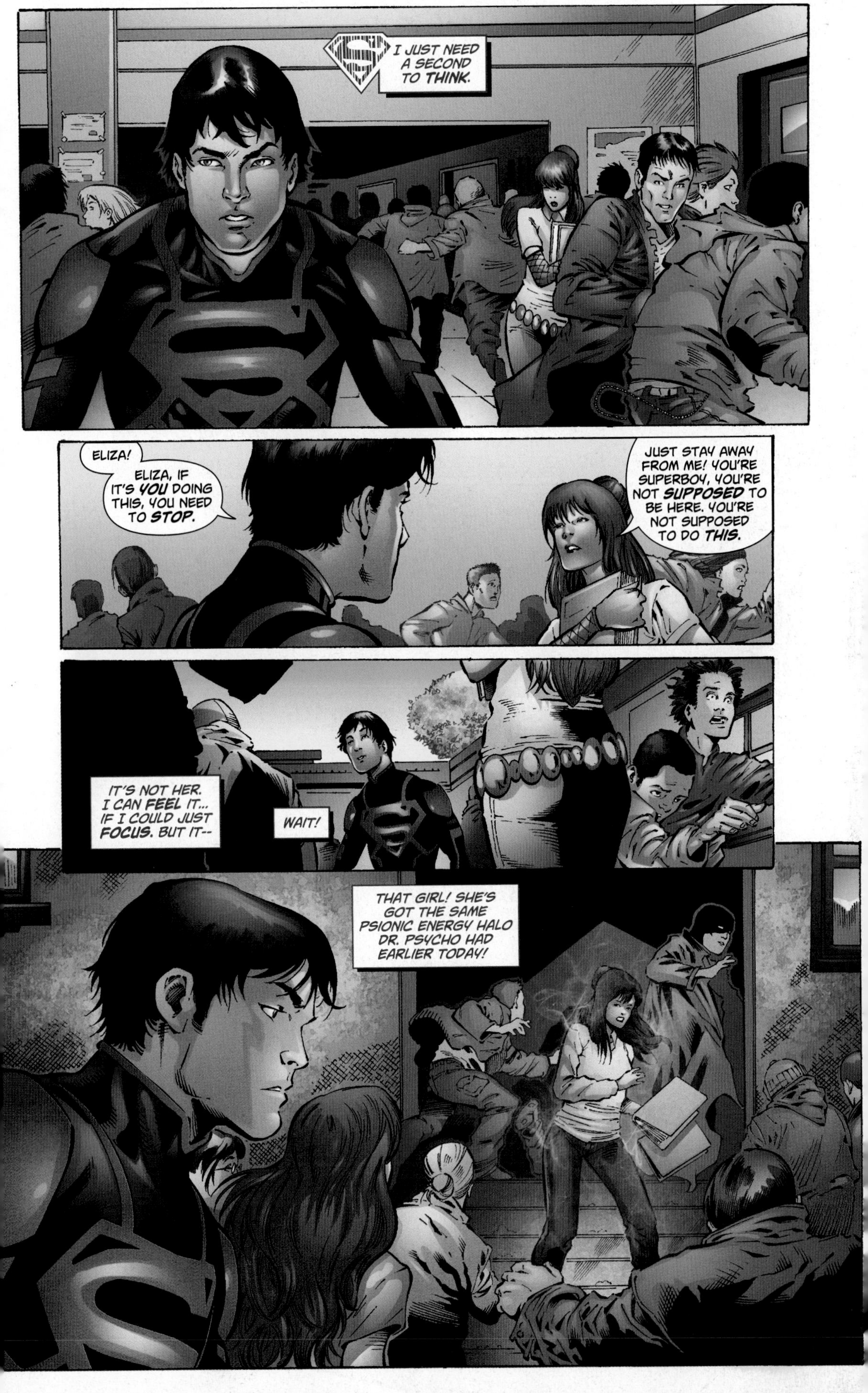
I JUST NEED A SECOND TO THINK.
ELIZA!
ELIZA, IF IT'S YOU DOING THIS, YOU NEED TO STOP.
JUST STAY AWAY FROM ME! YOU'RE SUPERBOY, YOU'RE NOT SUPPOSED TO BE HERE. YOU'RE NOT SUPPOSED TO DO THIS.
IT'S NOT HER. I CAN FEEL IT... IF I COULD JUST FOCUS. BUT IT--
WAIT!
THAT GIRL! SHE'S GOT THE SAME PSIONIC ENERGY HALO DR. PSYCHO HAD EARLIER TODAY!

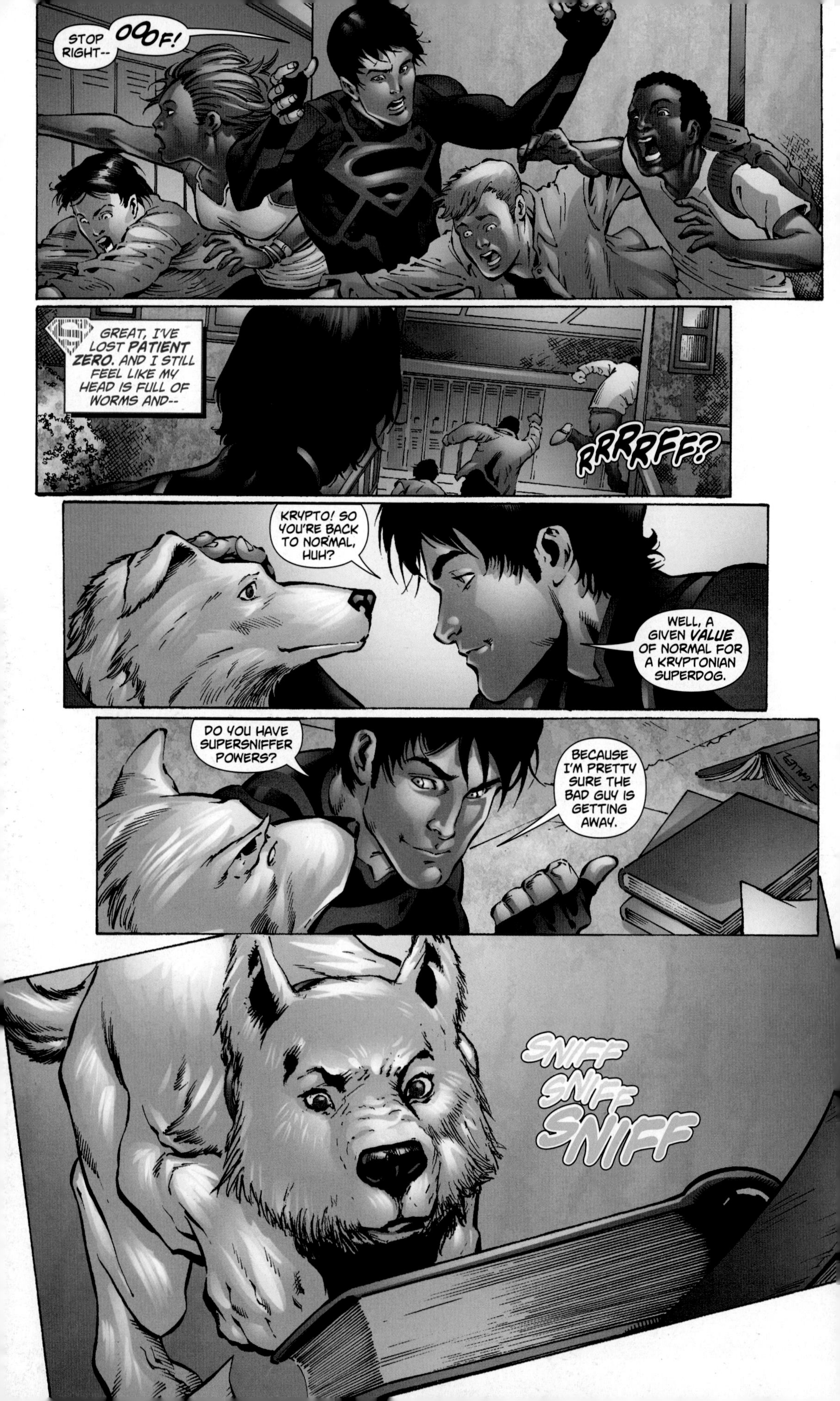
STOP RIGHT--
OOOF!
GREAT, I'VE LOST PATIENT ZERO. AND I STILL FEEL LIKE MY HEAD IS FULL OF WORMS AND--
RRRRFF?
KRYPTO! SO YOU'RE BACK TO NORMAL, HUH?
WELL, A GIVEN VALUE OF NORMAL FOR A KRYPTONIAN SUPERDOG.
DO YOU HAVE SUPERSNIFFER POWERS?
BECAUSE I'M PRETTY SURE THE BAD GUY IS GETTING AWAY.
SNIFF
SNIFF
SNIFF

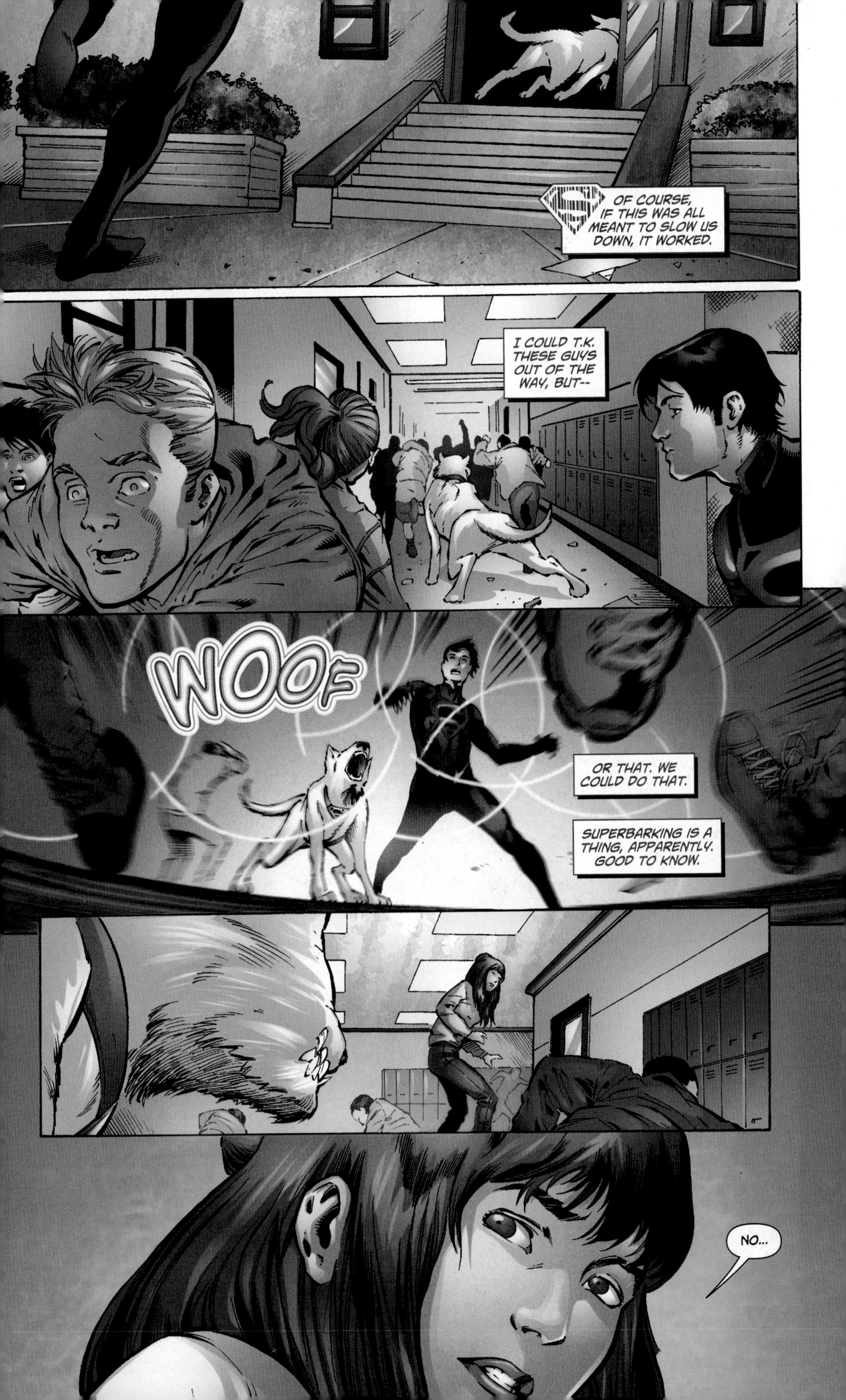
OF COURSE, IF THIS WAS ALL MEANT TO SLOW US DOWN, IT WORKED.
I COULD T.K. THESE GUYS OUT OF THE WAY, BUT--
WOOF
OR THAT. WE COULD DO THAT.
SUPERBARKING IS A THING, APPARENTLY. GOOD TO KNOW.
NO...

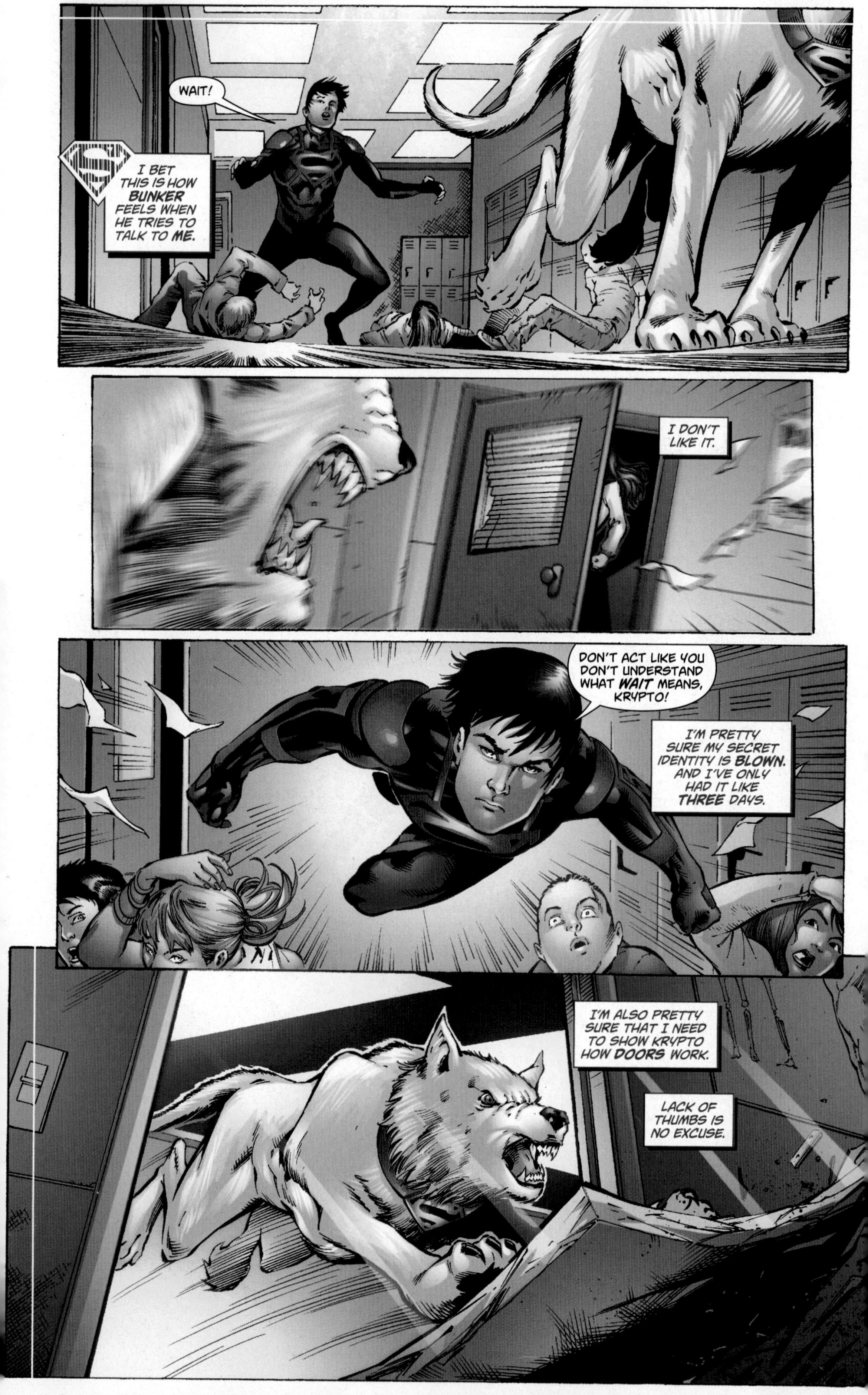
WAIT!
I BET THIS IS HOW BUNKER FEELS WHEN HE TRIES TO TALK TO ME.
I DON'T LIKE IT.
DON'T ACT LIKE YOU DON'T UNDERSTAND WHAT WAIT MEANS, KRYPTO!
I'M PRETTY SURE MY SECRET IDENTITY IS BLOWN. AND I'VE ONLY HAD IT LIKE THREE DAYS.
I'M ALSO PRETTY SURE THAT I NEED TO SHOW KRYPTO HOW DOORS WORK.
LACK OF THUMBS IS NO EXCUSE.

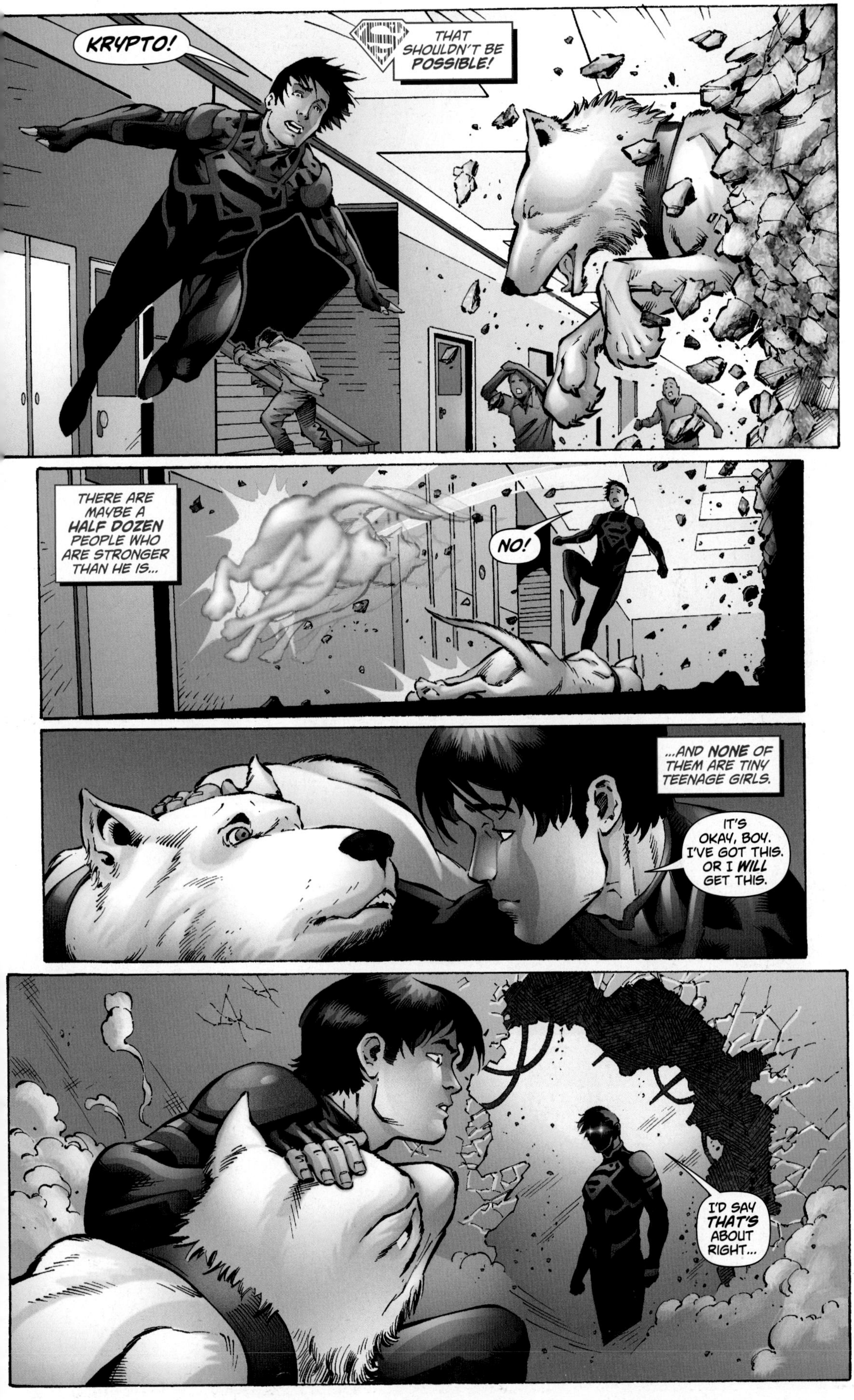
KRYPTO!
THAT SHOULDN'T BE POSSIBLE!
THERE ARE MAYBE A HALF DOZEN PEOPLE WHO ARE STRONGER THAN HE IS...
NO!
...AND NONE OF THEM ARE TINY TEENAGE GIRLS.
IT'S OKAY, BOY. I'VE GOT THIS. OR I WILL GET THIS.
I'D SAY THAT'S ABOUT RIGHT...

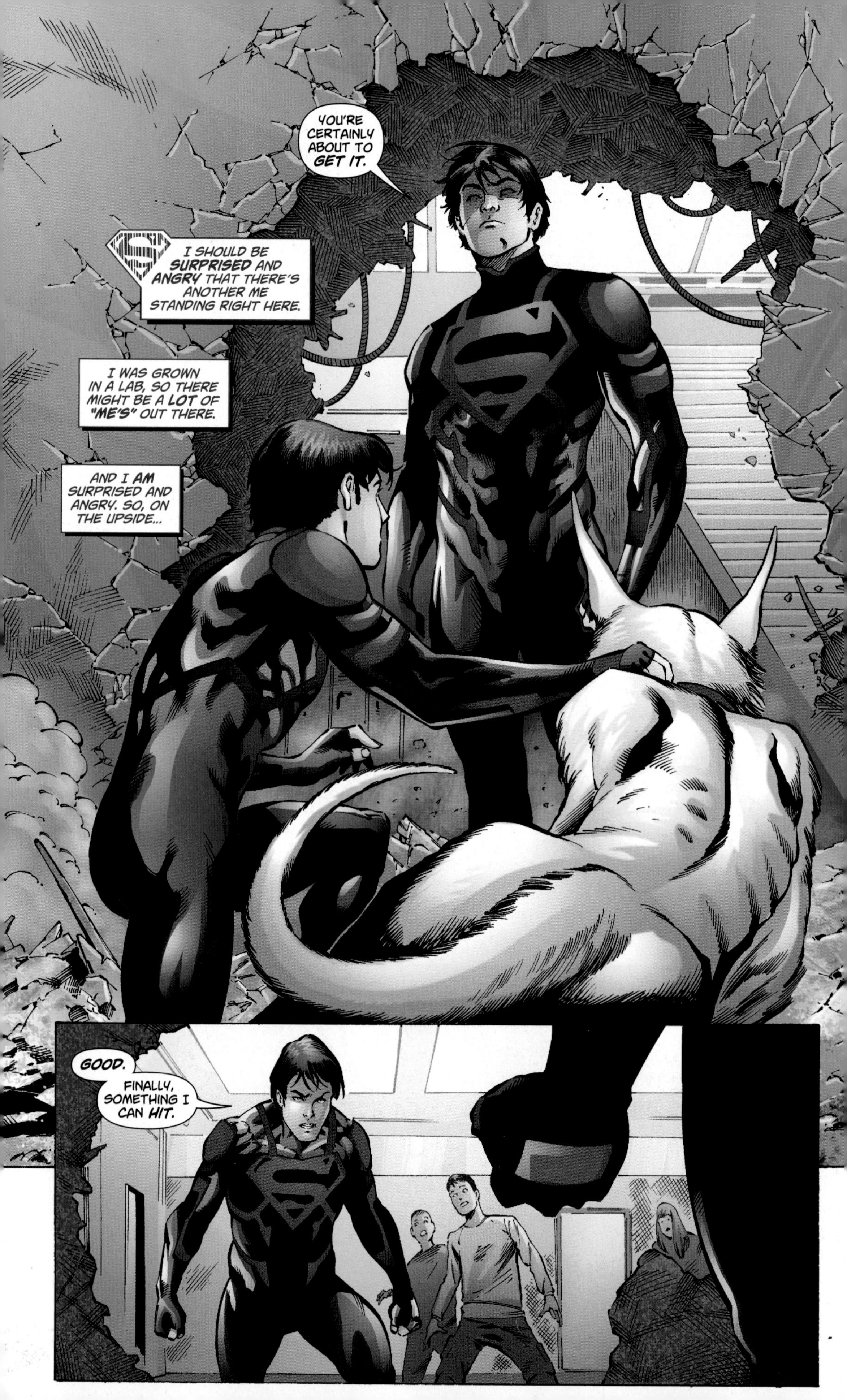
YOU'RE CERTAINLY ABOUT TO GET IT.
I SHOULD BE SURPRISED AND ANGRY THAT THERE'S ANOTHER ME STANDING RIGHT HERE.
I WAS GROWN IN A LAB, SO THERE MIGHT BE A LOT OF "ME'S" OUT THERE.
AND I AM SURPRISED AND ANGRY. SO, ON THE UPSIDE...
GOOD.
FINALLY, SOMETHING I CAN HIT.

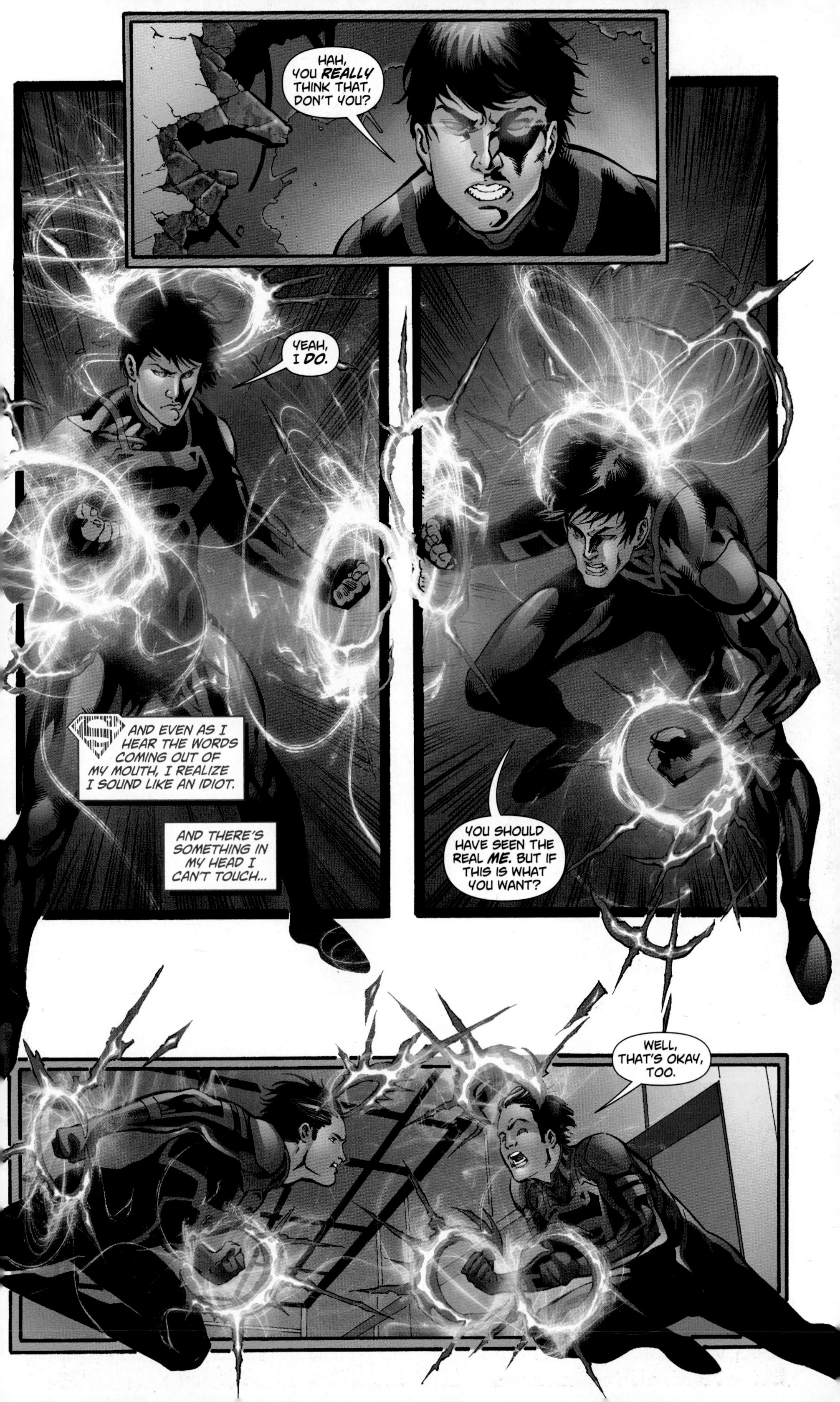
HAH, YOU REALLY THINK THAT, DON'T YOU?
YEAH, I DO.
AND EVEN AS I HEAR THE WORDS COMING OUT OF MY MOUTH, I REALIZE I SOUND LIKE AN IDIOT.
AND THERE'S SOMETHING IN MY HEAD I CAN'T TOUCH...
YOU SHOULD HAVE SEEN THE REAL ME. BUT IF THIS IS WHAT YOU WANT?
WELL, THAT'S OKAY, TOO.

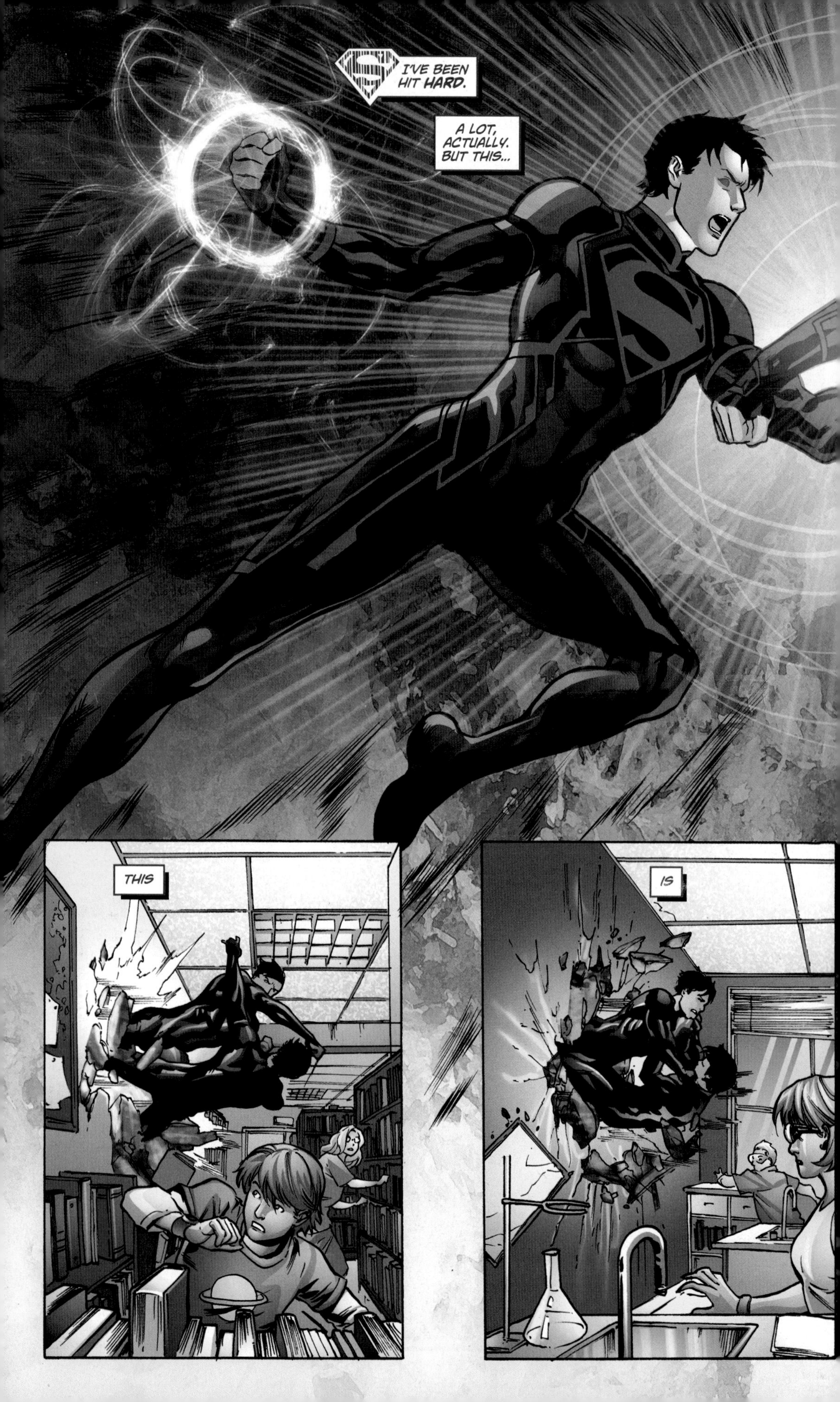

I'VE BEEN HIT HARD.
A LOT, ACTUALLY. BUT THIS...
THIS
IS

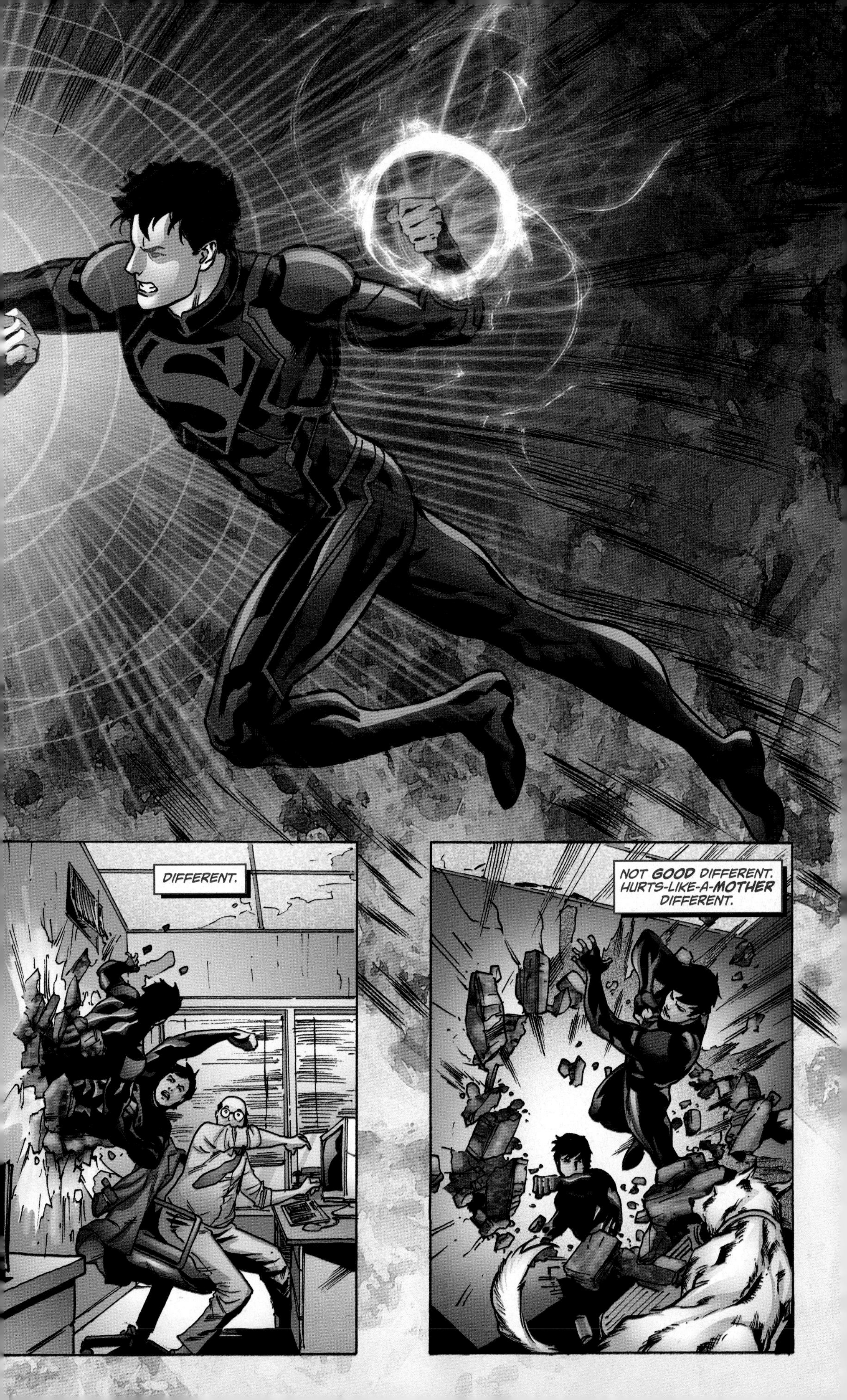
DIFFERENT.
NOT GOOD DIFFERENT. HURTS-LIKE-A-MOTHER DIFFERENT.

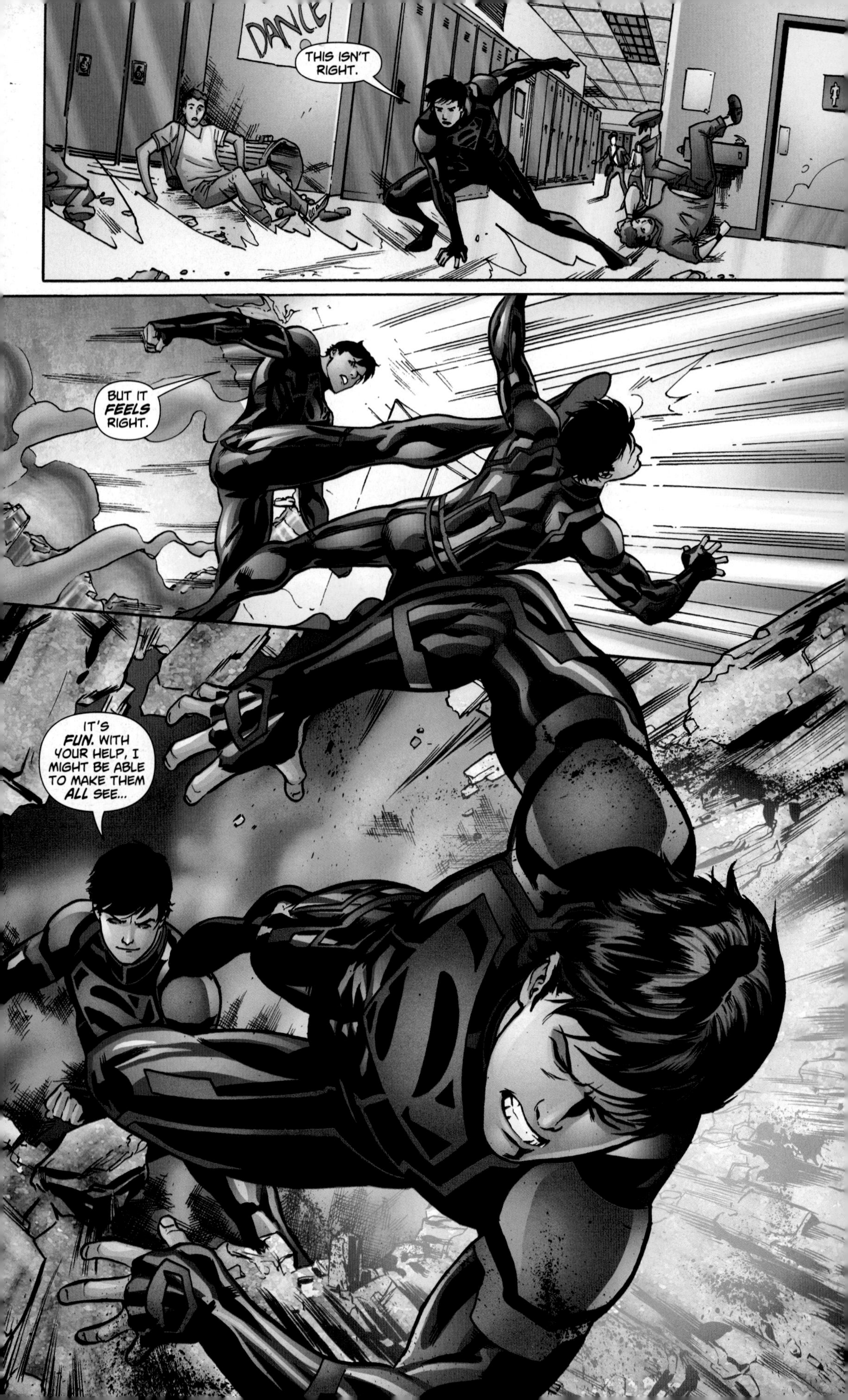
DANCE
THIS ISN'T RIGHT.
BUT IT FEELS RIGHT.
IT'S FUN. WITH YOUR HELP, I MIGHT BE ABLE TO MAKE THEM ALL SEE...

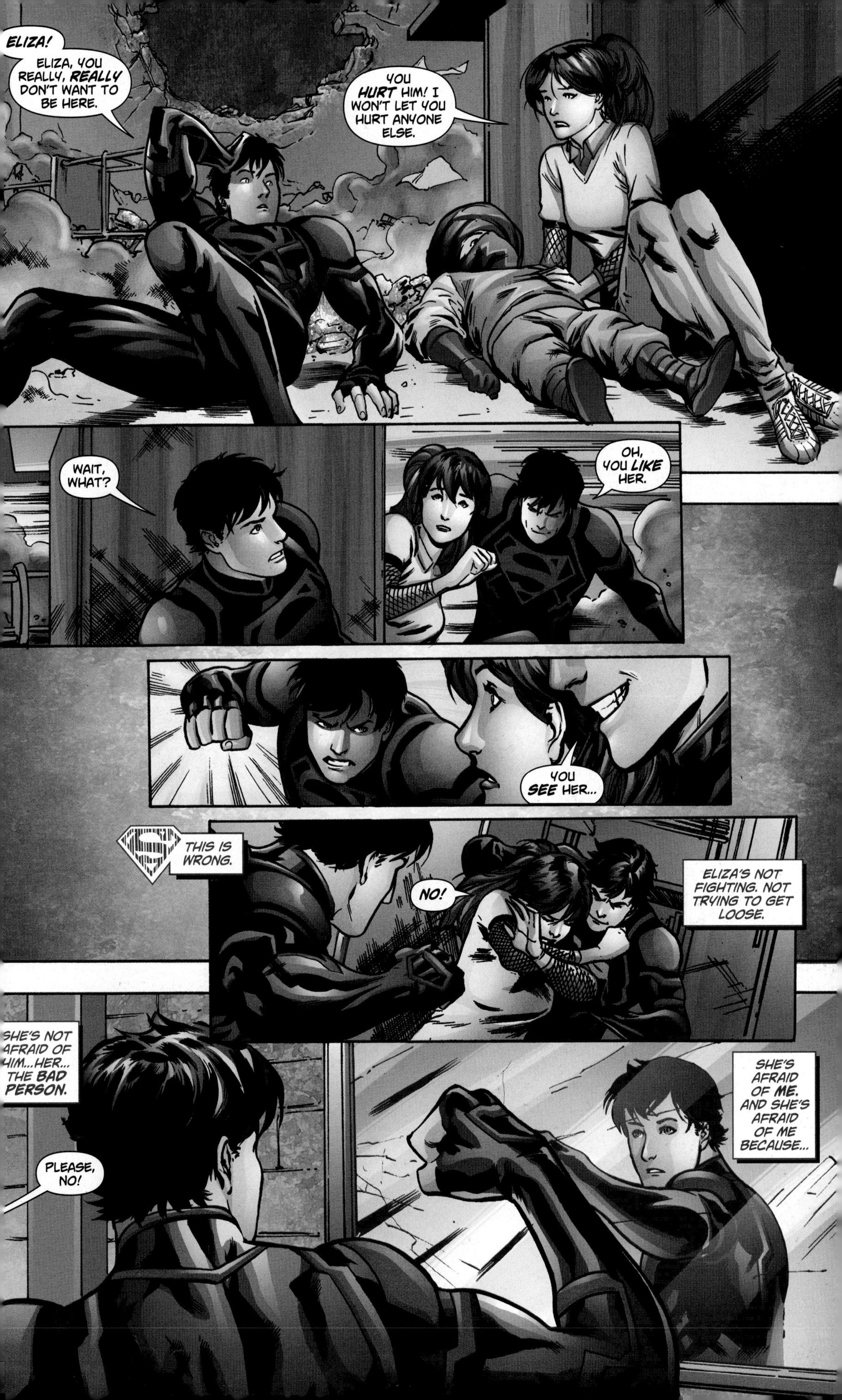

ELIZA!
ELIZA, YOU REALLY, REALLY DON'T WANT TO BE HERE.
YOU HURT HIM! I WON'T LET YOU HURT ANYONE ELSE.
WAIT, WHAT?
OH, YOU LIKE HER.
YOU SEE HER...
THIS IS WRONG.
NO!
ELIZA'S NOT FIGHTING. NOT TRYING TO GET LOOSE.
SHE'S NOT AFRAID OF HIM...HER... THE BAD PERSON.
PLEASE, NO!
SHE'S AFRAID OF ME. AND SHE'S AFRAID OF ME BECAUSE...

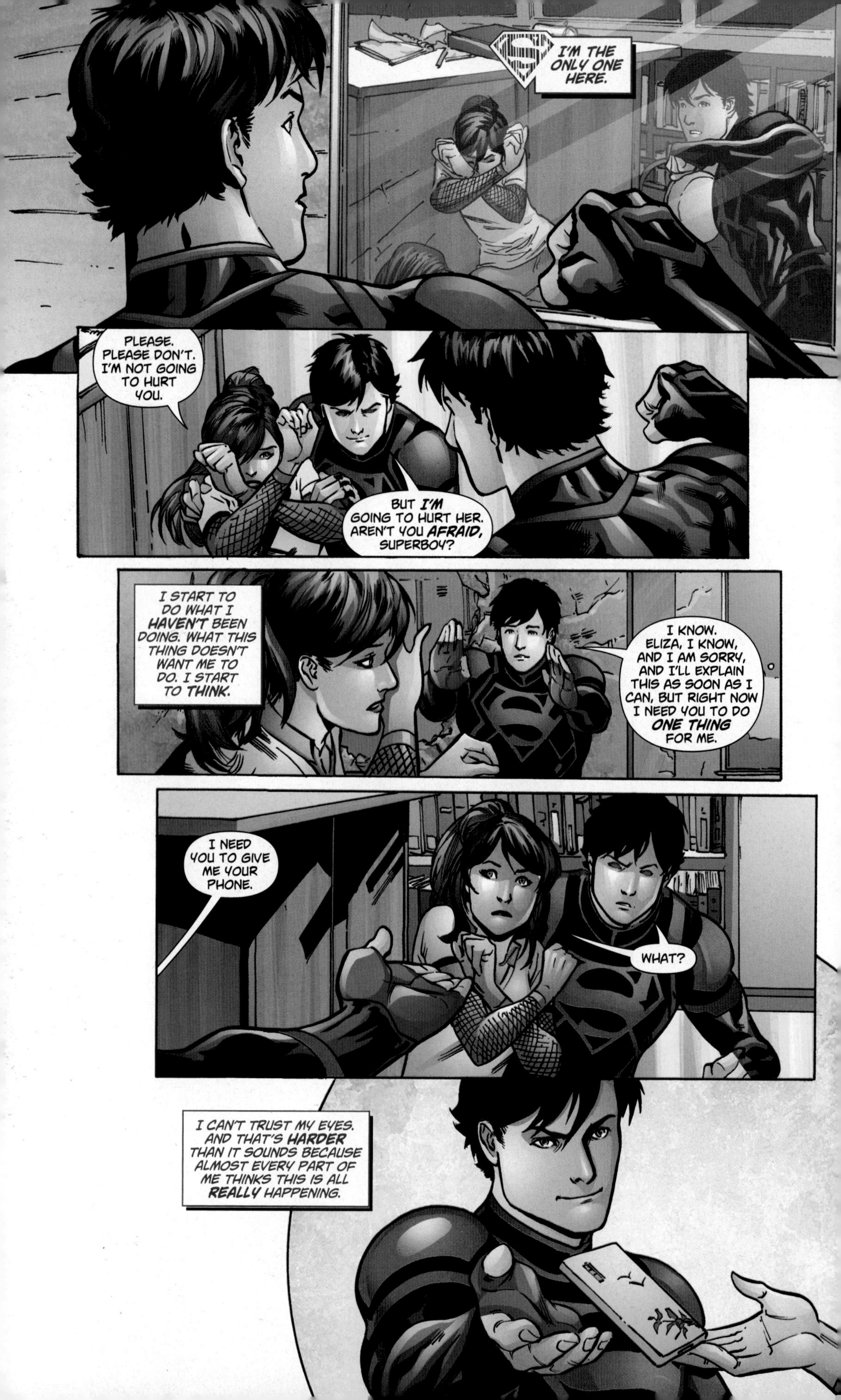
I'M THE ONLY ONE HERE.
PLEASE. PLEASE DON'T. I'M NOT GOING TO HURT YOU.
BUT I'M GOING TO HURT HER. AREN'T YOU AFRAID, SUPERBOY?
I START TO DO WHAT I HAVEN'T BEEN DOING. WHAT THIS THING DOESN'T WANT ME TO DO. I START TO THINK.
I KNOW. ELIZA, I KNOW, AND I AM SORRY, AND I'LL EXPLAIN THIS AS SOON AS I CAN, BUT RIGHT NOW I NEED YOU TO DO ONE THING FOR ME.
I NEED YOU TO GIVE ME YOUR PHONE.
WHAT?
I CAN'T TRUST MY EYES. AND THAT'S HARDER THAN IT SOUNDS BECAUSE ALMOST EVERY PART OF ME THINKS THIS IS ALL REALLY HAPPENING.

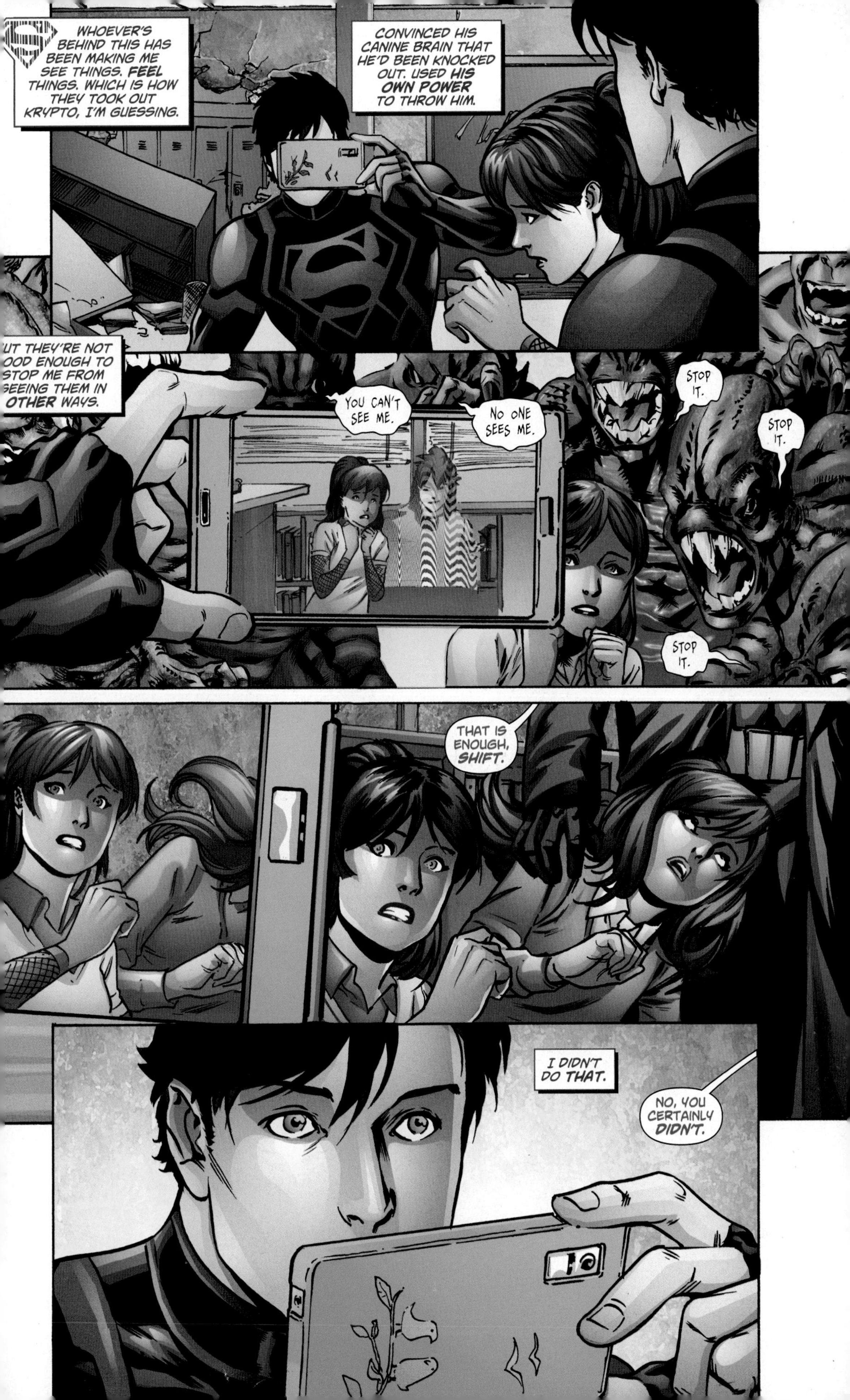
WHOEVER'S BEHIND THIS HAS BEEN MAKING ME SEE THINGS. FEEL THINGS. WHICH IS HOW THEY TOOK OUT KRYPTO, I'M GUESSING.
CONVINCED HIS CANINE BRAIN THAT HE'D BEEN KNOCKED OUT. USED HIS OWN POWER TO THROW HIM.
UT THEY'RE NOT OOD ENOUGH TO STOP ME FROM EEING THEM IN OTHER WAYS.
YOU CAN'T SEE ME.
NO ONE SEES ME.
STOP IT.
STOP IT.
STOP IT.
THAT IS ENOUGH, SHIFT.
I DIDN'T DO THAT.
NO, YOU CERTAINLY DIDN'T.

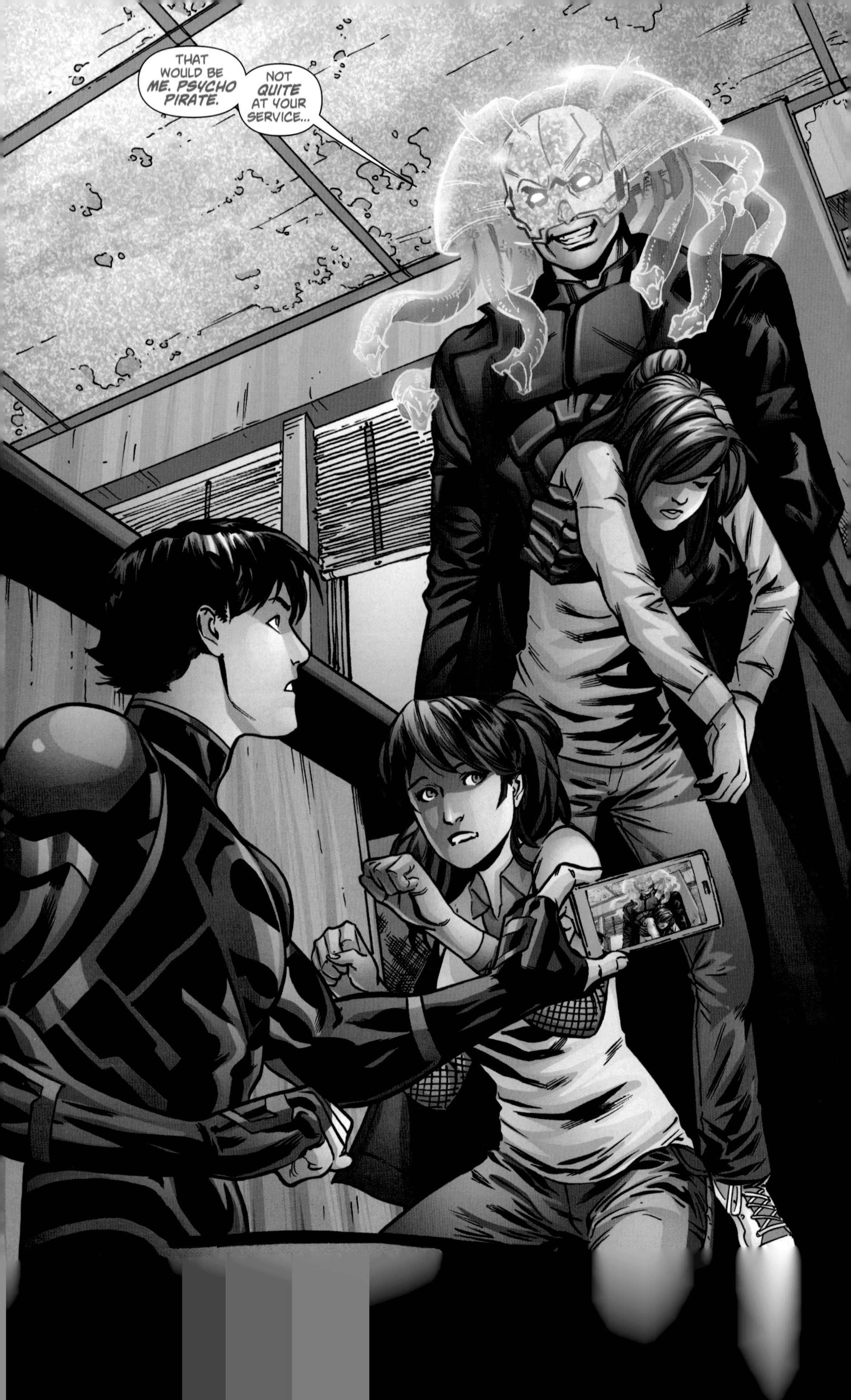
THAT WOULD BE ME. PSYCHO PIRATE.
NOT QUITE AT YOUR SERVICE...

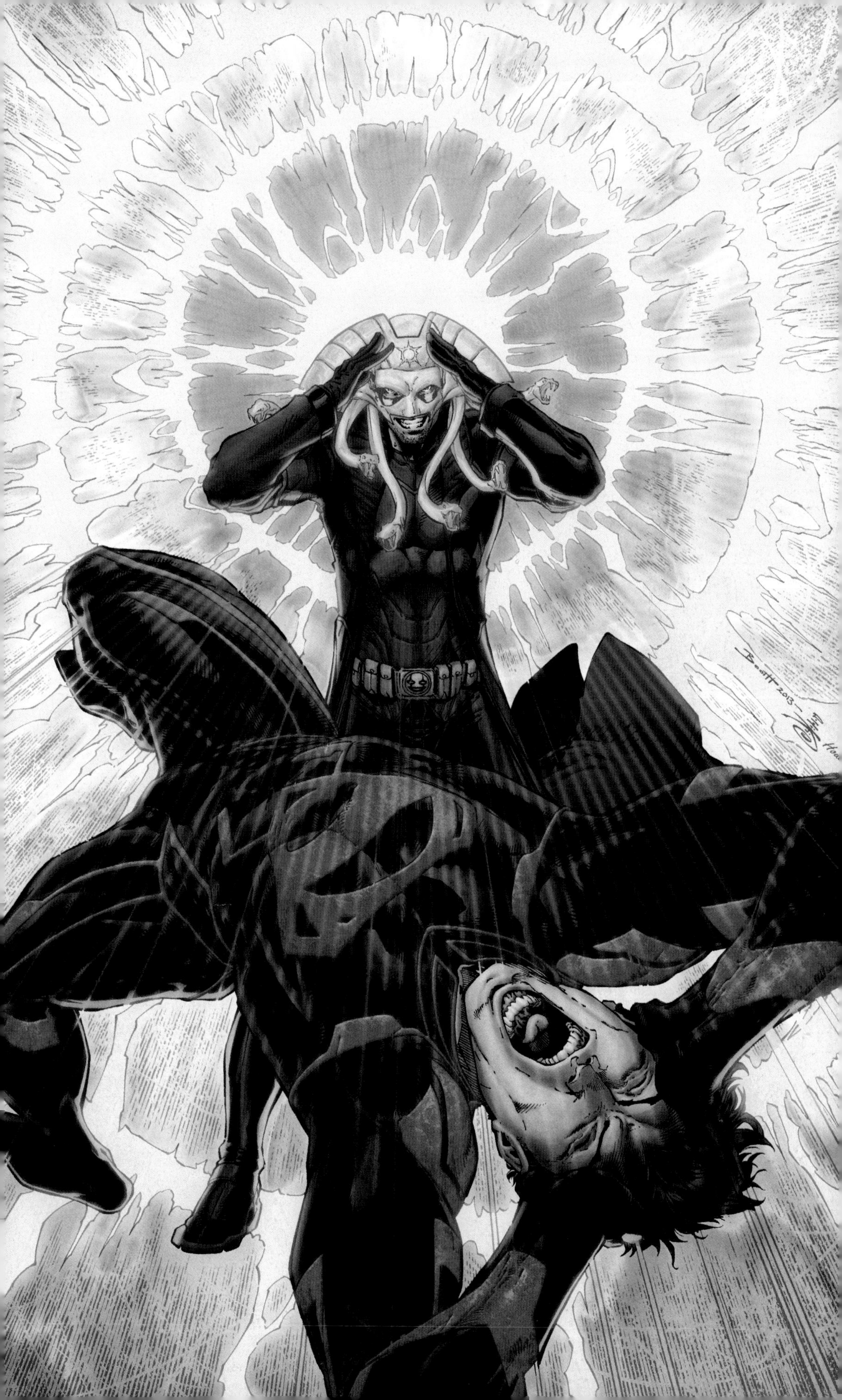

SECRETS AND ORIGINS

JUSTIN JORDAN writer **ROBSON ROCHA** penciller **DAN GREEN** inker cover art by **BRETT BOOTH, NORM RAPMUND & ANDREW DALHOUS**

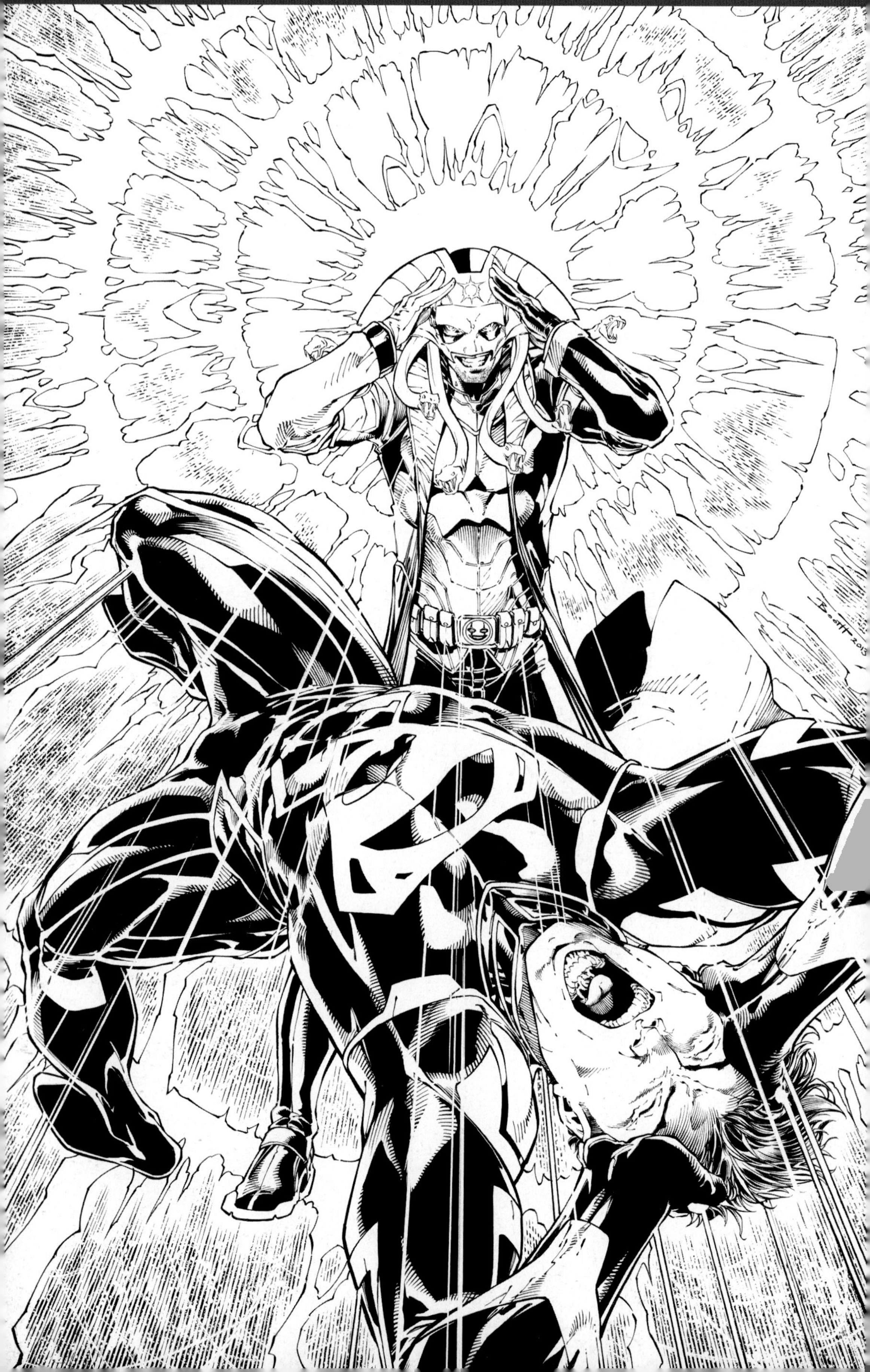

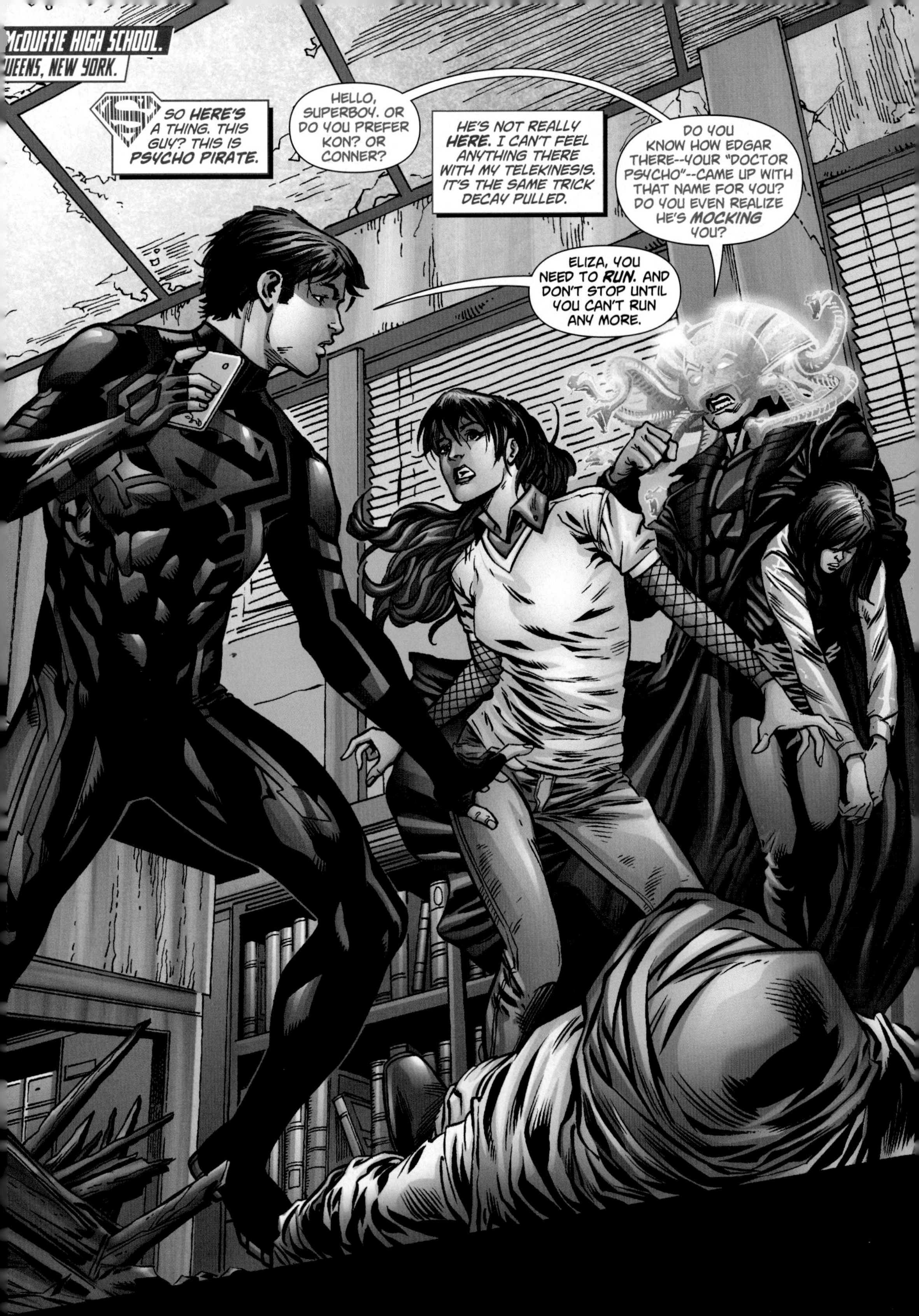
McDUFFIE HIGH SCHOOL.
QUEENS, NEW YORK.
SO HERE'S A THING. THIS GUY? THIS IS PSYCHO PIRATE.
HELLO, SUPERBOY. OR DO YOU PREFER KON? OR CONNER?
HE'S NOT REALLY HERE. I CAN'T FEEL ANYTHING THERE WITH MY TELEKINESIS. IT'S THE SAME TRICK DECAY PULLED.
DO YOU KNOW HOW EDGAR THERE--YOUR "DOCTOR PSYCHO"--CAME UP WITH THAT NAME FOR YOU? DO YOU EVEN REALIZE HE'S MOCKING YOU?
ELIZA, YOU NEED TO RUN. AND DON'T STOP UNTIL YOU CAN'T RUN ANY MORE.

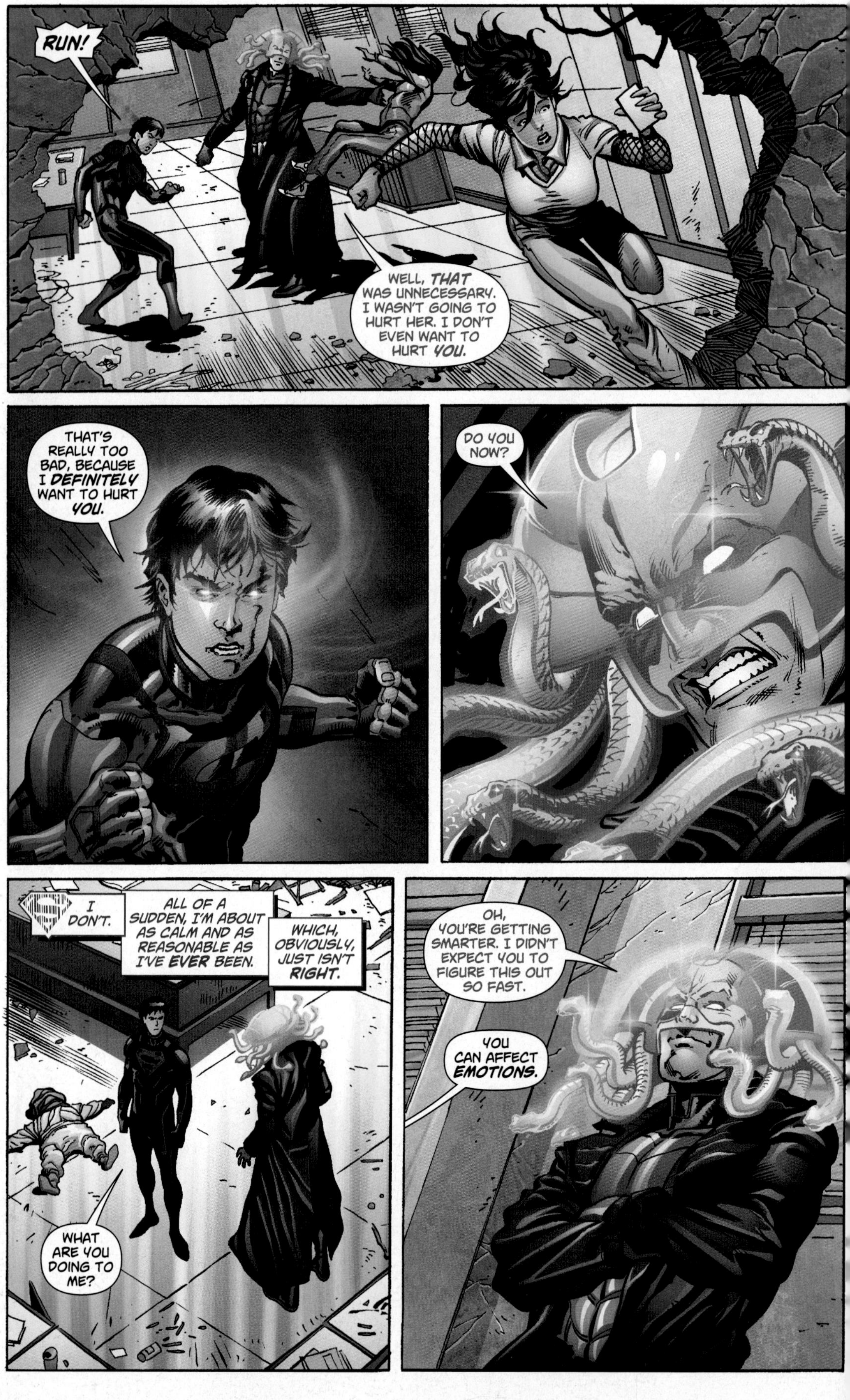
RUN!
WELL, THAT WAS UNNECESSARY. I WASN'T GOING TO HURT HER. I DON'T EVEN WANT TO HURT YOU.
THAT'S REALLY TOO BAD, BECAUSE I DEFINITELY WANT TO HURT YOU.
DO YOU NOW?
I DON'T.
ALL OF A SUDDEN, I'M ABOUT AS CALM AND AS REASONABLE AS I'VE EVER BEEN.
WHICH, OBVIOUSLY, JUST ISN'T RIGHT.
WHAT ARE YOU DOING TO ME?
OH, YOU'RE GETTING SMARTER. I DIDN'T EXPECT YOU TO FIGURE THIS OUT SO FAST.
YOU CAN AFFECT EMOTIONS.

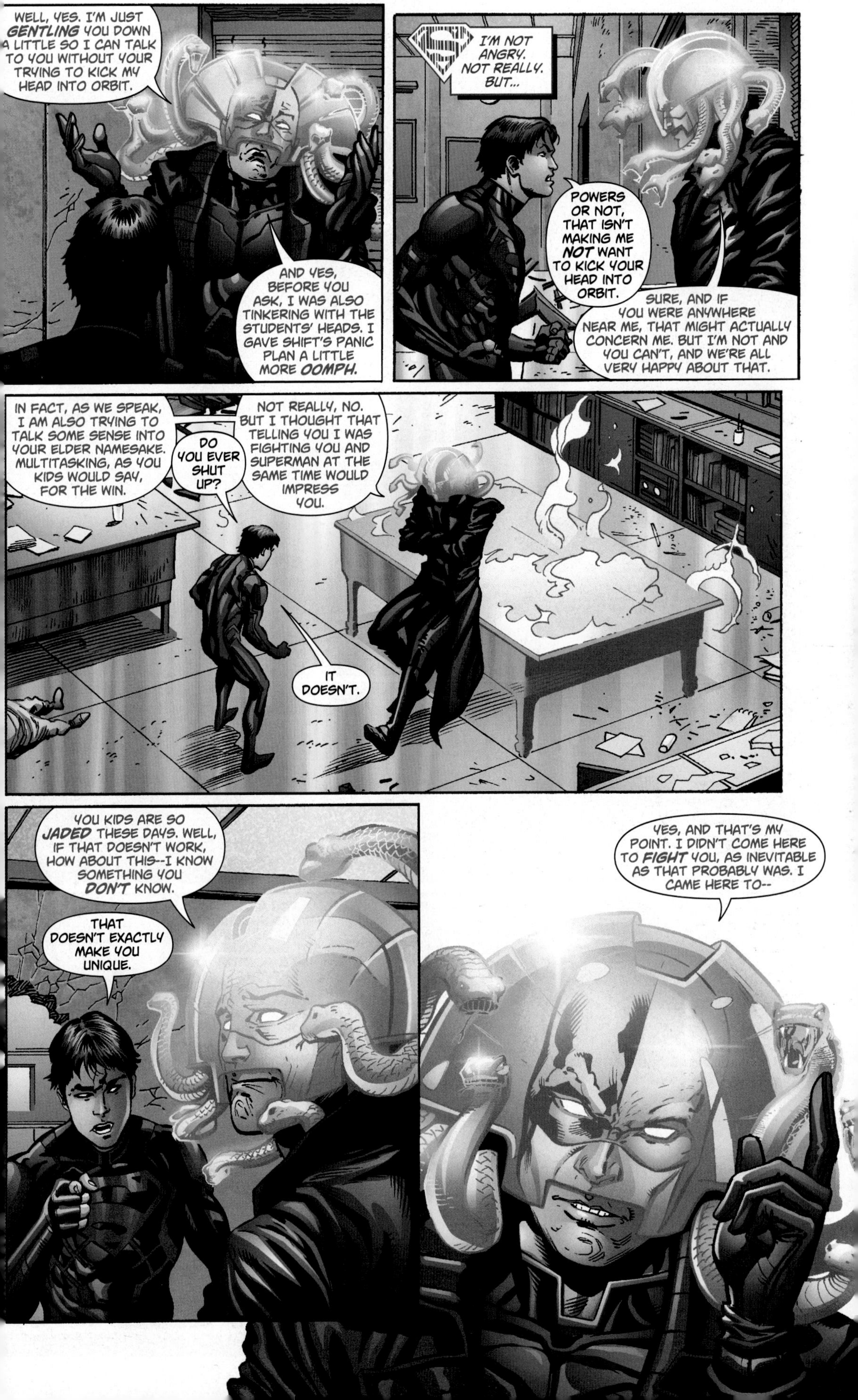

WELL, YES. I'M JUST GENTLING YOU DOWN A LITTLE SO I CAN TALK TO YOU WITHOUT YOUR TRYING TO KICK MY HEAD INTO ORBIT.
AND YES, BEFORE YOU ASK, I WAS ALSO TINKERING WITH THE STUDENTS' HEADS. I GAVE SHIFT'S PANIC PLAN A LITTLE MORE OOMPH.
I'M NOT ANGRY. NOT REALLY. BUT...
POWERS OR NOT, THAT ISN'T MAKING ME NOT WANT TO KICK YOUR HEAD INTO ORBIT.
SURE, AND IF YOU WERE ANYWHERE NEAR ME, THAT MIGHT ACTUALLY CONCERN ME. BUT I'M NOT AND YOU CAN'T, AND WE'RE ALL VERY HAPPY ABOUT THAT.
IN FACT, AS WE SPEAK, I AM ALSO TRYING TO TALK SOME SENSE INTO YOUR ELDER NAMESAKE. MULTITASKING, AS YOU KIDS WOULD SAY, FOR THE WIN.
DO YOU EVER SHUT UP?
NOT REALLY, NO. BUT I THOUGHT THAT TELLING YOU I WAS FIGHTING YOU AND SUPERMAN AT THE SAME TIME WOULD IMPRESS YOU.
IT DOESN'T.
YOU KIDS ARE SO JADED THESE DAYS. WELL, IF THAT DOESN'T WORK, HOW ABOUT THIS--I KNOW SOMETHING YOU DON'T KNOW.
THAT DOESN'T EXACTLY MAKE YOU UNIQUE.
YES, AND THAT'S MY POINT. I DIDN'T COME HERE TO FIGHT YOU, AS INEVITABLE AS THAT PROBABLY WAS. I CAME HERE TO--

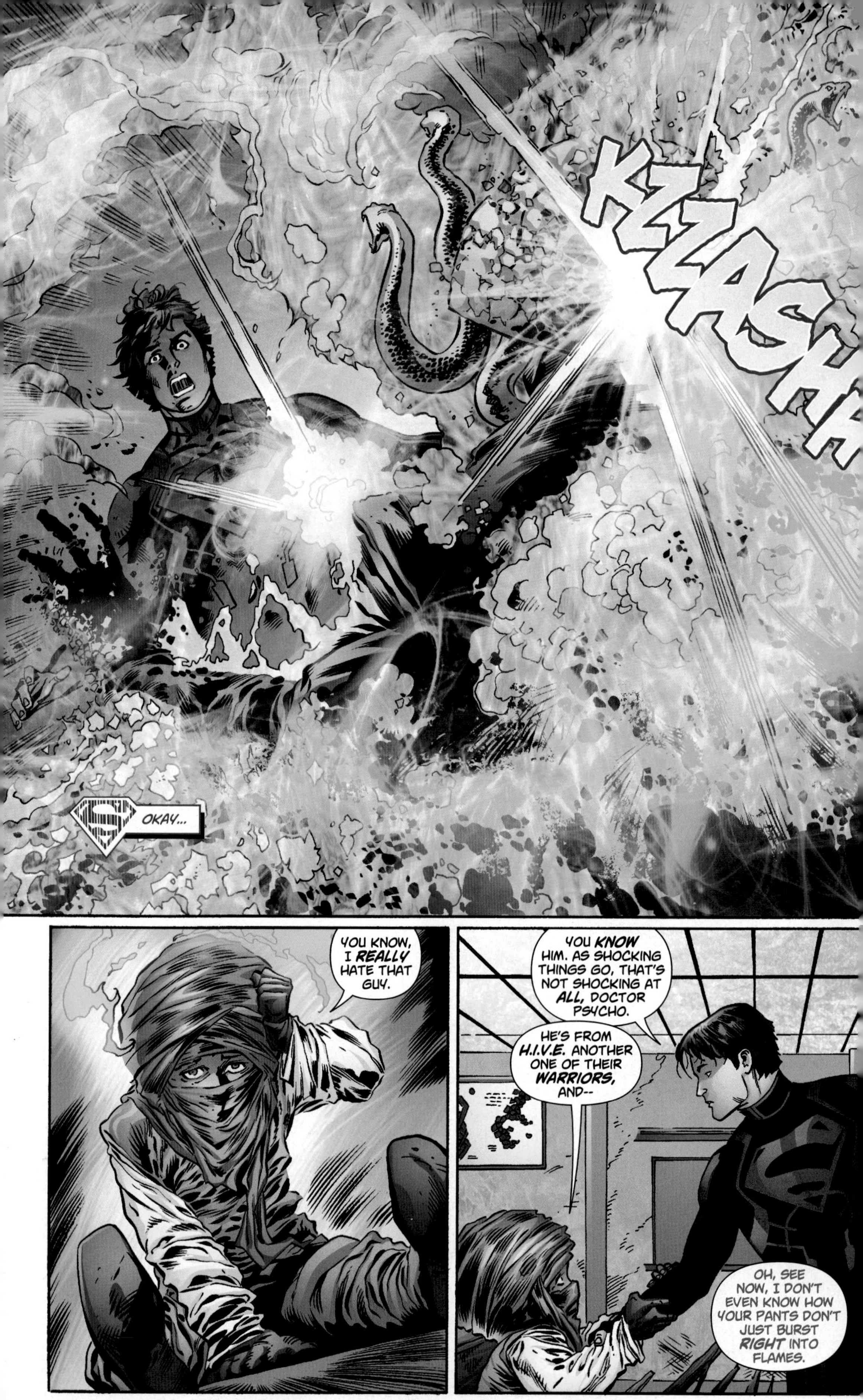
KZZASHH
OKAY...
YOU KNOW, I REALLY HATE THAT GUY.
YOU KNOW HIM. AS SHOCKING THINGS GO, THAT'S NOT SHOCKING AT ALL, DOCTOR PSYCHO.
HE'S FROM H.I.V.E. ANOTHER ONE OF THEIR WARRIORS, AND--
OH, SEE NOW, I DON'T EVEN KNOW HOW YOUR PANTS DON'T JUST BURST RIGHT INTO FLAMES.

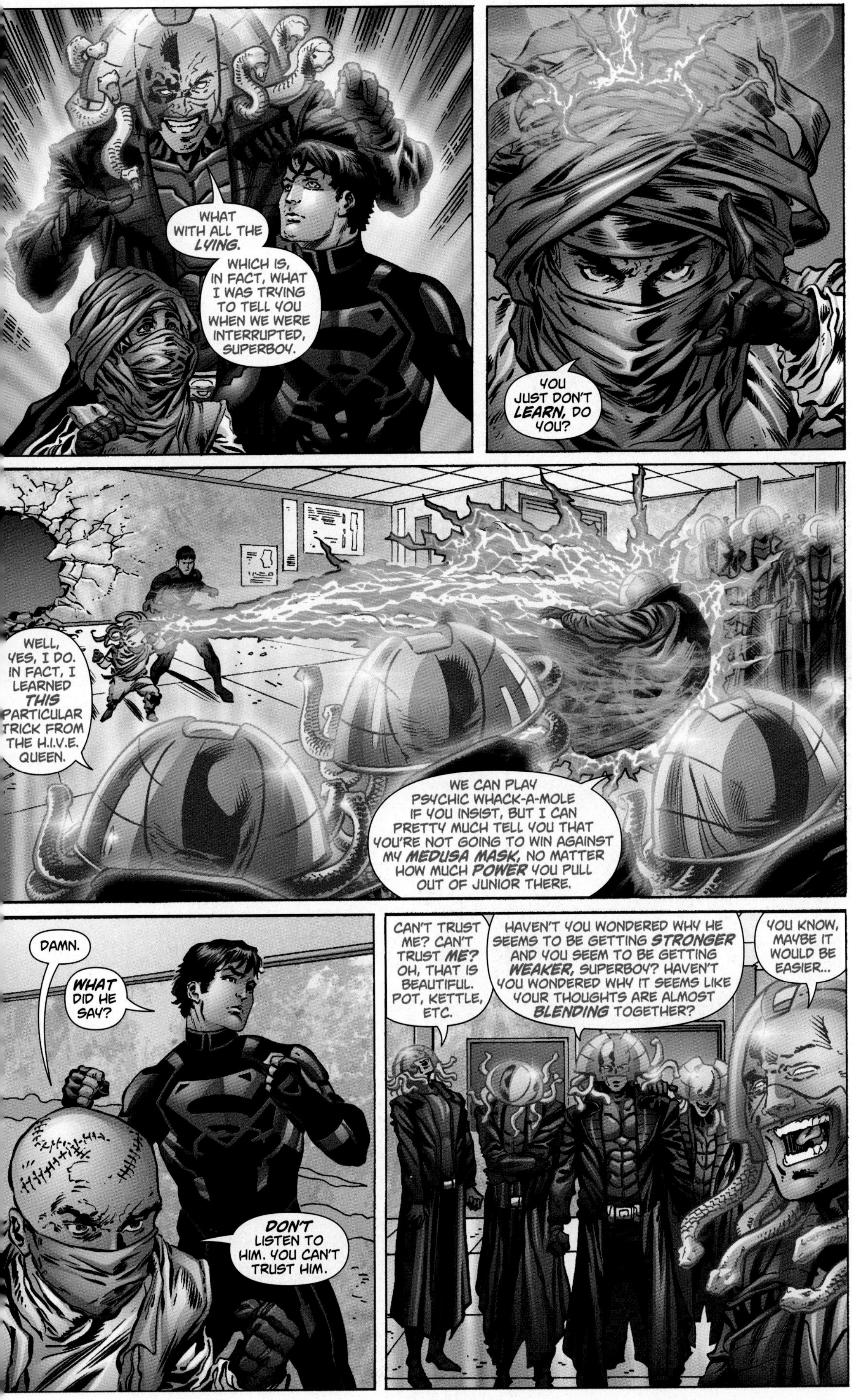

WHAT WITH ALL THE LYING.
WHICH IS, IN FACT, WHAT I WAS TRYING TO TELL YOU WHEN WE WERE INTERRUPTED, SUPERBOY.
YOU JUST DON'T LEARN, DO YOU?
WELL, YES, I DO. IN FACT, I LEARNED THIS PARTICULAR TRICK FROM THE H.I.V.E. QUEEN.
WE CAN PLAY PSYCHIC WHACK-A-MOLE IF YOU INSIST, BUT I CAN PRETTY MUCH TELL YOU THAT YOU'RE NOT GOING TO WIN AGAINST MY MEDUSA MASK, NO MATTER HOW MUCH POWER YOU PULL OUT OF JUNIOR THERE.
DAMN.
WHAT DID HE SAY?
DON'T LISTEN TO HIM. YOU CAN'T TRUST HIM.
CAN'T TRUST ME? CAN'T TRUST ME? OH, THAT IS BEAUTIFUL. POT, KETTLE, ETC.
HAVEN'T YOU WONDERED WHY HE SEEMS TO BE GETTING STRONGER AND YOU SEEM TO BE GETTING WEAKER, SUPERBOY? HAVEN'T YOU WONDERED WHY IT SEEMS LIKE YOUR THOUGHTS ARE ALMOST BLENDING TOGETHER?
YOU KNOW, MAYBE IT WOULD BE EASIER...

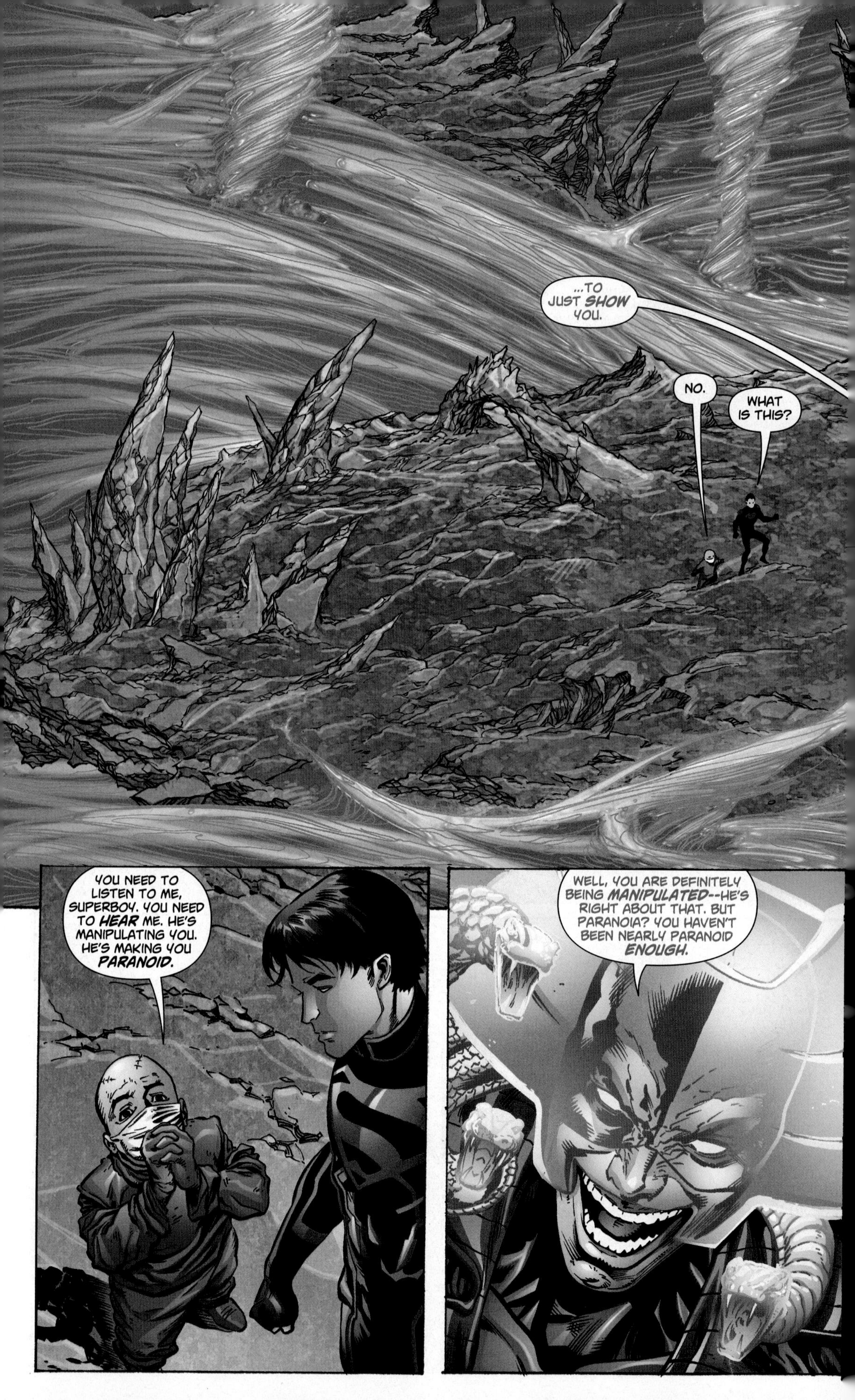
...TO JUST SHOW YOU.
NO.
WHAT IS THIS?
YOU NEED TO LISTEN TO ME, SUPERBOY. YOU NEED TO HEAR ME. HE'S MANIPULATING YOU. HE'S MAKING YOU PARANOID.
WELL, YOU ARE DEFINITELY BEING MANIPULATED--HE'S RIGHT ABOUT THAT. BUT PARANOIA? YOU HAVEN'T BEEN NEARLY PARANOID ENOUGH.

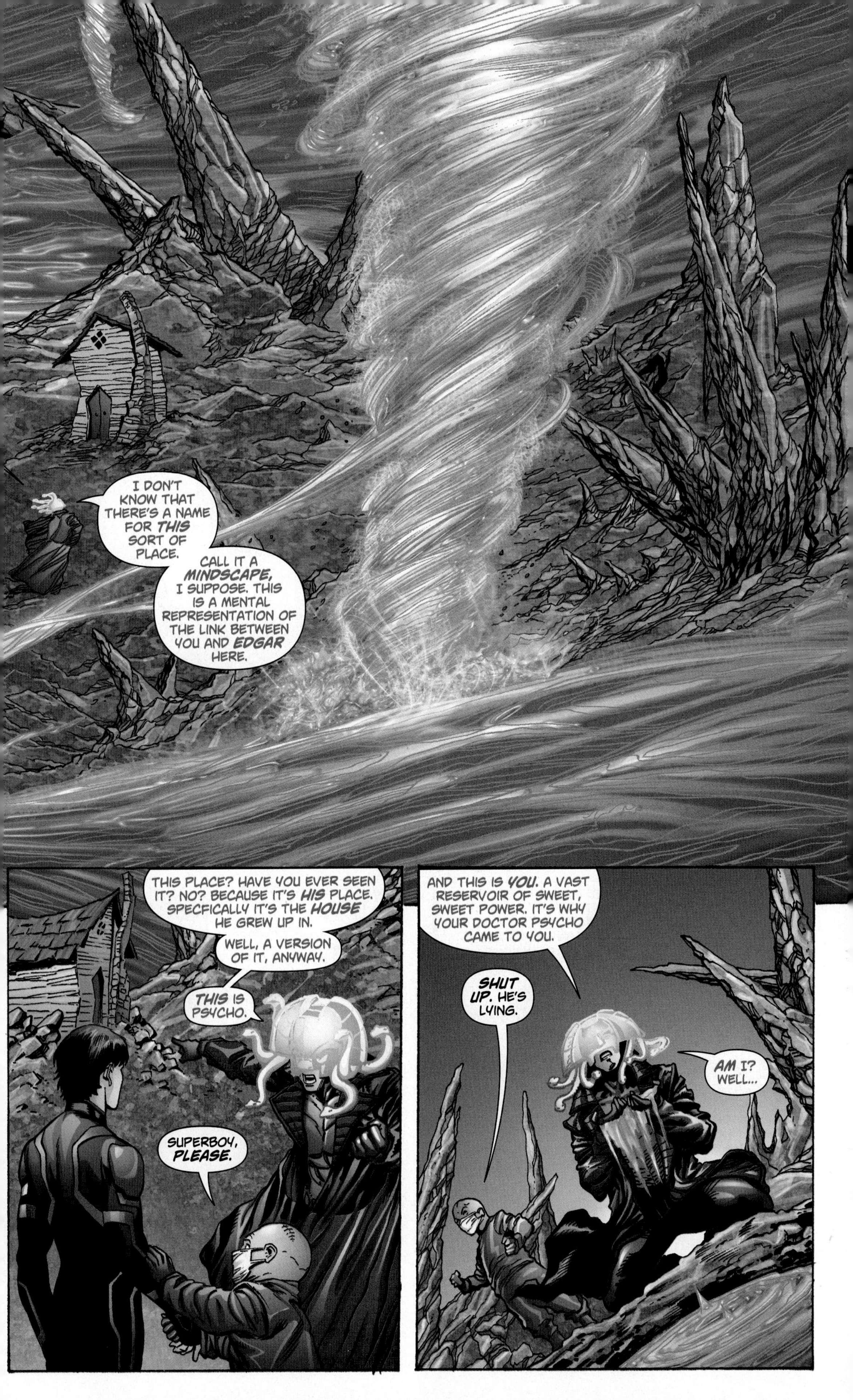
I DON'T KNOW THAT THERE'S A NAME FOR THIS SORT OF PLACE.
CALL IT A MINDSCAPE, I SUPPOSE. THIS IS A MENTAL REPRESENTATION OF THE LINK BETWEEN YOU AND EDGAR HERE.
THIS PLACE? HAVE YOU EVER SEEN IT? NO? BECAUSE IT'S HIS PLACE. SPECFICALLY IT'S THE HOUSE HE GREW UP IN.
WELL, A VERSION OF IT, ANYWAY.
THIS IS PSYCHO.
SUPERBOY, PLEASE.
AND THIS IS YOU. A VAST RESERVOIR OF SWEET, SWEET POWER. IT'S WHY YOUR DOCTOR PSYCHO CAME TO YOU.
SHUT UP. HE'S LYING.
AM I? WELL...

"...LET'S JUST *SEE* ABOUT THAT."

"I DON'T *WANT* TO *SEE* THIS."

"I DON'T *BLAME* YOU. BUT SUPERBOY NEEDS TO SEE THIS.

"THIS IS THE STORY OF A BOY NAMED EDGAR...

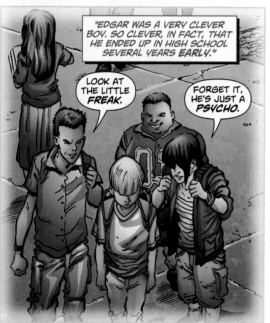

"EDGAR WAS A VERY CLEVER BOY. SO CLEVER, IN FACT, THAT HE ENDED UP IN HIGH SCHOOL SEVERAL YEARS *EARLY*."

LOOK AT THE LITTLE *FREAK.*

FORGET IT, HE'S JUST A *PSYCHO.*

"WHAT EDGAR WAS *NOT,* WAS *POPULAR.* EVERY DAY HE LOOKED FORWARD TO GOING HOME TO HIS LOVING FAMILY."

WHAT ARE YOU DOING HERE?

WHAT ARE YOU *DOING* IN OUR *HOUSE?*

"UNTIL THE DAY THEY *FORGOT* HE EXISTED.

"THERE WAS NO RECORD OF HIM AT SCHOOL OR IN ANY SYSTEM. IT WAS AS IF YOUNG EDGAR NEVER *EXISTED.*

"IT WAS AS IF SOMEONE HAD *WIPED* HIS EXISTENCE CLEAN FROM THE MINDS AND MEMORIES OF EVERYONE WHO KNEW HIM.

"WHICH, OF COURSE, SOMEONE *HAD.*

"EDGAR WAS SUPPOSED TO HAVE BEEN TAKEN FOR PSYCHIATRIC EVALUATION TO FIND OUT *WHY* HE INSISTED THESE PEOPLE WERE HIS PARENTS AND THAT HIS SCHOOL SHOULD KNOW HIM.

"*SUPPOSED* TO HAVE BEEN."

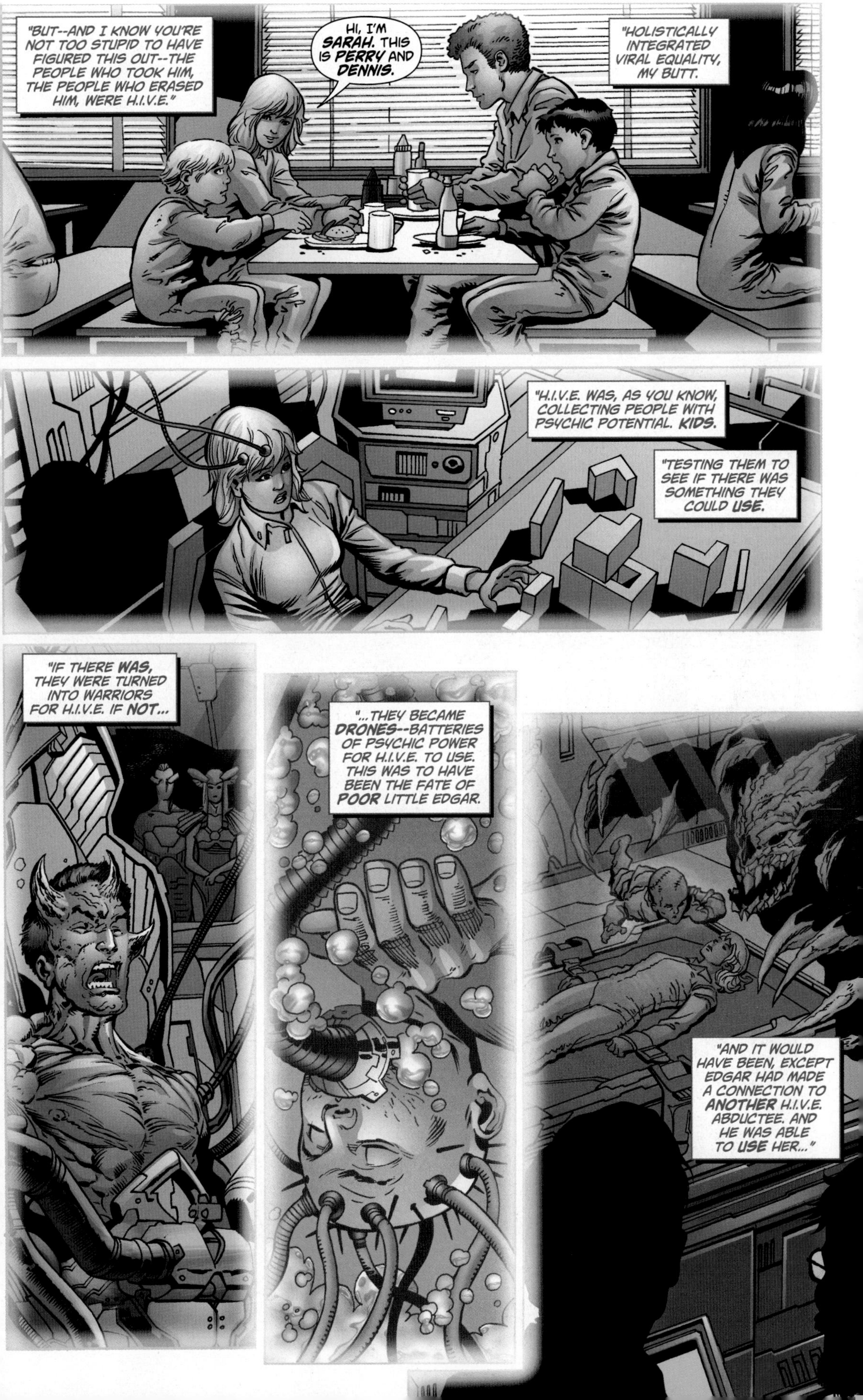
"BUT--AND I KNOW YOU'RE NOT TOO STUPID TO HAVE FIGURED THIS OUT--THE PEOPLE WHO TOOK HIM, THE PEOPLE WHO ERASED HIM, WERE H.I.V.E."
HI, I'M SARAH. THIS IS PERRY AND DENNIS.
"HOLISTICALLY INTEGRATED VIRAL EQUALITY, MY BUTT.
"H.I.V.E. WAS, AS YOU KNOW, COLLECTING PEOPLE WITH PSYCHIC POTENTIAL. KIDS.
"TESTING THEM TO SEE IF THERE WAS SOMETHING THEY COULD USE.
"IF THERE WAS, THEY WERE TURNED INTO WARRIORS FOR H.I.V.E. IF NOT...
"...THEY BECAME DRONES--BATTERIES OF PSYCHIC POWER FOR H.I.V.E. TO USE. THIS WAS TO HAVE BEEN THE FATE OF POOR LITTLE EDGAR.
"AND IT WOULD HAVE BEEN, EXCEPT EDGAR HAD MADE A CONNECTION TO ANOTHER H.I.V.E. ABDUCTEE. AND HE WAS ABLE TO USE HER..."

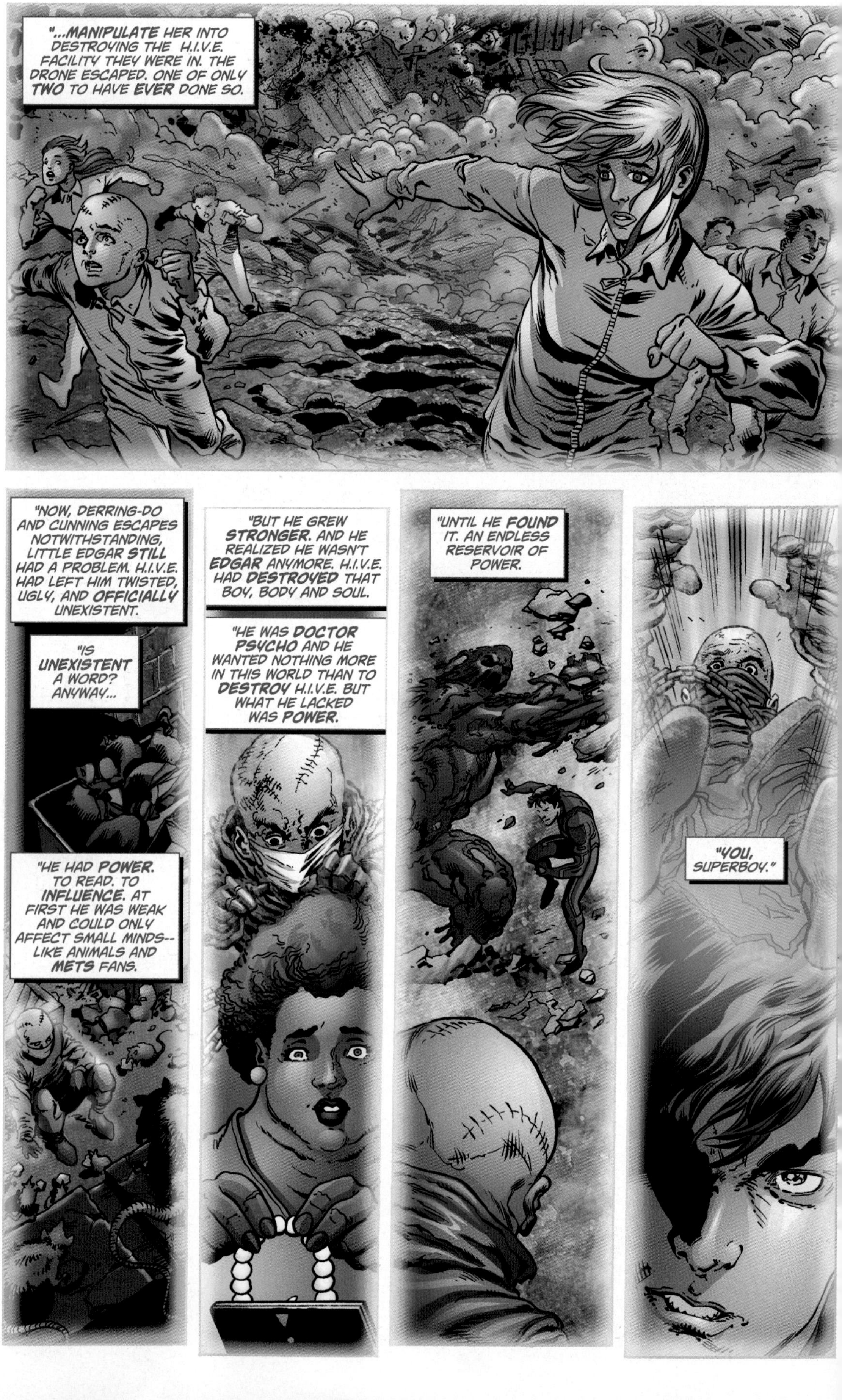
"...MANIPULATE HER INTO DESTROYING THE H.I.V.E. FACILITY THEY WERE IN. THE DRONE ESCAPED. ONE OF ONLY TWO TO HAVE EVER DONE SO.
"NOW, DERRING-DO AND CUNNING ESCAPES NOTWITHSTANDING, LITTLE EDGAR STILL HAD A PROBLEM. H.I.V.E. HAD LEFT HIM TWISTED, UGLY, AND OFFICIALLY UNEXISTENT.
"IS UNEXISTENT A WORD? ANYWAY...
"HE HAD POWER. TO READ. TO INFLUENCE. AT FIRST HE WAS WEAK AND COULD ONLY AFFECT SMALL MINDS--LIKE ANIMALS AND METS FANS.
"BUT HE GREW STRONGER. AND HE REALIZED HE WASN'T EDGAR ANYMORE. H.I.V.E. HAD DESTROYED THAT BOY, BODY AND SOUL.
"HE WAS DOCTOR PSYCHO AND HE WANTED NOTHING MORE IN THIS WORLD THAN TO DESTROY H.I.V.E. BUT WHAT HE LACKED WAS POWER.
"UNTIL HE FOUND IT. AN ENDLESS RESERVOIR OF POWER.
"YOU, SUPERBOY."

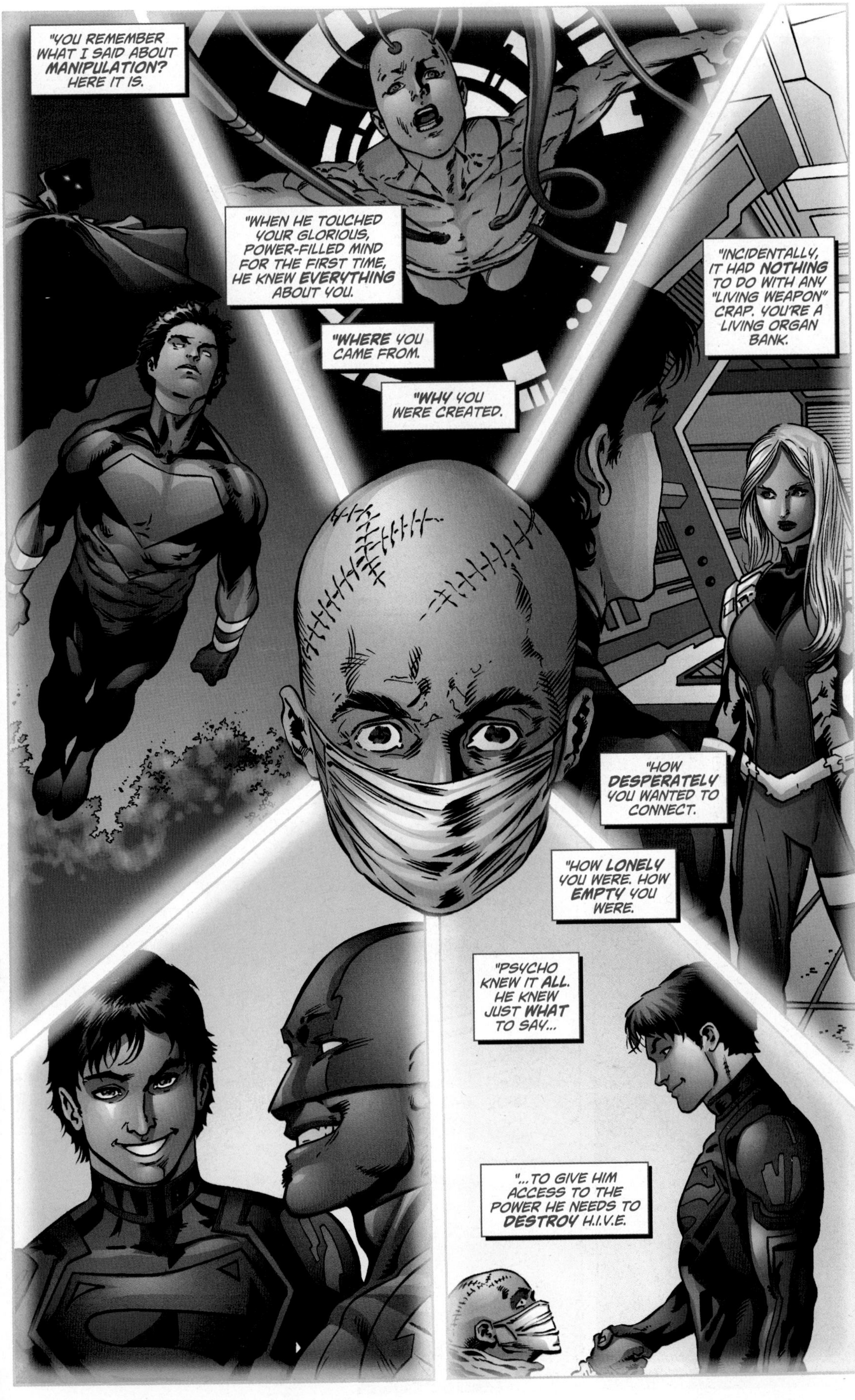
"YOU REMEMBER WHAT I SAID ABOUT MANIPULATION? HERE IT IS.
"WHEN HE TOUCHED YOUR GLORIOUS, POWER-FILLED MIND FOR THE FIRST TIME, HE KNEW EVERYTHING ABOUT YOU.
"WHERE YOU CAME FROM.
"WHY YOU WERE CREATED.
"INCIDENTALLY, IT HAD NOTHING TO DO WITH ANY "LIVING WEAPON" CRAP. YOU'RE A LIVING ORGAN BANK.
"HOW DESPERATELY YOU WANTED TO CONNECT.
"HOW LONELY YOU WERE. HOW EMPTY YOU WERE.
"PSYCHO KNEW IT ALL. HE KNEW JUST WHAT TO SAY...
"...TO GIVE HIM ACCESS TO THE POWER HE NEEDS TO DESTROY H.I.V.E.

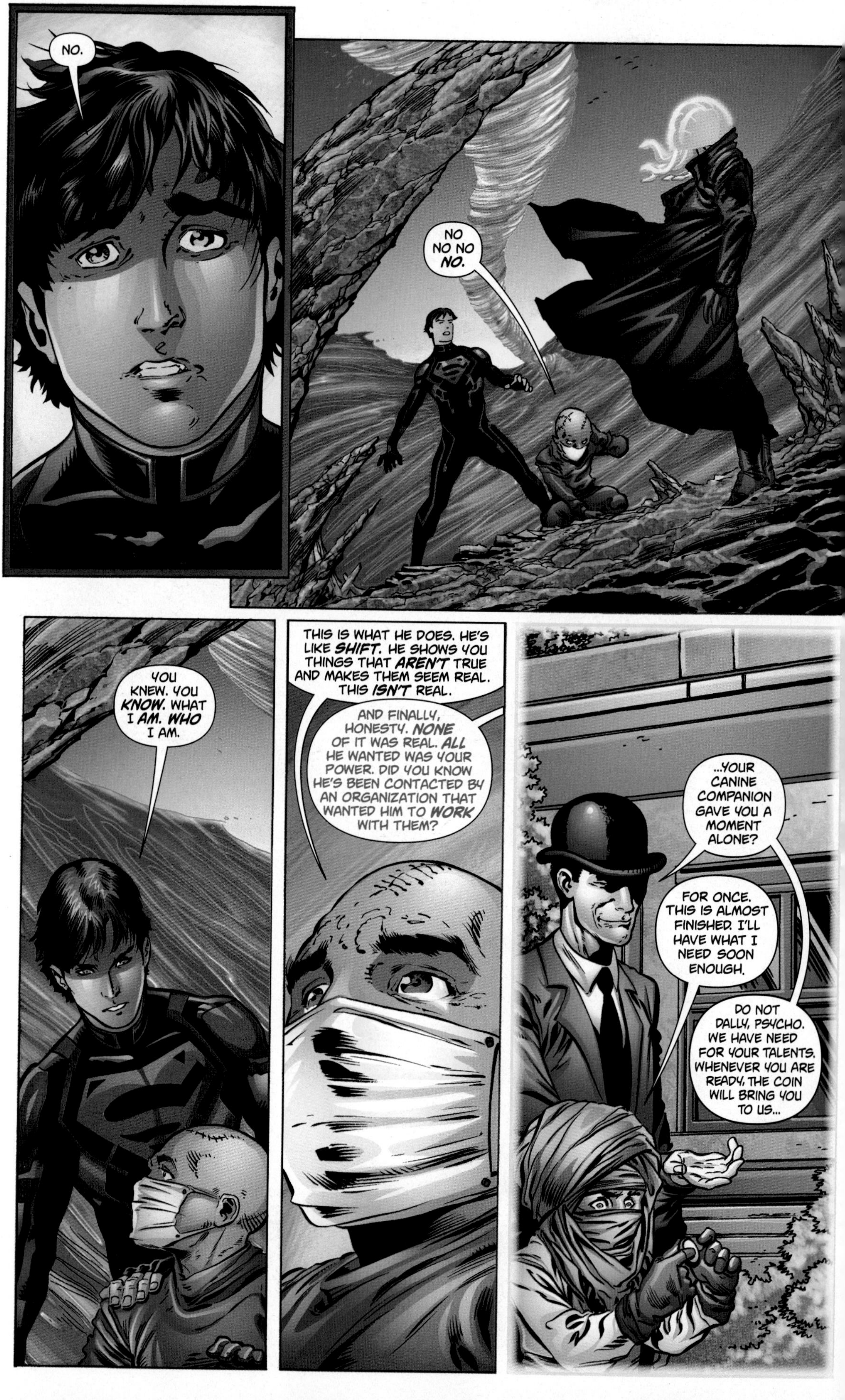
NO.
NO NO NO NO.
YOU KNEW. YOU KNOW. WHAT I AM. WHO I AM.
THIS IS WHAT HE DOES. HE'S LIKE SHIFT. HE SHOWS YOU THINGS THAT AREN'T TRUE AND MAKES THEM SEEM REAL. THIS ISN'T REAL.
AND FINALLY, HONESTY. NONE OF IT WAS REAL. ALL HE WANTED WAS YOUR POWER. DID YOU KNOW HE'S BEEN CONTACTED BY AN ORGANIZATION THAT WANTED HIM TO WORK WITH THEM?
...YOUR CANINE COMPANION GAVE YOU A MOMENT ALONE?
FOR ONCE. THIS IS ALMOST FINISHED. I'LL HAVE WHAT I NEED SOON ENOUGH.
DO NOT DALLY, PSYCHO. WE HAVE NEED FOR YOUR TALENTS. WHENEVER YOU ARE READY, THE COIN WILL BRING YOU TO US...

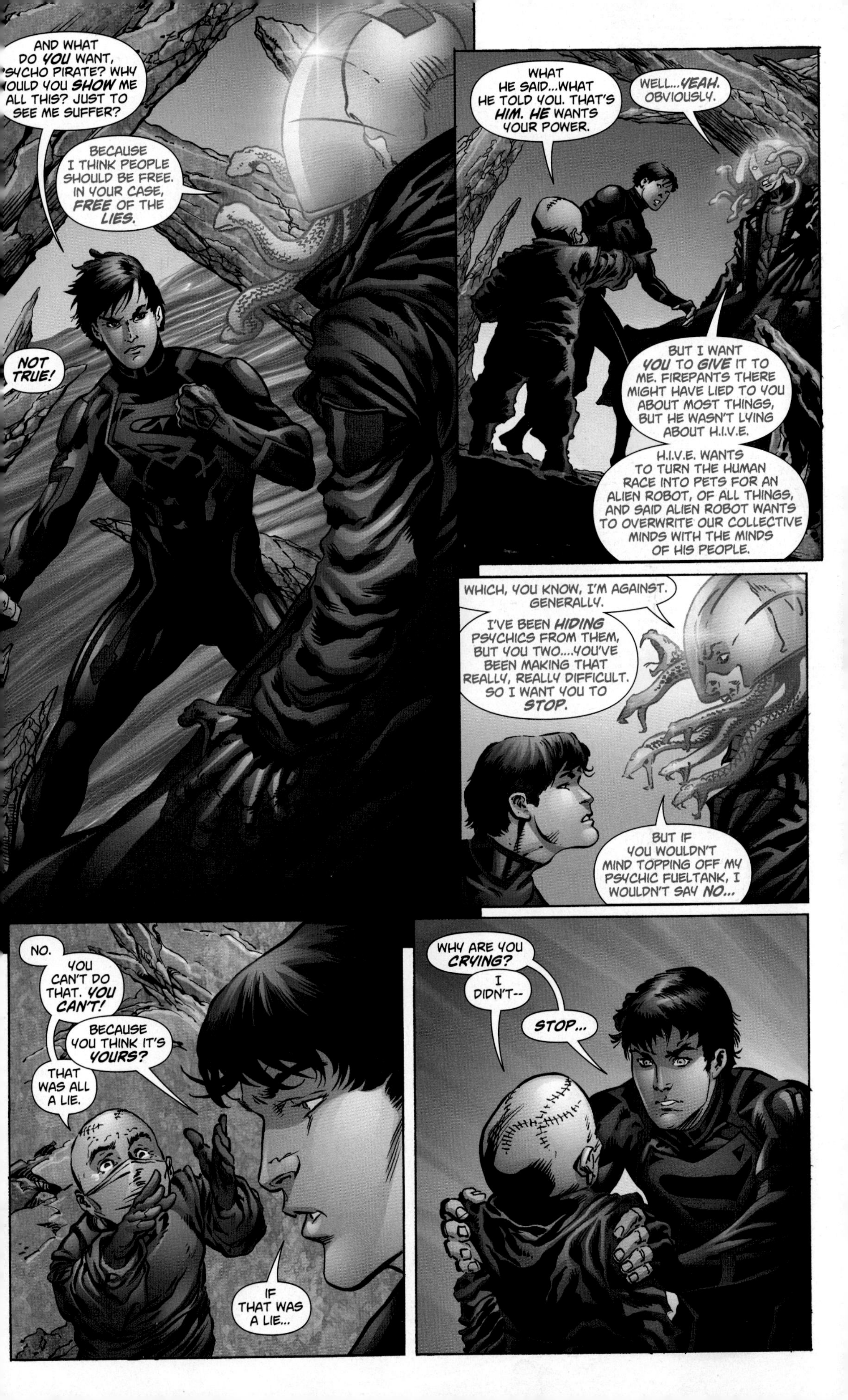
AND WHAT DO YOU WANT, SYCHO PIRATE? WHY OULD YOU SHOW ME ALL THIS? JUST TO SEE ME SUFFER?
BECAUSE I THINK PEOPLE SHOULD BE FREE. IN YOUR CASE, FREE OF THE LIES.
NOT TRUE!
WHAT HE SAID...WHAT HE TOLD YOU. THAT'S HIM. HE WANTS YOUR POWER.
WELL...YEAH. OBVIOUSLY.
BUT I WANT YOU TO GIVE IT TO ME. FIREPANTS THERE MIGHT HAVE LIED TO YOU ABOUT MOST THINGS, BUT HE WASN'T LYING ABOUT H.I.V.E.
H.I.V.E. WANTS TO TURN THE HUMAN RACE INTO PETS FOR AN ALIEN ROBOT, OF ALL THINGS, AND SAID ALIEN ROBOT WANTS TO OVERWRITE OUR COLLECTIVE MINDS WITH THE MINDS OF HIS PEOPLE.
WHICH, YOU KNOW, I'M AGAINST. GENERALLY.
I'VE BEEN HIDING PSYCHICS FROM THEM, BUT YOU TWO....YOU'VE BEEN MAKING THAT REALLY, REALLY DIFFICULT. SO I WANT YOU TO STOP.
BUT IF YOU WOULDN'T MIND TOPPING OFF MY PSYCHIC FUELTANK, I WOULDN'T SAY NO...
NO.
YOU CAN'T DO THAT. YOU CAN'T!
BECAUSE YOU THINK IT'S YOURS?
THAT WAS ALL A LIE.
IF THAT WAS A LIE...
WHY ARE YOU CRYING?
I DIDN'T--
STOP...

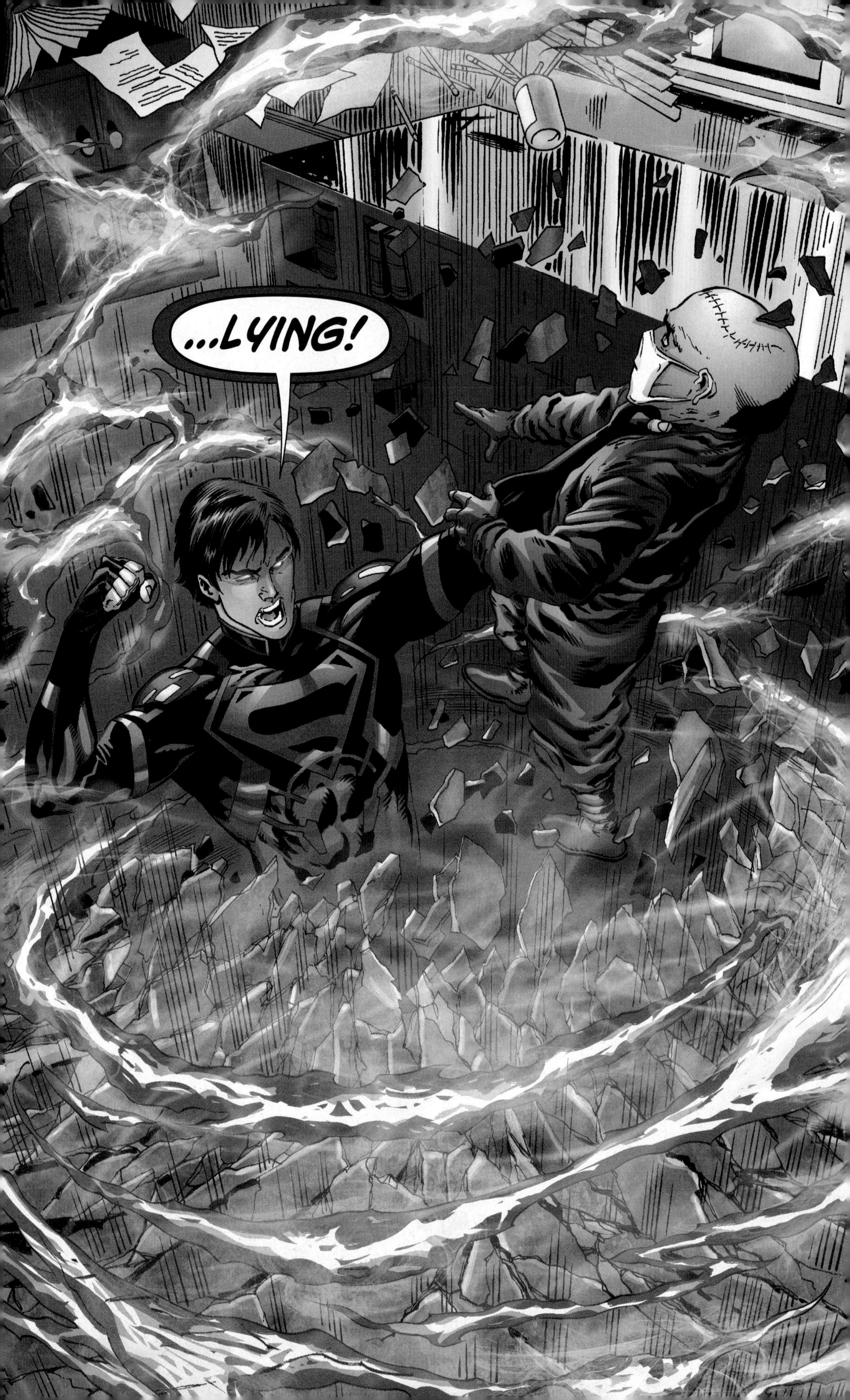
...LYING!

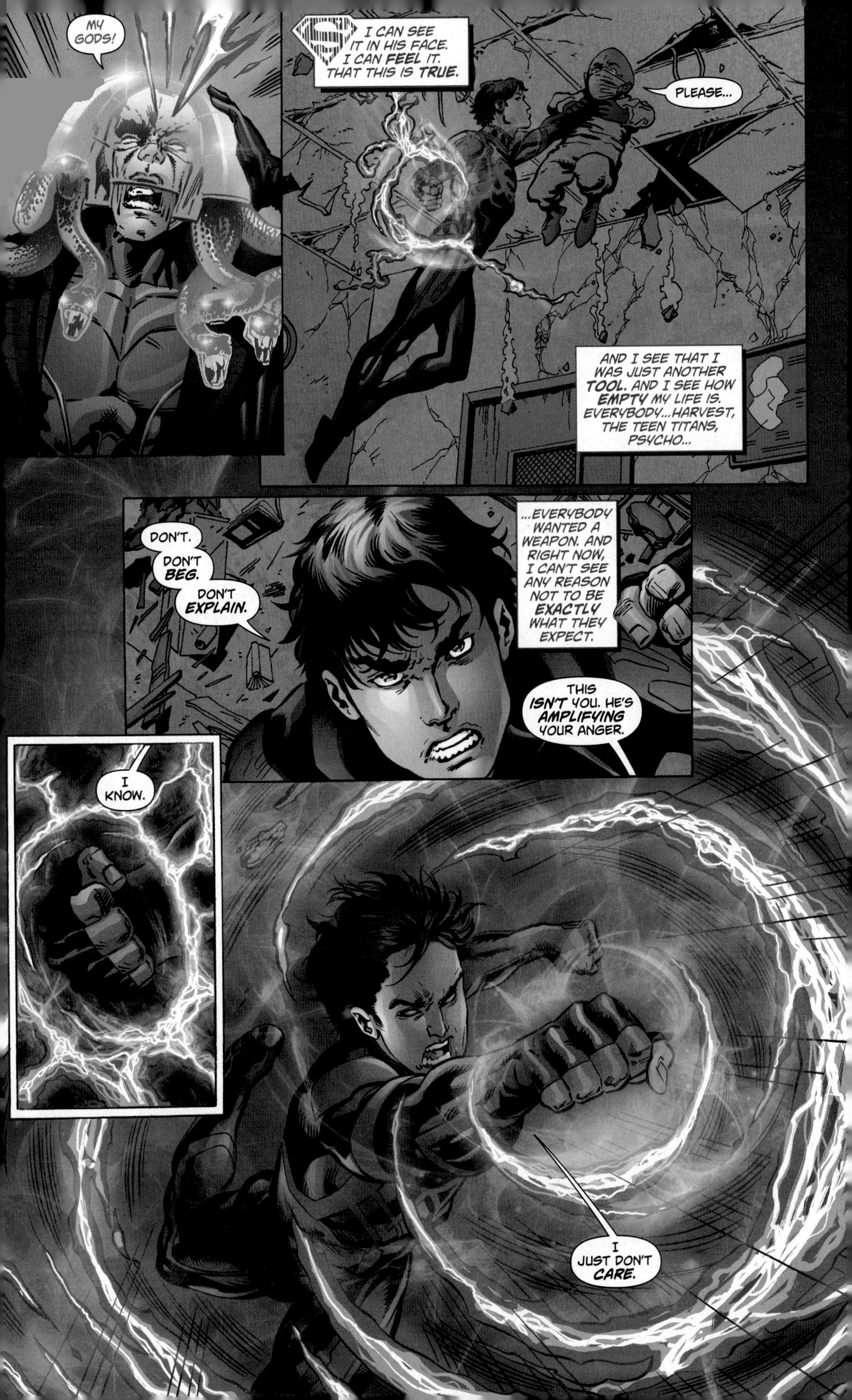
MY GODS!
I CAN SEE IT IN HIS FACE. I CAN FEEL IT. THAT THIS IS TRUE.
PLEASE...
AND I SEE THAT I WAS JUST ANOTHER TOOL. AND I SEE HOW EMPTY MY LIFE IS. EVERYBODY...HARVEST, THE TEEN TITANS, PSYCHO...
DON'T.
DON'T BEG.
DON'T EXPLAIN.
...EVERYBODY WANTED A WEAPON. AND RIGHT NOW, I CAN'T SEE ANY REASON NOT TO BE EXACTLY WHAT THEY EXPECT.
THIS ISN'T YOU. HE'S AMPLIFYING YOUR ANGER.
I KNOW.
I JUST DON'T CARE.

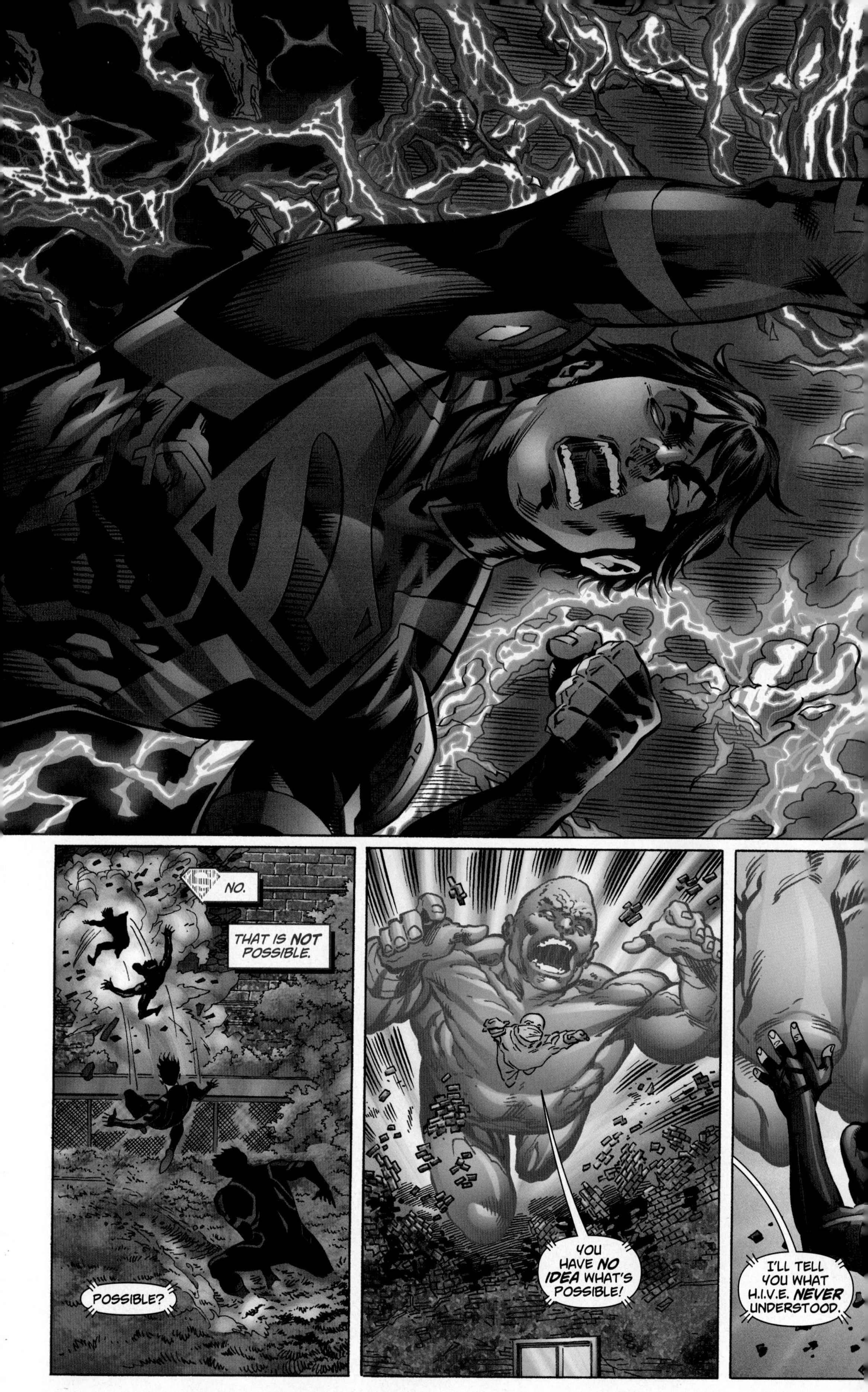
NO.
THAT IS NOT POSSIBLE.
POSSIBLE?
YOU HAVE NO IDEA WHAT'S POSSIBLE!
I'LL TELL YOU WHAT H.I.V.E. NEVER UNDERSTOOD.

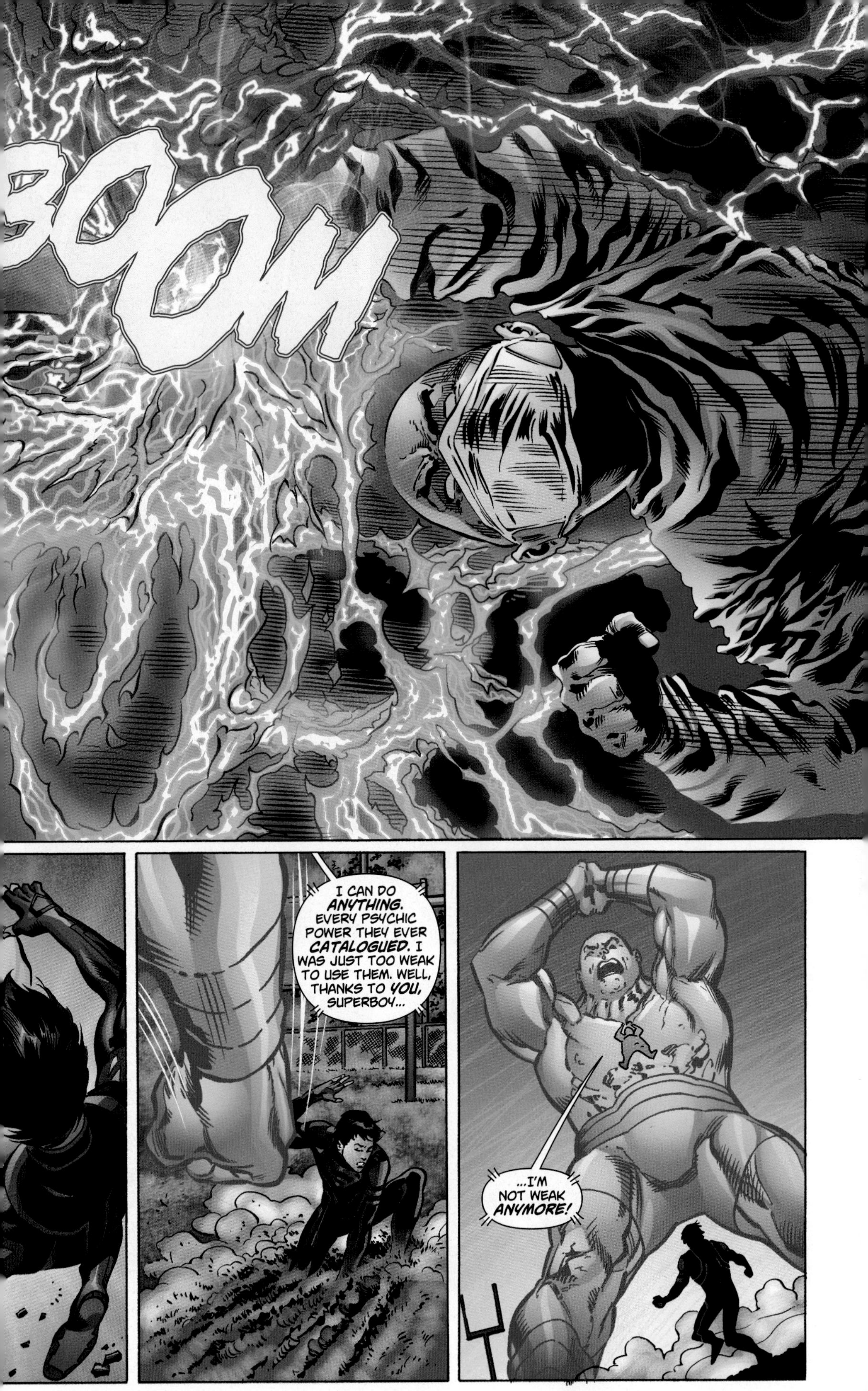
BOOM
I CAN DO ANYTHING. EVERY PSYCHIC POWER THEY EVER CATALOGUED. I WAS JUST TOO WEAK TO USE THEM. WELL, THANKS TO YOU, SUPERBOY...
...I'M NOT WEAK ANYMORE!

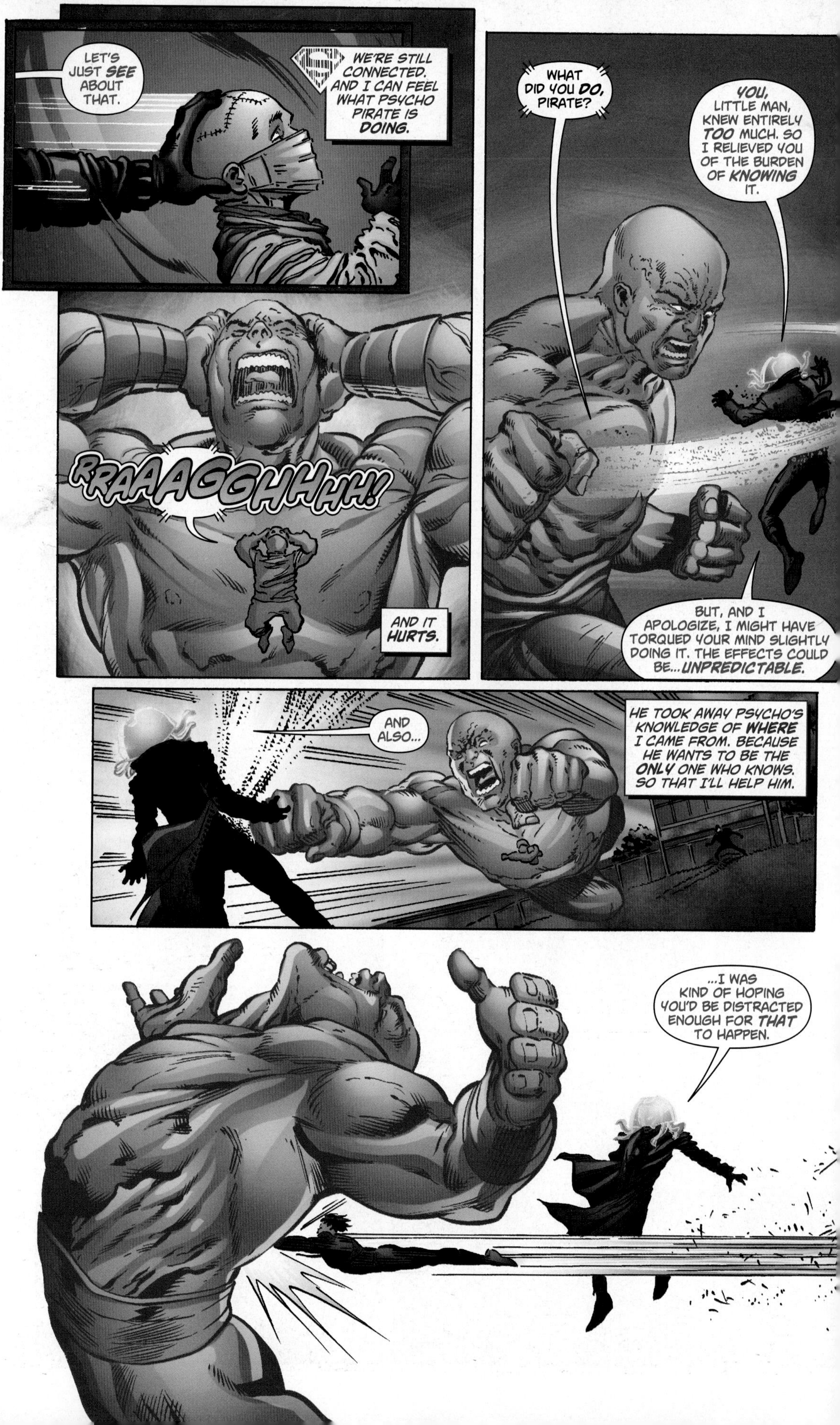
LET'S JUST SEE ABOUT THAT.
WE'RE STILL CONNECTED. AND I CAN FEEL WHAT PSYCHO PIRATE IS DOING.
WHAT DID YOU DO, PIRATE?
YOU, LITTLE MAN, KNEW ENTIRELY TOO MUCH. SO I RELIEVED YOU OF THE BURDEN OF KNOWING IT.
RRAAAGGHHHHH!
AND IT HURTS.
BUT, AND I APOLOGIZE, I MIGHT HAVE TORQUED YOUR MIND SLIGHTLY DOING IT. THE EFFECTS COULD BE...UNPREDICTABLE.
AND ALSO...
HE TOOK AWAY PSYCHO'S KNOWLEDGE OF WHERE I CAME FROM. BECAUSE HE WANTS TO BE THE ONLY ONE WHO KNOWS. SO THAT I'LL HELP HIM.
...I WAS KIND OF HOPING YOU'D BE DISTRACTED ENOUGH FOR THAT TO HAPPEN.

I KNOW THAT PSYCHO PIRATE IS AMPLIFYING MY RAGE. USING ME AS A WEAPON AGAINST PSYCHO.

I KNOW. AND I LET HIM.

I WILL NOT LET YOU HAVE IT ALL. I WILL TAKE IT FROM YOU. I WILL HAVE THIS POWER.

NO... TOO...TOO MUCH. I...

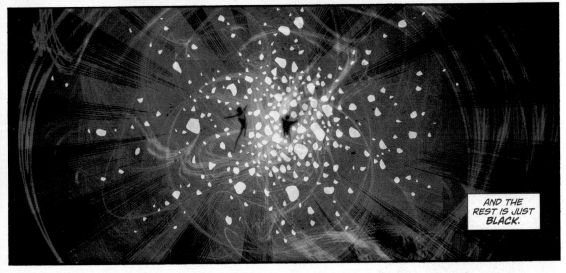

AND THE REST IS JUST BLACK.

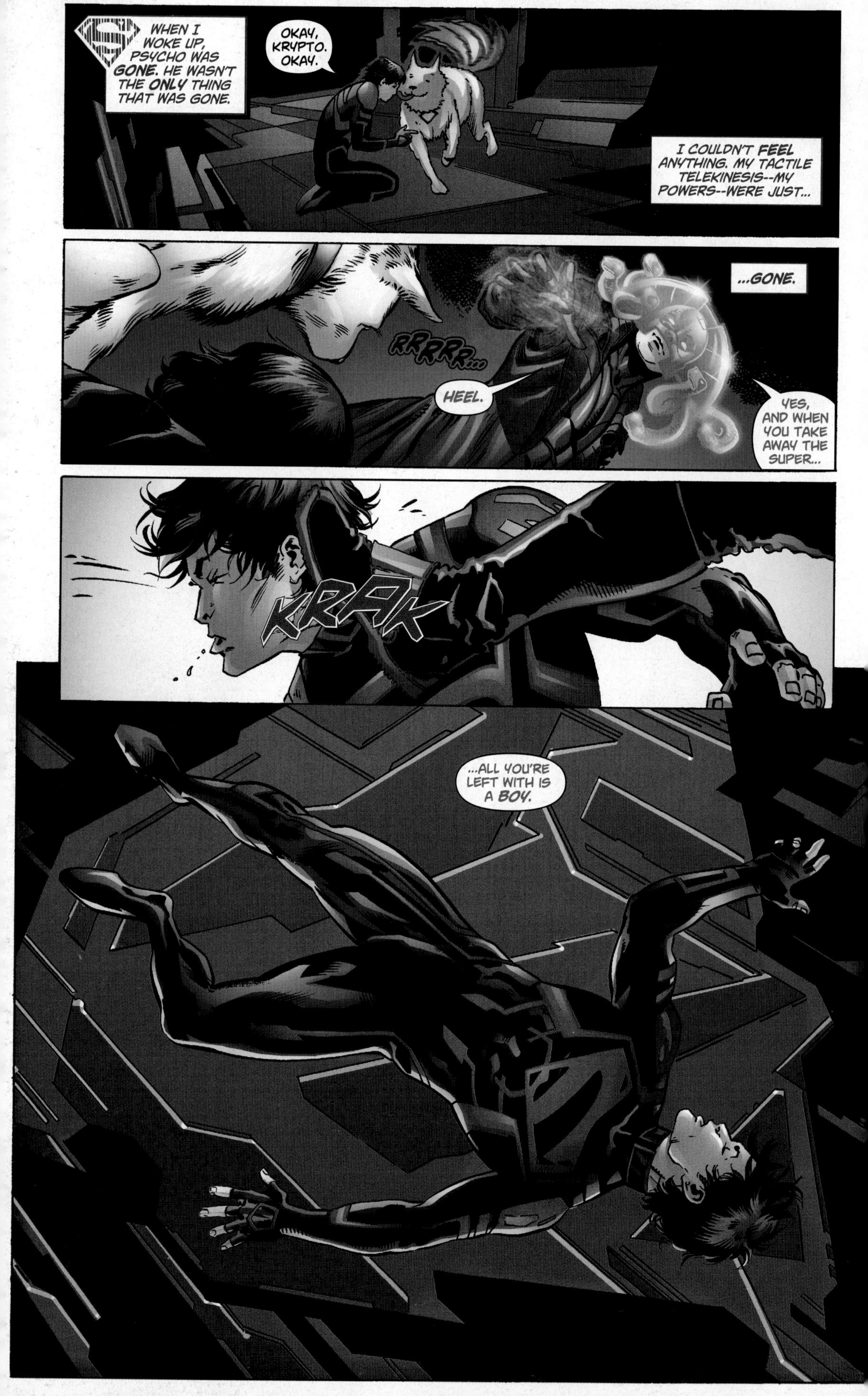
WHEN I WOKE UP, PSYCHO WAS GONE. HE WASN'T THE ONLY THING THAT WAS GONE.
OKAY, KRYPTO. OKAY.
I COULDN'T FEEL ANYTHING. MY TACTILE TELEKINESIS--MY POWERS--WERE JUST...
...GONE.
RRRRR...
HEEL.
YES, AND WHEN YOU TAKE AWAY THE SUPER...
KRAK
...ALL YOU'RE LEFT WITH IS A BOY.

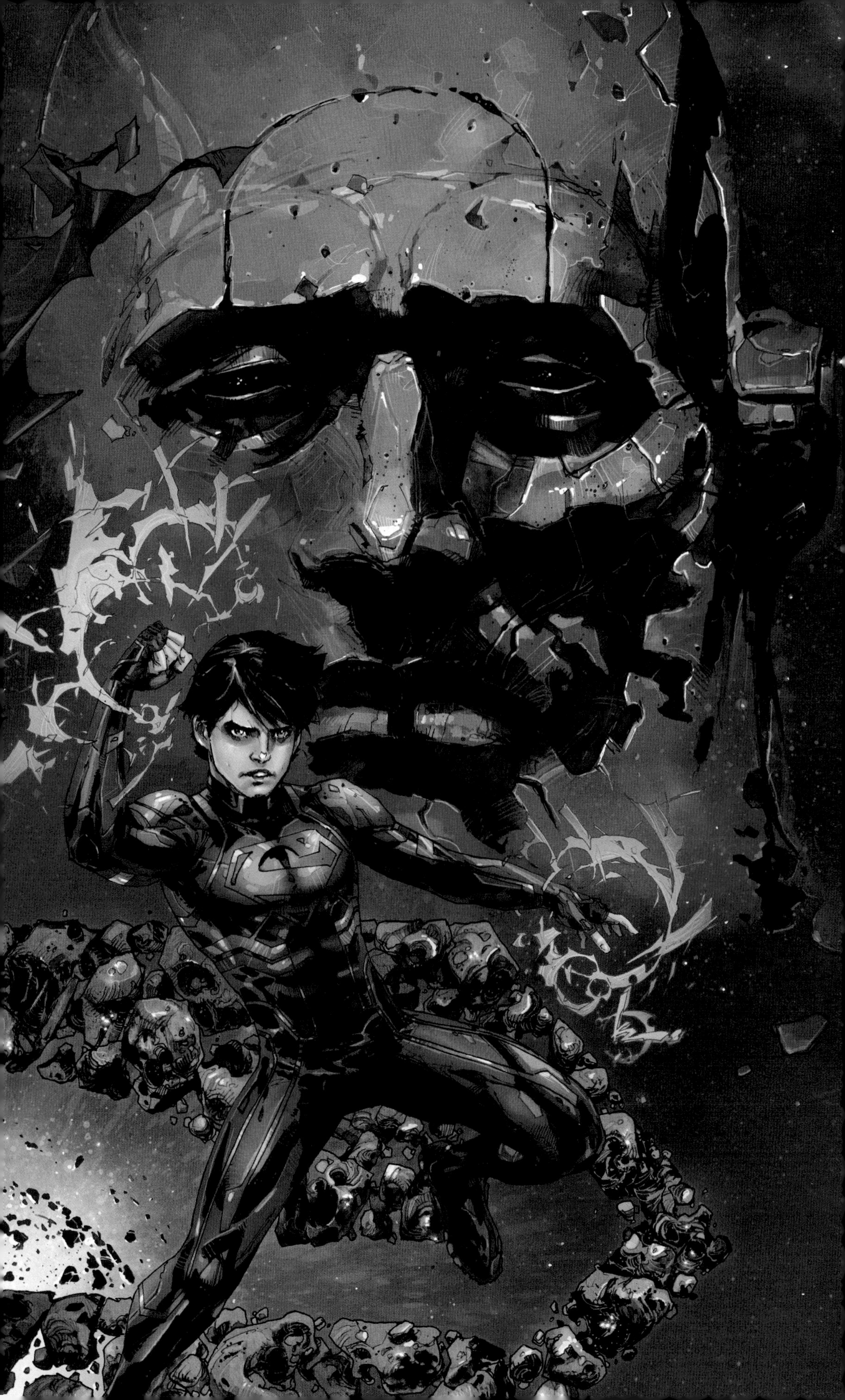

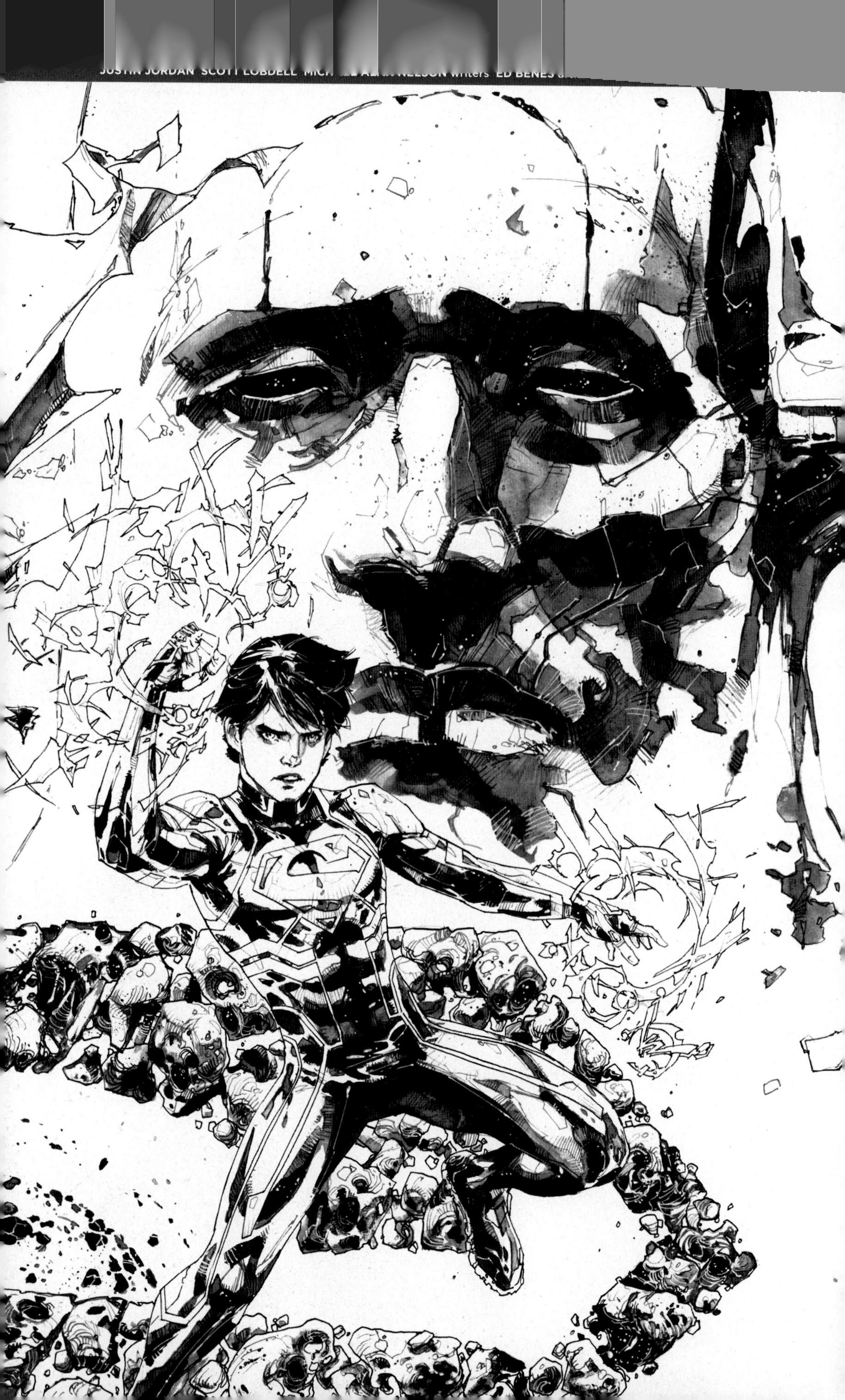
JUSTIN JORDAN SCOTT LOBDELL
writers

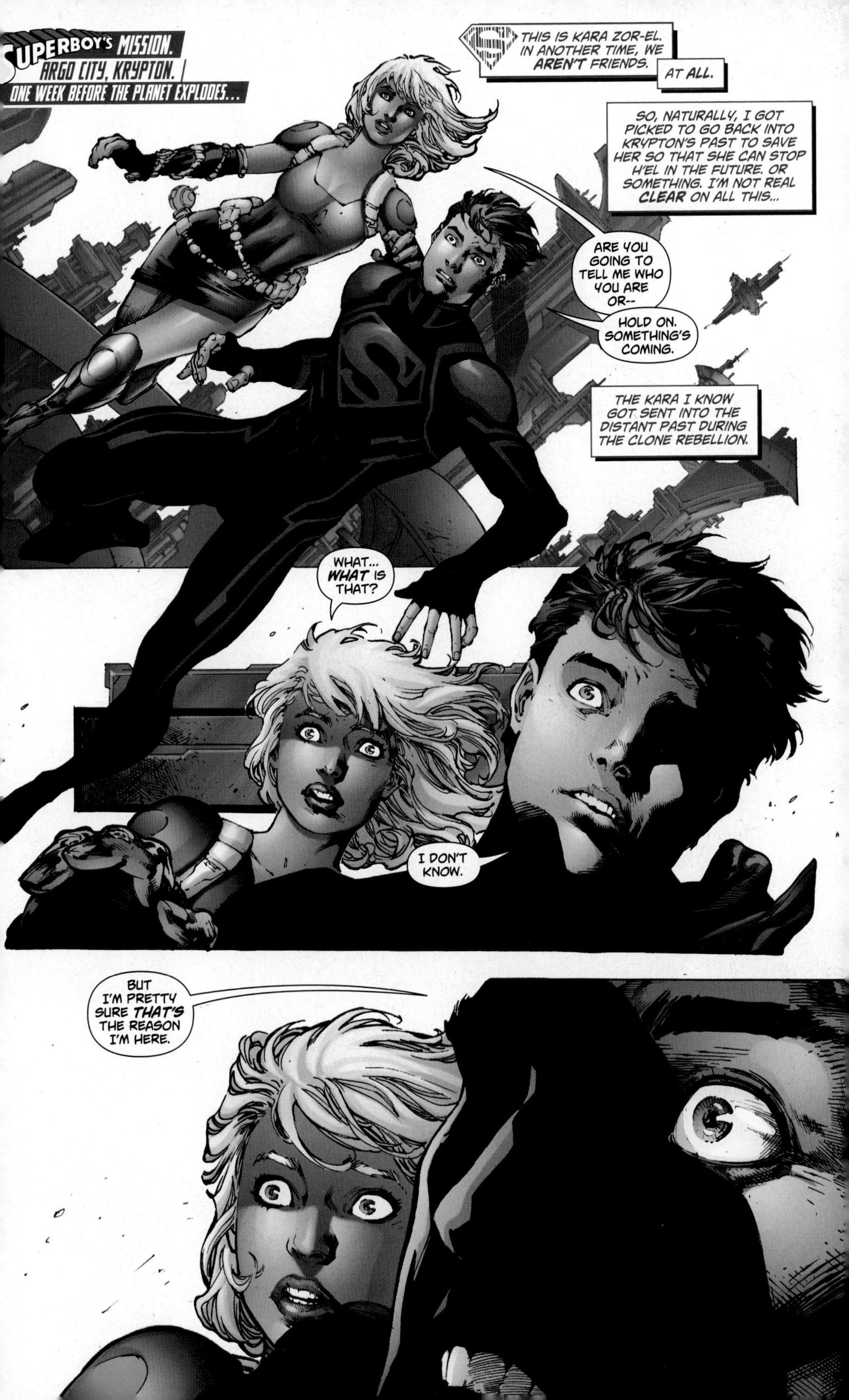
SUPERBOY'S MISSION.
ARGO CITY, KRYPTON.
ONE WEEK BEFORE THE PLANET EXPLODES...
THIS IS KARA ZOR-EL. IN ANOTHER TIME, WE AREN'T FRIENDS.
AT ALL.
SO, NATURALLY, I GOT PICKED TO GO BACK INTO KRYPTON'S PAST TO SAVE HER SO THAT SHE CAN STOP H'EL IN THE FUTURE. OR SOMETHING. I'M NOT REAL CLEAR ON ALL THIS...
ARE YOU GOING TO TELL ME WHO YOU ARE OR--
HOLD ON. SOMETHING'S COMING.
THE KARA I KNOW GOT SENT INTO THE DISTANT PAST DURING THE CLONE REBELLION.
WHAT... WHAT IS THAT?
I DON'T KNOW.
BUT I'M PRETTY SURE THAT'S THE REASON I'M HERE.

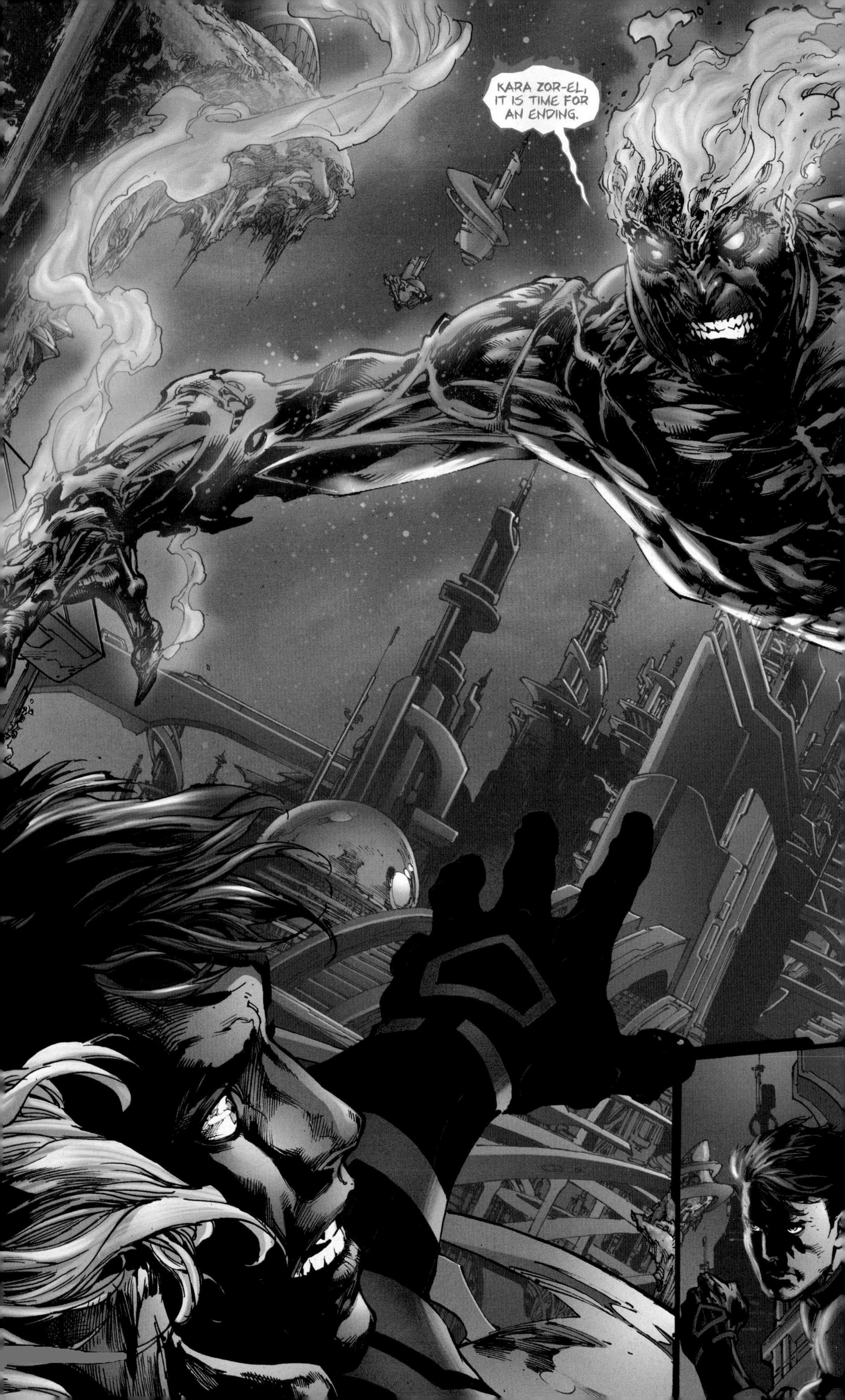
KARA ZOR-EL, IT IS TIME FOR AN ENDING.

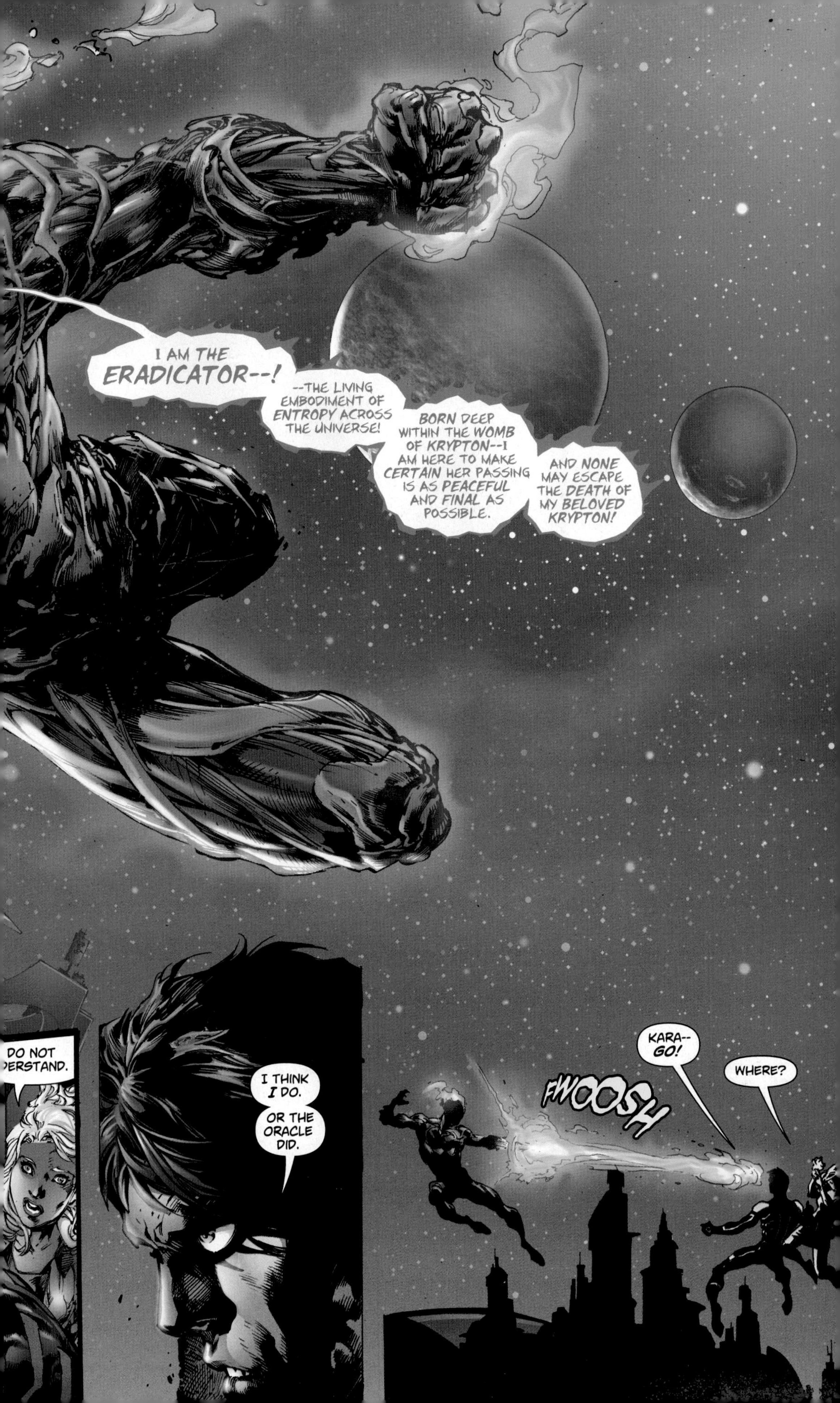
I AM THE ERADICATOR--!
--THE LIVING EMBODIMENT OF ENTROPY ACROSS THE UNIVERSE!
BORN DEEP WITHIN THE WOMB OF KRYPTON--I AM HERE TO MAKE CERTAIN HER PASSING IS AS PEACEFUL AND FINAL AS POSSIBLE.
AND NONE MAY ESCAPE THE DEATH OF MY BELOVED KRYPTON!
DO NOT
ERSTAND.
I THINK I DO.
OR THE ORACLE DID.
FWOOSH
KARA-- GO!
WHERE?

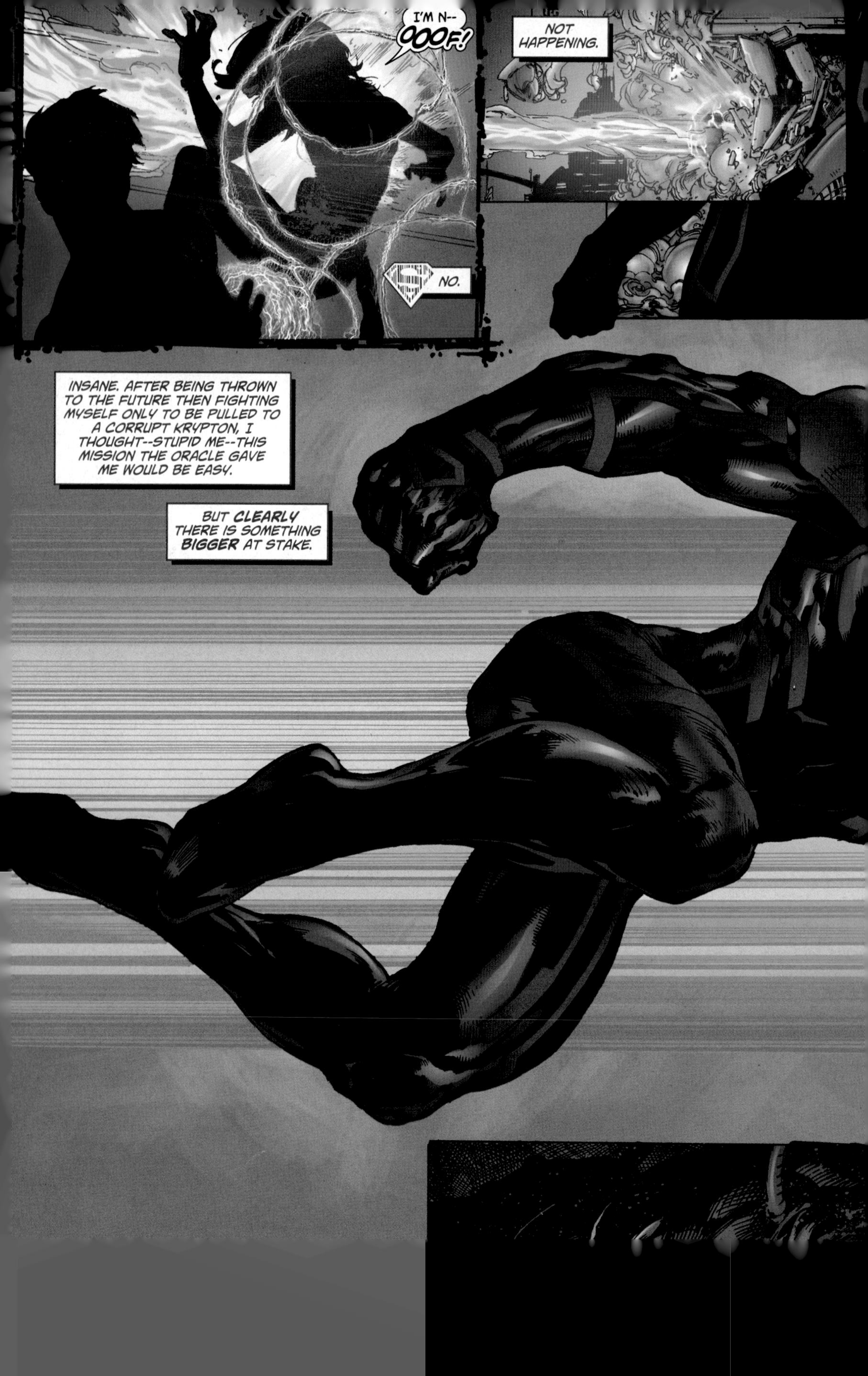
I'M N--
OOOF!
NO.
NOT HAPPENING.
INSANE. AFTER BEING THROWN TO THE FUTURE THEN FIGHTING MYSELF ONLY TO BE PULLED TO A CORRUPT KRYPTON, I THOUGHT--STUPID ME--THIS MISSION THE ORACLE GAVE ME WOULD BE EASY.
BUT CLEARLY THERE IS SOMETHING BIGGER AT STAKE.

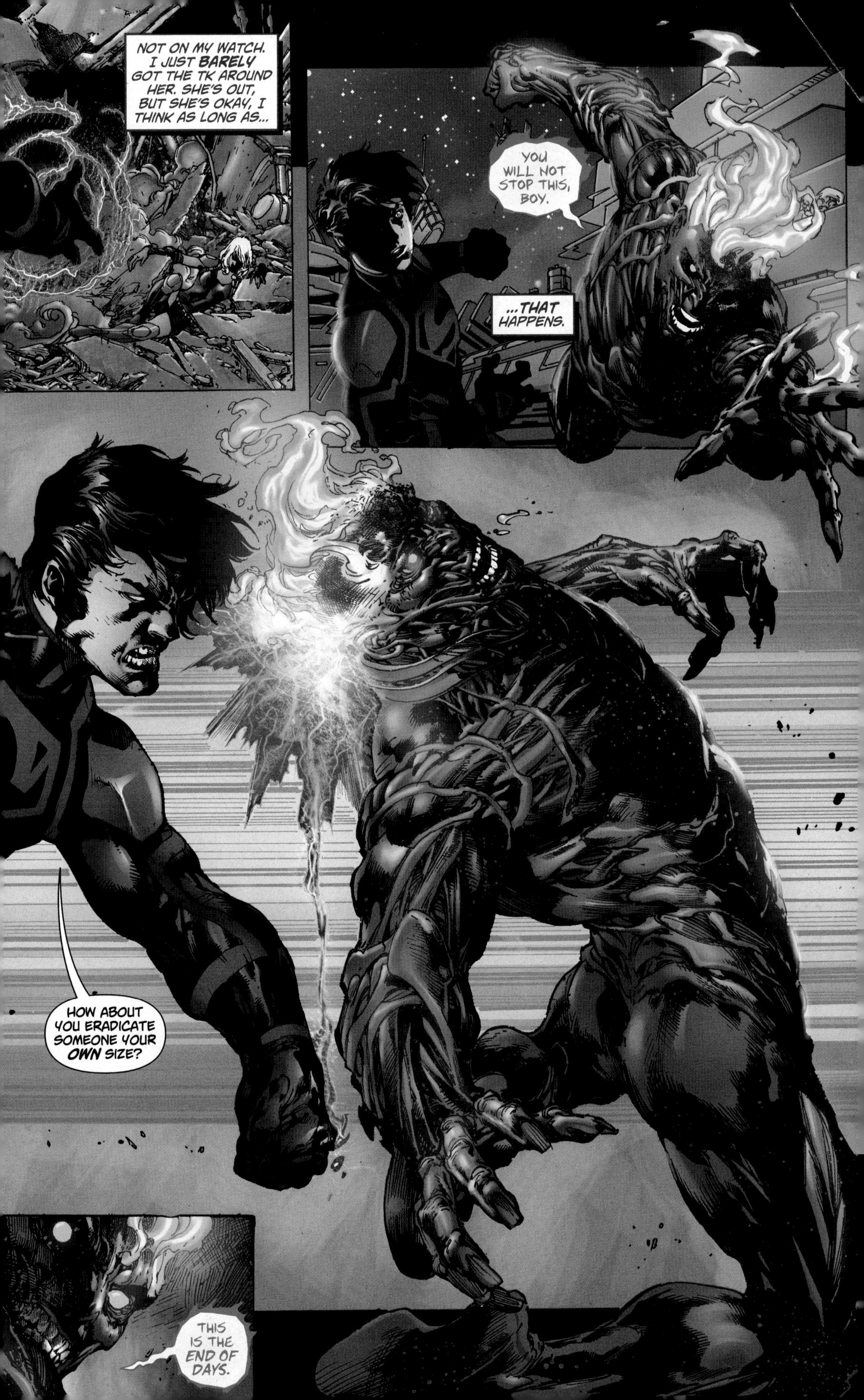
NOT ON MY WATCH. I JUST BARELY GOT THE TK AROUND HER. SHE'S OUT, BUT SHE'S OKAY, I THINK AS LONG AS...
YOU WILL NOT STOP THIS, BOY.
...THAT HAPPENS.
HOW ABOUT YOU ERADICATE SOMEONE YOUR OWN SIZE?
THIS IS THE END OF DAYS.

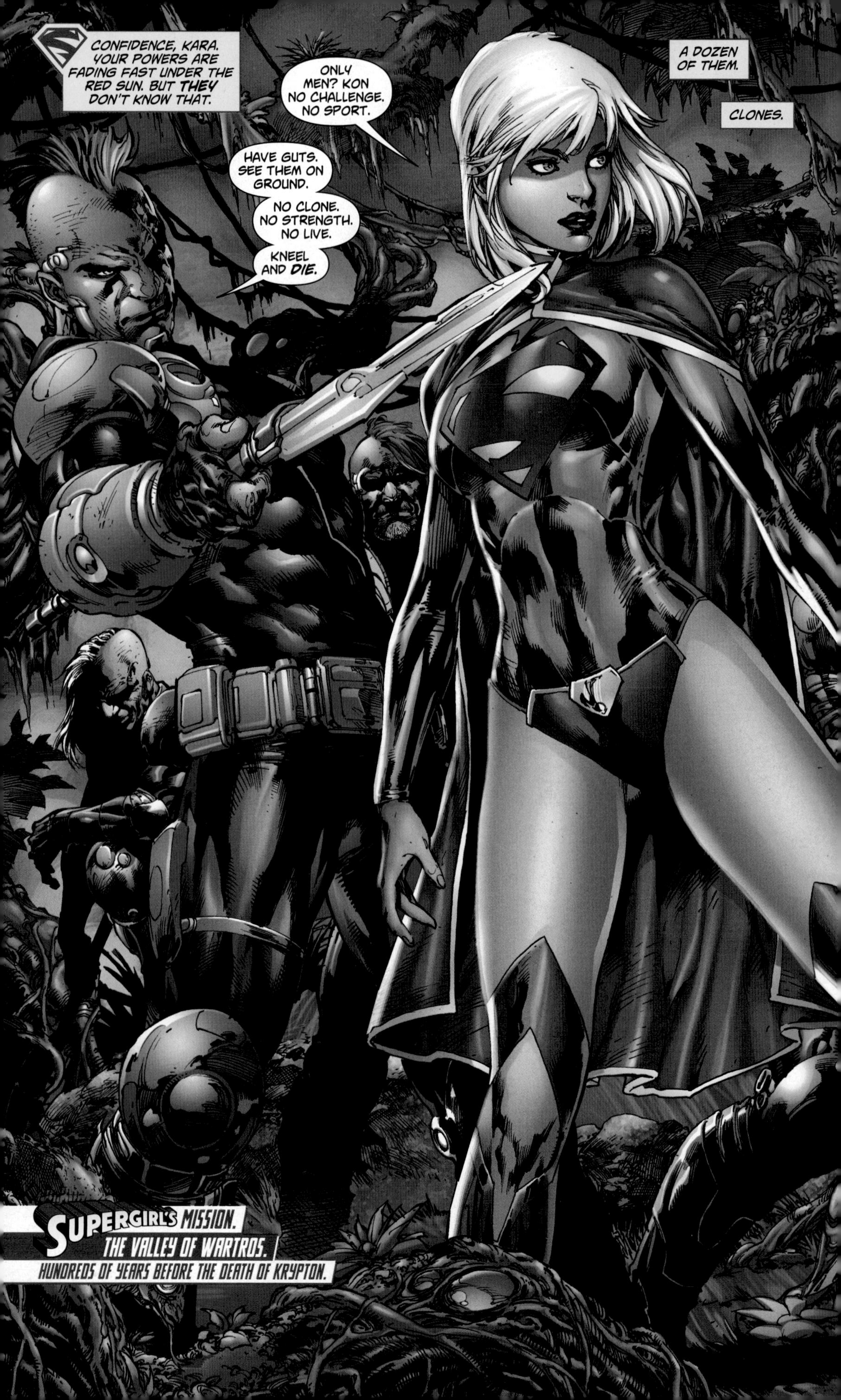
CONFIDENCE, KARA. YOUR POWERS ARE FADING FAST UNDER THE RED SUN. BUT **THEY** DON'T KNOW THAT.
ONLY MEN? KON NO CHALLENGE. NO SPORT.
HAVE GUTS. SEE THEM ON GROUND.
NO CLONE. NO STRENGTH. NO LIVE.
KNEEL AND **DIE**.
A DOZEN OF THEM.
CLONES.
SUPERGIRL'S MISSION.
THE VALLEY OF WARTROS.
HUNDREDS OF YEARS BEFORE THE DEATH OF KRYPTON.

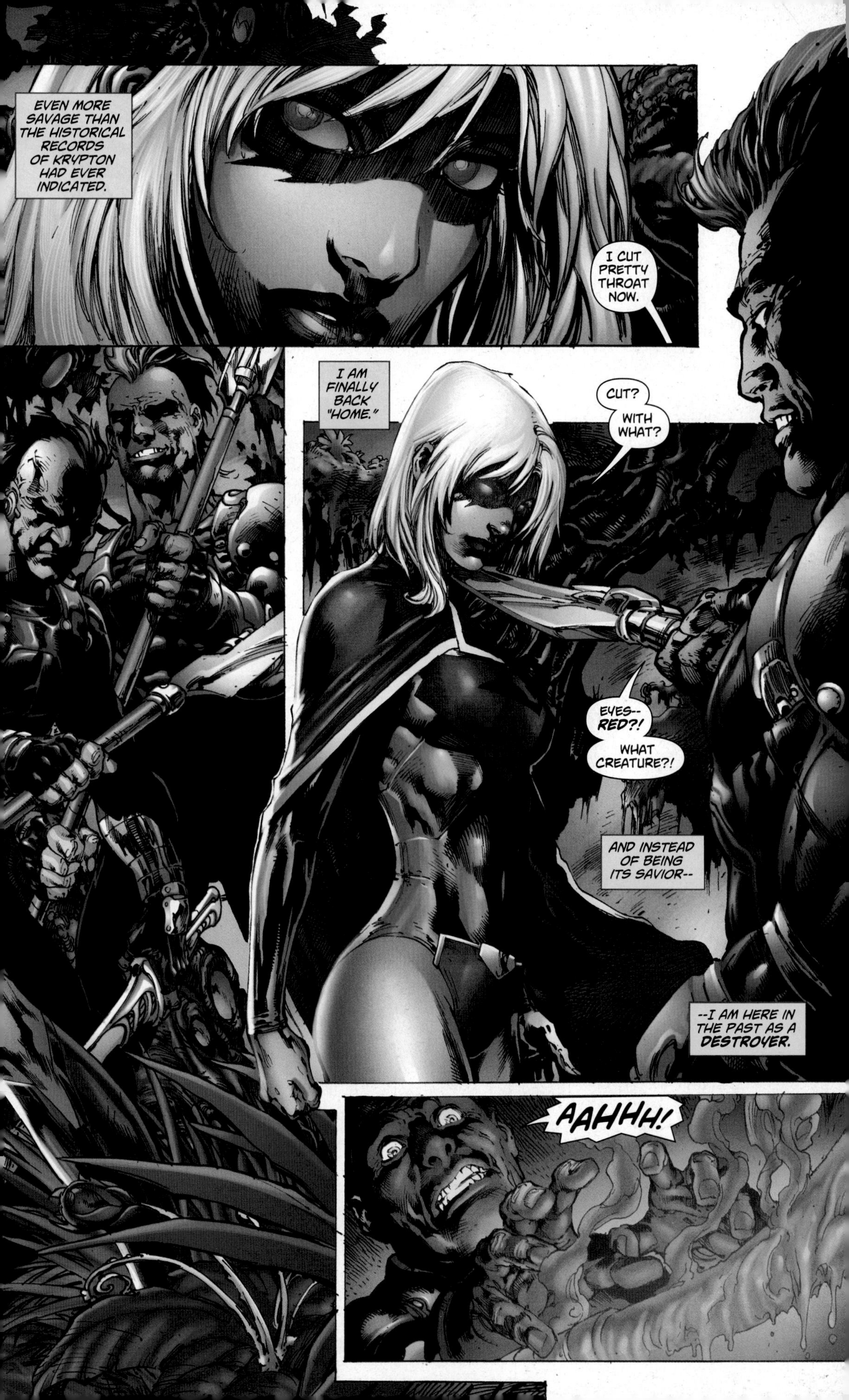
EVEN MORE SAVAGE THAN THE HISTORICAL RECORDS OF KRYPTON HAD EVER INDICATED.
I CUT PRETTY THROAT NOW.
I AM FINALLY BACK "HOME."
CUT? WITH WHAT?
EYES-- RED?!
WHAT CREATURE?!
AND INSTEAD OF BEING ITS SAVIOR--
--I AM HERE IN THE PAST AS A DESTROYER.
AAHHH!

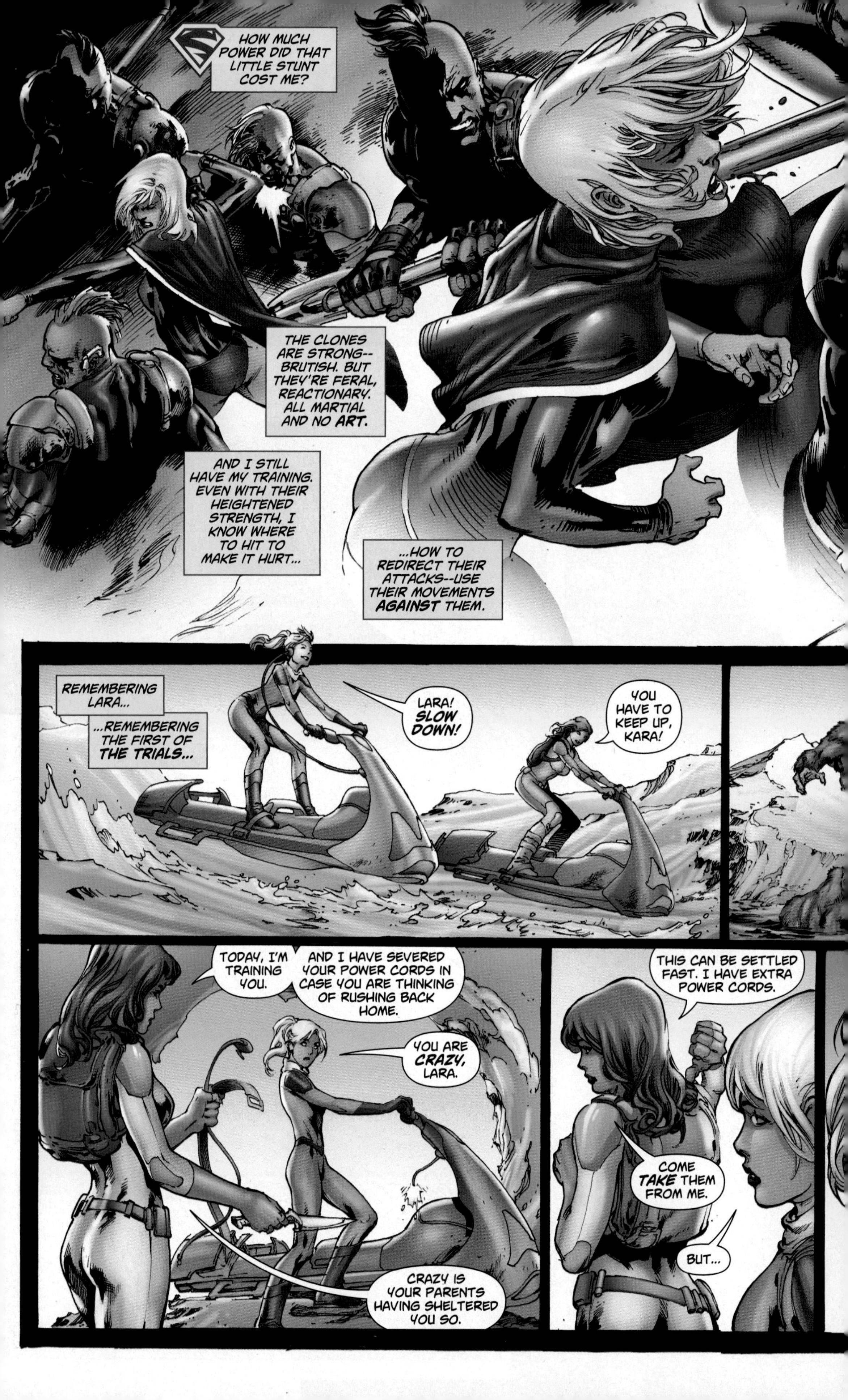
HOW MUCH POWER DID THAT LITTLE STUNT COST ME?
THE CLONES ARE STRONG-- BRUTISH. BUT THEY'RE FERAL, REACTIONARY. ALL MARTIAL AND NO ART.
AND I STILL HAVE MY TRAINING. EVEN WITH THEIR HEIGHTENED STRENGTH, I KNOW WHERE TO HIT TO MAKE IT HURT...
...HOW TO REDIRECT THEIR ATTACKS--USE THEIR MOVEMENTS AGAINST THEM.
REMEMBERING LARA...
...REMEMBERING THE FIRST OF THE TRIALS...
LARA! SLOW DOWN!
YOU HAVE TO KEEP UP, KARA!
TODAY, I'M TRAINING YOU.
AND I HAVE SEVERED YOUR POWER CORDS IN CASE YOU ARE THINKING OF RUSHING BACK HOME.
YOU ARE CRAZY, LARA.
CRAZY IS YOUR PARENTS HAVING SHELTERED YOU SO.
THIS CAN BE SETTLED FAST. I HAVE EXTRA POWER CORDS.
COME TAKE THEM FROM ME.
BUT...

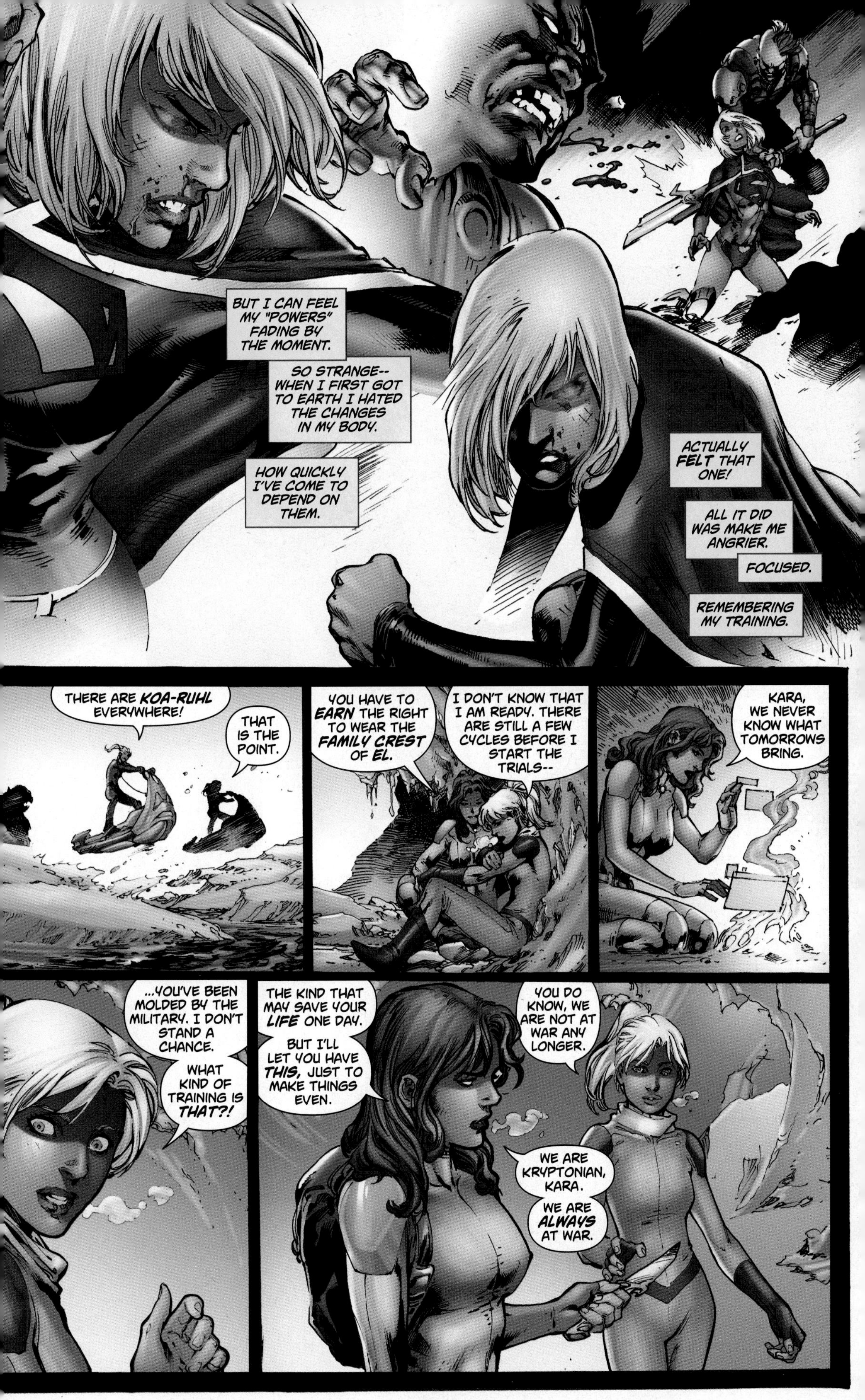

BUT I CAN FEEL MY "POWERS" FADING BY THE MOMENT.
SO STRANGE-- WHEN I FIRST GOT TO EARTH I HATED THE CHANGES IN MY BODY.
HOW QUICKLY I'VE COME TO DEPEND ON THEM.
ACTUALLY FELT THAT ONE!
ALL IT DID WAS MAKE ME ANGRIER.
FOCUSED.
REMEMBERING MY TRAINING.
THERE ARE KOA-RUHL EVERYWHERE!
THAT IS THE POINT.
YOU HAVE TO EARN THE RIGHT TO WEAR THE FAMILY CREST OF EL.
I DON'T KNOW THAT I AM READY. THERE ARE STILL A FEW CYCLES BEFORE I START THE TRIALS--
KARA, WE NEVER KNOW WHAT TOMORROWS BRING.
...YOU'VE BEEN MOLDED BY THE MILITARY. I DON'T STAND A CHANCE.
WHAT KIND OF TRAINING IS THAT?!
THE KIND THAT MAY SAVE YOUR LIFE ONE DAY.
BUT I'LL LET YOU HAVE THIS, JUST TO MAKE THINGS EVEN.
YOU DO KNOW, WE ARE NOT AT WAR ANY LONGER.
WE ARE KRYPTONIAN, KARA.
WE ARE ALWAYS AT WAR.

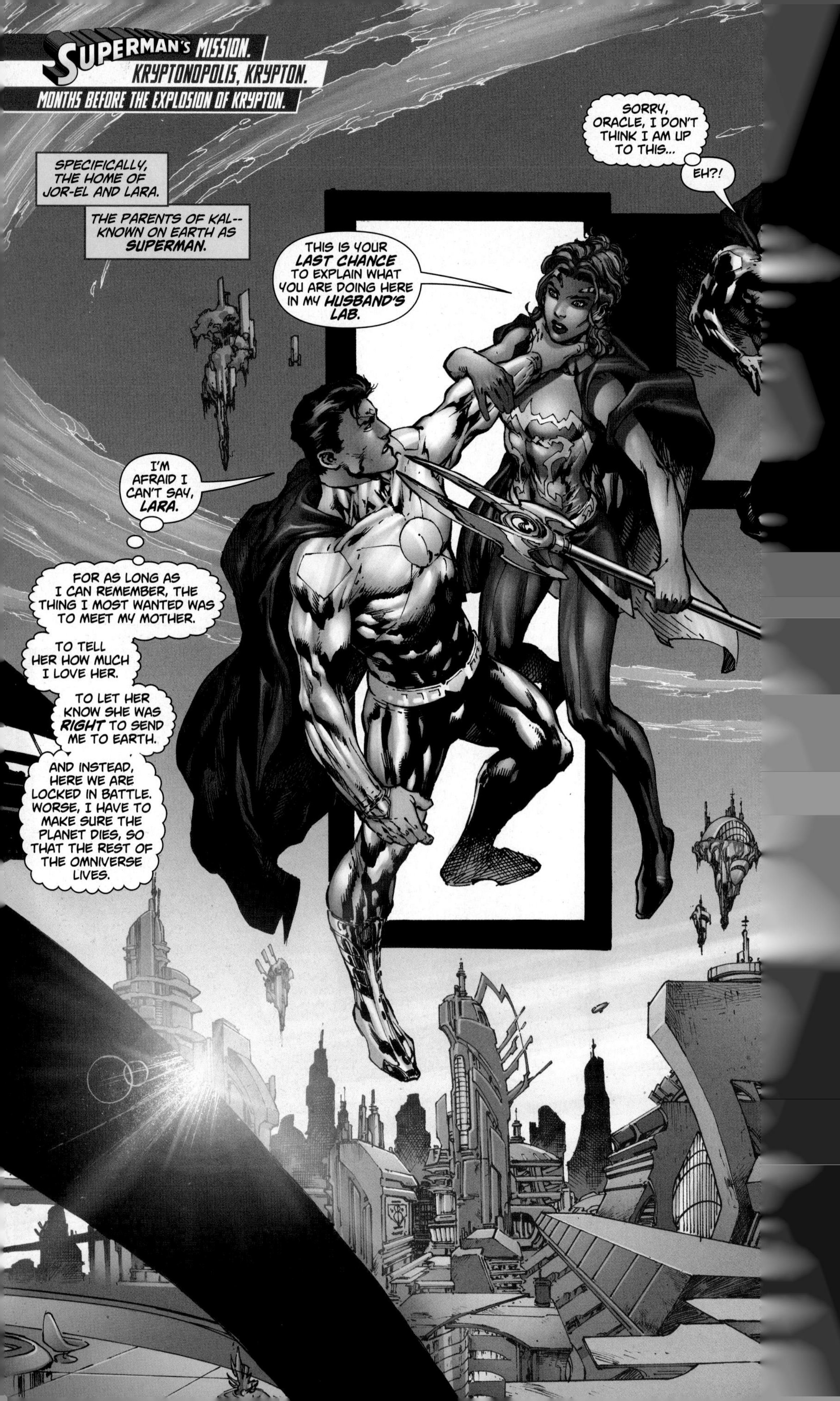
SUPERMAN'S MISSION.
KRYPTONOPOLIS, KRYPTON.
MONTHS BEFORE THE EXPLOSION OF KRYPTON.
SPECIFICALLY, THE HOME OF JOR-EL AND LARA.
THE PARENTS OF KAL-- KNOWN ON EARTH AS SUPERMAN.
SORRY, ORACLE, I DON'T THINK I AM UP TO THIS...
EH?!
THIS IS YOUR LAST CHANCE TO EXPLAIN WHAT YOU ARE DOING HERE IN MY HUSBAND'S LAB.
I'M AFRAID I CAN'T SAY, LARA.
FOR AS LONG AS I CAN REMEMBER, THE THING I MOST WANTED WAS TO MEET MY MOTHER.
TO TELL HER HOW MUCH I LOVE HER.
TO LET HER KNOW SHE WAS RIGHT TO SEND ME TO EARTH.
AND INSTEAD, HERE WE ARE LOCKED IN BATTLE. WORSE, I HAVE TO MAKE SURE THE PLANET DIES, SO THAT THE REST OF THE OMNIVERSE LIVES.

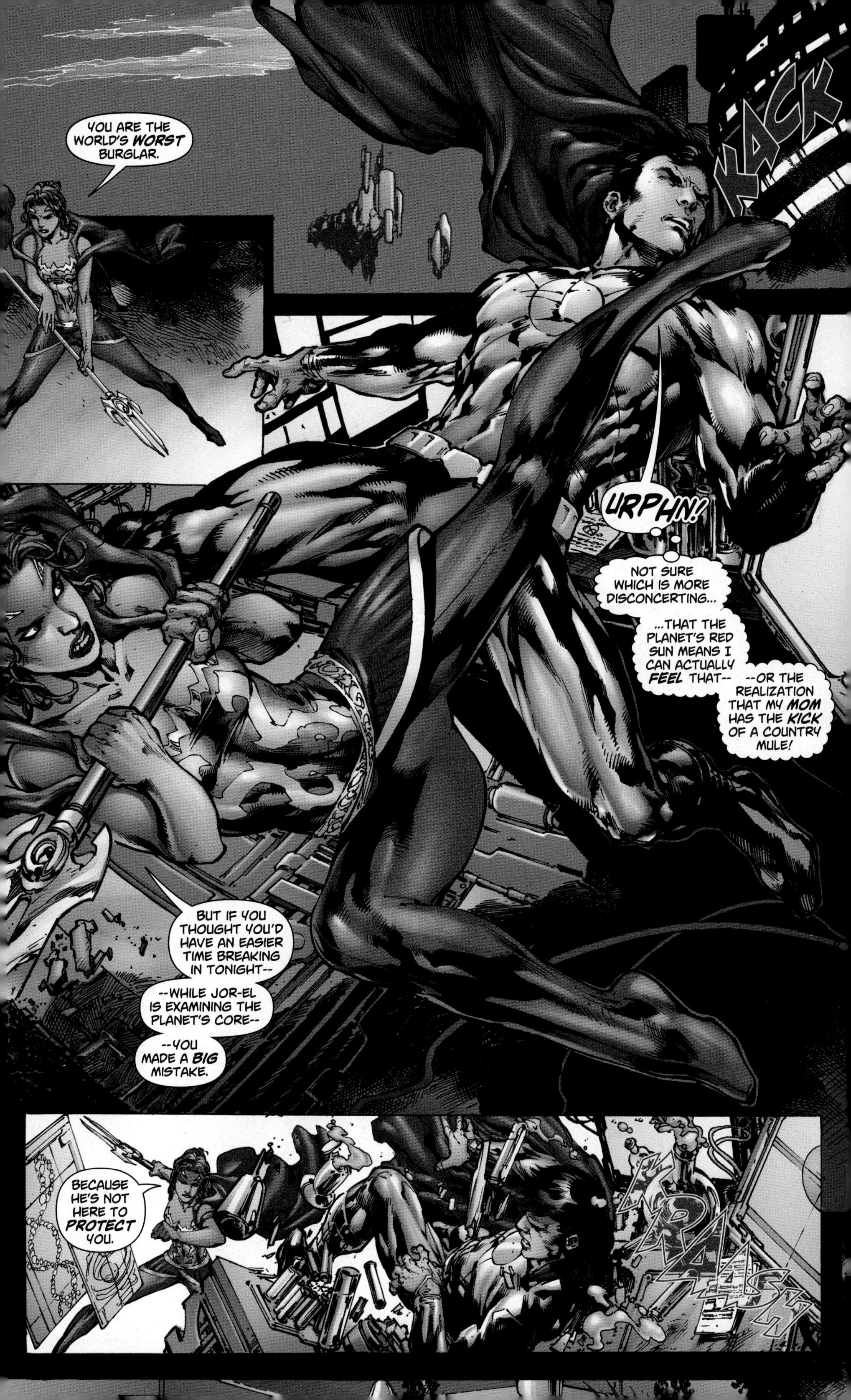

KRACK
YOU ARE THE WORLD'S WORST BURGLAR.
URPHN!
NOT SURE WHICH IS MORE DISCONCERTING...
...THAT THE PLANET'S RED SUN MEANS I CAN ACTUALLY FEEL THAT--
--OR THE REALIZATION THAT MY MOM HAS THE KICK OF A COUNTRY MULE!
BUT IF YOU THOUGHT YOU'D HAVE AN EASIER TIME BREAKING IN TONIGHT--
--WHILE JOR-EL IS EXAMINING THE PLANET'S CORE--
--YOU MADE A BIG MISTAKE.
BECAUSE HE'S NOT HERE TO PROTECT YOU.
KRAASH

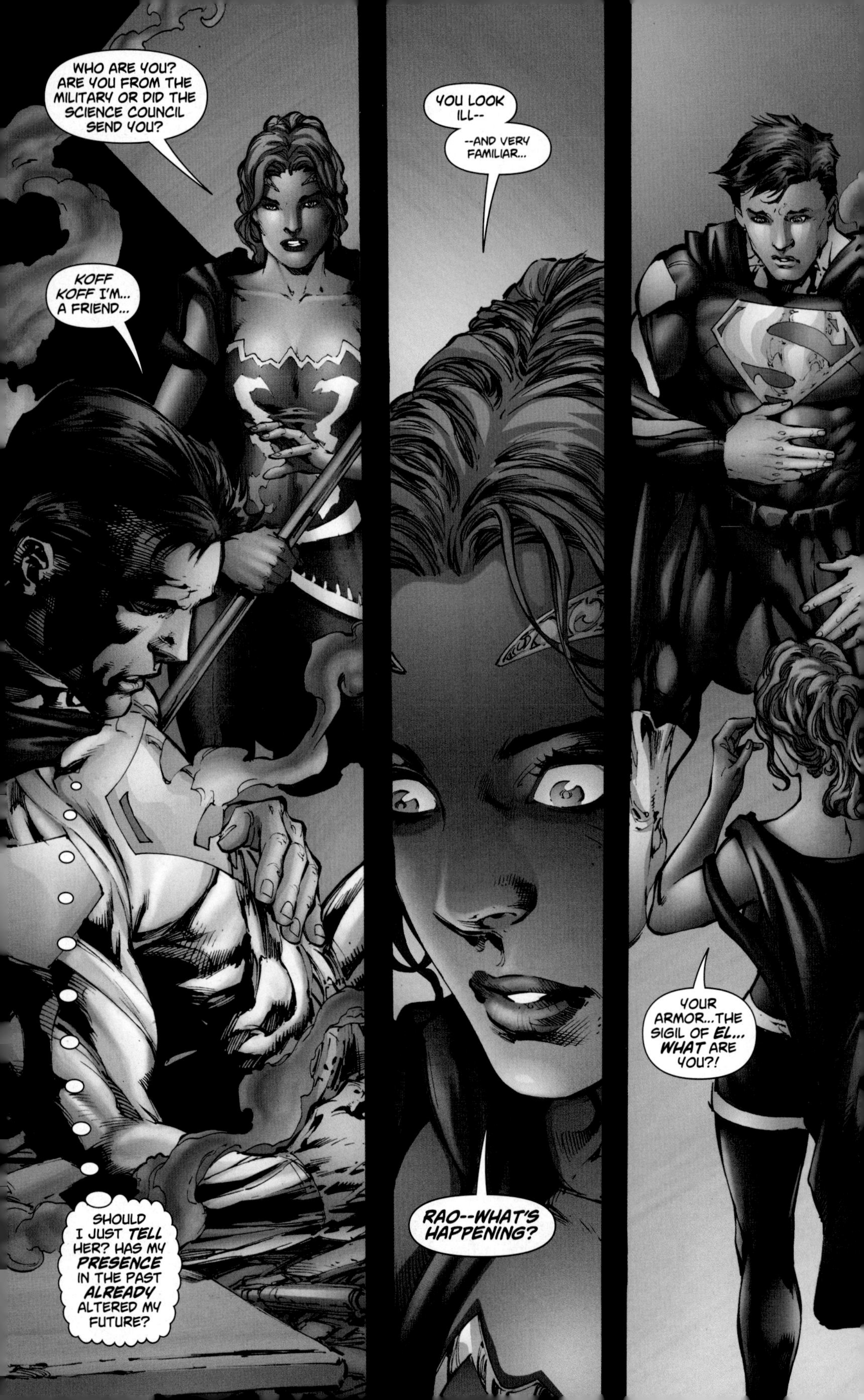
WHO ARE YOU? ARE YOU FROM THE MILITARY OR DID THE SCIENCE COUNCIL SEND YOU?
KOFF KOFF I'M... A FRIEND...
SHOULD I JUST TELL HER? HAS MY PRESENCE IN THE PAST ALREADY ALTERED MY FUTURE?
YOU LOOK ILL--
--AND VERY FAMILIAR...
RAO--WHAT'S HAPPENING?
YOUR ARMOR...THE SIGIL OF EL... WHAT ARE YOU?!

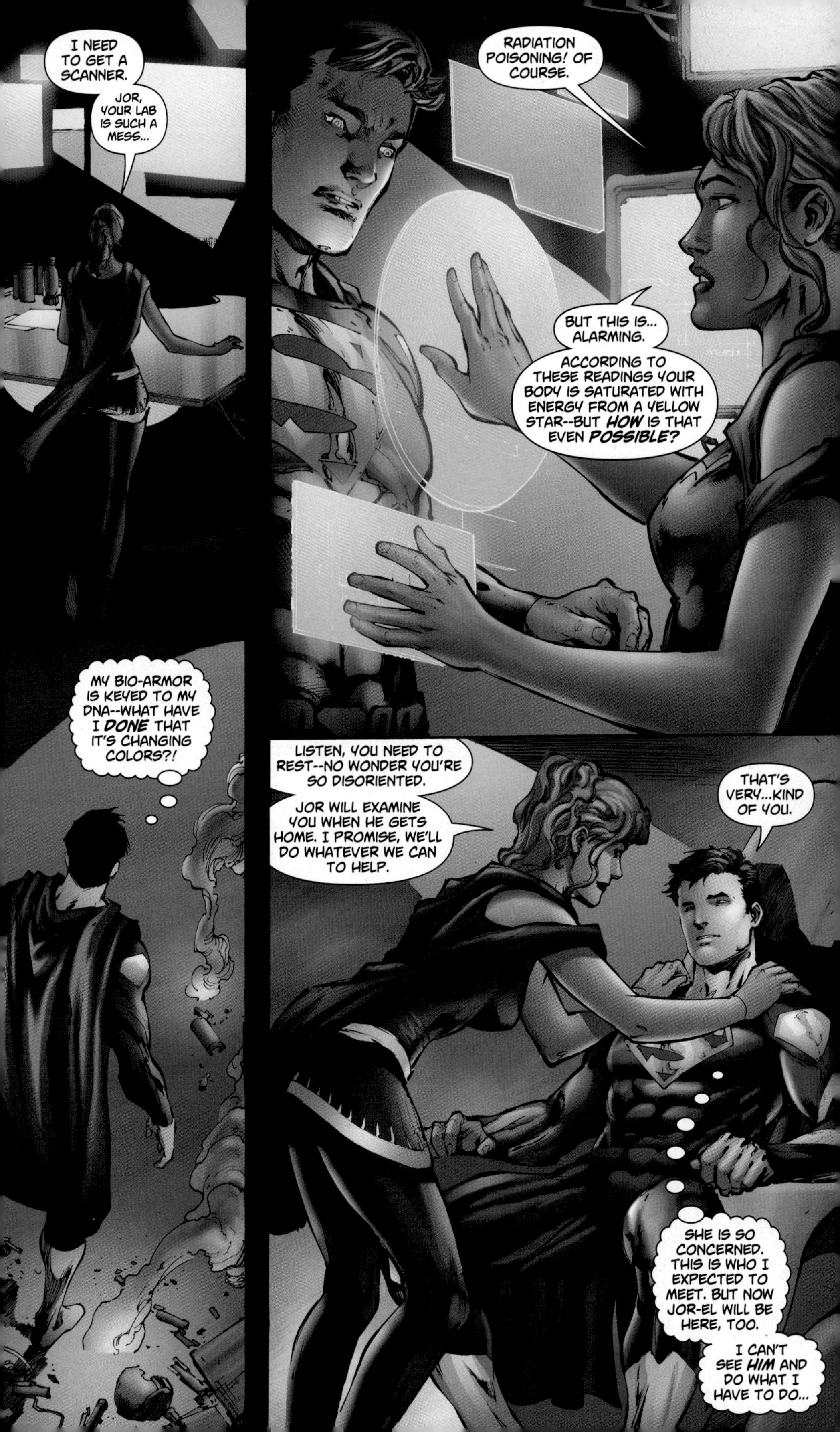
I NEED TO GET A SCANNER.
JOR, YOUR LAB IS SUCH A MESS...
RADIATION POISONING! OF COURSE.
BUT THIS IS... ALARMING.
ACCORDING TO THESE READINGS YOUR BODY IS SATURATED WITH ENERGY FROM A YELLOW STAR--BUT **HOW** IS THAT EVEN ***POSSIBLE?***
MY BIO-ARMOR IS KEYED TO MY DNA--WHAT HAVE I ***DONE*** THAT IT'S CHANGING COLORS?!
LISTEN, YOU NEED TO REST--NO WONDER YOU'RE SO DISORIENTED.
JOR WILL EXAMINE YOU WHEN HE GETS HOME. I PROMISE, WE'LL DO WHATEVER WE CAN TO HELP.
THAT'S VERY...KIND OF YOU.
SHE IS SO CONCERNED. THIS IS WHO I EXPECTED TO MEET. BUT NOW JOR-EL WILL BE HERE, TOO.
I CAN'T SEE ***HIM*** AND DO WHAT I HAVE TO DO...

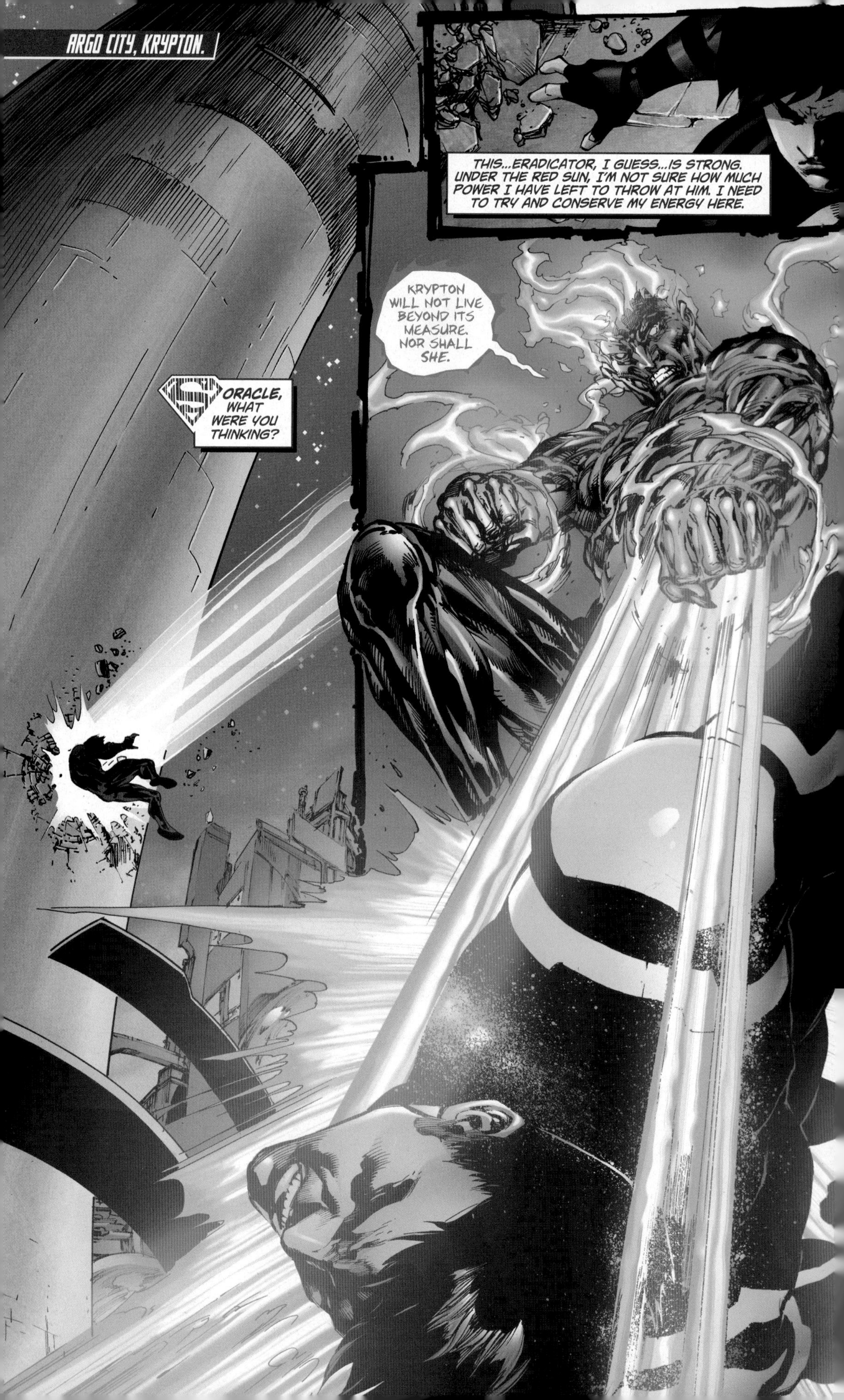
ARGO CITY, KRYPTON.
THIS...ERADICATOR, I GUESS...IS STRONG. UNDER THE RED SUN, I'M NOT SURE HOW MUCH POWER I HAVE LEFT TO THROW AT HIM. I NEED TO TRY AND CONSERVE MY ENERGY HERE.
KRYPTON WILL NOT LIVE BEYOND ITS MEASURE. NOR SHALL SHE.
ORACLE, WHAT WERE YOU THINKING?

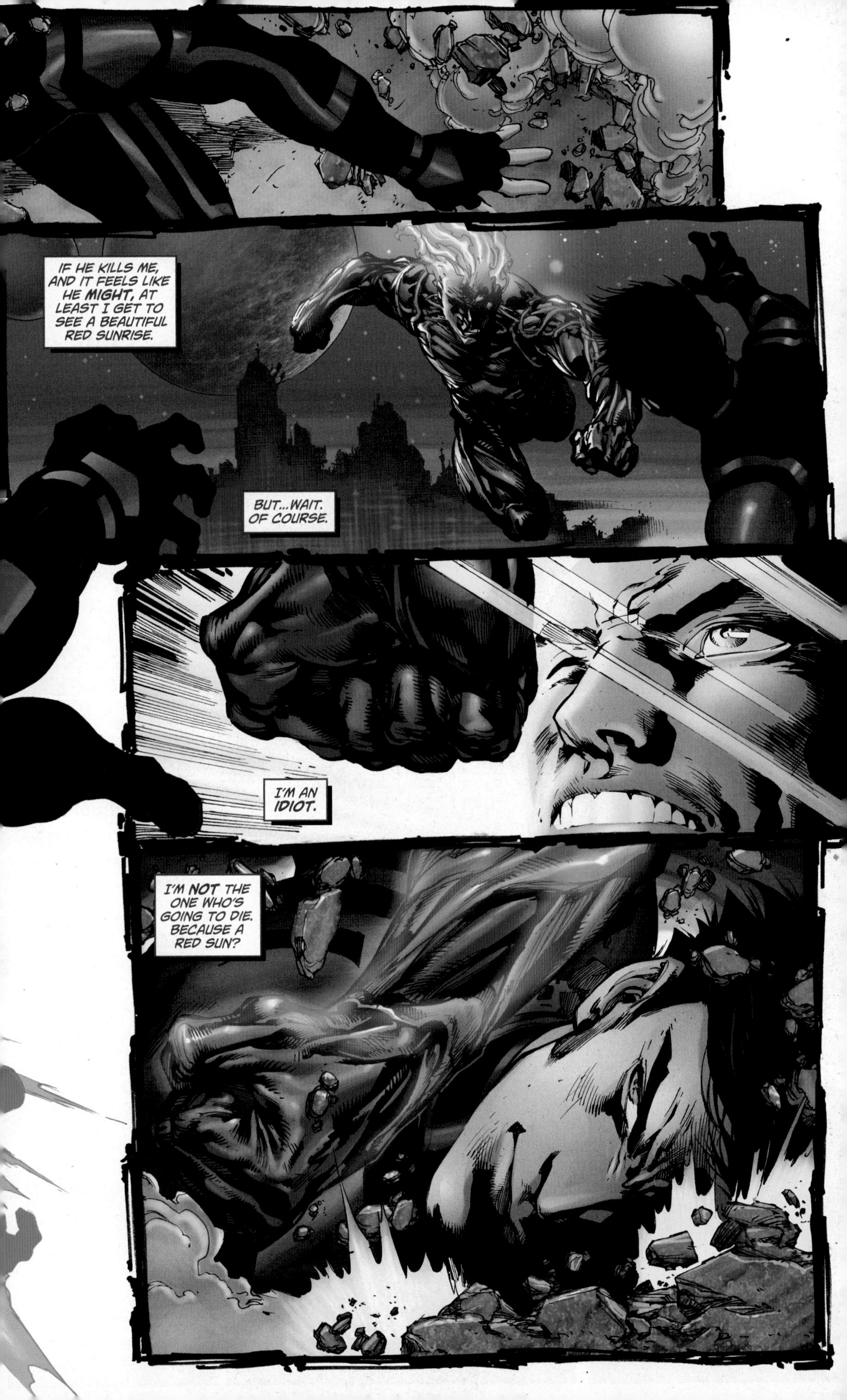
IF HE KILLS ME, AND IT FEELS LIKE HE MIGHT, AT LEAST I GET TO SEE A BEAUTIFUL RED SUNRISE.
BUT...WAIT. OF COURSE.
I'M AN IDIOT.
I'M NOT THE ONE WHO'S GOING TO DIE. BECAUSE A RED SUN?

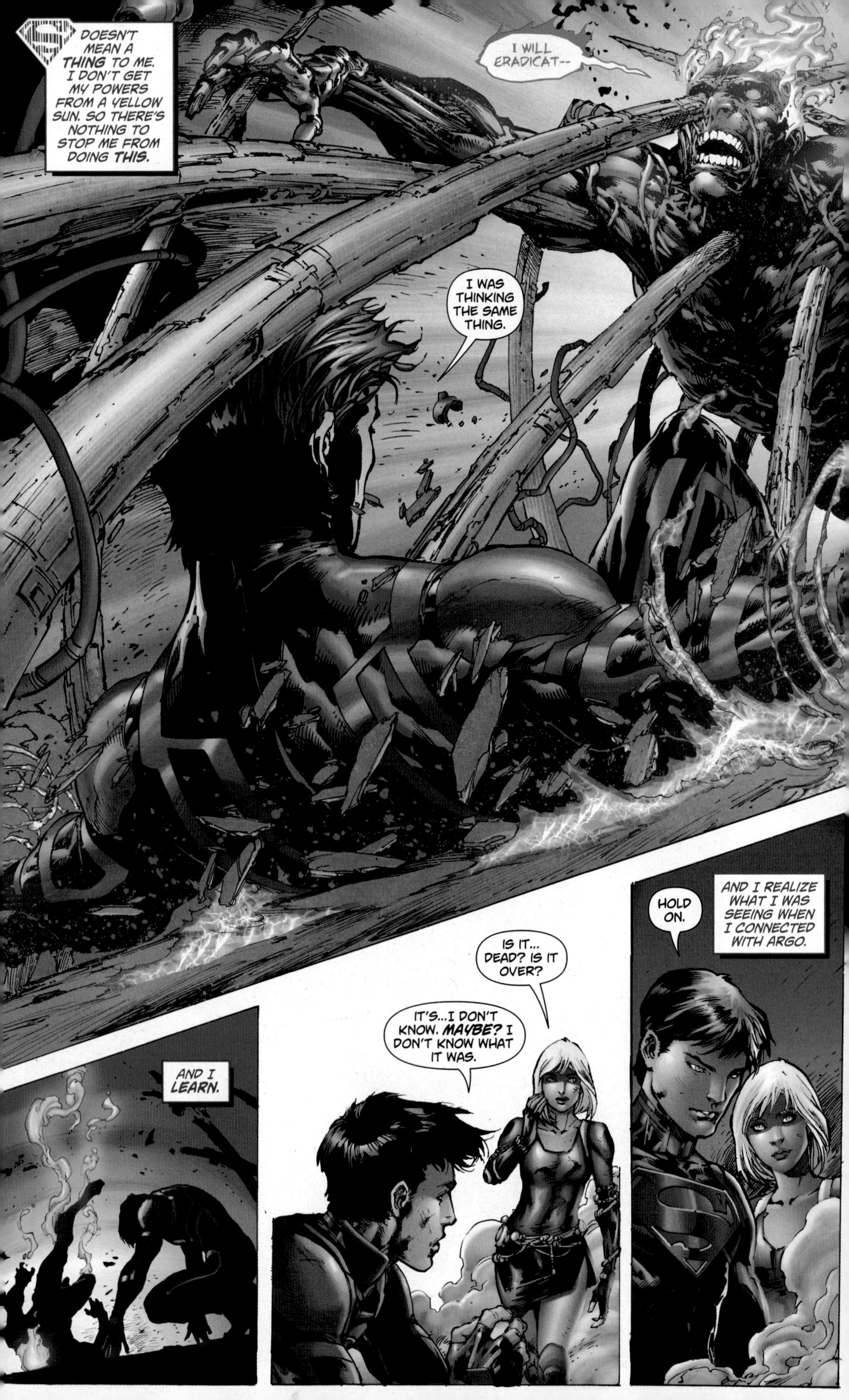
DOESN'T MEAN A THING TO ME. I DON'T GET MY POWERS FROM A YELLOW SUN. SO THERE'S NOTHING TO STOP ME FROM DOING THIS.
I WILL ERADICAT--
I WAS THINKING THE SAME THING.
AND I LEARN.
IS IT... DEAD? IS IT OVER?
IT'S...I DON'T KNOW. MAYBE? I DON'T KNOW WHAT IT WAS.
HOLD ON.
AND I REALIZE WHAT I WAS SEEING WHEN I CONNECTED WITH ARGO.

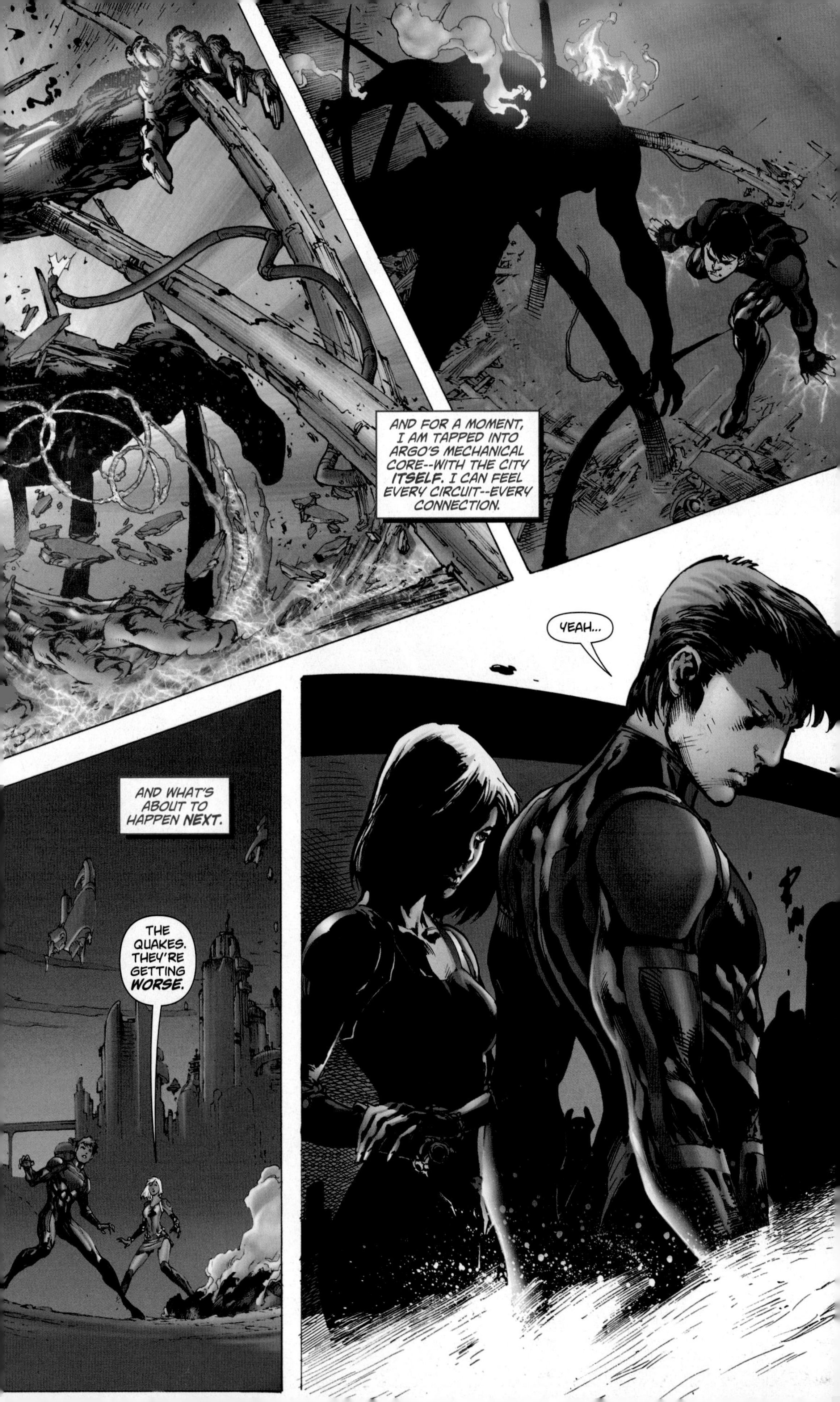
AND FOR A MOMENT, I AM TAPPED INTO ARGO'S MECHANICAL CORE--WITH THE CITY ITSELF. I CAN FEEL EVERY CIRCUIT--EVERY CONNECTION.
AND WHAT'S ABOUT TO HAPPEN NEXT.
THE QUAKES. THEY'RE GETTING WORSE.
YEAH...

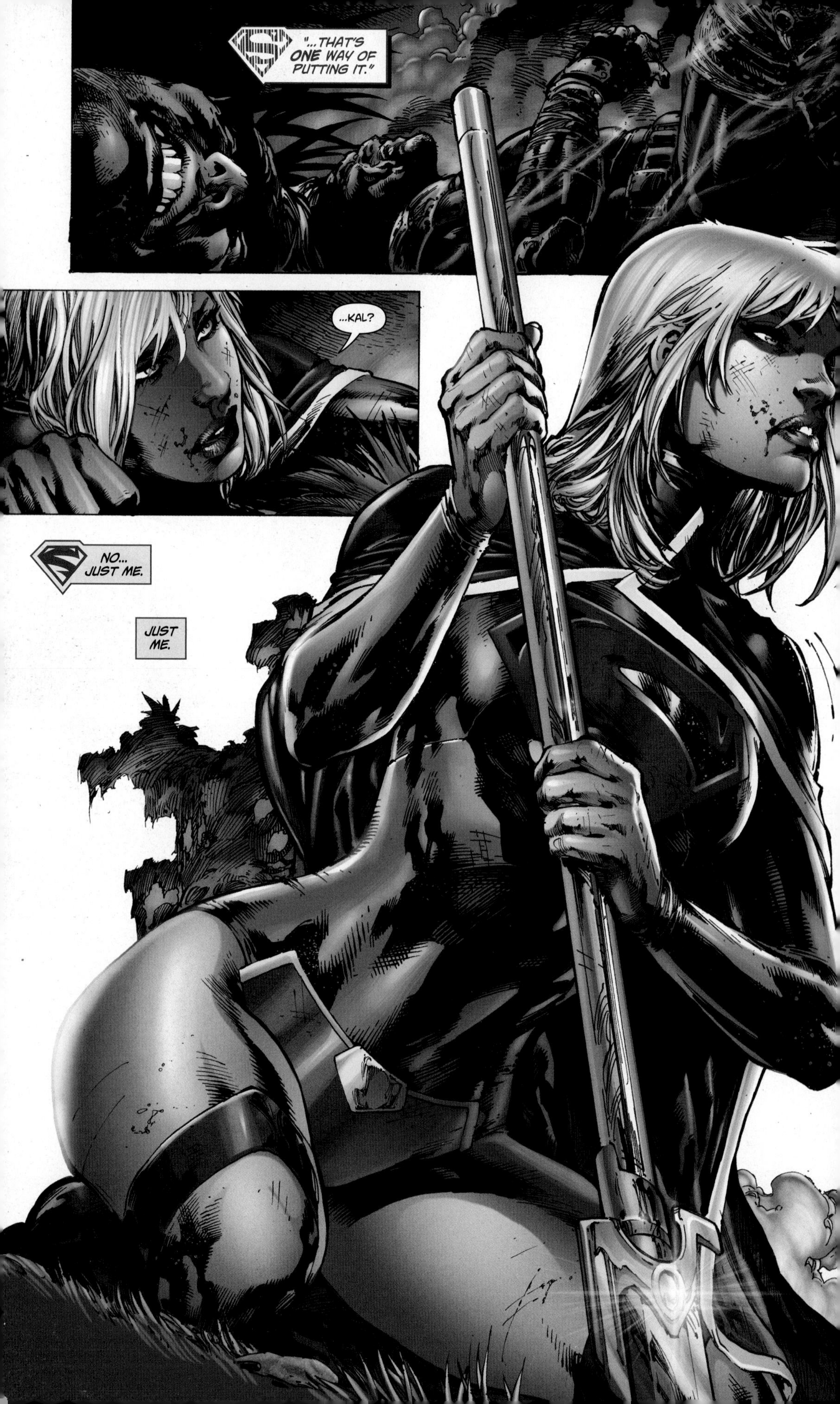
"...THAT'S ONE WAY OF PUTTING IT."
...KAL?
NO... JUST ME.
JUST ME.

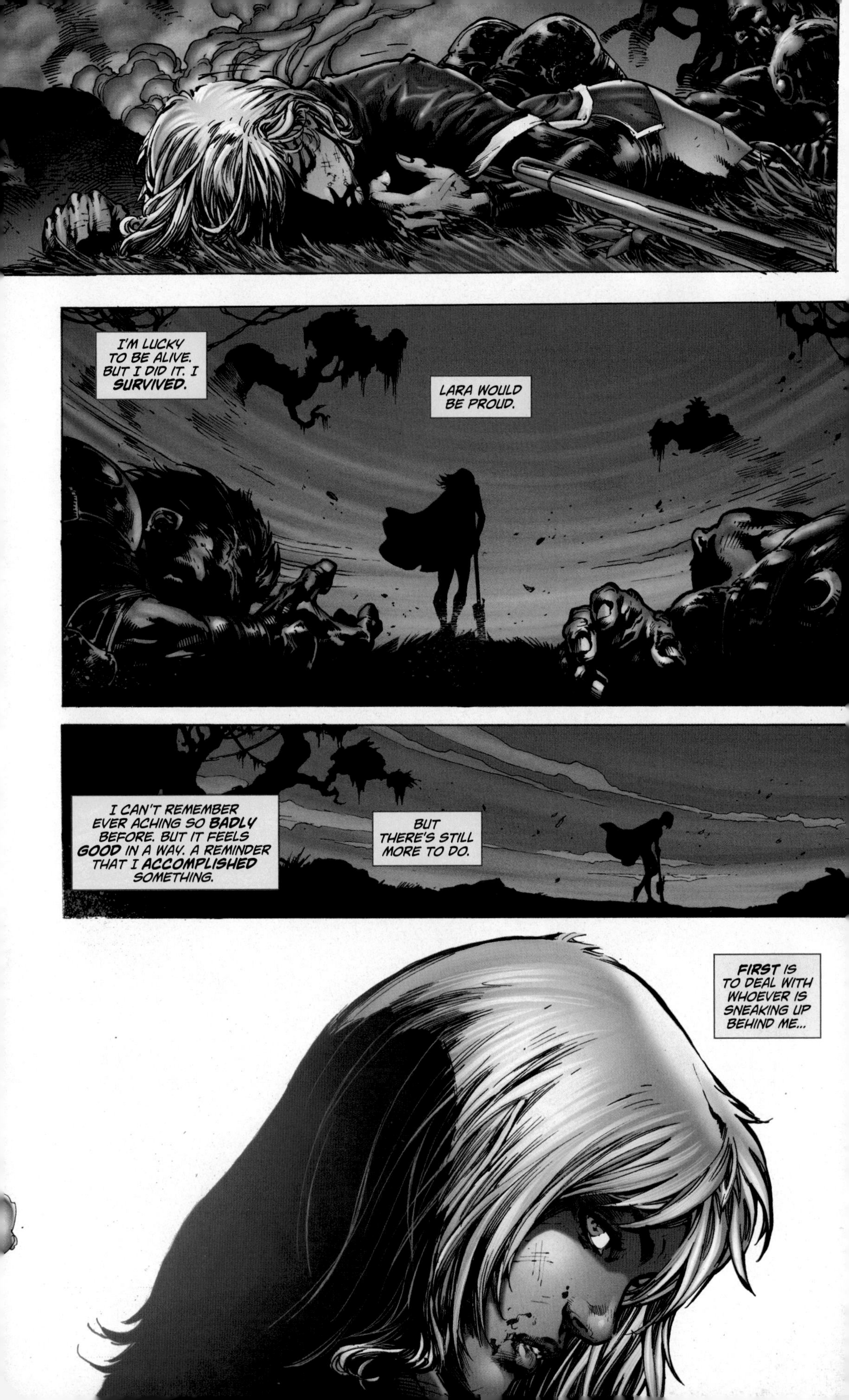
I'M LUCKY TO BE ALIVE. BUT I DID IT. I SURVIVED.
LARA WOULD BE PROUD.
I CAN'T REMEMBER EVER ACHING SO BADLY BEFORE. BUT IT FEELS GOOD IN A WAY. A REMINDER THAT I ACCOMPLISHED SOMETHING.
BUT THERE'S STILL MORE TO DO.
FIRST IS TO DEAL WITH WHOEVER IS SNEAKING UP BEHIND ME...

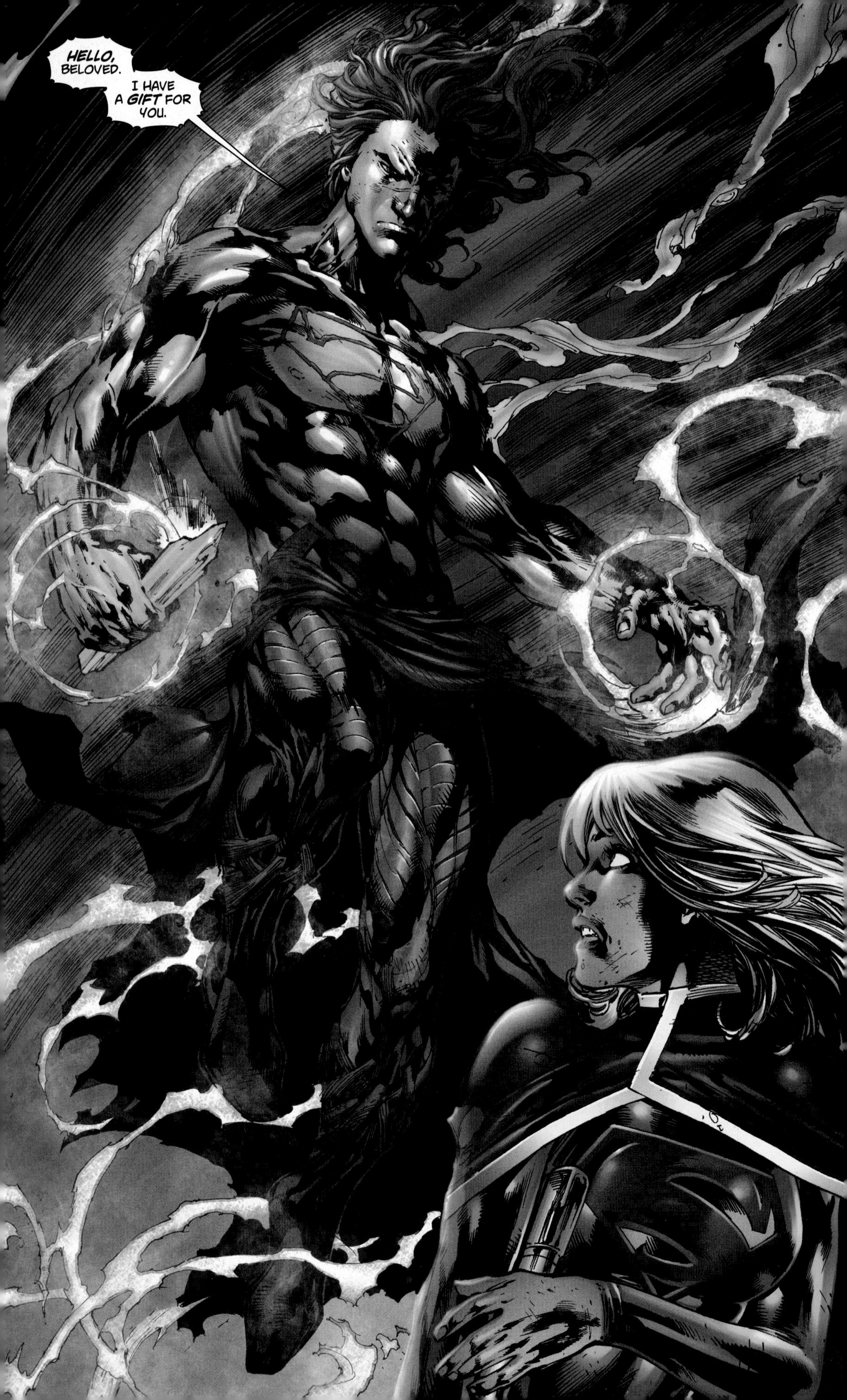
HELLO, BELOVED.
I HAVE A GIFT FOR YOU.

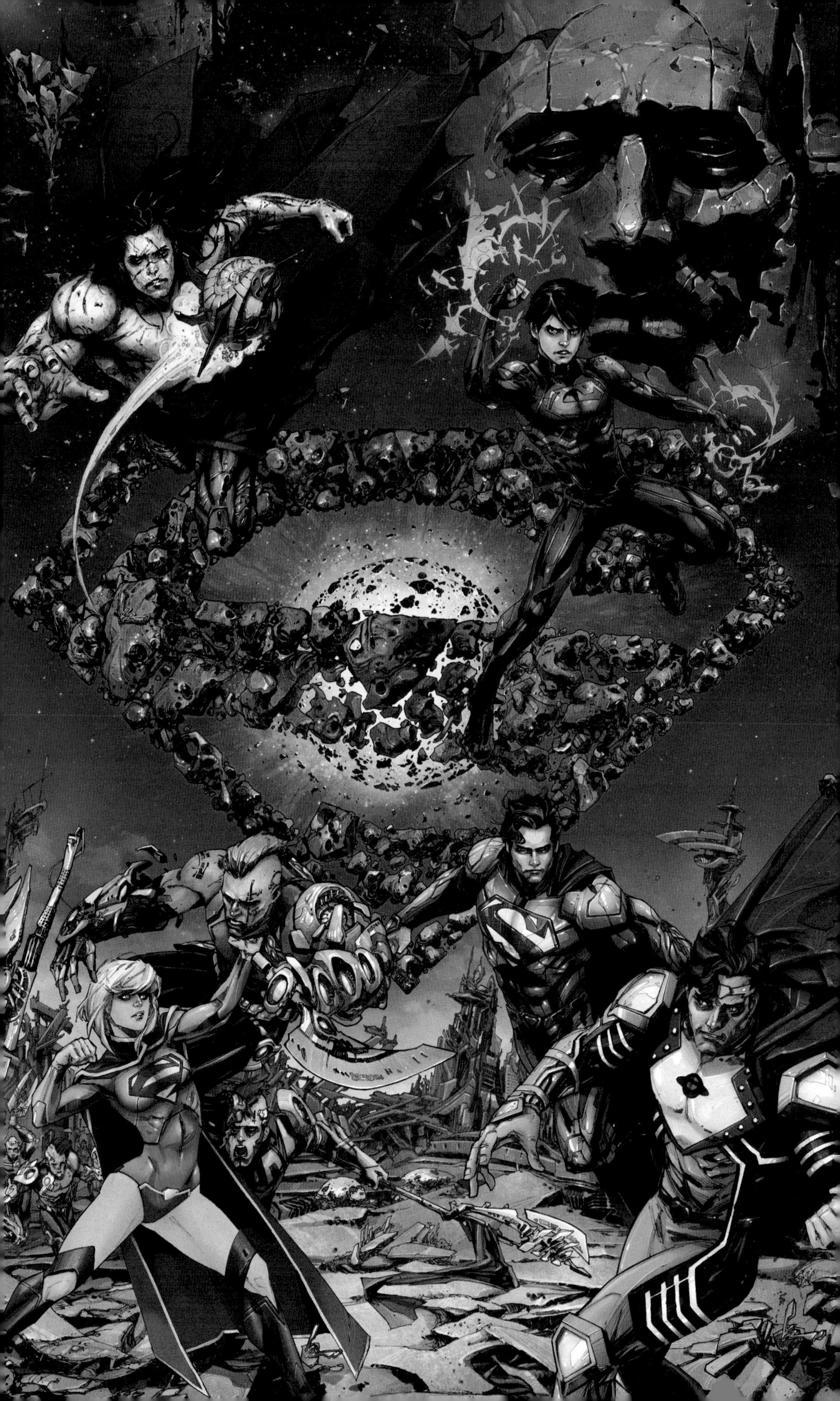

KRYPTON RETURNS: PART 4

SCOTT LOBDELL writer KENNETH ROCAFORT artist cover art by KENNETH ROCAFORT

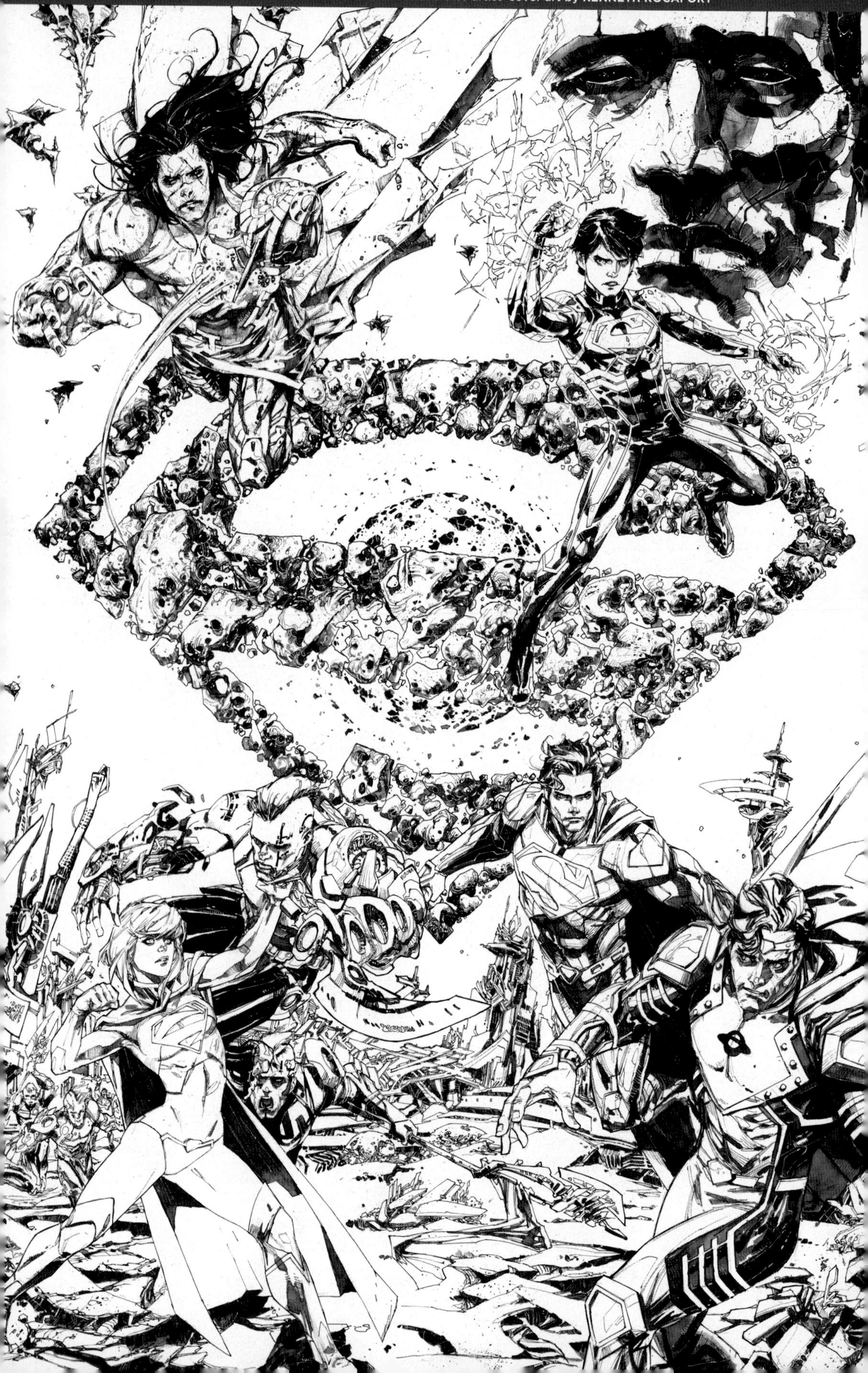

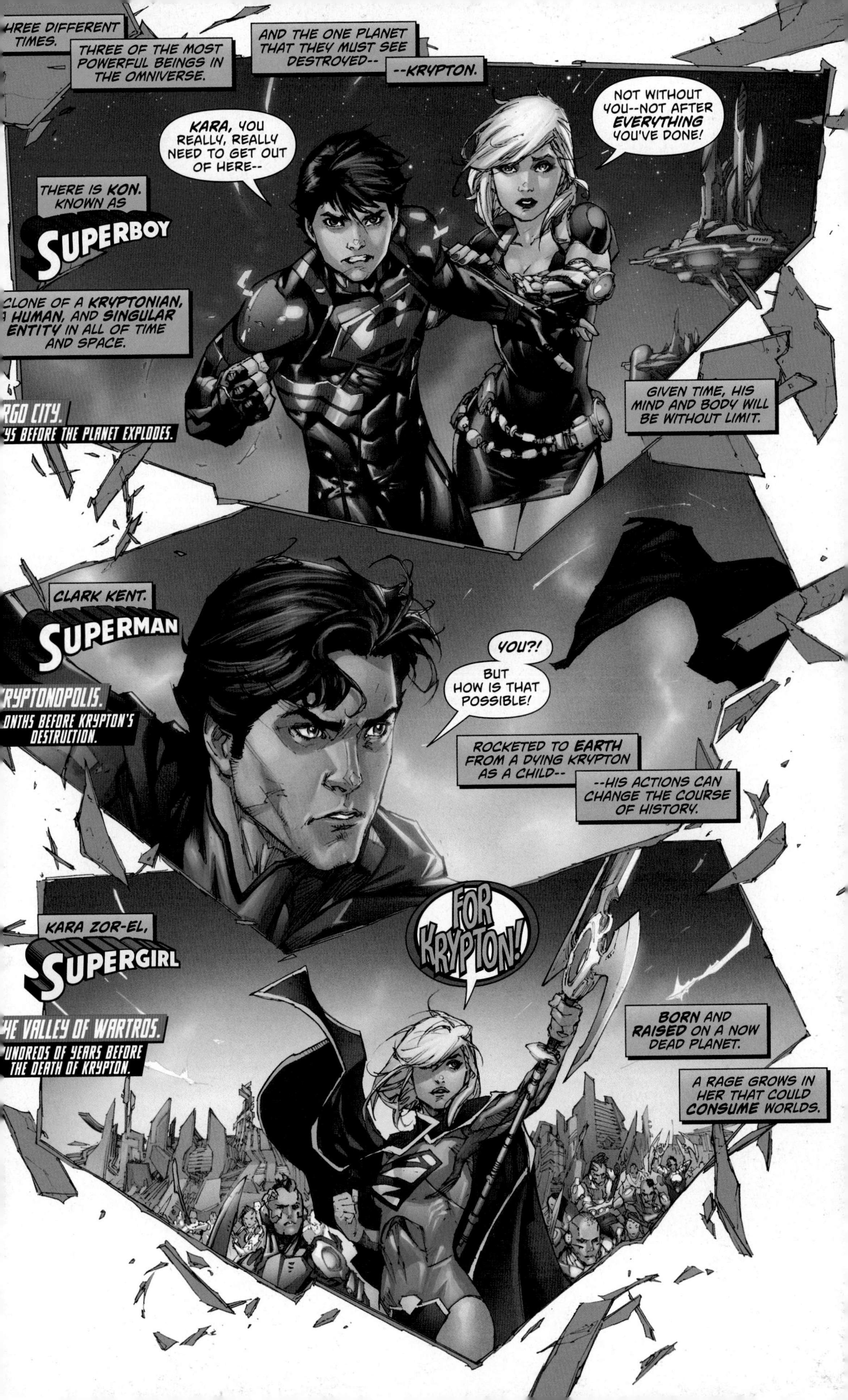

HREE DIFFERENT TIMES.
THREE OF THE MOST POWERFUL BEINGS IN THE OMNIVERSE.
AND THE ONE PLANET THAT THEY MUST SEE DESTROYED--
--KRYPTON.
RGO CITY.
YS BEFORE THE PLANET EXPLODES.
KARA, YOU REALLY, REALLY NEED TO GET OUT OF HERE--
NOT WITHOUT YOU--NOT AFTER EVERYTHING YOU'VE DONE!
THERE IS KON. KNOWN AS
SUPERBOY
CLONE OF A KRYPTONIAN, HUMAN, AND SINGULAR ENTITY IN ALL OF TIME AND SPACE.
GIVEN TIME, HIS MIND AND BODY WILL BE WITHOUT LIMIT.
CLARK KENT.
SUPERMAN
RYPTONOPOLIS.
ONTHS BEFORE KRYPTON'S DESTRUCTION.
YOU?!
BUT HOW IS THAT POSSIBLE!
ROCKETED TO EARTH FROM A DYING KRYPTON AS A CHILD--
--HIS ACTIONS CAN CHANGE THE COURSE OF HISTORY.
KARA ZOR-EL,
SUPERGIRL
HE VALLEY OF WARTROS.
UNDREDS OF YEARS BEFORE THE DEATH OF KRYPTON.
FOR KRYPTON!
BORN AND RAISED ON A NOW DEAD PLANET.
A RAGE GROWS IN HER THAT COULD CONSUME WORLDS.

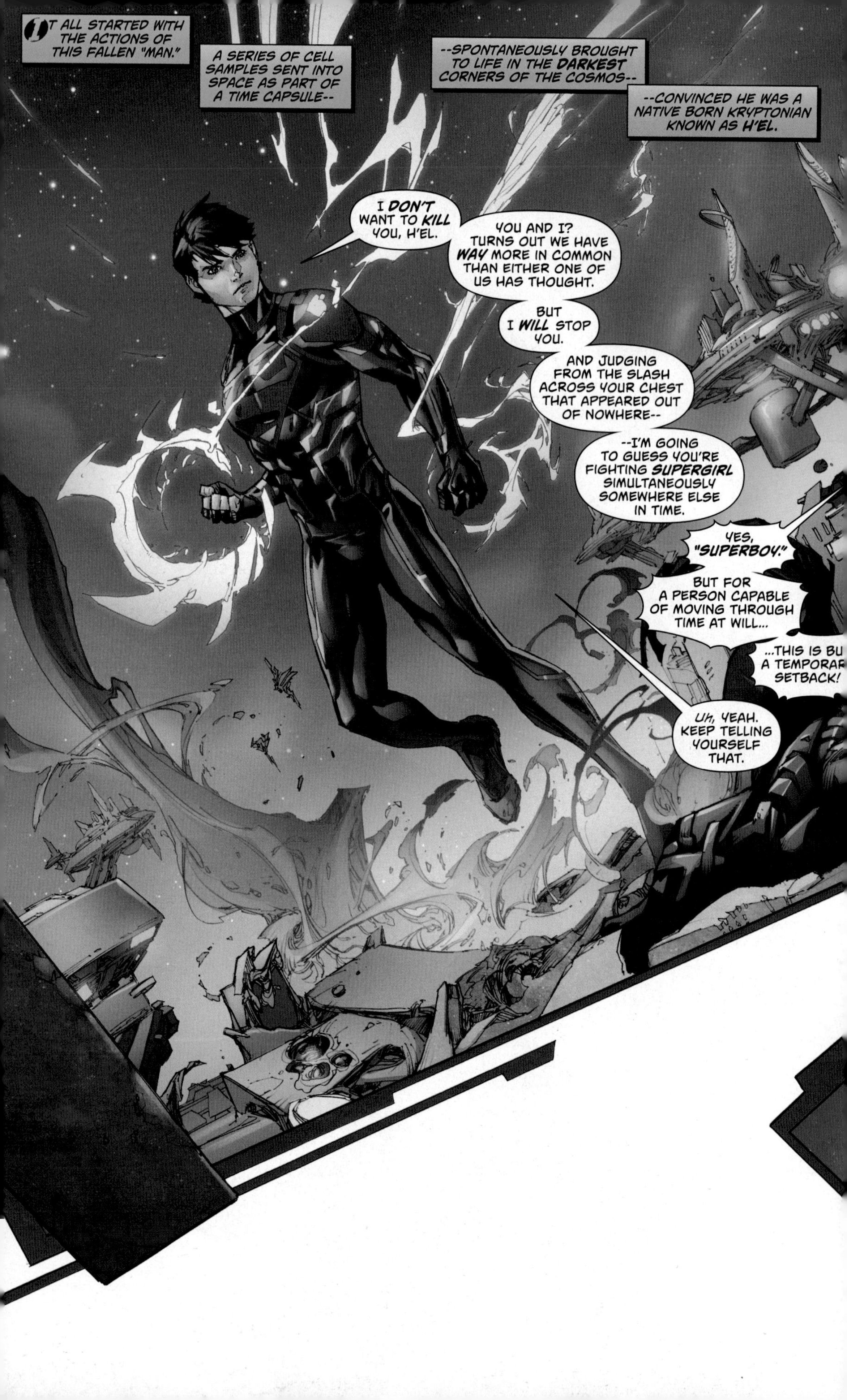
IT ALL STARTED WITH THE ACTIONS OF THIS FALLEN "MAN."
A SERIES OF CELL SAMPLES SENT INTO SPACE AS PART OF A TIME CAPSULE--
--SPONTANEOUSLY BROUGHT TO LIFE IN THE DARKEST CORNERS OF THE COSMOS--
--CONVINCED HE WAS A NATIVE BORN KRYPTONIAN KNOWN AS H'EL.
I DON'T WANT TO KILL YOU, H'EL.
YOU AND I? TURNS OUT WE HAVE WAY MORE IN COMMON THAN EITHER ONE OF US HAS THOUGHT.
BUT I WILL STOP YOU.
AND JUDGING FROM THE SLASH ACROSS YOUR CHEST THAT APPEARED OUT OF NOWHERE--
--I'M GOING TO GUESS YOU'RE FIGHTING SUPERGIRL SIMULTANEOUSLY SOMEWHERE ELSE IN TIME.
YES, "SUPERBOY."
BUT FOR A PERSON CAPABLE OF MOVING THROUGH TIME AT WILL...
...THIS IS BU A TEMPORAR SETBACK!
UH, YEAH. KEEP TELLING YOURSELF THAT.

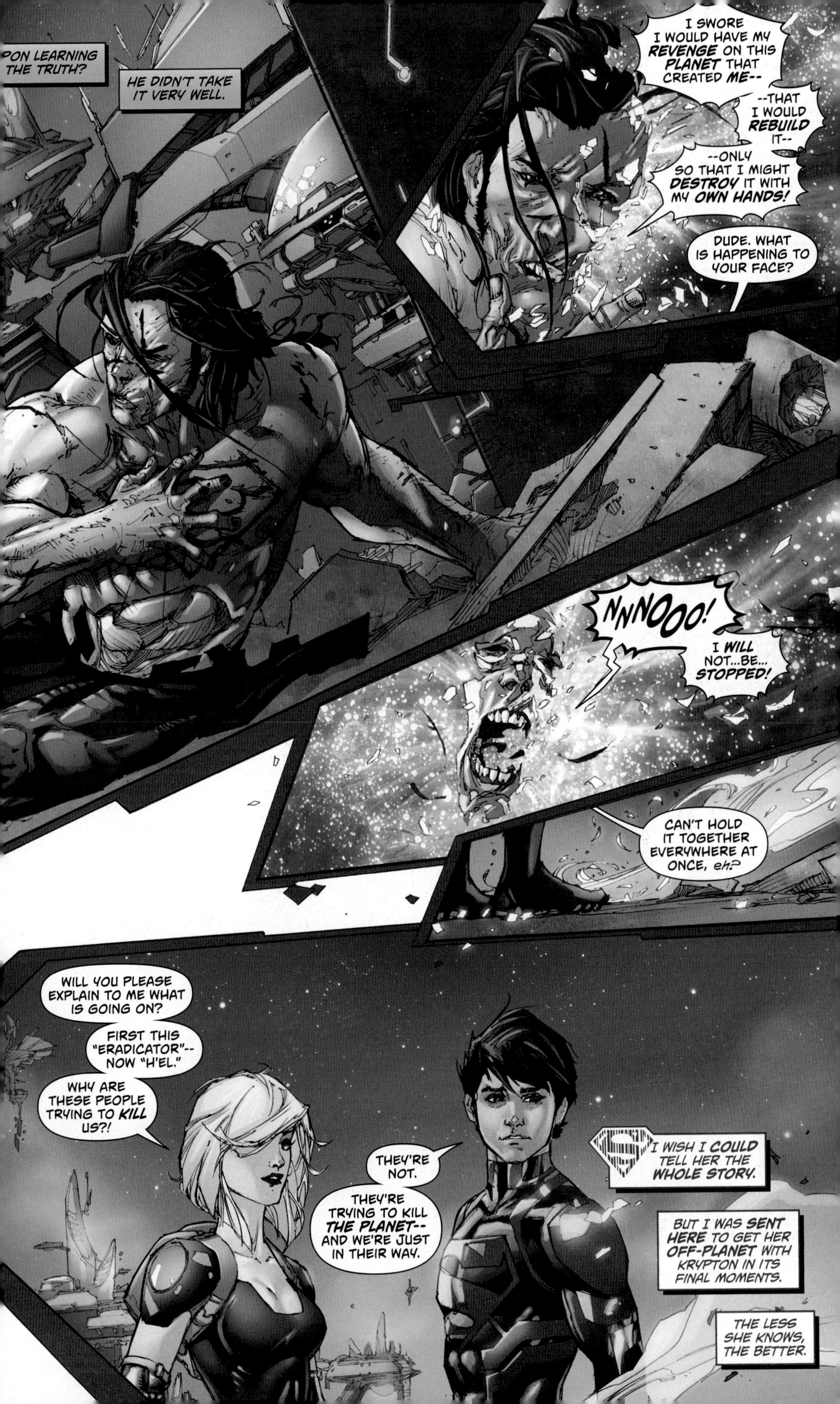

PON LEARNING THE TRUTH?
HE DIDN'T TAKE IT VERY WELL.
I SWORE I WOULD HAVE MY REVENGE ON THIS PLANET THAT CREATED ME--
--THAT I WOULD REBUILD IT--
--ONLY SO THAT I MIGHT DESTROY IT WITH MY OWN HANDS!
DUDE. WHAT IS HAPPENING TO YOUR FACE?
NNNOOO!
I WILL NOT...BE... STOPPED!
CAN'T HOLD IT TOGETHER EVERYWHERE AT ONCE, eh?
WILL YOU PLEASE EXPLAIN TO ME WHAT IS GOING ON?
FIRST THIS "ERADICATOR"-- NOW "H'EL."
WHY ARE THESE PEOPLE TRYING TO KILL US?!
THEY'RE NOT.
THEY'RE TRYING TO KILL THE PLANET-- AND WE'RE JUST IN THEIR WAY.
I WISH I COULD TELL HER THE WHOLE STORY.
BUT I WAS SENT HERE TO GET HER OFF-PLANET WITH KRYPTON IN ITS FINAL MOMENTS.
THE LESS SHE KNOWS, THE BETTER.

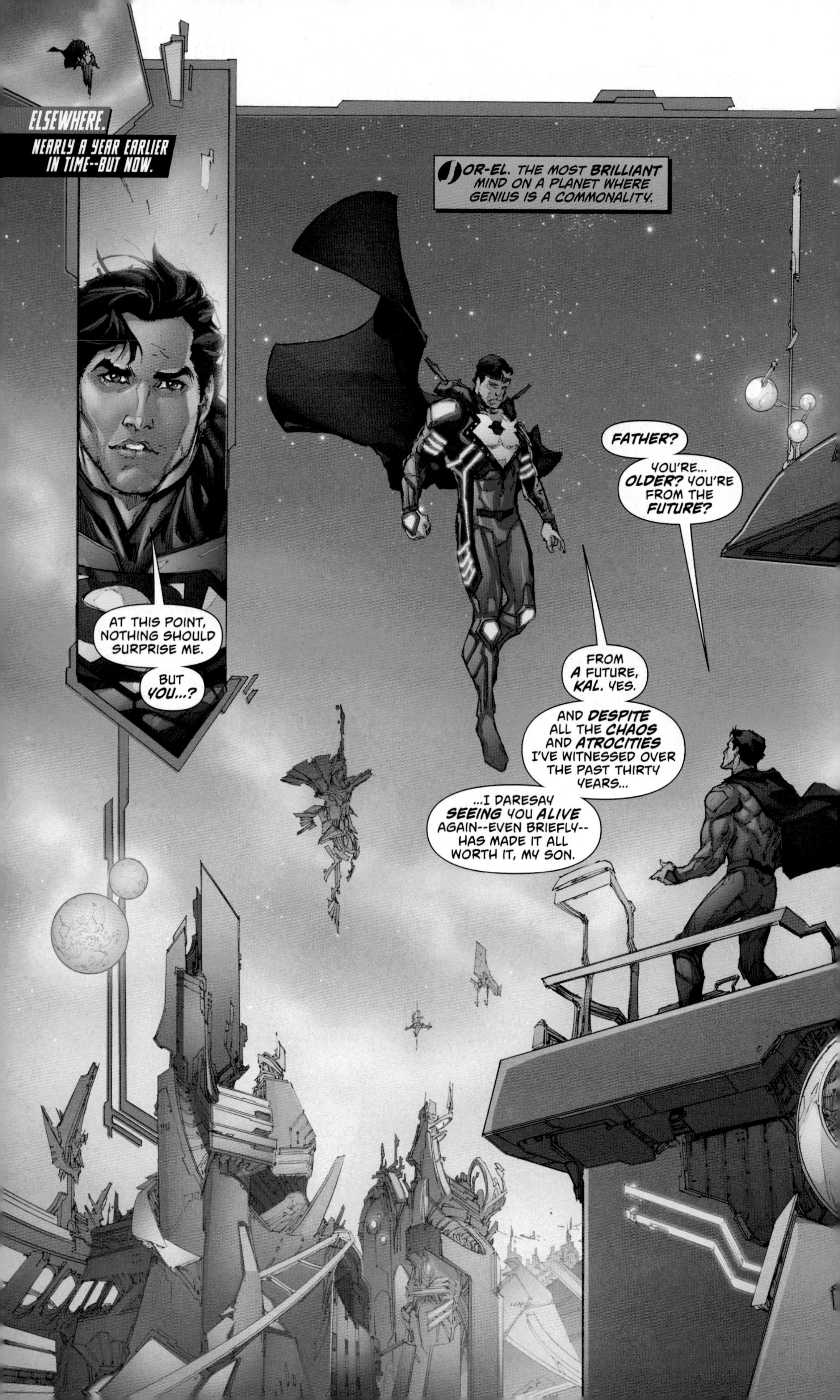
ELSEWHERE.
NEARLY A YEAR EARLIER IN TIME--BUT NOW.
JOR-EL. THE MOST BRILLIANT MIND ON A PLANET WHERE GENIUS IS A COMMONALITY.
AT THIS POINT, NOTHING SHOULD SURPRISE ME.
BUT YOU...?
FATHER?
YOU'RE... OLDER? YOU'RE FROM THE FUTURE?
FROM A FUTURE, KAL. YES.
AND DESPITE ALL THE CHAOS AND ATROCITIES I'VE WITNESSED OVER THE PAST THIRTY YEARS...
...I DARESAY SEEING YOU ALIVE AGAIN--EVEN BRIEFLY--HAS MADE IT ALL WORTH IT, MY SON.

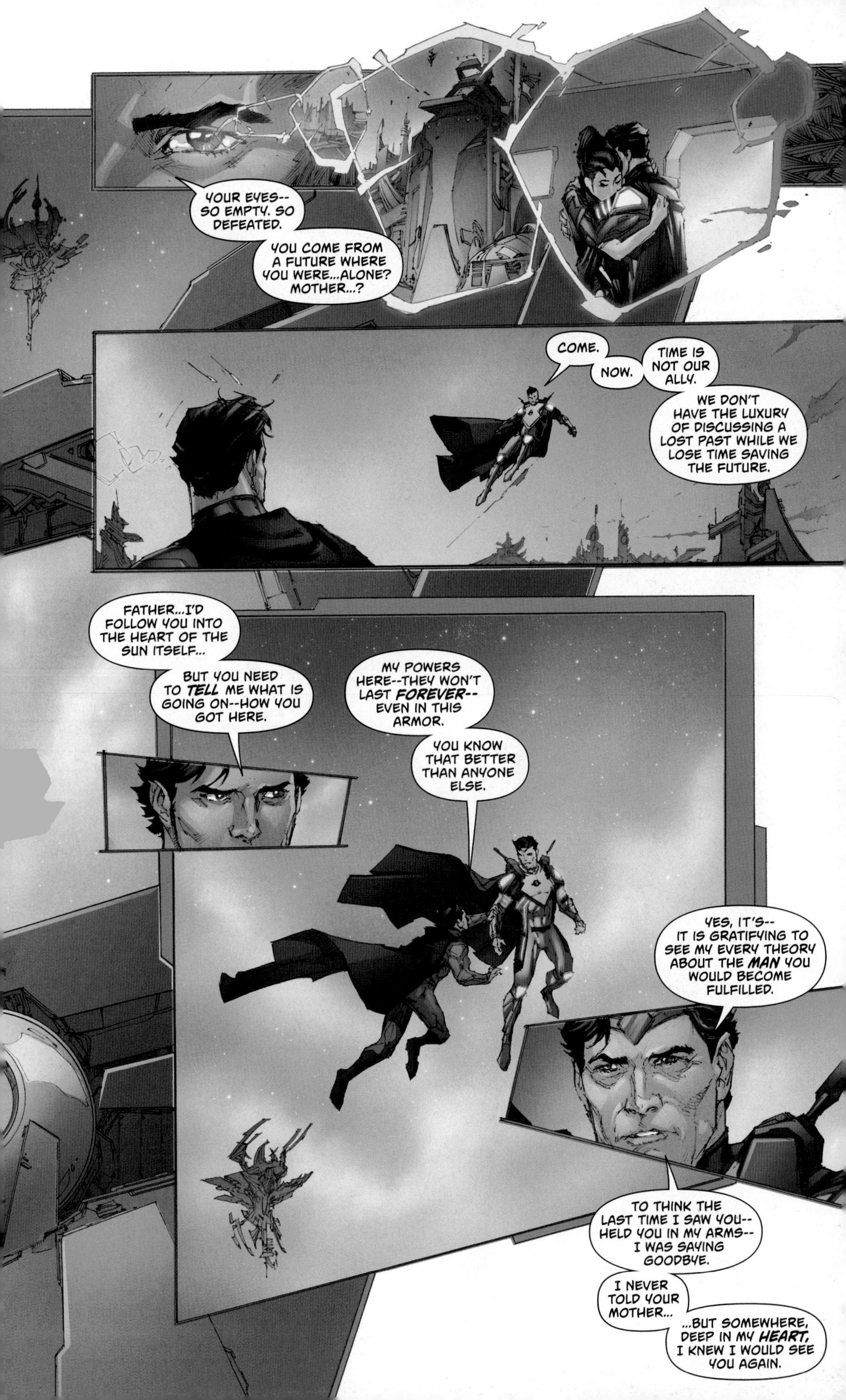
YOUR EYES--
SO EMPTY. SO
DEFEATED.
YOU COME FROM
A FUTURE WHERE
YOU WERE...ALONE?
MOTHER...?
COME.
NOW.
TIME IS
NOT OUR
ALLY.
WE DON'T
HAVE THE LUXURY
OF DISCUSSING A
LOST PAST WHILE WE
LOSE TIME SAVING
THE FUTURE.
FATHER...I'D
FOLLOW YOU INTO
THE HEART OF THE
SUN ITSELF...
BUT YOU NEED
TO **TELL** ME WHAT IS
GOING ON--HOW YOU
GOT HERE.
MY POWERS
HERE--THEY WON'T
LAST **FOREVER**--
EVEN IN THIS
ARMOR.
YOU KNOW
THAT BETTER
THAN ANYONE
ELSE.
YES, IT'S--
IT IS GRATIFYING TO
SEE MY EVERY THEORY
ABOUT THE **MAN** YOU
WOULD BECOME
FULFILLED.
TO THINK THE
LAST TIME I SAW YOU--
HELD YOU IN MY ARMS--
I WAS SAYING
GOODBYE.
I NEVER
TOLD YOUR
MOTHER...
...BUT SOMEWHERE,
DEEP IN MY **HEART,**
I KNEW I WOULD SEE
YOU AGAIN.

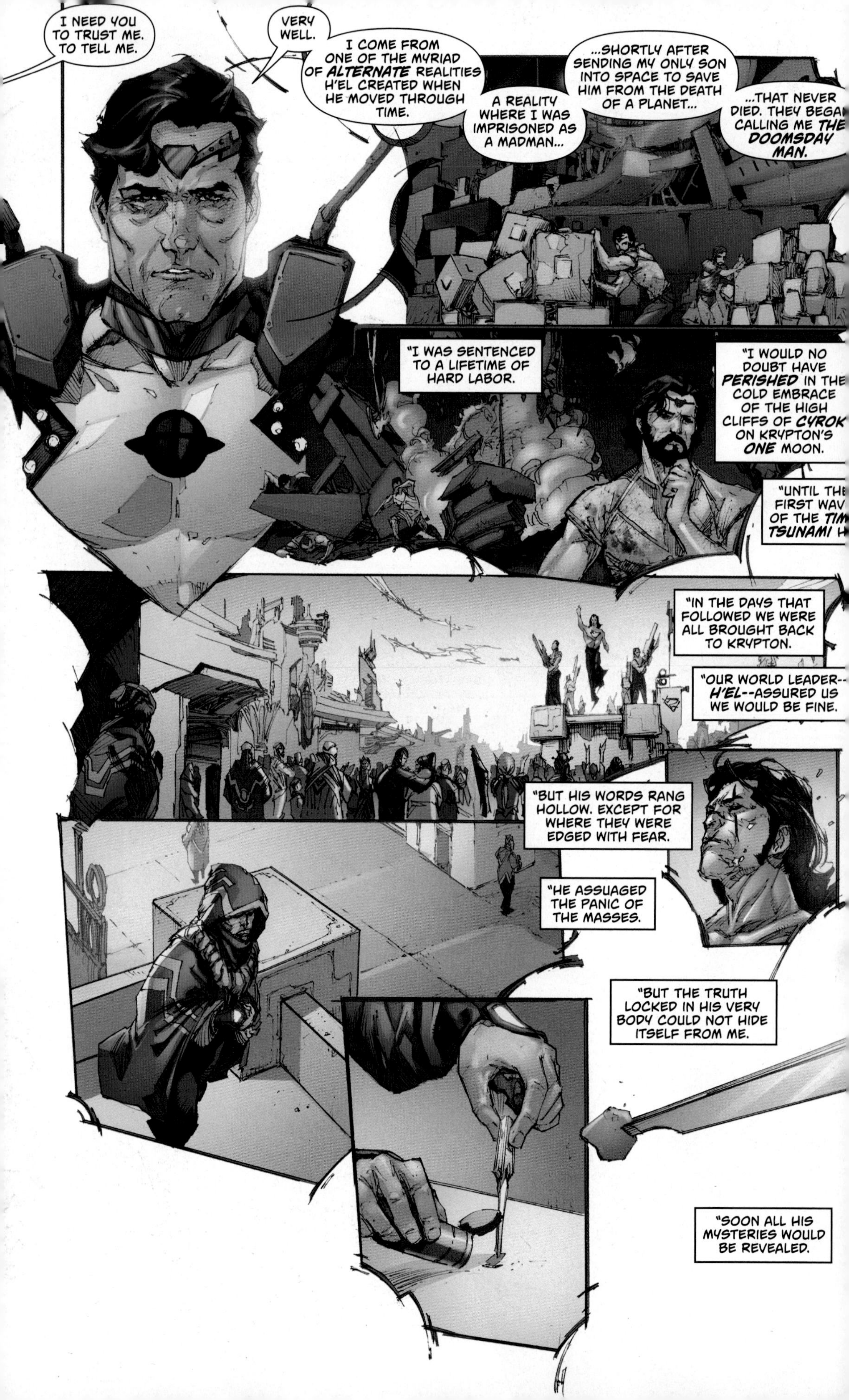
I NEED YOU TO TRUST ME. TO TELL ME.
VERY WELL.
I COME FROM ONE OF THE MYRIAD OF ALTERNATE REALITIES H'EL CREATED WHEN HE MOVED THROUGH TIME.
A REALITY WHERE I WAS IMPRISONED AS A MADMAN...
...SHORTLY AFTER SENDING MY ONLY SON INTO SPACE TO SAVE HIM FROM THE DEATH OF A PLANET...
...THAT NEVER DIED. THEY BEGA CALLING ME THE DOOMSDAY MAN.
"I WAS SENTENCED TO A LIFETIME OF HARD LABOR.
"I WOULD NO DOUBT HAVE PERISHED IN THE COLD EMBRACE OF THE HIGH CLIFFS OF CYROK ON KRYPTON'S ONE MOON.
"UNTIL TH FIRST WAV OF THE TIM TSUNAMI H
"IN THE DAYS THAT FOLLOWED WE WERE ALL BROUGHT BACK TO KRYPTON.
"OUR WORLD LEADER--H'EL--ASSURED US WE WOULD BE FINE.
"BUT HIS WORDS RANG HOLLOW. EXCEPT FOR WHERE THEY WERE EDGED WITH FEAR.
"HE ASSUAGED THE PANIC OF THE MASSES.
"BUT THE TRUTH LOCKED IN HIS VERY BODY COULD NOT HIDE ITSELF FROM ME.
"SOON ALL HIS MYSTERIES WOULD BE REVEALED.

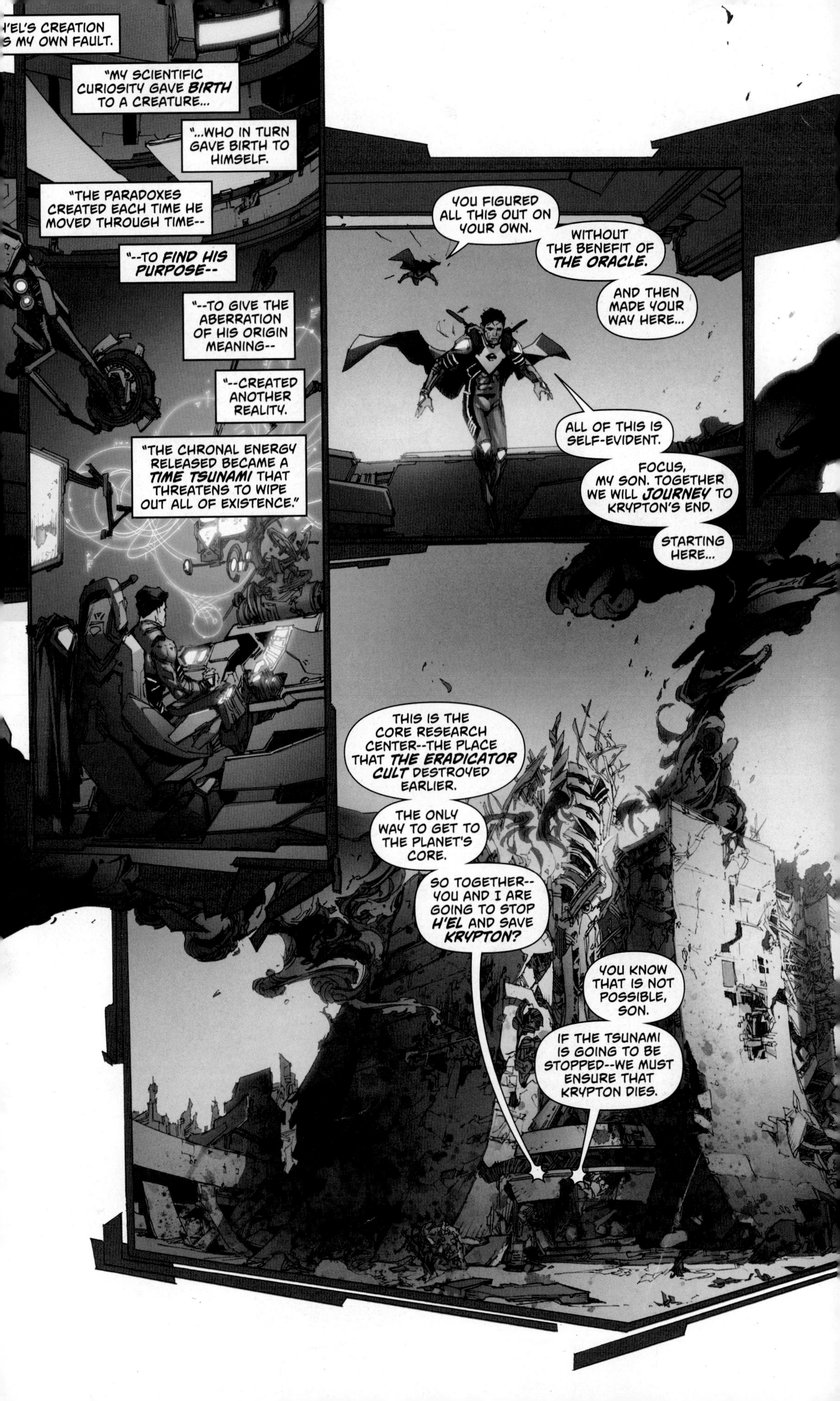
H'EL'S CREATION
S MY OWN FAULT.
"MY SCIENTIFIC CURIOSITY GAVE BIRTH TO A CREATURE...
"...WHO IN TURN GAVE BIRTH TO HIMSELF.
"THE PARADOXES CREATED EACH TIME HE MOVED THROUGH TIME--
"--TO FIND HIS PURPOSE--
"--TO GIVE THE ABERRATION OF HIS ORIGIN MEANING--
"--CREATED ANOTHER REALITY.
"THE CHRONAL ENERGY RELEASED BECAME A TIME TSUNAMI THAT THREATENS TO WIPE OUT ALL OF EXISTENCE."
YOU FIGURED ALL THIS OUT ON YOUR OWN.
WITHOUT THE BENEFIT OF THE ORACLE.
AND THEN MADE YOUR WAY HERE...
ALL OF THIS IS SELF-EVIDENT.
FOCUS, MY SON. TOGETHER WE WILL JOURNEY TO KRYPTON'S END.
STARTING HERE...
THIS IS THE CORE RESEARCH CENTER--THE PLACE THAT THE ERADICATOR CULT DESTROYED EARLIER.
THE ONLY WAY TO GET TO THE PLANET'S CORE.
SO TOGETHER--YOU AND I ARE GOING TO STOP H'EL AND SAVE KRYPTON?
YOU KNOW THAT IS NOT POSSIBLE, SON.
IF THE TSUNAMI IS GOING TO BE STOPPED--WE MUST ENSURE THAT KRYPTON DIES.

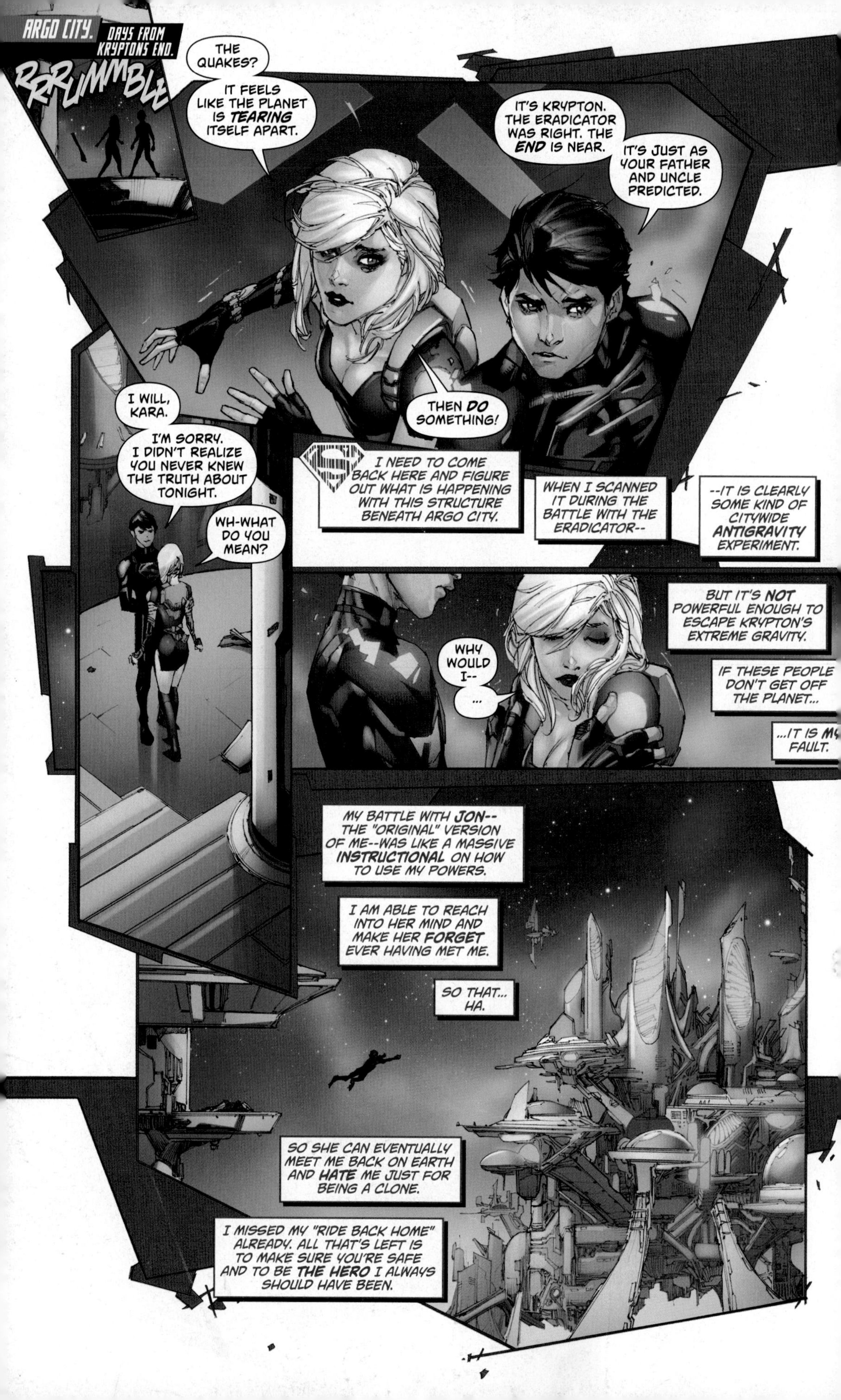
ARGO CITY. DAYS FROM KRYPTONS END.
RRRUMMBLE
THE QUAKES?
IT FEELS LIKE THE PLANET IS **TEARING** ITSELF APART.
IT'S KRYPTON. THE ERADICATOR WAS RIGHT. THE **END** IS NEAR.
IT'S JUST AS YOUR FATHER AND UNCLE PREDICTED.
THEN **DO** SOMETHING!
I WILL, KARA.
I'M SORRY. I DIDN'T REALIZE YOU NEVER KNEW THE TRUTH ABOUT TONIGHT.
WH-WHAT DO YOU MEAN?
I NEED TO COME BACK HERE AND FIGURE OUT WHAT IS HAPPENING WITH THIS STRUCTURE BENEATH ARGO CITY.
WHEN I SCANNED IT DURING THE BATTLE WITH THE ERADICATOR--
--IT IS CLEARLY SOME KIND OF CITYWIDE **ANTIGRAVITY** EXPERIMENT.
BUT IT'S **NOT** POWERFUL ENOUGH TO ESCAPE KRYPTON'S EXTREME GRAVITY.
WHY WOULD I-- ...
IF THESE PEOPLE DON'T GET OFF THE PLANET...
...IT IS MY FAULT.
MY BATTLE WITH **JON**-- THE "ORIGINAL" VERSION OF ME--WAS LIKE A MASSIVE **INSTRUCTIONAL** ON HOW TO USE MY POWERS.
I AM ABLE TO REACH INTO HER MIND AND MAKE HER **FORGET** EVER HAVING MET ME.
SO THAT... HA.
SO SHE CAN EVENTUALLY MEET ME BACK ON EARTH AND **HATE** ME JUST FOR BEING A CLONE.
I MISSED MY "RIDE BACK HOME" ALREADY. ALL THAT'S LEFT IS TO MAKE SURE YOU'RE SAFE AND TO BE **THE HERO** I ALWAYS SHOULD HAVE BEEN.

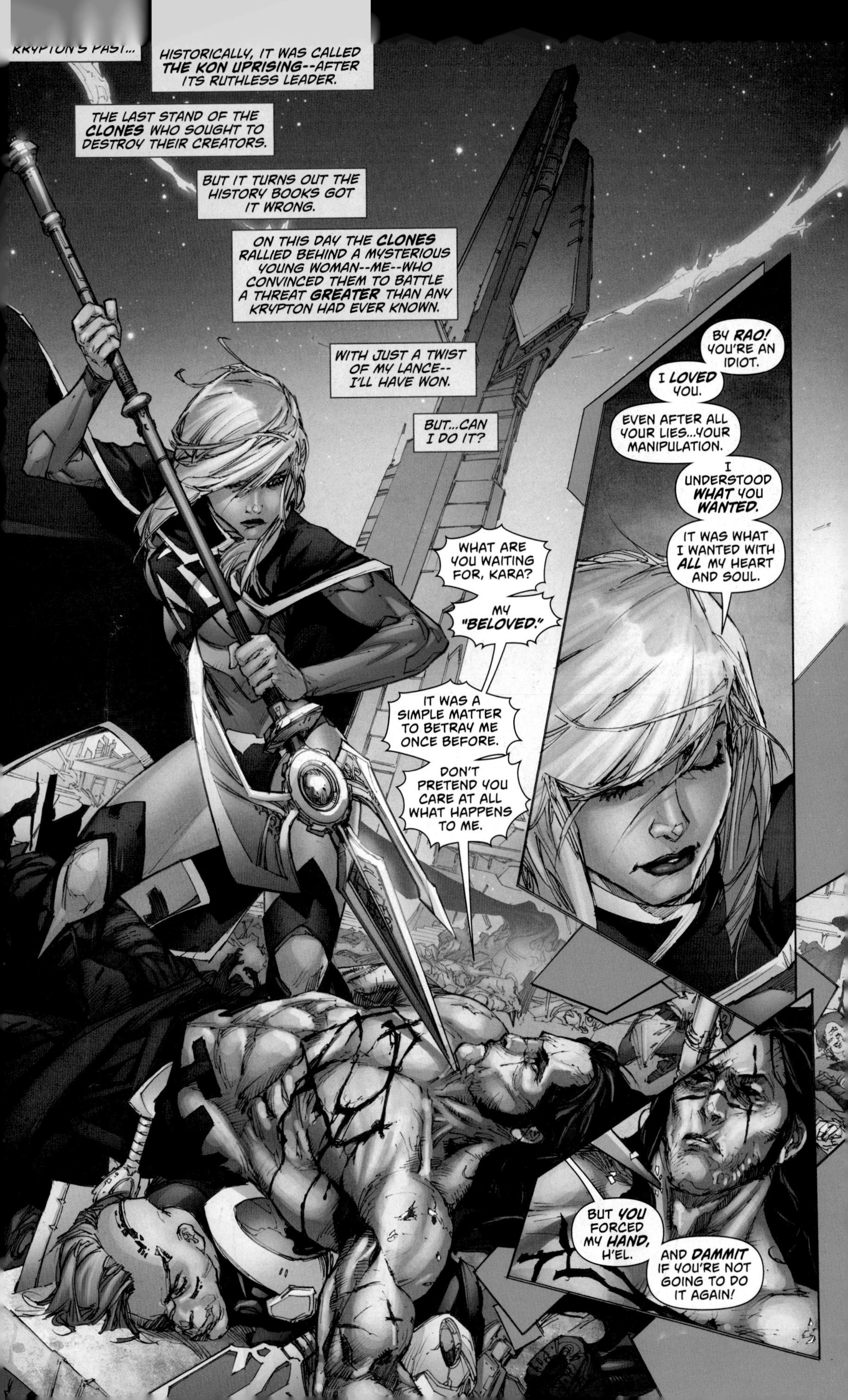
KRYPTON'S PAST...
HISTORICALLY, IT WAS CALLED THE KON UPRISING--AFTER ITS RUTHLESS LEADER.
THE LAST STAND OF THE CLONES WHO SOUGHT TO DESTROY THEIR CREATORS.
BUT IT TURNS OUT THE HISTORY BOOKS GOT IT WRONG.
ON THIS DAY THE CLONES RALLIED BEHIND A MYSTERIOUS YOUNG WOMAN--ME--WHO CONVINCED THEM TO BATTLE A THREAT GREATER THAN ANY KRYPTON HAD EVER KNOWN.
WITH JUST A TWIST OF MY LANCE--I'LL HAVE WON.
BUT...CAN I DO IT?
WHAT ARE YOU WAITING FOR, KARA?
MY "BELOVED."
IT WAS A SIMPLE MATTER TO BETRAY ME ONCE BEFORE.
DON'T PRETEND YOU CARE AT ALL WHAT HAPPENS TO ME.
BY RAO! YOU'RE AN IDIOT.
I LOVED YOU.
EVEN AFTER ALL YOUR LIES...YOUR MANIPULATION.
I UNDERSTOOD WHAT YOU WANTED.
IT WAS WHAT I WANTED WITH ALL MY HEART AND SOUL.
BUT YOU FORCED MY HAND, H'EL.
AND DAMMIT IF YOU'RE NOT GOING TO DO IT AGAIN!

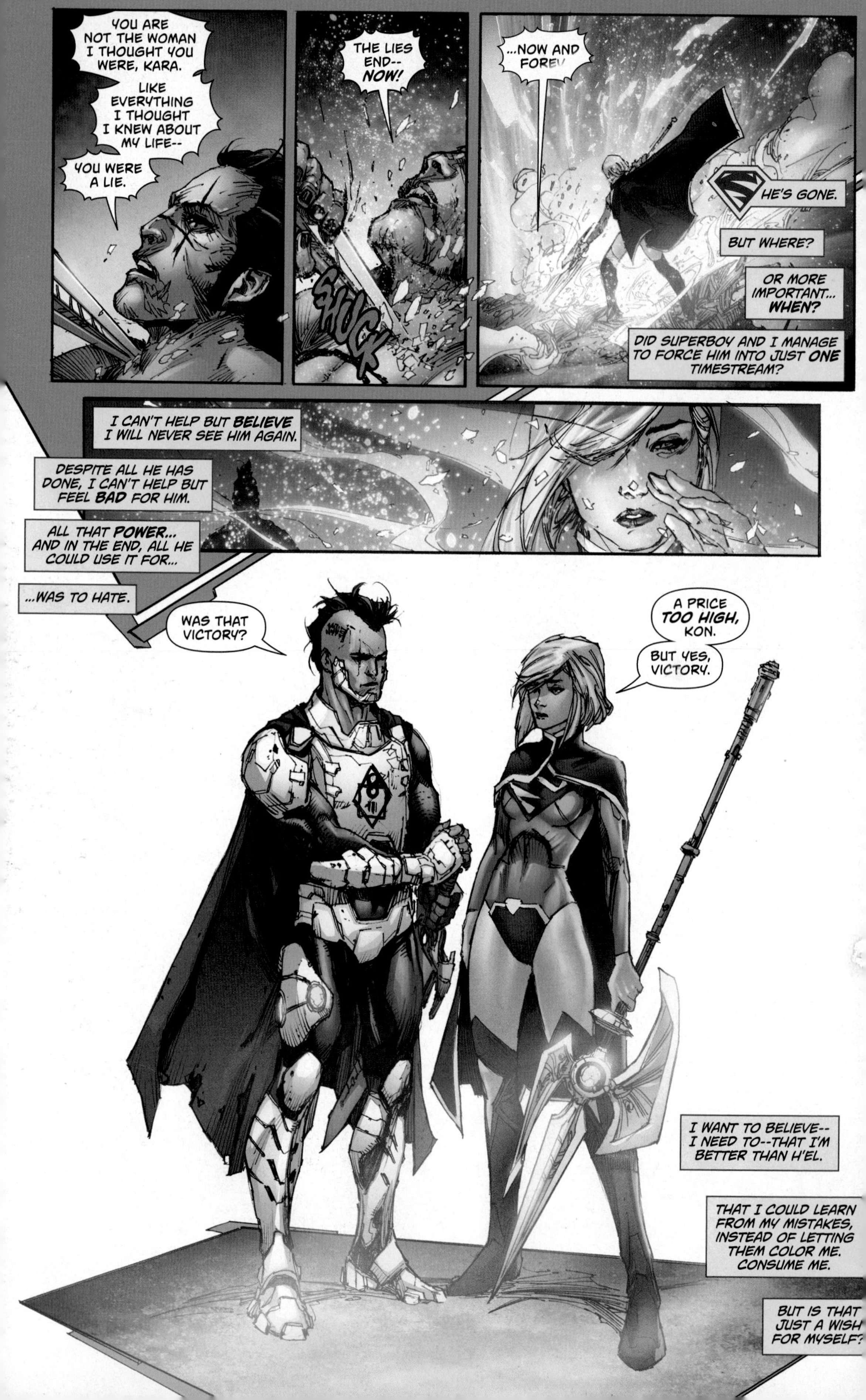

YOU ARE NOT THE WOMAN I THOUGHT YOU WERE, KARA.
LIKE EVERYTHING I THOUGHT I KNEW ABOUT MY LIFE--
YOU WERE A LIE.
THE LIES END-- NOW!
SHUCK
...NOW AND FOREV
HE'S GONE.
BUT WHERE?
OR MORE IMPORTANT... WHEN?
DID SUPERBOY AND I MANAGE TO FORCE HIM INTO JUST ONE TIMESTREAM?
I CAN'T HELP BUT BELIEVE I WILL NEVER SEE HIM AGAIN.
DESPITE ALL HE HAS DONE, I CAN'T HELP BUT FEEL BAD FOR HIM.
ALL THAT POWER... AND IN THE END, ALL HE COULD USE IT FOR...
...WAS TO HATE.
WAS THAT VICTORY?
A PRICE TOO HIGH, KON.
BUT YES, VICTORY.
I WANT TO BELIEVE-- I NEED TO--THAT I'M BETTER THAN H'EL.
THAT I COULD LEARN FROM MY MISTAKES, INSTEAD OF LETTING THEM COLOR ME. CONSUME ME.
BUT IS THAT JUST A WISH FOR MYSELF?

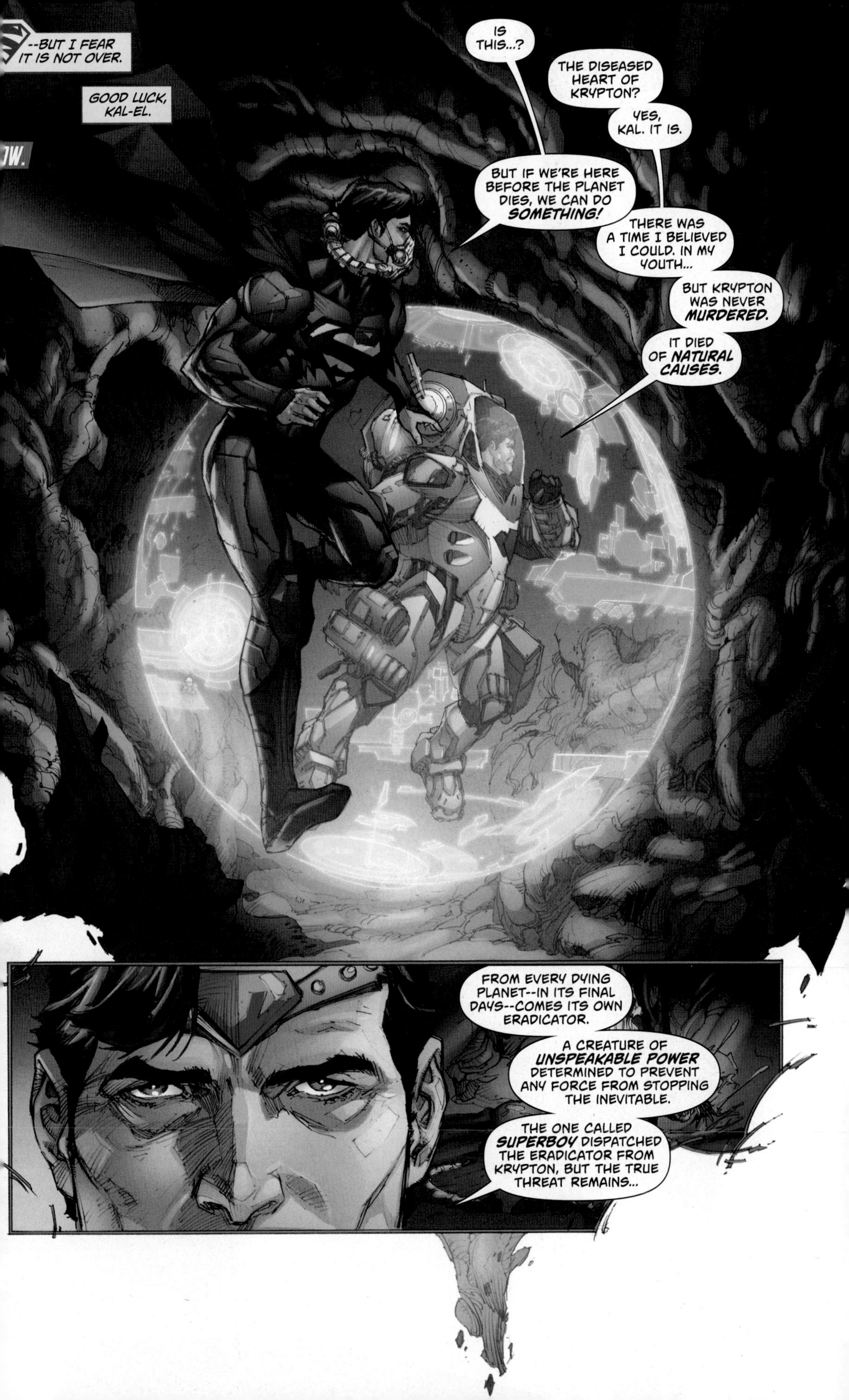
--BUT I FEAR IT IS NOT OVER.
GOOD LUCK, KAL-EL.
IS THIS...?
THE DISEASED HEART OF KRYPTON?
YES, KAL. IT IS.
BUT IF WE'RE HERE BEFORE THE PLANET DIES, WE CAN DO SOMETHING!
THERE WAS A TIME I BELIEVED I COULD. IN MY YOUTH...
BUT KRYPTON WAS NEVER MURDERED.
IT DIED OF NATURAL CAUSES.
FROM EVERY DYING PLANET--IN ITS FINAL DAYS--COMES ITS OWN ERADICATOR.
A CREATURE OF UNSPEAKABLE POWER DETERMINED TO PREVENT ANY FORCE FROM STOPPING THE INEVITABLE.
THE ONE CALLED SUPERBOY DISPATCHED THE ERADICATOR FROM KRYPTON, BUT THE TRUE THREAT REMAINS...

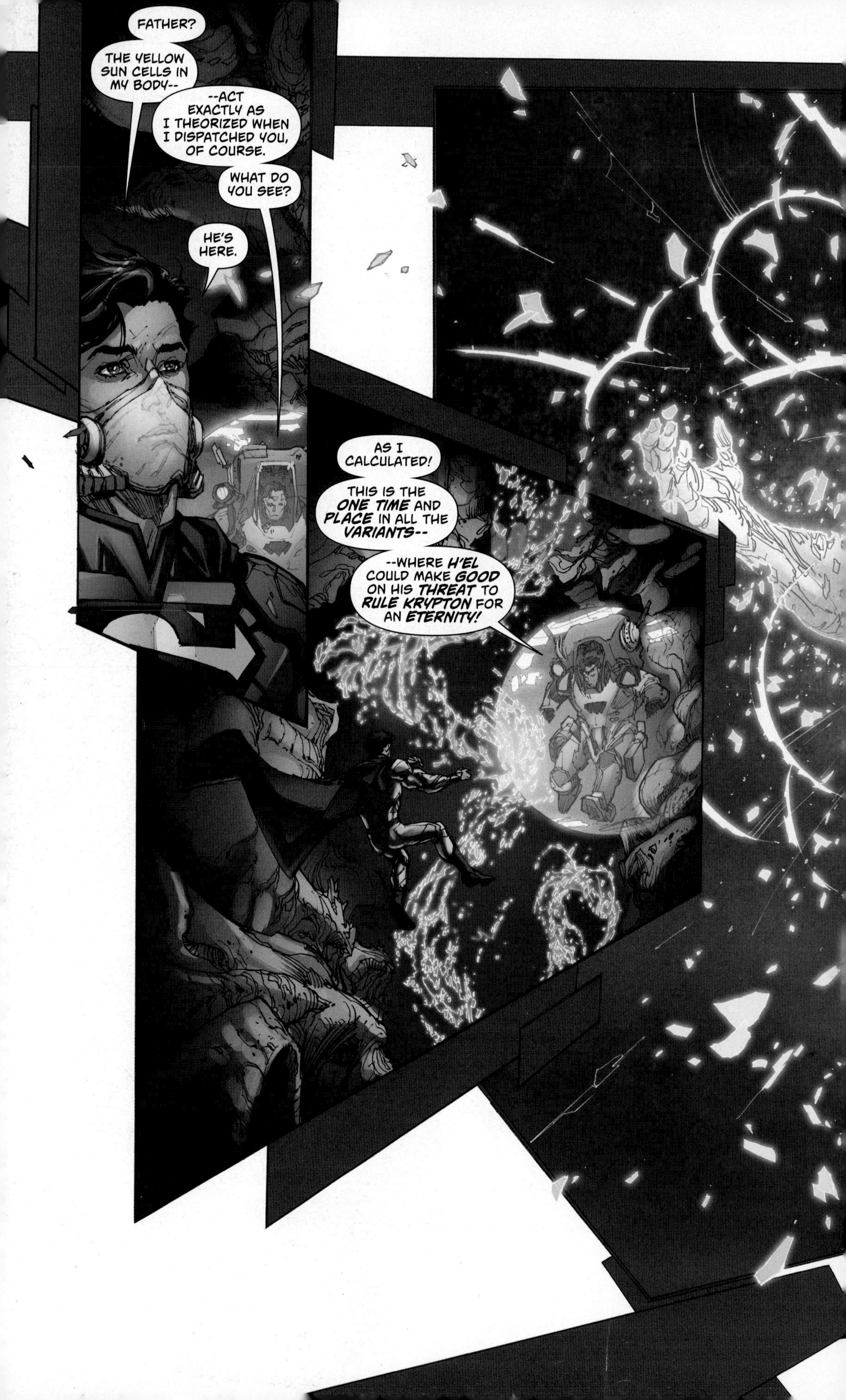
FATHER?
THE YELLOW SUN CELLS IN MY BODY--
--ACT EXACTLY AS I THEORIZED WHEN I DISPATCHED YOU, OF COURSE.
WHAT DO YOU SEE?
HE'S HERE.
AS I CALCULATED!
THIS IS THE ONE TIME AND PLACE IN ALL THE VARIANTS--
--WHERE H'EL COULD MAKE GOOD ON HIS THREAT TO RULE KRYPTON FOR AN ETERNITY!

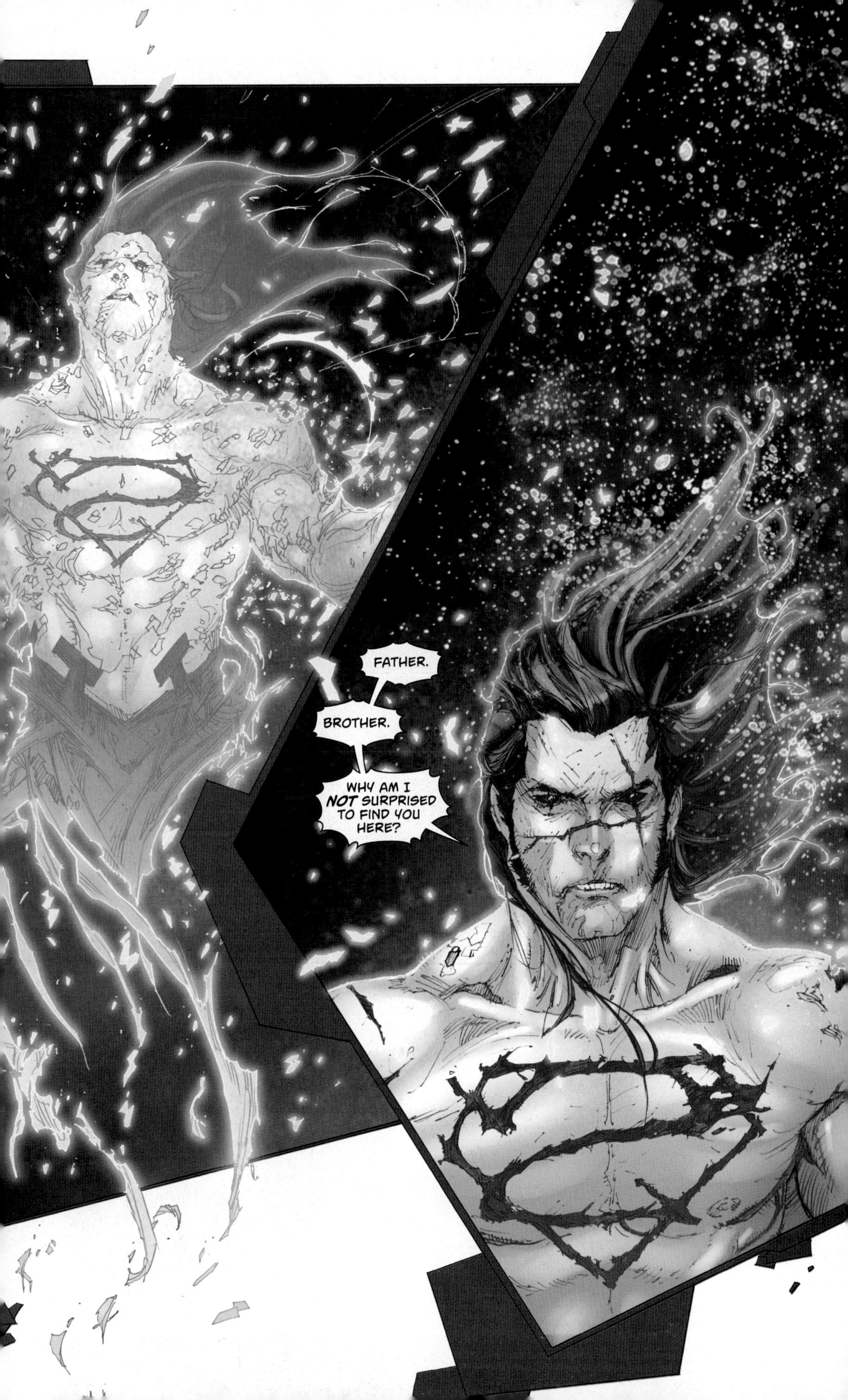
FATHER.
BROTHER.
WHY AM I *NOT* SURPRISED TO FIND YOU HERE?

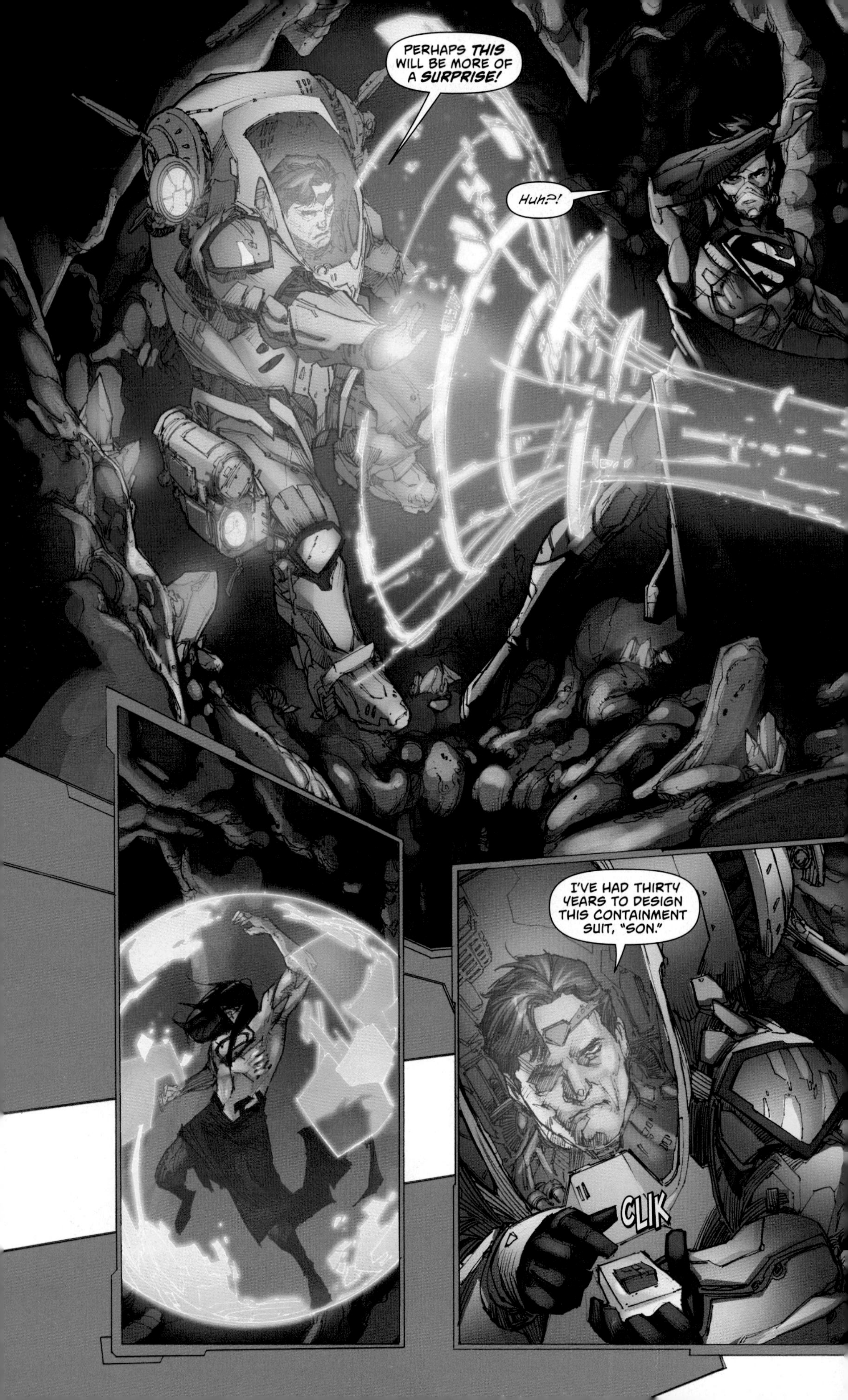
PERHAPS THIS WILL BE MORE OF A SURPRISE!
Huh?!
I'VE HAD THIRTY YEARS TO DESIGN THIS CONTAINMENT SUIT, "SON."
CLIK

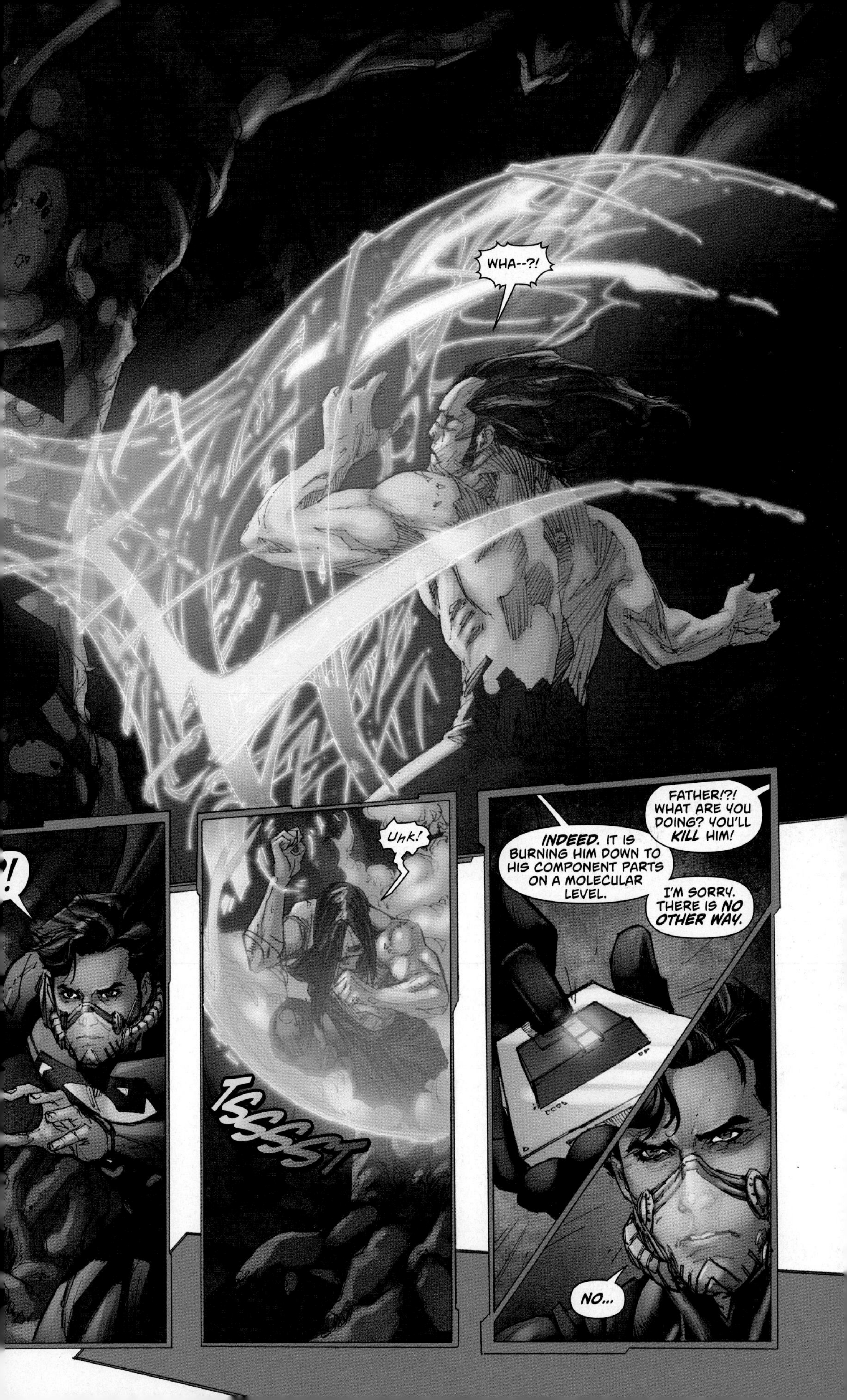
WHA--?!
?!
Uhk!
TSSSSST
INDEED. IT IS BURNING HIM DOWN TO HIS COMPONENT PARTS ON A MOLECULAR LEVEL.
FATHER!?! WHAT ARE YOU DOING? YOU'LL KILL HIM!
I'M SORRY. THERE IS NO OTHER WAY.
NO...

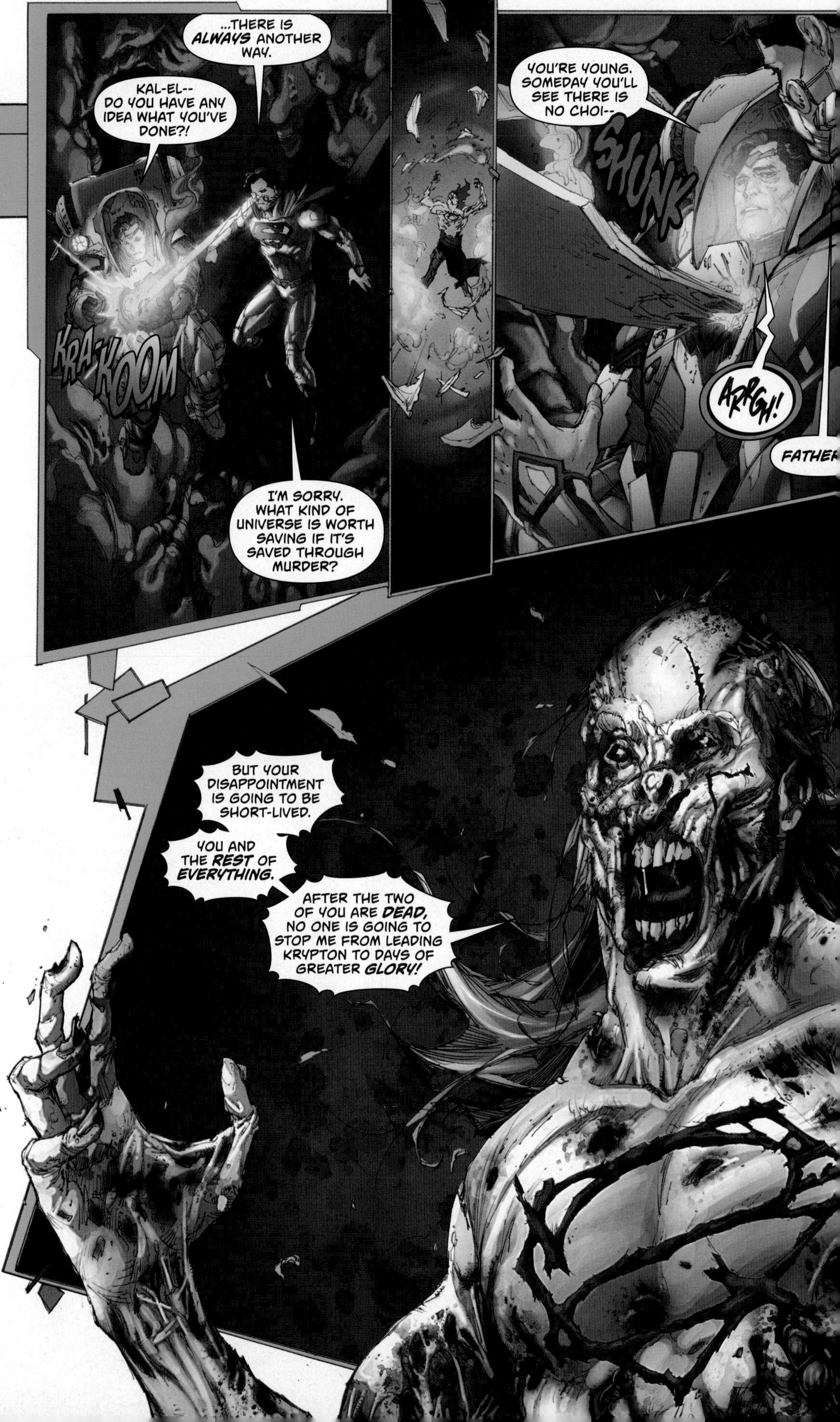
KAL-EL-- DO YOU HAVE ANY IDEA WHAT YOU'VE DONE?!
...THERE IS ALWAYS ANOTHER WAY.
KRA-KOOM
I'M SORRY. WHAT KIND OF UNIVERSE IS WORTH SAVING IF IT'S SAVED THROUGH MURDER?
YOU'RE YOUNG. SOMEDAY YOU'LL SEE THERE IS NO CHOI--
SHUNK
ARRGH!
FATHER
BUT YOUR DISAPPOINTMENT IS GOING TO BE SHORT-LIVED.
YOU AND THE REST OF EVERYTHING.
AFTER THE TWO OF YOU ARE DEAD, NO ONE IS GOING TO STOP ME FROM LEADING KRYPTON TO DAYS OF GREATER GLORY!

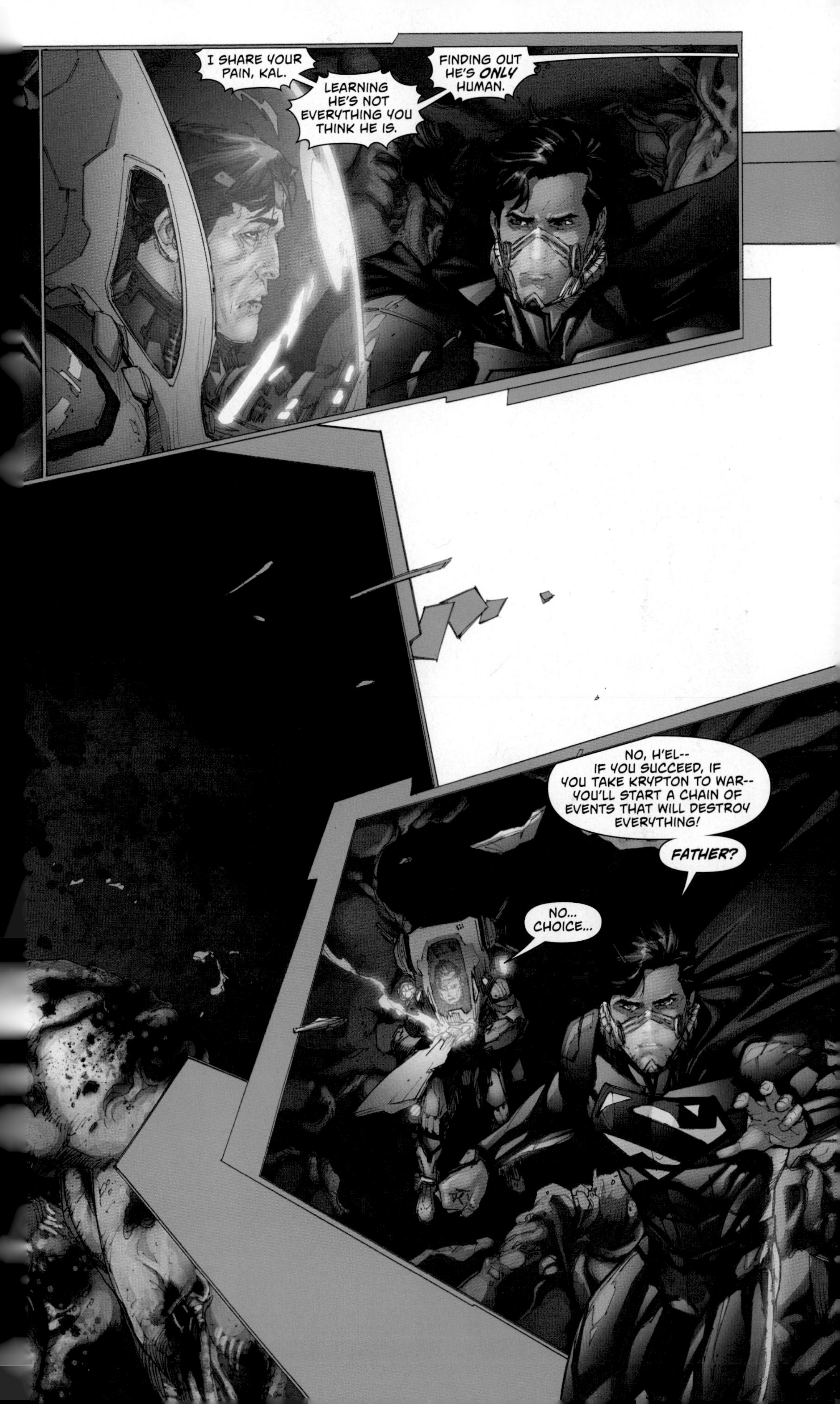
I SHARE YOUR PAIN, KAL.
LEARNING HE'S NOT EVERYTHING YOU THINK HE IS.
FINDING OUT HE'S *ONLY* HUMAN.
NO, H'EL-- IF YOU SUCCEED, IF YOU TAKE KRYPTON TO WAR-- YOU'LL START A CHAIN OF EVENTS THAT WILL DESTROY EVERYTHING!
FATHER?
NO... CHOICE...

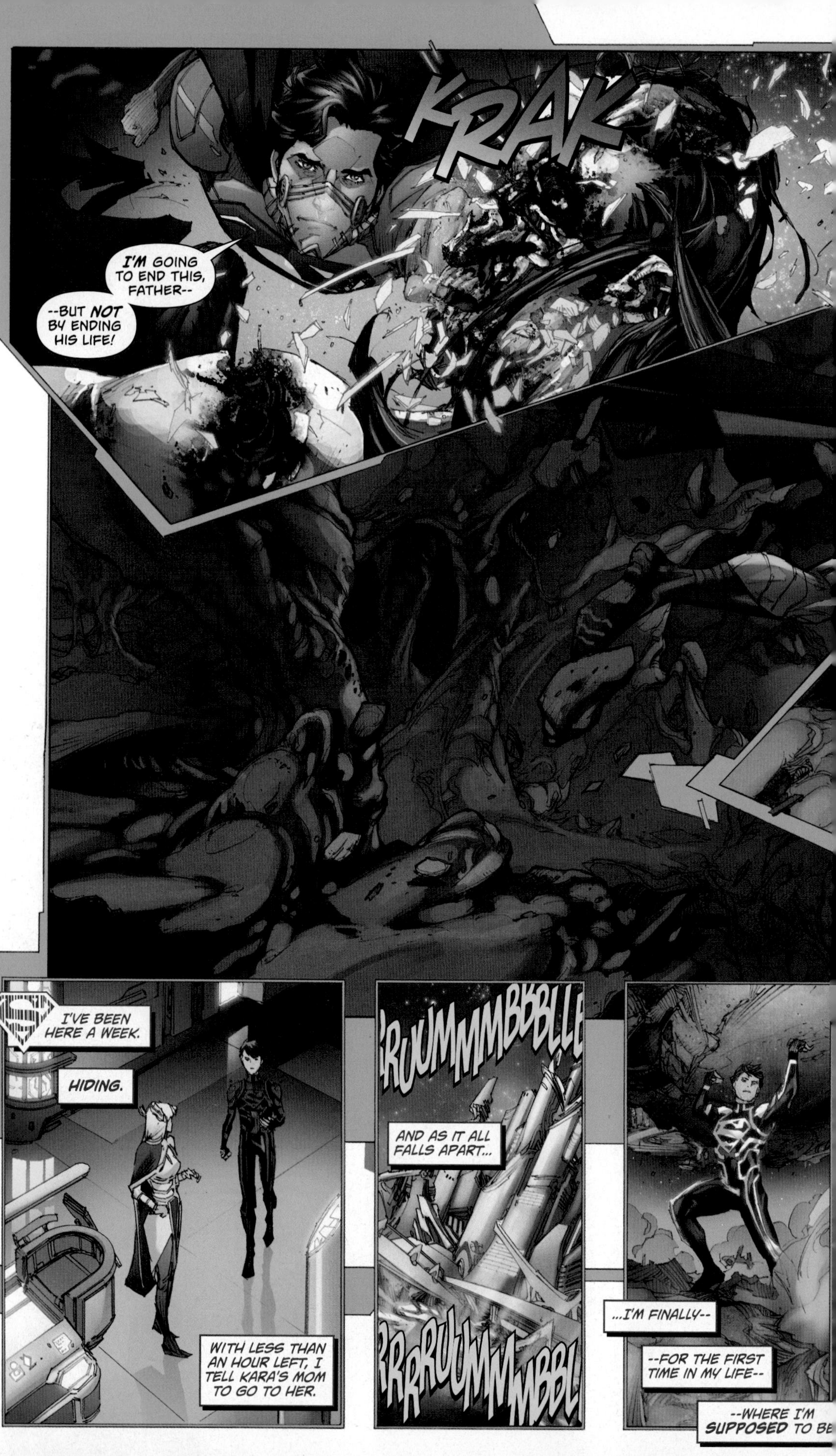
KRAK
I'M GOING TO END THIS, FATHER--
--BUT NOT BY ENDING HIS LIFE!
I'VE BEEN HERE A WEEK.
HIDING.
WITH LESS THAN AN HOUR LEFT, I TELL KARA'S MOM TO GO TO HER.
RRUUMMMMBBBLLE
AND AS IT ALL FALLS APART...
RRRRUUMMMBBL
...I'M FINALLY--
--FOR THE FIRST TIME IN MY LIFE--
--WHERE I'M SUPPOSED TO BE

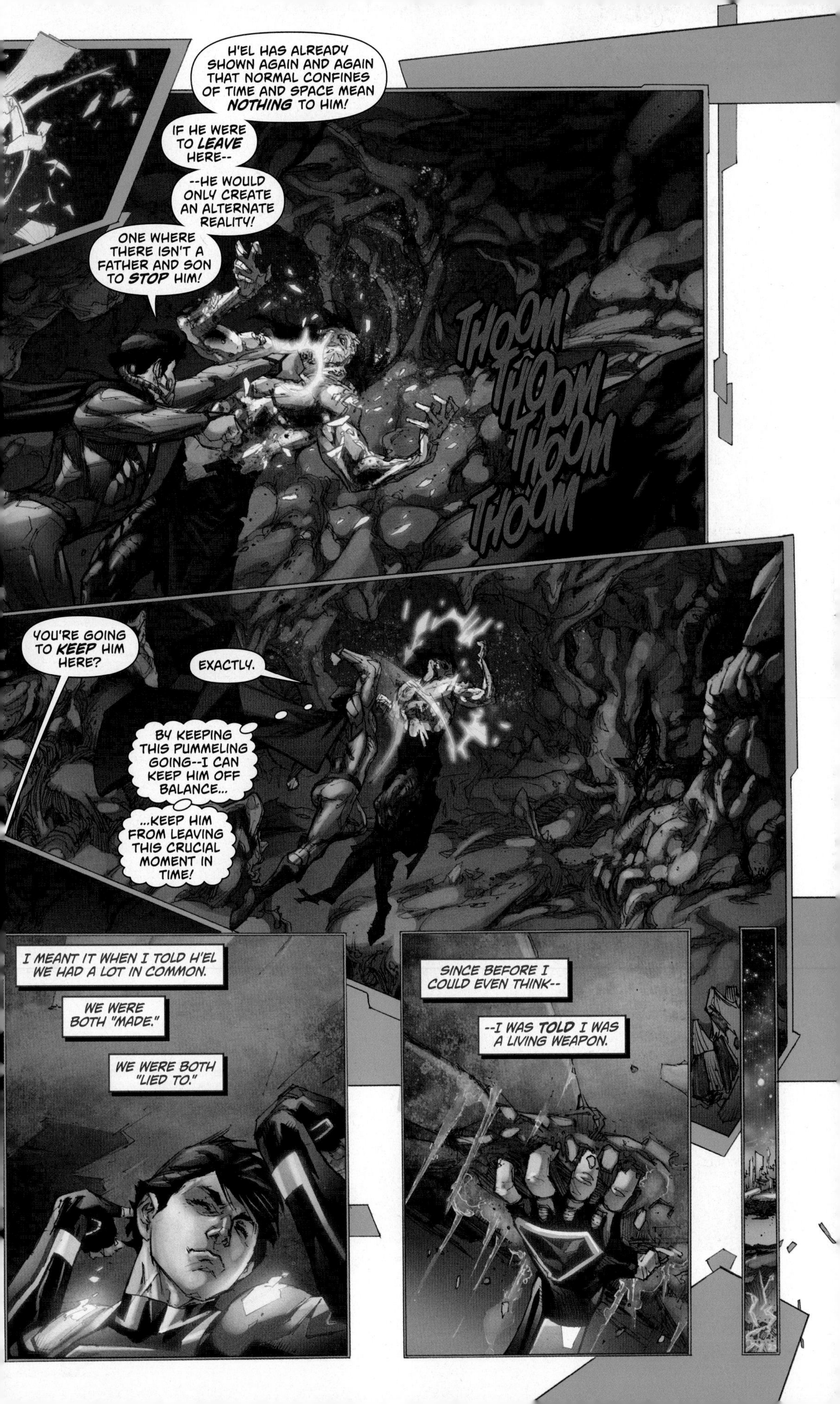
H'EL HAS ALREADY SHOWN AGAIN AND AGAIN THAT NORMAL CONFINES OF TIME AND SPACE MEAN NOTHING TO HIM!
IF HE WERE TO LEAVE HERE--
--HE WOULD ONLY CREATE AN ALTERNATE REALITY!
ONE WHERE THERE ISN'T A FATHER AND SON TO STOP HIM!
THOOM THOOM THOOM THOOM
YOU'RE GOING TO KEEP HIM HERE?
EXACTLY.
BY KEEPING THIS PUMMELING GOING--I CAN KEEP HIM OFF BALANCE...
...KEEP HIM FROM LEAVING THIS CRUCIAL MOMENT IN TIME!
I MEANT IT WHEN I TOLD H'EL WE HAD A LOT IN COMMON.
WE WERE BOTH "MADE."
WE WERE BOTH "LIED TO."
SINCE BEFORE I COULD EVEN THINK--
--I WAS TOLD I WAS A LIVING WEAPON.

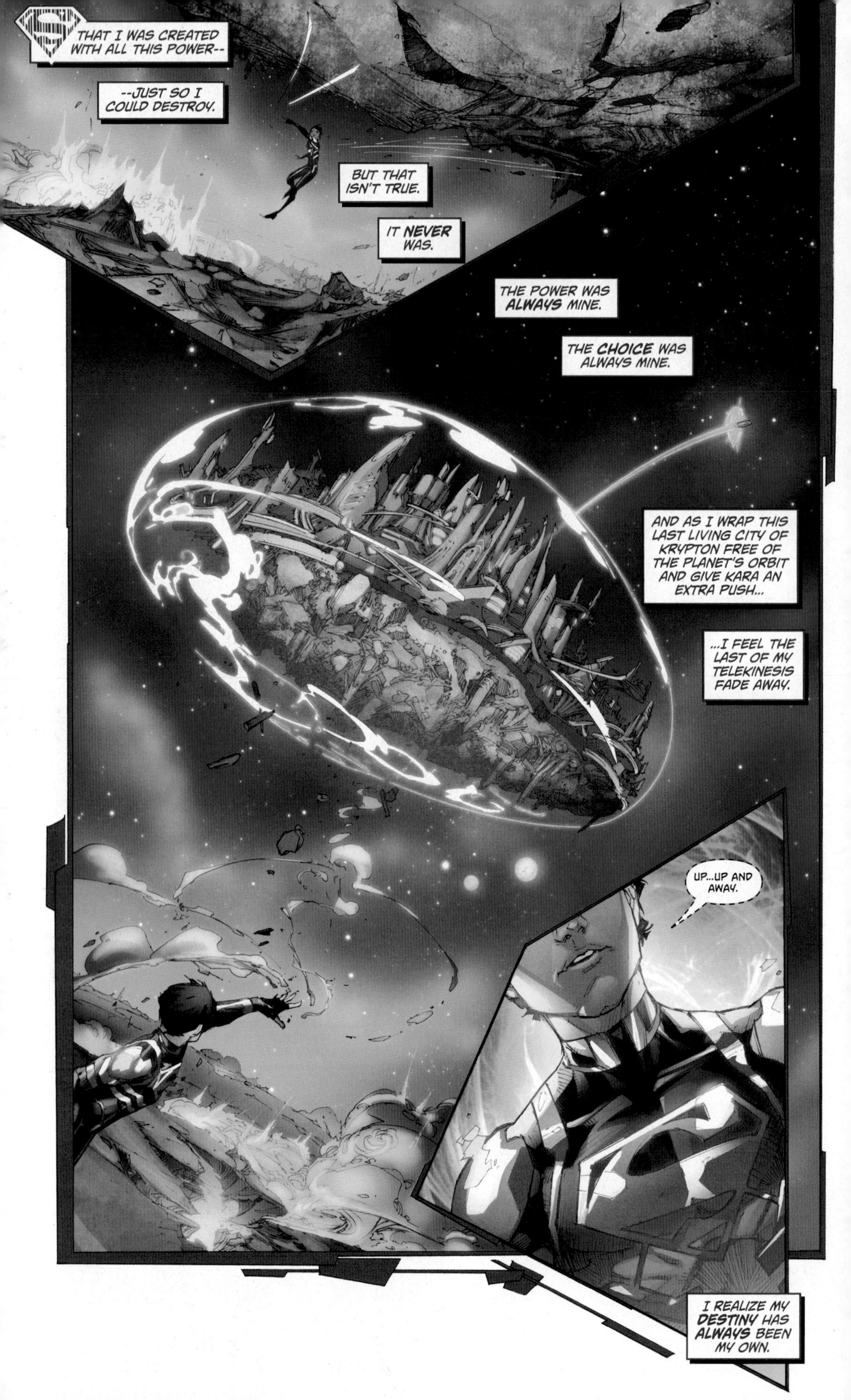

THAT I WAS CREATED WITH ALL THIS POWER--
--JUST SO I COULD DESTROY.
BUT THAT ISN'T TRUE.
IT NEVER WAS.
THE POWER WAS ALWAYS MINE.
THE CHOICE WAS ALWAYS MINE.
AND AS I WRAP THIS LAST LIVING CITY OF KRYPTON FREE OF THE PLANET'S ORBIT AND GIVE KARA AN EXTRA PUSH...
...I FEEL THE LAST OF MY TELEKINESIS FADE AWAY.
UP...UP AND AWAY.
I REALIZE MY DESTINY HAS ALWAYS BEEN MY OWN.

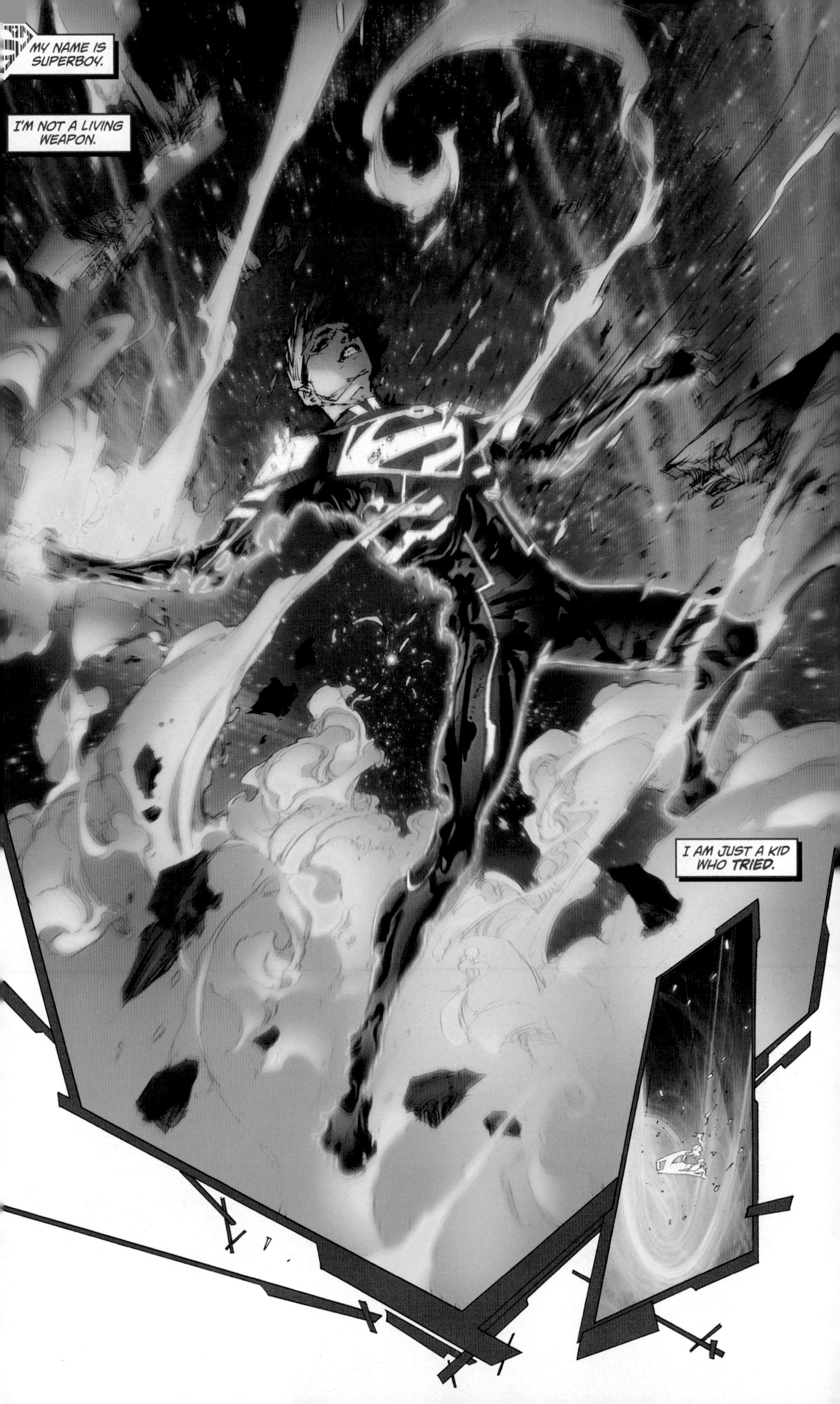
MY NAME IS SUPERBOY.
I'M NOT A LIVING WEAPON.
I AM JUST A KID WHO TRIED.

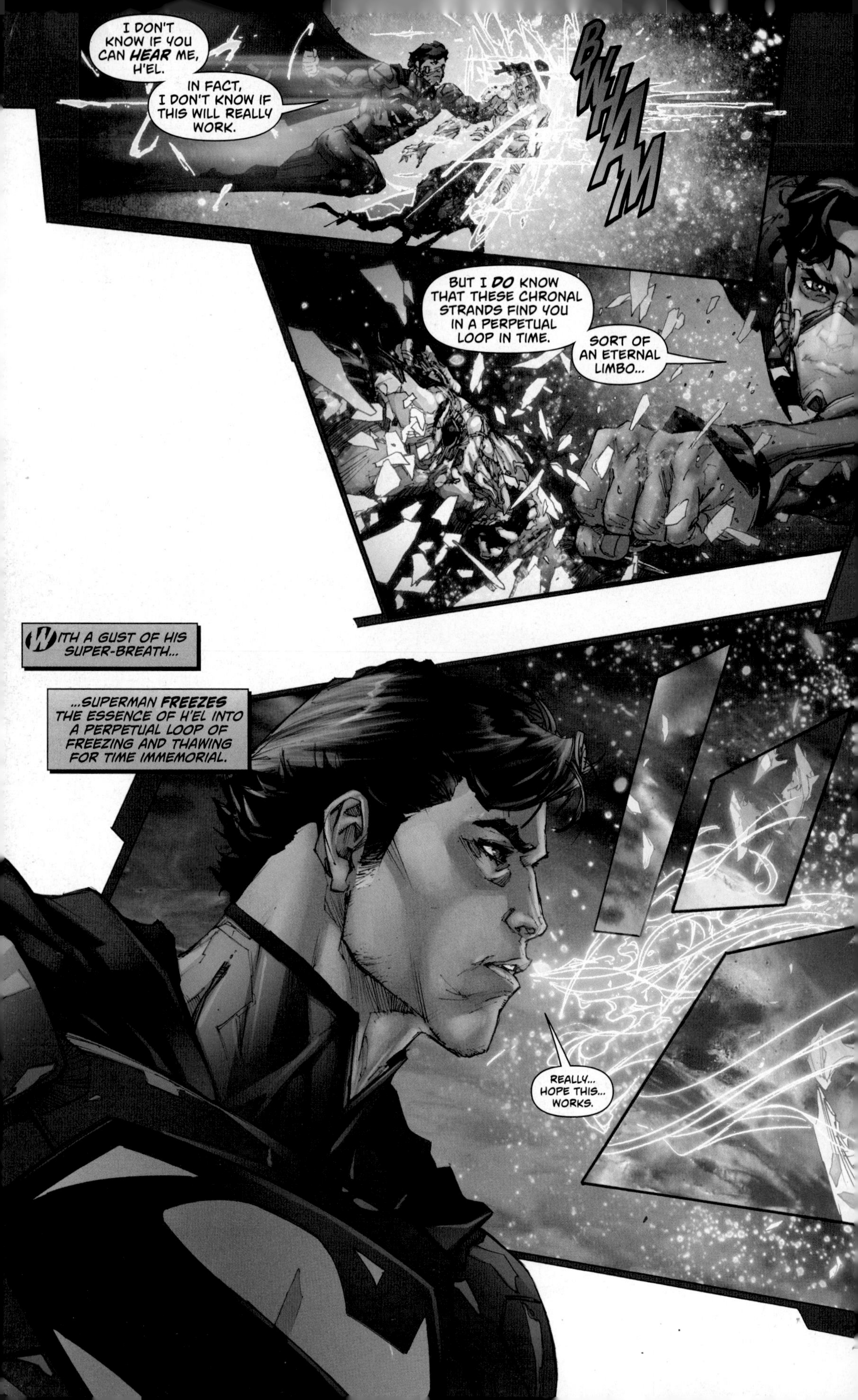
I DON'T KNOW IF YOU CAN HEAR ME, H'EL.
IN FACT, I DON'T KNOW IF THIS WILL REALLY WORK.
BWHAM
BUT I DO KNOW THAT THESE CHRONAL STRANDS FIND YOU IN A PERPETUAL LOOP IN TIME.
SORT OF AN ETERNAL LIMBO...
WITH A GUST OF HIS SUPER-BREATH...
...SUPERMAN FREEZES THE ESSENCE OF H'EL INTO A PERPETUAL LOOP OF FREEZING AND THAWING FOR TIME IMMEMORIAL.
REALLY... HOPE THIS... WORKS.

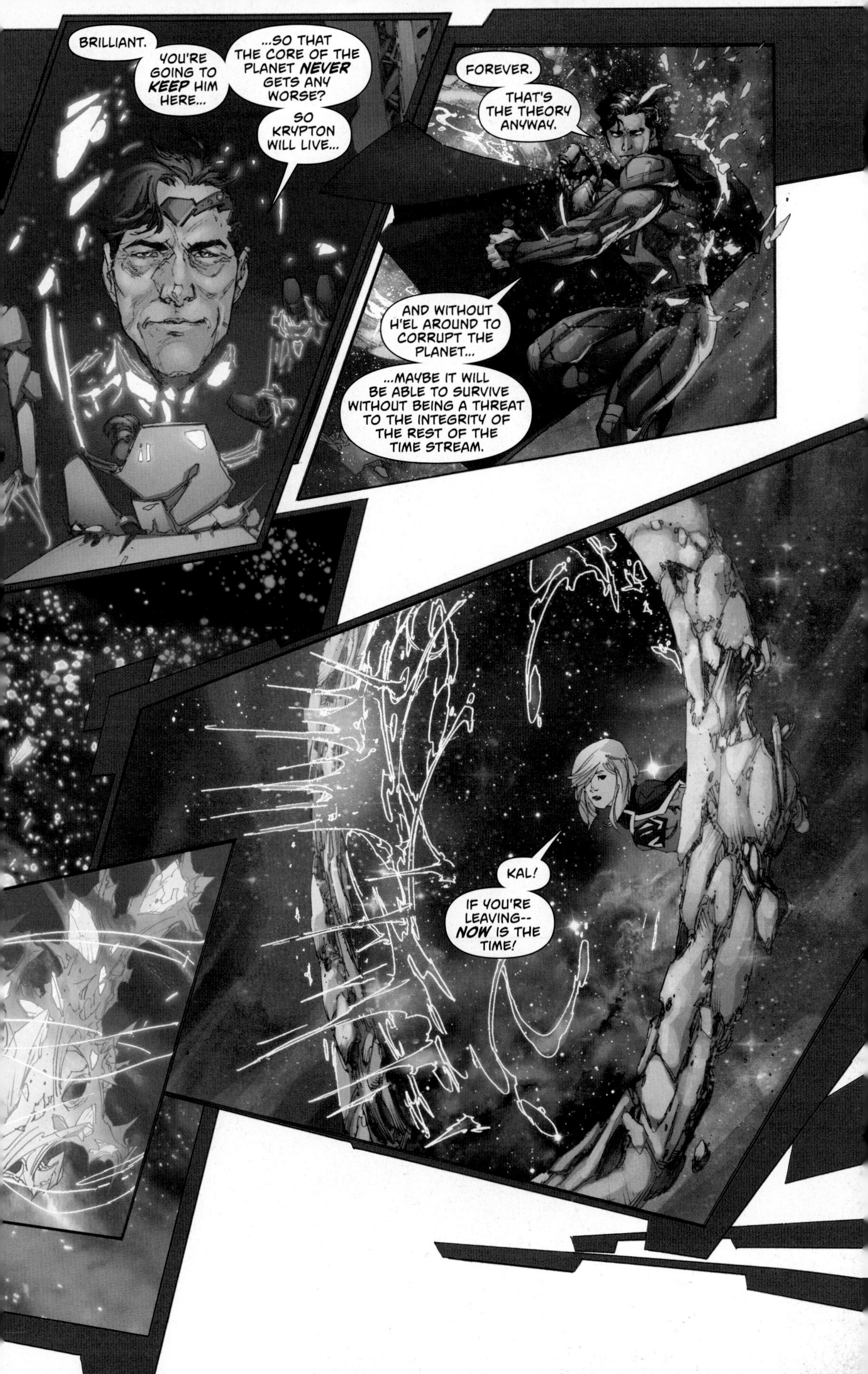
BRILLIANT.
YOU'RE GOING TO ***KEEP*** HIM HERE...
...SO THAT THE CORE OF THE PLANET ***NEVER*** GETS ANY WORSE?
SO KRYPTON WILL LIVE...
FOREVER.
THAT'S THE THEORY ANYWAY.
AND WITHOUT H'EL AROUND TO CORRUPT THE PLANET...
...MAYBE IT WILL BE ABLE TO SURVIVE WITHOUT BEING A THREAT TO THE INTEGRITY OF THE REST OF THE TIME STREAM.
KAL!
IF YOU'RE LEAVING-- ***NOW*** IS THE TIME!

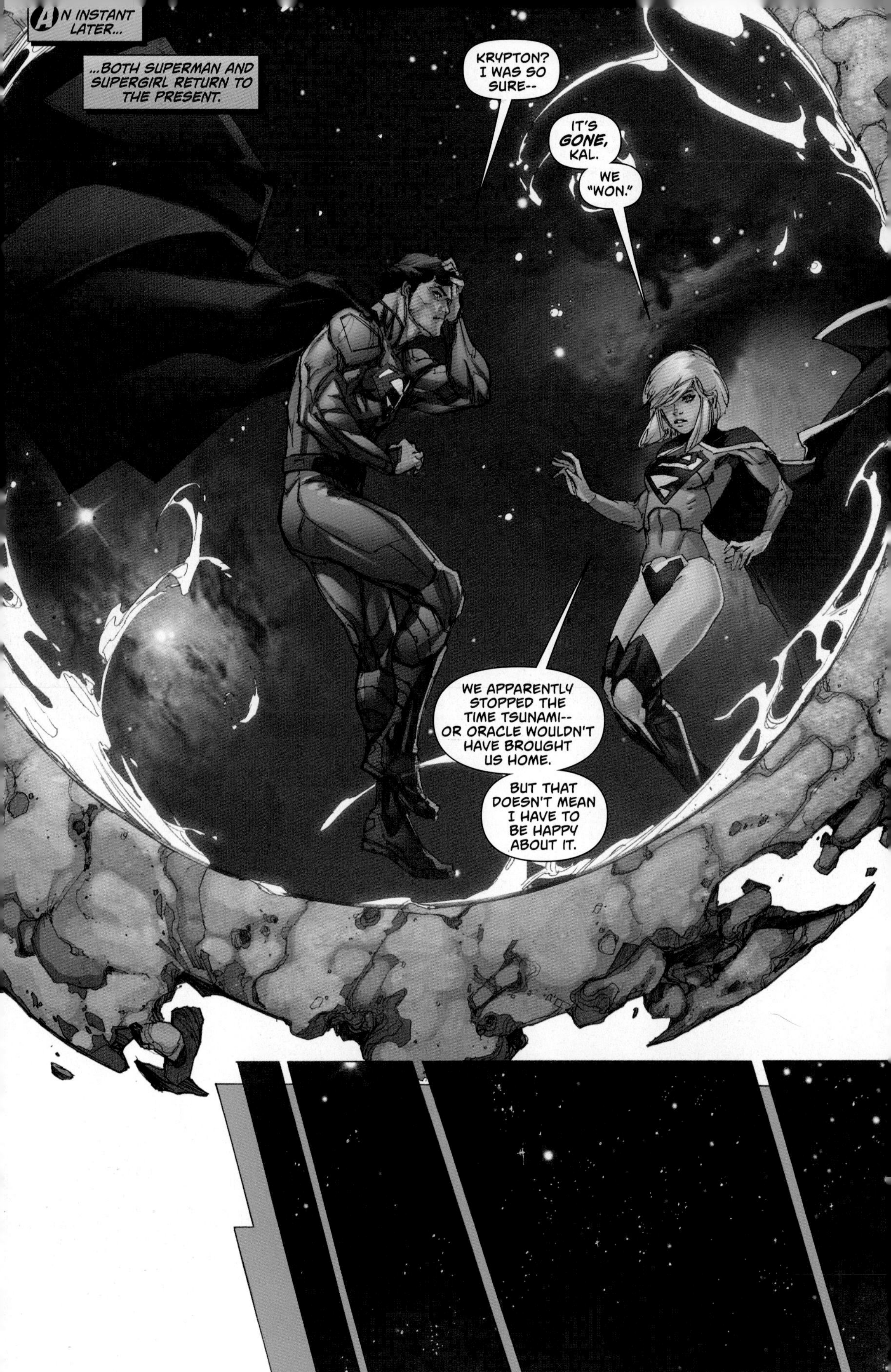
AN INSTANT LATER...
...BOTH SUPERMAN AND SUPERGIRL RETURN TO THE PRESENT.
KRYPTON? I WAS SO SURE--
IT'S GONE, KAL.
WE "WON."
WE APPARENTLY STOPPED THE TIME TSUNAMI-- OR ORACLE WOULDN'T HAVE BROUGHT US HOME.
BUT THAT DOESN'T MEAN I HAVE TO BE HAPPY ABOUT IT.

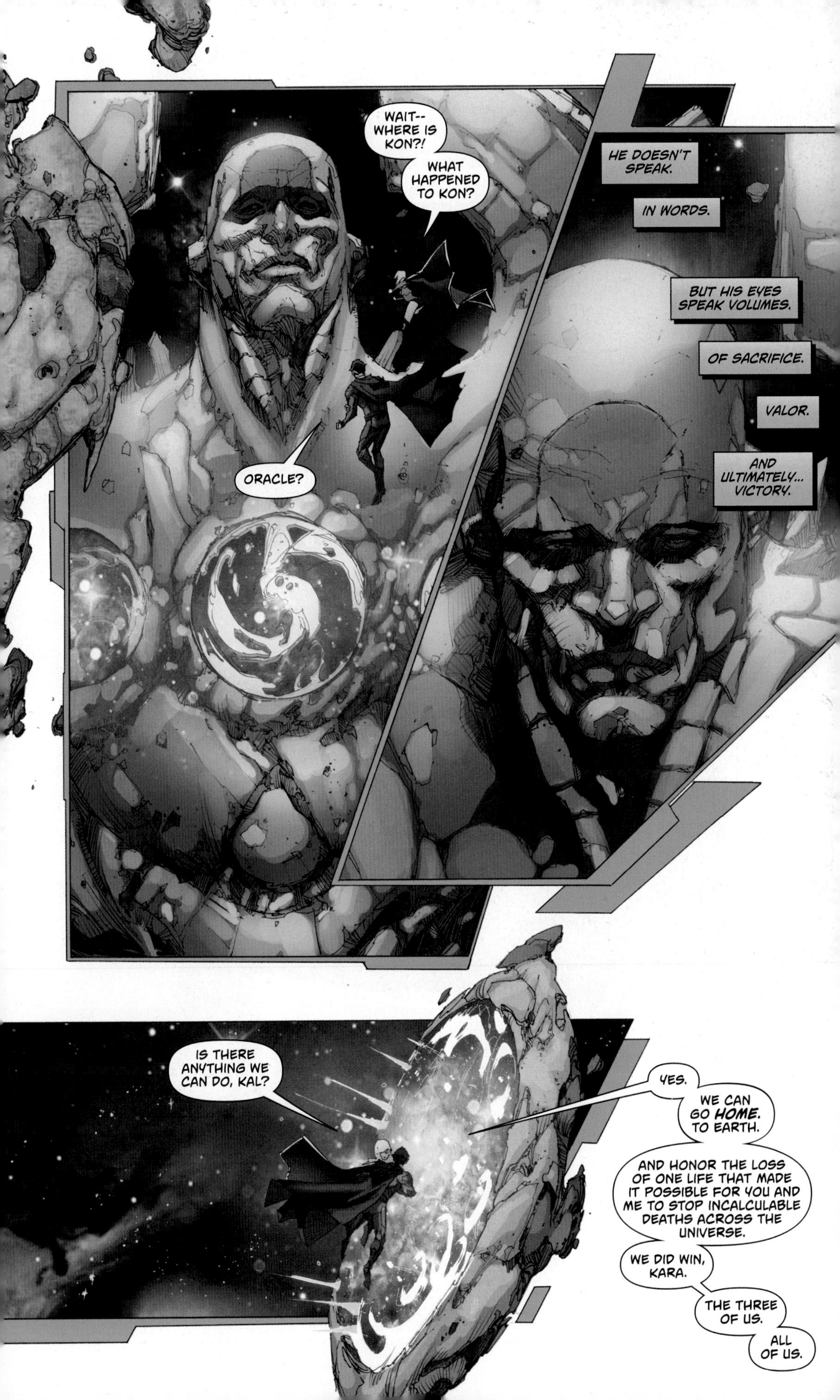
WAIT-- WHERE IS KON?!
WHAT HAPPENED TO KON?
ORACLE?
HE DOESN'T SPEAK.
IN WORDS.
BUT HIS EYES SPEAK VOLUMES.
OF SACRIFICE.
VALOR.
AND ULTIMATELY... VICTORY.
IS THERE ANYTHING WE CAN DO, KAL?
YES.
WE CAN GO **HOME**. TO EARTH.
AND HONOR THE LOSS OF ONE LIFE THAT MADE IT POSSIBLE FOR YOU AND ME TO STOP INCALCULABLE DEATHS ACROSS THE UNIVERSE.
WE DID WIN, KARA.
THE THREE OF US.
ALL OF US.

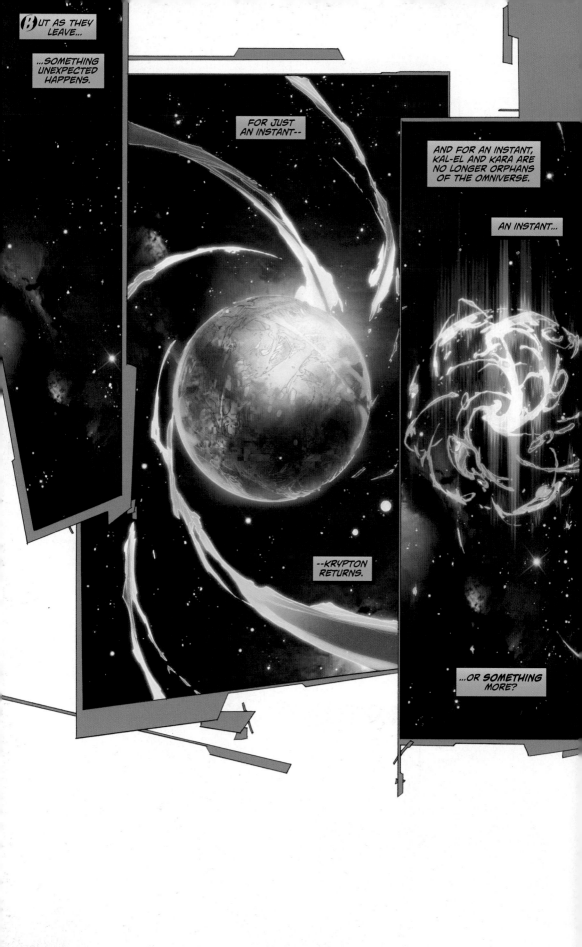

BUT AS THEY LEAVE...

...SOMETHING UNEXPECTED HAPPENS.

FOR JUST AN INSTANT--

AND FOR AN INSTANT, KAL-EL AND KARA ARE NO LONGER ORPHANS OF THE OMNIVERSE.

AN INSTANT...

--KRYPTON RETURNS.

...OR SOMETHING MORE?

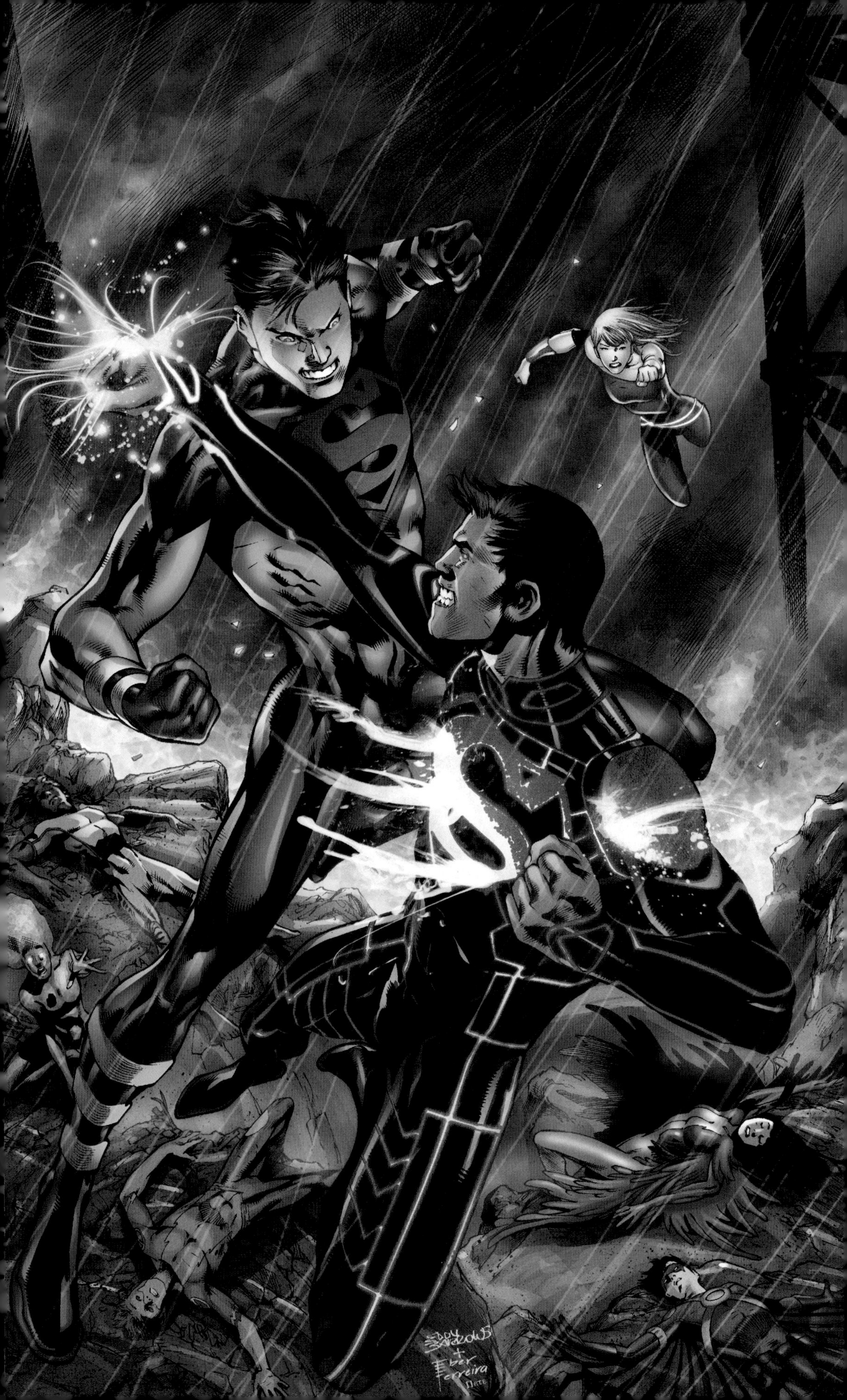

cover art by **EDDY BARROWS, EBER FERRIERA & PETE PANTAZIS**

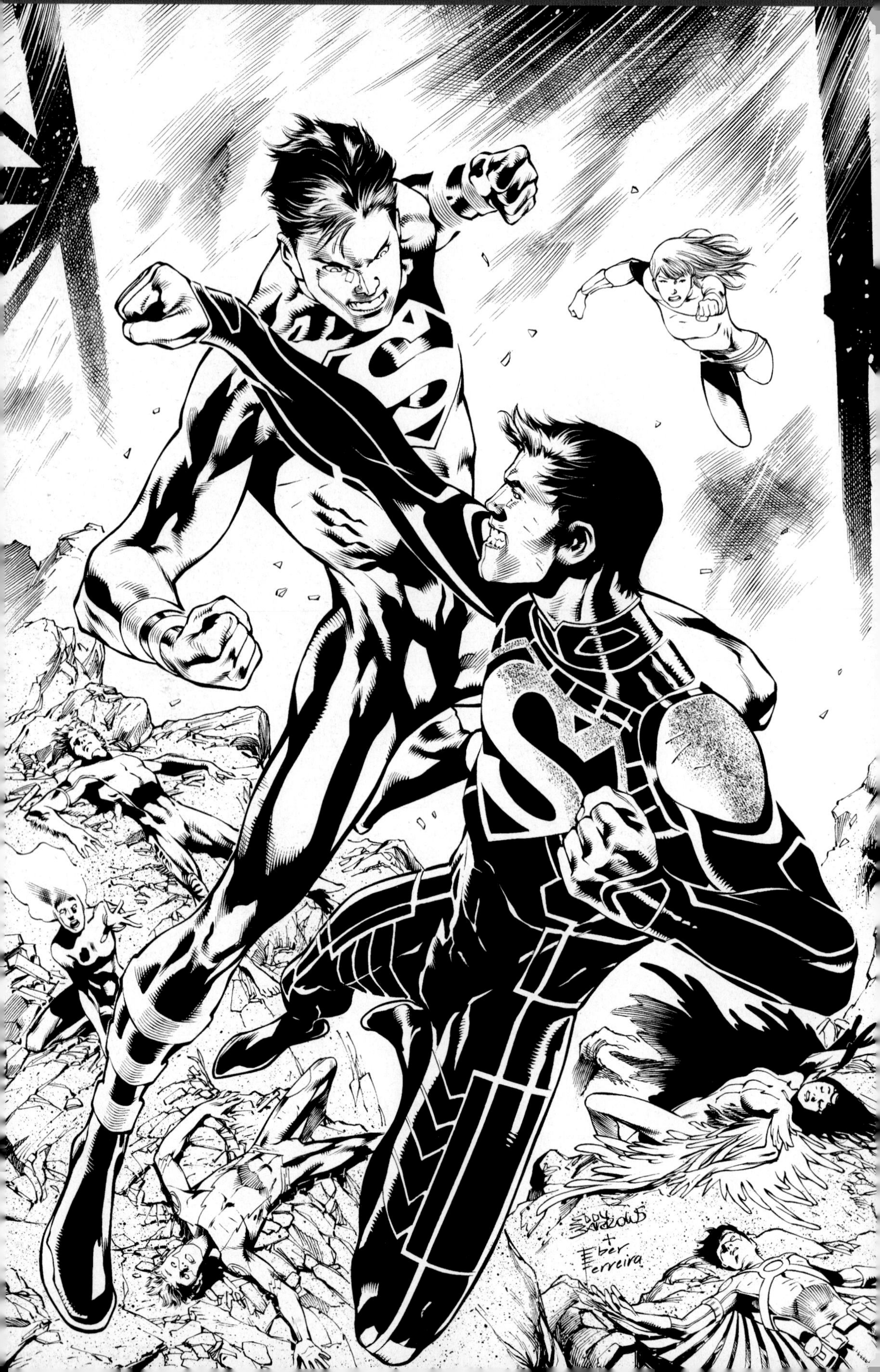

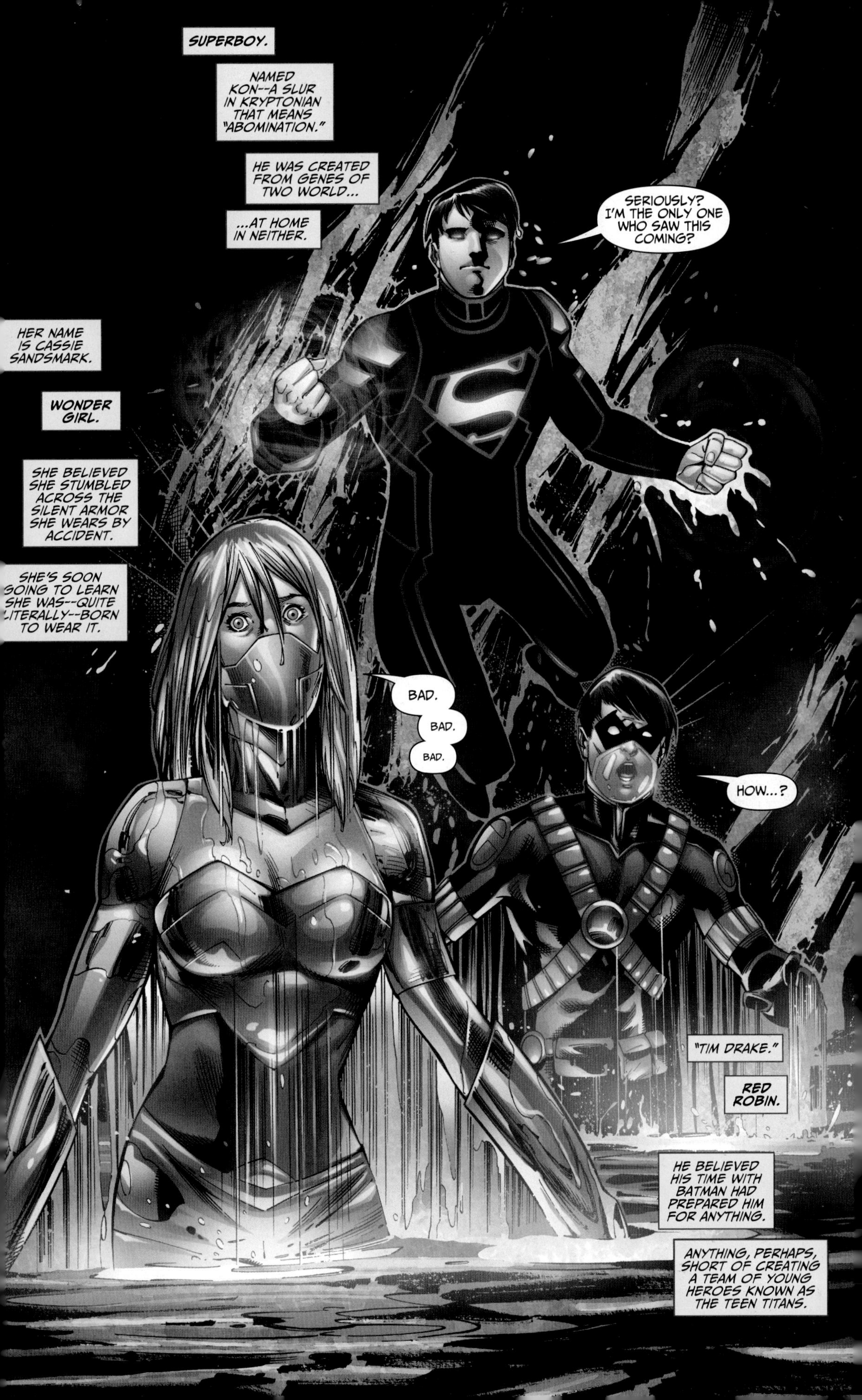

SUPERBOY.
NAMED KON--A SLUR IN KRYPTONIAN THAT MEANS "ABOMINATION."
HE WAS CREATED FROM GENES OF TWO WORLD...
...AT HOME IN NEITHER.
SERIOUSLY? I'M THE ONLY ONE WHO SAW THIS COMING?
HER NAME IS CASSIE SANDSMARK.
WONDER GIRL.
SHE BELIEVED SHE STUMBLED ACROSS THE SILENT ARMOR SHE WEARS BY ACCIDENT.
SHE'S SOON GOING TO LEARN SHE WAS--QUITE LITERALLY--BORN TO WEAR IT.
BAD.
BAD.
BAD.
HOW...?
"TIM DRAKE."
RED ROBIN.
HE BELIEVED HIS TIME WITH BATMAN HAD PREPARED HIM FOR ANYTHING.
ANYTHING, PERHAPS, SHORT OF CREATING A TEAM OF YOUNG HEROES KNOWN AS THE TEEN TITANS.

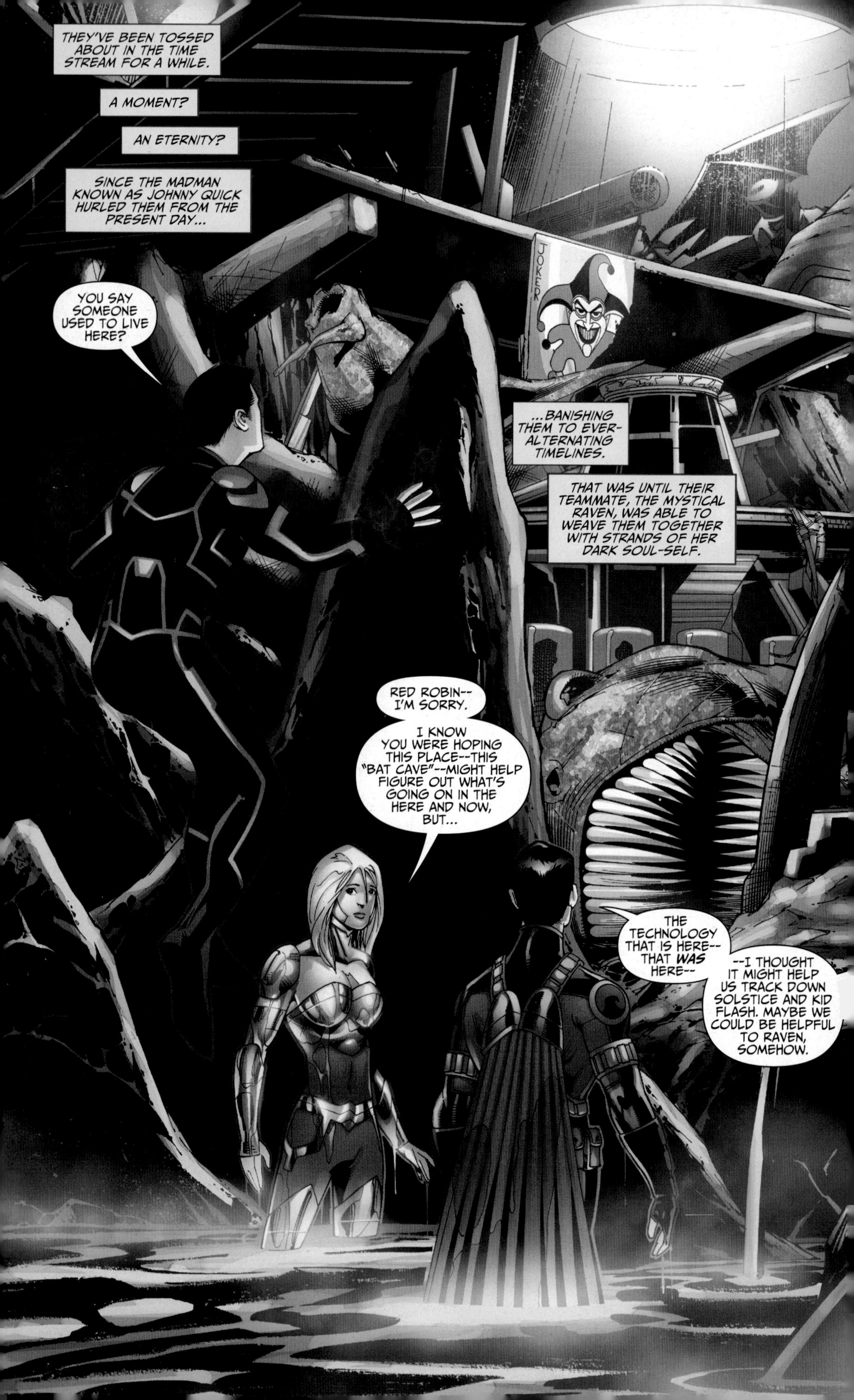
THEY'VE BEEN TOSSED ABOUT IN THE TIME STREAM FOR A WHILE.
A MOMENT?
AN ETERNITY?
SINCE THE MADMAN KNOWN AS JOHNNY QUICK HURLED THEM FROM THE PRESENT DAY...
YOU SAY SOMEONE USED TO LIVE HERE?
JOKER
...BANISHING THEM TO EVER-ALTERNATING TIMELINES.
THAT WAS UNTIL THEIR TEAMMATE, THE MYSTICAL RAVEN, WAS ABLE TO WEAVE THEM TOGETHER WITH STRANDS OF HER DARK SOUL-SELF.
RED ROBIN-- I'M SORRY.
I KNOW YOU WERE HOPING THIS PLACE--THIS "BAT CAVE"--MIGHT HELP FIGURE OUT WHAT'S GOING ON IN THE HERE AND NOW, BUT...
THE TECHNOLOGY THAT IS HERE-- THAT **WAS** HERE--
--I THOUGHT IT MIGHT HELP US TRACK DOWN SOLSTICE AND KID FLASH. MAYBE WE COULD BE HELPFUL TO RAVEN, SOMEHOW.

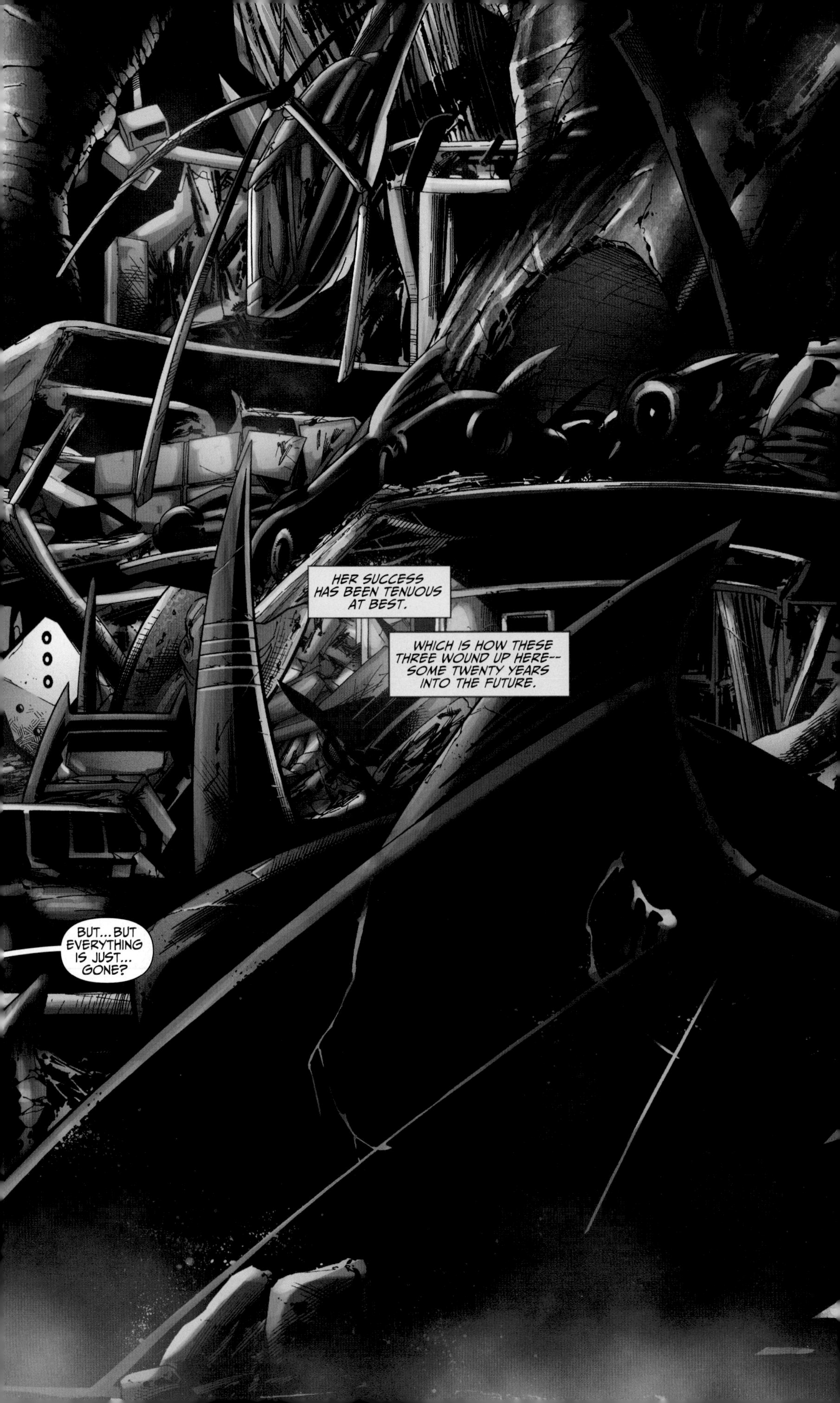
HER SUCCESS HAS BEEN TENUOUS AT BEST.
WHICH IS HOW THESE THREE WOUND UP HERE-- SOME TWENTY YEARS INTO THE FUTURE.
BUT...BUT EVERYTHING IS JUST... GONE?

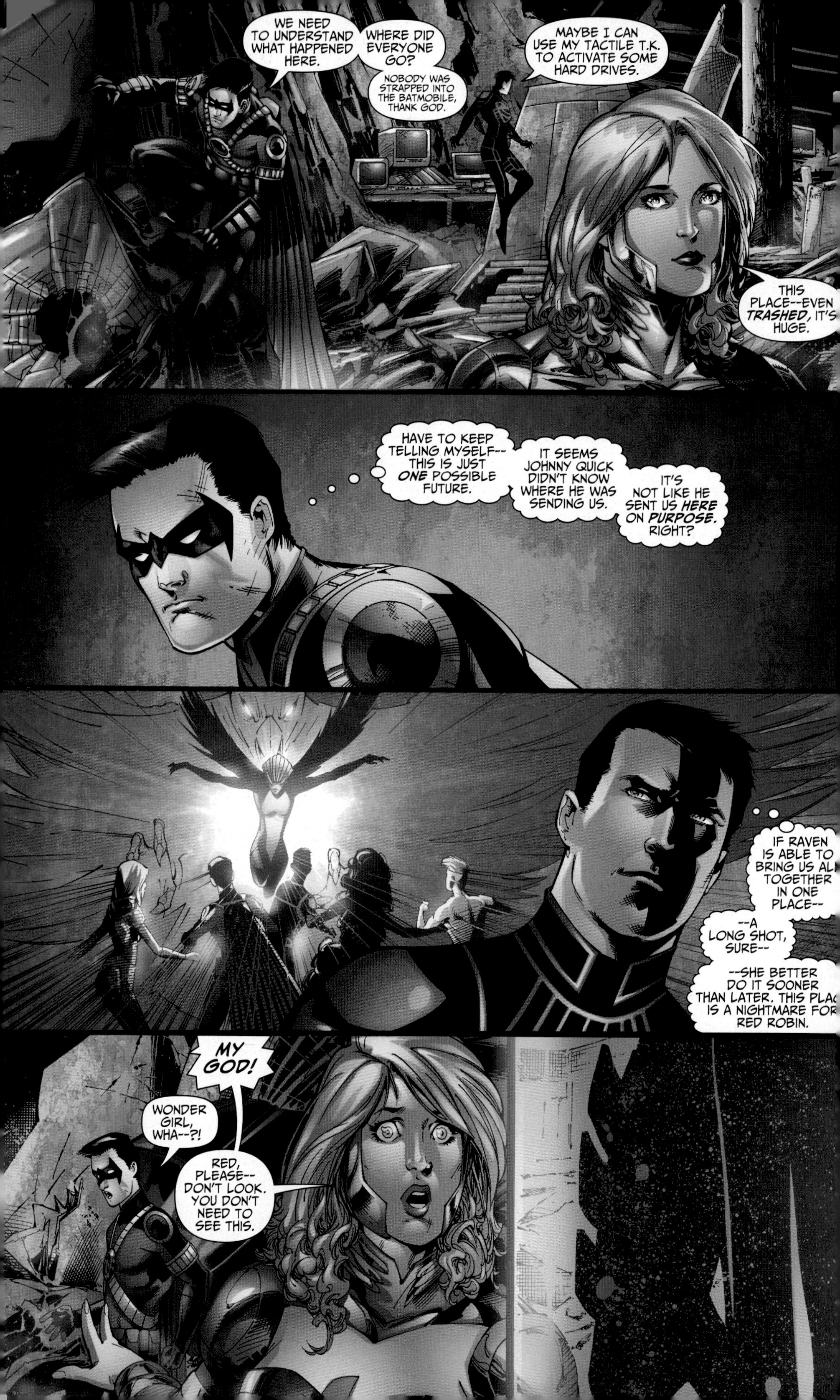

WE NEED TO UNDERSTAND WHAT HAPPENED HERE.
WHERE DID EVERYONE GO?
NOBODY WAS STRAPPED INTO THE BATMOBILE, THANK GOD.
MAYBE I CAN USE MY TACTILE T.K. TO ACTIVATE SOME HARD DRIVES.
THIS PLACE--EVEN TRASHED, IT'S HUGE.
HAVE TO KEEP TELLING MYSELF-- THIS IS JUST ONE POSSIBLE FUTURE.
IT SEEMS JOHNNY QUICK DIDN'T KNOW WHERE HE WAS SENDING US.
IT'S NOT LIKE HE SENT US HERE ON PURPOSE. RIGHT?
IF RAVEN IS ABLE TO BRING US AL TOGETHER IN ONE PLACE--
--A LONG SHOT, SURE--
--SHE BETTER DO IT SOONER THAN LATER. THIS PLAC IS A NIGHTMARE FOR RED ROBIN.
MY GOD!
WONDER GIRL, WHA--?!
RED, PLEASE-- DON'T LOOK. YOU DON'T NEED TO SEE THIS.

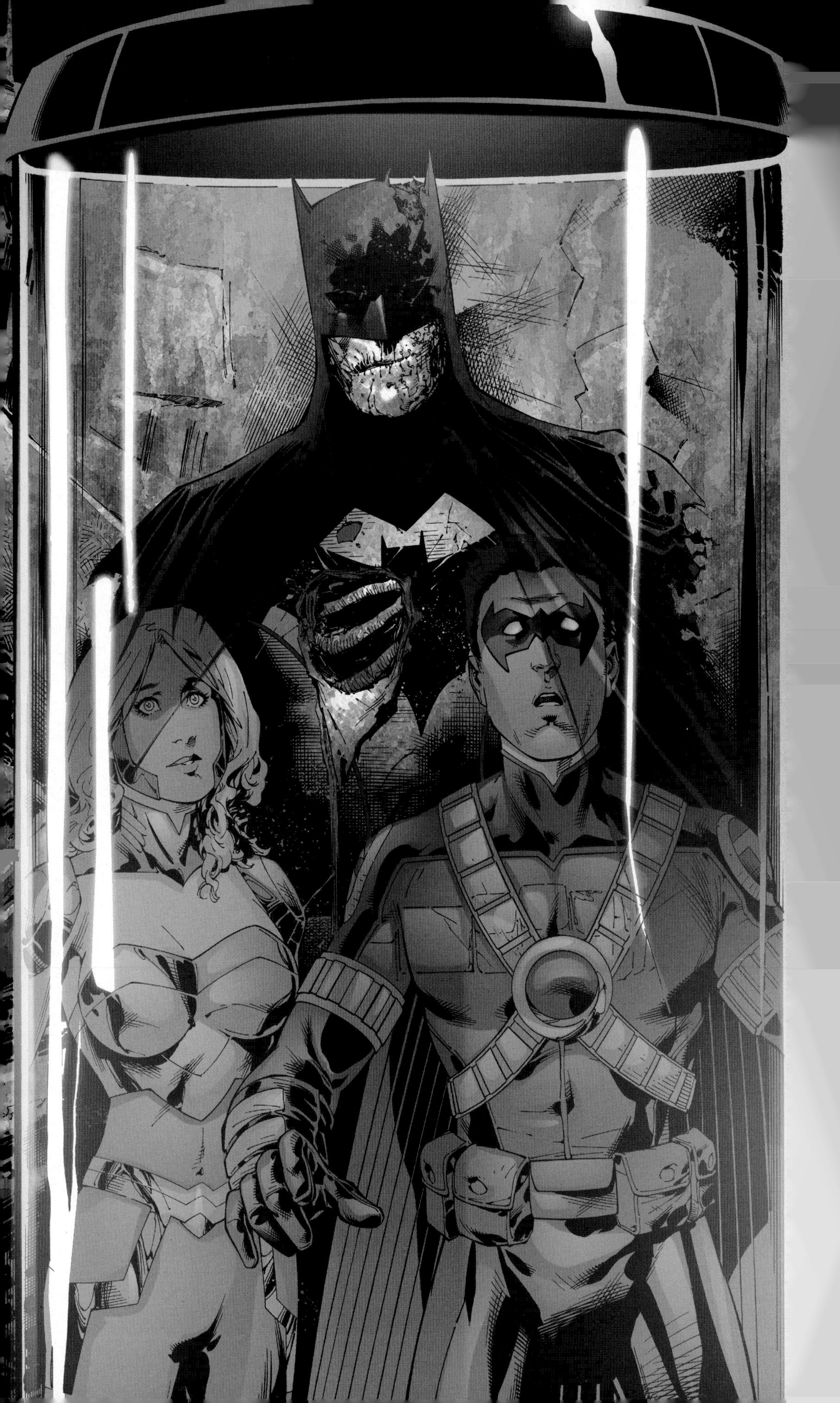

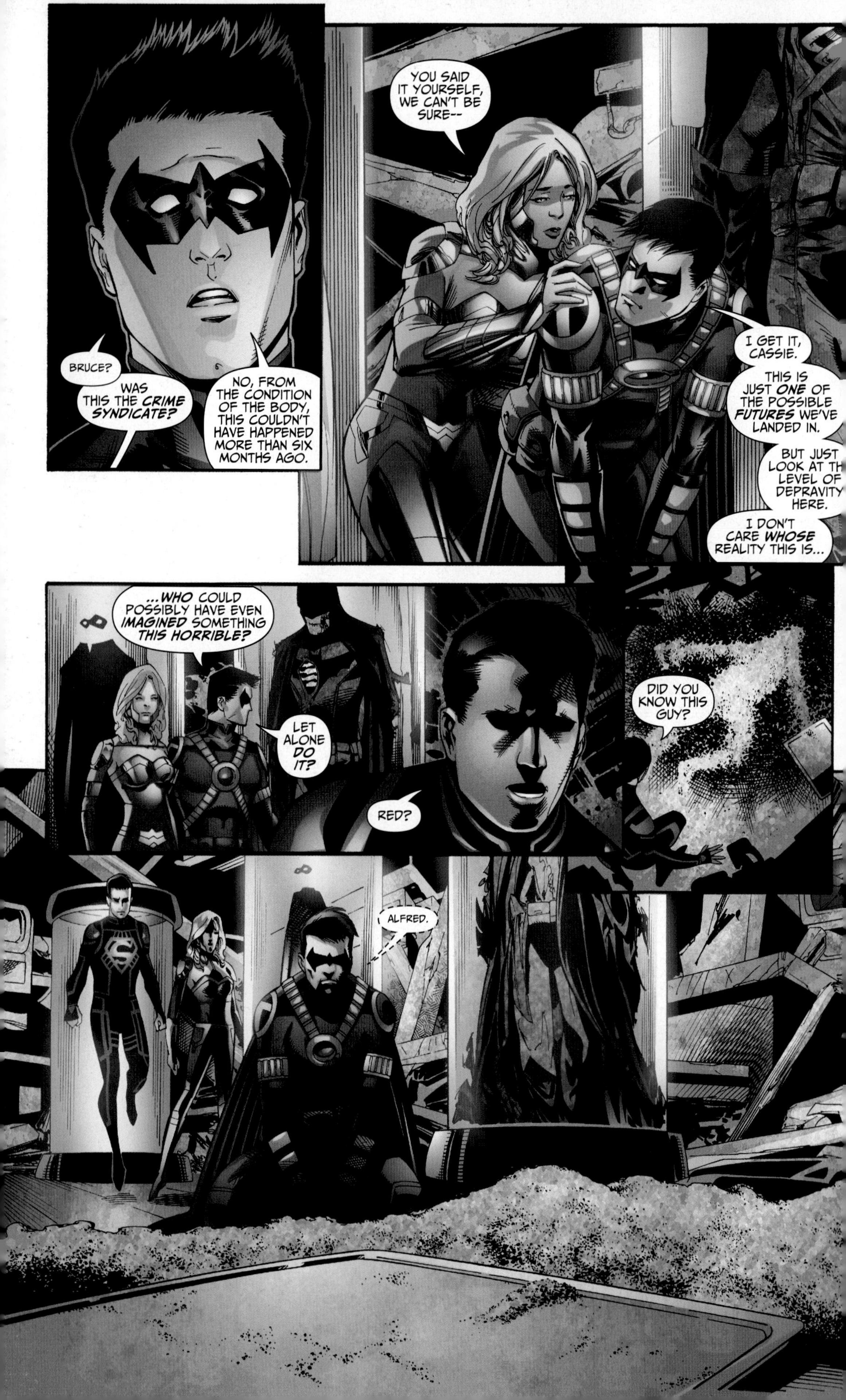
BRUCE?
WAS THIS THE CRIME SYNDICATE?
NO, FROM THE CONDITION OF THE BODY, THIS COULDN'T HAVE HAPPENED MORE THAN SIX MONTHS AGO.
YOU SAID IT YOURSELF, WE CAN'T BE SURE--
I GET IT, CASSIE.
THIS IS JUST ONE OF THE POSSIBLE FUTURES WE'VE LANDED IN.
BUT JUST LOOK AT TH LEVEL OF DEPRAVITY HERE.
I DON'T CARE WHOSE REALITY THIS IS...
...WHO COULD POSSIBLY HAVE EVEN IMAGINED SOMETHING THIS HORRIBLE?
LET ALONE DO IT?
DID YOU KNOW THIS GUY?
RED?
ALFRED.

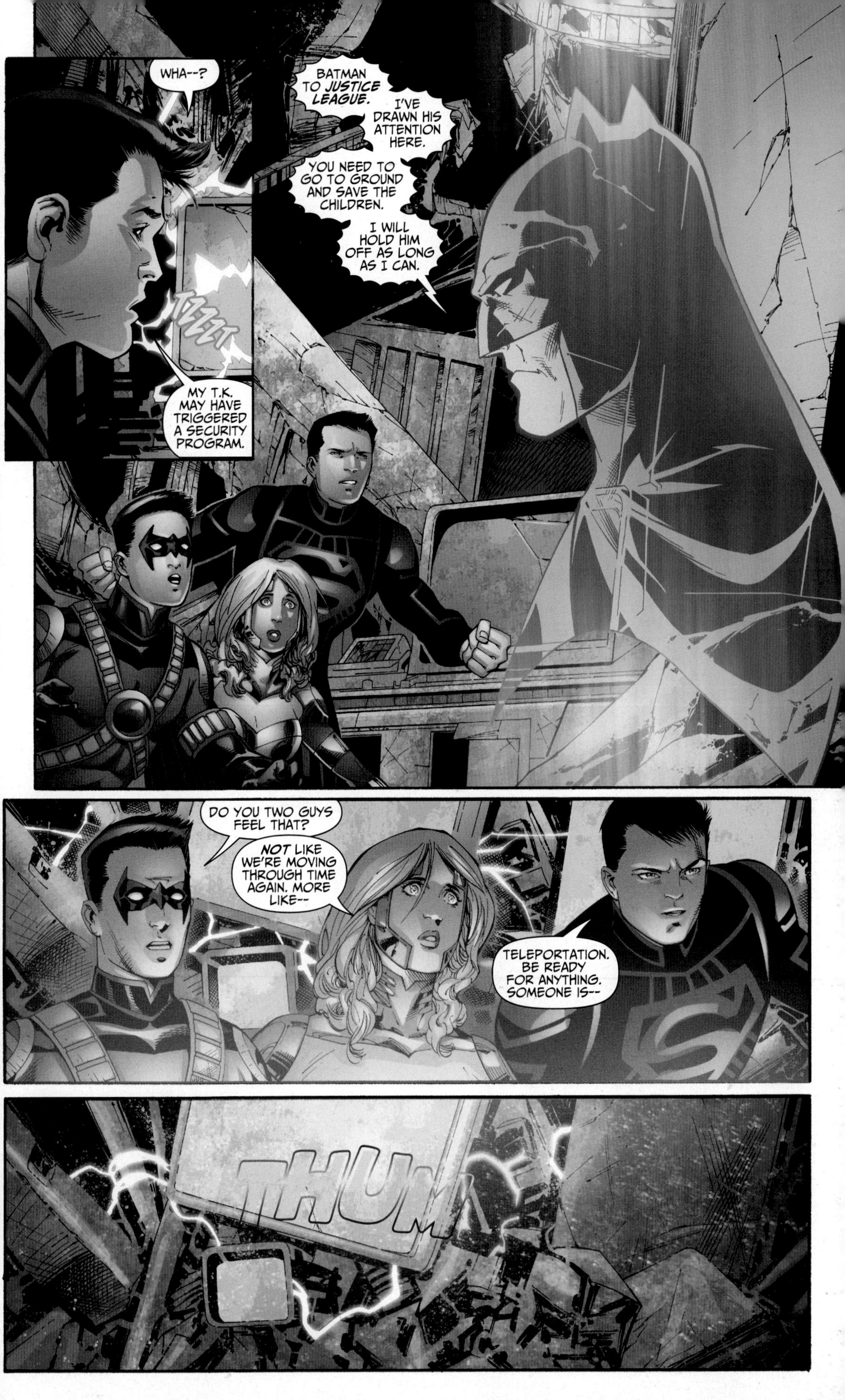
WHA--?
BATMAN TO JUSTICE LEAGUE.
I'VE DRAWN HIS ATTENTION HERE.
YOU NEED TO GO TO GROUND AND SAVE THE CHILDREN.
I WILL HOLD HIM OFF AS LONG AS I CAN.
TZZZT
MY T.K. MAY HAVE TRIGGERED A SECURITY PROGRAM.
DO YOU TWO GUYS FEEL THAT?
NOT LIKE WE'RE MOVING THROUGH TIME AGAIN. MORE LIKE--
TELEPORTATION. BE READY FOR ANYTHING. SOMEONE IS--
THUM

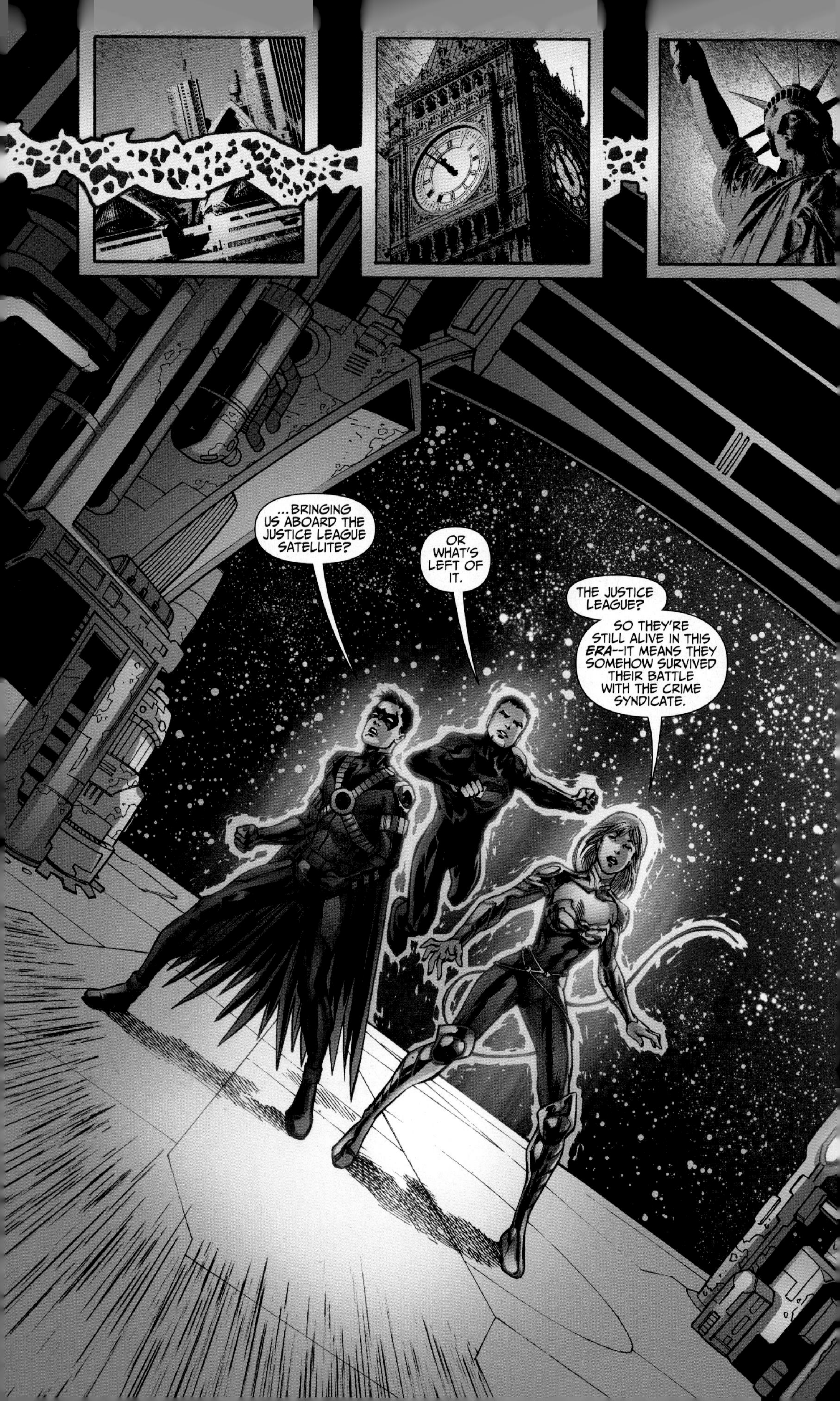
...BRINGING US ABOARD THE JUSTICE LEAGUE SATELLITE?
OR WHAT'S LEFT OF IT.
THE JUSTICE LEAGUE?
SO THEY'RE STILL ALIVE IN THIS ERA--IT MEANS THEY SOMEHOW SURVIVED THEIR BATTLE WITH THE CRIME SYNDICATE.

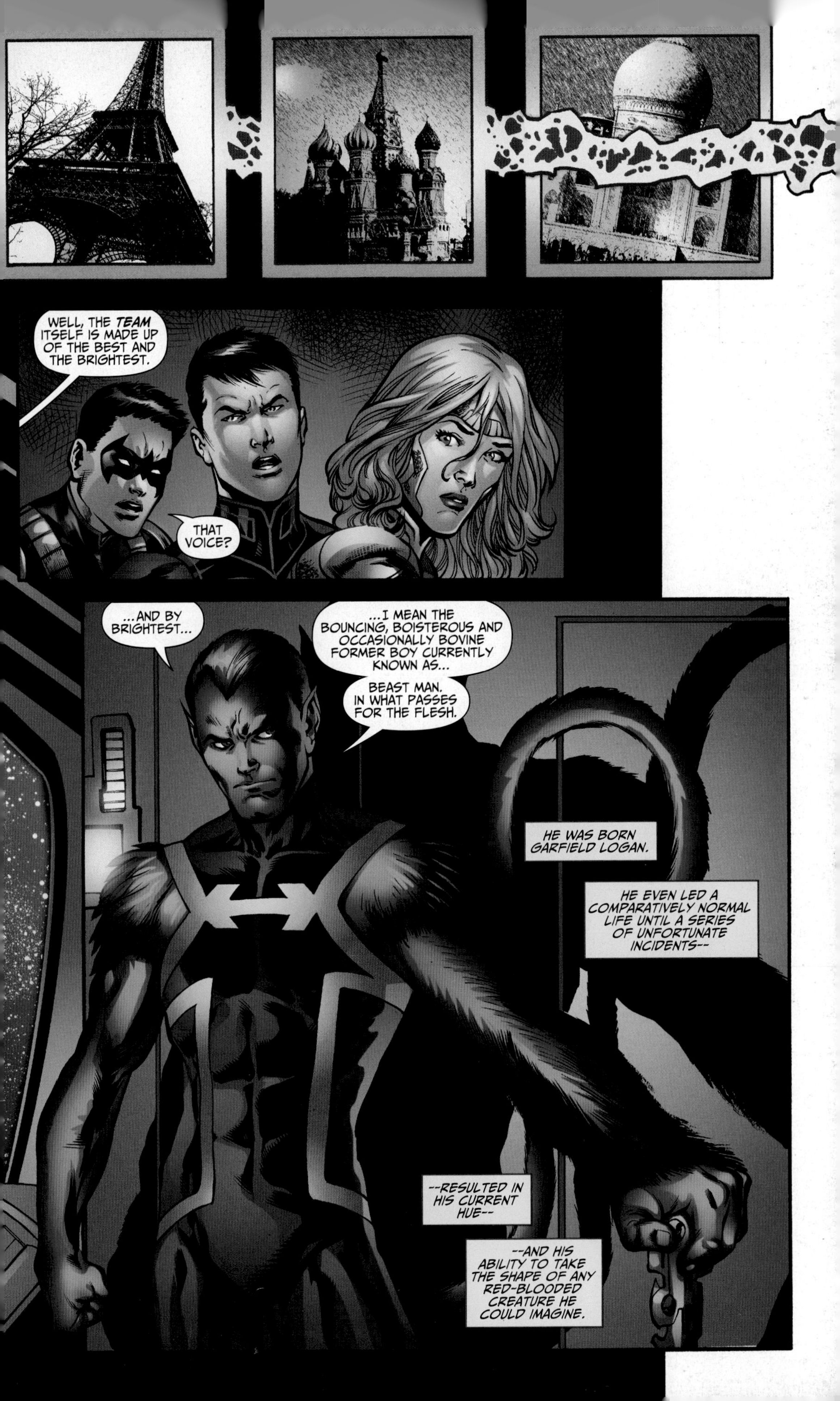
WELL, THE TEAM ITSELF IS MADE UP OF THE BEST AND THE BRIGHTEST.
THAT VOICE?
...AND BY BRIGHTEST...
...I MEAN THE BOUNCING, BOISTEROUS AND OCCASIONALLY BOVINE FORMER BOY CURRENTLY KNOWN AS...
BEAST MAN. IN WHAT PASSES FOR THE FLESH.
HE WAS BORN GARFIELD LOGAN.
HE EVEN LED A COMPARATIVELY NORMAL LIFE UNTIL A SERIES OF UNFORTUNATE INCIDENTS--
--RESULTED IN HIS CURRENT HUE--
--AND HIS ABILITY TO TAKE THE SHAPE OF ANY RED-BLOODED CREATURE HE COULD IMAGINE.

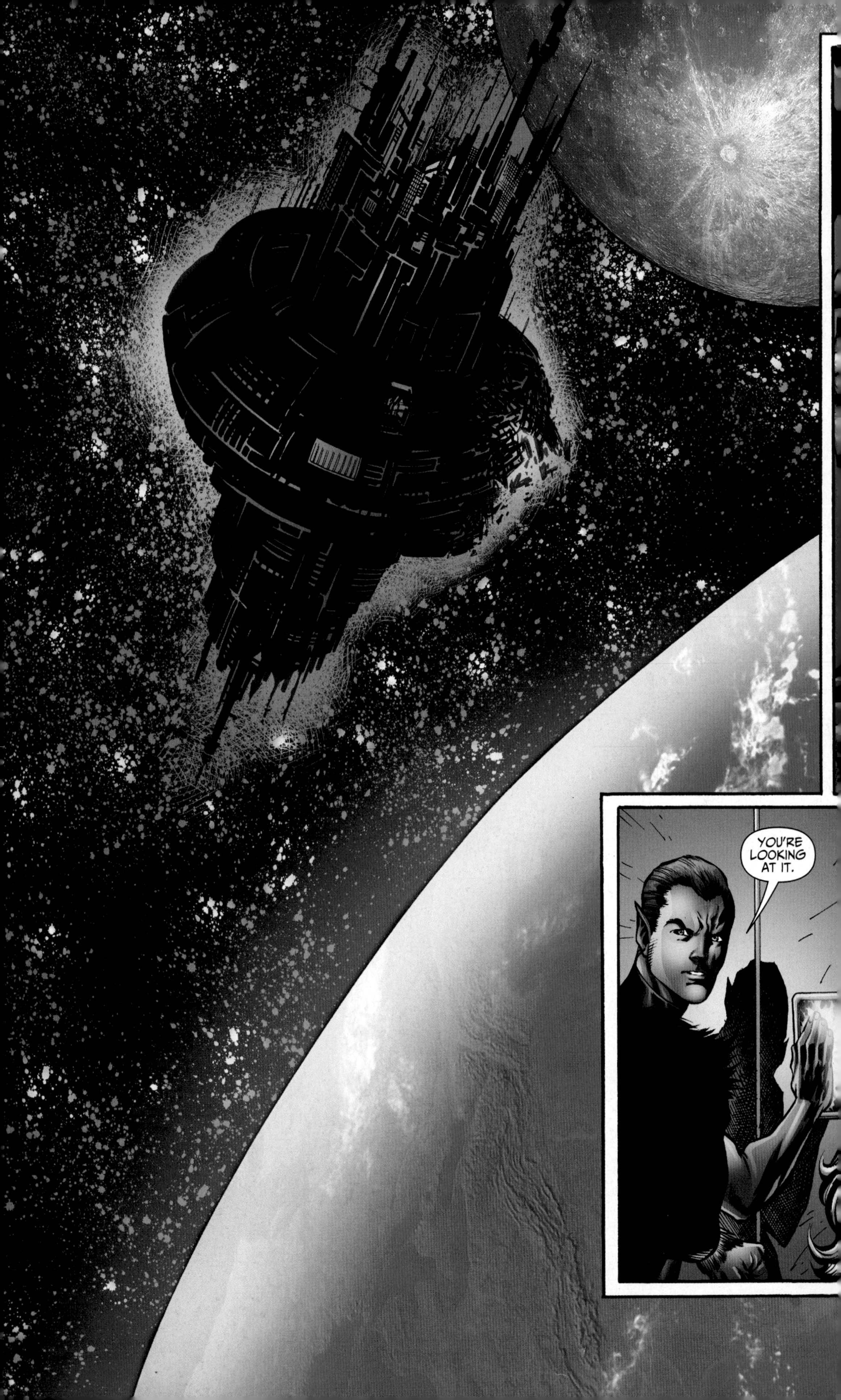
YOU'RE LOOKING AT IT.

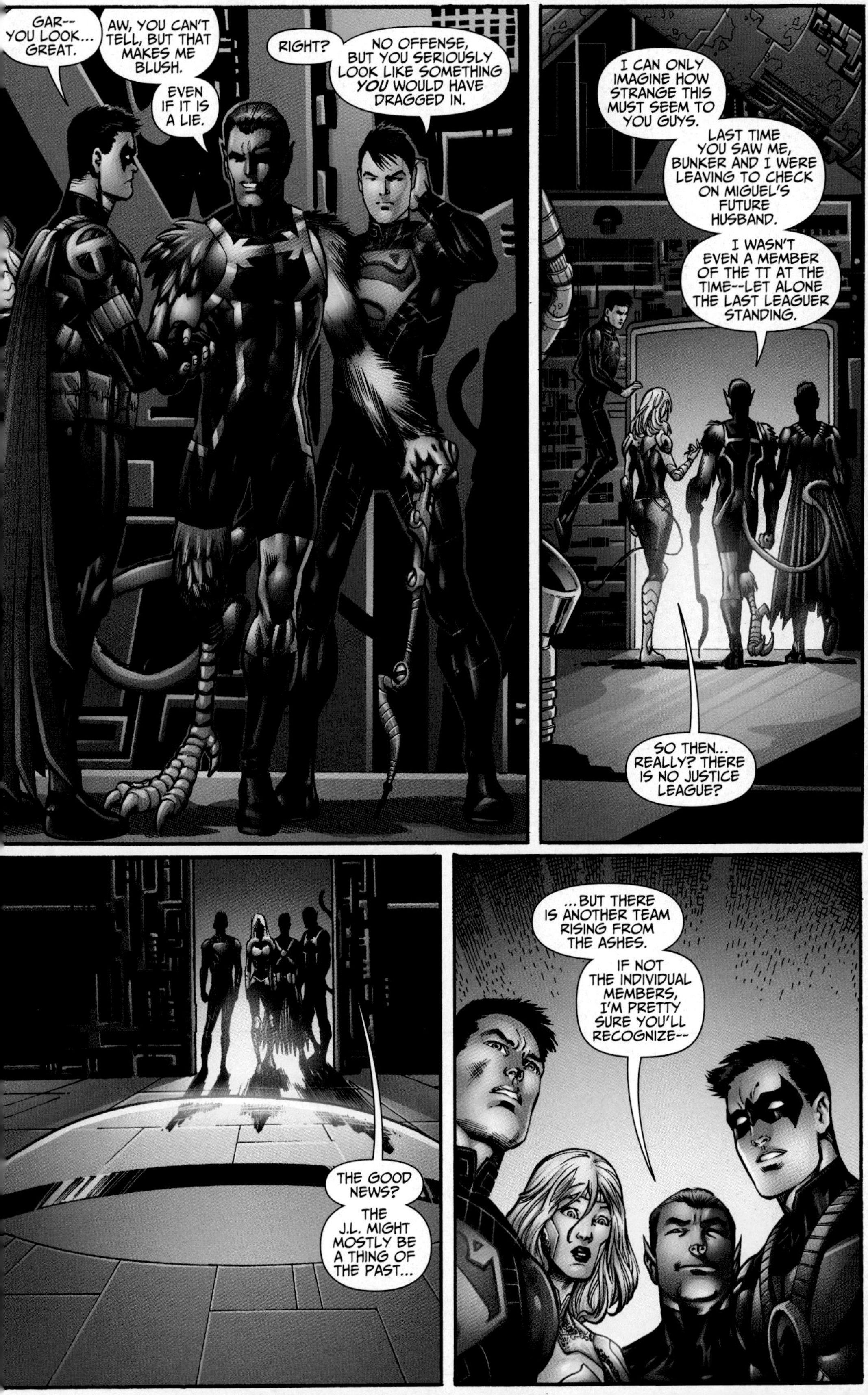
GAR-- YOU LOOK... GREAT.
AW, YOU CAN'T TELL, BUT THAT MAKES ME BLUSH.
EVEN IF IT IS A LIE.
RIGHT?
NO OFFENSE, BUT YOU SERIOUSLY LOOK LIKE SOMETHING YOU WOULD HAVE DRAGGED IN.
I CAN ONLY IMAGINE HOW STRANGE THIS MUST SEEM TO YOU GUYS.
LAST TIME YOU SAW ME, BUNKER AND I WERE LEAVING TO CHECK ON MIGUEL'S FUTURE HUSBAND.
I WASN'T EVEN A MEMBER OF THE TT AT THE TIME--LET ALONE THE LAST LEAGUER STANDING.
SO THEN... REALLY? THERE IS NO JUSTICE LEAGUE?
THE GOOD NEWS?
THE J.L. MIGHT MOSTLY BE A THING OF THE PAST...
...BUT THERE IS ANOTHER TEAM RISING FROM THE ASHES.
IF NOT THE INDIVIDUAL MEMBERS, I'M PRETTY SURE YOU'LL RECOGNIZE--

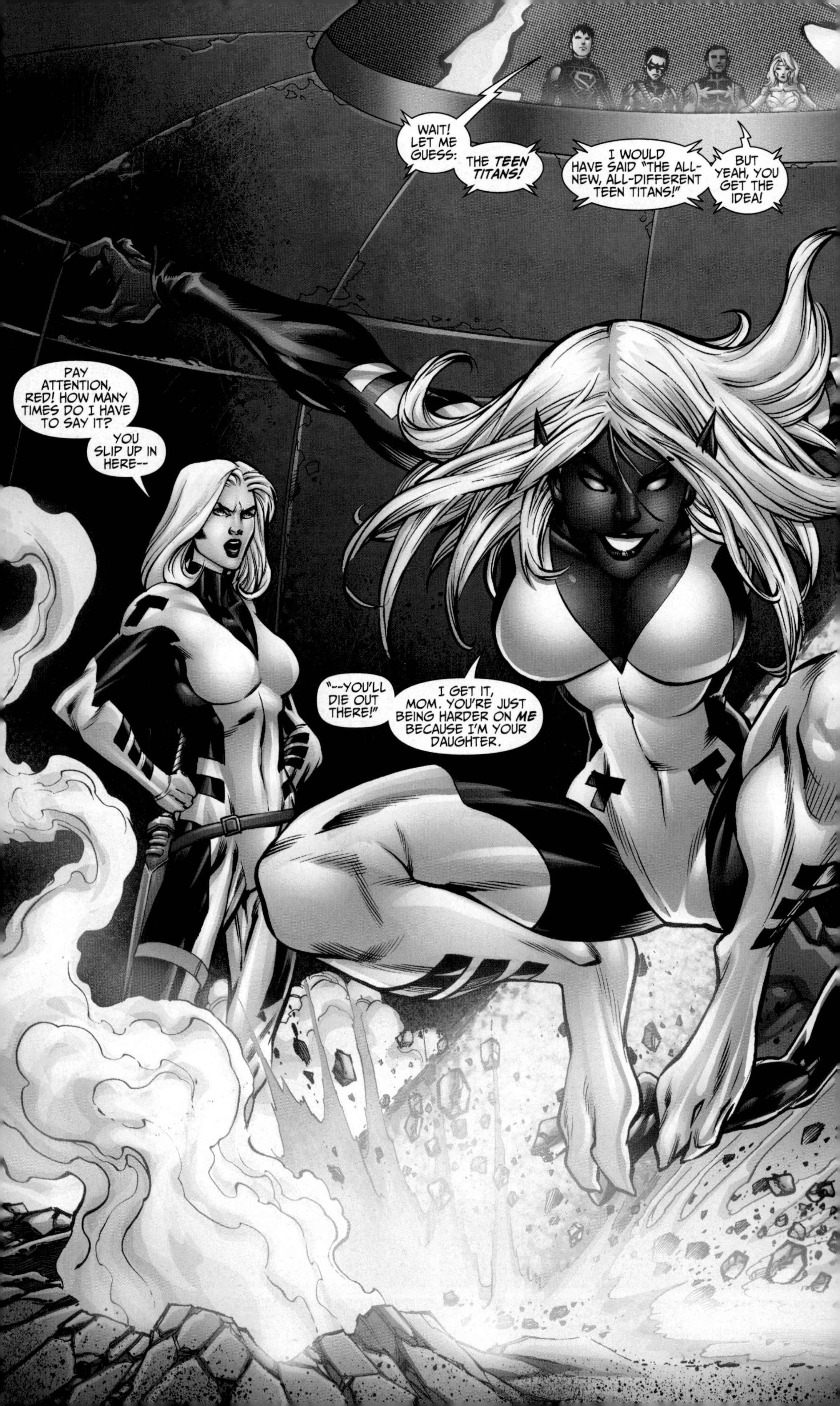

WAIT! LET ME GUESS:
THE *TEEN TITANS!*
I WOULD HAVE SAID "THE ALL-NEW, ALL-DIFFERENT TEEN TITANS!"
BUT YEAH, YOU GET THE IDEA!
PAY ATTENTION, RED! HOW MANY TIMES DO I HAVE TO SAY IT?
YOU SLIP UP IN HERE--
"--YOU'LL DIE OUT THERE!"
I GET IT, MOM. YOU'RE JUST BEING HARDER ON *ME* BECAUSE I'M YOUR DAUGHTER.

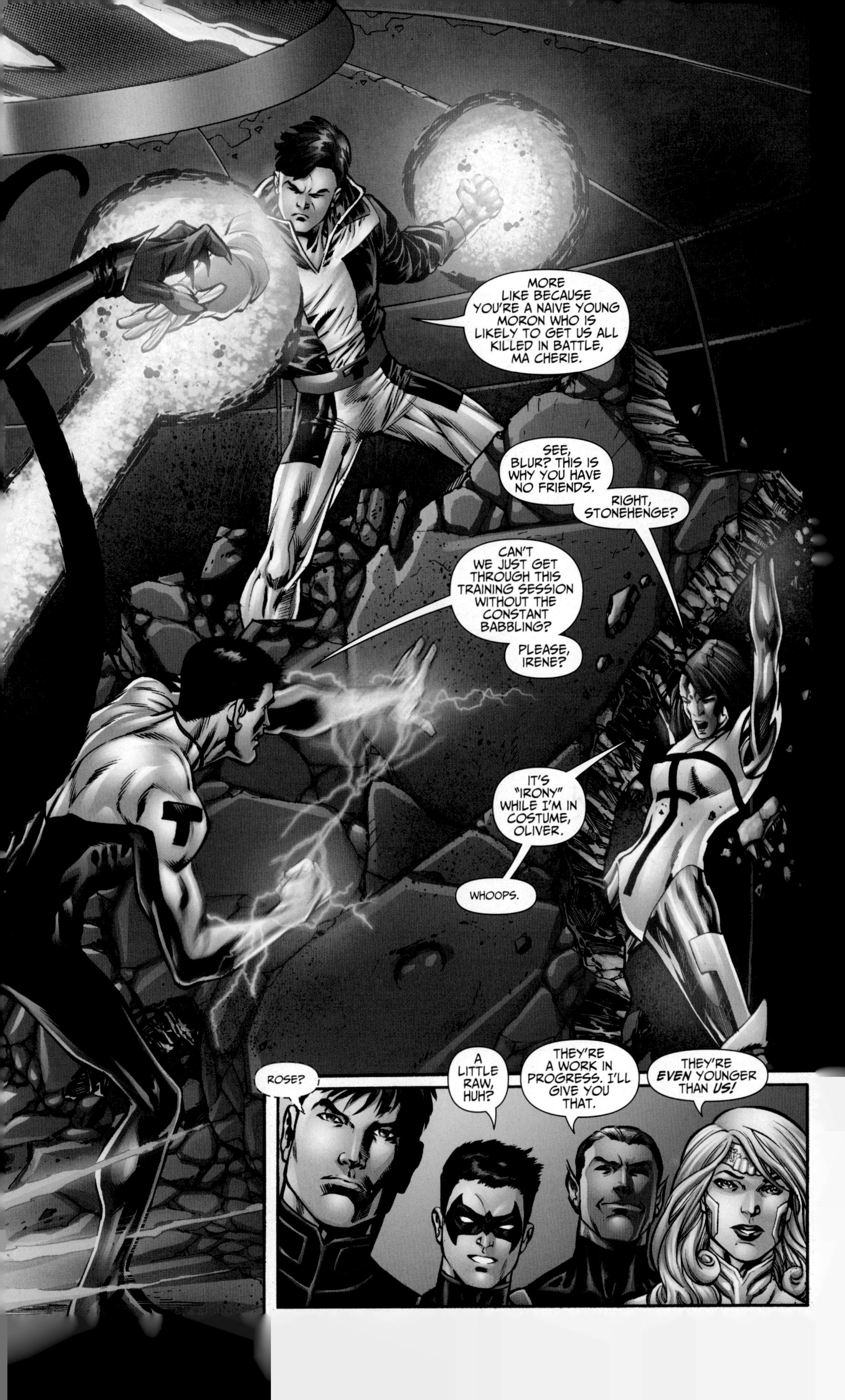
MORE LIKE BECAUSE YOU'RE A NAIVE YOUNG MORON WHO IS LIKELY TO GET US ALL KILLED IN BATTLE, MA CHERIE.
SEE, BLUR? THIS IS WHY YOU HAVE NO FRIENDS.
RIGHT, STONEHENGE?
CAN'T WE JUST GET THROUGH THIS TRAINING SESSION WITHOUT THE CONSTANT BABBLING?
PLEASE, IRENE?
IT'S "IRONY" WHILE I'M IN COSTUME, OLIVER.
WHOOPS.
ROSE?
A LITTLE RAW, HUH?
THEY'RE A WORK IN PROGRESS. I'LL GIVE YOU THAT.
THEY'RE *EVEN* YOUNGER THAN *US!*

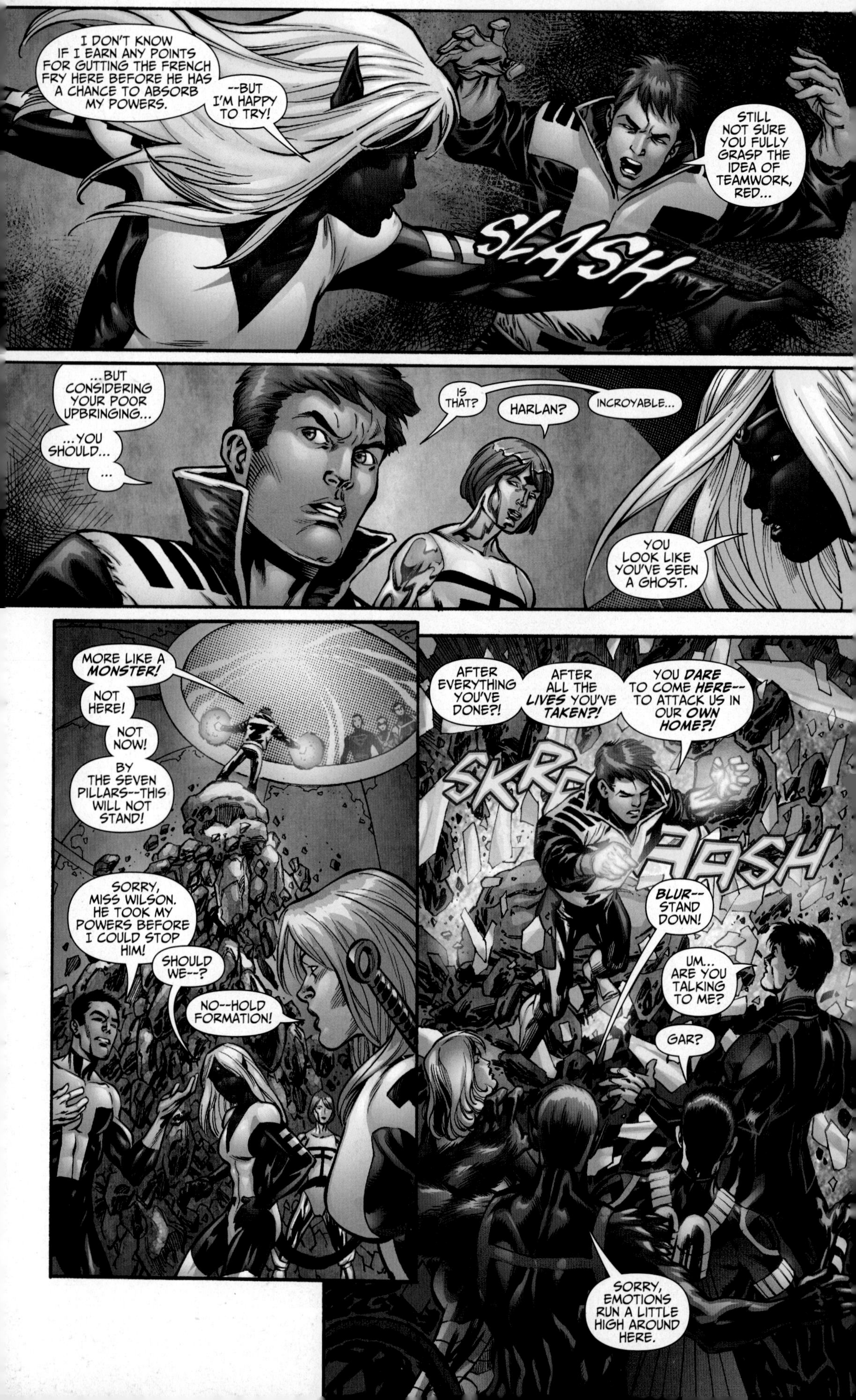
I DON'T KNOW IF I EARN ANY POINTS FOR GUTTING THE FRENCH FRY HERE BEFORE HE HAS A CHANCE TO ABSORB MY POWERS.
--BUT I'M HAPPY TO TRY!
STILL NOT SURE YOU FULLY GRASP THE IDEA OF TEAMWORK, RED...
SLASH
...BUT CONSIDERING YOUR POOR UPBRINGING...
...YOU SHOULD...
...
IS THAT?
HARLAN?
INCROYABLE...
YOU LOOK LIKE YOU'VE SEEN A GHOST.
MORE LIKE A MONSTER!
NOT HERE!
NOT NOW!
BY THE SEVEN PILLARS--THIS WILL NOT STAND!
SORRY, MISS WILSON. HE TOOK MY POWERS BEFORE I COULD STOP HIM!
SHOULD WE--?
NO--HOLD FORMATION!
AFTER EVERYTHING YOU'VE DONE?!
AFTER ALL THE LIVES YOU'VE TAKEN?!
YOU DARE TO COME HERE--TO ATTACK US IN OUR OWN HOME?!
BLUR--STAND DOWN!
UM... ARE YOU TALKING TO ME?
GAR?
SORRY, EMOTIONS RUN A LITTLE HIGH AROUND HERE.

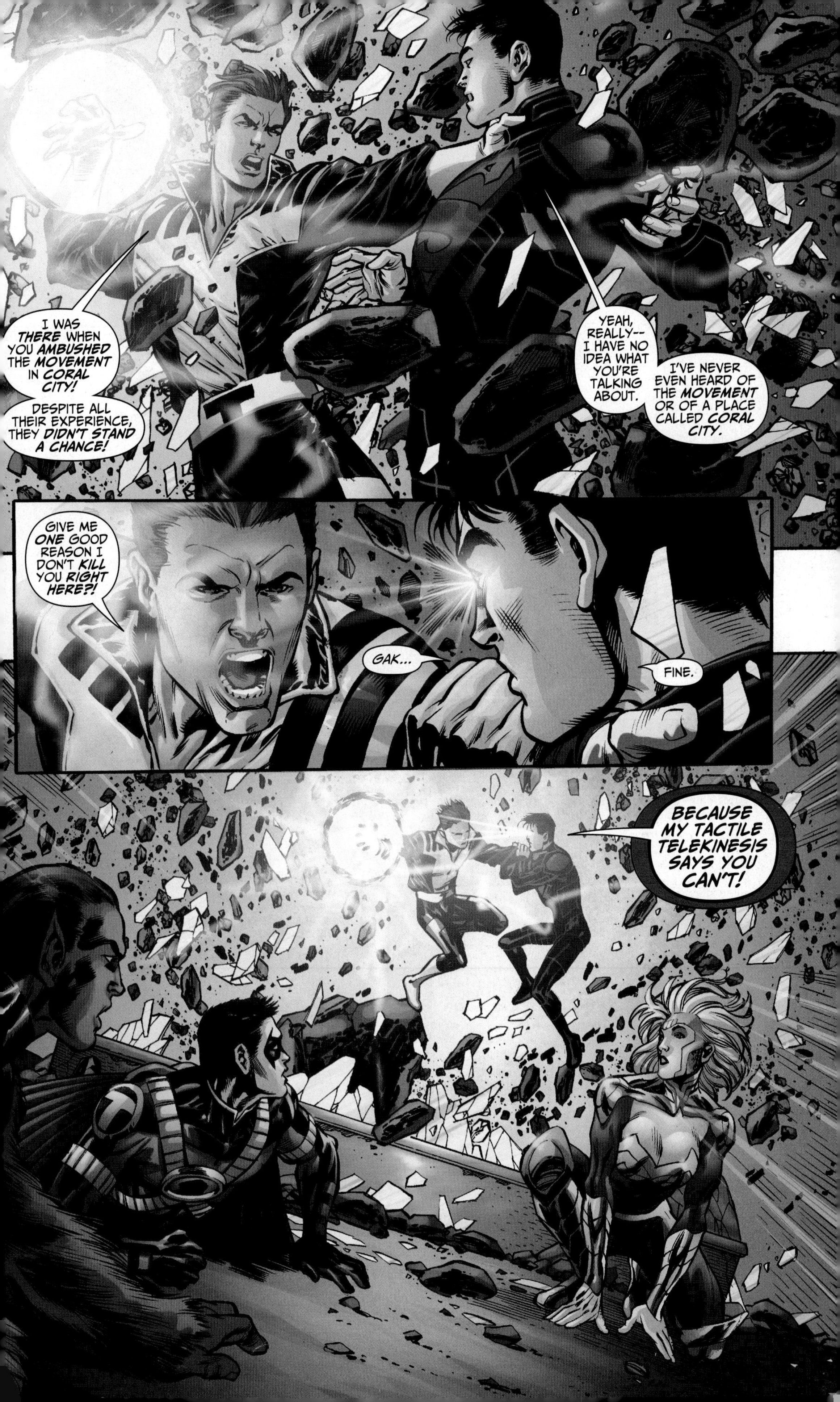
I WAS THERE WHEN YOU AMBUSHED THE MOVEMENT IN CORAL CITY!
DESPITE ALL THEIR EXPERIENCE, THEY DIDN'T STAND A CHANCE!
YEAH, REALLY-- I HAVE NO IDEA WHAT YOU'RE TALKING ABOUT.
I'VE NEVER EVEN HEARD OF THE MOVEMENT OR OF A PLACE CALLED CORAL CITY.
GIVE ME ONE GOOD REASON I DON'T KILL YOU RIGHT HERE?!
GAK...
FINE.
BECAUSE MY TACTILE TELEKINESIS SAYS YOU CAN'T!

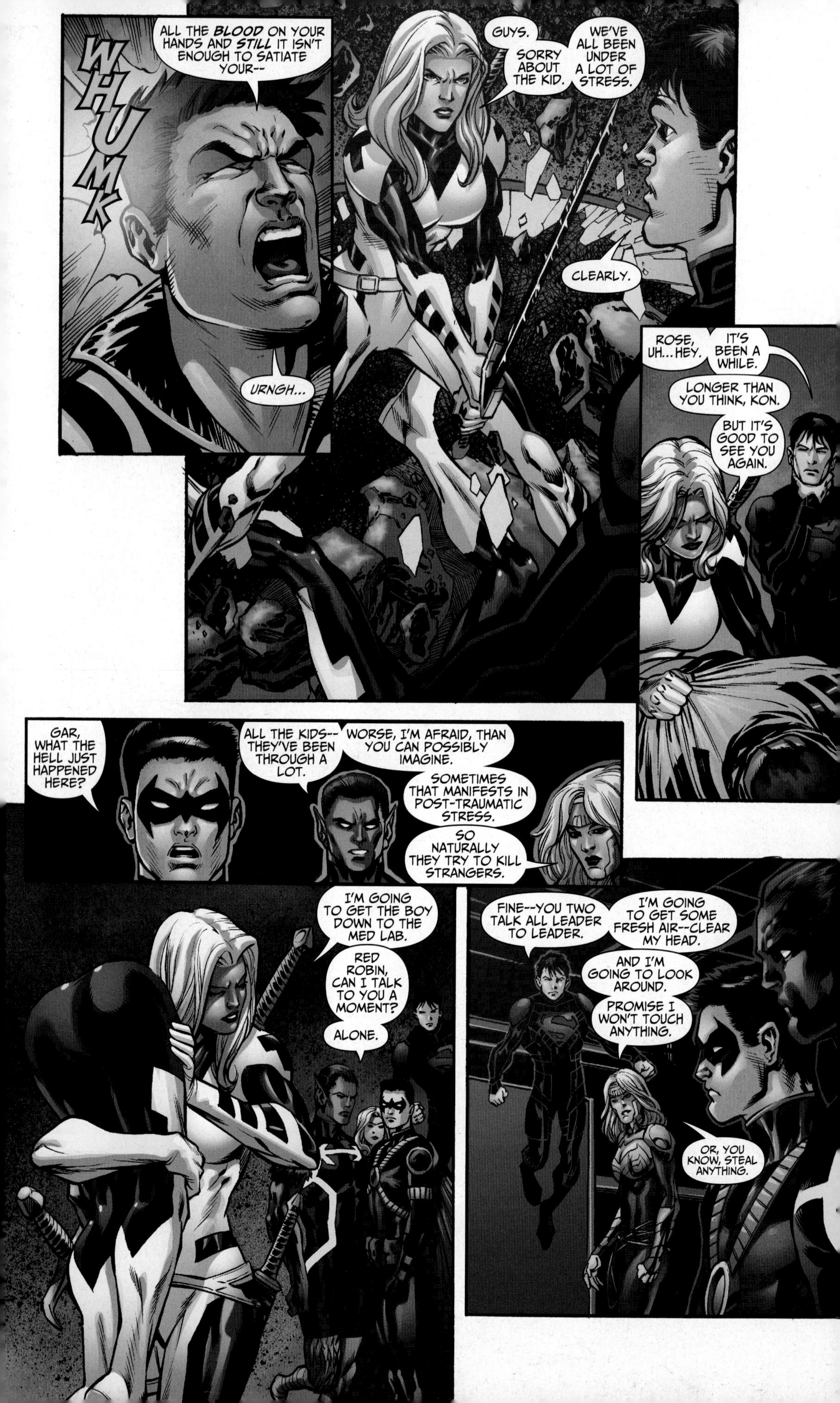
WHUMK
ALL THE *BLOOD* ON YOUR HANDS AND *STILL* IT ISN'T ENOUGH TO SATIATE YOUR--
URNGH...
GUYS.
SORRY ABOUT THE KID.
WE'VE ALL BEEN UNDER A LOT OF STRESS.
CLEARLY.
ROSE, UH...HEY.
IT'S BEEN A WHILE.
LONGER THAN YOU THINK, KON.
BUT IT'S GOOD TO SEE YOU AGAIN.
GAR, WHAT THE HELL JUST HAPPENED HERE?
ALL THE KIDS-- THEY'VE BEEN THROUGH A LOT.
WORSE, I'M AFRAID, THAN YOU CAN POSSIBLY IMAGINE.
SOMETIMES THAT MANIFESTS IN POST-TRAUMATIC STRESS.
SO NATURALLY THEY TRY TO KILL STRANGERS.
I'M GOING TO GET THE BOY DOWN TO THE MED LAB.
RED ROBIN, CAN I TALK TO YOU A MOMENT?
ALONE.
FINE--YOU TWO TALK ALL LEADER TO LEADER.
I'M GOING TO GET SOME FRESH AIR--CLEAR MY HEAD.
AND I'M GOING TO LOOK AROUND.
PROMISE I WON'T TOUCH ANYTHING.
OR, YOU KNOW, STEAL ANYTHING.

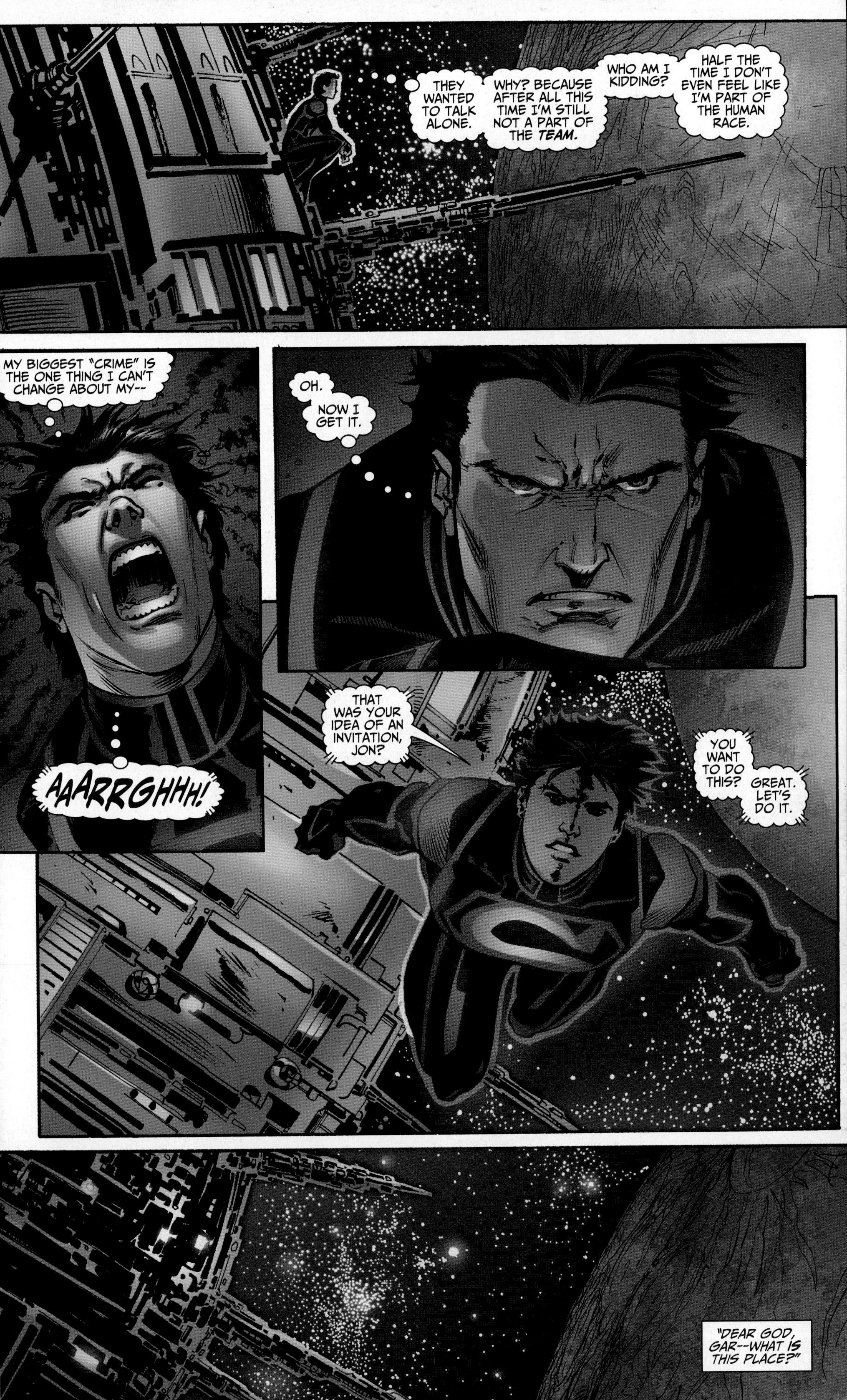
THEY WANTED TO TALK ALONE.
WHY? BECAUSE AFTER ALL THIS TIME I'M STILL NOT A PART OF THE *TEAM.*
WHO AM I KIDDING?
HALF THE TIME I DON'T EVEN FEEL LIKE I'M PART OF THE HUMAN RACE.
MY BIGGEST "CRIME" IS THE ONE THING I CAN'T CHANGE ABOUT MY--
AAARRGHHH!
OH.
NOW I GET IT.
THAT WAS YOUR IDEA OF AN INVITATION, JON?
YOU WANT TO DO THIS?
GREAT. LET'S DO IT.
"DEAR GOD, GAR--WHAT IS THIS PLACE?"

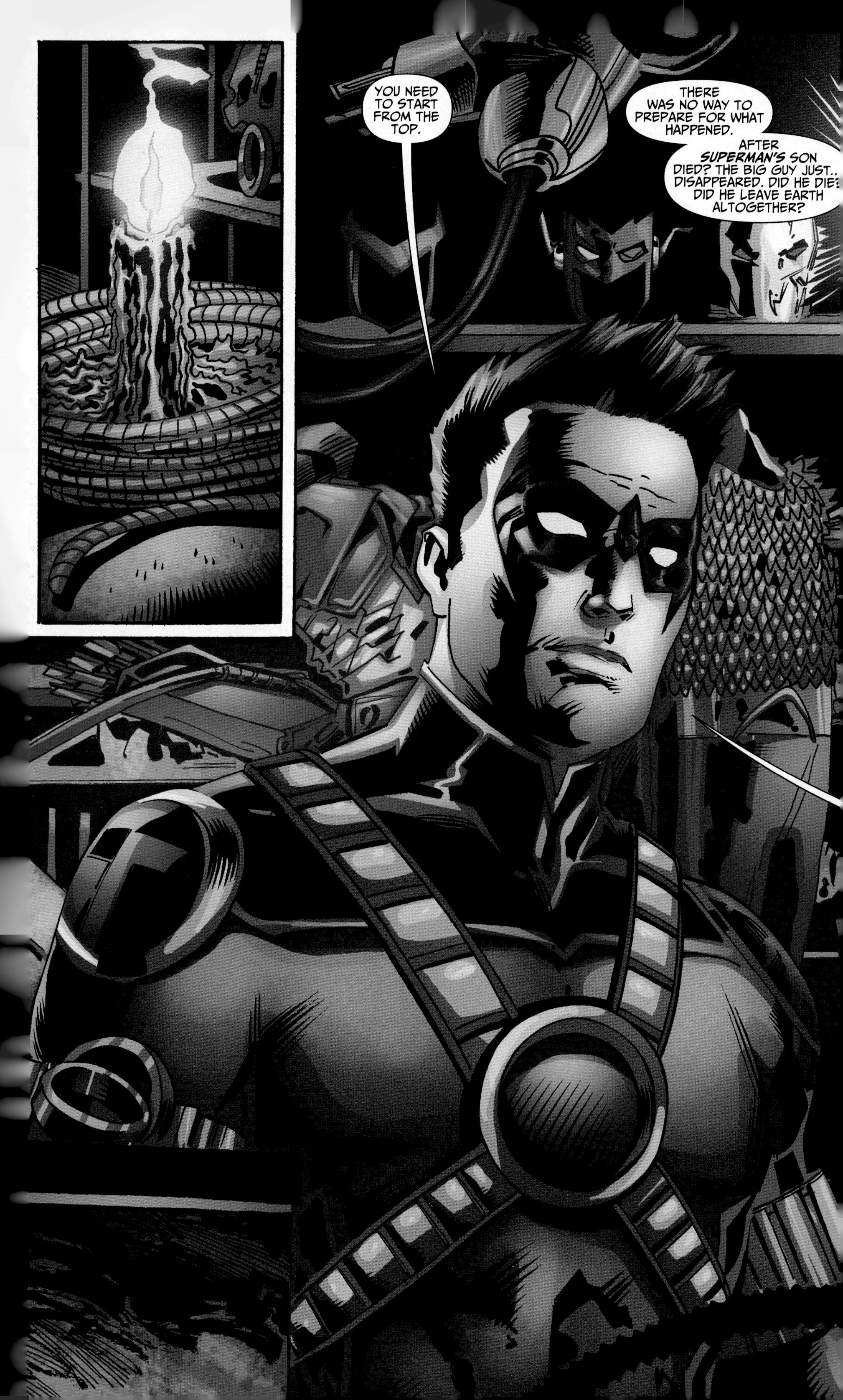
YOU NEED TO START FROM THE TOP.
THERE WAS NO WAY TO PREPARE FOR WHAT HAPPENED.
AFTER *SUPERMAN'S* SON DIED? THE BIG GUY JUST.. DISAPPEARED. DID HE DIE? DID HE LEAVE EARTH ALTOGETHER?

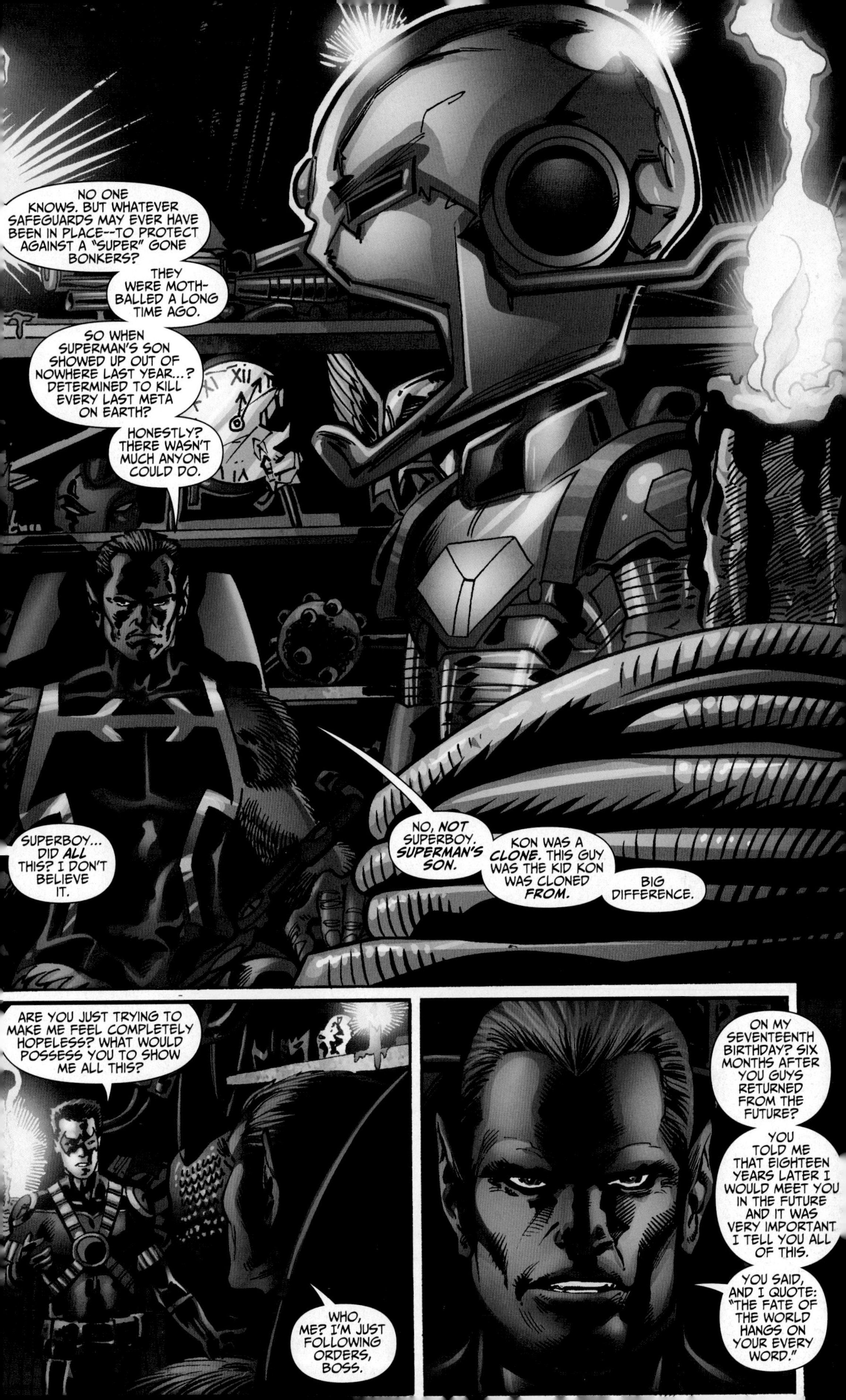
NO ONE KNOWS. BUT WHATEVER SAFEGUARDS MAY EVER HAVE BEEN IN PLACE--TO PROTECT AGAINST A "SUPER" GONE BONKERS?
THEY WERE MOTH-BALLED A LONG TIME AGO.
SO WHEN SUPERMAN'S SON SHOWED UP OUT OF NOWHERE LAST YEAR...? DETERMINED TO KILL EVERY LAST META ON EARTH?
HONESTLY? THERE WASN'T MUCH ANYONE COULD DO.
SUPERBOY... DID ALL THIS? I DON'T BELIEVE IT.
NO, NOT SUPERBOY. SUPERMAN'S SON.
KON WAS A CLONE. THIS GUY WAS THE KID KON WAS CLONED FROM.
BIG DIFFERENCE.
ARE YOU JUST TRYING TO MAKE ME FEEL COMPLETELY HOPELESS? WHAT WOULD POSSESS YOU TO SHOW ME ALL THIS?
WHO, ME? I'M JUST FOLLOWING ORDERS, BOSS.
ON MY SEVENTEENTH BIRTHDAY? SIX MONTHS AFTER YOU GUYS RETURNED FROM THE FUTURE?
YOU TOLD ME THAT EIGHTEEN YEARS LATER I WOULD MEET YOU IN THE FUTURE AND IT WAS VERY IMPORTANT I TELL YOU ALL OF THIS.
YOU SAID, AND I QUOTE: "THE FATE OF THE WORLD HANGS ON YOUR EVERY WORD."

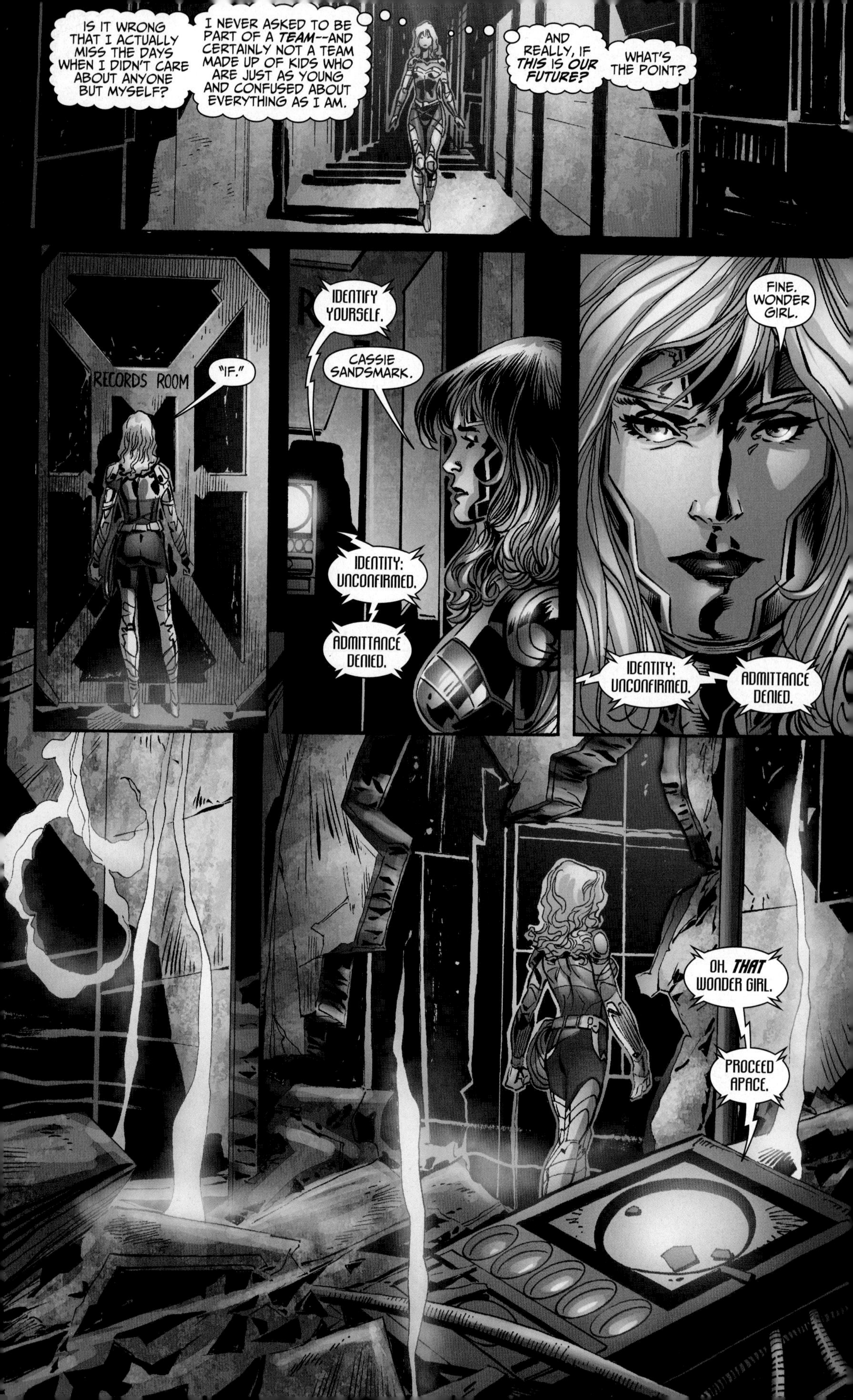
IS IT WRONG THAT I ACTUALLY MISS THE DAYS WHEN I DIDN'T CARE ABOUT ANYONE BUT MYSELF?
I NEVER ASKED TO BE PART OF A TEAM--AND CERTAINLY NOT A TEAM MADE UP OF KIDS WHO ARE JUST AS YOUNG AND CONFUSED ABOUT EVERYTHING AS I AM.
AND REALLY, IF THIS IS OUR FUTURE?
WHAT'S THE POINT?
RECORDS ROOM
"IF."
IDENTIFY YOURSELF.
CASSIE SANDSMARK.
IDENTITY: UNCONFIRMED.
ADMITTANCE DENIED.
FINE. WONDER GIRL.
IDENTITY: UNCONFIRMED.
ADMITTANCE DENIED.
OH. THAT WONDER GIRL.
PROCEED APACE.

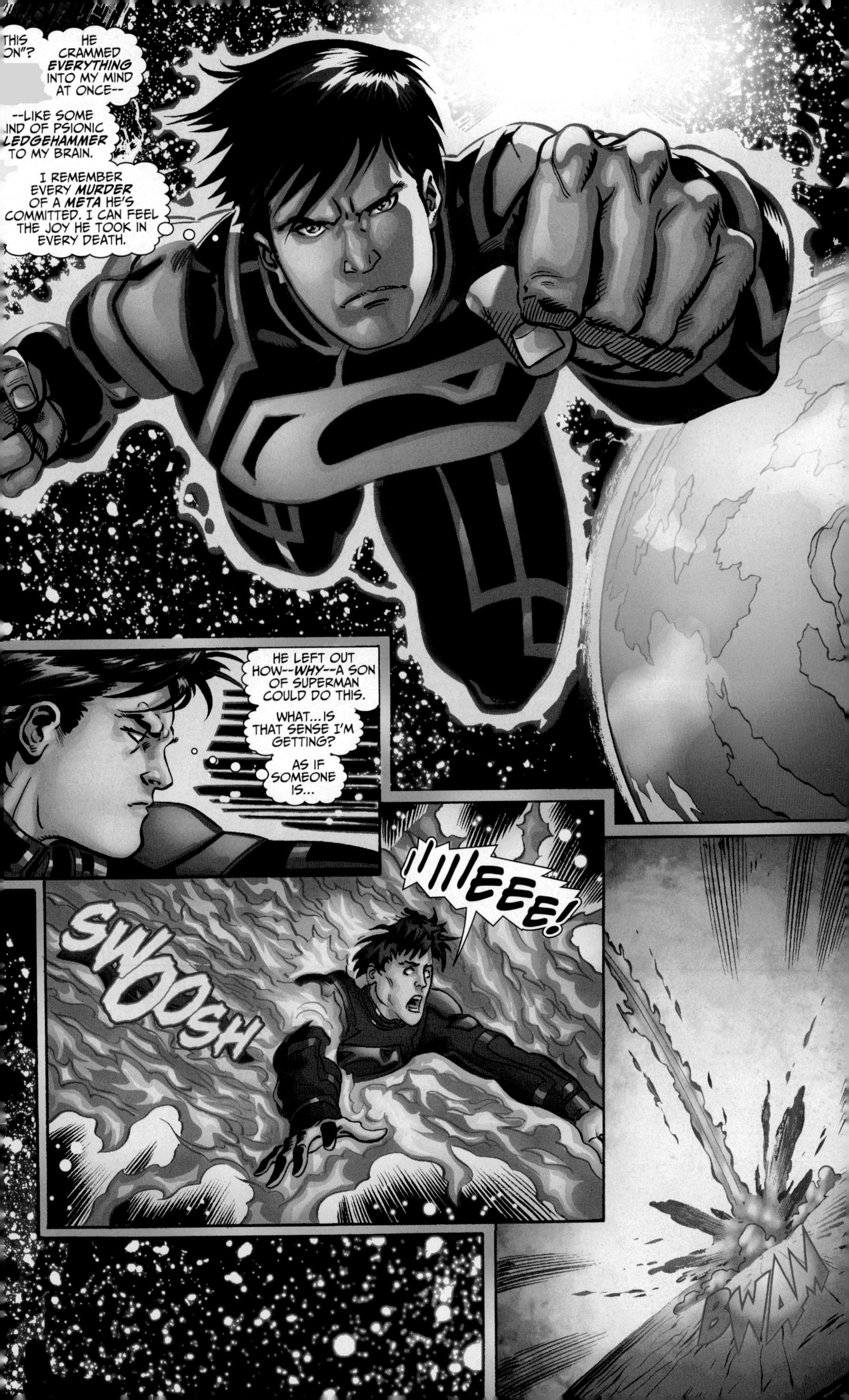

THIS
ON"?
HE CRAMMED EVERYTHING INTO MY MIND AT ONCE--
--LIKE SOME
IND OF PSIONIC
LEDGEHAMMER
TO MY BRAIN.
I REMEMBER EVERY MURDER OF A META HE'S COMMITTED. I CAN FEEL THE JOY HE TOOK IN EVERY DEATH.
HE LEFT OUT HOW--WHY--A SON OF SUPERMAN COULD DO THIS.
WHAT...IS THAT SENSE I'M GETTING?
AS IF SOMEONE IS...
IIIIEEEE!
SWOOSH
BWAM

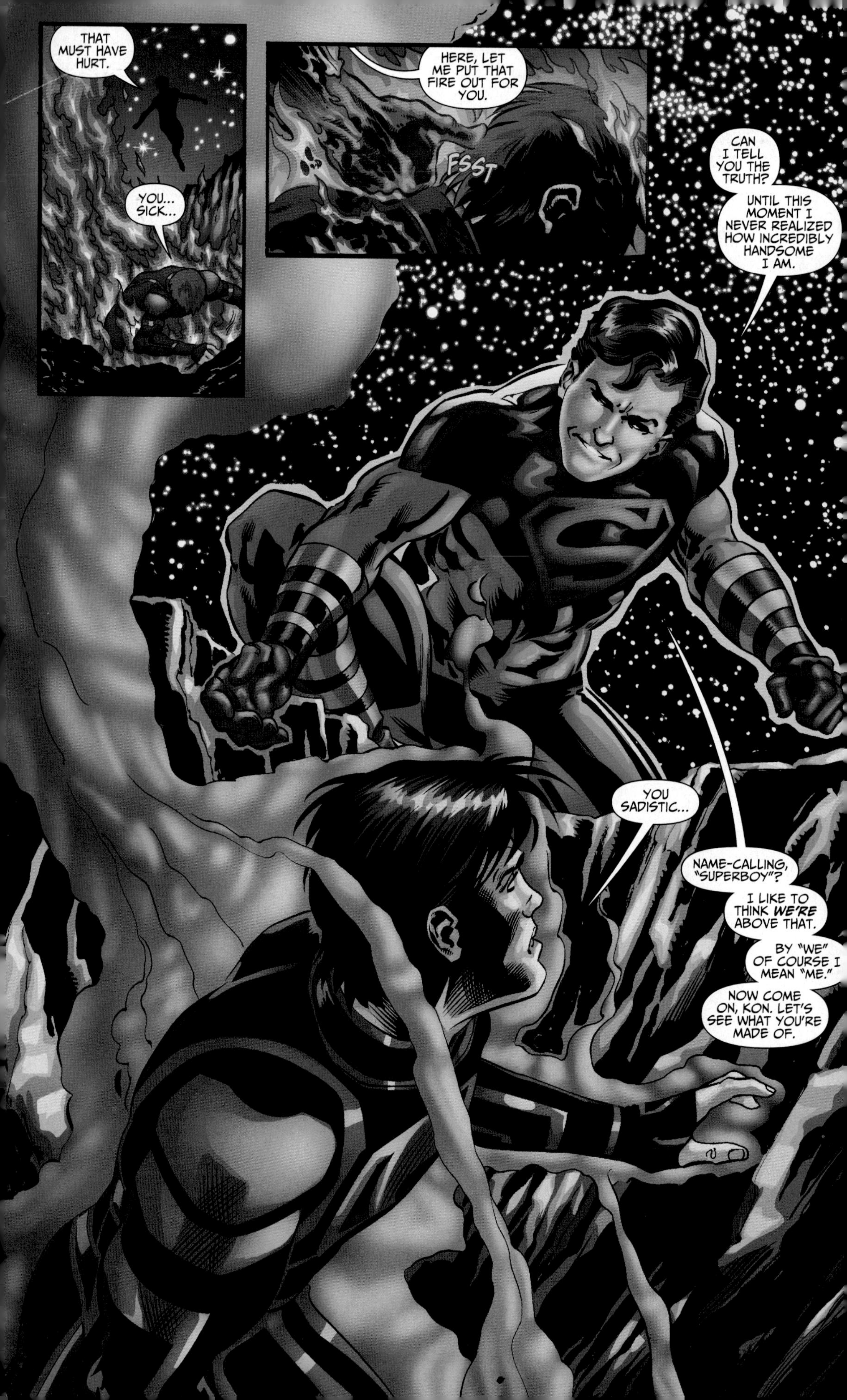
THAT MUST HAVE HURT.
YOU... SICK...
HERE, LET ME PUT THAT FIRE OUT FOR YOU.
FSST
CAN I TELL YOU THE TRUTH?
UNTIL THIS MOMENT I NEVER REALIZED HOW INCREDIBLY HANDSOME I AM.
YOU SADISTIC...
NAME-CALLING, "SUPERBOY"?
I LIKE TO THINK *WE'RE* ABOVE THAT.
BY "WE" OF COURSE I MEAN "ME."
NOW COME ON, KON. LET'S SEE WHAT YOU'RE MADE OF.

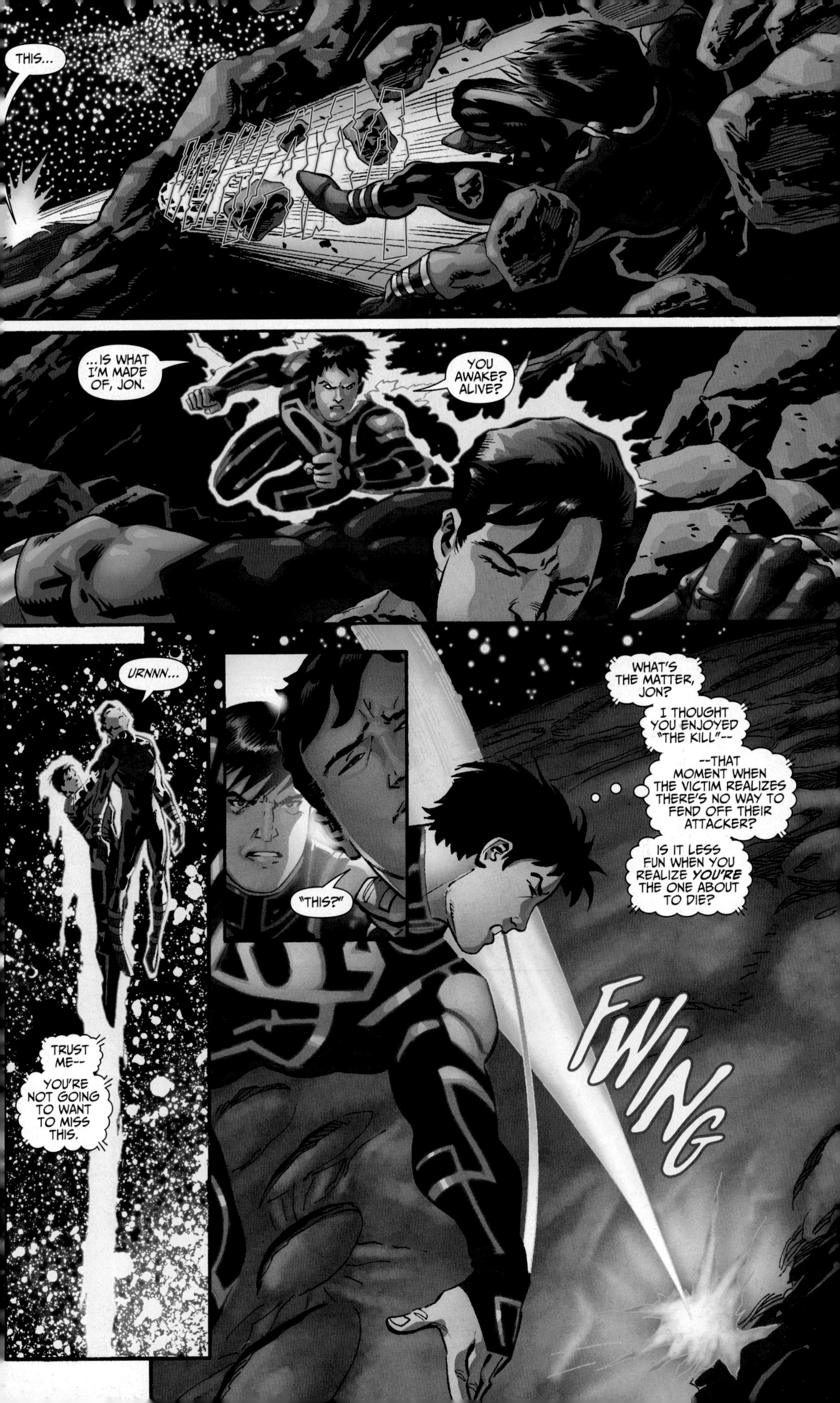

THIS...
...IS WHAT I'M MADE OF, JON.
YOU AWAKE? ALIVE?
URNNN...
"THIS?"
WHAT'S THE MATTER, JON?
I THOUGHT YOU ENJOYED "THE KILL"--
--THAT MOMENT WHEN THE VICTIM REALIZES THERE'S NO WAY TO FEND OFF THEIR ATTACKER?
IS IT LESS FUN WHEN YOU REALIZE YOU'RE THE ONE ABOUT TO DIE?
TRUST ME--
YOU'RE NOT GOING TO WANT TO MISS THIS.
FWING

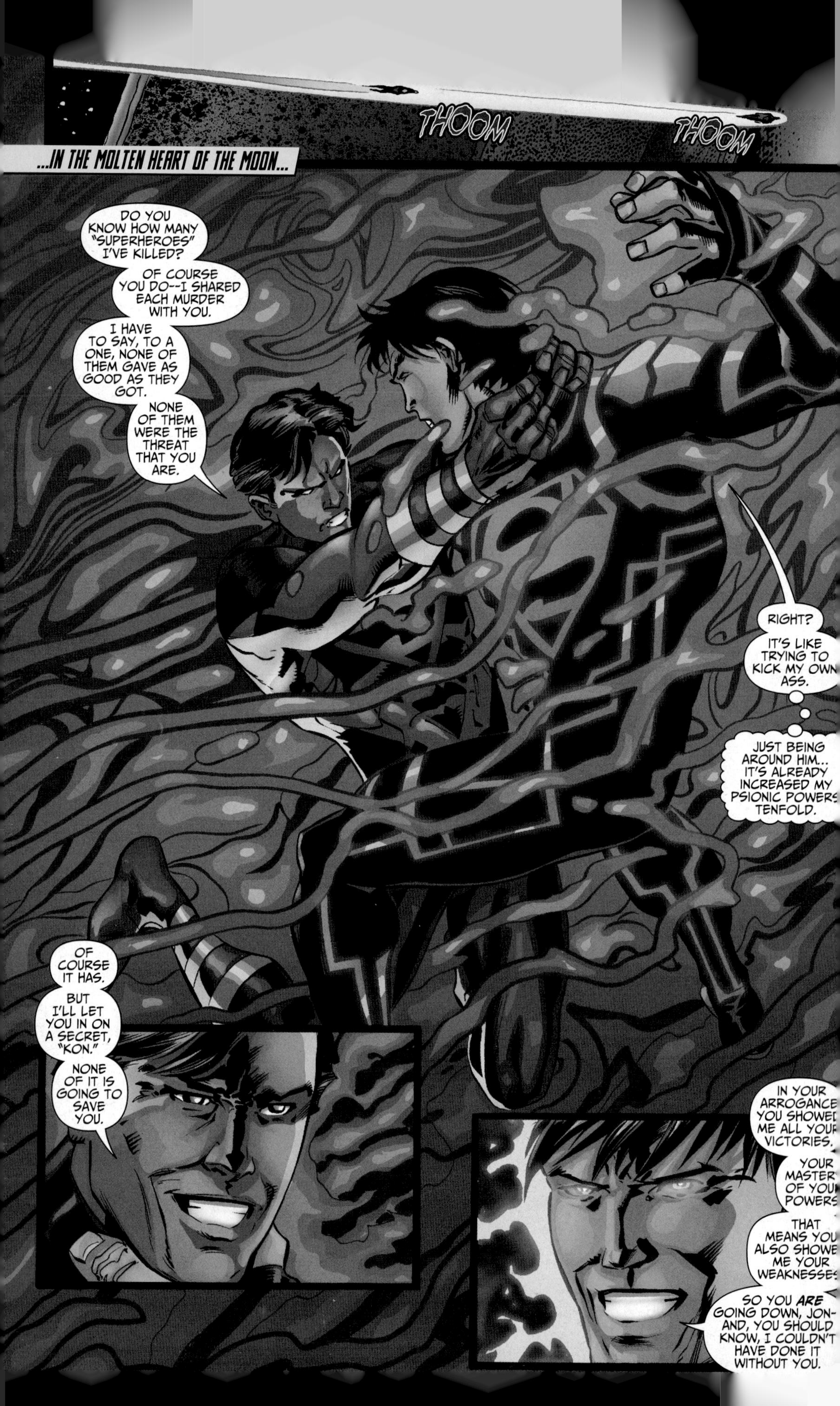
THOOM
THOOM
...IN THE MOLTEN HEART OF THE MOON...
DO YOU KNOW HOW MANY "SUPERHEROES" I'VE KILLED?
OF COURSE YOU DO--I SHARED EACH MURDER WITH YOU.
I HAVE TO SAY, TO A ONE, NONE OF THEM GAVE AS GOOD AS THEY GOT.
NONE OF THEM WERE THE THREAT THAT YOU ARE.
RIGHT?
IT'S LIKE TRYING TO KICK MY OWN ASS.
JUST BEING AROUND HIM... IT'S ALREADY INCREASED MY PSIONIC POWERS TENFOLD.
OF COURSE IT HAS.
BUT I'LL LET YOU IN ON A SECRET, "KON."
NONE OF IT IS GOING TO SAVE YOU.
IN YOUR ARROGANCE YOU SHOWED ME ALL YOUR VICTORIES.
YOUR MASTERY OF YOUR POWERS.
THAT MEANS YOU ALSO SHOWED ME YOUR WEAKNESSES.
SO YOU ARE GOING DOWN, JON-AND, YOU SHOULD KNOW, I COULDN'T HAVE DONE IT WITHOUT YOU.

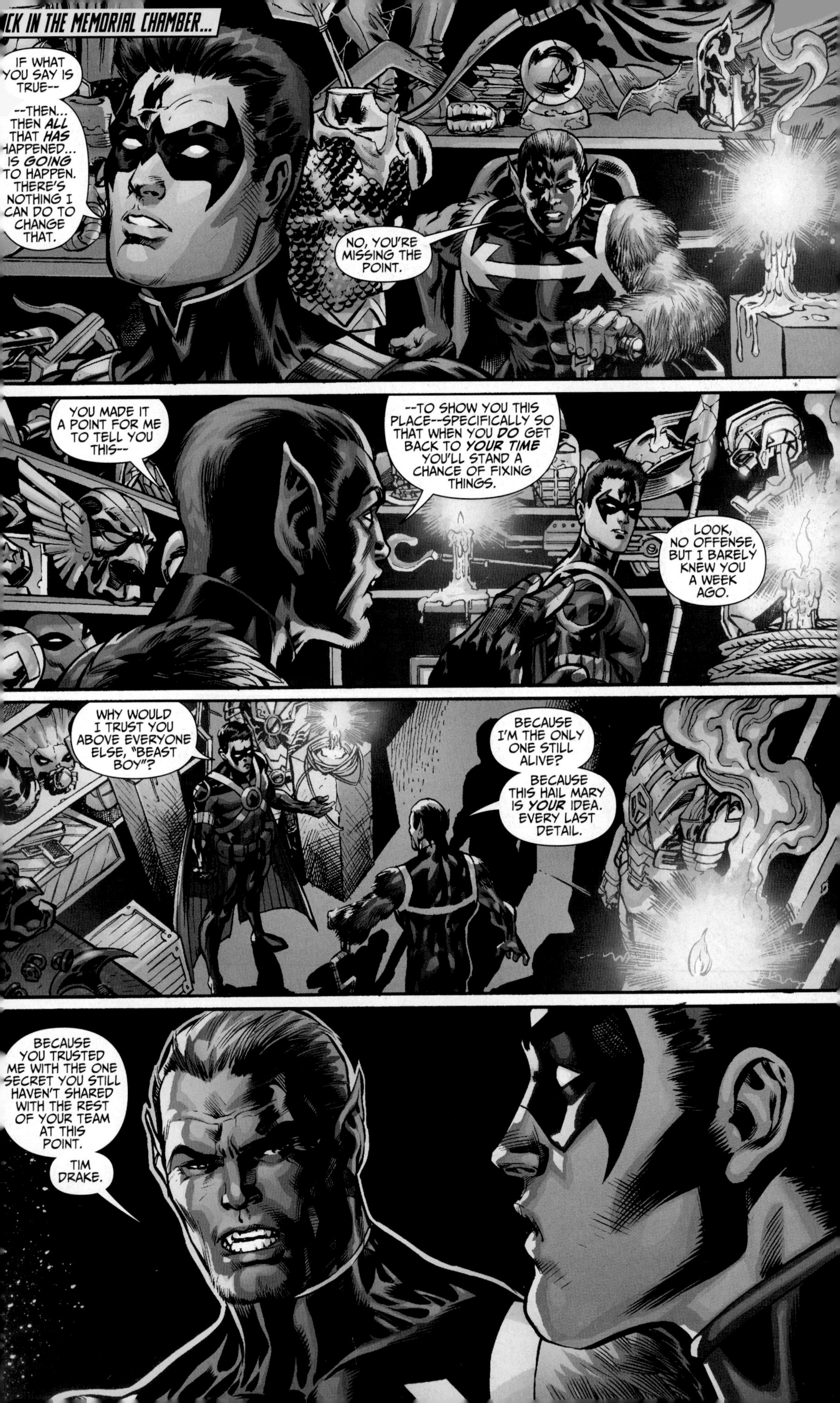

CK IN THE MEMORIAL CHAMBER...
IF WHAT YOU SAY IS TRUE--
--THEN... THEN ALL THAT HAS HAPPENED... IS GOING TO HAPPEN. THERE'S NOTHING I CAN DO TO CHANGE THAT.
NO, YOU'RE MISSING THE POINT.
YOU MADE IT A POINT FOR ME TO TELL YOU THIS--
--TO SHOW YOU THIS PLACE--SPECIFICALLY SO THAT WHEN YOU DO GET BACK TO YOUR TIME YOU'LL STAND A CHANCE OF FIXING THINGS.
LOOK, NO OFFENSE, BUT I BARELY KNEW YOU A WEEK AGO.
WHY WOULD I TRUST YOU ABOVE EVERYONE ELSE, "BEAST BOY"?
BECAUSE I'M THE ONLY ONE STILL ALIVE?
BECAUSE THIS HAIL MARY IS YOUR IDEA. EVERY LAST DETAIL.
BECAUSE YOU TRUSTED ME WITH THE ONE SECRET YOU STILL HAVEN'T SHARED WITH THE REST OF YOUR TEAM AT THIS POINT.
TIM DRAKE.

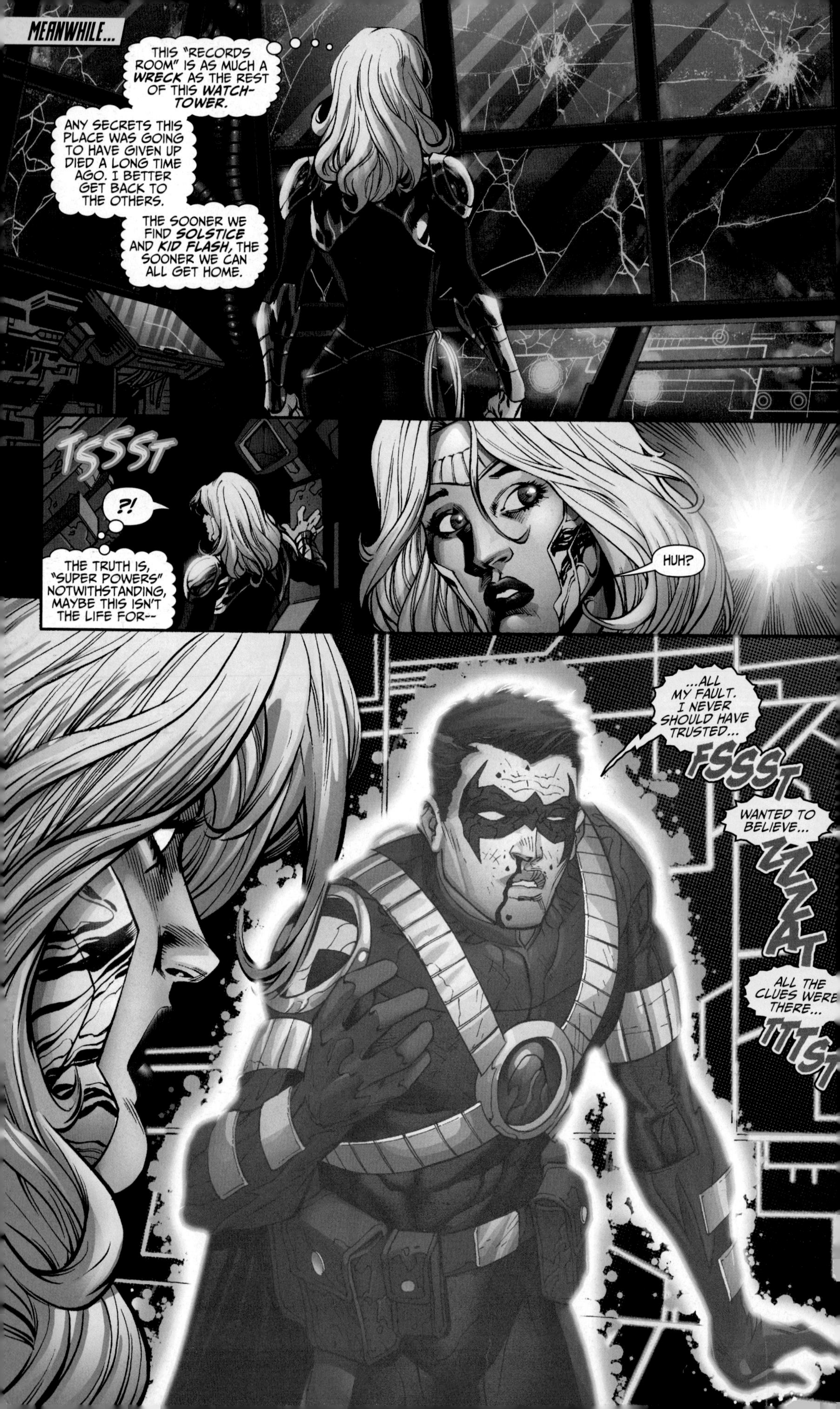
MEANWHILE...
THIS "RECORDS ROOM" IS AS MUCH A WRECK AS THE REST OF THIS WATCH-TOWER.
ANY SECRETS THIS PLACE WAS GOING TO HAVE GIVEN UP DIED A LONG TIME AGO. I BETTER GET BACK TO THE OTHERS.
THE SOONER WE FIND SOLSTICE AND KID FLASH, THE SOONER WE CAN ALL GET HOME.
TSSST
?!
THE TRUTH IS, "SUPER POWERS" NOTWITHSTANDING, MAYBE THIS ISN'T THE LIFE FOR--
HUH?
...ALL MY FAULT. I NEVER SHOULD HAVE TRUSTED...
FSSST
WANTED TO BELIEVE...
ZZZAT
ALL THE CLUES WERE THERE...
TTTST

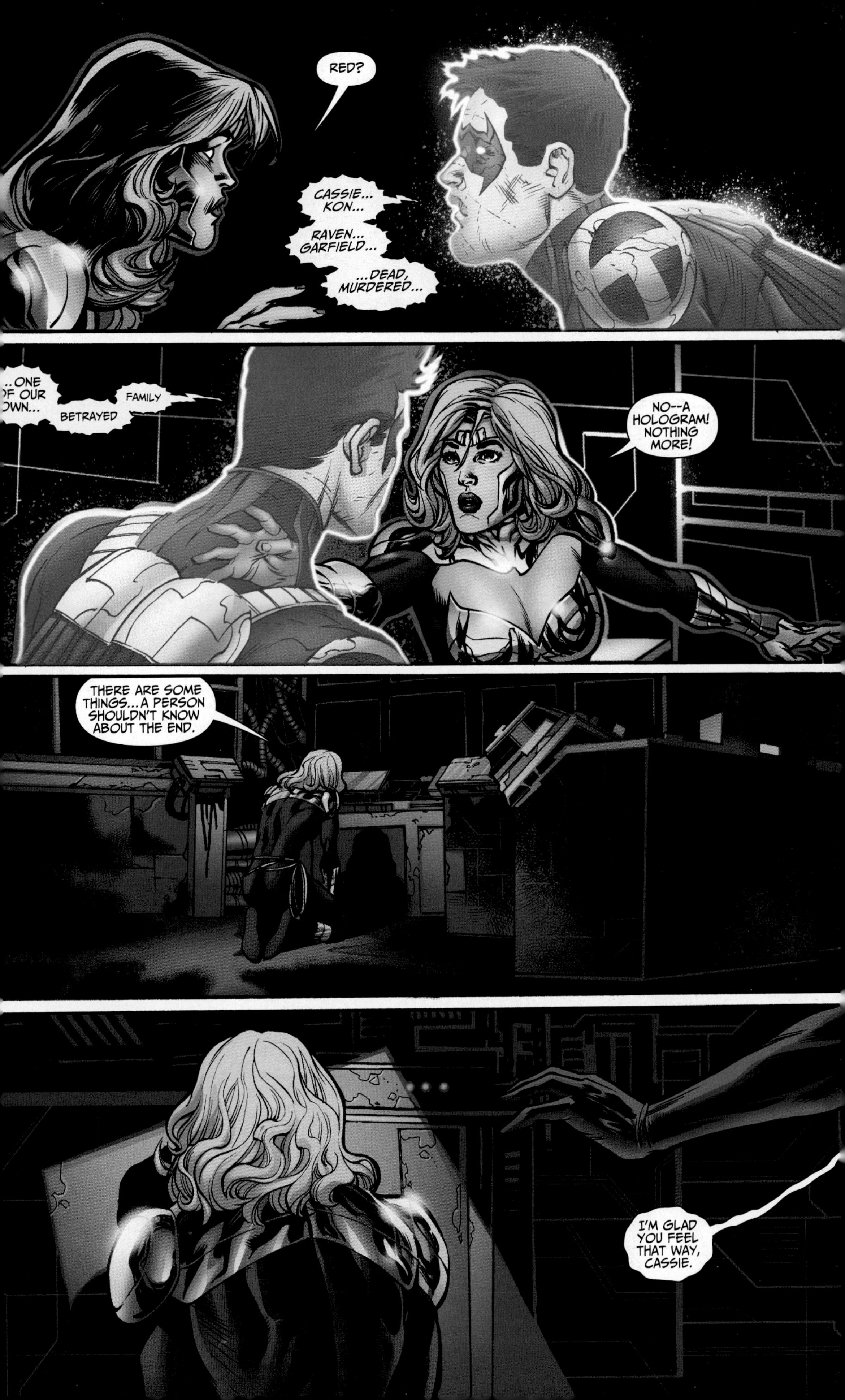
RED?
CASSIE... KON...
RAVEN... GARFIELD...
...DEAD, MURDERED...
..ONE OF OUR OWN...
BETRAYED
FAMILY
NO--A HOLOGRAM! NOTHING MORE!
THERE ARE SOME THINGS...A PERSON SHOULDN'T KNOW ABOUT THE END.
I'M GLAD YOU FEEL THAT WAY, CASSIE.

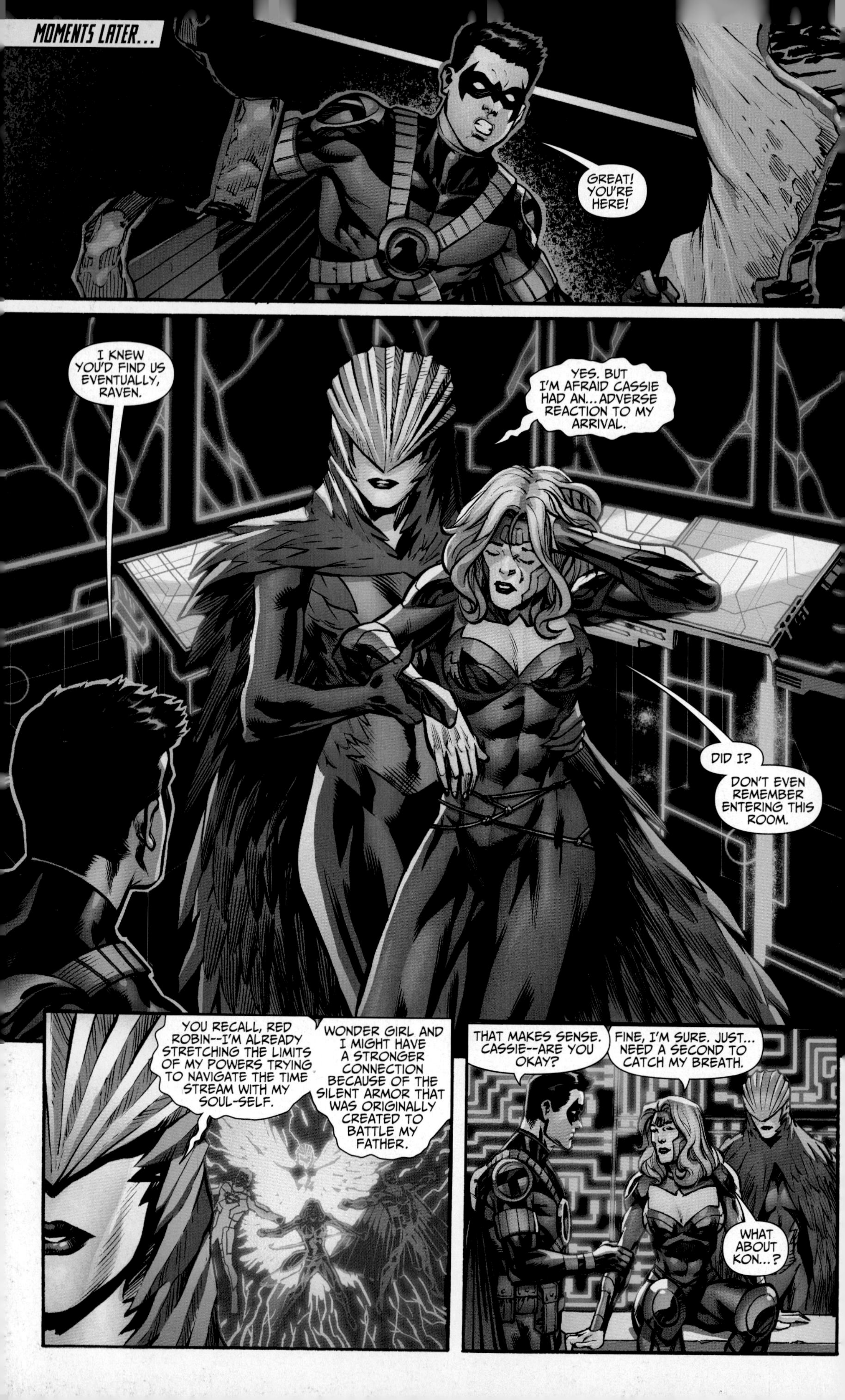
MOMENTS LATER...
GREAT! YOU'RE HERE!
I KNEW YOU'D FIND US EVENTUALLY, RAVEN.
YES. BUT I'M AFRAID CASSIE HAD AN...ADVERSE REACTION TO MY ARRIVAL.
DID I?
DON'T EVEN REMEMBER ENTERING THIS ROOM.
YOU RECALL, RED ROBIN--I'M ALREADY STRETCHING THE LIMITS OF MY POWERS TRYING TO NAVIGATE THE TIME STREAM WITH MY SOUL-SELF.
WONDER GIRL AND I MIGHT HAVE A STRONGER CONNECTION BECAUSE OF THE SILENT ARMOR THAT WAS ORIGINALLY CREATED TO BATTLE MY FATHER.
THAT MAKES SENSE. CASSIE--ARE YOU OKAY?
FINE, I'M SURE. JUST... NEED A SECOND TO CATCH MY BREATH.
WHAT ABOUT KON...?

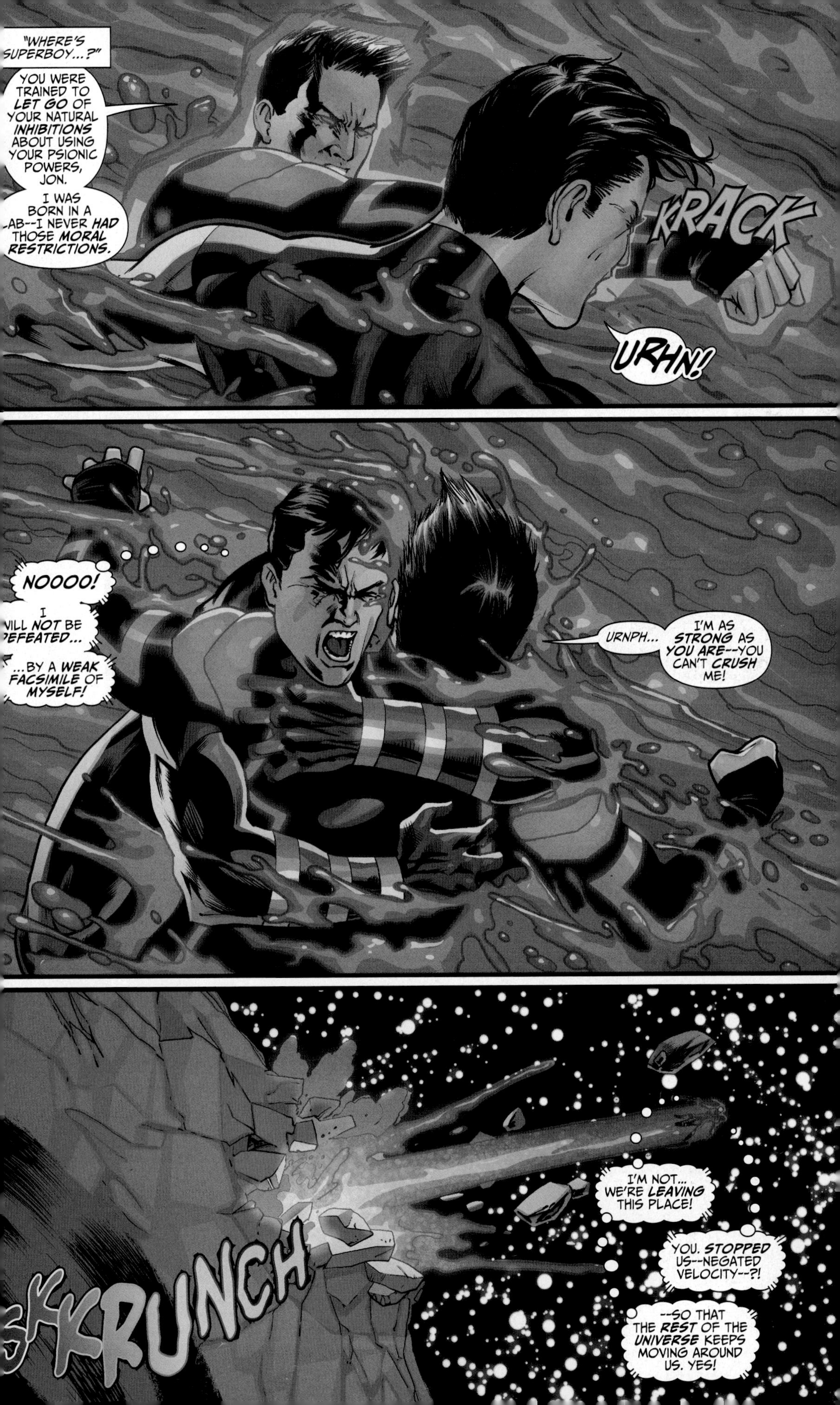
"WHERE'S SUPERBOY...?"
YOU WERE TRAINED TO LET GO OF YOUR NATURAL INHIBITIONS ABOUT USING YOUR PSIONIC POWERS, JON.
I WAS BORN IN A LAB--I NEVER HAD THOSE MORAL RESTRICTIONS.
KRACK
URHN!
NOOOO!
I WILL NOT BE DEFEATED...
...BY A WEAK FACSIMILE OF MYSELF!
URNPH...
I'M AS STRONG AS YOU ARE--YOU CAN'T CRUSH ME!
SKKRUNCH
I'M NOT... WE'RE LEAVING THIS PLACE!
YOU. STOPPED US--NEGATED VELOCITY--?!
--SO THAT THE REST OF THE UNIVERSE KEEPS MOVING AROUND US. YES!

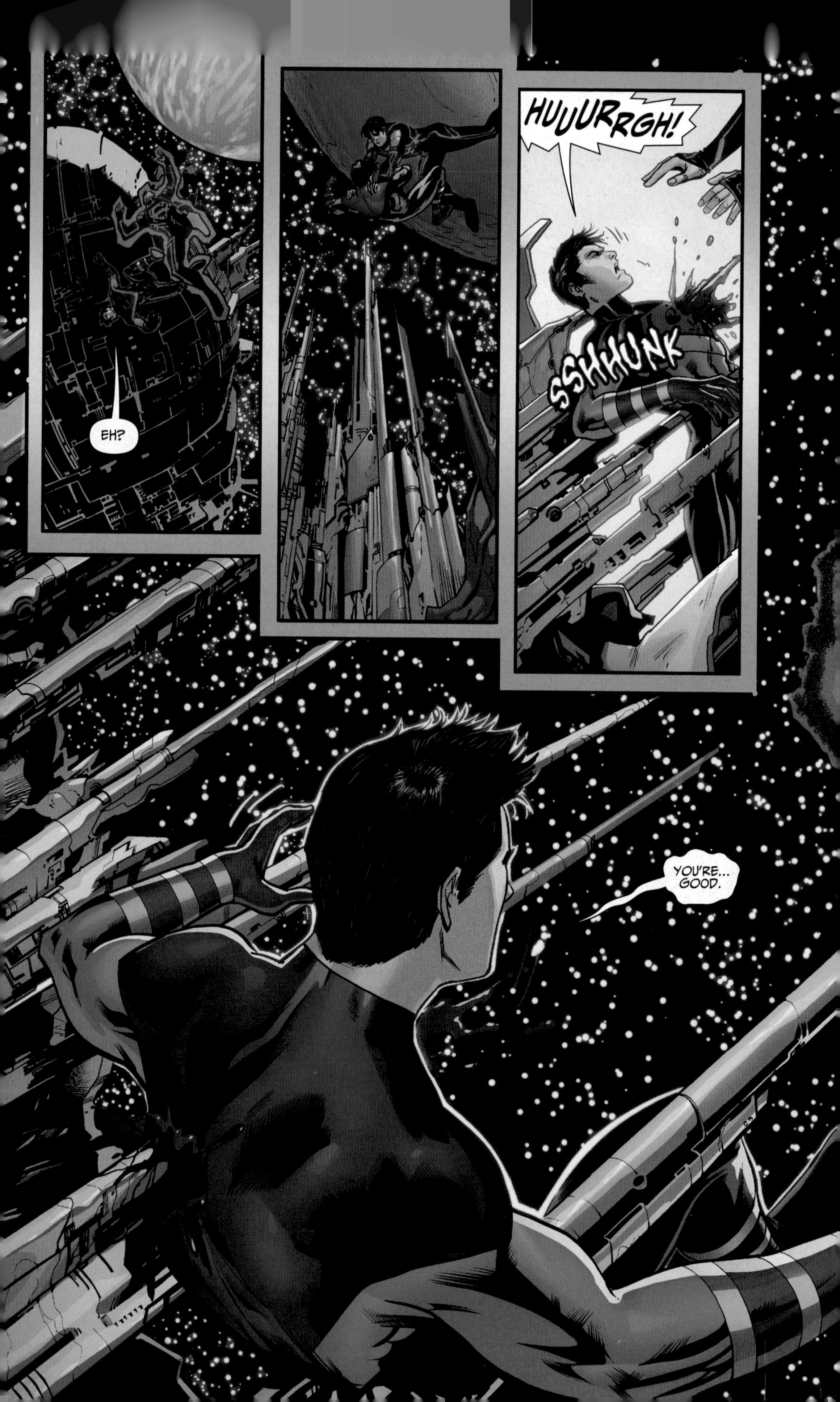
EH?
HUUURRGH!
SSHHUNK
YOU'RE... GOOD.

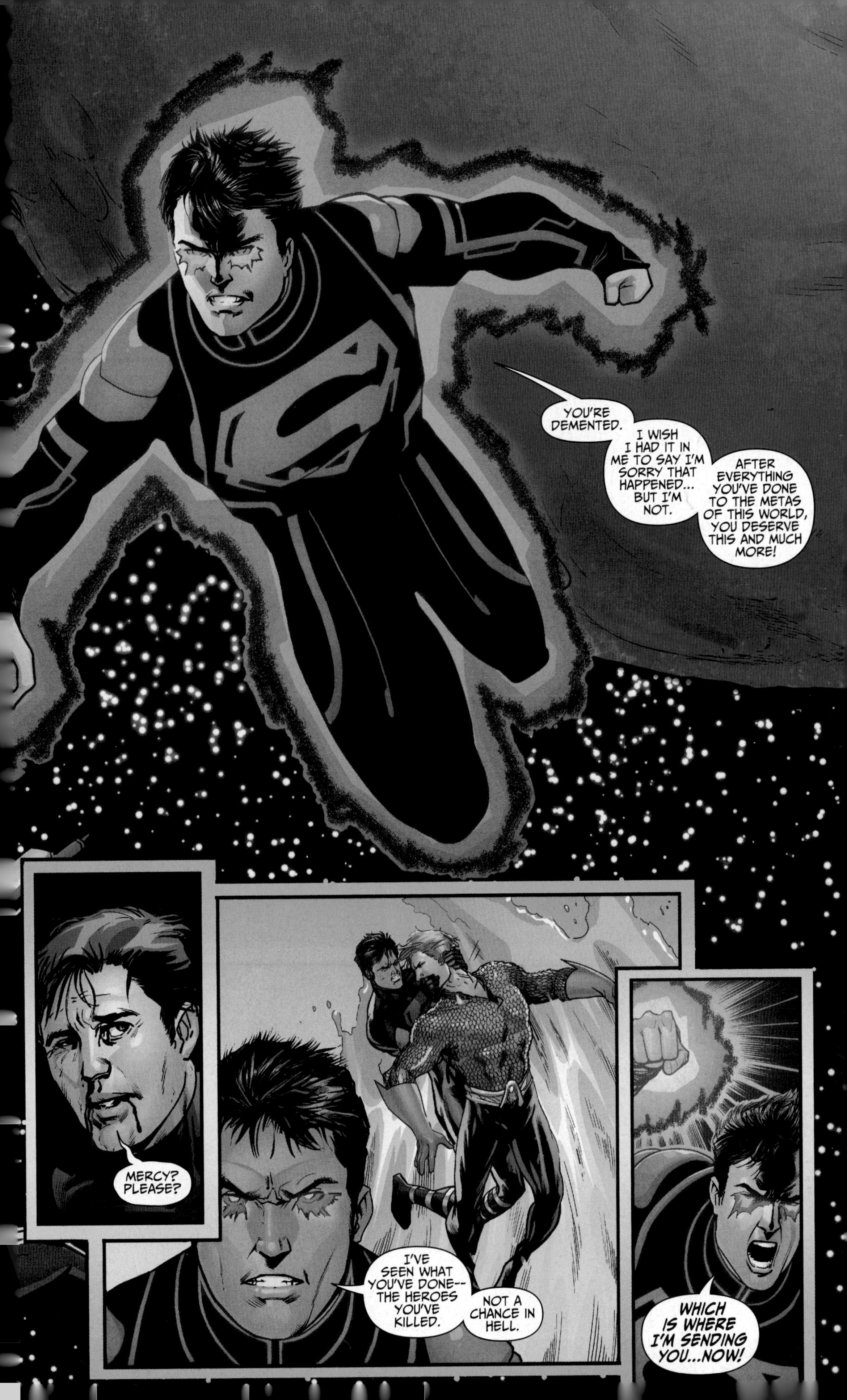
YOU'RE DEMENTED.
I WISH I HAD IT IN ME TO SAY I'M SORRY THAT HAPPENED... BUT I'M NOT.
AFTER EVERYTHING YOU'VE DONE TO THE METAS OF THIS WORLD, YOU DESERVE THIS AND MUCH MORE!
MERCY? PLEASE?
I'VE SEEN WHAT YOU'VE DONE-- THE HEROES YOU'VE KILLED.
NOT A CHANCE IN HELL.
WHICH IS WHERE I'M SENDING YOU...NOW!

WHA--?!

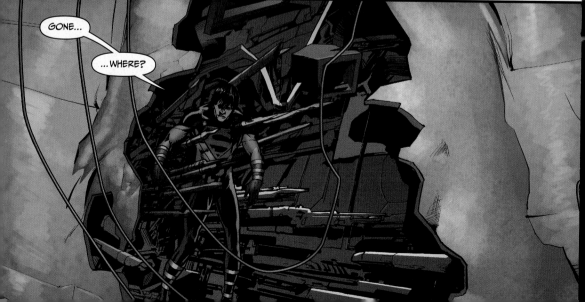

GONE...

...WHERE?

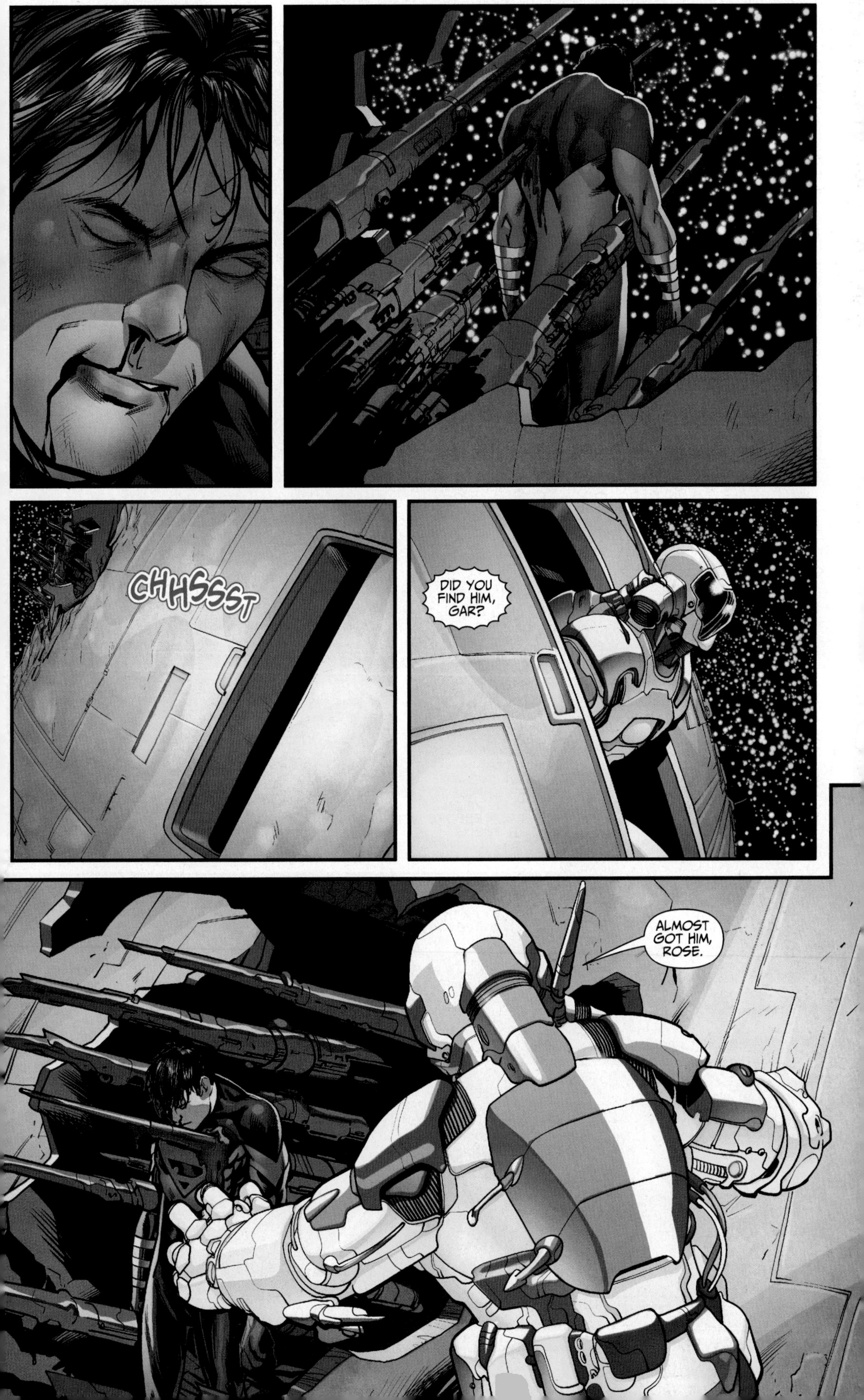
CHHSSST
DID YOU FIND HIM, GAR?
ALMOST GOT HIM, ROSE.

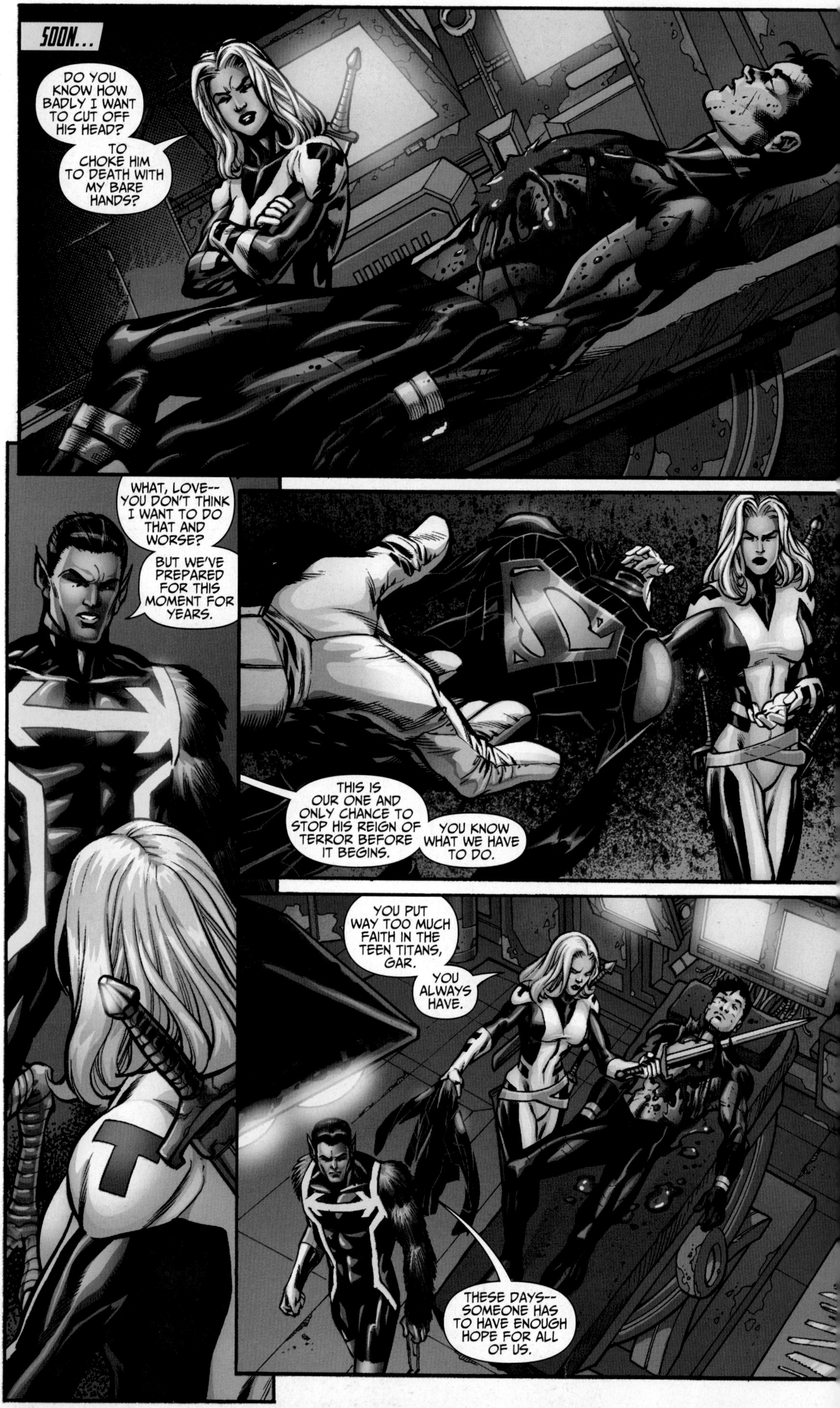
SOON...
DO YOU KNOW HOW BADLY I WANT TO CUT OFF HIS HEAD?
TO CHOKE HIM TO DEATH WITH MY BARE HANDS?
WHAT, LOVE-- YOU DON'T THINK I WANT TO DO THAT AND WORSE?
BUT WE'VE PREPARED FOR THIS MOMENT FOR YEARS.
THIS IS OUR ONE AND ONLY CHANCE TO STOP HIS REIGN OF TERROR BEFORE IT BEGINS.
YOU KNOW WHAT WE HAVE TO DO.
YOU PUT WAY TOO MUCH FAITH IN THE TEEN TITANS, GAR.
YOU ALWAYS HAVE.
THESE DAYS-- SOMEONE HAS TO HAVE ENOUGH HOPE FOR ALL OF US.

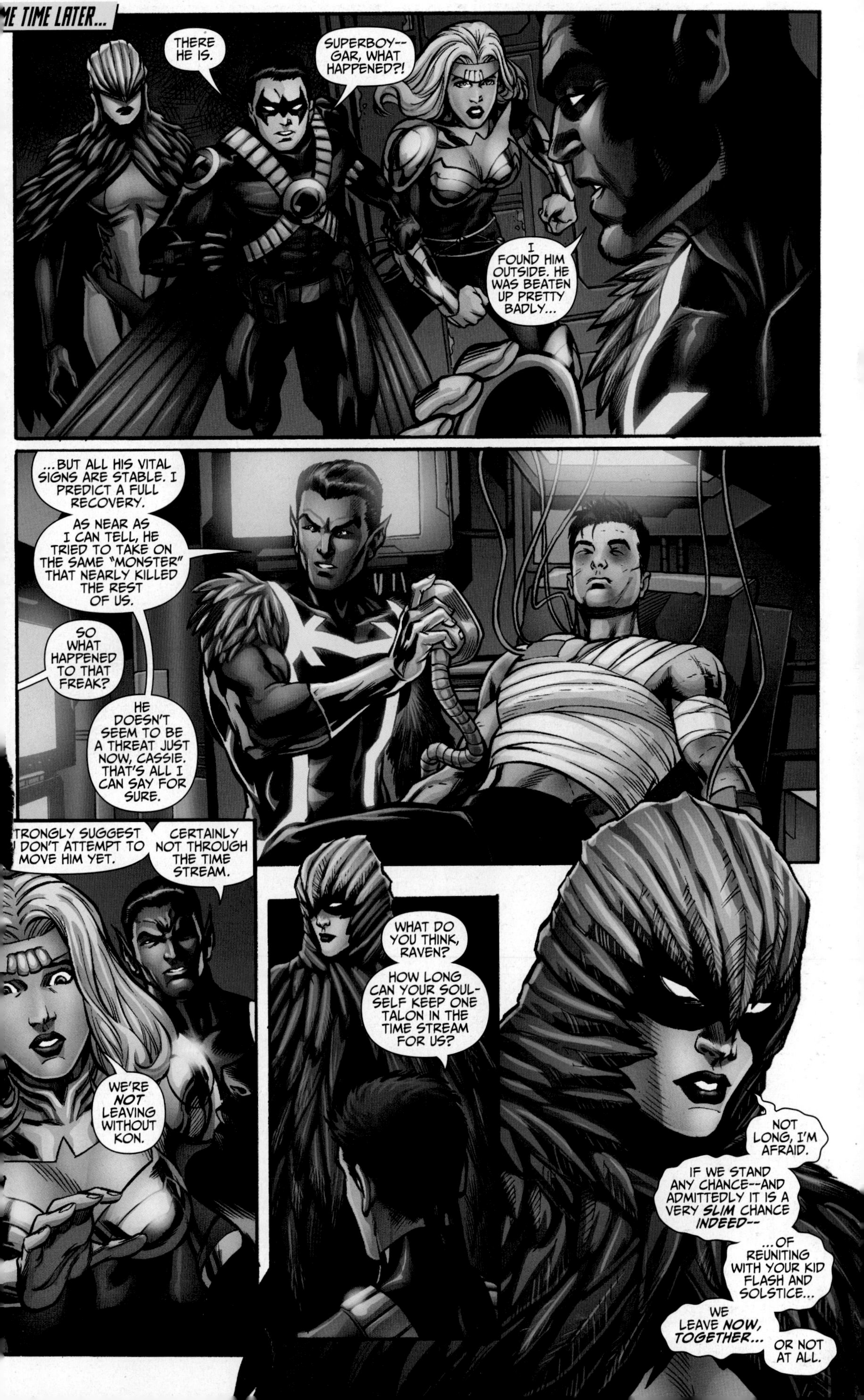
ME TIME LATER...
THERE HE IS.
SUPERBOY-- GAR, WHAT HAPPENED?!
I FOUND HIM OUTSIDE. HE WAS BEATEN UP PRETTY BADLY...
...BUT ALL HIS VITAL SIGNS ARE STABLE. I PREDICT A FULL RECOVERY.
AS NEAR AS I CAN TELL, HE TRIED TO TAKE ON THE SAME "MONSTER" THAT NEARLY KILLED THE REST OF US.
SO WHAT HAPPENED TO THAT FREAK?
HE DOESN'T SEEM TO BE A THREAT JUST NOW, CASSIE. THAT'S ALL I CAN SAY FOR SURE.
TRONGLY SUGGEST DON'T ATTEMPT TO MOVE HIM YET.
CERTAINLY NOT THROUGH THE TIME STREAM.
WE'RE NOT LEAVING WITHOUT KON.
WHAT DO YOU THINK, RAVEN?
HOW LONG CAN YOUR SOUL-SELF KEEP ONE TALON IN THE TIME STREAM FOR US?
NOT LONG, I'M AFRAID.
IF WE STAND ANY CHANCE--AND ADMITTEDLY IT IS A VERY SLIM CHANCE INDEED--
...OF REUNITING WITH YOUR KID FLASH AND SOLSTICE...
WE LEAVE NOW, TOGETHER...
OR NOT AT ALL.

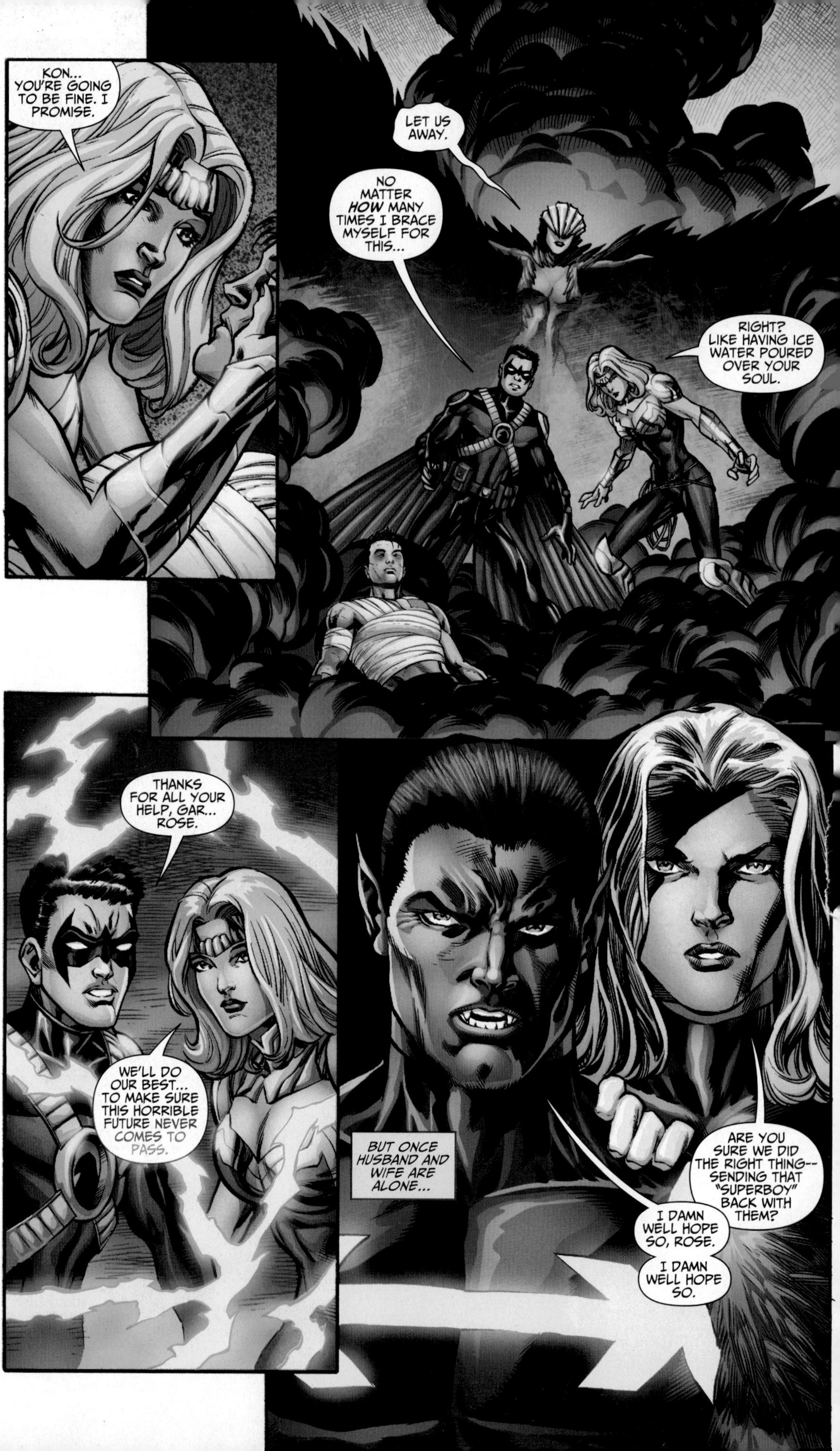

KON... YOU'RE GOING TO BE FINE. I PROMISE.
LET US AWAY.
NO MATTER *HOW* MANY TIMES I BRACE MYSELF FOR THIS...
RIGHT? LIKE HAVING ICE WATER POURED OVER YOUR SOUL.
THANKS FOR ALL YOUR HELP, GAR... ROSE.
WE'LL DO OUR BEST... TO MAKE SURE THIS HORRIBLE FUTURE NEVER COMES TO PASS.
BUT ONCE HUSBAND AND WIFE ARE ALONE...
ARE YOU SURE WE DID THE RIGHT THING--SENDING THAT "SUPERBOY" BACK WITH THEM?
I DAMN WELL HOPE SO, ROSE.
I DAMN WELL HOPE SO.

ERADICATOR BY ED BENES

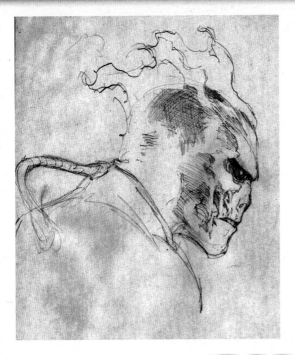

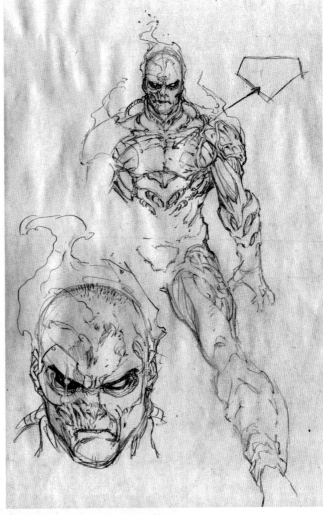

DECAY, DREADNAUGHT & PSIPHON BY R.B. SILVA

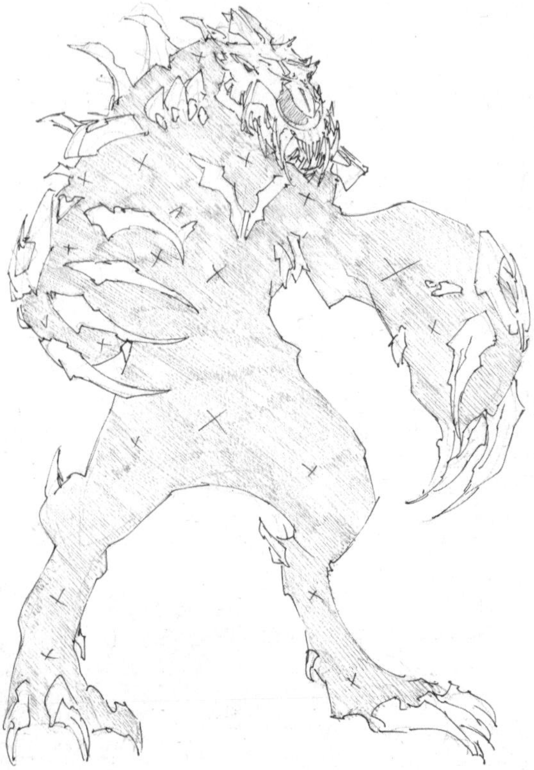

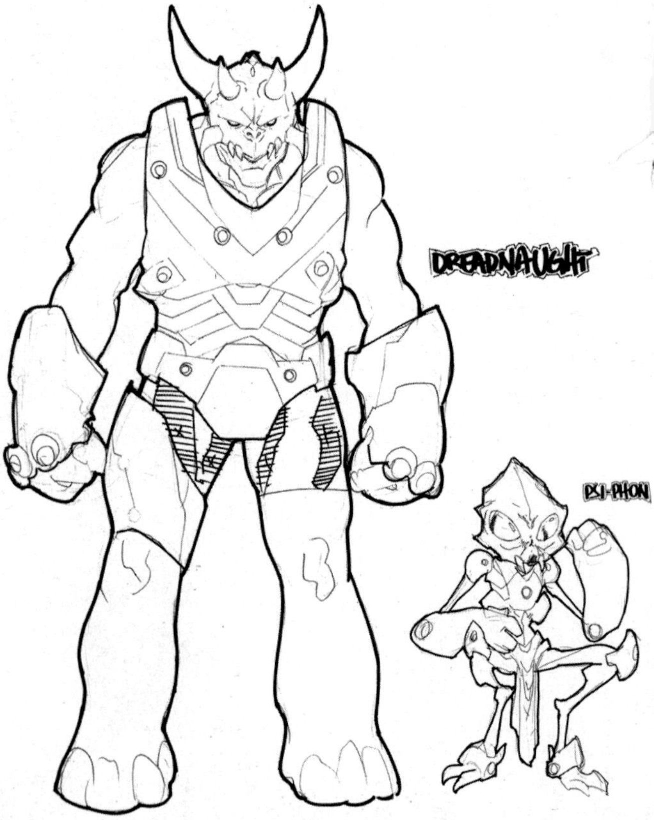

DREADNAUGHT
PSI-PHON

START AT THE BEGINNING!

SUPERMAN: ACTION COMICS VOLUME 1: SUPERMAN AND THE MEN OF STEEL

SUPERMAN VOLUME 1: WHAT PRICE TOMORROW?

GEORGE *PEREZ* JESUS *MERINO* NICOLA *SCOTT*

SUPERGIRL VOLUME 1: THE LAST DAUGHTER OF KRYPTON

MICHAEL *GREEN* MIKE *JOHNSON* MAHMUD *ASRAR*

SUPERBOY VOLUME 1: INCUBATION

SCOTT *LOBDELL* R.B. *SILVA* ROB *LEAN*

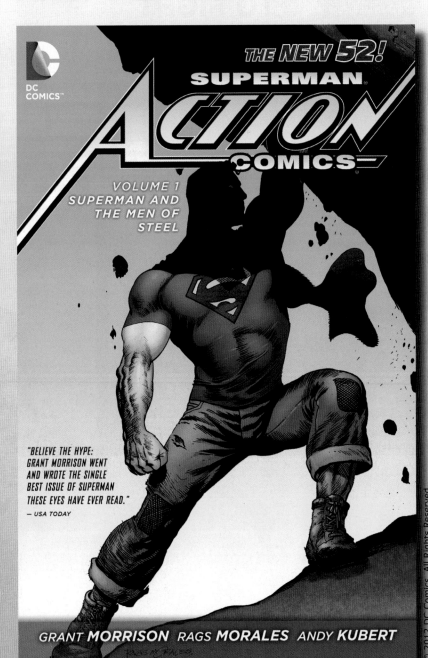

THE NEW 52!
DC COMICS™

SUPERMAN
ACTION COMICS

VOLUME 1
SUPERMAN AND THE MEN OF STEEL

"BELIEVE THE HYPE: GRANT MORRISON WENT AND WROTE THE SINGLE BEST ISSUE OF SUPERMAN THESE EYES HAVE EVER READ."
— USA TODAY

GRANT **MORRISON** RAGS **MORALES** ANDY **KUBERT**

START AT THE BEGINNING!

TEEN TITANS
VOLUME 1: IT'S OUR RIGHT TO FIGHT

**TEEN TITANS
VOL. 2: THE CULLING**

**TEEN TITANS VOL. 3:
DEATH OF THE FAMILY**

**THE CULLING: RISE OF
THE RAVAGERS**

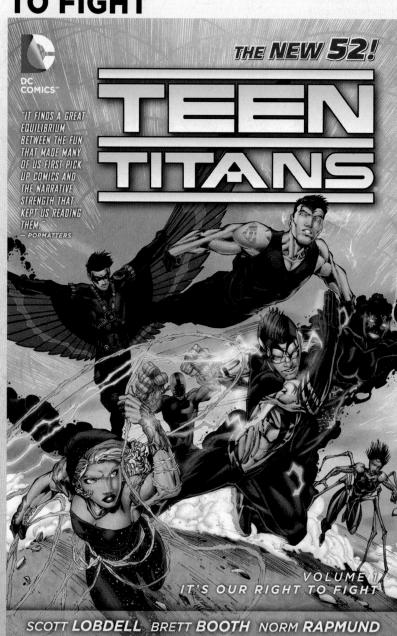

THE NEW 52!

DC COMICS™

*"IT FINDS A GREAT
EQUILIBRIUM
BETWEEN THE FUN
THAT MADE MANY
OF US FIRST PICK
UP COMICS AND
THE NARRATIVE
STRENGTH THAT
KEPT US READING
THEM."*
— POPMATTERS

TEEN TITANS

**VOLUME 1
IT'S OUR RIGHT TO FIGHT**

SCOTT **LOBDELL** BRETT **BOOTH** NORM **RAPMUND**

"An invigorating, entertaining and modern take on the Man of Steel."
—VARIETY

"Grade: A-."
—ENTERTAINMENT WEEKLY

FROM THE WRITER OF *JUSTICE LEAGUE* & *GREEN LANTERN*

GEOFF JOHNS

with GARY FRANK

SUPERMAN: THE LAST SON OF KRYPTON

with RICHARD DONNER & ADAM KUBERT

with GARY FRANK

SUPERMAN: BRAINIAC

GEOFF **JOHNS** GARY **FRANK** JON **SIBAL**

SUPERMAN SECRET ORIGIN

INTRODUCTION BY DAVID S. GOYER

with GARY FRANK

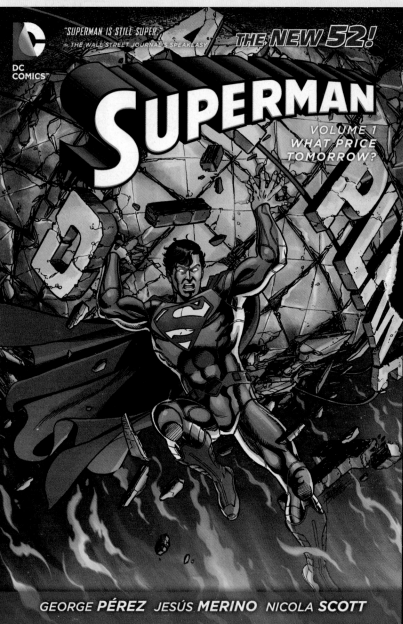

Foreword

Interest in the craft of pottery—a unique blend of art and science—has grown steadily for most of this century. Certain events have accelerated the rate of this growth such as the return of Bernard Leach from Japan in 1920, and the awakening of people's enthusiasm for the more enduring arts which took place after the last war. Today there seems no abatement to the quest for genuine craftsmanship. Books have appeared at an increasing rate recently, but in my opinion many have tended to be too general in scope to be of real value to what is now becoming a well-informed readership. Harry Fraser, in choosing to concentrate on glazes, has tackled a most intriguing and often baffling area. No one is, or should be, satisfied with all the glazes he uses; everyone would like to know more about them. So a book on glazing is always welcome.

Harry Fraser has for some time now shown that he is more than just sympathetic to the craft potter's world. He has listened to the craftsmen who use the materials and the tools of pottery so as to try to do something about improving their manufacture and distribution. He has, moreover, an industrial background, having held positions in production, technical and general management, so that he is in a position to bring industrial potters and craft potters together. Both need to share their experiences, and the craft potter can learn from industry's technical and scientific researches in order to further his own different aims.

Happily too, within the selected field of glazing for the craft potter, the range of his book is wide, and the style simple so that although some of the material is highly technical no beginner need be daunted by the subjects dealt with. Many familiar aspects, such as glaze calculation, have of course been included, but they need to be restated clearly and simply as Harry Fraser does until they are easily understood. But more importantly he has added much new material on several subjects, grinding mills, deflocculation, and poisons in glazes to name just a few. The earlier chapters on basic chemistry and raw materials may introduce these fascinating aspects of ceramics to some people and coax them into more specialized reading. On the other hand, the chapters on colours, curing glaze faults, and of course the recipes themselves will set others on a more practical path.

I believe there is interest and information here for all those concerned with pottery, be they professional craftsmen, teachers or students wanting a comprehensive introduction to glazes and glazing. Harry Fraser's book is a welcome addition to the potter's library.

MICHAEL CASSON

Acknowledgements

I would like to express my gratitude to several friends and associates including Philip Robinson of Staffordshire University for provision of photomicrographs; Michael Casson, David Leach and Harry Stringer for photographs and other assistance and especially to Gordon Slinn who so helpfully assisted with information and checking of the original manuscript in 1972.

My thanks are also due to Podmore and Sons Ltd, British Ceramic Research, Portmeirion Potteries Ltd, Waterford Wedgwood (UK) plc, and William Boulton Ltd for the use of material from *The World of Geology* by Peter Cattermole.

In addition my thanks are due to those many others who have provided photographs for the 1998 edition including Peter Lane David Frith, Bridget Drakeford, Lawrence Carter Louise Darby, Nick Caiger-Smith, Derek Emms, Daphne Carnegy, Rita Broadley, Stephen Course, Petra Tilley, Edward Hughes and Jane Elmer-Smith.

And last but not least, a special vote of thanks to Linda Lambert, my editor at A & C Black Publishers for her helpful advice and patience.

Stoke-on-Trent HARRY FRASER
1998

Contents

1. Introduction, classification and technique

INTRODUCTION

Pottery is made of Earth, shaped with the aid of Water, dried in Air, and made durable by Fire. It therefore provides the perfect combination of what the ancient scholars thought were the four primaries from which the world was made. Even today there remains much logic in this belief, for pottery clays and glazes constantly demonstrate their close affinity with nature and with the volcanic minerals from which the Earth's crust is constructed.

It has been claimed that pottery was the first synthetic material discovered by man: an artificial stone produced by burning clay in an open fire, and pottery has been of value to man in countless ways since the dawn of his history. The durability of the pottery objects he used has provided an index to our heritage—a mirror to our civilization with which modern man has been able to find out more about himself and his environment at any point in recorded history.

Today it would be hard to imagine the consequences of a world without ceramics; a world without bricks, tiles, pottery and the refractories necessary to withstand the high temperatures in the smelting of metals and the melting of glass.

It is said that pottery made the birth of glass possible, since, with the aid of pottery crucibles that were sufficiently refractory to withstand attack, impure glass was produced as early as 12 000 B.C. It is an interesting theory that although a glaze is merely a coating of glass on the pottery, the development of glazes may have preceded the invention of glass in its own right.

Our knowledge of ways to form glazes on pottery certainly dates back to at least 5 000 B.C. Glazed objects were made in various parts of the world long before the development of any scientific knowledge of chemistry and consequently the processes involved must have been simple and the raw materials easily obtained. The results that were achieved were often of a very high quality but were achieved by empirical methods rather than by an application of scientific knowledge or theory. The first glazed ware was almost certainly produced by the Egyptians, who mixed soluble sodium compounds into the clay from which they fashioned ornaments, beads and sculptures to produce objects which we now refer to as Egyptian paste. During the drying process, the soluble salts naturally migrated with the water to the surface of the object. There a scum was formed, which melted to form a glass upon firing. Eventually, however, the Egyptians were to develop separate glazes which were made, applied, and fired much as we do today.

Pottery is glazed for a variety of reasons depending upon the product. Functional pottery (i.e. cups, saucers, etc.) made from a pottery clay which is porous to a greater or lesser degree when fired, is glazed to render the outer surface completely impermeable to the foodstuffs which the pottery is designed to carry. In addition to this, a smooth glaze surface is usually desirable even over completely vitreous bodies so that the pottery can be cleaned much more easily. A satisfactory glaze coat can also influence the strength of the pottery. Glazing, however, is often done purely for decorative effect either directly as in the use of an artistic, coloured or crackle glaze on ornamental pottery, or indirectly to mask the unattractive colour of the fired clay body—as in the use of white opaque glazes on vitreous china sanitary ware.

The usual technique of pottery production is to carry out a firing of the clay ware to produce biscuit pottery and then to apply the glaze, followed by a further firing termed the glost firing. With certain glaze/body combinations, however, satisfactorily glazed pottery can be produced by a once-firing process in which the glaze is applied directly to the clay ware followed by a glost (i.e. glaze) firing which serves to develop both the glaze and the clay body at the same time. It is by no means easy to produce a satisfactory product by the once-fired process and consequently, although the practice is widespread in the pottery industry, it is very unusual amongst craft potters.

CLASSIFICATION

There are numerous types of glazes if one includes the major chemical variations and the different types of pottery bodies to which glazes can be applied. Consequently there are various ways in which pottery glazes can be classified. The usual glaze classifications are: (*a*) lead glazes, (*b*) leadless glazes. This is an obvious classification but can only be applied to glazes having firing ranges up to about 1160°C (2120°F) since above this temperature lead oxide tends to volatilize increasingly readily. Consequently glazes compounded to mature at above 1160°C (2120°F) are inevitably of the leadless type.

Another classification sometimes used in industry is that based on the ware to which it is applied, i.e. terra cotta, earthenware, parian, bone china, vitreous china, stoneware. Since, however, a very large number of glazes fall into these categories, such a classification is not a practical one.

A more logical classification, and one often used, is to classify glazes according to the effect produced on the finished article such as: transparent, opaque, matt, semi-matt, satin vellum, crackle.

Satin vellum glazes are glazes which have a type of semi-matt surface in which the effect produced is particularly fine producing a satin sheen. Crackle glazes, of course, are those which are deliberately compounded to produce marked crazing or cracking of the glaze.

The most common method of classifying glazes nowadays is to base the classification on the maturing range (i.e. firing temperature) of the glaze, as follows—

(*a*) Raku glazes—generally maturing below 900°C (1650°F).
(*b*) Majolica glazes—maturing in the range of approx. 900–1050°C (1650–1920°F).
(*c*) Earthenware glazes—maturing between 1020 and 1160°C (1870–2120°F).
(*d*) Stoneware glazes—maturing between 1200 and 1300°C (2190–2370°F).
(*e*) Porcelain glazes—generally maturing in the range 1220–1450°C (2230–2640°F).

It would be useful at this juncture to review this method of glaze classification in a little more detail by considering the pottery produced at each of the firing ranges. It will also be helpful in that some of the glazes will be referred to by maturing range in later chapters.

Raku

The Raku process involves the rapid firing of an invariably heavily grogged clay which will withstand the stresses involved in rapid drying, firing and cooling. The pottery may be once-fired or, more usually, fired both biscuit and glost, and the firing temperature is traditionally within the range 750–900°C (1380–1650°F).

The pots are placed into a kiln which often comprises little more than a saggar (i.e. a refractory box) partly embedded in a coke fire although simple intermittent kilns fired by electricity, oil or gas have been constructed. The pots, placed directly into the hot, glowing kiln with metal tongs, are left until they begin to glow and are then withdrawn using the tongs. Immediately upon removal from the kiln the glazed pot is quenched in oil, or buried in sawdust or wrapped in grass etc. in order to obtain unusual colouring effects by a reducing action on the constituents of the still-molten glaze. Alternatively the pots can be left to cool naturally or can be quenched in water in which case the normal oxidized effect is obtained.

The pottery produced is primitive but the

process is of appreciable value in teaching, since the complete pottery process—from the forming operation to the finished pot, can be demonstrated in a matter of a few hours instead of over a period of days.

Terra cotta

Terra cotta clays are naturally occurring clays containing about 9 per cent of iron oxide which produces the characteristic red-brown fired colour. Extensive deposits occur throughout the world, a notable one being the Etruria marl deposit at Stoke-on-Trent. They are porous when fired within the range 1 020–1 100°C (1 870–2 010°F), this being the usual glost (glaze) firing range in which a satisfactory coefficient of expansion (*see* Chapter 2) is developed to give good craze-resistance.

Earthenware

This is the name given to blended pottery clays which develop satisfactory craze-resistance when

Fig. 1
Raku pot by Harry Stringer
Wax resist applied to light-coloured body followed by transparent lead glaze. Carbon from smoke subsequently entering the exposed body produced the attractive dark patches.

Fig. 2
16-inch earthenware fish dish (iron pigments) and lustre bowl by Alan Caiger-Smith

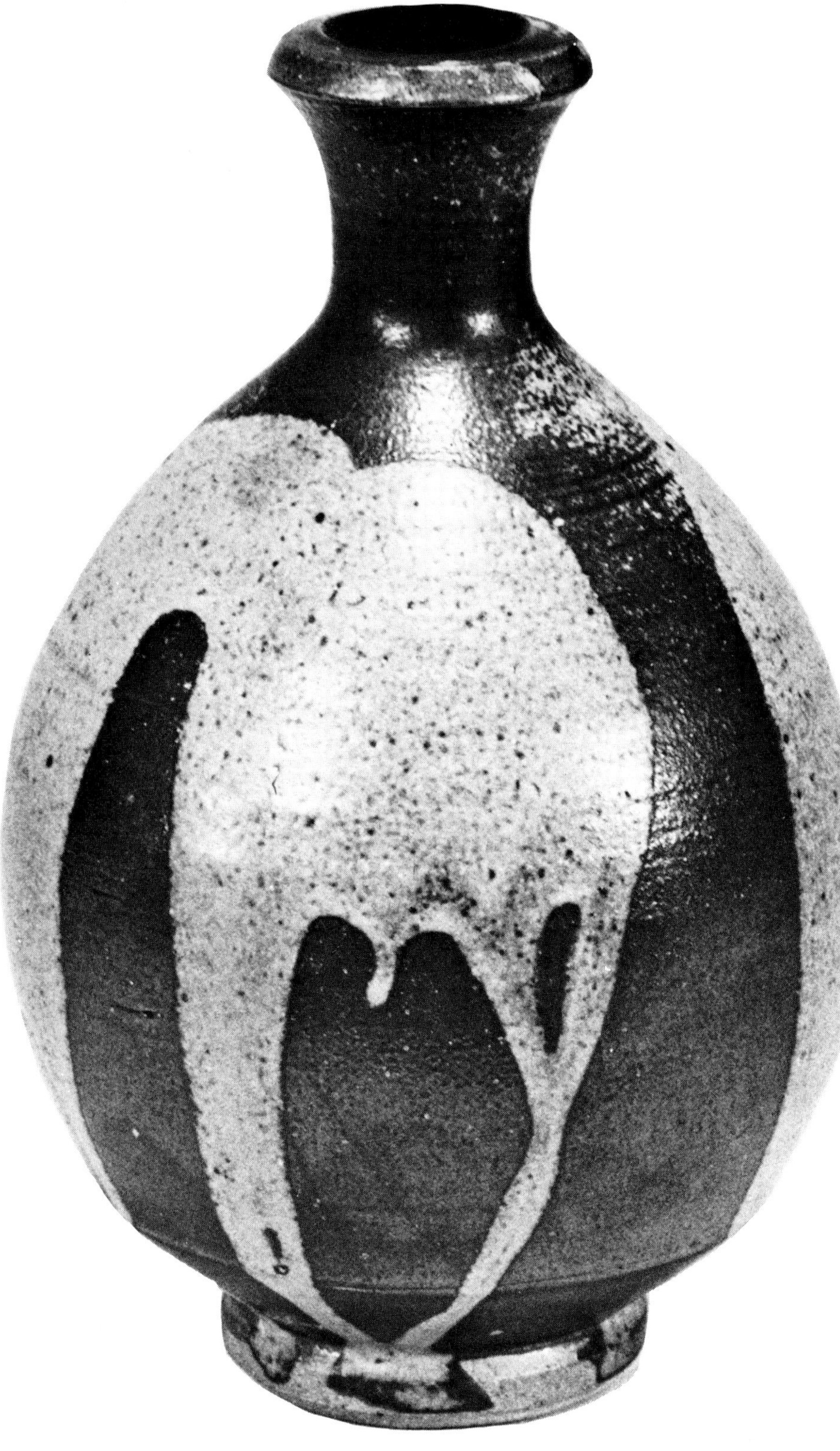

Fig. 3
Stoneware lamp base by Derek Emms
Oak-ash glaze applied thinly, then pattern poured with thick glaze. Fired 1 300°C, reduction.

fired within the range 1 100–1 160°C (2 010–2 120°F). The pottery body is porous over this range and usually fires white or ivory (especially industrial earthenware) but may be buff or red. Craft potters often biscuit fire at a low temperature (900–1 080°C) (1 650–1 980°F) followed by a glost firing at a higher temperature (1 100–1 160°C) (2 010–2 120°F), but the industrial practice is invariably to biscuit fire at the full maturing range of the body (i.e. 1 100–1 160°C) followed by a lower glost firing usually within the range (1 020–1 060°C) (1 870–1 940°F). The reasons for the different firing techniques are various and are given in *Kilns and Kiln Firing for the Craft Potter* (H. Fraser), but the important aspect is that earthenware pottery, at some point in its production, must be fired above cone 1 (1 100°C) (2 010°F) otherwise crazing of the glaze is likely to occur.

Stoneware

Stoneware is the name given to pottery which matures in the range of about 1 200–1 300°C (2 190–2 370°F). It is characterized by a plastic body which is vitrified or nearly so (although stoneware sewer pipes have a porosity figure often around 10 per cent) and which is usually grey or buff or brown in colour, the principal constituents of the body being ball clays and/or fireclays. Stoneware glazes maturing in this range are commonly fired under reduction conditions to obtain certain characteristic effects from the presence of copper and/or iron oxides present in the glaze, or to encourage iron in the body to 'bleed' through the glaze layer. Reduction firing of stoneware glazes is not, however, essential nor is it desirable for many stoneware glazes and much beautiful oxidized stoneware pottery has been and is being produced—notably by Hans Coper and Lucie Rie.

Porcelain

The name 'porcelain' is said to be derived from the Italian *porcella*, literally 'little pig', a Mediterranean sea-snail whose shell is noted for its whiteness and translucency. This derivation indicates the nature of porcelain bodies which are vitrified, white, and translucent, i.e. they allow light partly to pass through them.

Porcelain bodies are usually based on china clays to which feldspar is added to provide a flux, and flint or quartz to promote stability, hardness, and a better 'glaze fit'.

Purists would say that the firing range is traditionally within the range 1 300–1 450°C (2 370–2 640°F), i.e. higher than for stoneware. Highly plastic porcelain bodies such as Potclay 1 147 and 1 149 bodies have incidentally been developed which show all the qualities of porcelain but which mature in the 1 220–1 280°C (2 230–2 340°F) region. Consequently one can classify porcelain glazes as maturing somewhere within the 1 220–1 450°C (2 230–2 640°F) range.

An exception is the English variety of porcelain incorporating calcined ox bones and known as 'bone china' or to give it the more elegant name preferred by the connoisseur, 'bone porcelain'. Its production is largely confined to the industry where it is biscuit fired to its vitrification point (around 1 240°C (2 270°F)) but is glazed with a transparent glaze and glost fired at about 1 020–1 060°C (1 870–1 940°F).

Fig. 4
Porcelain pot by Eileen Lewenstein
Cut with needle and double-glazed with matt white beneath and green glaze over.

DIFFERENCES IN TECHNIQUE

When clay ware is fired the clay body decomposes under the effect of heat, liberating gases from the burning away of volatiles—mainly carbonaceous material, and steam from the liberation of water present in the clay crystal. Although most of the water has been driven away at $350°C$ ($660°F$), vapour may still be detected up to $900°C$ ($1650°F$). Carbonaceous material and other volatiles usually remain up to $900-1100°C$ ($1650-2010°F$) or higher—especially with stoneware bodies and with rapid firing cycles.

Naturally, if the biscuit pottery is refired to a lower temperature than that of its first firing then the amount of further decomposition which takes place will be negligible. If, however, the second firing exceeds the temperature of the first then the body will begin to decompose still further, liberating gases which, if the pot is glazed, have to bubble through the glaze layer.

In the production of earthenware or other porous pottery the industrial potter desires to obtain a smooth glaze covering free of pinholes or other glaze blemishes so that, in the case of functional pottery, the glazed surface is quite impervious. This is assisted by glost firing at a temperature lower than the biscuit firing as a result of which the ware remains inert during the glost firing resulting in little risk of warping. This, in turn, permits use of pin cranks on to which glazed dishes, plates or saucers (of similar shape and diameter) can be stacked thus providing a tighter packing of ware into the kiln. Also, of course, a warped biscuit piece is less loss than a warped glost one. The industrial potter therefore biscuit fires earthenware to the maturing range of the clay, i.e. $1100-1160°C$ ($2010-2120°F$) and then uses glazes which demand a lower glaze firing of around $1050°C$ ($1920°F$).

Earthenware biscuit fired to its full maturing range is, however, relatively vitreous, i.e. non-porous (except for certain types of ovenware bodies), and consequently an efficient dipping technique is demanded to prevent glaze 'runs' from developing on the dipped pot; also, the glaze slip has to be more carefully adjusted than would be necessary if the ware to be dipped had high porosity. With quite vitreous biscuit ware such as industrial vitreous china and bone china (fired at around $1240°C$ ($2260°F$)) the glaze is commonly applied by spraying to overcome the negligible porosity.

The difficulties encountered in the application of glazes to articles of relatively low porosity have caused most craft potters to adopt a different firing technique to that of the industry. The craft potter generally biscuit fires clay ware up to a point at which most of the volatiles have been burned away but at which little consolidation has taken place so that the biscuit pottery has very high porosity. This equates with a biscuit firing range of around $960-1080°C$ ($1760-1980°F$) for earthenware and $960-1140°C$ ($1760-2080°F$) for stoneware (which at the lower limit, nevertheless often biscuit fires to a pink colour due to unburnt carbon). Such high biscuit porosity enables the glaze to be easily applied by dipping (due to high water absorption), resulting in a firm but even coat, this ease of application being the principal reason why the low biscuit/high glost technique is adopted.

The glaze used on this low-fired biscuit ware is one which matures at the firing range of the clay, so that the glost firing serves to develop both the body and the glaze at the same time. Thus for earthenware a glaze will be selected which matures at $1100-1160°C$ ($2010-2120°F$) and for stoneware at $1200-1300°C$ ($2190-2370°F$). However, once the temperature of the glost fire exceeds that of the biscuit, the body itself begins to decompose still further and gases are given off which have to bubble through the glaze layer. This produces bubbles in the glaze which burst upon reaching the surface producing pinholes or small craters. In order to allow more time for these bubble craters to dissipate it is necessary to 'soak' the pottery, i.e. to hold the kiln at the glaze firing temperature for half an hour (or longer) so that the craters have an opportunity to heal themselves before the glaze becomes too viscous as it cools.

The quality and texture of stoneware and porcelain glazes are, incidentally, often enhanced by the gases which inevitably bubble through from the biscuit ware and also by the reactions which take place between the glaze and the decomposing body. Indeed, much stoneware pottery owes its success and appeal to the glaze effects brought about by a high temperature glost firing.

In the case of earthenware there is no doubt that the industrial technique generally results in a smoother and glossier glaze surface and increased craze-resistance—but glaze application problems may be difficult for the craft potter to overcome. In addition to this the more technical approach of the industry often results in earthenware which has a more clinical appearance: the glaze and body tend to appear more as two completely separate entities and less as one being a sympathetic extension of the other.

REDUCTION

Reduction firing and reduction glazes have become very popular in the production of stoneware and porcelain. The fact that the classic achievements of the ancient Chinese potters consisted largely of pottery fired under reduction conditions has given the technique a prestige sanctioned by the best work of the past and has set a standard which the modern potter often seeks to emulate.

The theory of reduction firing is simple. When any carbonaceous material is burned, the carbon it contains combines with oxygen present in the air to form the gas carbon dioxide. If the amount of material being burned is greater than the amount of air available to ensure complete combustion then inadequate combustion takes place resulting in the formation of carbon (often seen as black smoke) and carbon monoxide gas. At the high temperatures reached in pottery kilns, such free carbon and carbon monoxide are chemically active and will seize oxygen from any available source including that contained by certain of the oxides in ceramic materials. When oxygen is extracted from certain materials in this

Fig. 5
Stoneware bowl (fired under reduction conditions) by John Davies
Mottled effect produced by the activated iron bleeding through the glaze from the grog in the stoneware body can be readily seen. P.1037 clay with P.2227 glaze plus $\frac{1}{4}$ per cent cobalt.

Fig. 6
Stoneware pot (oxidized firing) 18 inches high by Hans Coper

way they are said to be reduced and this reduction in the amount of oxygen in the material
may affect its colour.

Copper oxide, for example, can be reduced to
the form which gives a red colour instead of the
usual green; red iron oxide (haematite), instead
of producing browns, will give greys and black
after its reduction to the black iron oxide (mag-
netite). Under reduction firing conditions, clay
bodies fire to a greyer, darker colour than they
otherwise would, owing to reduction of the iron
oxides they contain. Localized concentrations of
iron oxide such as result from the addition to a
clay of a buff grog which contains a high proportion of iron oxide, or an iron-bearing sand,
cause pronounced dark-coloured specks in the
clay during firing. These, owing to the increased
chemical activity of the iron, tend to combine
with and 'bleed' through the glaze layer, producing a speckled glaze.

Reducing atmospheres can be generated inside

electric kilns by the deliberate introduction of
carbonaceous material such as charcoal, moth
balls, oil or gas into the firing chamber during
the firing process, although this shortens element
life appreciably. Unless carbon is introduced in
this way, the kiln atmosphere during the firing
process of any normal electric kiln is inevitably
oxidizing or neutral and reduction effects are
not obtained.

Reducing atmospheres are, however, very
easily generated in kilns fired by solid fuels, oil
or gas, simply by reducing the amount of air fed
into the kiln to less than is required for the full
combustion of the fuel. Indeed, with the more
primitive kilns, reduction is a natural, almost
inevitable occurrence, hard to prevent rather
than hard to achieve, and the magnificent reduction effects obtained by the early Chinese
potters were probably a natural consequence of
the way they fired their kilns.

2. Basic chemistry, structure and properties of glazes

ELEMENTS, COMPOUNDS AND MIXTURES

All materials are made up of elements, the building blocks which can be built or coupled together to form each of the various materials around us. There are altogether 103 different elements but only about 40 are commonly encountered in ceramics. They are chemically expressed in the form of symbols, e.g. Al for aluminium, Si for silicon, O for oxygen, Pb for lead, H for hydrogen, etc.

When atoms of different elements combine together a new material, i.e. a 'compound' is formed. For example, two atoms of hydrogen plus one atom of oxygen can combine to form the compound water. This can be expressed chemically as $H + H + O = H_2O$ (water). The grouping together of the chemical element symbols to denote the compound is referred to as the formula and all compounds can be chemically expressed in this way, e.g. silica = SiO_2, clay = $Al_2O_3 . 2SiO_2 . 2H_2O$. In this way the symbols of the various elements provide the alphabet of the language of chemistry.

The smallest possible whole part of an element is an atom. The element hydrogen (H) has the lightest weight of any element and it was, therefore, given an atomic weight of 1. All other elements were given an atomic weight which denoted the number of times one atom of that element was heavier than one atom of hydrogen, e.g. carbon had an atomic weight of 12 (i.e. 12 times heavier than hydrogen), silicon an atomic weight of 28, oxygen an atomic weight of 16, etc. In 1961 carbon of atomic weight 12 was adopted as the standard in place of hydrogen, but this does not affect the approximate values.

The smallest possible portion of a compound is a molecule, this molecule being made up of a combination of one or more atoms of one or more elements. If the atomic weights of each of the elements in the formula of the compound are added together we obtain the molecular weight of the compound concerned. Thus water (H_2O) has a molecular weight of $1 \times 2 + 16 = 18$.

It is important to note that chemical compounds can only be formed when elements combine together in fixed proportions. If the same elements combine together in different ratios then a different compound is formed for each ratio which occurs. Materials which are loosely mixed together are referred to as mixtures, i.e. their constituents are not chemically bonded together and the ratio of the various materials to each other is variable. Air is a mixture.

SOLUTIONS AND SOLUBILITY

In any general consideration of the properties of glazes and glasses it is important to review the basic principles of solutions and solubility.

A solution can be defined as a molecular mixture of two or more substances. Thus when sugar is completely dissolved in water the separate particles in the solution consist of molecules of sugar and water and it will remain as a solution indefinitely unless the water is evaporated away, when the sugar will reform crystals from its molecules.

A mixture of sand with water, however, is a suspension and not a solution. In a suspension the individual particles of the material mixed with the liquid are not reduced in size down to the constituent molecules: they remain floating in the liquid for a while, completely unaltered, and then gradually settle out under their own weight. Thus a mixture of glaze and water is a suspension since the glaze particles are insoluble in water: they remain quite inert and do not break down into their constituent molecules, i.e. they do not dissolve.

In a solution the substance present in the larger amount, i.e. the dissolving agent, is usually referred to as the solvent and the substance dissolved in it as the solute. At any given temperature the solute, regardless of the material, has a definite degree of solubility in the solvent. As a general rule, the higher the temperature of a liquid the more solid it will dissolve. The opposite, however, is true when a gas is dissolved in a liquid. In this latter case the higher the temperature of the liquid the less the quantity of gas which can be dissolved.

When a solvent at a fixed temperature will not dissolve any more solute, the solution is said to be saturated. In this condition no further solute can be dissolved, any further addition merely remaining unaltered until, in the case of a solid dissolved in a liquid, the temperature of the solvent is increased. If, however, a saturated solution of a solid in a liquid is cooled to a lower temperature the solvent becomes incapable of holding so much solute in solution with the result that some of the solute will separate out of the solution in the form of crystals of the original solute.

This process of crystallization from a saturated solution is responsible for the formation of many of the earth's minerals which crystallized out of molten rock-forming materials as the earth cooled. It is also the phenomenon causing devitrification (crystallization) of transparent pottery glazes and the formation of crystals necessary in the formation of matt and certain opaque glazes.

CRYSTALLOGRAPHY AND STRUCTURE

When compounds are formed it should not be considered that the compound is constructed of countless molecules each of which is formed to its chemical formula as a completely separate indivi-

dual unit. With silica (SiO_2) for example, one should not consider this to be constructed of countless atoms of silicon each of which is combined with two atoms of oxygen, but more as a network or pattern of silicon and oxygen atoms which are combined together and present in the ratio of one to two. The network is three-dimensional and continuous and forms particles which are referred to as crystals. The network itself is referred to as the crystal lattice.

If this network is composed in an orderly fashion, having set distances and angles between the individual atoms, then the final network will form itself into a distinctive shape. In the case of a crystal of rock salt (*see* Fig. 7) the atoms are arranged to form cells which are of cubic shape. The rock salt crystal is also cubic, being built up of a large number of the cells which are stacked together—much as a large cube may be built with small building blocks.

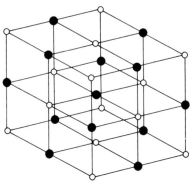

Fig. 7
Salt (NaCl) crystal

All minerals in fact are crystalline materials and each mineral has an individual crystal shape which is always the same no matter what the conditions of its formation, a study of the crystal shape being one way in which minerals can be identified.

The fact that a mineral is crystalline prevents it from appearing transparent, since light attempting to pass through it is reflected or refracted by the faces of the individual crystals. It is therefore obvious that transparent glazes must have a somewhat different structure to that of the usual solid materials.

Glazes and glasses do in fact have a different structure to that of crystalline materials. Natural materials such as clays, feldspars, etc. used as constituents of glazes are crystalline but the glaze melts upon firing with the result that the various glaze materials combine together to form new compounds. These new compounds are essentially silicates, being formed by the molten materials dissolving the silica present in all glazes to form a solution.

It has been mentioned earlier that when a saturated solution is cooled, less of the dissolved material can be retained in solution, with the result that crystals of the material are formed. This formation of crystals, however, will only take place as long as the solution is sufficiently fluid to allow the molecules to orientate themselves to form the crystal lattice. In the case of glasses and glazes, these are normally comparatively viscous when molten and consequently the formation of crystals of the various minerals dissolved in the glaze takes place with difficulty owing to the viscosity of the melt. As the glaze cools it becomes progressively more viscous and eventually becomes rigid thus firmly fixing the molecules in position before the crystallization can take place. Glazes are therefore commonly referred to as solid solutions since the random arrangement of the atoms and molecules is similar at room temperature to the random arrangement when the glaze was a molten liquid. Since liquids,

glasses and glazes have this random arrangement of the atoms and molecules they cannot show any definite crystal form.

This random network theory was first proposed by Zachariasen, who concluded that whereas crystalline materials possessed a three-dimensional symmetrical arrangement of the atoms which was repeated at regular intervals, glass structures have a three-dimensional random arrangement of the atoms, the pattern not being repeated at regular distances throughout the glass (*see* Fig. 8).

The random network structure, incidentally, is also thought to be responsible for the low thermal expansion of glasses and glazes, since this would permit some adjustment or packing of the molecules without changing the volume.

Glazes can consequently be defined as glasses, which are supercooled liquids of high viscosity at ordinary temperatures. They therefore exhibit the normal physical and chemical properties of glasses, being hard, impermeable to gases and liquids, and almost or completely insoluble except in strong acids or bases. Like glasses they are not definite chemical compounds but are mixtures of complex silicates and borates.

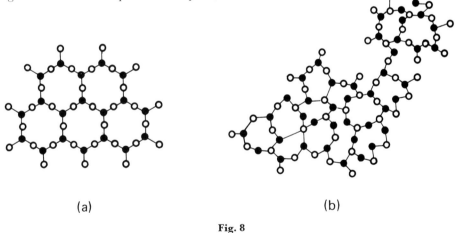

(a)　　　　　　　　　　　　(b)

Fig. 8
Crystal lattice structures
(*a*) is the rigid structure of crystalline silica. (*b*) is the more random structure characteristic of glazes and glasses.

COEFFICIENT OF EXPANSION

An important property of the fired glaze is its degree of expansion when subjected to heat. This can be measured in the laboratory by firing a glaze sample to its maturing range then carefully measuring its expansion when heated over a certain temperature range (usually room temperature to 500°C (930°F)). The increase in length of the sample at 500°C is then expressed as a percentage of the length at room temperature and is referred to as the coefficient of expansion or 'expansion' of the glaze. It serves to give an indication of the craze-resistance properties of the glaze: if too much expansion is developed then crazing of the glaze on the body may result; if insufficient expansion is developed then peeling may occur.

The term 'glaze fit' is often used to refer to the difference between the expansion of the glaze and that of the body on to which it is applied. A good glaze fit is one in which there is no risk of crazing or peeling.

STRENGTH OF GLAZES AND GLAZED POTTERY

The supposed tensile strength of a glass or glaze can theoretically be calculated but there is always a large discrepancy between the calculated and actual strengths, the actual strength being some 200 times less than the calculated one. In addition to this the spread of breaking loads for a group of samples of the same glass is great.

These factors led to the Griffith theory, in which it was proposed that all glasses contain minute flaws or cracks which act as stress multipliers and that therefore the strength of a glass is determined by the number or gravity of these flaws (particularly those on the surface).

In the glass industry, sulphur gases are sometimes introduced into the furnaces. This removes some of the high-expansion alkalis from the glass surface, leaving an excess of silica and thus increasing the compression of the surface glass,

the durability, and the strength. The same could theoretically be done with glazes but the side effects such as risk of scumming would outweigh any slight advantage to be gained.

The strength of a glazed ceramic object is therefore dependent to a certain degree upon the state of its surface. In this way there is an analogy between ceramics and metals for it is well known that the strength of a metal can be increased by polishing its surface.

Provided that the glaze suits the body, i.e. the glaze has a similar or lower coefficient of expansion than the body on to which it is applied there is no doubt that the glazed article is stronger than the same article unglazed. However, if the coefficient of expansion of the glaze is greater than that of the body, in which case the glaze is in a state of tension and is not craze-resistant, then the reverse may obtain, i.e. the glazed article may have less strength than the unglazed one. It is therefore likely that strongly alkaline glazes will actually reduce the tensile strength of pottery articles to which they are applied. Certainly it can easily be demonstrated that when a glaze is under compression in relation to the pottery body, the article will tolerate a much greater pressure load before breaking than if the glaze were under tension.

Glazes in a high state of compression (i.e. highly craze-resistant ones) may cause shapes such as cylinders to fracture along the vertical axis. In actual fact, however, the forces needed to cause fracture due to a compressive stress must be appreciable, for a glass or glaze can withstand a very much greater compressive than tensile force. It is for this reason that crazing of the glaze layer is a much more common fault than is peeling of the glaze.

In addition, the length of time for which pressure is applied to glazed articles is important. Glasses and glazed articles seem to fatigue quickly and they will often fail to withstand over a longer period of time a load they can safely withstand over a short period. The apparent reduction in mechanical strength may be as much as 40 per cent.

3. Effect of heat

When glasses are heated they progressively soften and fuse. Technically one cannot describe the process as a melting process since melting refers to the conversion of a solid to a liquid phase (such as the melting of ice to water), the melting point being the temperature at which the two phases are in equilibrium. The term solid in this context implies a regular internal geometrical arrangement of atoms in a lattice structure in contrast to the imperfect or random network arrangement of the atoms in a liquid and in a glass.

Fusion is the culmination of several conditions operating in sequence or simultaneously to produce a fluid melt at a higher temperature. In addition to the effect of high temperature, chemical decomposition and combination, diffusion, and solution formation, all contribute in the fusion process.

SINTERING

A very important process in the early stages is sintering. This is a process whereby heat converts a powder into a cohesive mass without developing a glassy phase. What in fact happens is that the corners and contact surfaces of the

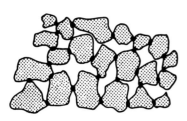

Fig. 9
Sintering
Adhesion at contact points only

particles soften, thus causing the particles to stick to each other (*see* Fig. 9).

The temperature at which sintering begins is well below the melting-point of a pure substance or the fusion temperature range of a mixture. Vitrification does not occur at all and consequently the mass lacks strength and is usually in a friable condition. The fact that glazes generally are finely ground and therefore consist of fine particles which have relatively large surfaces, high surface energy, and low melting points, helps to promote the sintering process.

THE FUSION PROCESS

Under the effect of heat the lattice structure is loosened and further stresses are set up by the differential thermal expansions of the various materials present. These stresses cause minute fractures, reducing the size of the particles and increasing the exposed surface so that they react more readily. The edges and corners of the lattices are also gradually exposed through abrasion, and fissures appear in the particles which permit the entrance and diffusion of the smaller ions and atoms. The formation of eutectics (i.e. mixtures which have a fusion temperature lower than that of any of their constituents), gradually takes place and with the development of the liquid phase, the more refractory particles are surrounded and are gradually taken into solution in the liquid phase.

Under the influence of heat many materials dissociate, i.e. disintegrate into two or more substances solely through the action of heat. Obvious examples include the dehydration of the clays liberating water vapour, and the dissociation of

13

the various carbonates, sulphates, oxides etc. When a glazed body is fired the gases which are produced by dissociation are supplemented by gases which are liberated from the clay or biscuit body on to which the glaze has been applied, by gases absorbed from the kiln atmosphere, by the liberation of gases adsorbed on the surfaces of particles of the glaze materials, and, particularly, by the release of air present in the voids between the glaze particles. These gases then pass into and through the fusing glaze layer producing an effective stirring action which helps to make the glaze more homogeneous. Inevitably this will be a very slow action when the viscosity of the fusing glaze is very high but it is accelerated as the glaze

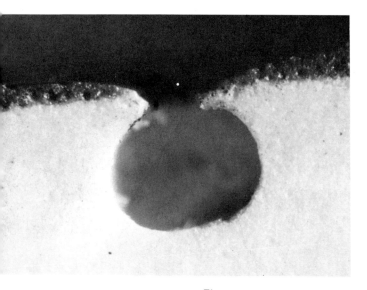

Fig. 10
Transverse section through glaze pinhole
The pinhole in the glaze arises from the large cavity in the body which was caused by an air bubble in the casting slip. Note the smaller, spherical bubbles in the glaze. Oblique incident light × 40 (half plate).
(By courtesy of North Staffs Polytechnic)

becomes more fluid with increasing temperature. In actual fact the bubbling action caused by these escaping gases may be very vigorous, the glaze surface bubbling like boiling tar or treacle.

When the glaze becomes sufficiently fluid, convection currents increase and become an important factor in promoting homogeneity throughout the glaze.

THE FLUID STATE

It has been stated that glazes are supercooled liquids and that therefore they possess physical properties in the rigid state which are more or less a continuation of those in the fluid state.

The viscosity of a glaze consequently alters gradually from a rigid condition at room temperature to that of a thin fluid at a high temperature.

The viscosity of a glaze at high temperature is an extremely important characteristic and can be affected not only by the temperature but also by the time for which the glaze is exposed to heat. It depends also upon the nature of the materials used in compounding the glaze. The rate and uniformity of the fusion process depends upon that portion of the glaze which fuses at the lower temperature, surrounding, penetrating, and dissolving the more refractory particles.

As these particles are taken into solution the process is accelerated by the agitation of the liberated gases bubbling through the glaze layer as has been mentioned earlier. In the manufacture of glass bottles, window glass, etc. it is usual for certain chemical compounds to be added to the molten glass batch to 'sweep' away the gas bubbles which have been liberated by the fusing action, as otherwise the manufactured articles may be contaminated with bubbles, blisters and pinholes (*see* Fig. 10).

However, since the layer of glaze on pottery is very thin, the same result can be obtained by ensuring that the firing temperature is sufficiently high to reduce the viscosity to a level at which the bubbles will easily escape owing to their natural buoyancy, or by 'soaking' the glaze, i.e. maintaining the temperature for a short while at maximum firing temperature so as to give time for the bubbles to work their way through the glaze layer. Any bubbles not released from the glaze may cause the glaze after firing to have an orange-peel or dimpled surface owing to the glaze surface above the bubbles sinking as the bubbles shrink during cooling.

The uniformity of thickness of the matured glaze depends upon the viscosity. If the glaze is

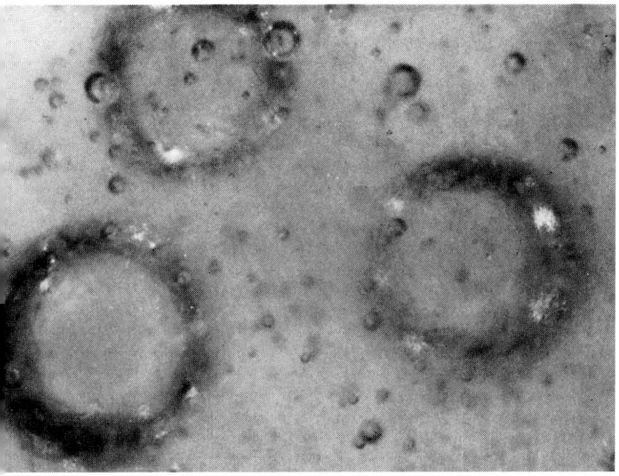

(a) at 1 070°C

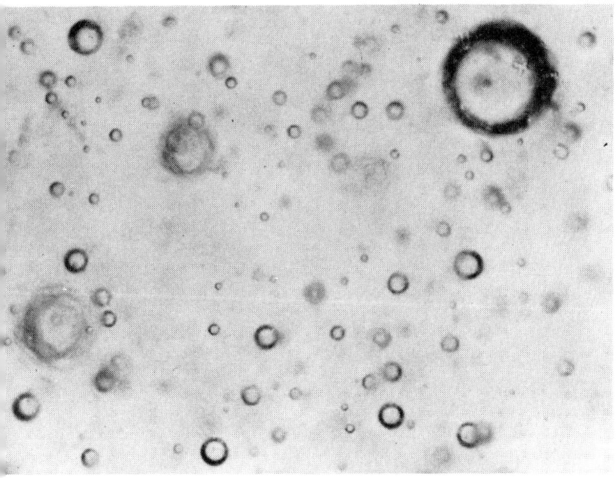

(b) at 1 100°C

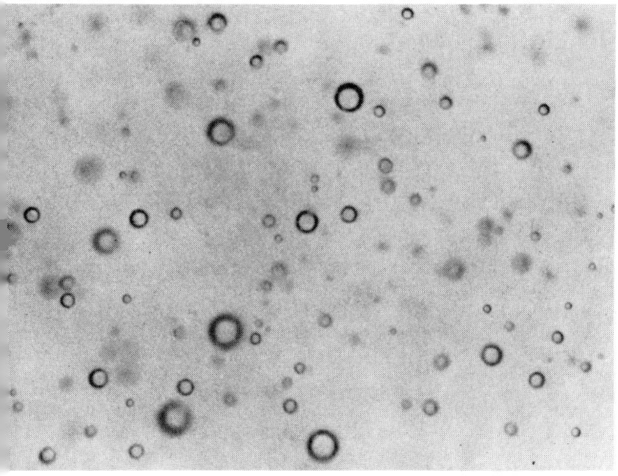

(c) at 1 190°C

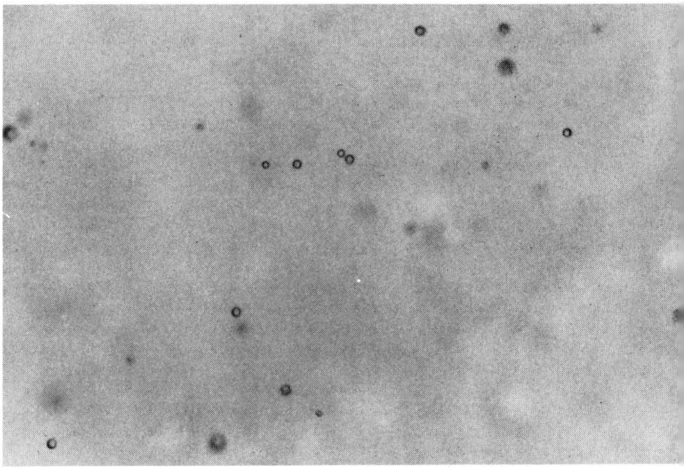

(d) at 1 230°C

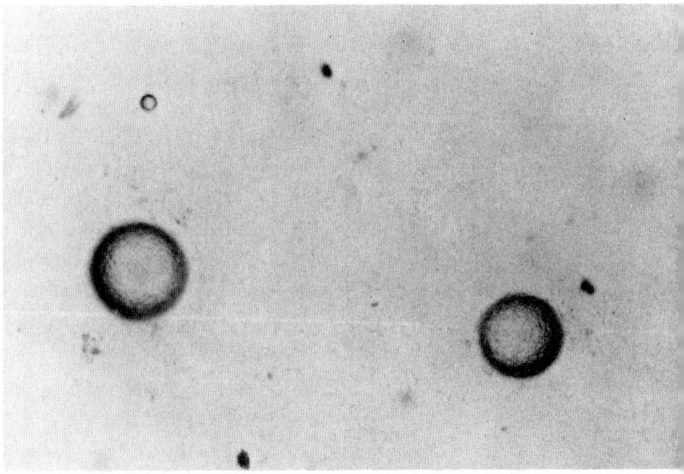

(e) at 1 260°C

Fig. 11
Maturing of a glaze

A series of photomicrographs displaying the clearing of gas bubbles with increasing fluidity as the glaze matures. Note also the clearing of crystalline matter, which gives *(a)* its hazy appearance and which later becomes dissolved and, in *(e)*, the formation of new bubbles due to overfiring. Reflected light, crossed polars × 128 (half plate).

(By courtesy of North Staffs Polytechnic)

too fluid, it will drain away from vertical or inclined surfaces and collect in the hollows and recesses. A very fluid glaze covering a coloured decoration often causes a displacement of the decorated pattern or a smearing of the detail owing to the movement of the molten glaze.

Glazes which are very fluid cannot be satisfactorily fused over highly porous bodies. This is because the very fluid glaze penetrates too far and too quickly below the surface of the body. It may in fact happen that the porous body soaks up the more fusible portions of the glaze, leaving the more refractory portions isolated on the surface as an immature coating. Glazes suitable for once-firing processes therefore have to possess late-fusing properties.

The viscosity of a glaze has a restraining influence which limits or prevents the formation of visible crystals as the glaze cools. Without this restraint nearly all glazes would devitrify (i.e. crystallize) during cooling, and consequently transparent glazes would be extremely difficult to obtain.

In this connexion alumina is of extreme importance to the ceramist, for its presence in pottery glazes increases the viscosity and stability of the glazes, preventing devitrification from occurring. Magnesia also increases glaze viscosity as do zirconia and zircon. Additions of over 15 per cent of lime also increase the viscosity very rapidly, especially at the higher temperatures. Compounds of lead, sodium, potassium and boron all decrease the viscosity, i.e. increase fluidity.

VOLATILIZATION

All the constituents of a glaze are volatile to a certain degree depending particularly upon the temperature, the kiln atmosphere, the vapour pressure of each constituent, and the duration of the firing. Glazes which contain an appreciable amount of lead are particularly liable to suffer from the effects of volatilization with the result that the glossy glazes are not as shiny as they should be. One way of helping to prevent this is by placing the pots having the more susceptible glazes in saggars (i.e. fireclay boxes). These have the effect of confining the vapours given off by the glazes and preventing an excessive amount of vapour from escaping. Another method is to fill a saucer or similar receptacle with a volatile glaze in an attempt to saturate the kiln atmosphere with glaze vapour, thus reducing the degree of volatilization of the glazes on the pots. The loss by volatilization is always greatest wherever the pottery has been fired in a large free space, at the higher temperatures, and from the thickest deposits.

Incidentally, the well-known effects of volatilization are illustrated by the effects of a white glaze opacified with tin fired in close proximity to a pot containing chromium oxide in its glaze composition. A combination of chromium and tin produces a characteristic pink colour referred to as chrome-tin pink, and owing to volatilization the tin-opacified white pots often show a pink tinge after firing.

Similarly, a glaze containing zinc oxide in close proximity in the same kiln to one containing chromium may show an unpleasant brownish discoloration due to a combination of chromium and zinc.

SURFACE TENSION

The force of surface tension results from the fact that any one molecule situated well within the mass of a liquid, such as *A* in Fig. 12, has the forces of attraction of neighbouring molecules distributed uniformly round it in all directions

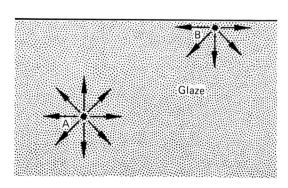

Fig. 12
Surface tension

whereas any molecule such as *B* situated near the surface is acted upon by forces of attraction which are mainly acting downwards and away from the surface.

These internal forces, which influence molten glazes as well as liquids at room temperatures, act as an inward attraction which exerts a pull on the liquid surface as though the liquid was enclosed in a tough elastic membrane and causes small quantities of the liquid to form into globules on horizontal surfaces. If the mass of the liquid is small the drop will become more or less spherical, since a sphere has the minimum surface area for a given volume. However, the larger the drop the more the sphere will be distorted (due to the increased effect of gravity with increased mass) and the shape of the drop will become flatter, progressing to a rounded disc and eventually to a thin flat layer with a slightly thickened edge.

One natural effect of surface tension is to strengthen the surface slightly in comparison to the glaze interior, the surface skin tending to be harder and glossier than the interior.

With increasing temperature the increased energy and movement of the glaze molecules causes a reduction in the effect of surface tension and thus any liquid droplets tend to flatten and flow into each other. However, the ability of the glaze to 'wet' the surface of the body on which it is applied and thus to flow is dependent also upon the force of adhesion at the body/glaze junction or interface and this varies slightly with different bodies. Consequently the temperature needed to cause a glaze to flow just sufficiently to cover a body surface may vary slightly with different bodies.

Other factors influence glaze flow on bodies, notably the smoothness or otherwise of the body surface. A roughened surface acts as a 'key' to retard the flow of the glaze over it, whereas a smoother body allows the glaze to flow more easily.

The optimum firing range of a glaze may therefore vary slightly from one body to another, owing to difference in body smoothness and in adhesion at the body/glaze interface, causing, for example, the same glaze to flow more freely on porcelain than on stoneware.

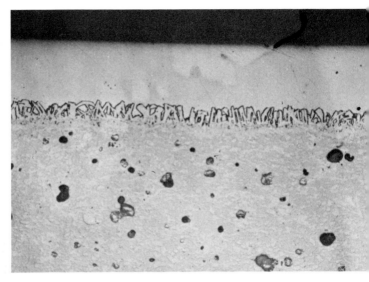

Fig. 13(a)
Transverse section through porcelain
Shows buffer layout containing crystals of anorthite formed by reaction of glaze and body. Reflected light × 128 (half plate). Etched 10 per cent. HF 15 seconds.
(By courtesy of North Staffs Polytechnic)

Fig. 13(b)
Buffer layer on bone china
This reaction layer is non-crystalline. The upper layer has been forced to the surface of the glaze by gas bubbles and this piece had the appearance of being underglazed. Reflected light × 128 (half plate). Etched 10 per cent. HF 15 seconds.
(By courtesy of North Staffs Polytechnic)

THE BUFFER LAYER

During firing the glaze attacks the clay or biscuit surface; evidence of this is readily seen by magnification of a cross-section of the glaze/body interface, but sometimes the results of the glaze attack can be seen by the unaided eye as a corroded body surface beneath the glaze. This combination at the interface of the glaze and body results in a merging of the two, forming a layer known as the buffer layer or reaction layer.

A natural consequence of buffer layer formation is the dissolving action of the glaze upon any 'impurities' at the body surface. If the impurity contains a colouring pigment, as with an iron-bearing grog for example, then the action of the glaze produces a rather larger speck or blotch of colour in the glaze as the impurity is dissolved into it. In general glazes may become very slightly coloured by any body pigmentation and a transparent raw lead glaze on a terra cotta or fireclay body will itself become very slightly honey-coloured in comparison to the same glaze on a white body.

The higher the temperature to which the glaze is fired, the stronger the buffer layer formation. This is largely why high-temperature glazes are frequently very much more coloured or speckled by body combination.

A further, and very important factor, is that wares which have good buffer layer formation also have much greater resistance to the stresses which cause crazing and peeling of the glaze. Consequently the high-fired wares, such as stoneware and porcelain, and wares which have been refired, generally have greater resistance to these faults than do low-fired products, where the buffer layer is less well developed.

COOLING CONSIDERATIONS

When a pure substance in a molten state is gradually cooled, a temperature will eventually be reached at which crystallization will occur. At this point the temperature will remain static until the crystalline stage has been completed, this interruption in the cooling curve being due to the compensating effect of the heat of crystalliza-

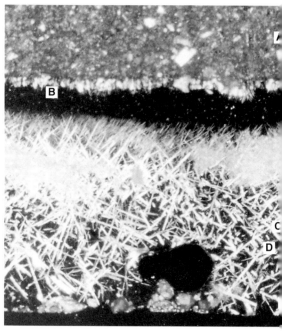

Fig. 14(a)
Transverse section of rutile glaze
(A) Chunks of rutile which have not dissolved; (B) needle crystals of rutile which have crystallized during cooling; (C) glaze with no rutile crystals; (D) buffer layer; (E) body, the white pieces at the bottom of the quartz. Transmitted light, crossed polars x 100 (half plate).

Fig. 14(b)
Haematite crystals in iron-adventurine glaze
Extensive crystal build-up due to composition and slow cooling conditions.

tion which is liberated. In contrast to this, transparent glazes pass from one state to another in a virtually continuous and gradual process so that there is little evolution of heat or retardation of cooling, i.e. there is a gradual stiffening of the liquid until the viscosity or stickiness becomes so great that the behaviour is that of a solid. Even with very crystalline glazes the natural interruption of the cooling curve is usually very slight.

In all cases—whether with pure substances or glazes—the actual size of any crystals which are developed depends upon several factors but particularly upon the rate of cooling.

The formation of igneous rocks shows interesting examples of the influence of cooling rate. An important difference between granite and basalt for example, apart from chemical divergence, is that granite is of much coarser grain than the lava, basalt. This is because lava cools rather quickly at the surface of the Earth (which is cold relative to the hot lava material) and there is insufficient time for good crystals to grow before the magma solidifies. On the other hand, granite and similar coarse-grained igneous rocks contain abundant large, well-formed crystals which had time to grow in a slowly cooling magma that never reached the Earth's surface. The fact that the intrusive granite is often found exposed on the surface of the Earth is simply due to the removal of the overlying rocks by ice, wind and rain.

True matt glazes, opaque glazes produced by crystal formation, and all other crystalline glazes must, therefore, be cooled slowly over their molten phase, so as to allow sufficient time for the necessary crystallization to take place. With zircon-opacified glazes, for example, and especially those where the zircon is introduced in fritted form, rapid cooling may cause the glaze to become rigid before the zircon has had sufficient opportunity to precipitate fully from glaze solution. Consequently the glaze may fire transparent or semi-opaque instead of opaque. Similarly, a rapid cooling cycle may cause other opaque glazes to become clear and matt glazes to become glossy.

The molten phase can be considered to be from the maturing range down to about 900°C (1 650°F) for high-temperature glazes, down to about 750°C (1 380°F) for earthenware ones, and a little lower for low-temperature glazes. However, by far the most critical range is the first 200°C (390°F) or so below the maturing point of the glaze.

Glossy transparent glazes need to be cooled rapidly over their molten phase for optimum gloss. Not only does a rapid cooling cycle minimize the crystallization (devitrification) of glazes but it also reduces the time interval during which loss of gloss can occur through volatilization.

Any stresses created by a rapid cooling of the glaze down to its liquidus point (i.e. the point at which it can be regarded as having changed from a liquid to a solid) will be dissipated owing to the molten or plastic nature of the glaze. Below this point, cooling can be as rapid as the pottery body will allow. In practice, care has to be taken to cool the kiln reasonably slowly much below the liquidus point, otherwise the silica inversions (*see* pp. 107–9) at 573°C (1 063°F) and 225°C (440°F) may cause cracking (dunting) (*see* pp. 112–3) if cooling is too rapid.

4. Composition and formula

We have seen from Chapter 2 that glazes and glasses consist essentially of silica and that this is because silica, and the silicates which are formed from silica, have the property of solidifying from a molten state without recrystallizing. This glass-forming property, without which glasses and glazes could not be produced, is not however confined to silica but is possessed by certain other materials such as germania (GeO_2), antimony oxide (Sb_2O_3), boric oxide (B_2O_3), arsenic pentoxide (AsO_5) and phosphorus pentoxide (P_2O_5).

Silica alone in fact would make an excellent glaze, but it is too refractory (melting point $1713°C$ ($3115°F$)) and so fluxes have to be added to reduce the fusion range to a suitable level for the particular clay on which the glaze is to be used. When glazes are heated, these fluxes melt and surround the particles of the glass-former (silica) which is gradually melted and taken into solution. The presence of alumina, which is also taken into solution, preserves a gradual and viscous melt.

Each of the constituents of a glaze, expressed as the oxides they form when fired, can be set out in the form of a glaze formula so that the overall chemical make-up of the glaze can quickly be seen. As glazes are of variable composition (they are mixtures of compounds), the oxide constituents are not shown consecutively in a long molecular chain which would imply a fixed chemical composition but are arrayed separately, one below the other, the molecular amount of each oxide present being denoted by a prefix which is referred to as the molecular equivalent (more about this later).

The chemical compounds shown in a glaze formula are traditionally divided into three columns: a column on the left for the alkaline oxides of metals, which are referred to as the 'bases' or 'basic' oxides, a column on the right for the acidic or non-metallic oxides referred to as the 'acids' or 'acidic' oxides, and a column between the two for the intermediate or 'amphoteric' oxides which are chemically neutral between the basic and the acidic oxides.

In order that glaze formulae can more easily be compared it is customary during calculation to adjust arithmetically the amount of the oxides expressed in any formula so that the sum of the molecular equivalents of each of the basic oxides totals unity, i.e. 1.0. The actual ratio of the various oxides to each other is not, of course, altered in any way. When the sum of the bases has been adjusted to unity it becomes much simpler to compare one formula with another and, in particular, to compare the ratios of the bases, amphoterics, and acids with each other since these ratios largely determine how a glaze will behave.

The great German ceramist Hermann Seger carried out much research into the importance of the ratios of the groups to each other and listed three ratios which are of outstanding importance to the potter when compounding glazes. They are as follows.

1. The ratio of the bases to acids is normally in the proportion of 1 to 2 in the case of majolica and other soft glazes, about 1 to 2.5 for earthenware glazes, and about 1 to 4 and upwards for stoneware and porcelain glazes.

2. The ratio of alumina to silica is normally kept in the proportion of 1/5th to 1/10th.

3. The amount of boric oxide present is normally about 1/10th that of silica.

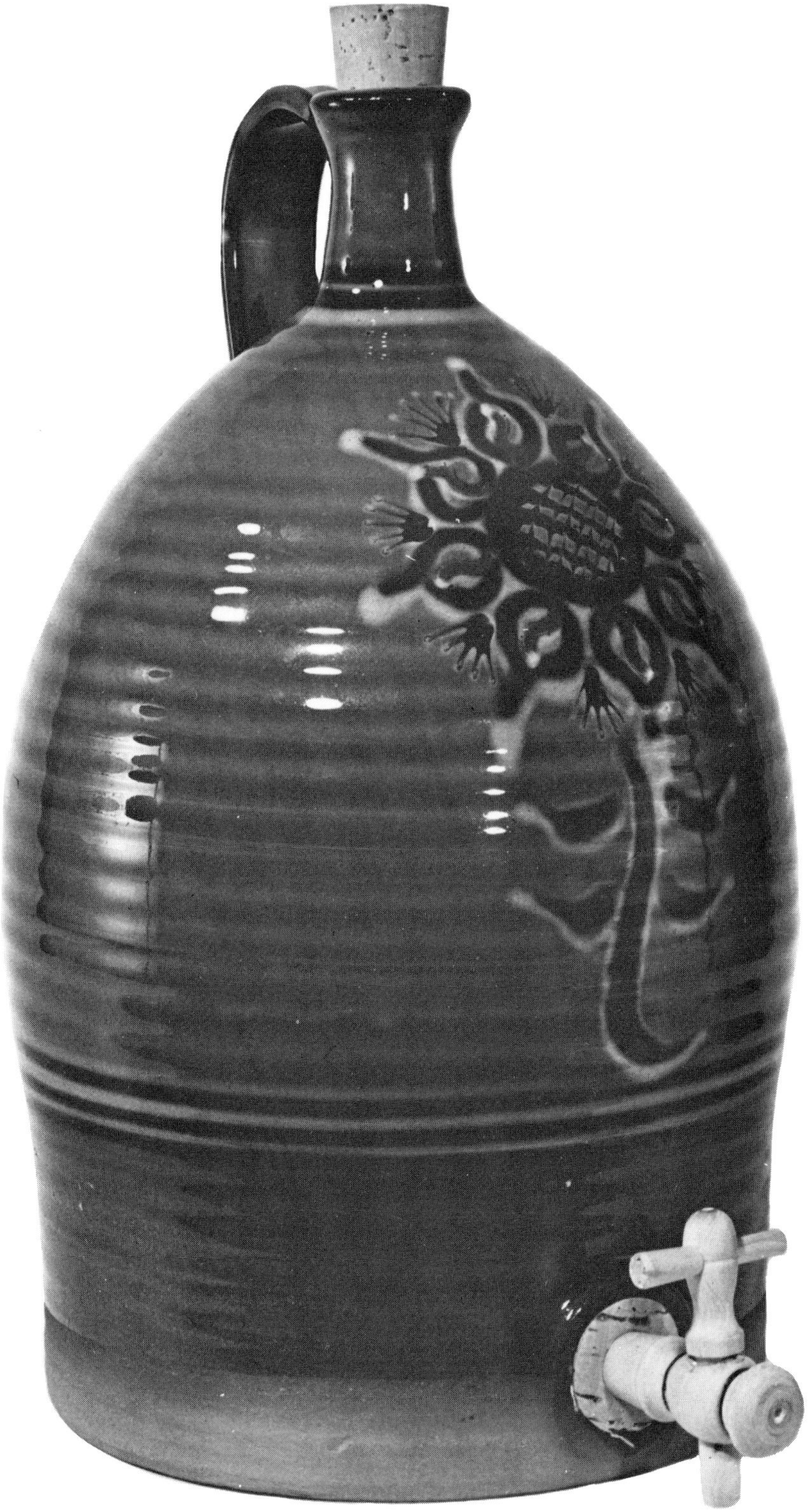

Fig. 15
Slipware cider jar by Alan Frewin
Decoration by black slip with white slip over the black and brushed away in places to expose the black. The centre of the flower combed with red slip and inside of petals sgraffito. Honey-coloured glaze from lead monosilicate and clay. Once fired.

These ratios are often referred to as the 'Seger' ratios and their validity will be seen from two formulae given below, one being an earthenware and one a stoneware glaze.

Earthenware

$$\left.\begin{array}{l} 0\cdot5 \ PbO \\ 0\cdot2 \ K_2O \\ 0\cdot2 \ Na_2O \\ 0\cdot1 \ CaO \end{array}\right\} 0\cdot3 \ Al_2O_3 \left\{\begin{array}{l} 2\cdot5 \ SiO_2 \\ 0\cdot25 \ B_2O_3 \end{array}\right.$$

Stoneware

$$\left.\begin{array}{l} 0\cdot5 \ CaO \\ 0\cdot2 \ MgO \\ 0\cdot3 \ ZnO \end{array}\right\} 0\cdot6 \ Al_2O_3. \ 5\cdot0 \ SiO_2$$

A further examination of the above formulae shows the interesting fact that each of the bases has only one atom of oxygen (O) in each molecule, e.g. one atom of oxygen only is present in CaO, PbO, Na_2O etc. To replace Ca, Pb, Na, and the other elements from which basic oxides can be formed, the ceramist can substitute the letter 'R', this being the only letter of the alphabet which is not given to any particular chemical element. Each of the bases in a glaze formula can then be classified as the 'RO or R_2O' group since each element (R) has only one atom of oxygen (O) in the molecule. Similarly the amphoterics (Al_2O_3) can be classified as being the 'R_2O_3' group and the acids (SiO_2) as being the 'RO_2' group. There are exceptions—notably boric oxide B_2O_3, which is usually regarded as an acidic oxide but which, because of its R_2O_3 structure, could be classified as an amphoteric oxide; indeed, it is the usual practice in the U.S.A. to regard B_2O_3 as an amphoteric oxide. The common opacifiers SnO_2 (tin oxide), ZrO_2 (zirconia) and TiO_2 (titania) owing to their RO_2 structure are generally classified in the acid group. This method of classifying glaze constituents is often used to determine in which of the three glaze groups a particular oxide should be included.

It is important to remember that the degree of fluxing power varies enormously with the type of flux being used and, in particular, with the firing range of the glaze. Lime (CaO) for ex-

ample, is a very useful flux in high-temperature glazes but in glazes maturing below 1 100°C (2 010°F) it tends to act more as a refractory material. Barium oxide, zinc oxide and magnesium oxide are also better suited to high-temperature glazes. Lead oxide on the other hand, is best suited to the earthenware range as at temperatures much higher than 1 180°C (2 160°F) lead oxide begins to volatilize from the glaze layer.

Increasing the number of fluxes used in a glaze will tend to reduce its firing temperature owing to the additional eutectics formed.

The ceramist is frequently required to produce glazes which can be fired at as low a temperature as possible consistent with obtaining satisfactory craze-resistance. However, the expansion characteristics of the clay body as well as its elasticity determine to a certain degree the type of glaze which can be used. Consequently most of the glazes in the majolica range are lead-containing or low-solubility glazes, since leadless glazes in the low-temperature range do not give good craze-resistance. In this connexion, although additions of the alkaline oxides such as the oxides of sodium, potassium and lithium, markedly lower the viscosity and therefore the firing temperature of glazes, they also increase the glaze expansion and therefore make the glaze more prone to crazing, especially when above 0·5 molecular part is present in the formula. This, in fact, is the reason why strongly alkaline glazes (used, for example, to produce Persian or turquoise blue from the addition of copper) inevitably show poor craze-resistance. Consequently the alkaline oxides are to be avoided wherever possible when one wishes to reduce firing temperature without affecting craze-resistance.

In contrast, glazes having a high silica content produce a large amount of silicates which have low expansion properties, and, therefore, give good craze-resistance. If, however, the glaze is underfired, a lesser amount of silicates may be developed which will make the glaze less craze-resistant. Similarly if the silica content is not so finely ground as normal, the larger particles will take longer to dissolve under the same firing conditions. This too may cause insufficient silicate development and thus lower craze-resistance.

5. The constituent oxides

We have seen from the previous chapter that the constituents of pottery glazes can be grouped into three categories—

(*a*) The basic oxides which combine with silica or boric oxide to form silicates and borates which are the basis of pottery glazes. The basic oxides are exclusively fluxes and include the very fluid and notably alkaline oxides of sodium and potassium as well as the more refractory fluxes such as lime.

(*b*) The amphoteric or neutral oxides. Alumina is the only commonly used amphoteric oxide.

(*c*) The acidic oxides such as silica and boric oxide.

Let us now look at the three groups in more detail by examining the characteristics of the various oxides in each group and noting how each oxide is introduced into the glaze recipe. The major raw materials used to supply most of the glaze constituents will be dealt with in chapter six.

THE BASIC OXIDES

Lead oxide (PbO)
Lead oxide is one of the most widely used fluxes for low- and medium-temperature glazes. It is a vigorous flux and reacts easily with silica to form low-melting lead silicates, which form stable glasses without additional oxides.

The lead silicates alone form good glazes in the moderate temperature range. Lead glazes are noted for their high refractive index which results in a brilliant lustrous glaze surface and a vivid colour response from pigments in or under the glaze. Further characteristics of lead glazes which make them popular are that they have long firing ranges and they do not overfire or underfire as easily as leadless glazes; they are also less sensitive to slight changes in the glaze composition which might result from poor preparation. In addition, lead glazes generally exhibit good craze-resistance and may easily be rendered transparent, white, coloured, matt or textured by making appropriate alterations to the glaze recipe.

Lead in a glaze is present as PbO but could be introduced as red lead (Pb_3O_4), lead carbonate ($PbCO_3$), white lead ($2PbCO_3 . Pb(OH)_2$), galena (PbS) or litharge (PbO). Great care has to be taken when handling raw lead compounds, however, owing to their toxic nature (*see* Chapter 8) and consequently it is now usual for the craft potter, and compulsory for the factory, to introduce lead in the form of a lead frit—usually lead bisilicate frit ($PbO . 2SiO_2$) or lead sesquisilicate frit ($PbO . 1.5SiO_2$).

Lead is not often used in glazes maturing above 1180°C since above this temperature the lead tends increasingly to vaporize giving loss of gloss. This effect is particularly pronounced when the lead is introduced as a raw lead constituent instead of in the form of a lead frit. The only other disadvantage of lead as a flux apart from its toxicity is that it can be easily reduced if the ware comes into contact with flame or smoke. This may result in blistering of the glaze and a grey discoloration.

Potassium oxide (Potash, K_2O); **Sodium oxide** (Soda, Na_2O)
The principal sources of potassium and sodium found in the earth's crust are the potash and soda feldspars, these feldspars being used in glazes principally because of the fluxing action of the

K_2O and Na_2O they contain. Feldspars (and similar minerals such as Cornish stone and nepheline syenite) are particularly useful, because they introduce potash and soda in an insoluble form. Most other raw materials containing these alkalis are soluble in water and therefore cannot be satisfactorily used in glazes without being fritted (*see* Chapter 8). Potassium carbonate (pearl ash, K_2CO_3), for example, is water-soluble as also are potassium nitrate (saltpetre, KNO_3), sodium chloride (salt, $NaCl$), sodium carbonate (soda ash, Na_2CO_3) and borax ($Na_2B_4O_7 \cdot 10H_2O$). Consequently, when these materials are used to introduce soda or potash they are fritted to convert them into an insoluble form.

Potash and soda are the principal alkaline oxides and because of this both materials are often used as the basic fluxes in strongly alkaline glazes. They are very vigorous fluxes but possess a high coefficient of expansion and consequently seriously reduce the craze-resistance of glazes in which they are incorporated. Potash is often preferred to soda because it produces a more brilliant glaze than soda, especially when lead is present. It also gives a slightly longer firing range than soda. In low-temperature glazes the potash content may be as high as 25 per cent.

Na_2O, soda, is similar in its action to potash, these two oxides being the most powerful fluxes for silica. As a flux, Na_2O is more powerful pound for pound than K_2O and produces a more fluid liquid. A ternary eutectic containing 70 per cent silica, 23 per cent potash and 7 per cent soda melts at only $540°C$ ($1000°F$). This shows the tremendous fluxing powers of these oxides with respect to silica and also the effect of the eutectic between K_2O and Na_2O. Soda is generally used only in the very low-temperature glazes where the effect of its fluxing power is required.

Strongly alkaline glazes containing high proportions of potassium, sodium or lithium oxide are noted for their unusual and exciting colour response to the introduction of copper, cobalt, manganese and iron. The addition of copper, for example, gives a vivid electric blue or turquoise blue characteristic of much of the Persian and Egyptian pottery of antiquity.

Calcium oxide (Lime, CaO)

Calcium oxide is one of the principal fluxes of medium- and high-temperature glazes. In glazes maturing at temperatures below $1100°C$ ($2010°F$) it tends to act more as a refractory than as a flux but it is a powerful flux at high temperatures when it produces very fluid liquids. If lime is present in excess or if the liquid is too fluid it will devitrify easily, forming crystals of calcium feldspar and thus giving a matt glaze unless the alumina content is increased to compensate. It is a common flux in glazes—especially in stoneware and porcelain glazes where it is often the principal flux.

Calcium oxide is usually introduced into glazes in the form of whiting (calcium carbonate, $CaCO_3$). Whiting dissociates upon heating liberating carbon dioxide gas which can cause bubbling and blistering of the glaze surface (especially in low-temperature glazes) and consequently a longer than usual 'soaking' period or a slower firing cycle may be necessary. Dolomite is also used extensively as a means of introducing lime when the glaze recipe also includes magnesia. Other materials used to introduce lime are anorthite—the lime feldspar, fluorspar (calcium fluoride, CaF_2) if a very small amount of lime is required, and colemanite ($CaO \cdot 1·3B_2O_3 \cdot 2·75H_2O$) or a calcium borate frit if the glaze recipe also includes boric oxide.

Zinc oxide (ZnO)

Zinc oxide is introduced into glazes as the oxide and is used as an auxiliary flux especially in glazes of the leadless type. It is not a powerful flux and tends to act as a refractory in glazes maturing below $1050°C$ ($1920°F$). A particularly useful property of zinc oxide, however, is the relative ease with which zinc silicate crystallizes from molten glazes during cooling to produce a crystalline and matt surface. Consequently zinc oxide is a common constituent of matt glazes and of matting mixtures. The so-called Bristol glazes represent attempts to replace lead oxide by zinc oxide when the poisonous nature of raw lead compounds had become a health hazard in the growing pottery industry.

Zinc oxide has a marked effect on the colours produced by several colouring oxides. It tends to have a depressing effect when used with iron, the colours tending to be dull, but it accentuates the brilliance of greens obtained from copper. When chromium colours are used in conjunction with a zinc-bearing glaze a dull, khaki-brown colour results.

Magnesium oxide (Magnesia, MgO)

Magnesia is only useful as a secondary flux in glazes maturing over $1150°C$ ($2100°F$) but is commonly used as a secondary flux in high-temperature glazes when it becomes a very vigorous flux, strongly increasing fluidity. If present in large amounts, it will produce an attractive smooth, buttery opaque surface. Magnesia lowers the coefficient of expansion of the melt to a greater degree than any other base.

Magnesia is introduced in the form of magnesium carbonate ($MgCO_3$), as talc ($3MgO . 4SiO_2 . H_2O$) or as dolomite ($CaCO_3 . MgCO_3$). The mineral magnesite ($MgCO_3$) is used extensively in the industry especially when producing frits containing magnesia. A mixture of lime and magnesia such as is produced when dolomite is used is not as refractory as either oxide used alone.

Barium oxide (Baryta, BaO)

Barium oxide, like the oxides of calcium and magnesium is essentially a high-temperature flux, its fluxing action becoming evident only in glazes maturing above $1130°C$ ($2070°F$). It produces beautiful satiny matt glazes at high temperatures but an excess produces a rough fired glaze surface. It is best introduced directly into glazes in the form of precipitated barium carbonate ($BaCO_3$). The natural but impure minerals witherite ($BaCO_3$) and barytes ($BaSO_4$) are, however, also used in the industry to introduce barium oxide into frits.

Lithium oxide (Li$_2$O)

Lithium oxide has a fluxing action and colour response similar to that of potash and soda, but has the advantage of a much lower expansion and consequently can be used to produce alkaline glazes with a much higher craze-resistance than

is possible by the use of potash or soda. Lithium is seldom used in glaze compositions, however, because of its expense. It can be introduced in the form of lithium carbonate ($LiCO_3$) or as the minerals petalite, lepidolite or spodumene.

Strontium oxide (SrO)

Strontium is not commonly used as a flux since it has generally similar properties to calcium oxide but is appreciably more expensive. It is, however, slightly more fusible than calcium and therefore can be substituted when a more fluid melt is desired in a glaze at a given temperature.

THE AMPHOTERIC OXIDES

Aluminium oxide (Alumina, Al$_2$O$_3$)

Simple mixtures of fluxes and silica will produce glazes but these are unsatisfactory because they tend to melt fairly suddenly and they produce very fluid melts which would tend to run off the pot during firing and also tend to crystallize (devitrify) easily during cooling. Additions of alumina make glazes more stable by making the melt much more viscous, thus deterring devitrification and causing a more gradual change from the solid to the liquid phase as the glaze melts. In this way the molten glaze can be caused to remain viscous over a range of temperatures up to one or two hundred degrees above the point at which the glaze would otherwise have run off the pot.

Alumina has a melting point of $2050°C$ ($3720°F$) and therefore makes glazes more refractory but at the same time it imparts great durability and resistance. As a general rule the percentage of alumina increases as the firing temperature increases. The presence and amount of alumina provides the most conspicuous difference between a glaze and a glass, glazes invariably containing a much greater percentage. The important role alumina plays in glaze construction and properties is reflected by the fact that its value is regarded as being second in importance only to that of silica.

The source of the alumina required for a glaze is influenced by the glaze firing temperature. In low-fired glazes the alumina usually comes from feldspar which is considered as a refractory in these glazes. In earthenware, stoneware and porcelain glazes the alumina is commonly introduced in the form of china clay, alumina hydrate ($Al_2O_3 . 3H_2O$) or calcined alumina (Al_2O_3). China clay having a theoretical composition of $Al_2O_3 . 2SiO_2 . 2H_2O$ also introduces silica and is particularly useful because of its assistance in maintaining glazes in suspension during dipping.

Alumina is both acidic and basic in behaviour because it can combine with both of the acidic oxides SiO_2 and B_2O_3 as well as the bases. For this reason it is referred to as an intermediate or amphoteric oxide.

Boric oxide (B_2O_3)
In the U.S.A. it is the usual practice to regard boric oxide as an amphoteric oxide, but in the U.K. it is classified with the acidic oxides (q.v.).

THE ACIDIC OXIDES

Boric oxide (B_2O_3)
In order to produce a low-temperature glaze a large amount of flux is necessary to fuse and dissolve the essential glass-forming oxide which is usually silica. If lead oxide is not to be used we must fall back on the oxides of potassium, sodium, calcium, lithium, etc., but a high proportion of these oxides is not desirable owing to the unsatisfactory side effects. High quantities of the very alkaline potassium and sodium oxides, for example, cause very poor craze-resistance in the finished glaze, while high amounts of the other oxides cause a matt or dimpled fired surface or raise the cost of the glaze considerably.

One way, however, to reduce the firing temperature is to substitute some of the silica by the other glass-forming agent—boric oxide, which, unlike silica, is a flux. Boric oxide has a good low-temperature fluxing action and owing to the low expansion characteristics of the borates which it forms in the fired glaze it produces good craze-resistance.

When used in quantities larger than 15 per cent, however, its effect on craze-resistance is reversed; large quantities also lower the resistance of the glaze to acid and water attack. Boric

oxide makes glazes a little more prone to devitrification—especially over terra cotta bodies which, because of their relatively high lime content, allow crystals of calcium borate to form in the fired glaze if it is cooled too slowly, resulting in a milky, bluish discoloration.

B_2O_3 usually has to be introduced into glazes in the form of a frit since the common materials used to introduce boric oxide, namely borax ($Na_2B_4O_7 . 10H_2O$) and boric acid ($B_2O_3 . 3H_2O$) are soluble in water. B_2O_3 can, however, be introduced by the use of the mineral colemanite which is insoluble but which tends to vary in composition.

Silica (SiO_2)
Silica is the fundamental oxide of glasses and glazes and is undoubtedly the most important ceramic material. It is therefore fortunate for the ceramist that 60 per cent of the Earth's crust consists of silica, often in a readily accessible and pure form.

Pottery glazes consist mainly of silica, the other glaze ingredients being used solely to modify the glaze in some way such as lowering the firing temperature, producing a matt surface, or producing opacity. The viscosity of the melt and thus the maturing range of the glaze depends upon the amount of silica present and in low-fired glazes the ratio of silica to fluxes will be about 2 : 1 increasing to about 10 : 1 for high-temperature porcelain or stoneware glazes.

As a general rule, increasing the silica content of a glaze will

(*a*) raise the maturing range by making the melt more refractory,

(*b*) increase the viscosity of the melt (i.e. reduce fluidity),

(*c*) increase the resistance of the fired glaze to chemical attack,

(*d*) increase the hardness and strength of the fired glaze (The greater silica content of stoneware and porcelain glazes is responsible for their generally greater hardness and durability in comparison to low-temperature glazes.),

(*e*) reduce the coefficient of expansion and thus improve craze-resistance.

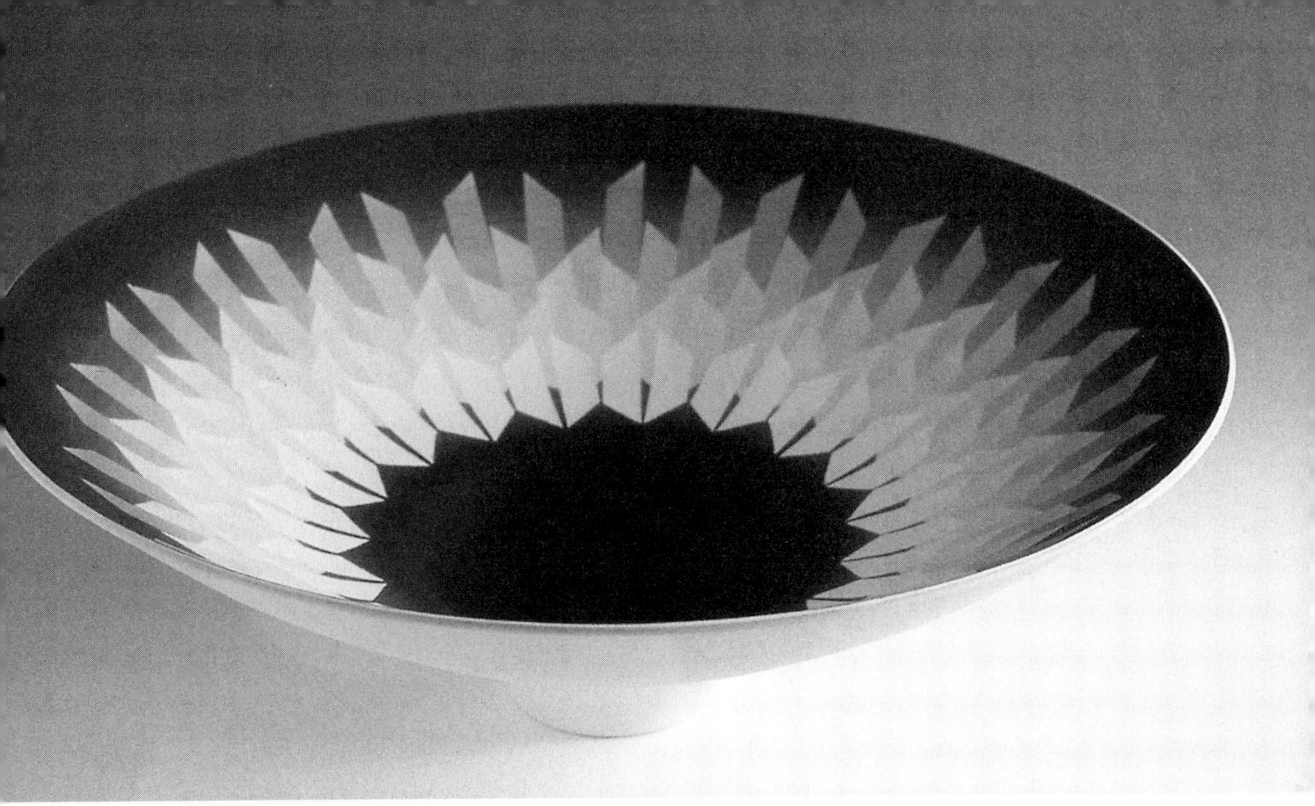

Fig I6
Porcelain bowl by Peter Lane
Thrown and turned in HF1149 porcelain body with airbrushed ceramic stains over paper resists applied to the bisque and thinly applied transparent glaze.

Fig. 17
Oxide-decorated stoneware bowl by Derek Emms

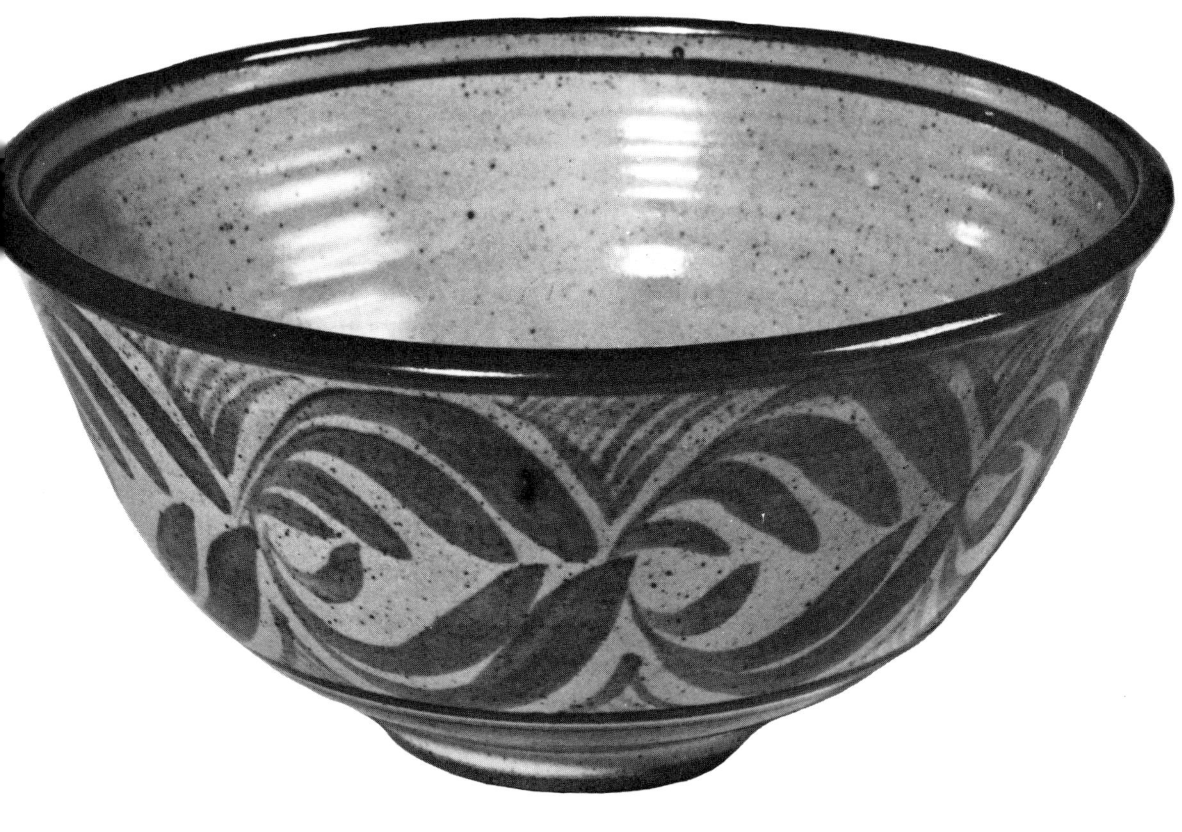

Fig. 18
Translucent porcelain bowl by Victor Margrie
Semi-matt zinc glaze with shiny talc crackle glaze painted over.
Fired cone 8, reduced between cone 06 and 7.

Silica of high purity may be obtained directly from a variety of sources, the chief of which are rock crystal, sandstone and flint. Rock crystal results from silica dissolved or suspended in water which is then deposited in fissures in rocks through which the water passes. Veins of pure quartz produced in this way are very commonly found in siliceous rocks. Sands and sandstones represent the ultimate product of the decomposition of igneous rocks which have gradually eroded and lost the associated bases which have been removed by solution. Flint is obtained either from pure nodules of silica formed out of the metamorphosed skeletons of sponges and located among the chalk deposits of south-east England or from extensive silica deposits, especially in Belgium, formed from finely ground sands, the particles of which have been cemented together.

Silica is introduced indirectly into glazes by the use of china clay $(Al_2O_3 . 2SiO_2 . 2H_2O)$, feldspar, Cornish stone or nepheline syenite. The usual practice is to introduce as much clay as is necessary to provide the required amount of alumina, then to use one of the other materials or a direct source to introduce the further amount of silica required in the glaze formula.

The effect that silica has in making melts more refractory and viscous is of interest to geologists and vulcanologists also. Siliceous magmas are very viscous and may congeal within a volcano, stopping the flow of further magma from the vent. It was this phenomenon of siliceous magma which built up such fantastic pressure behind the plug of Mont Pelée that it was forcibly blown out in a huge explosion and followed by an uprush of hot gaseous magma that swamped the nearby town of St Pierre, Martinique, in 1902.

6. The raw materials

The popular conception of a rock is that of a hard, compact substance such as granite; however not all rocks are of this type and the geologist would include in his classification of 'rock', materials of a different consistency such as beach sand, layers of pebbles and the various types of clay. The fundamental components of rocks are minerals—substances which are usually silicates, oxides and carbonates of the more abundant elements within the Earth's crust. Thus quartz, a familiar mineral, is silicon dioxide (silica), calcite is calcium carbonate, and haematite, iron oxide. There are a large number of known mineral species but only a very few are really abundant in rocks and of these the principal rock-forming ones are the silicates.

The geologist classifies rocks into three main categories—

1. IGNEOUS ROCKS

These are rocks which originate from magmas—molten mixtures of minerals, often rich in gases, found deep below the surface. If magmas cool beneath the surface they form *intrusive* rocks such as the granites. Magmas reaching the surface form *extrusive* rocks such as the spectacular volcanic rocks—basalt, obsidian, etc.

2. SEDIMENTARY ROCKS

These are formed from igneous rocks which have been eroded by running water, wind, waves, currents, ice and gravity, the eroded particles usually being moved from their place of origin to a new place of deposition where they may consolidate. Sandstones, shales and many clays are formed in this way. Other sedimentary rocks are of chemical or organic origin such as the limestones.

3. METAMORPHIC ROCKS

These are rocks which have been changed. The changes may be barely visible or may be so great that it is impossible to determine what the original rock once was. Metamorphism results from heat, pressure, or permeation by other substances such as gases or fluids from igneous material.

The igneous rocks are of particular interest to the ceramist and of these, granite has special significance since this rock directly or indirectly provides many of the potter's materials. A close examination of granite will show it to consist of three different kinds of crystals which will be identified as feldspar, quartz and mica.

The famous china clay deposits in Cornwall resulted from attack by hot acid gases containing dissolved fluorine and bromine from the Earth's interior upon the feldspar present in the granite. This hypogenic action, as it is called, resulted in the removal of some of the flux content by converting it into more soluble compounds which were eventually leached away. Erosion also continually takes place from above by dilute carbonic acid in the form of rainwater and this either accelerates the conversion process or is in itself directly responsible for the breakdown of the feldspar to clay. An indication of this last process is given by the scheme below—

The salts of potassium, sodium and calcium are dissolved out of the granite mass and carried away to the sea from which they may be removed

$$K_2O.Al_2O_3.6SiO_2 \quad + \quad 2H_2CO_3 \quad = \quad Al_2O_3.2SiO_2.2H_2O \quad + \quad K_2CO_3 \quad + \quad 4SiO_2 \quad + \quad CO_2$$

or $Na_2O.Al_2O_3.6SiO_2$ or Na_2CO_3

| Feldspar | Carbonic acid | China clay | Carbonate | Silicate | Gas |

by precipitation to form valuable deposits of potash, soda, limestone etc.

Where decomposition of the granite is only slight, some of the flux is retained by the feldspar, the granite mass then becoming a source of Cornish (Cornwall) stone.

In many parts of the world the granite has been eroded and the constituent minerals of feldspar, quartz and mica carried away. The particles of each mineral naturally tend to settle out of suspension at different rates owing to their different specific gravities and this frequently results in separate deposits of feldspar, one of the ceramist's most useful raw materials. The feldspar deposits ultimately decay to form clays, as was shown earlier.

Feldspar

Feldspar is a general name given to an abundant group of minerals of very varied composition but of similar crystalline structure. If the group were considered a single mineral (and there is good reason for this), it would be by far the most common mineral—five times as common as quartz. Feldspars are found in nearly all igneous rocks and in rocks formed from them. Granites contain approximately 60 per cent of feldspar. Deposits occur widely, but especially in Scandinavia, Canada and the U.S.A. Small deposits occur in Cornwall and the north of Scotland.

All the varieties of feldspar are aluminium silicates combined with potassium oxide, sodium oxide, calcium oxide, barium oxide or lithium oxide or, more usually a combination of them all. The different varieties of feldspar are each classified according to whichever of the basic oxides is dominant. For example, feldspar containing a preponderance of potassium oxide is commonly referred to as potash feldspar or orthoclase but it should be appreciated that this is an over-simplification since at least one of the other basic oxides is almost always present. The principal feldspars are the following—

Orthoclase (potash feldspar) $K_2O \cdot Al_2O_3 \cdot 6SiO_2$
Microcline (potash feldspar) $K_2O \cdot Al_2O_3 \cdot 6SiO_2$
Albite (soda feldspar) $Na_2O \cdot Al_2O_3 \cdot 6SiO_2$
Anorthite (lime feldspar) $CaO \cdot Al_2O_3 \cdot 2SiO_2$

It will be seen that feldspars are virtually complete glazes in themselves, possessing a flux, alumina, and silica and it is therefore natural that feldspar is very frequently the dominant mineral in stoneware and porcelain glazes. Feldspar is also the most commonly used flux for pottery bodies.

From the chemical point of view, the potash feldspars (orthoclase and microcline) are put into one group. The other group, containing what the geologist refers to as plagioclase feldspars, begins with albite and ends with anorthite. Between these are feldspars that are difficult to identify because they contain varying proportions of sodium and calcium, as oligoclase, andesite and labradorite. Rarer feldspars with barium and other metals are also known to occur.

Cornish (or Cornwall) stone

Cornish stone is a peculiar, virtually iron-free form of granite located in the south-west of England and often used in Britain as an alternative to feldspar. It is sometimes referred to as china-stone which is probably derived from the fact that the Chinese used a similar variety of stone, referred to as petuntse.

Cornish stone contains one or more varieties of feldspar (usually orthoclase and albite), china clay, mica, quartz and fluorspar (calcium fluoride) which gives the rock its purplish or bluish colour and a greater fusibility. It is of very variable composition and is commonly graded into four classes which, decreasing in china clay content and increasing in fluorspar content and fusibility are: dry white, medium white, mild purple and hard purple. In an attempt to produce a consistent product it is, however, usual to use a mixed grade. Owing to the fact that the total flux content of mixed stone is around 7 per cent, it is not so fusible as a feldspar which has a flux content of approximately 16 per cent.

A typical formula for Cornish stone might be

$$\left.\begin{matrix} 0{\cdot}40\ K_2O \\ 0{\cdot}28\ Na_2O \\ 0{\cdot}26\ CaO \\ 0{\cdot}06\ MgO \end{matrix}\right\} 1{\cdot}35\ Al_2O_3 \cdot 9{\cdot}0\ SiO_2$$

Cornish stone therefore, like feldspar, introduces

the alkaline fluxes potash, soda and lime into a glaze, but more alumina and silica than is introduced by feldspar.

Nepheline syenite

Nepheline syenite is composed mainly of potash feldspar with some mica or hornblende but little or no quartz. It is slightly more fusible than feldspar as it contains an unusually high amount of soda and potash in relation to the amount of silica present. It is commonly expressed by the formula

$$\left.\begin{array}{r} 0{\cdot}25\ K_2O \\ 0{\cdot}75\ Na_2O \end{array}\right\} 1{\cdot}1\ Al_2O_3 \cdot 4{\cdot}65\ SiO_2$$

Basalt

Basalt is solidified lava, extensive deposits of which exist throughout the world. As would be expected it is variable in composition from one deposit to another but may be quite consistent in composition within the same deposit. In total the rock is about half feldspar, half ferromagnesian minerals.

Basalt provides a very useful flux in high-temperature glazes, being slightly more fusible than feldspar. Owing to its high iron content it is particularly useful in the production of brown or black glazes such as the tenmoku types and in fact may produce a dark brown glaze by itself at around 1 250°C (2 280°F). Glazes containing high amounts of basalt sometimes glisten owing to a tendency to crystallize, and they also tend to have a short firing range (both properties are due to the low alumina content). Basalt nevertheless is an interesting and useful glaze constituent. A typical analysis would be SiO_2 48·6%, Al_2O_3 14·1%, Fe_2O_3 11·2%, MgO 10·3%, CaO 7·9%, K_2O 2·4%, TiO_2 0·6%, MnO 1·6%, P_2O_5 0·3%, loss 3·8%.

China clay

As has been detailed earlier in this chapter, china clay or kaolin as it is commonly called, results from the decomposition of the feldspar present in granite. The gradual decomposition of the feldspar may begin at the top of the granite mass from the action of very dilute carbonic acid (rainwater) or, as in the case of the invaluable Cornish deposits, by hypogenic action of hot acid gases from below the granite mass. The mixture of china clay, mica and quartz comprising the decomposed granite is extracted from the cliff face by washing with powerful water jets, the extracted material then being passed into settling tanks where the mixture settles out in order of specific gravity and particle size, the china clay settling out last of all to give a relatively pure deposit.

China clay provides both alumina and silica, and as both of these materials are very refractory, it is natural that additions of china clay raise the glaze firing temperature. China clay or kaolin also greatly assists in making glazes suspend better in water. It is expressed by the formula $Al_2O_3 \cdot 2SiO_2 \cdot 2H_2O$.

Dolomite

Dolomite is an abundant, naturally occurring sedimentary rock containing approximately 54 per cent calcium carbonate and 46 per cent magnesium carbonate when pure, but in fact pure deposits are rare.

Dolomite is often formed by simple chemical precipitation from bicarbonates of calcium and magnesium in water solution, other deposits being formed by magnesium carbonate solutions reacting with limestone. It is a cheap and convenient mineral to use whenever both magnesia and lime are required in the glaze composition and tends to produce a slightly lower temperature fusion than does a synthetically produced mixture. When dolomite is fired, about 48 per cent of its weight is lost as carbon dioxide gas (CO_2).

Whiting

Whiting is a finely ground form of calcium carbonate, $CaCO_3$, which may be in the form of limestone, marble, calcite or chalk. It is therefore commonly used to introduce lime into glaze recipes.

Magnesite

The principal source of magnesia, MgO, is the mineral magnesite, $MgCO_3$, which contains about 48 per cent MgO and 52 per cent CO_2 when pure, but in nature often contains some iron oxide. It occurs as a replacement in limestone or dolomite due to the action of percolating magnesia-bearing waters, as veins in high magnesia rocks such as serpentine, or separately as beds of white sedimentary rock. It is frequently used as an alternative to chemically precipitated magnesium carbonate as a source of magnesia in glazes.

Talc

Talc is a widespread metamorphic rock formed by alteration of other magnesium-bearing minerals. It has the formula $3MgO \cdot 4SiO_2 \cdot H_2O$ but sometimes contains impurities of iron oxide, alumina, the alkalis and lime.

Fluorspar

Fluorspar or fluorite has the formula CaF_2 and occurs as a crystalline rock. Large deposits are rare but it is a common constituent of sedimentary and igneous rocks. It introduces calcium and is a powerful flux but the fluorine content can be troublesome in transparent glazes since the presence of more than 2 per cent of fluorine in the glaze melt can produce opalescence owing to the formation of immiscible fluorine-concentrated droplets.

Colemanite

Colemanite is often referred to as borocalcite or hydrated calcium borate. It is represented by the formula $2CaO \cdot 3B_2O_3 \cdot 5H_2O$ and is a natural mineral introducing both calcium and boric oxide in an insoluble form. It is in fact the only way of introducing boric oxide in an insoluble form except by making use of a borax frit. Owing to the combination of lime and boric oxide, glazes containing large amounts of colemanite tend to devitrify easily, resulting in the formation of calcium borate crystals which may produce a milky or bluish-white opalescent colour.

When colemanite is calcined it loses approximately 27 per cent of its weight through release of water. This tends to ta. e place relatively suddenly and may cause bubbling or spitting of the glaze if the colemanite content is high. For this reason, and because colemanite is of variable composition, the industry tends to use colemanite largely as a frit constituent, perhaps introducing it into glazes as a calcium borate frit.

Cryolite

Cryolite is sodium aluminium fluoride Na_3AlF_6. It is a rare mineral found in Greenland and Colorado and because of its rarity artificial cryolite is produced. It is an interesting material because it makes sodium oxide available in a natural and unfritted form. It is useful in preparing alkaline glazes but the fluorine content may cause pitting or pinholing of the glaze owing to volatilization.

Potassium carbonate

This is often referred to as pearl ash and has the formula K_2CO_3. It is used as a source of potassium but is soluble in water and is therefore usually introduced into glazes in the form of an alkaline frit constituent.

Magnesium carbonate

This is used in glazes as a source of magnesium oxide in quantities up to 10 per cent. Large amounts may cause pitting or crawling owing to volatilization. The formula is $MgCO_3$.

Zinc oxide

Zinc oxide is the only readily available source of zinc for glazes and in small quantities is a useful secondary flux.

Borax

Borax has the formula $Na_2O \cdot 2B_2O_3 \cdot 10H_2O$ and is therefore a source of both sodium and boric oxide in glazes. As was mentioned in the previous chapter, boric oxide is particularly useful in low-temperature leadless glazes. Borax is, however, soluble in water and consequently it is normally introduced in the form of a frit. It was originally obtained from deposits of volcanic origin but now comes mostly from brines and dry lake beds. The largest and most famous deposit occurs in the Death Valley region of California.

Galena

Galena has the formula PbS, being lead sulphide, and is a heavy, brittle, silvery-grey mineral found

Fig. 19
Porcelain tea pot by David Leach

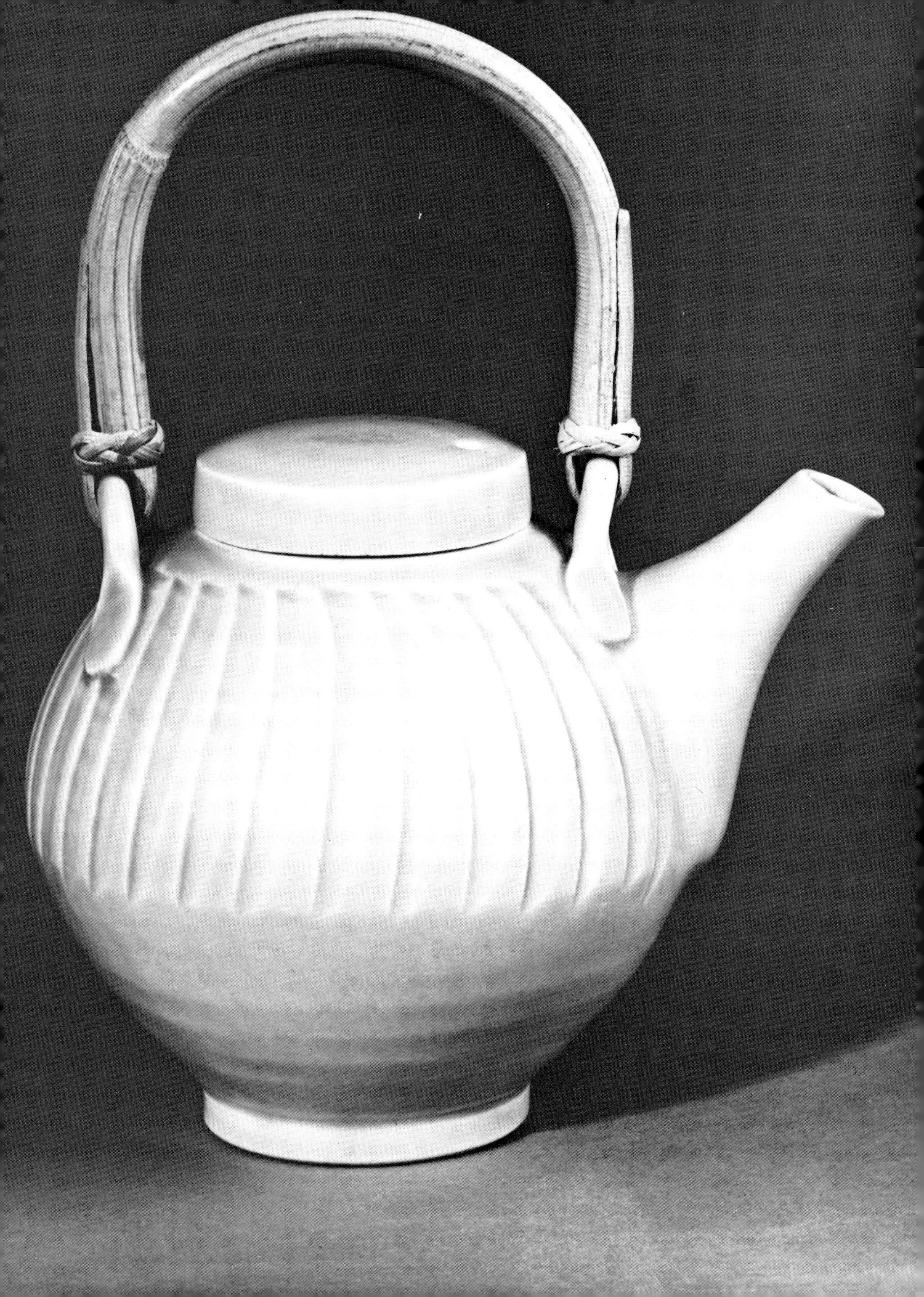

in veins, pockets and replacement deposits in carbonate rocks. It was the basis of many mediaeval glazes but is now normally used only as a frit constituent. Galena is not quite so potentially dangerous, however, as other raw lead compounds since it does not readily dissolve in the stomach juices.

Lead carbonate (White lead, $2PbCO_3 . Pb(OH)_2$); **Lead oxide** (Red lead, Pb_3O_4); **Lead oxide** (Litharge, yellow lead, PbO)

These are very powerful fluxes in pottery glazes. However, owing to their toxic nature they are prohibited from being used in factories as a

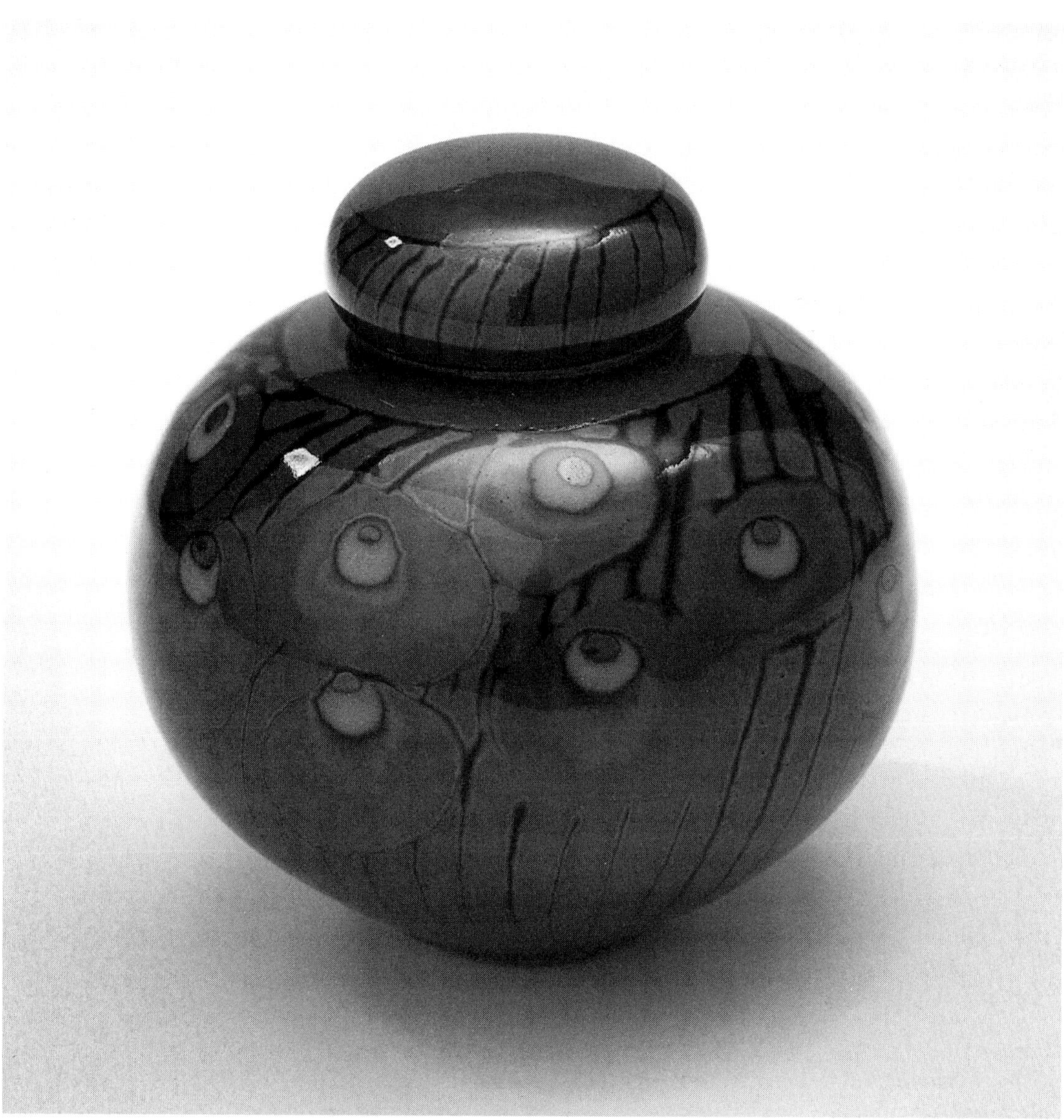

Fig. 20
Ginger jar by David Frith
Wax motif, celadon and kala overglaze.

direct glaze constituent, and in schools etc. their use is permitted only for special work under supervision. Consequently PbO is usually introduced into glazes as a lead frit.

Lepidolite

Lepidolite is a lithium mica with potassium and fluorine and is very variable in composition. It is sometimes used in glazes as a secondary flux to provide a source of lithium oxide. An excess amount can cause pitting and pinholing through volatilization.

It is commonly represented by the formula

$$\left.\begin{array}{l} 0{\cdot}503\ Li_2O \\ 0{\cdot}369\ K_2O \\ 0{\cdot}128\ Na_2O \end{array}\right\} 1{\cdot}04\ Al_2O_3 \,.\, 3{\cdot}76\ SiO_2$$

Petalite

This is similar to lepidolite but slightly more refractory and is used as a secondary flux in high-temperature porcelain and stoneware glazes. Its formula is $Li_2O \,.\, Al_2O_3 \,.\, 8SiO_2$.

Quartz

Quartz is one of the most common minerals in the Earth's crust and as the chemical, silica, SiO_2, it forms an important part of most igneous rocks and provides the potter with his most important material. Quartzite and some sandstones are almost 100 per cent quartz and these materials are commonly ground and used directly as a source of silica in glazes. Flint, another form of silica occurring as grey, black or brown nodules in chalk deposits and thought to be derived from the skeletons of sponges, is also widely used as a source of silica, the hard nodules being calcined to make them more friable before they are ground. It is a very refractory material having a melting point of 1 713°C (3 115°F).

Alumina

Calcined alumina, having the formula Al_2O_3, is sometimes used as a direct source of alumina in glazes. It does not, however, assist in suspending glazes as would china clay—which is the usual way of introducing alumina. In glazes which possess a high clay content it can be useful as a part replacement of the clay thus reducing shrinkage and tendency to crawl. Alumina increases the molten viscosity of glazes thus increasing the firing range and reducing the tendency of the glaze to crystallize on cooling. Its refractoriness (melting point 2 050°C (3 720°F)) makes it useful for the production of bat washes etc. in which case it is best introduced in the form of alumina hydrate, $Al(OH)_3$.

Wood ash

When plants and trees are burned their ashes will frequently be found to contain a combination of materials which fuse or melt at stoneware temperatures and which produce delicate colour shades due to traces of certain colouring oxides. The problem is that a lot of wood is needed to produce a little ash and furthermore the ashes of plants and trees tend to differ in their composition from one to another and with the type of soil in which growth took place. According to Rhodes, however, ashes are likely to have a composition within the following limits—

Alumina	10–15 per cent
Silica	30–70 per cent
Potash	up to 15 per cent
Lime	up to 30 per cent

with traces of iron, phosphorus, magnesium and other elements

Most ashes will fuse at around cones 8–10 but by themselves produce a thin unattractive glass. Therefore wood ash is usually mixed with feldspar, clay and other materials, the ash content being in the region of 10–60 per cent by weight (very much more by volume as the ash is so light in weight). It is usual to stir the ash in an excess of water and allow it to stand overnight in order to dissolve much of the soluble material which can then be discarded by decanting off the surplus water. To obtain a reliable ash composition and performance it is advisable to wash the ash several times in this way, each washing operation removing a little more of the soluble material. As this is predominantly of fluxes, the washing results in the ash becoming more refractory. The ash is then sieved and dried.

7. Glaze calculations

'When you can measure what you are speaking about, and express it in numbers, you know something about it, but when you cannot measure it, when you cannot express it in numbers, your knowledge is of a meagre and unsatisfactory kind; it may be the beginning of knowledge, but you have scarcely, in your thoughts, advanced to the stage of Science whatever the matter may be.' LORD KELVIN

MOLECULAR AND FORMULA WEIGHT

In a previous chapter we have seen that the molecular weight of a compound can be calculated by adding together the atomic weights of the combined elements. Thus water, H_2O, is given a molecular weight of 18 since it is regarded as consisting of two hydrogen atoms (atomic weight 1) and one oxygen atom (atomic weight 16). It is known that water has hydrogen:oxygen atoms in the ratio of 2:1 but suppose some water was composed of H_4O_2? The molecular weight would then be 36! In fact there is much evidence to show that several distinct types of water molecules exist which can be given the formulae H_4O_2, H_6O_3, etc.

Although with certain compounds the precise formula can be determined experimentally, very often the formula of a compound cannot be stated with an exact degree of certainty, and in these cases it is the standard practice to assume that the molecule of a compound has the simplest possible formula. The molecular weight is then calculated from this assigned formula.

In order to differentiate between these compounds where the formula is assumed and those where the precise formula can be determined experimentally, some chemists use the term 'molecular weight' only for the latter, and in all other cases refer to 'formula weight'.

Both terms are, however, in general use to refer to the sum of the atoms contained in the assigned formula of the molecule of a chemical compound and for simplicity we will in this section use the term molecular weight throughout.

Importance of molecular formulae

A knowledge of the molecular formula and molecular weight of a substance enables the ceramist to determine the change in weight of certain materials due to oxidation or reduction or loss of chemically combined water. For example, if one ton of china clay is calcined to 1 100°C (2 010°F) the loss in weight due to loss of water can be calculated quite easily—

Formula of china clay Al_2O_3 . $2SiO_2$. $2H_2O$
Molecular weight $102 + 120 + 36 = 258$

258 tons of china clay will lose 36 tons on calcination

1 ton of china clay will lose $\dfrac{36}{258} \times 2\,240$ lb $= 312 \cdot 6$ lb

We have seen from earlier chapters that it is customary to compare glazes by comparison of their molecular formulae. However, although the molecular formula provides an excellent picture of the overall make-up of a glaze, and an indication of its firing range and properties, it does not immediately tell us the recipe by which that particular glaze may be made. Let us therefore consider the relationship between the composition or analysis of a material and its formula.

Relationship between percentage composition and formula

The percentage composition of china clay is given as

Silica	SiO_2	= 46·51 per cent
Alumina	Al_2O_3	= 39·53 per cent
Water	H_2O	= 13·96 per cent

The molecular formula can be calculated by dividing each oxide by its molecular weight, thus—

SiO_2	$46{\cdot}51 \div 60 = 0{\cdot}775$
Al_2O_3	$39{\cdot}53 \div 102 = 0{\cdot}387$
H_2O	$13{\cdot}96 \div 18 = 0{\cdot}775$

Dividing throughout by the smallest number (0·387) the empirical formula (simplest formula) is

$$Al_2O_3 . 2SiO_2 . 2H_2O$$

Therefore the molecular formula for china clay is

$$Al_2O_3 . 2SiO_2 . 2H_2O$$

Similar principles apply in calculating the molecular formula of a glaze from its percentage composition.

A simple glaze has the following percentage composition—

PbO	= 63·9 per cent
Al_2O_3	= 5·87 per cent
SiO_2	= 30·23 per cent

Dividing the percentage composition of each oxide by its molecular weight the ratio becomes

$$\frac{63{\cdot}90}{223} PbO : \frac{5{\cdot}87}{102} Al_2O_3 : \frac{30{\cdot}23}{60} SiO_2$$
$$= 0{\cdot}287\ PbO : 0{\cdot}058\ Al_2O_3 : 0{\cdot}504\ SiO_2$$

In calculating the empirical formula, each molecular part would have been divided by the smallest number (in this case 0·058).

However, in ceramics a convention is adopted with glazes, namely that 'THE SUM OF THE BASIC OXIDES BE EQUAL TO UNITY'.

In this calculation the basic oxide is PbO and dividing throughout by 0·287 the glaze formula becomes

$$1\ PbO : 0{\cdot}202\ Al_2O_3 : 1{\cdot}756\ SiO_2$$

Given the formula, calculate the percentage composition

The reverse procedure to that shown in the previous problem is shown below.

Given the formula of a glaze as

$$\left.\begin{matrix} 0{\cdot}6\ PbO \\ 0{\cdot}4\ Na_2O \end{matrix}\right\} 0{\cdot}25\ Al_2O_3 \left\{\begin{matrix} 1{\cdot}9\ SiO_2 \\ 0{\cdot}4\ B_2O_3 \end{matrix}\right.$$

calculate the percentage composition.

PbO	$0{\cdot}6 \times 223$	=	133·8
Na_2O	$0{\cdot}4 \times 62$	=	24·8
Al_2O_3	$0{\cdot}25 \times 102$	=	25·5
SiO_2	$1{\cdot}90 \times 60$	=	144·0
B_2O_3	$0{\cdot}40 \times 70$	=	28·0
			326·1

326·1 represents the molecular weight (formula weight) of the glaze. By multiplying throughout by $\frac{100}{326{\cdot}1}$ the percentage composition is

PbO	41·04
Na_2O	7·59
Al_2O_3	7·82
SiO_2	34·96
B_2O_3	8·59

It can be seen in the above calculation that MOLECULAR WEIGHT × MOLECULAR PARTS = PARTS BY WEIGHT.

For example, using sodium oxide, Na_2O,

Molecular weight	= 62
Molecular parts	= 0·4
and their product	= 24·8 (parts by weight)

This relationship is used throughout glaze calculations.

CALCULATIONS INVOLVING RECIPES

It has been shown that the chemical analysis of a glaze can be written in terms of a molecular formula. Also, that, given the molecular formula of a glaze, the percentage composition may be calculated.

All the previous calculations involve the preparation of glazes from the actual oxides contained in the formula and indeed, on a small scale in the laboratory it is possible to weigh out the respective oxides (PbO, Al_2O_3, etc.), and to make the glaze. The percentage composition then becomes the actual working recipe of the glaze.

For larger-scale production, however, it is both

uneconomical and impractical to manufacture glazes from raw oxides and interest therefore centres on calculations involving glazes compounded from raw materials such as china clay, feldspar, frits, etc.

Formula-to-recipe conversion

Let us now consider a simple glaze having the formula

$$PbO \,.\, 0{\cdot}25\ Al_2O_3 \,.\, 2{\cdot}5\ SiO_2$$

We can see that this has one base only—lead oxide, and that since this is a powerful flux and the base:silica ratio is 1:2·5 the glaze will probably mature in the low earthenware region, i.e. 1 000–1 080°C (1 830–1 980°F).

A complete list of raw material formulae and molecular weights is given on pages 134–6 but for simplicity of reference for the following calculations some of the data are repeated here as follows—

		Molecular weight
Litharge	PbO	223
Flint	SiO_2	60
China clay	$Al_2O_3 . 2SiO_2 . 2H_2O$	258
Feldspar	$K_2O . Al_2O_3 . 6SiO_2$	556
Lead bisilicate	$PbO . 2SiO_2$	343
Lead sesquisilicate	$PbO . 1{\cdot}5\ SiO_2$	313
Whiting	$CaCO_3$	100
Zinc oxide	ZnO	81

CONVERSION PROCEDURE

The rule is simply to multiply the molecular units (sometimes called the 'molecular equivalent') of each oxide in the formula by the molecular weight of the selected raw material used to introduce the oxide.

In the glaze formula given above there is one molecular unit of lead oxide (PbO), 0·25 molecular unit of alumina (Al_2O_3) and 2·5 molecular units of silica (SiO_2). We can use several alternative materials to introduce these oxides into the recipe but for the purposes of the following calculation we will use litharge to supply the lead oxide, clay to supply the alumina and some silica, and flint to supply the rest of the silica. A chart similar to the one below may be used to aid the calculation.

The calculation procedure is as follows.

One molecular part of litharge introduces the required one molecular unit of PbO. Multiplying the molecular parts by the molecular weight we get $1 \times 223 = 223$ parts by weight of litharge.

The next item in the formula is the 0·25 unit of alumina for which it is usual to use clay—which is given the formula $Al_2O_3 . 2SiO_2 . 2H_2O$. The H_2O can be ignored since this will disappear during firing but since clay contains twice as much silica as alumina (i.e. $Al_2O_3 . 2SiO_2$) the use of clay will introduce into the recipe an amount of silica equivalent to twice the introduced amount of alumina. This, however, is no problem since glazes always contain much more silica than alumina.

0·25 molecular part of clay therefore introduces the required amount of alumina and twice this amount of silica. Multiplying the molecular parts by the molecular weight we get $0{\cdot}25 \times 258 = 64{\cdot}5$ parts by weight of clay.

0·50 unit of silica has been introduced by the clay and so we now have altogether, one unit of lead oxide, 0·25 of alumina and 0·50 of silica. Since the formula requires 2·50 units of silica we need a further 2·0 parts of silica only to satisfy

Glaze formula $PbO . 0{\cdot}25\ Al_2O_3 . 2{\cdot}5\ SiO_2$

Glaze oxides introduced			*Raw material*	*Molecular parts*	*Molecular weight*	*Recipe parts by weight*
PbO	*Al_2O_3*	*SiO_2*				
1·0			Litharge	1	223	223
	0·25	0·50	Clay	0·25	258	64·5
		2·00	Silica	2	60	120
1·0	0·25	2·50				

Glaze formula $PbO \cdot 0{\cdot}25\ Al_2O_3 \cdot 2{\cdot}5\ SiO_2$

PbO	*Al_2O_3*	*SiO_2*	*Raw material*	*Molecular parts*	*Molecular weight*	*Recipe parts by weight*
1·0		2·0	Lead bisilicate	1	343	343
	0·25	0·50	Clay	0·25	258	64·5
1·0	0·25	2·50				

the formula and flint is used to do this.

Multiplying the molecular parts by the molecular weight we get $2 \times 60 = 120$ parts by weight of flint.

We now have a recipe—

223 parts of litharge	i.e.	54·7 per cent
64·5 parts of clay	i.e.	15·8 per cent
120 parts of flint	i.e.	29·5 per cent

In view of the raw lead content of the above ecipe its use could not be permitted in factories and would be severely restricted in educational establishments. To overcome this difficulty we can calculate a new recipe for the same formula but using a lead bisilicate frit instead of lead oxide. Above (top of page) is a recipe incorporating lead bisilicate frit, calculated to the same formula.

In this case the lead bisilicate ($PbO \cdot 2SiO_2$) satisfies the lead oxide requirements and also introduces twice this amount of silica. Use of flint is not necessary since the combination of the silica introduced by the lead bisilicate frit with that introduced by the clay is just sufficient to satisfy the formula. If lead sesquisilicate ($PbO \cdot 1{\cdot}5\ SiO_2$) had been used instead of the bisilicate, then sufficient silica to satisfy the formula would not have been introduced by the frit and the clay, and addition of flint (0·50 molecular part) would have been required.

We therefore have two recipes; one raw lead and one low-solubility, both of which have the same formula and therefore in theory give exactly the same glaze. In practice however there is usually a slight difference on account of impurities in the materials or variation in eutectic formation and a slight final adjustment based on the fired result may be necessary if one is used as a direct replacement for the other.

Suppose we now look at a further example and select a stoneware glaze which has the following molecular formula—

$$\left.\begin{matrix} 0{\cdot}4\ K_2O \\ 0{\cdot}4\ CaO \\ 0{\cdot}2\ ZnO \end{matrix}\right\} 0{\cdot}50\ Al_2O_3 \cdot\ 4{\cdot}2\ SiO_2$$

In this instance the percentage composition figures have, of course, been obtained by dividing the parts by weight figures by 400·2 (*see* below).

Recipe-to-formula conversion

This is a little more difficult than converting formula to recipe but it should present no problems if the calculation is done methodically. Such calculations are very useful in enabling one

K_2O	*CaO*	*ZnO*	*Al_2O_3*	*SiO_2*	*Material*	*Molecular parts*	*Molecular weight*	*Parts by weight*	*% weight*
0·40			0·40	2·40	Feldspar	0·40	556	222·2	55·5
	0·40				Whiting	0·40	100	40·0	10·0
		0·20			Zinc oxide	0·20	81	16·2	4·0
			0·10	0·20	Clay	0·10	258	25·8	6·5
				1·60	Silica (flint)	1·60	60	96·0	24·0
0·4	0·4	0·2	0·5	4·2				400·2	100·0

to calculate a formula from any recipe, thus providing a greater understanding of the glaze and a means of directly comparing it with others.

The basic principles of calculation can be summarized as follows—

(*a*) Determine the molecular formula and molecular weight of each recipe ingredient.

(*b*) Divide the parts by weight by the molecular weight to determine the molecular parts of each ingredient (the percentage composition figures can be regarded as the parts by weight data).

(*c*) Where the molecular formula of an ingredient contains more than one oxide, use the molecular parts (calculated above) to determine the molecular amount of each oxide.

(*d*) Use the chart to display the molecular amounts of each oxide introduced by each material in the recipe and add together any amounts of the same oxide so as to give a total molecular amount of each oxide.

(*e*) Divide the molecular amount of each oxide by the sum of the molecular amounts of the basic oxides so that they can be set out as a formula, the sum of the bases totalling unity.

Let us now calculate back to the formula from the recipe of the glaze listed earlier in this chapter, i.e. the low-solubility glaze having the recipe

> 223 parts of litharge or 54·7 per cent
> 64·5 parts of clay or 15·8 per cent
> 120 parts of flint or 29·5 per cent

It would not matter whether we began with the parts by weight figures or whether we regarded the percentage figures as being the parts by weight figures since both will produce the same formula when calculated back. However, for consistency we will in this instance use the parts by weight figures.

Incidentally, for recipe-to-formula calculations the introduced oxides will be listed at the right-hand side of the chart instead of on the left. This does not matter of course but may be an aid to neatness with complex recipes where one cannot easily tell at once how many oxide columns will be needed in the chart (*see* below).

The method of calculation is as follows—

(*a*) The molecular formulae and molecular weights of the recipe ingredients are

Litharge, PbO   Molecular weight 223
Clay, $Al_2O_3 . 2SiO_2 . 2H_2O$ Molecular weight 258
Flint, SiO_2 Molecular weight 60

(*b*) Divide the parts by weight by the molecular weight to obtain the molecular parts.

223 parts by weight litharge ÷ 223 = 1·0 molecular part
64·5　,,　　,,　　,, clay　　÷ 258 = 0·25　　,,　　part
120　,,　　,,　　,, flint　　÷ 60　= 2·0　　,,　　parts

(*c*) Where the molecular formula contains more than one oxide, use the molecular parts to determine the molecular amount of each oxide. Litharge and flint each introduce only one oxide. Clay, however, introduces silica as well as alumina in the ratio 2:1, therefore a molecular amount of 0·50 molecule of silica must be added to the chart in addition to 0·25 of alumina.

(*d*) The chart has been set out below.

(*e*) The basic oxides total unity and no further adjustment is necessary. However, had we used the percentage composition figures then some adjustment would have been necessary.

Material	Molecular weight	Parts by weight	Molecular parts	PbO	Al_2O_3	SiO_2
Litharge	223	223	1	1·0		
Clay	258	64·5	0·25		0·25	0·50
Flint	60	120	2·0			2·00
				1·0	0·25	2·50

A more difficult example

Frequently we can obtain a more accurate analysis of certain materials to replace the theoretical analysis and this will enable us to increase the accuracy of calculation. The feldspar family is a notable example. Potash feldspar is allotted a molecular formula of $K_2O \cdot Al_2O_3 \cdot 6SiO_2$ but this is an over-simplification and, as was pointed out in Chapter 6 most potash feldspars are so called because potash is the predominant, but not the only, flux. Suppose we discover that the molecular formula of our feldspar is actually

$$\left.\begin{matrix} 0{\cdot}72\ K_2O \\ 0{\cdot}28\ Na_2O \end{matrix}\right\} 1{\cdot}13\ Al_2O_3 \quad 7{\cdot}8\ SiO_2$$

the molecular weight of which is 670·0.

We will now carry out a further recipe-to-formula calculation using the above feldspar in a recipe comprising

222·2 parts feldspar
40·0 parts whiting
16·2 parts zinc oxide
25·8 parts clay
96·0 parts flint

Below, the calculated molecular part (0·33) of feldspar is multiplied by the molecular amount of each oxide in the feldspar formula—exactly as one would have done if the theoretical formula instead of the actual formula had been used. We therefore multiply 0·33 molecular part by 0·72 K_2O to give 0·238 in the chart, by 0·28 Na_2O to give 0·09, by 1·13 Al_2O_3 to give 0·37 and by 7·8 SiO_2 to give 2·58.

When the molecular amounts of each oxide introduced by each recipe ingredient have been determined, it is discovered in this instance that the sum of all the bases adds up to 0·93 whereas we need them to total unity. For this reason we therefore multiply throughout by $\frac{100}{93} = 1{\cdot}08$ and arrange as formula as follows—

$$\left.\begin{matrix} 0{\cdot}257\ K_2O \\ 0{\cdot}097\ Na_2O \\ 0{\cdot}432\ CaO \\ 0{\cdot}216\ ZnO \end{matrix}\right\} 0{\cdot}507\ Al_2O_3 \cdot\ 4{\cdot}73\ SiO_2$$

It will be interesting to compare this molecular formula with that used in the calculation on page 39. Note that the recipe is the same in each case, the slight difference in the molecular formula being due solely to the fact that one calculation included the theoretical formula of feldspar whereas the other was based on an actual analysis of the feldspar in use.

A useful glaze calculator is illustrated in Fig. 21.

Material	*Molecular parts*	*Molecular weight*	*Parts by weight*	K_2O	Na_2O	CaO	ZnO	Al_2O_3	SiO_2
Feldspar	0·33	670	222·2	0·238	0·09			0·37	2·58
Whiting	0·40	100	40·0			0·40			
Zinc oxide	0·20	81	16·2				0·20		
Clay	0·10	258	25·8					0·10	0·20
Flint	1·60	60	96·0						1·60
				0·238	0·09	0·40	0·20	0·47	4·38

bases add up to 0·93

RAPID GLAZE CALCULATOR
Colin Pearson & Dennis Healing
Ceramic Calculators
Marston Magna
Yeovil Somerset
England
© COPYRIGHT 1969
MOLECULAR WEIGHT MATERIALS
776 White Lead (basic)
685 Red Lead
667 Average Cornish Stone
556 Potash Felspar
524 Soda Felspar
462 Average Nepheline–Syenite
412 Colemanite
382 Borax
378 Talc
343 Ideal Lead Bisilicate
313 Ideal Lead Sesquisilicate
310 Bone Ash
258 China Clay
233 Barium sulphate
223 Lead oxide
210 Cryolite
197 Barium carbonate
184 Dolomite
160 Ferric oxide
153 Barium oxide
148 Strontium carbonate
138 Potassium carbonate
124 Boracic Acid
102 Alumina
100 Calcium carbonate, Whiting
94 Potassium oxide
84 Magnesium carbonate
81 Zinc oxide
80 Titanium oxide
74 Lithium carbonate
72 Ferrous oxide
70 Boric oxide
62 Sodium oxide
60 Silica
56 Calcium oxide
40 Magnesium oxide
30 Lithium oxide
EQUIVALENT WEIGHTS
White Lead 258
Red Lead 228
Colemanite 206
Cryolite 420
Bone Ash 103
MOLECULAR PARTS
MOLECULAR WEIGHTS
RECIPE WEIGHTS
A
B
C
D
U
200 %
P3241

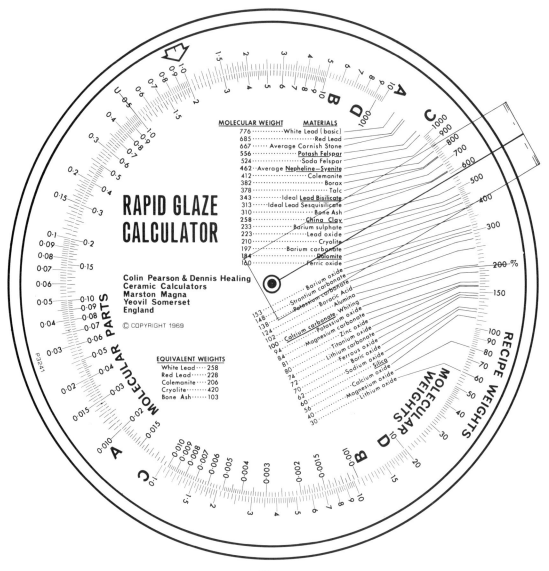

Fig. 21

Rapid glaze calculator designed by Colin Pearson and Dennis Healing

An instrument, based on slide-rule principles, designed to facilitate the rapid calculation of recipe to formula and vice versa. The face is inscribed with useful data.

Several software programs for PCs running on MS Windows operating systems are now available to facilitate recipe to formula and formula to recipe calculations. In the United Kingdom, *The Glaze Workbook* by David Hewitt is very good and ideal for both the craft potter and student as is *Glaze Calculation for Studio Potters* by Dr Chris Hogg.

In North America, *Insight* by Tony Hansen, *Hyperglaze* by Richard Burkett and *Glazechem* by Robert J. Wilt are popular. *Matrix* produced in New Zealand by Lawrence Ewing is also well recommended.

CALCULATIONS INVOLVING FRITTED GLAZES

EXAMPLE

The recipe of a glaze is

Borax frit	60
Lead frit	30
China clay	10

The lead frit is $PbO \cdot 2SiO_2$.

The borax frit formula is

$$\left.\begin{matrix} 0{\cdot}6\ CaO \\ 0{\cdot}3\ Na_2O \\ 0{\cdot}1\ K_2O \end{matrix}\right\} 0{\cdot}18\ Al_2O_3 \left\{\begin{matrix} 2{\cdot}06\ SiO_2 \\ 0{\cdot}60\ B_2O_3 \end{matrix}\right.$$

Calculate the formula of the glaze.

Method

The molecular weight of the borax frit is calculated in the usual way—

$$\begin{array}{lll} CaO & 0{\cdot}6 \times 56 & = 33{\cdot}6 \\ Na_2O & 0{\cdot}3 \times 62 & = 18{\cdot}6 \\ K_2O & 0{\cdot}1 \times 94 & = 9{\cdot}4 \\ Al_2O_3 & 0{\cdot}18 \times 102 & = 18{\cdot}4 \\ SiO_2 & 2{\cdot}06 \times 60 & = 123{\cdot}6 \\ B_2O_3 & 0{\cdot}60 \times 70 & = 42{\cdot}0 \\ \hline & & 245{\cdot}6 \end{array}$$

$60 \div 245{\cdot}6 = 0{\cdot}244$, and since 1 molecule of borax frit brings in 0·6 CaO, then 0·244 molecule of borax frit will bring in $0{\cdot}6 \times 0{\cdot}244 = 0{\cdot}146$ molecular part CaO. The molecular parts for other oxides are calculated on a similar basis in the chart below.

The sum of the basic oxides = 0·33. We bring the sum to unity by dividing throughout by 0·33 which results in the following molecular formula—

$$\left.\begin{matrix} 0{\cdot}442\ CaO \\ 0{\cdot}221\ Na_2O \\ 0{\cdot}073\ K_2O \\ 0{\cdot}264\ PbO \end{matrix}\right\} 0{\cdot}25\ Al_2O_3 \left\{\begin{matrix} 2{\cdot}288\ SiO_2 \\ 0{\cdot}442\ B_2O_3 \end{matrix}\right.$$

Material	*Molecular weight*	*Molecular parts*	*Parts by weight*	*PbO*	*CaO*	*NaO_2*	*K_2O*	*Al_2O_3*	*SiO_2*	*B_2O_3*
Borax frit	245·6	0·244	60		0·146	0·073	0·024	0·044	0·503	0·146
Lead frit	343·0	0·087	30	0·087					0·174	
China clay	258·0	0·039	10					0·039	0·078	
				0·087	0·146	0·073	0·024	0·083	0·755	0·146

8. Frits and Processing

THE NECESSITY FOR FRITTING

We have seen that lead is an extremely useful constituent of ceramic glazes, for it provides a low melting temperature and a low viscosity in the molten glaze with a reasonably low coefficient of expansion and a high refractive index which produces very glossy smooth glazes.

Lead has been used in glazes for many hundreds of years and was originally introduced as lead sulphide or galena. This was later discontinued in favour of lead carbonate, i.e. white lead which, owing to its flaky structure, suspended better in glazes than the oxides and sulphides of lead which because of their granular structure tended to settle out of suspension quickly. Unfortunately, however, the oxides and carbonates of lead are readily soluble in the gastric juices of the stomach from where they are taken into the bloodstream, the lead compounds accumulating until a certain concentration is reached when the characteristic symptoms of lead poisoning appear.

There were 200 deaths from lead poisoning in the British pottery industry in the year 1900. These were invariably due to ingestion via the mouth and nose of small quantities of glaze over a period of time.

In an attempt to overcome the problem, regulations were introduced which enforced stricter standards of hygiene—notably laws which demanded the use of protective clothing and which forbade smoking and eating in any workshops where raw lead compounds were used. In addition, responsibility was brought to the employer to ensure that the floors of dipping shops etc. were washed daily. It became compulsory for lead compounds to be handled only in a damp condition, in order to suppress dust, and respirators had to be used by anyone handling or mixing raw lead compounds.

Many factories attempted to discontinue the use of lead completely and to rely entirely on leadless glazes. This, however, met with limited success and so efforts were concentrated on attempts to convert the lead compounds into a form which would not be soluble in the gastric juices and would therefore be unable to introduce dissolved lead into the bloodstream of the operatives. Success was eventually achieved by the process of fritting (*see* page 45), in which the lead oxide was combined with silica (and sometimes other glaze constituents) to form lead silicate, lead bisilicate or lead sequisilicate frits depending upon the ratio of lead oxide to silica used during the fritting process.

In addition to fritting soluble lead compounds to convert them to a form which is virtually insoluble in human gastric juice, fritting is also used to convert water-soluble constituents of pottery glazes into an insoluble form. Any materials which are soluble in water cannot be incorporated satisfactorily into glazes, since they partly or completely dissolve and pass with the water into the pottery body during the glaze application process, instead of remaining with the glaze coating on the pottery surface. As the water is evaporated away during subsequent drying, most of the dissolved material passes back through the pores of the pot, through the glaze layer, and forms a deposit of crystals on the surface of the unfired glaze layer. Soluble materials therefore cannot be evenly dispersed in glazes since they 'un-mix' themselves after the glaze has been applied. Furthermore, since the amount which actually dissolves varies with the material, with the water temperature and with the length of time the material is present in the water, one does not know what proportion of the material is dissolved. If, however, the water-soluble constituent is converted by a fritting operation into an insoluble form (usually a silicate) then it can be incorporated satisfactorily into the glaze recipe.

Several potentially useful materials are sol-
uble in water. Borax, for example, is very useful for introducing both sodium and boric oxides into glazes but borax is water-soluble and consequently it is usual to frit the borax content of a glaze with some of the other glaze constituents so that the borax is introduced in the form of a borax frit. Similarly, potassium oxide, introduced in the form of potassium carbonate (pearl ash) and sodium oxide, introduced in the form of sodium carbonate (soda ash) are also very soluble in water but are useful in the production of alkaline or crackle glazes. These materials are therefore normally introduced in the form of an alkaline frit in which most of the flux content consists of potassium and sodium oxides.

There are a number of companies that produce a wide range of lead frits, borax frits and alkaline frits, and publish recipes of most of these in which the chemical make-up of the frits can be readily seen.

Fig. 22
Continuous frit kiln
(By courtesy of Podmore & Sons Ltd)

THE FRITTING PROCESS

Fritting can be done either continuously or in an intermittent frit kiln. Continuous fritting obviously is only undertaken where large quantities of a particular type of frit are required. In the continuous process the pre-mixed ingredients are fed at a constant rate into one end of a box-shaped kiln which is lined with refractory bricks and heated by powerful gas or oil burners which directly impinge on to the frit materials thus melting them. The firing conditions are then adjusted so that the molten frit overflows from the kiln at the same rate as the equivalent amount of raw material is introduced. This, therefore, results in a constant stream of molten frit flowing out of the kiln. The molten frit can then be either quenched in water to give a granulated product or passed through water-cooled rollers, cold air

position in one end of the cylinder and made to fire into the kiln to melt the frit materials, the exhaust gases passing through the opposite end of the cylinder and via a duct into a chimney. As the melting process proceeds, the cylinder is rocked to and fro through an arc of about 70° to facilitate thorough mixing of the frit batch. When a test sample removed on a poker indicates that the materials have been thoroughly melted together to form a bubble-free frit, the charge is

Fig. 23
Intermittent frit kiln being discharged
(By courtesy of Podmore & Sons Ltd)

jets and flails which result in a flake-like product. The frit is then taken away by screw feeds or conveyor belts to hoppers from which it is later taken and passed into the grinding mills.

Many frits, however, are made in intermittent kilns which are often of the rotary type. These consist of a steel cylinder lined with suitable refractories and mounted horizontally and rotated by a gear mechanism. After the frit materials have been introduced, the burner is secured in

removed by rotating the cylinder until the molten material pours out into a large tank full of water. This is manually stirred with a long steel poker to break up the frit and prevent the formation of large lumps. The molten frit falling into the water bath is one of the most spectacular sights in the pottery industry.

The fritting temperature, incidentally, varies with the frit but is generally in the range 1 100–1 200°C (2 010–2 190°F).

LEAD SOLUBILITY TESTS

The lead content of a frit can be very high. With a lead bisilicate frit, for example, the lead oxide content is approximately 65 per cent and with a lead sesquisilicate frit approximately 71 per cent. However, as the lead is intended to be present as a more or less insoluble compound it is important to ensure that the actual degree of solubility is within a certain defined limit. In Britain, Government regulations stipulate that any lead-containing glaze used in a pottery factory must not yield more than 5 per cent of its dry weight of soluble lead (calculated as PbO) when treated with 0·25 per cent hydrochloric acid at room temperature. The content of hydrochloric acid in the gastric juice is actually 0·17 per cent, but 0·25 per cent hydrochloric acid is used in the solubility test so as to compensate for the fact that the acid in the body is at blood temperature. Full details of the lead solubility test are given in Appendix 2. Glaze powders which pass this test are referred to as low-solubility glazes, and it is the enforced replacement in factories of raw lead glazes by low-solubility glazes that has largely been responsible for the dramatic reduction in the incidence of lead poisoning in the industry. It is important to bear in mind that the maximum permissible lead content (of low-solubility glazes) varies with different countries; for example, Germany has a 1 per cent and Holland a 2·5 per cent limit.

The solubility of a lead frit depends not only upon the lead content but obviously also upon the temperature at which the test is carried out and especially upon the particle size of the ground frit. The finer a frit is ground the greater will be its solubility owing to the greater surface area of the ground particles in relation to their mass. Finely ground frits are therefore more toxic than frits which are not so finely ground.

A method of physically reducing the solubility of lead frits by coating the ground particles with a very thin layer of an impervious and insoluble material has been developed. This technique, which is now protected by patent, consists in grinding the frit and then adding a stabilized silicone ester in a suitable solvent. On drying out, the ester polymerizes, and thus each particle of frit is coated with a very thin film which is impervious to, and insoluble in, dilute acids. As this film consists essentially of silica, the chemical properties of the frit are not affected by the coating process; moreover, if the coated frit is subjected to further grinding, the increase in solubility of the particles is roughly proportional to the new surface exposed showing that the protective film is not readily removed by grinding.

Sir Thomas Thorpe gave his name to an empirical ratio—Thorpe's ratio—which was subsequently simplified by J. W. Mellor (as below) and which has served as a guide to estimate whether a glaze will conform to the British low-solubility regulations for glaze powders. The ratio is

$$\frac{\text{Total mol. equivalents of bases and alumina}}{\text{Total mol. equivalents of acid}}$$

To conform to the low-solubility regulations the result should not exceed 0·5.

It has been proved that TiO_2 and Al_2O_3 markedly reduce lead solubility whilst K_2O and B_2O_3 increase it. Owing to its usual effect on lead solubility boric oxide is generally not included in the composition of lead frits but the maxim does not always hold true and several lead borosilicate frits have been produced which contain high amounts of lead yet which are of low solubility and which have surprisingly low thermal expansions.

FRITTING ON A STUDIO SCALE

Fritting can be done on a small scale by weighing out the required amount of the various materials in the complete recipe, dry mixing them together, and heating the mixture in a crucible, which could be made from a suitable clay biscuited at a temperature in excess of the maturing temperature of the frit. It is best to leave out part of any clay content of the glaze recipe for introduction at the milling stage so that it will assist in glaze suspension (which it will not do if fritted).

The crucible must be heated strongly until the contents melt. A good melting action will be attained at around 1 130°C (2 070°F) for lead glazes and from 1 180°C (2 160°F) to 1 200°C (2 190°F) for borax and alkaline glazes. As the melting process takes place it will be accompanied by the generation of many gas bubbles, and heating should be prolonged for about half an hour after the fritting temperature has been reached so as to allow a thorough fritting action to take place, resulting in the water-soluble materials being dissolved and taken into glaze solution.

Heating a crucible half full of frit to this temperature range is not a simple operation, since heating in open air with bunsen burners or in a bed of coke in raku fashion will not allow a sufficiently high temperature to be obtained. A small electric kiln can be used, the crucible being lifted out with tongs after the required temperature has been reached and the kiln switched off, but this procedure is not recommended as it is too easy to make a frightful mess inside the kiln. The best procedure is to construct a small but simple top-loading furnace fired by a gas or oil burner and built from refractory materials or refractory insulation bricks.

When the frit is sufficiently molten it is poured out into a bath of water which causes it to solidify and break up. The frit particles then have to be ground. This is best done either in an ordinary ball mill or Op-po mill until the particle size is sufficiently fine to leave less than 1 per cent residue on a 120- or 200-mesh sieve (200-mesh is obviously better). Grinding with a mortar and pestle is possible but laborious.

Glazes prepared in this way, i.e. in fully fritted form, will not usually contain any soluble materials. It should, however, be borne in mind that fritted glazes usually have a markedly lower firing range than the equivalent raw glaze, owing to the formation of eutectics during fritting.

A word of warning! A crucible of molten frit at a temperature of around 1 100°C (2 010°F) must be treated with respect: therefore use a good pair of tongs, heat-resistant gloves and goggles. Take care also when pouring the frit into water as this action is accompanied by much spitting and spattering as the frit comes into contact with the water.

OTHER MATERIALS OF CONCERN

By converting raw lead constituents into a relatively safe lead frit such as lead bisilicate we do not completely remove all hazardous materials from glaze blends. There are certain other materials which must be treated with caution.

Antimony oxide and barium carbonate (used in rat poisons) in particular must be handled with care with proper attention to washing and personal hygiene, since both materials are very poisonous. In addition, boric acid and borax are significantly toxic as also are colouring agents such as cadmium selenium stains, liquid gold lustres (these are often prepared in a highly toxic liquid amalgam of mercury) and many on-glaze enamels. Exposure over a period to chromium oxide can cause severe skin irritation whilst prolonged exposure to depleted uranium oxide has been known to cause kidney damage, also nickel oxide is carcinogenic. Exposure over a period to siliceous dust may cause silicosis and since a high percentage of clay and glaze consists of silica it is important to avoid unnecessary creation of clay or glaze dust in the pottery room. This involves the adoption of sensible techniques and good housekeeping. Flint or quartz in dry powdered form should be avoided wherever possible.

The removal of all so-called 'toxic' materials would be an instant remedy. It would also remove several extremely useful materials for which there are no safe substitutes. It is therefore very important to keep the situation in true perspective. School physics and biology departments contain hazards at least equal to those in pottery departments; so do the wood-working, metalwork and some art and craft departments—not to mention the chemistry department which contains a variety of chemicals infinitely more toxic than those materials normally encountered in the pottery department. Given proper attention to personal and departmental hygiene, with instruction and supervision by those responsible for students, there is no reason why any difficulties should be encountered by the potter or pottery teacher during a normal lifetime.

9. Acid-resistance and lead release

In the previous chapter fritting was discussed and it was explained that the lead compounds were by this process converted to a safe form in order to protect the potter, i.e. the person actually handling the unfired glaze powders.

However, it is possible, under certain conditions, for lead (and other potentially toxic metallic compounds) to be extracted from the *fired* glaze surface by the action of certain acids present in foods, drinks and preservatives, and as a result of occasional reports of illness arising from foodstuffs contaminated in this way there has been much recent interest in the acid-resistance properties of glazes generally, and the potential toxicity of certain types. It must, however, be stressed that this presents a quite separate problem from that discussed in the previous chapter since the acid-resistance of a fired glaze has little relationship to the properties of the unfired powder.

The following acids are among those found in foodstuffs—

(a) Citric acid—present in fruit juices, especially lemon juice.

(b) Malic acid—present in apple juice.

(c) Succinic acid—present in coffee and whisky.

(d) Acetic acid—present in vinegar.

When these acids, or foods containing them, are brought into contact with fired glazes they will, in time, produce signs of attack on the glaze. The degree of attack may be so small as to be incapable of measurement and can therefore be ignored; on the other hand, certain types of fired glaze may be attacked to a very appreciable degree and this may well result in a situation where toxic amounts of metallic compounds are dissolved out of the fired glaze (which may or may not show visual evidence of attack).

The metallic compounds of main concern are those of lead, barium, zinc, antimony, selenium and cadmium. Of these, lead, antimony, cadmium and zinc present the biggest problem but particularly lead since it is such a common glaze constituent and cannot be replaced in low-temperature glazes by any other flux without adversely affecting the glaze brilliance, colour response, craze-resistance or maturing range.

Acid-resistance tests have been introduced in certain countries, notably U.S.A., Finland and Germany, to check whether or not the amount of undesirable metallic compounds released from a glazed article by acid attack is below defined limits. The results are normally expressed as milligrammes per square decimetre of surface area, although in the American test the result is expressed in parts per million. One part per million is equivalent to one milligramme per litre.

The limit of lead allowed in the American test is 7 parts per million which is approximately equal to 0.7 mg/dm^2. The permissible level, however, does vary with different countries. Finland for example has a maximum level of 0.6 mg/dm^2, Germany imposes a maximum level of 1.5 mg/dm^2.

In the German test, the fired article is filled with a 4 per cent solution of acetic acid and is allowed to stand at room temperature for 24 hours. After this period the concentration of the undesirable metal (usually lead, but may be antimony, cadmium or zinc) is determined and expressed in terms of release in milligrammes per square decimetre.

It is likely that Britain too will impose similar regulations in the near future but the precise form that the British test will take has not yet been determined. Any test should logically take into consideration the following factors—

(*a*) Nature of the acid
(*b*) Time of contact
(*c*) Temperature of contact
(*d*) Area of contact
(*e*) Units in which to express the result
(*f*) Sampling technique

It will be appreciated that the presence of certain metallic compounds in any foodstuff must not be assumed to have arisen from the plate or vessel used to contain it, since pollution from other sources must be taken into account. For this reason it is pointless to attempt to test a fired glaze by carrying out an analysis on any foodstuff in contact with the glaze. Any test must be consistent and involve reagents which will not in themselves introduce the elements the test is designed to detect. Furthermore, of the organic acids previously listed, citric acid exerts a much stronger leaching action than the others (and, incidentally, has a greater leaching action than a mineral acid such as hydrochloric acid of similar concentration) and the acid used in the test should therefore logically be related to the actual use of the articles to be tested.

These are some of the reasons why the sampling technique and nature of the acid to be used in any test are of importance. Consequently it is likely that cooking vessels—casseroles etc.—will be tested with oils and cooking fats and storage vessels used for wines and spirits etc. will be tested with acetic, succinic, malic or citric acids whereas table-ware would logically be tested with acetic acid.

It has been reported that an indication of whether any article is suspect may, however, be gained in the home or studio by putting 2 oz of white vinegar in the fired pot to be tested and leaving this to stand at room temperature for about 12 hours. About 1/8 of a teaspoonful of liver of sulphur should then be dissolved in about 2 oz of hot water. The vinegar from the pot under test should then be poured into a clean glass and a similar amount of clean, fresh vinegar poured into another glass. Two teaspoonfuls of the sulphur solution are then added to each glass which will result in a white cloudy precipitate being formed in the fresh vinegar. A precipitate will also be formed in the test vinegar and if this is tinged a tan or brownish colour then it is possible that heavy metals which have been leached out of the fired glaze are present in the precipitate. In such a case the glaze concerned requires more accurate analysis before being used on the inside of any foodstuff container.

One point that must, however, be emphasized is that a very large number of acid-resistance tests on pottery have recently been made in Britain following publicity given to the topic. In each case, tests made on fired commercial low-solubility glazes revealed that every sample passed the test easily with a very wide margin of safety—an average figure of 0.15 mg/dm^2 being obtained under the Finnish test (generally the most stringent one).

The problem of pottery decorated with on-glaze enamels (and transfers) is more severe than that of undecorated ware or ware decorated under the glaze—this, of course, being due to lead released from the flux used in the enamel. Nevertheless, although the amount of metal released by acid attack on the enamel is always higher than that released from the glaze, the fact that on-glaze decoration is usually confined to a very small area of the total ware surface does reduce the problem, since testing is logically related to the total ware surface or a major part of it. Obviously, the greater the degree of on-glaze decoration, the greater the risk of the metal release figures nearing the test limit.

It has, incidentally, been shown that if on-glaze enamels are underfired their lead-release properties are higher, on account of the increased surface exposed and the relatively unstable flux layer. It can be shown that as the firing temperature nears the correct $750°C$ ($1380°F$) mark, the lead-release figure progressively decreases, the decoration sinking into the glaze and producing an overall composition which is more resistant to attack. Similarly, 'soaking' the ware for a longer period, or refiring, tends to increase the acid-resistance of enamels.

Owing to the toxic nature of raw lead compounds it is compulsory for the pottery factory to introduce any lead required in a glaze in the form of a lead frit and there is much evidence to show that lead introduced in this form provides a greater acid-resistance in the fired glaze than does an equivalent amount of lead introduced 'raw' as white lead, litharge, etc. Coated frits (*see* page 47) may have some slight advantage over normal frits from an acid-resistance point of view.

It can be concluded that commercial low-solubility glazes can be regarded as quite safe provided that they are fired to the prescribed maturing temperature. Lead glazes prepared from raw lead compounds instead of from low-solubility frits may, however, be subject to considerable acid attack (especially if underfired) yielding potentially toxic quantities of lead. Crystalline or 'artistic' glazes, particularly those containing metallic compounds in crystalline form deposited on the surface of the glaze, are also liable to acid attack as are glazes, whether lead or leadless, containing certain metal oxides —notably copper. This appears to make the crystal lattice of the glaze unstable, so that the glaze can be attacked more easily. These types of glaze should not therefore be used for surfaces which are likely to come into contact with foodstuffs if the glaze concerned contains a significant amount of a potentially toxic metal.

Additions of boron, raw lead, copper, potassium and sodium will increase the solubility of any lead present in a glaze whilst additions of calcium, titanium, silica and alumina generally reduce solubility. In the case of copper it is reported that even a small addition may reduce the acid-resistance of a glaze by up to 200 times. Low-solubility glazes which are otherwise safe can therefore yield dangerous amounts of lead if copper is added to them. Stoneware and porcelain glazes, of course, can be considered quite safe due to the invariable absence of the 'toxic' metals

and the extra resistance imparted by their high silica content.

Although the problem of acid-resistance of fired glaze surfaces is obviously a very important one in as much as it directly affects our daily health, it is important to view the problem with a just sense of proportion. It is difficult to conceive a more resistant alternative to ceramics for foodstuff containers. Certainly, vessels made of aluminium, pewter, copper and certain glasses and plastics will very readily be attacked by dilute acids and alkalis. Although certain glazes such as those already mentioned can yield toxic concentrations of lead and other metals under the action of dilute acids, the majority of commercial glazes are quite safe and indeed, for many applications in which acid-resistance is of vital importance such as in the chemical industry, glazed containers are often insisted upon in preference to other types to contain acids much more corrosive than those encountered in the household.

During this century there has been a dramatic reduction in the incidence of lead poisoning owing to a better understanding of the problems involved, better hygiene, and, in the case of the potter, by the use of frits in place of raw lead compounds.

There exist many other, and probably more important, sources of contamination of foodstuffs by lead. Notorious examples are the use of lead compounds in petrol which, following combustion, become liberated in the atmosphere, and the use of certain types of water softeners which tend to remove the protective scum which forms on the inside of lead pipes through which water passes. Insecticides containing lead must also be considered a hazard since the use of these (and lead deposited from other sources such as exhaust fumes) tend naturally to contaminate foodstuffs with the result that there is a certain amount of lead present in virtually all foods that we eat. An average meal is said to contain 0·3–0·5 mg of lead.

It is perhaps interesting to recall that lead poisoning has been claimed to be the major influence in the decline of the Roman civilization. At that time lead was used, in the form of lead acetate, for food preservation; grape syrup was cooked in leaden vessels and grapes were preserved for a year simply by placing in rainwater boiled down to one-third volume in leaden receptacles. Similar uses were known in Greece and ancient statements exist that certain Greek wines produced sterility, miscarriage, headache, etc. (all symptoms of lead poisoning). To support this theory it is claimed that lead has been found in bones of well-to-do classes of the 'classical' period of Roman and Greek history but not in bones from before or after that period, nor in bones of the poor.

10. Opacifiers

OPACITY

It has been mentioned earlier that all crystalline minerals are opaque owing to refraction and scattering of the light by the crystal faces. This is why it is difficult to obtain matt transparent glazes, since the crystal development normally necessary for the production of the matt finish causes scattering of the light falling upon the glaze with the result that the glaze is slightly opaque.

Glazes which become completely molten when fired to their maturing temperature to form a smooth bubble-free glass and which do not crystallize out during cooling are generally transparent and this can be considered to be the normal state of glazes. However, if the glaze contains suspended particles of a material which has a different refractive index (the ability to bend light) from the glassy matrix, then the light rays will be diffused and the glaze appear opaque. These facts indicate the two principal means by which glazes can be rendered opaque, namely,

(a) The interference with light penetration by the suspension in the glaze of undissolved particles or crystals, i.e. by crystal deposition.

(b) The diffusion of light rays by particles at the surface or suspended in the glaze such as gas bubbles.

To produce opacity by crystal deposition an opacifier is added to the glaze. This produces a dispersion of minute opaque crystals in the glaze (otherwise a completely transparent glass) during the firing process. Opacifiers can be inert, i.e. they remain as solid particles during the complete firing process of the glaze on to the body; or they can be of the recrystallized type, in which the opacifier is dissolved by the glaze during the

firing process and then thrown out of solution as the glaze cools, i.e. exactly as crystalline glazes are produced. Tin oxide is the commonest of the inert opacifiers and titania is typical of the recrystallized types. Zircon (zirconium silicate) combines both processes, some material being taken into solution and recrystallizing during cooling, whilst the rest remains inert during the firing process. Slow cooling of the glaze is essential with opacifiers of the recrystallized type, since rapid cooling may hinder or prevent recrystallization.

Opacification by the formation of gas bubbles is very unpredictable. The glazes tend to be unstable, and they have low abrasion resistance.

Opacity results from the difference between the refractive index of the opacifier and the glassy matrix. The important factor is not the particular refractive index of the suspended opacifier but the magnitude of the difference between the suspension and the matrix. The refractive indices of some of the commonest opacifiers are shown in the table below. These can be compared with the refractive index of a clear glaze, i.e. 1·5–1·6 for a leadless, and 1·8–1·9 for a lead glaze.

Titanium dioxide	2·5–2·9
Zirconium oxide (zirconia)	2·13–2·2
Tin oxide	1·99–2·09
Zirconium silicate (zircon)	1·94
Calcium fluoride	1·43
Air bubbles	1·00

If all other factors are equal, the degree of opacification is directly proportional to the difference in refractivity of the two phases (i.e. the opacifier and the glaze). The ratio of opacifier to glass, the solubility of the opacifier in the glass and the dispersion of the opacifier throughout the glass also influence the degree of opacification as do the size, shape and orientation of the opacifier crystals.

The size of the particles is a very important factor and it can easily be demonstrated that, within certain limitations, the finer the particle size of the opacifier the greater will be the opacity obtained from the same weight of material. It is for this reason that zirconia and zircon opacifiers are ground so very finely (ultra-fine) by the manufacturers. Tin oxide and titania are of course of extremely fine particle size since they are chemically precipitated materials. Grinding to reduce their particle size still further is unnecessary.

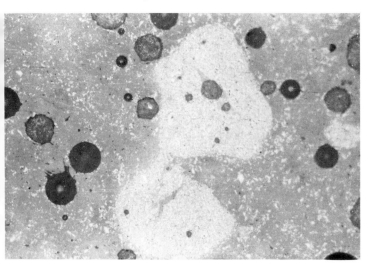

Fig. 24
Zircon aggregate in glaze

The ratio of surface to weight for ultra-fine particles is very much higher than for normally ground particles and this results in greatly increased surface activity and thereby increased chemical activity. Unfortunately, however, the particles not only become highly active towards other substances but also develop a high affinity for each other. This results in the formation of very tight agglomerates (i.e. batches of tightly packed undispersed opacifier particles) which are almost indistinguishable in properties from the coarser particles from which the finely ground material was produced. As these aggregates also

exhibit an average index of refraction intermediate between that of the opacifier and the glassy matrix, reduced opacification may result. The photomicrograph shown in Fig. 24 is taken from a polished section of a glaze opacified with a superfine grade of zircon (Podmore Superzon). It can be seen quite clearly that the zircon has not been completely dispersed and large agglomerates still remain.

Although one obtains a more efficient opacifier by reducing the particle size it is essential to disperse the particles thoroughly throughout the glaze in order to achieve optimum opacification.

DISPERSION OF THE OPACIFIER

Dispersion is influenced considerably by processing technique. In particular, opacifiers actually ground together with the other raw materials from which a glaze is prepared tend to be much more thoroughly dispersed than opacifiers merely stirred into the prepared powder or slop glaze. Indeed, this is why commercial concerns usually grind the opacifier with the other glaze ingredients and, in the case of fritted glazes, zircon-opacified, add the zircon to the frit batch. Craft potters, however, do not usually have the facilities to grind their own glazes and therefore purchase either the glaze in ground form or the ground raw materials from which to prepare the glaze. If the glaze is transparent and a white glaze is desired, this means that the opacifier has to be added to the prepared glaze (followed by the water addition). In this case very thorough stirring is necessary to disperse the opacifier properly. Sieving the slop glaze twice also helps to achieve a satisfactory level of dispersion.

Ultra-fine zircon can more easily be mixed into a glaze if during grinding the zircon is processed so that each ultra-fine particle becomes covered with a thin film of siliceous clay. 'Disperzon' opacifier is of this type. When added to a prepared glaze it will disperse much more easily with the same degree of stirring, owing to swelling of the clay film which forces the particles apart.

In all cases it is best to allow the fully prepared glaze to stand for at least several hours, followed by a further stirring before it is put into use.

MATERIALS USED AS OPACIFIERS

Tin oxide

The oldest, best, and most widely used opacifier is tin oxide, (SnO_2). It is very dependable and produces a 'soft' white opacity—often referred to as a 'blue-white'.

The solubility of tin oxide in the glaze melt is low, tin oxide therefore being regarded as an 'inert' type of opacifier; consequently the opacity it produces is not diminished readily by rapid cooling—as is the case with opacifiers of the re-crystallizing type. It has a noticeable refractory effect on glazes and a negligible or slightly beneficial influence on craze-resistance. One disadvantage of tin oxide is that in contact with chromium a pink tinge (chrome-tin pink) may result, this frequently occurring when chromium pigments are used under or on the glaze as in the maiolica technique.

An addition of around 7–10 per cent to transparent glazes is needed to achieve full opacity. It is reported, however, that the substitution of zircon or zirconia for part of the silica in a tin-opacified glaze may increase the opacity and gloss beyond that which could be expected from the use of tin oxide alone.

Unfortunately for the potter the cost of tin oxide has increased enormously in recent years and consequently other, cheaper opacifiers—especially zircon—have become increasingly popular.

Zircon

Zirconium silicate ($ZrSiO_4$) or zircon, occurs in small quantities in many igneous rocks but especially in granites, pegmatites and nepheline syenite. Erosion of the parent rock by natural agencies provides the alluvial deposits from which practically all commercial zircon is derived. Very good deposits occur in Australia in the form of beach sands.

To make the zircon suitable as an opacifier it is necessary to grind it to a consistent and very fine particle size without impairing its chemical purity. Consequently grinding is frequently car-ried out in Vibro-Energy mills (*see* page 79) using zircon-grinding media. Maximum opacity is given by the form of zircon with the smallest particle size but since the cost of the opacifier is increased by finer grinding various grades of zircon opacifier are marketed, e.g. Cookson Zircosil 15, Zircosil 5 and Zircosil 1 (listed in decreasing order of particle size – i.e. Zircosil 1 is finest). Zircopax, a product mentioned in several American books is a zircon opacifier.

Zircon is more soluble in the glaze than is tin oxide and therefore more of the zircon remains dissolved in the glaze matrix. For this reason it is necessary to use about twice as much zircon by weight as tin oxide to achieve a similar level of opacification. Consequently it is usual to add about 12–15 per cent of zircon to a transparent glaze to obtain full opacity. There is, incidentally, a threshold value of a few per cent below which no opacity is apparent. Zircon acts both as an inert and as a recrystallizing type of opacifier. For successful opacity, however, as little zircon as possible should be taken into solution and for this reason there should be minimum potash and soda in the glaze and a careful balance of silica and alumina—a ratio of 10 : 1 giving the best results.

Zircon produces a harsher white colour than that obtained with tin oxide. It is an extremely refractory material, being stable up to 1 700°C (3 090°F), and therefore makes glazes more refractory. It also has a low expansion and hence appreciably increases craze-resistance. Substituting zircon for tin oxide as a glaze opacifier will therefore increase the craze-resistance, make the glaze more refractory and promote a harsher white appearance. The viscosity and surface tension will also be increased, making the glaze more likely to crawl.

Additions of 10–25 per cent make the glaze surface exceedingly hard and scratch-resistant. With still larger additions, separation occurs, producing small 'islands' of crystals in the glassy matrix and when stains are added this results in a mottled appearance due to preferential absorption of the stain by the matrix.

Zircon has previously been regarded as an inferior substitute for tin oxide but in its modern forms it has its own intrinsic value as a ceramic material. It is useful not only as an opacifier but also to provide the excellent physical properties characteristic of zircon glazes, e.g. their good craze-resistance, hardness, and colour-stabilization properties. These latter properties are thought to be derived from the small amount of zircon which remains dissolved in the glaze.

Zirconium oxide

Commonly referred to as zirconia (ZrO_2), zirconium oxide is usually the finely ground and chemically purified natural mineral, baddeleyite, extensive deposits of which occur in Transvaal, South Africa. Zirconia from this source often has a grey colour but on heating to about 500–600°C 930–1110°F) the grey colour begins to fade, the material becoming practically white at 800–1000°C (1470–1830°F). Zirconium oxide produced by chemical precipitation methods is always white in colour.

Zirconia has a slightly higher index of refraction than zircon and for this reason might be regarded as a more efficient opacifier. The difference, however, is marginal and is completely outweighed by the appreciably higher cost of zirconia; consequently zircon is by far the more commonly used opacifier. Its opacifying properties, as would be expected, are very similar to those of zircon. Like zircon it is liable to give clear white patches with medium- and high-temperature glazes containing boric oxide, the best results being obtained from glazes with a high content of lime and alumina and a low boric oxide content.

Other opacifiers

Titania (TiO_2), antimony oxide (Sb_2O_3), bone ash (calcium phosphate) ($Ca_3(PO_4)_2$) and calcium fluoride (CaF_2), are sometimes used as opacifiers. For various reasons each can be considered inferior to tin oxide or zircon for the opacification of glazes.

Titania, as has previously been mentioned, is dissolved by the glaze during melting and is then precipitated out of the glaze during cooling. Slow cooling is therefore essential so that proper recrystallization can take place. The fired colour is usually creamish and the glaze surface matt or semi-matt owing to the coarse nature of the crystals.

Antimony oxide may be used as an opacifier for low- and medium-temperature glazes. In combination with lead it will give an opaque yellow due to formation of lead antimoniate.

Bone ash is reported to give good opacity up to cone 11 but there is high risk of pinholes and blisters (due to volatilization), and crawling. Nevertheless, an addition of up to 5 per cent is often used to opacify stoneware celadon glazes.

11. Colour in ceramic glazes

The colour shown by any object is due to reflection from it of those wavelengths of light which produce the particular colour that we see, the wavelengths which produce the other colours of the spectrum being absorbed by the object concerned.

Glazes may be coloured by the addition of colouring oxides or by the use of prepared stains —these being specially fritted combinations of colouring oxides with other materials.

THE COLOURING OXIDES

The basic oxides generally used are those of iron, cobalt, copper, chromium, manganese, nickel, vanadium and also to a lesser extent, antimony, rutile and ilmenite. Each of these provides a characteristic range of colour tones as detailed below but it must be recognized that the colour response varies with the type of glaze, the firing temperature, and the kiln atmosphere.

Iron oxide (Fe_2O_3)

This is found in almost all raw materials. The celadons of Chinese times were reduced iron oxide which tends to give greyish greens and blues. The colour range given by iron oxide is quite broad, covering many shades of honey or brown-yellow through shades of brown, red-brown, and black and, under reduction conditions, greys, grey-blues and greens, and black. In lead glazes, iron oxides will tend to produce rather warmer colours than in leadless glazes and certainly very much more vivid. Alkaline glazes give cooler tints, not so vivid as the lead glazes but brighter than the leadless ones.

Iron earths such as yellow ochre etc. contain up to about 60 per cent iron oxide and are very variable in composition but are useful for producing the lighter tints—honey, yellow or yellow-browns in oxidation atmosphere. Most terra cotta clays contain about 7–10 per cent of iron oxide and are often incorporated in glazes as a replacement for separate additions of clay and iron oxide.

'Natural' red iron oxide (haematite) is generally used to produce browns which tend to be rather greyer and cooler than the redder browns produced by the chemically precipitated red iron oxide.

Ferrous iron, or black iron oxide (FeO) will generally give the same colour as the red oxide but owing to the fact that there is more iron present in relation to oxygen than with the red oxides, the colours obtained are generally darker or murkier.

Under oxidizing or neutral firing conditions much of the black iron oxide does in fact change to the red oxide during the firing operation. Under reducing conditions black can be obtained from most forms of iron oxide if sufficient is present. Red iron oxides tend to disperse more readily than the black oxides and this is why they are generally preferred for colouring glazes.

Iron oxides are quite vigorous fluxes and will quite noticeably reduce the firing ranges of any glazes in the middle- and high-temperature range into which they are incorporated—and especially so under reduction firing conditions. Reduction firing often causes any iron present in the body to become increasingly more reactive and to form vitrified, dark-coloured specks which may combine with and produce a continuation of the speck into the glaze layer from the body beneath.

The colours produced by iron oxide are somewhat muted in the presence of tin oxide, the combination tending to produce cream colours instead of browns; although browns and, in the case of lead glazes, red-browns will show where the glaze is thin. Zinc oxide tends to produce a rather dull combination with iron oxide in any glaze and there is no doubt that the best colours with iron oxide are produced in a zinc-free, lead glaze. Titania (TiO_2) in glazes seems to act as a catalyst and considerably increases the colouring power of any iron pigmentation, but lime (CaO) exerts a pronounced bleaching action on iron pigments, thus reducing their colouring power (although lime is desirable for reduced iron celadons). In very high-lead glazes a large addition of iron oxide (about 11 per cent) together with the presence of ilmenite and a slow cooling rate can produce the beautiful aventurine glazes in which the iron crystallizes out in the glaze solution and produces 'flitters' of iron showing gold, red and brown crystals.

Because of the variety of colours they produce and their stability up to high temperatures iron oxides are the most useful ceramic pigments.

Cobalt oxide (Co_3O_4)

Cobalt oxide is by far the most powerful pigment available to the potter. In the production of white-firing earthenware bodies a quantity of 1 part in 100 000 parts of the body is often added so as to cancel out the colouring effect of the small amount of iron and titania present in the clays used in the body recipe. If the earthenware body is overfired, however, the cobalt content tends to become over-active and produces a grey colour which is why overfired white earthenware bodies often appear grey instead of white.

In glazes, an addition of 0·2 per cent will give a definite blue, 1–2 per cent a medium strong blue, 2–4 per cent a dark blue and more than this a pronounced inky-blue or black colour. The brilliance of the colour is emphasized in lead glazes and especially so in alkaline ones. One disadvantage of cobalt oxide is that because of its intense colouring power a minute speck will produce a very definite speck in the fired glaze. This problem can be minimized by using cobalt in the form of cobalt carbonate, which has an extremely fine particle size.

'Zaffre' and 'smalt' are mentioned by some authorities. Zaffre is a calcined ore of cobalt and contains 7–10 per cent cobalt. 'Smalt' is a blue stain produced from a frit of cobalt ore and sand.

Since blue is probably the most popular decorative colour cobalt is perhaps the most valuable source of pottery colour. It is widely used in the preparation of other shades and in fact is an essential constituent of good black colours (except iridium blacks). A brilliant black cannot be obtained without the use of a substantial proportion of cobalt oxide in the colour.

Copper oxide (CuO)

Copper oxide is generally used to produce apple-greens in glazes fired under oxidizing or neutral firing conditions. Under reduction conditions a red colour can be obtained which is known as 'ox-blood' or 'sang-de-boeuf'. It is a reasonably strong colouring pigment and additions over about 6 per cent may produce a metallic finish due to precipitation of the copper out of solution to give a blackish metallic film.

In strongly alkaline glazes an addition of 3–5 per cent of copper oxide gives an attractive turquoise-blue colour. Zinc and boric oxide counteract this effect.

Above cone 03 (1 040°C (1 900°F)) copper oxide volatilizes increasingly rapidly and can influence the colour of other glazed pieces.

Additions of copper oxide tend to reduce the acid-resistance of fired glazes and may result in a large amount of any lead present being leached out. Because of its fluxing power, copper—like cobalt and iron—will reduce the firing range of any glaze into which it is introduced.

Chromium oxide (Cr_2O_3)

Chrome generally gives a green colour, somewhat darker than the green of copper. In glazes of very high lead content and low alumina content, a brilliant orange-red colour can sometimes be obtained with an addition of 1–2 per cent of chromium oxide. In combination with zinc, chromium will give a dull-brown colour instead of green. Zinc glazes over a chromium underglaze decoration will cause the decoration to become brown.

In combination with tin the well-known

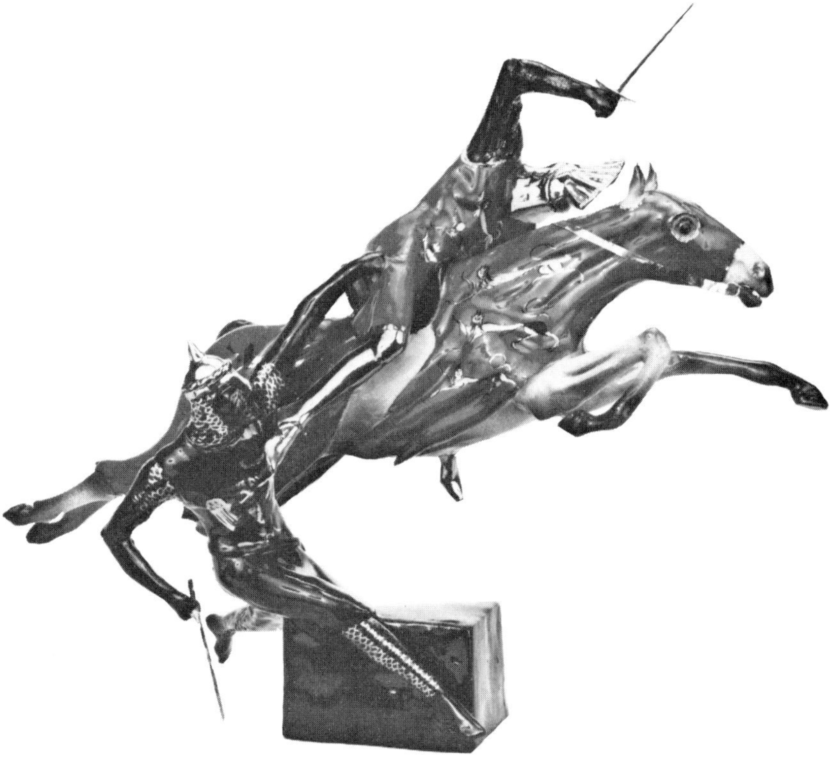

Fig. 25
Knight and Saracen by Michael Sutty
In terra cotta and bone china. Enamels used on biscuit and on transparent glaze, with lustres on the enamels. Biscuit, glost and five enamel firings.

Fig. 26
Lidded jars by Louise Darby

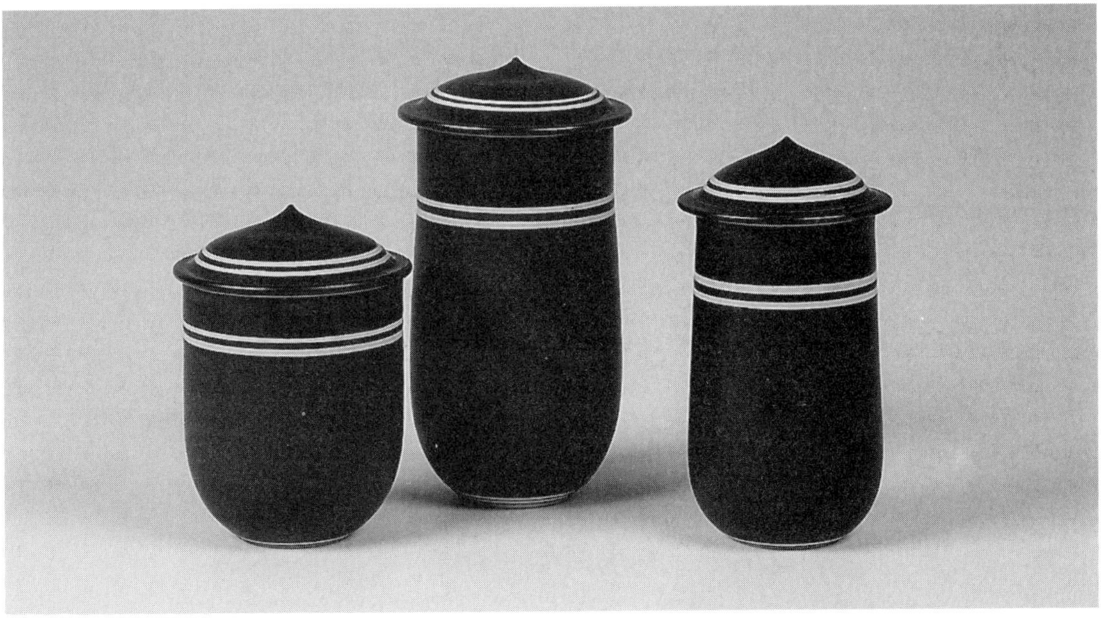

chrome-tin pinks can be obtained. About 1 per cent of chromium oxide is sufficient to produce the pink tint. At temperatures above cone 7, chromium oxide becomes increasingly volatile and the vapour produced may cause any tin-glazed pottery in the same kiln to become flashed with a pinkish or brownish discoloration due to this chrome-tin combination.

Nickel oxide (NiO)

Additions of nickel oxide to glazes tend to produce rather muted khaki-brown or green-brown colours but the tint obtained is not consistent. It is very useful, however, as a modifying agent to adjust the tint given by other colouring pigments, an example being a combination of nickel and chromium to produce pleasant, soft grey-greens.

Owing to its refractoriness, nickel oxide will raise the maturing range of glazes if introduced in large amounts. It also changes its state of oxidation during firing, as does manganese, and the gas bubbles released may cause bubbling or blistering. A further problem is that crystals of nickel silicate may form during cooling, causing a rough glaze surface.

Manganese dioxide (MnO_2)

Manganese dioxide is one of the least powerful colouring oxides. Additions of manganese tend to give a medium or dark brown colour and sepia browns can be produced in this way. A plum or slightly purplish plum colour will be obtained from an 8 per cent addition to a lead glaze and a rather more purple tint in highly alkaline ones. About 5 per cent of iron oxide plus 1 or 2 per cent of manganese dioxide is often used to produce a deep honey or Rockingham brown in medium- or low-temperature glazes.

In all cases the manganese dioxide breaks down under the effect of heat to produce manganese oxide in accordance with the equation $3MnO_2 = Mn_3O_4 + O_2$. The oxygen released may cause bubbling and blistering of the glaze. This can produce an attractive result if the manganese glaze is covered by another glaze of a different colour. Use of the carbonate instead of the dioxide gives a smoother colour, less prone to specking.

Vanadium pentoxide (V_2O_5)

Vanadium pentoxide added directly to a lead glaze will tend to produce a cream-yellow tint, often spangled with darker brown-yellow patches. If vanadium is added directly to a tin glaze a similar colour is obtained but added to transparent leadless glazes there is often a lack of colour. In all cases the colour obtained from direct additions is not so satisfactory as that obtained with prepared stains containing vanadium, which are noted for their stability. Calcined combinations of vanadium and tin produce good cream-yellow stains whilst vanadium/zircon produces a good turquoise blue. The yellow and blue can then be blended to produce a range of stable greens.

Antimony oxide (Sb_2O_3)

Until the development of vanadium/tin yellows, antimony oxide was the principal base for yellow colours.

In lead glaze a good yellow is obtained from the formation of lead antimoniate (Naples Yellow) which, however, is not stable above $1100°C$ ($2010°F$). The yellow cannot be satisfactorily obtained in glazes with low lead contents or in alkaline glazes.

Antimony oxide is very poisonous and must be carefully handled.

Rutile

Rutile, the ore of titanium, is a black mineral found in metamorphic rocks and in Australian beach sands. Rutile deposits usually contain some iron oxide and the combination results in a buff colour being obtained from additions of rutile to glazes (but blue-white under reduction).

During cooling of the glaze, the rutile very easily crystallizes out of glaze solution to produce a mottled effect. The degree of crystallization will be appreciably increased by the addition to the glaze of a small amount of ilmenite, which tends to act as a 'seed' around which the rutile crystals readily form. Titania has a similar effect. The rutile crystals produce a matt or semi-matt finish to the glaze. A very attractive rutile glaze can, incidentally, be made from Podmore lead sesquisilicate frit to which is added 7 per cent of rutile and 1 per cent of ilmenite.

Rutile has a modifying effect on the colour of any glazes containing iron, copper, cobalt or chromium, giving attractively textured and greying tones to the colours.

Ilmenite

Ilmenite is iron titanate. It produces an effect similar to that of black iron oxide (due to the high iron content of the ilmenite). When coarsely ground (about 40–60 mesh), ilmenite can be used to produce speckles in glazes and bodies. When finely ground it may increase the tendency of other materials to crystallize from glaze solution (especially with rutile as mentioned previously).

Oxide combinations

Some of the more attractive tints result when two or more oxides are used in combination. For an illustration of this one has only to look at the subtle colours which may result when cobalt is blended with iron, manganese, vanadium etc. and compare these with the stark, primitive blue of cobalt oxide alone.

In general, the colour which results from a combination of two different oxides is predictable, i.e. is a proportional mixture of the characteristic colour of each constituent. There are, however, a few notable exceptions such as the pink from chrome/tin, the khaki-brown from chrome/nickel, the grey from nickel/manganese, the grey-blue from nickel/cobalt and the grey-brown from nickel/vanadium. Methodical exploration of oxide combinations may be facilitated by use of the 'line-blend' approach detailed on page 103.

Combination may, however, arise as the natural consequence of the interaction of one layer with another, such as occurs when a coloured glaze is applied over a differently pigmented glaze or underslip and the two are fired together. The combination may be slight and the colour unpredictable, depending largely on the thickness of the covering glaze, but the use of this technique often results in an unusual breakthrough of the lower colour through the upper

one, especially at high temperatures, producing a random marking or veining of the glaze which can be extremely attractive. Underslips containing large amounts of iron oxide (up to 20 per cent) are often used with good results.

Fig. 27
Stoneware goblet by Colin Pearson
Glaze covers iron underslip which breaks through to produce attractive brown markings.

Where this type of effect is required, oxides are to be preferred to stains as the colouring pigments. The fact that certain oxides break down and liberate large volumes of gas results in a pronounced stirring action, causing the lower glaze to bleed through more vigorously in comparison to glazes coloured with prepared stains, which tend to be a little more placid.

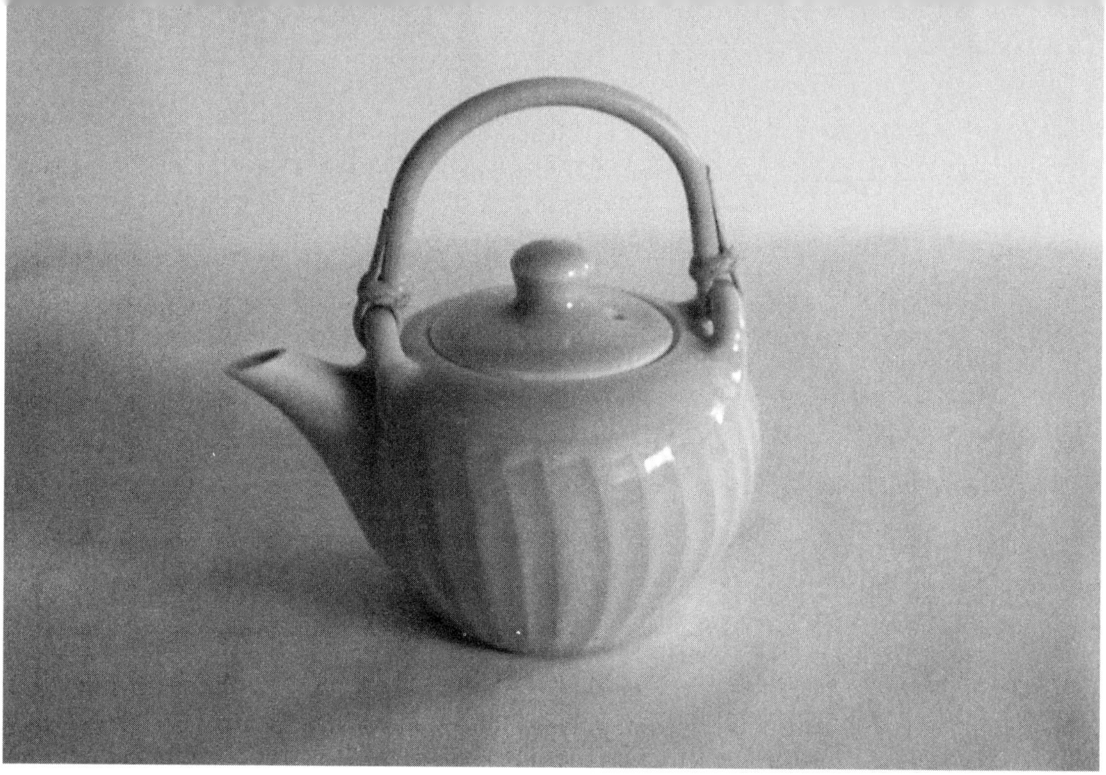

Fig. 28
Teapot by Derek Emms

Fig. 29
Maiolica dishes
Decorated by Ann Wynn Reeves with copper and iron oxides and use of wax resist. 17 × 13 inches.
(By courtesy of Kenneth Clark Pottery)

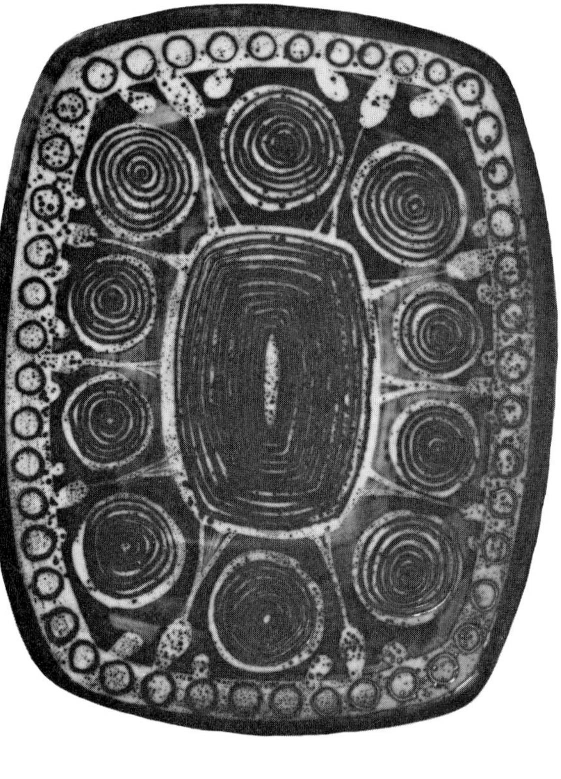

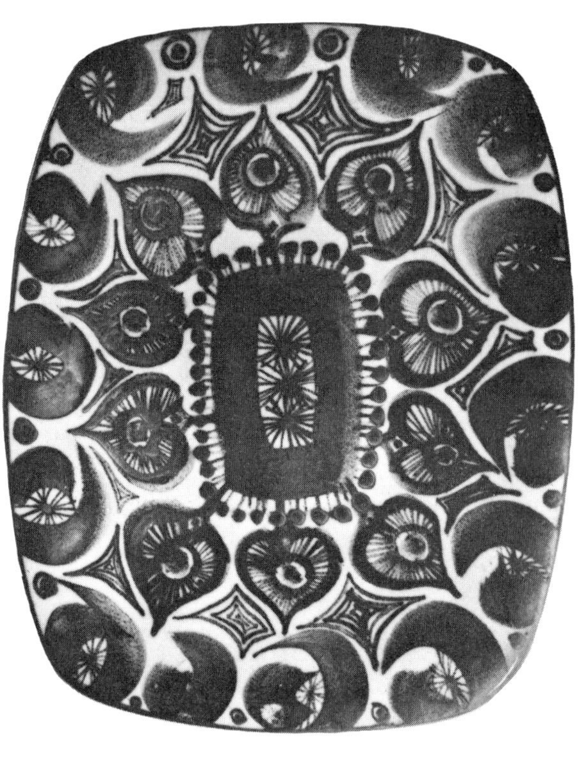

PREPARED STAINS

Certain colours can only be obtained when the constituent materials are actually calcined or fritted together—examples being the vivid red colours which can be produced from fritted mixtures of cadmium and selenium oxides, and the high-temperature pinks obtained from iron and zirconium. In addition to this there may be undesirable side effects associated with the use of certain oxides: for example, the very refractory nature of manganese dioxide and its dissociation during firing may cause problems under certain conditions, whilst many raw pigments, especially the ochres, may contain a high percentage of soluble salts.

Prepared stains are mixtures of colouring pigments (usually oxides) with other materials, the mixture then being calcined to combine it chemically, followed by fine grinding and washing to remove soluble salts. The use of prepared stains provides the potter with a wider palette of colouring pigments, which are usually more predictable and stable over a certain temperature range than the raw oxides used alone. However, although certain stains may be excellent, even at stoneware temperatures, others may have an ingredient which limits the firing range to a lower level and this must be taken into account.

The actual colour produced by the oxide constituents of the stain may be varied by the incorporation into the stain of modifiers such as nickel oxide, diluents to lighten the colour, such as flint and alumina, and fluxes to reduces the temperature needed to cause the ingredients to combine. The final colour results from the colouring oxides actually dissolving into the host material, the colouring ion becoming latched into the crystal lattice and being surrounded by oxygen atoms. Usually the ion is surrounded by either two or four oxygen atoms, i.e. is in a two-coordination or four-coordination arrangement; with certain combinations there is a six-coordination arrangement. The principal sources of colours are as follows.

Blues

Blues are obtained mainly from cobalt and vanadium oxides. With cobalt the blues are developed from the four-coordinated state; in the six-coordinated state, pinks can be produced but these have yet to be properly developed. A stable blue known as matt blue is produced by calcining cobalt and alumina to form cobalt aluminate which has a spinel structure. Mazarine blue is cobalt silicate.

The vanadium blues (including turquoise) are produced from mixtures of zirconia, silica and vanadium with an alkaline halide such as sodium fluoride. The vanadium ion is thus locked in a zircon lattice, producing a good blue in the four-coordinated state and a yellow when six-coordinated. Pinks can be obtained from this system by using iron instead of vanadium and a very good clear yellow by substituting praseodymium for vanadium.

Greens

Chromium oxide is the most commonly used base for green stains but these are also often produced by mixing the blues and yellows obtained from vanadium or by using copper oxide.

Yellows

Praseodymium is often used to produce a good yellow, stable at high temperatures. Yellows are also commonly produced with a mixture of tin and vanadium which is calcined at $1200°C$ ($2190°F$) or higher. The well-known Naples Yellow is produced from lead antimonate but this is unsatisfactory beyond the earthenware range.

Lead chromates are sometimes used but these are not stable and decompose at low temperatures. Uranium oxide (U_3O_8) has been used for yellow glazes as also have molybdenum, and a combination of rutile/zinc.

Pinks

One of the most useful pinks can be produced by an iron/zircon mixture which is calcined at $800°C$ ($1470°F$) and which produces a pink, stable at stoneware temperatures. A mixture of manganese dioxide and alumina, calcined at $1300°C$ ($2370°F$), has also been used to produce good pink colours. In this case the host lattice is corundum with manganese latched in.

Pinks are also commonly produced by calcined mixtures of chromium and tin oxides although the presence of lime is said to be necessary to obtain really good pinks with this system. A calcined mixture of chrome and alumina can be used to obtain a ruby colour but this has not yet been properly developed. Similarly, cobalt compounds in highly alkaline glazes may produce pink colours but these are very unstable.

Reds

The best reds are obtained from calcined mixtures of selenium and cadmium oxides, both of which are relatively expensive. Very good scarlets and crimsons can be obtained from this stain which is, incidentally, unusual in being white in unfired colour. Selenium/cadmium reds unfortunately are not stable much above $1060°C$ ($1940°F$). They are very susceptible to localized reduction conditions or lead vapour, causing black spots in the fired glaze. A tiny splash of copper glaze will produce a similar effect. Tomato-red colours can be produced from uranium oxide in lead glazes. These are now uncommon owing to difficulty in obtaining uranium oxide, although a depleted form is more readily obtainable.

Browns

These are obtained generally by mixing chromium and iron compounds with the addition of modifiers such as manganese dioxide, zinc oxide, nickel oxide, uranium oxide, antimony oxide, titanium dioxide and alumina.

Browns can be also produced from manganese dioxide and iron oxides, separately or in combination. Manganese dioxide, like other oxides such as cobalt oxide, has the ability to alter its state of oxidation during heating, subsequently liberating part of its oxygen content when the temperature rises above a certain limit. This liberated gas may be the cause of bubbles or blisters being produced in the molten glaze. Problems of this kind can be avoided by calcining a mixture of the colouring oxide with a suitable host lattice. This is one of the principal reasons why a prepared stain may be preferred to a raw oxide.

Blacks and greys

Blacks and greys can be obtained from mixtures of iron, cobalt and manganese, although nickel, chromium and copper oxide are sometimes also introduced. About 2–3 per cent each of any three of these oxides will yield a black colour in most glazes.

UNDERGLAZE COLOURS

Underglaze colours, which may sometimes be used as an alternative to glaze stains, usually consist not only of the pigmentary oxide or mixture of oxides, but also a flux to bind the colour to the body surface, accessory materials to modify the colour and refractory materials to control the fusibility. The industrial practice is to 'harden-on' the colour on the biscuit pottery surface by carrying out a firing at about $650°C$ ($1200°F$). This fixes the colour firmly into position and thus prevents displacement during dipping. At the same time the actual porosity of the hardened-on colour is similar to that of the unpainted areas of the biscuit ware, so that the glaze coating will be uniform overall.

COLOURED GLAZE PREPARATION AND CONTROL

As has been seen, coloured glazes may be produced either by the addition of colouring oxides or by the addition of prepared stains. Whichever pigments are used, a 200-mesh sieve should be used to screen the pigment after mixing with a little water and the pigment should then be thoroughly mixed into the glaze.

Naturally the precise tint of glaze colour which results depends to a certain degree upon the type of base glaze. Additions of colouring pigments to white glazes will obviously give a different shade from additions to a transparent glaze, white glazes producing more muted and paler shades. Use of a white base glaze generally produces a greater uniformity of colour—there is a reduced tendency to shading of the colour where glaze thickness varies. For the brightest colours, transparent base glazes must be used. In the low-

and medium-temperature range, lead glazes give much more vivid tints than leadless ones.

Some of the best glaze colours are obtained from mixtures of colouring oxides—or from mixtures of prepared stains. A point that should not be overlooked, however, is that the addition of colouring pigments may affect the maturing temperature of the glaze, depending upon the type of oxide and amount added. A good black glaze is often prepared by the addition of 2 per cent of cobalt, 2 per cent of manganese and 3 per cent

of iron but the combined addition (7 per cent) will significantly flux the glaze, reducing its firing temperature. This can be corrected by adding a little clay. Mirror-black glazes can be made by additions of copper oxide and iron oxide to lead glazes but such glazes are often not acid-resistant.

An excessive variety of colouring pigments tends to result in dark, drab colours; if all the colouring oxides, for example, were mixed together one would tend to obtain a drab grey tint.

12. Glaze types and effects

CRYSTALLINE GLAZES

Crystalline glazes can generally be regarded as those glazes which contain crystals produced as the glaze cools. In its liberal interpretation this definition obviously covers an enormous variety of glaze effects, so that glazes such as the aventurines, rutile glazes and matt glazes could be regarded as varieties of crystalline glaze. The various types of crystalline glaze, however, are normally classified according to the actual size of the crystals as being microcrystalline or macrocrystalline types.

Microcrystalline glazes

These are those in which the crystals are so small as to be incapable of detection by the unaided eye. Examples are satin-vellum and matt glazes formed by crystallization from solution of zinc, calcium or barium silicates and titanates.

Macrocrystalline glazes

These are those in which the crystals are sufficiently large to be readily detectable by the naked eye. This category includes the well-known crystalline glazes, where the glaze surface may be covered completely or partially with well-developed individual crystals which are clustered together, covering large areas. Alternatively, the crystals may be suspended in the glassy matrix below the surface, as with aventurine glazes.

As mentioned previously, the development of crystalline glazes depends very much upon the duration of the firing and in particular upon the speed of cooling whilst the glaze is molten. Other factors are important, such as the character of the solvent glaze—which should be low in alumina—and the type of materials used to form the crystals. Zinc, titanium and iron are the oxides most commonly used in macrocrystalline glazes. The addition of ilmenite to such glazes is very useful since this seems to act as a 'seeding' agent around which crystals more readily form. One problem with the use of crystalline glazes is that they often become very fluid when molten (owing to the small amount of alumina present) and may therefore flow very markedly on vertical surfaces. Although this may produce extremely attractive results, it may result in the pot becoming glued to the base upon which it is supported in the glost fire with resultant destruction of the piece. Consequently it is very advisable to place such pots on stilts and not flat upon the kiln shelves.

AVENTURINE GLAZES

These are transparent glazes which have crystals or spangles suspended in the glassy matrix. The crystals reflect light, resulting in a sparkling appearance—rather similar to the flitters of haematite (iron oxide) found in aventurine quartz, from which the glaze name is taken. Although aventurine glazes produced by crystals of iron oxide are by far the most common, such glazes have also been produced with chromium, copper and uranium.

By far the best aventurines are produced in lead glazes. A lead glaze will dissolve up to about 7 per cent of iron oxide under normal firing conditions. If a greater amount than this is added, the excess iron will crystallize out of solution under slow cooling conditions. The amount of iron, and the speed of cooling, are very critical: too much iron oxide results in a coarse, rough matt surface instead of the glossy surface characteristic of a good aventurine glaze. The correct amount of iron oxide seems to be around 11 per cent and the glaze should have a low alumina content.

Sufficient heat treatment to produce a good glass, followed by slow cooling conditions, is vital for proper development of the aventurine effect.

RUTILE GLAZES

Rutile, discussed on page 60, dissolves easily in glazes and then crystallizes out on cooling to form titania crystals. Iron, occurring naturally with the rutile, gives a light-brown colour to the glaze in which the titania crystals appear and so the resultant glaze is flecked owing to the buff-coloured titania crystals appearing in the brown matrix. The buff areas are matt whereas the matrix is glossy (provided that the base glaze is glossy). The best effects are produced in high-lead glazes to which 5–12 per cent of rutile is added. About 1 per cent of ilmenite assists in developing crystal formation by acting as a nucleating agent. The presence of zinc may produce yellow patches instead of brown.

Slow cooling is essential for the best results. Rapid cooling gives minimum titania crystal development resulting in a predominantly iron-brown glossy glaze. Very slow cooling produces a predominance of the titania crystals giving a matt, buff or off-white glaze. Generally, the greater the rutile content, the heavier the break-up. Interesting effects can be obtained by adding oxides or stains to rutile glazes and many of the so-called 'artistic' glazes are produced in this way.

MATT GLAZES

Since true matt glazes develop as a result of crystallization, matt glazes may be considered to be a variety of crystalline glaze. However, matt effects can also be produced by the presence in the fired glaze of undissolved material such as talc, bone, alumina or pitchers (i.e. ground biscuit ware), or, more commonly, by under-firing the glaze, but with these methods the

quality of the matt surface is not as good as with the true matts.

True matt glazes are produced by introducing appreciable quantities of zinc or calcium into the glaze so that crystals of zinc silicate are formed in the case of zinc matts and calcium silicate in the case of lime matts, the crystals being precipitated as the glaze cools from the maturing range. In high-temperature glazes barium is often used to produce smooth barium silicate matts. It is important that matt glazes are not overfired, since this tends to produce alumino-silicates instead of silicates, with reduced mattness. It is also important that the cooling rate be sufficiently slow to allow the crystals to form.

A popular way of producing a matt glaze is by adding 10–40 per cent of a matting agent, made up from a 50/50 mixture of zinc oxide and china clay. The china clay introduces alumina, which reduces the size of the zinc silicate crystals (these would otherwise be too large, causing an excessively rough surface) and also tends to make the glaze more refractory so that some mattness may also result from the glaze being underfired. Whiting could be substituted for zinc to produce a lime matt.

SATIN-VELLUM GLAZES

True matt glazes nevertheless tend to have a rough surface which is easily marked by metals (the glaze acting as an abrasive) and which is more difficult to clean than is a smoother glaze. For these reasons the much smoother semi-matt surface of the satin-vellum glaze may be preferred. Satin-vellum glazes have a most attractive satin sheen surface and are produced by addition of 4 per cent each of zinc, titanium and tin oxides to a glaze maturing in the majolica or low-earthenware region, i.e. up to 1 100°C (2 010°F).

FLOW GLAZES

Basically these are glazes which are very fusible and which are applied thickly on to a fired glaze surface, the ware then being fired again to the upper limit, or a little higher than the normal maturing temperature of the flow glaze, so that it sags or runs decoratively. Such glazes are normally applied on to rims or upper surfaces, the most suitable location being determined by considerations of the shape of the articles. Lead glazes are usually used and are often prepared using a glaze binder to increase viscosity and thus to obtain a good glaze pick-up. Very good results can be obtained if the fired glaze underneath is coloured or white and especially if the flow glaze contains rutile.

CRACKLE GLAZES

These are glazes which are designed to craze for decorative effect. Such glazes may be specially compounded to have a high coefficient of expansion—high amounts of soda or potash are often used to ensure this—or the firing conditions may be adjusted so that the pottery body is insufficiently fired, resulting in a poor glaze fit. This latter technique, in fact, is often the best, since by virtue of the fact that this mis-match between the glaze and the body is not so pronounced, the craze lines may be more evenly spaced.

One problem with crackle glazes is controlling the degree of crazing: glazes having too high a coefficient of expansion will craze too much, producing innumerable craze lines, often packed very closely together. Certain glazes, in fact, may be crazed so much that the glaze appears opaque or opalescent and the individual craze lines are difficult to detect. Earthenware can often be made to craze effectively by biscuit firing to 950°C (1 740°F) and using a glaze which matures in the region of 950–1 000°C (1 740–1 830°F).

The craze lines can afterwards be decorated if required by rubbing coloured inks into the craze cracks. If colouring pigments are rubbed into the cracks and the pottery refired then the position of the colouring pigment will often be shown as blurred lines in the glaze, new craze lines, in different locations, being formed during cooling.

Incidentally, many of the ancient Chinese pieces of pottery which are now so decoratively crazed were probably uncrazed originally, the craze lines forming some months, years or even centuries later.

VOLCANIC OR FROTH GLAZES

All glazes undergo bubbling and boiling during the fusion process and these bubbles can often be seen by inspection of the fusing glaze from the spy hole. Normally this bubbling action is allowed to subside by continuing fusion of the glaze followed by a soaking procedure during firing. If the bubbling is suddenly arrested by a rapid cooling of the glaze this bubbling effect can often be fixed into the glaze—the glaze bubbles solidifying before they have had an opportunity to subside. Raku glazes are frequently bubbled or frothed rather like pumice owing to this combination of insufficient firing and rapid cooling.

In order to magnify the bubbling for decorative effect, materials which rapidly decompose can be introduced into the glaze, producing large volumes of gas whilst the glaze is molten. Coarsely ground silicon carbide can be used for this purpose as also can barium sulphate.

The best results are obtained with low-temperature glazes and with rapid cooling conditions down to dull red heat. Naturally such glazes are somewhat unpredictable.

LUSTRE GLAZES

Lustre glazes produce a thin film of metal on the glaze surface as a result of the glaze being reduced. They are generally applied on to fired glaze surfaces but certain types of in-glaze lustre are used exactly as normal glazes. There are basically two kinds of lustre glaze: those which can be fired in oxidizing atmospheres but which incorporate a reducing agent in their composition, and those which must be fired under reducing atmosphere conditions in order to obtain the desired effect.

The former type contain metal resinates produced by heating the metallic salt with resin, the resinate then being dissolved in about twice its weight of a suitable oil such as lavender oil, with turpentine used as a thinner. Upon firing to a red heat—about 650–750°C (1 200–1 380°F), a thin film of the dissolved metal is deposited upon the surface of the fired glaze, the fire being oxidizing throughout. Such lustres can therefore be fired in the same fire as on-glaze enamels. Liquid bright gold is probably the most popular lustre of this type.

The latter type, which have to be fired under reduction conditions, do not contain any local reducing agent. With this type of lustre the metallic salt, such as copper carbonate, silver nitrate etc., is mixed with about three times its weight of an iron-bearing clay or ochre, with a binder to hold the film which is applied to the fired glaze. The ware is fired, oxidizing to about 750°C (1 380°F) but then reduced strongly for a soaking period of up to an hour, the reduction atmosphere being maintained until the ware passes to black heat. This type of lustre is more durable than the former type since the reduced metallic deposit extends into the glaze and is not confined to its surface. The ware may, however, require burnishing to obtain the true colour.

An alternative type of lustre fired under reduction conditions is one in which the glaze applied to the biscuit ware is made to produce a lustred effect. This is done by adding 2–14 per cent of the metallic salt to the glaze and firing in the normal way. The ware is then reheated to about 650–750°C (1 200–1 380°F) and reduced to produce the lustre. The best results with this method are obtained with low-firing lead borosilicate glazes containing zinc and tin oxides. The lead content should not be too high, otherwise the glaze may blacken owing to reduced lead.

LOCALIZED REDUCTION GLAZES

Reducing atmospheres in an electric kiln considerably shorten element life and consequently the ability to reduce a glaze whilst firing in an oxidizing atmosphere is of particular interest to potters firing by electricity.

In the section on lustre glazes the production of a metallic film by the use of oils and resins to reduce the glaze was discussed and consequently lustre glazes of this type can be regarded as localized reduction glazes. Such glazes, however, cannot be easily manufactured by the craft potter and interest is therefore directed to simpler means of obtaining a localized reduction effect—notably by the use of silicon carbide. When glazes are loaded with silicon carbide and fired, the silicon carbide oxidizes preferentially. If the firing cycle is correct and the right amount of silicon carbide is present, then metallic oxides present in the glaze will be reduced.

The silicon carbide should be as fine as possible but at least 200-mesh since the coarser the grade the greater the tendency to pitting, owing to violent bubbling of the glaze. Too much silicon carbide will result in a badly pinholed, greyish looking glaze; insufficient silicon carbide will not reduce the glaze. The firing cycle is important since a quantity of silicon carbide just sufficient to reduce a glaze will be insufficient if the firing cycle is lengthened, owing to the increased heat work. Speckled reds from reduced copper oxide can be obtained relatively easily but it is more difficult to obtain an even colour, or to obtain a reduced glaze free of the pitting and pinholing characteristic of the presence of silicon carbide.

A good starting range for experiments would be up to 5 per cent addition of copper or iron oxide and 3–8 per cent of silicon carbide to a leadless glaze, adjusting the quantity of silicon carbide as necessary.

SLIP GLAZES

This is the name given to glazes which are predominantly made from clay. Most low-temperature clays, such as the terra cottas, will melt and flow like a glaze if heated to a sufficiently high temperature. For most British red clays the firing range would have to be in excess of cone 10 (1 300°C, 2 370°F) to obtain a satisfactory glass, unless some additions of flux are made to the clay. Albany slip, a slip glaze popular with American potters, is a clay mined at Albany in the U.S.A. which is very low-firing and has a formula approximately as below

$$\left.\begin{array}{l} 0\cdot19\ K_2O \\ 0\cdot46\ CaO \\ 0\cdot35\ MgO \end{array}\right\} \left.\begin{array}{l} 0\cdot61\ Al_2O_3 \\ 0\cdot08\ Fe_2O_3 \end{array}\right\} 3\cdot97\ SiO_2$$

This clay which contains about 6 per cent of iron oxide and 1 per cent of titania, when used alone, fires through shades of beige at 1 000–1 080°C (1 830–1 980°F), becomes dark manganese brown at around 1 150°C (2 100°F), begins to form a glass at around 1 200°C (2 190°F) and at 1 250°C (2 280°F) gives a smooth, dark, treacle-brown colour. A mixture of Etruria marl (a terra-cotta clay, firing range 1 020–1 100°C (1 870–2 010°F) and 35–40 per cent of a borax frit (such as Podmore P. 2246 frit), seems to give a similar result. Inevitably, however, slip glazes are confined to the stoneware and porcelain range.

Slip glazes are best applied to leather-hard clay ware. Because of the high amount of clay contained in the slip, the high degree of contraction during drying of the slip glaze would cause it to flake away if applied to a biscuit surface. This flaking is minimized when the slip glaze is applied to leather-hard (or softer) ware since the glaze and the ware then shrink together. Indeed, slip glazes can be regarded as glassy engobes.

ONCE-FIRE GLAZES

Like slip glazes, these are applied to clay ware. They are often based upon standard glazes used for the normal two-firing technique but adjusted to make them compatible with a once-firing process. Many normal glazes cannot be used satisfactorily in the once-firing technique since they tend to fuse and flow a little too early with the result that the very fluid section of the glaze actually flows into the open pores of the body and is absorbed as though by blotting paper.

Once-fire glazes usually contain an appreciable amount of clay which assists in adhesion to the clay ware. A typical once-fire glaze which will make a good earthenware slip glaze would, for example, consist of 50 parts of lead bisilicate, 45 parts of clay and 5 parts of whiting. Once-fire glazes are sometimes termed 'raw' glazes but this term is more correctly used to describe glazes containing no frit, i.e. made completely of raw materials.

TERRA SIGILLATA

Terra sigillata is actually a type of slip glaze which is commonly seen on much of the attractive and classical wares of the Greeks and the Romans —especially Samian ware. It produces a dense, smooth, glassy surface which is usually brownish red but may be brown or yellow/brown in colour. Its surface, which is rather similar to that of Parian or Jasper ware, provides a good base for painted decoration.

Terra sigillata glaze is produced by separating and collecting only the extremely fine particles from a suspension of an iron-bearing clay such as Etruria marl in water. The clay should be mixed with water to form a thin suspension and then allowed to settle out. The surplus water on the surface can then be decanted away and the top 20 to 25 per cent only of the remaining slip removed for use. The remainder is discarded but the top layer which has been removed can then be used directly as terra sigillata, although to improve the quality some potters repeat the process. This top fraction will naturally consist only of the finest particles present in the original clay.

Terra sigillata must be applied very thinly to clay ware. Thick deposits readily crack owing to the high drying shrinkage of the clay film. To obtain the best fired colour it is usually necessary to fire at around 960°C (1 760°F) or lower: at higher temperatures the colour tends to become too dark and the surface not so attractive.

A result very similar to that obtained with terra sigillata can be obtained by burnishing a leather-hard or white-hard terra cotta pot prior to firing. This burnishing operation, which can be done with a polished boxwood modelling tool, results in a polishing of the surface by forcing any protruding particles into the interstices of the others. The very even, smooth surface is then similar to that produced by the tight packing which naturally results from the very small particles of terra sigillata.

RAKU GLAZES

The Raku procedure was described on page 2. Raku glazes are merely those which will mature at a low temperature, and although certain majolica glazes will do this it is usual to make up glazes which almost inevitably contain either a high amount of lead frit or raw lead. Raw lead

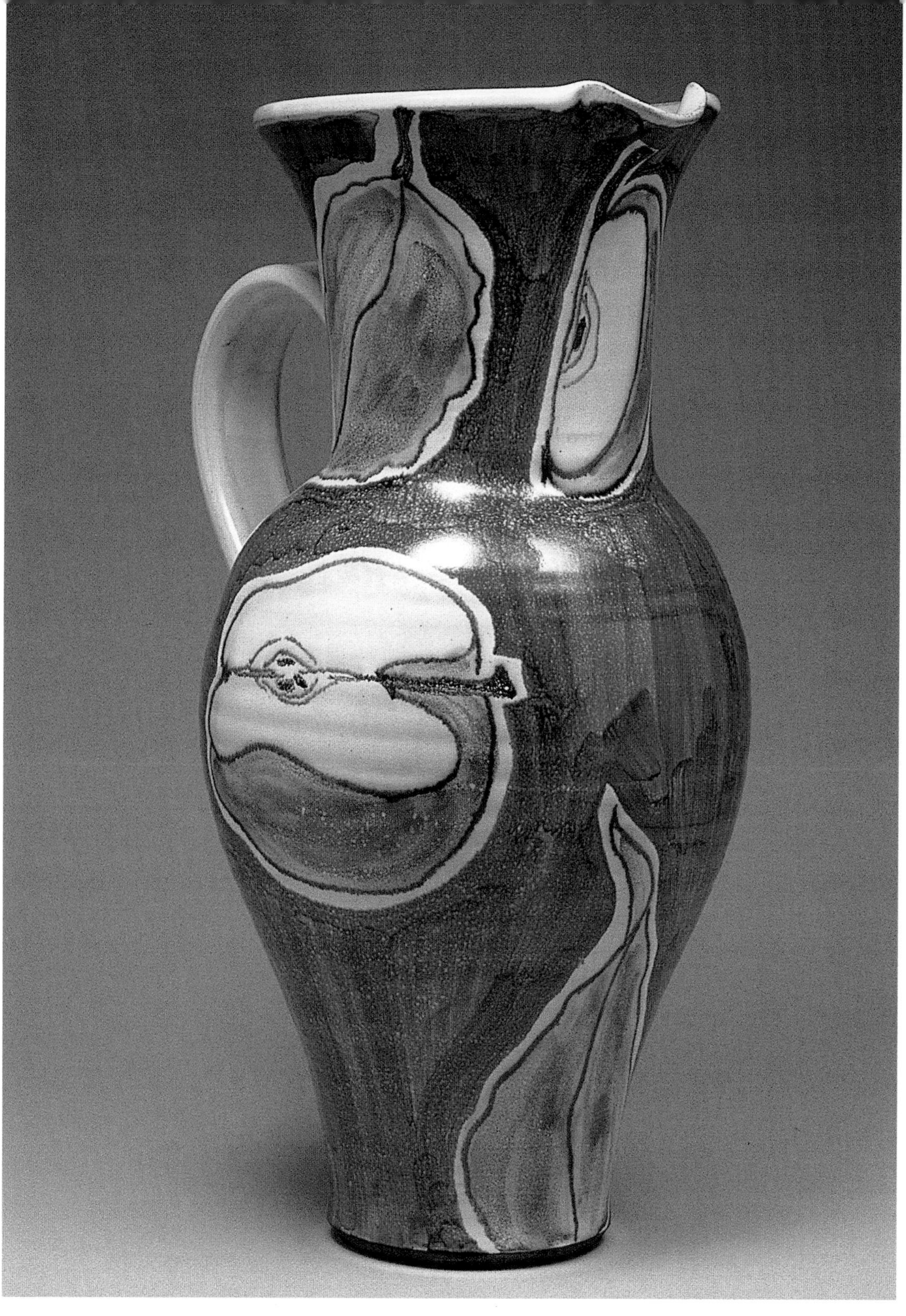

Hand thrown and painted tin-glazed maiolica earthenware jug by Daphne Carnegy
(Photograph by Stephen Brayne)

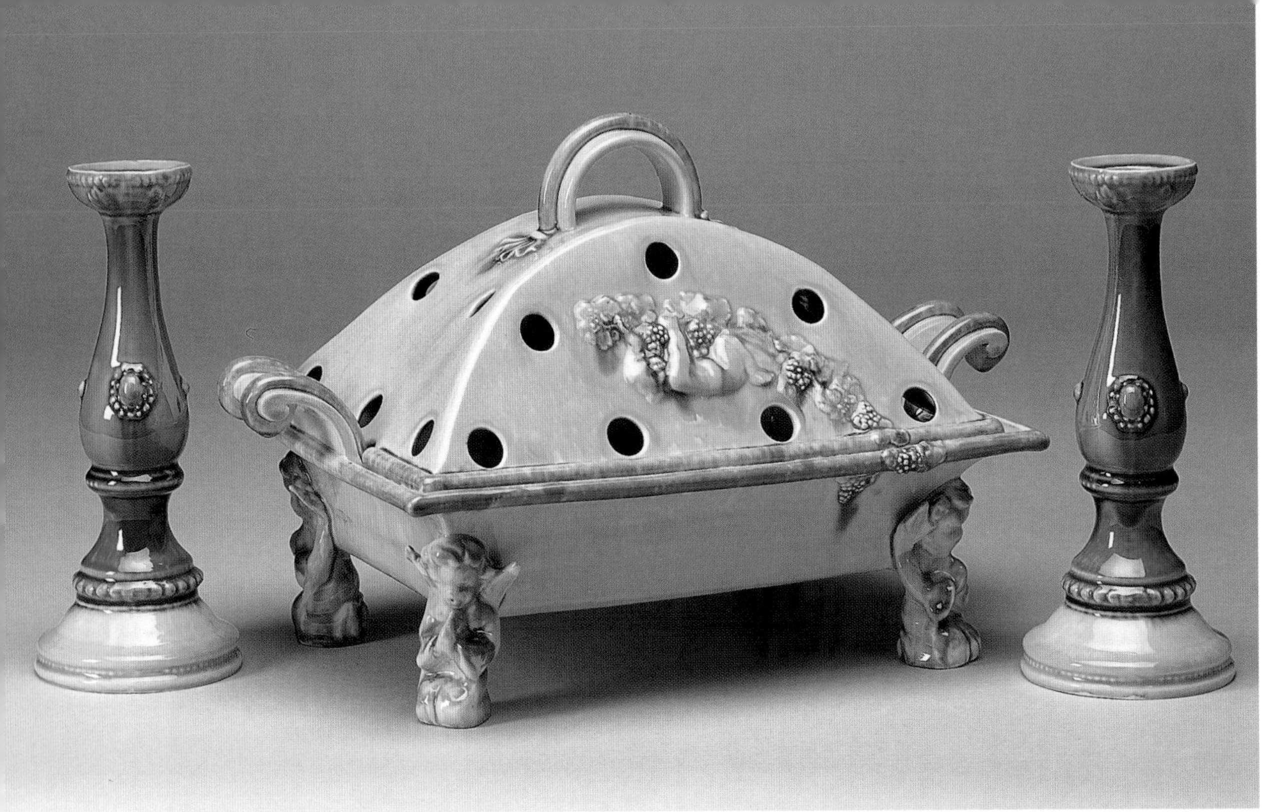

ABOVE
Lidded dish and candlesticks with coloured earthenware glazes by Rita Broadley

BELOW
Hand thrown earthenware platters and bowls decorated with slips and underglaze colours by Jane Elmer-Smith
The low solubility transparent glaze gives extra brightness and richness to the decoration.

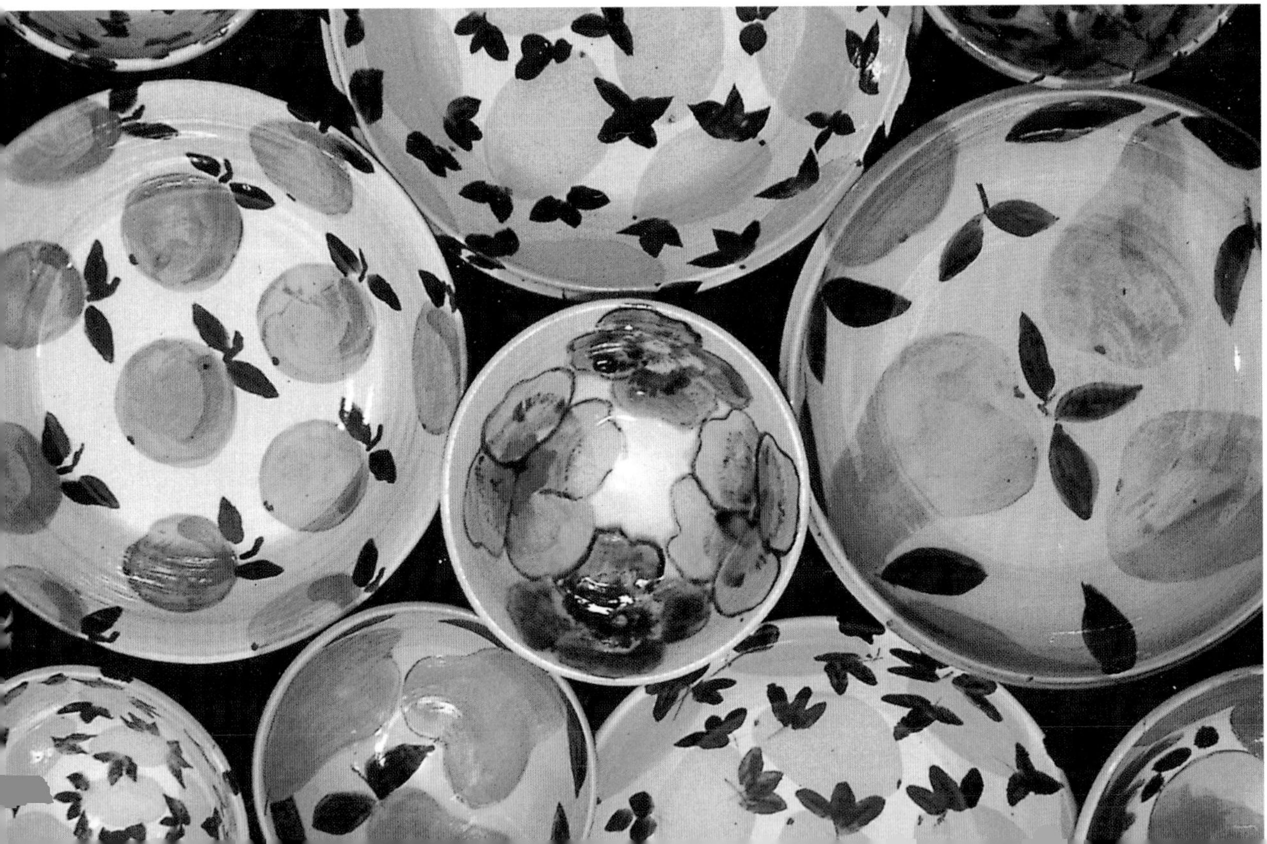

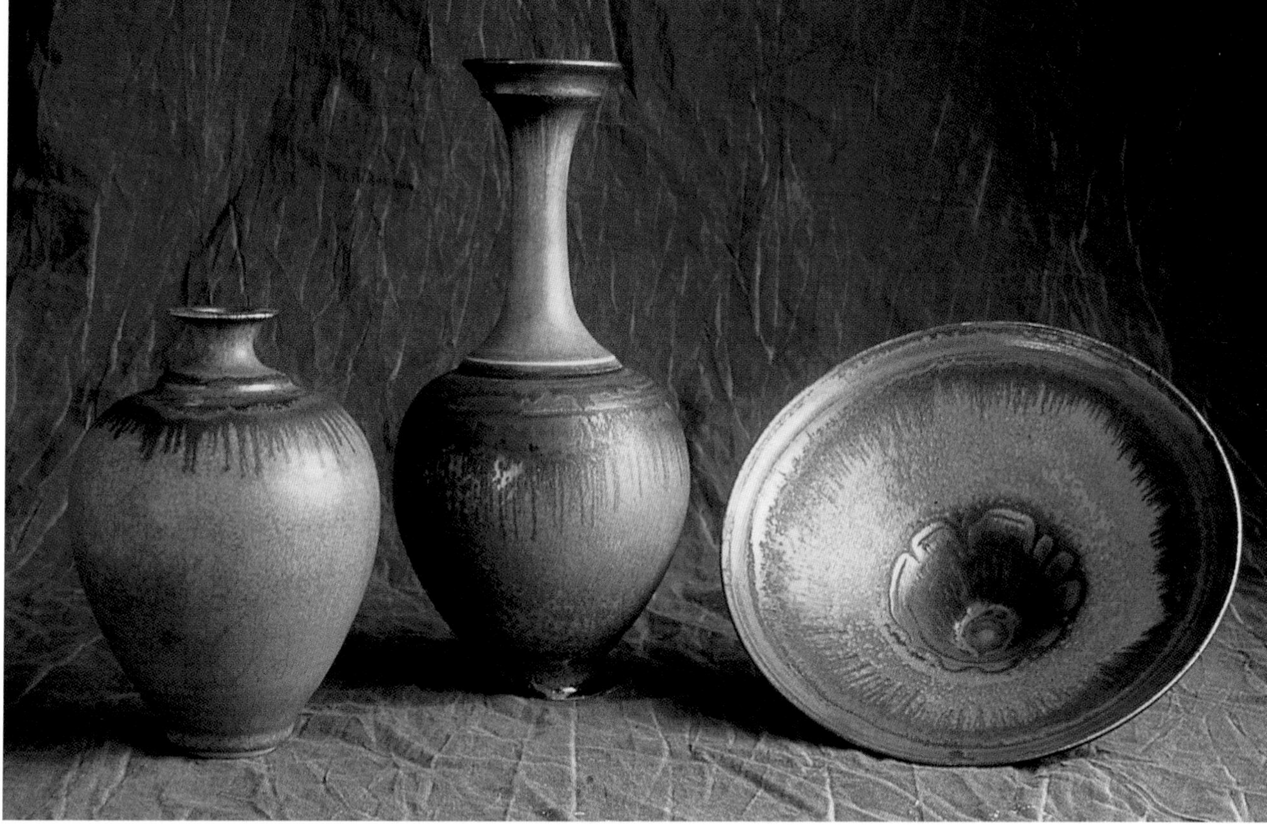

ABOVE
Porcelain vases and bowl by Bridget Drakeford
Copper glaze with bronze lustre.

BELOW
Porcelain bowl by Peter Lane
Thrown and turned in HF1149 porcelain body with air-brushed ceramic stains over paper resists applied to the bisque and thinly applied transparent glaze. This bowl is from his renowned 'Fractured Light' series.

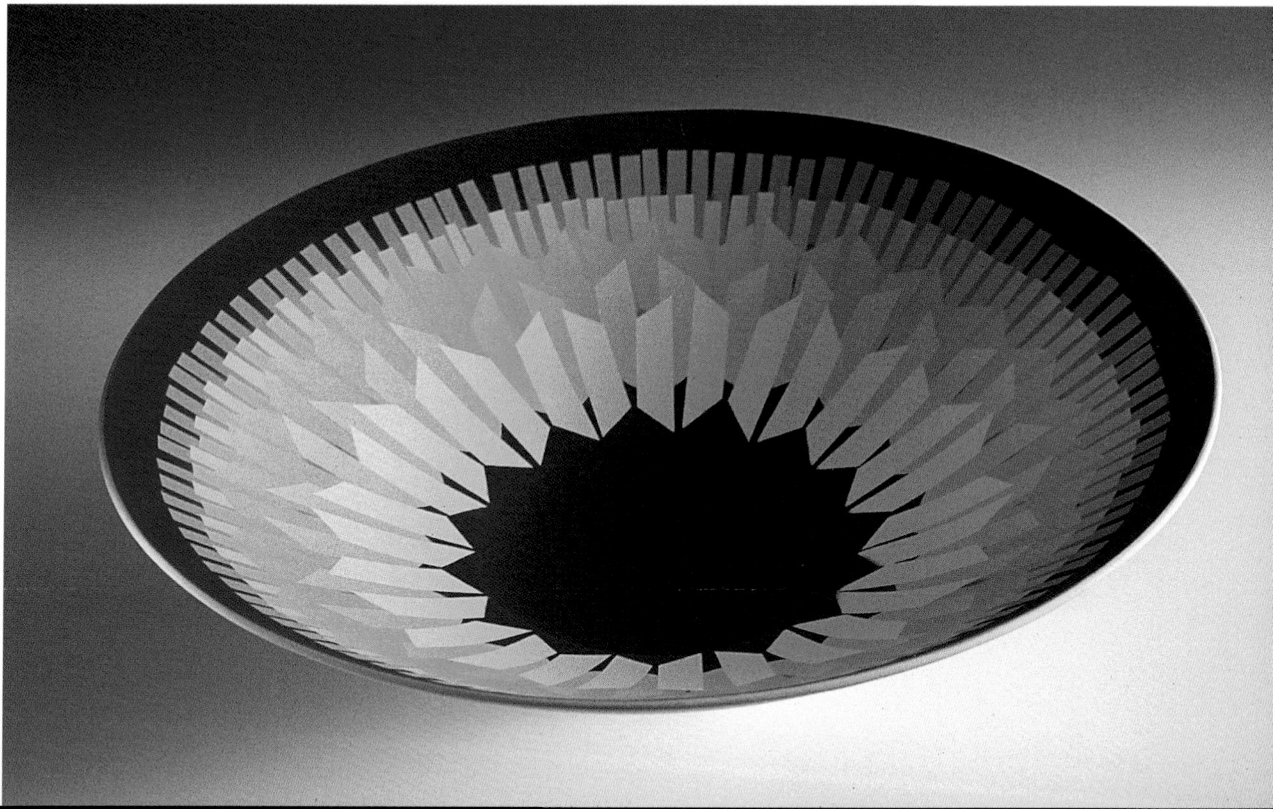

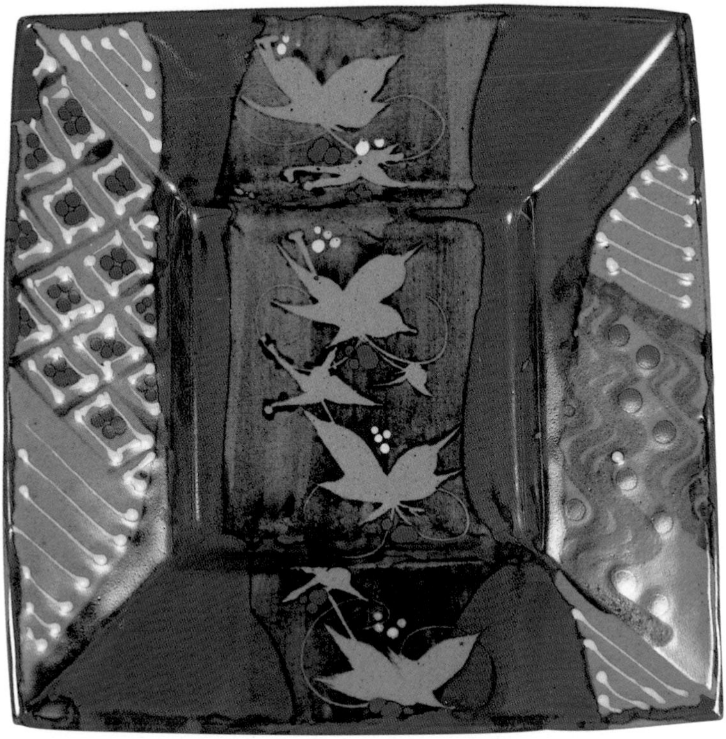

LEFT

Pressed square dish by David Frith

Celadon glaze, wax motif. Poured raku overglaze, painted and trailed pigments and glazes.

BELOW

Stoneware casserole with tenmoku glaze and applied decoration by Derek Emms

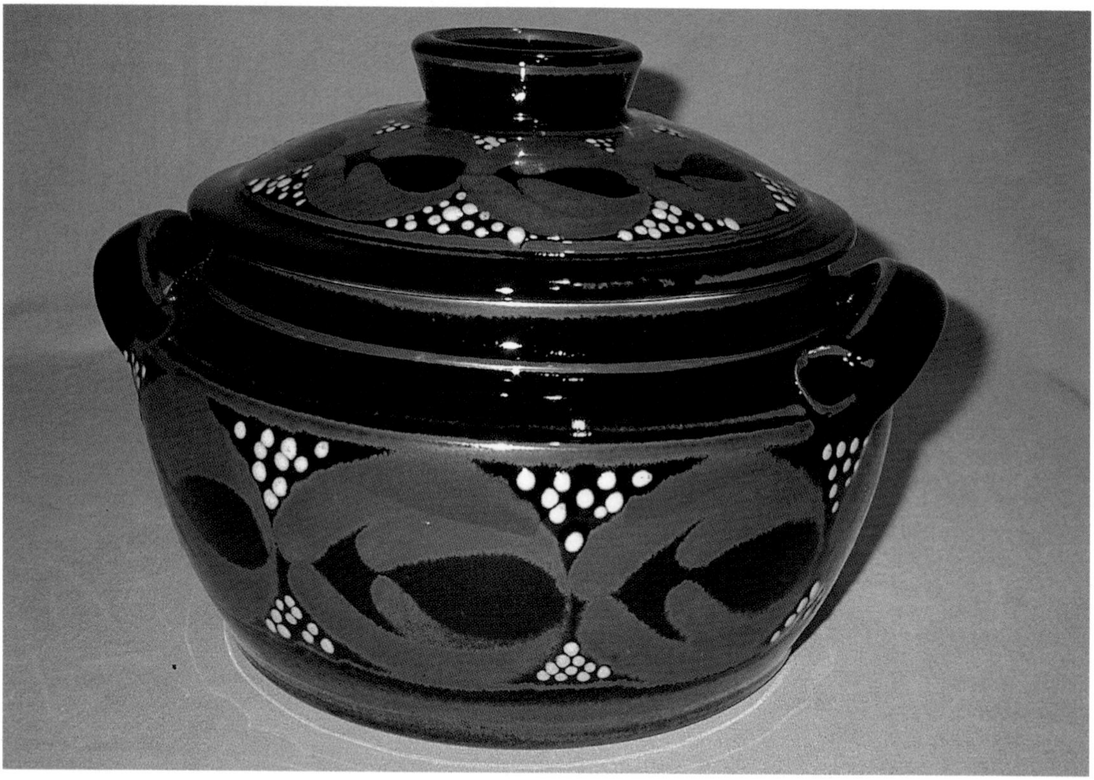

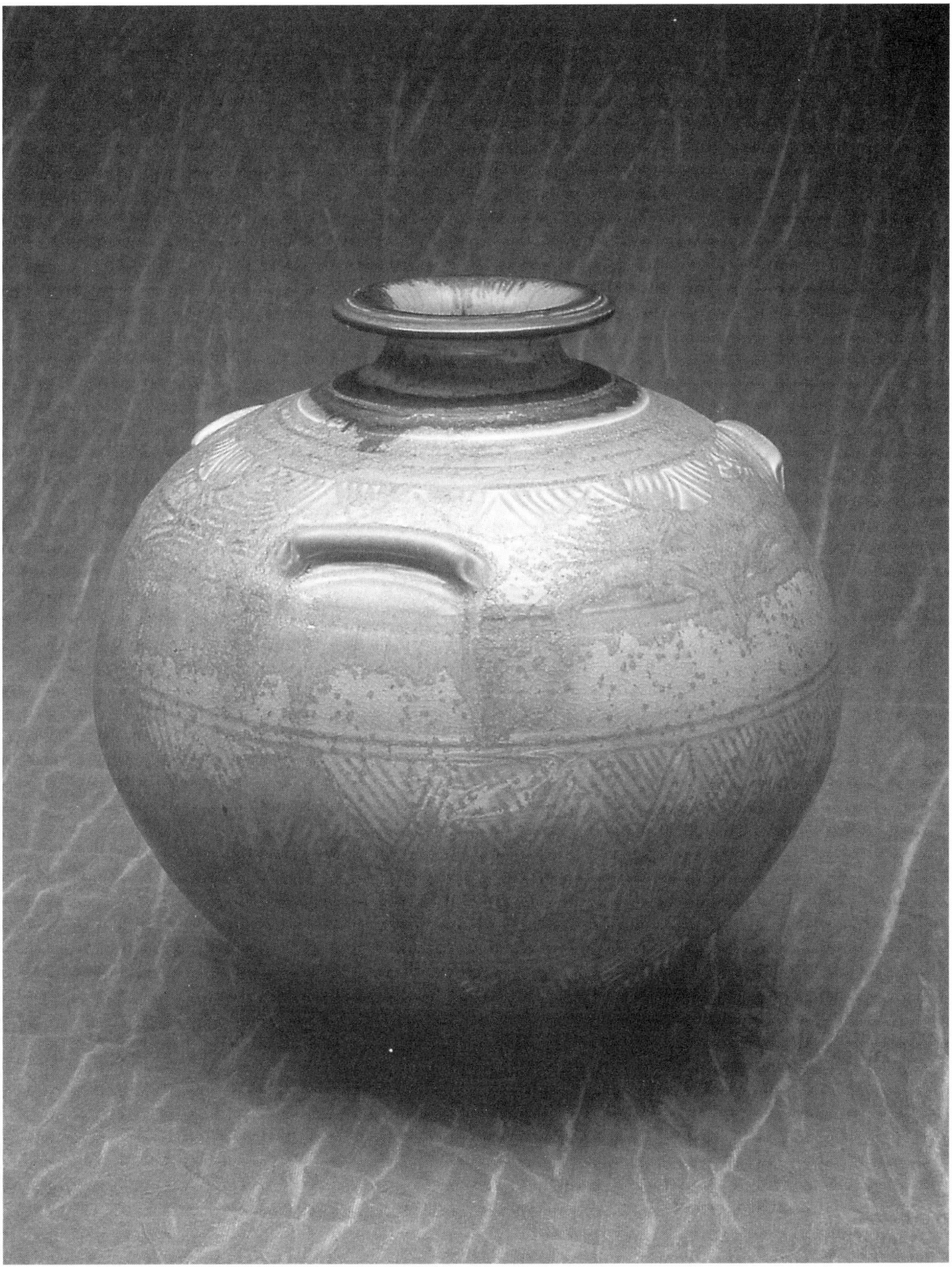

Fig. 30
Large vase, copper glaze with bronze, by Bridget Drakeford

glazes can be made to mature at a very low temperature but these do, of course, have the disadvantage of being toxic. An interesting Raku glaze has been developed from an alkaline frit by Harry Stringer of Taggs Yard in Barnes and the recipe for this is given on page 121.

Owing to the fact that the Raku body is under-fired, Raku glazes inevitably craze, this being accentuated by the fact that for best results Raku glazes are generally thickly applied. Reduction effects can be produced by dipping the red-hot glazed pot in oil or wrapping in grass etc.

ENGOBES

Engobes are clay slips applied to soft or leather-hard pottery to mask the colour of the clay body from which the pottery is made. Thus buff or greyish pottery may be covered with a white slip to make it appear more attractive or to provide a better contrast for subsequent decoration. Thus, although engobes are applied in the manner of glazes they are more properly classified as clays and, in fact, a glaze has to be applied subsequently to seal the engobe, as with other porous biscuit surfaces.

In theory an engobe should contain as much of the clay used in the body as the difference in colour permits so that shrinkage of the pot and its engobe may be similar both before and after firing. In actual practice, however, the engobe in slip form has to be applied to the pot which has already contracted to a certain degree. Consequently it is necessary for the slip to have a somewhat lower shrinkage rate than the ware body to which it has been applied. It is best to prepare the engobe as nearly as possible to the recipe for the body as the colour will allow but adding a little china clay if the body to which the engobe is to be applied is stoneware, or a flint/feldspar mix if the body is earthenware. A trial can then be carried out, applying the engobe to the ware whilst it is softer than the leather-hard condition if at all possible. If the engobe shrinks too much, some of the clay content should be replaced by calcined clay, china clay substituted for ball clay, or the non-plastic materials such as feldspar or flint increased.

Alternatively, a thinner coat should be applied, perhaps two very thin dips instead of one thicker one, or application of the slip carried out when the ware is softer. If on the other hand the engobe does not shrink enough then the clay content of the slip should be increased, perhaps binders added, or the slip applied when the ware is drier or soft biscuited. Leach (*A Potter's Book*) mentions the use of a white slip of 6 parts of china clay, 2 parts of ball clay, and 2 parts of feldspar on stoneware tiles biscuit-fired at 1 200°C (2 190°F).

Engobes which are darker than the body to which they are applied are easily produced by adding a suitable colouring pigment to a slip largely produced from the body as mentioned above. Engobes much whiter than the body to which they are applied are more difficult to produce. The lighter colour has to be obtained by using china clay, flint, alumina or other materials of a very light colour as a replacement or part replacement of the darker clay from which the engobe is made. The use of an opacifier such as tin or zircon would whiten the engobe but is no more effective than adding any other white-burning material such as flint.

Semi-opaque glazes may give extremely attractive results over coloured engobes and especially if the engobe contains a high amount of colouring oxides which have the effect of bleeding through the glaze layer.

VAPOUR GLAZING

The most common example of this is the practice of salt glazing in which rock salt or common salt is vaporized by throwing it on to the fires or into the path of a burner flame. The salt then volatilizes and, in the presence of steam, combines with the pottery body to form a very thin coat of sodium alumino-silicate glaze.

The decomposition of the salt under the action of heat and moisture is given by the equation

$$2NaCl + H_2O = 2HCl + Na_2O$$

The salt should be damp to assist in steam formation—indeed, some potters use a brine drip-feed into the path of the burner flames—and the kiln should have a good brick chimney or flue to take away the hydrochloric acid fumes and traces of chlorine gas which are formed. The salt vapour rapidly glazes the inside of the kiln as well as the ware and it is best to coat the inside walls of the kiln and the kiln furniture with a wash of zircon or a zircon/alumina mix. Salt glazing cannot be done in an electric kiln as damage is caused to the elements and brickwork.

Fig. 31
Round, covered porcelain box by Gwyn Hannsen
Pale celadon glaze inside, mottled grey outside. The pot was sprayed with a vitreous slip (feldspar and china clay) containing minute quantities of manganese and cobalt and slightly salted in a wood-fired kiln. Once-fired only. 8 cm dia, thrown.

The ware must not be too porous when salting commences, otherwise the vapour penetrates the body and the glaze tends to become dull.

A temperature of at least 1 060°C (1 940°F) but preferably in excess of 1 180°C (2 160°F) is necessary for the steam to react satisfactorily with the salt vapour. Consequently most salt glazing is done with stoneware bodies, the salt being introduced over the last 80°C (175°F) or so of the firing. However, salt glazing below stoneware temperatures is possible, especially if about 10–15 per cent of borax is mixed with the salt. Too low a temperature or too much salt may produce a white scum.

Whilst the salting is taking place the damper should be closed back slightly in order to keep the salt vapour in contact with the ware for the longest period possible before being carried away into the exhaust system. Very approximately 1/2 lb salt is necessary for each cubic foot of kiln capacity but the point at which sufficient salting has been carried out is usually determined by pulling draw trials out of the kiln on a poker, quickly cooling these and then examining them to see if sufficient glazing has taken place. The fired colour of the salt glaze depends upon the iron/titania content of the body, varying from white or buff (below 1 per cent) to dark brown (above 5 per cent). Some potters, however, use engobes to mask the body colour.

Salt glazing is useful on account of its cheapness and also for the craze-resistance of the glaze which arises from the thinness of the coat. One problem is that it may be difficult to glaze the inside surfaces of vases, deep bowls etc., and it is therefore sometimes necessary to glaze the insides of these objects separately with a standard glaze.

ASH GLAZES

Ashes are so variable in composition that the best means of introducing them into glazes is by a process of trial and error. A good starting point would be to use a simple formula of 40 per cent of feldspar, 40 per cent of wood ash, and 20 per cent of clay and then to see what happens when this mixture is fired to about 1 260°C (2 300°F). If it is too matt or underfired, the feldspar content should be increased or a quantity of colemanite, whiting, or perhaps a borax frit added. If the mixture is too shiny, silica or china clay can be introduced to make the melt more refractory.

The textures which result from the incorporation of wood ash may be interesting, unusual and, sometimes, beautiful, with subtle colour. Reduction firing conditions generally produce the more attractive results.

It is usual to wash the ash before use as was discussed on page 35.

CHUN GLAZES

Chun glazes are difficult to define and little is understood about the mechanism of their formation. They are semi-opalescent and the charac-

Fig. 32
15-inch diameter stoneware plate with overlapping glazes by Frank Hamer
The lightest glaze is a lime matt, the middle tone glaze is a dolomite and lime matt, and the dark
glaze a matt from iron oxide which burns through the other two. 1 200°C, oxidized.

teristic effect appears to form only in low-alumina glazes containing boron. This would seem to suggest that the effect may be due to devitrification, although one school of thought considers that the effect arises from the intermixing of two glass structures of slightly different refractive index; according to another the effect is due to the presence of phosphorus or fluorine resulting from the use of bone ash or fluorspar.

Most Chun glazes are of a bluish or greenish colour which is derived most commonly from the presence of a very small amount of iron oxide in combination with reduction firing conditions.

CALCIUM BORATE GLAZES

Glazes containing appreciable amounts of cole-manite or a calcium borate frit under conditions of slow cooling will recrystallize to produce an opalescent effect. This may be very beautiful, the opalescence appearing in unstained glazes as white 'fluffy' clouds dispersed in the fired glaze. If a stain has been used the calcium borate precipitate causing the opalescence is contrasted as a less intense colour in comparison to that of the glassy background.

Calcium borate frit is preferable to colemanite —or is desirable as a part replacement—owing to the tendency for glazes containing large amounts of colemanite to 'sputter' (*see* Chapter 6).

A typical glaze recipe producing a pleasant opalescent green at 1 100°C (2 010°F) is: calcium borate frit 60, china clay 10, potash feldspar 30, copper oxide 5.

13. Crushing and grinding

It is seldom possible to reduce large lumps of rock material to a fine powder in a single machine or in one operation, and reduction in size is therefore usually accomplished in two or more stages.

PRELIMINARY CRUSHING

The simplest and most common form of coarse crushing equipment is the jaw crusher and these machines can be designed to take large lumps of rock, reducing it to a size range of 1 to 3 inches in diameter.

forward motion of the jaw. Eventually the material falls through the gap between the jaws at the bottom.

Once the material has been reduced to a size range of 1 to 3 inches it can then be fed into an intermediate grinder where the material is reduced down to 1/8 inch or less. There are several types of intermediate grinding equipment such as pan grinders, rolls, hammer mills and disc crushers but the most popular type is the grinding pan.

Both wet and dry grinding pans are available

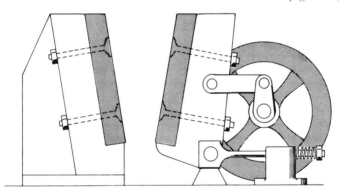

Fig. 33
Typical jaw crusher

As will be seen from the illustration in Fig. 33, a jaw crusher consists of two plates or jaws, one of which is fixed and approximately vertical, the other being moveable and forming a 'V' with the first. The moveable jaw is caused to approach and recede from the fixed jaw so that material fed between the jaws will be crushed by a squeezing action and fall further into the 'V' where it is reduced still further by the next

but the dry grinding pan is the most commonly used. It consists of two heavy rollers or wheels called 'mullers' which rest on a revolving platform or pan. Material to be crushed is introduced into the pan and this carries it under the heavy mullers which crush it. The speed of rotation of the pan is sufficient to cause the crushed material to be forced to the outer section of the pan where screen plates are fitted which allow sufficiently fine material to fall through. Coarser material is directed by a ploughshare back to the mullers for further grinding.

FINE GRINDING

This is the process of converting sand or gravel-sized material down to a fine powder.

General considerations

The activity of a material is proportional to specific surface, i.e. it is proportional to the exposed surface area of the material. The smaller the particle the greater the surface area of the particle in relation to its mass and the more reactive a material becomes. Glazes and other materials will therefore fuse more readily under the same degree of heat if more finely ground.

However, the finer a glaze is ground the 'dustier' and more expensive it becomes and, perhaps more important, the more likely it is to crawl, but on the other hand a glaze that is too coarse is difficult to keep in suspension. Potters, therefore, grind their glazes to a size range which is considered to be a happy medium. Much, however, depends upon the glaze. An alkaline frit glaze, for example, would probably be best ground only to 120-mesh since the increased solubility of the particles with smaller particle size could be very troublesome, causing reduced alkalinity and the frit to set hard. Similarly, fritted glazes are generally not ground so finely as raw ones since the frit solubility might be increased beyond the acceptable limits. Raw stoneware glazes on the other hand can generally be ground quite finely and this is desirable since the more finely ground flux content (usually feldspar) promotes a greater fluxing action.

For most glazes a reasonable average is to grind to less than 1 per cent retained on a 200-mesh screen. It is important to appreciate that the material passing through the screen will have no fine limit and the particles will have a size range varying from ultra-fine to 200-mesh.

At this point it will be useful to consider the unit of measurement of particle size. Specifying that a material is finer than a particular lawn size is a common and most useful practice, since

all potters quickly become accustomed to mentally relating lawn numbers to particle size, i.e. we remember from a visual inspection of a 200-mesh screen that the holes are very much finer than those of, say, 100-mesh, and by reference to a table giving aperture sizes of standard sieves we can obtain a measurement of the actual size of the average hole in the lawn and thus an indication of the size of the largest particles which pass through it.

The micron

When materials are ground into the ultra-fine range, i.e. less than approximately 300-mesh, we begin to enter a range of particle sizes where the use of screens is unusual. For this reason, and also because a more precise unit is obtained, ceramists generally adopt the micron as the unit of measurement, one micron being one-thousandth of a millimetre, i.e. 0·001 mm. It is commonly expressed by the Greek letter 'mu' (μ).

An indication of the size relationship of a micron is given by the following chart.

Particles just passing		
80-mesh	approx.	160 microns
120-mesh	approx.	110 microns
200-mesh	approx.	75 microns
300-mesh	approx.	50 microns
finest filter paper	less than	5 microns

Thus a particle passing a 200-mesh sieve may be referred to as being not larger than 75 microns in size.

In those applications, such as the grinding of glazes and frits, where the material has to be ground in the region of 120- to 300-mesh, it is usual to make use of ball mills. For grinding below 300-mesh (e.g. ultra-fine grinding of zircon opacifiers) the Vibro-Energy mill becomes the more practical and efficient proposition.

THE BALL MILL

This consists of a closed cylinder lined with blocks of silica rock (silex, chert or flint), porcelain, or, in the case of certain smaller mills, rubber lined. The mill is partly filled with flint pebbles or porcelain balls and the material to be ground, the grinding action being obtained by the impact

Fig. 34
Ball mill
(By courtesy of William Boulton Ltd)

Fig. 35
Ball mill action
Grinding is produced by the tumbling action of the pebbles or balls.
(*a*) Slow speed; (*b*) normal speed; (*c*) rapid speed.

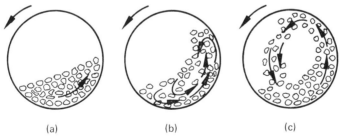

(a) (b) (c)

and abrasive action of the grinding media sliding and tumbling in the mill while it is being rotated.

If the ball mill is rotated at very slow speed the grinding charge will merely slide on the moving inner surface of the mill, wearing this rather than the material to be ground. If, however, the mill is rotated at high speed, the centrifugal force will cause the grinding charge to distribute uniformly over the inner lining of the mill and to be carried with it. If this high speed is gradually reduced a speed will be obtained at which the centrifugal force is not sufficient to carry the grinding media around the mill lining, the media rising to a maximum height and then cascading down to strike the layer of moving balls beneath (*see* Fig. 35).

It used to be considered that this was the most efficient milling speed but it is now recognized that a more efficient grinding action is obtained by rotating the mill at sufficient speed to cause a churning action of the grinding medium throughout the whole charge. This optimum speed has been found to be approximately 64–90 per cent of the *critical speed*, (i.e. the speed of rotation which is just sufficient to cause the grinding charge to ride with the mill lining). If the internal radius of the mill is measured in feet then the critical speed will be indicated by the formula

$$\frac{54 \cdot 19}{\sqrt{R}}$$

where R is the radius of the mill interior, in feet, less the radius of the grinding ball in feet.

The following table indicates the optimum speed of rotation for various sizes of mill.

Mill internal diameter (ft)	Rev/ min	Mill internal diameter (ft)	Rev/ min
0·75	56·5	3·06	24·8
1·0	49·0	4·06	20·0
1·65	38·0	5·05	18·0
2·38	28·3	6·52	16·0

Grinding charge

If the material to be ground is fairly coarse then grinding media up to about 2 in. in diameter may have to be used to break the material down initially, but if the material is reasonably fine then it will be ground more quickly the smaller the grinding media. It is usual to use mixed media varying from 2 in. down to $\frac{1}{2}$ in. or so in size, although with the smallest mills only the smaller sizes of media can be used satisfactorily.

The proportioning of grinding medium, material to be ground, and water is important. The media should occupy 50–55 per cent of the internal volume of the mill, the charge plus water occupying 20–25 per cent. However, the water and the material to be ground are mainly contained by the interstices between the individual pieces of grinding media and consequently

the mill is only some two-thirds full when fully charged. Grinding is usually commenced with equal volumes of water and material to be ground, the volume of the latter firstly being determined by dividing its weight by its specific gravity.

Grinding procedure

Since the softer materials require very little grinding whereas harder materials such as frits demand a much longer grinding operation, it is usual to grind any much harder fraction until about one-half to one hour before completion and then to add the remainder of the mill batch, i.e. the much softer material (china clay, whiting, etc.) plus any further water addition necessary to adjust the viscosity. This produces a faster total milling time than if all the batch were initially added to the mill. Naturally, with un-fritted glazes, such as most high-temperature ones where the hardness variation of the constituents is not so great, the whole of the mill batch may be charged into the mill initially, although it is still good practice to use less than the full amount of water, introducing the remainder when the desired fineness has been reached. Milling is then continued for $\frac{1}{4}$–$\frac{1}{2}$ hour to achieve thorough mixing. Most glazes can be milled down to less than 1 per cent on 200-mesh in 7–12 hours, raw glazes such as most stoneware ones being ground more quickly than fritted ones.

Materials which markedly increase viscosity, such as gums and other glaze binders should not be introduced into the mill since the increased viscosity which would result would seriously hinder grinding, owing to cushioning of the grinding action.

When grinding has finished, the charge is poured out on to a grid or coarse lawn which retains only the grinding media, the ground material passing through.

Drying out

The ground material is usually directed on to a drying bed such as those shown in Fig. 36. These are of brick and are heated from beneath by burners, the water being evaporated away until the glaze is dry when it is scooped or dug away and bagged. Owing to deterioration of the drying bed a hot spot may sometimes form which may sinter the glaze immediately above and cause it to form into very hard nodules or lumps.

Glaze milled in very small mills can, of course, be poured through a coarse screen (to catch the media) into a suitable receptacle and the surplus water decanted off after standing. The glaze can then be easily dried out.

ULTRA-FINE GRINDING

Rick's law states that the force required to break a particle by impact is proportional to the volume of the particle. This indicates that the force required to break a particle having a diameter of one micron (1/1 000 mm) is only one-millionth of that necessary to break a particle which will just pass a 150-mesh screen. It will therefore be appreciated that for ultra-fine grinding only very small forces are necessary and the use of force in excess of that which will just break the material merely results in wasted energy and a noisier operation. In order to obtain a high rate of output, these small forces must be applied at a very high rate, this being best achieved by the use of grinding media of large surface area vibrating at high frequency.

One other vitally important factor is that the grinding forces must be applied to thin layers of material (i.e. the forces should not be 'cushioned'), otherwise the particles merely move away from the point of impact and rearrange themselves without producing breakage.

The essential requirements for ultra-fine grinding by impact are therefore the application of very small impact forces at a high frequency rate to a thin layer of the material to be ground. These considerations led to the development of the Podmore-Boulton Vibro-Energy mill which is now in general use for ultra-fine grinding operations.

THE VIBRO-ENERGY MILL

Basically the Vibro-Energy mill consists of a grinding chamber and a vibrator. The grinding chamber is filled with small pieces of a very hard grinding medium such as sintered alumina or zircon in the form of half-inch cylinders and the material to be ground is introduced from the top to fill the voids between the grinding media.

The vibrator consists of a specially designed electric motor having a heavy shaft, at each end of which is fitted an 'out-of-balance' weight. The lower weight can be adjusted to vary the angle it makes with the top weight between 0 and 90° and serves to provide a powerful three-dimensional high-frequency vibration whilst the upper weight imparts a gyratory movement to the grinding media. Around the periphery of the grinding chamber are springs which provide a restoring force and also substantially damp out vibration of the mill base.

The grinding action is produced as the pieces of grinding medium impinge gently against each other. The pieces also tend to spin, which creates a certain amount of shear force but, more important, ensures that a cylindrical surface is maintained. The packed mass of grinding medium also slowly gyrates in the horizontal plane while in the vertical plane it rises in proximity to the outer wall and descends as it approaches the inner wall. This assists in distributing and mixing the material being ground.

The material to be ground should preferably be pre-ground to 80-mesh or finer. It is common for ultra-fine grinding to be approached in stages, i.e. the material from one mill is fed into one or more others, where it is progressively ground finer. The ground material is finally run off from the mill on to drying beds exactly like those used with the ball mill.

Vibro-Energy mills are, incidentally, also used for dry grinding of certain materials, the charge being fluidized by introducing compressed air at the base of the grinding chamber and the ground material being carried away by the air stream into a receiving hopper.

THE OP-PO MILL

For the craft potter or for the school or college wishing to produce small batches of glaze, perhaps to a special recipe or from rock material, it has become usual to use a small ball mill to grind

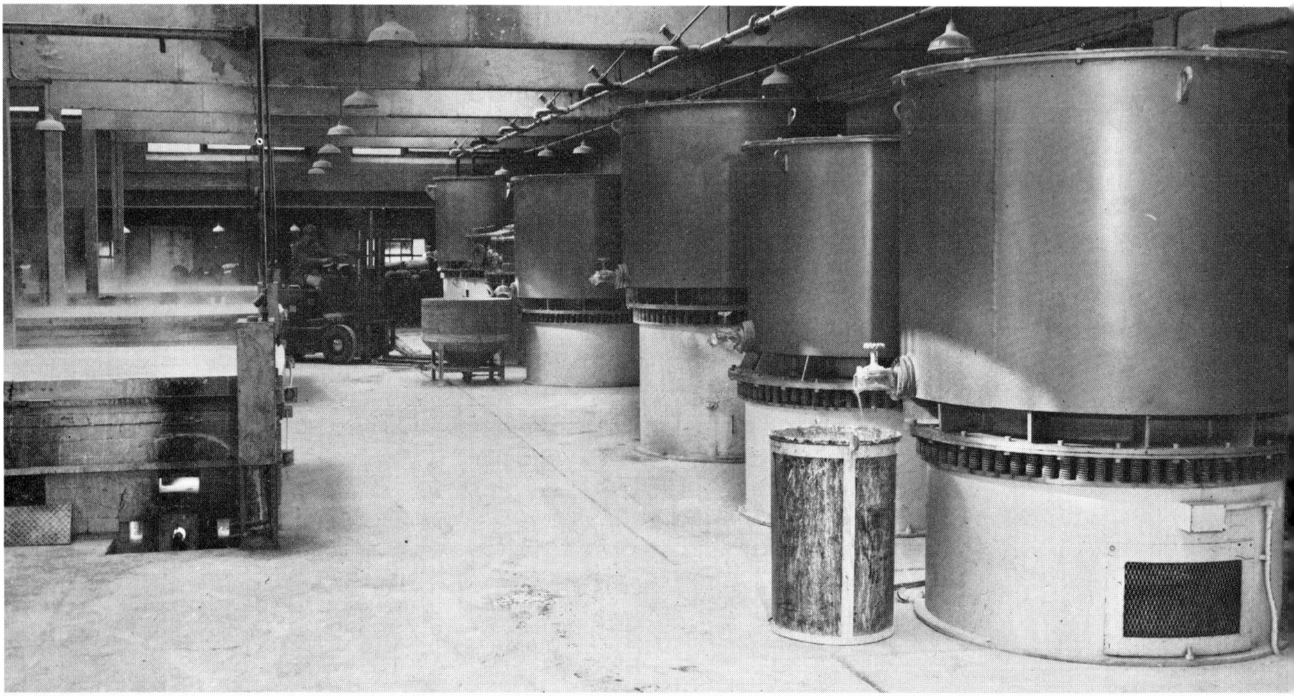

Fig. 36
A series of Vibro Energy mills
Note also the drying beds for the slop-ground material on the left of the photograph.
(By courtesy of Podmore & Sons Ltd)

Fig. 37
Vibro Energy mill layout
(By courtesy of Podmore & Sons Ltd)

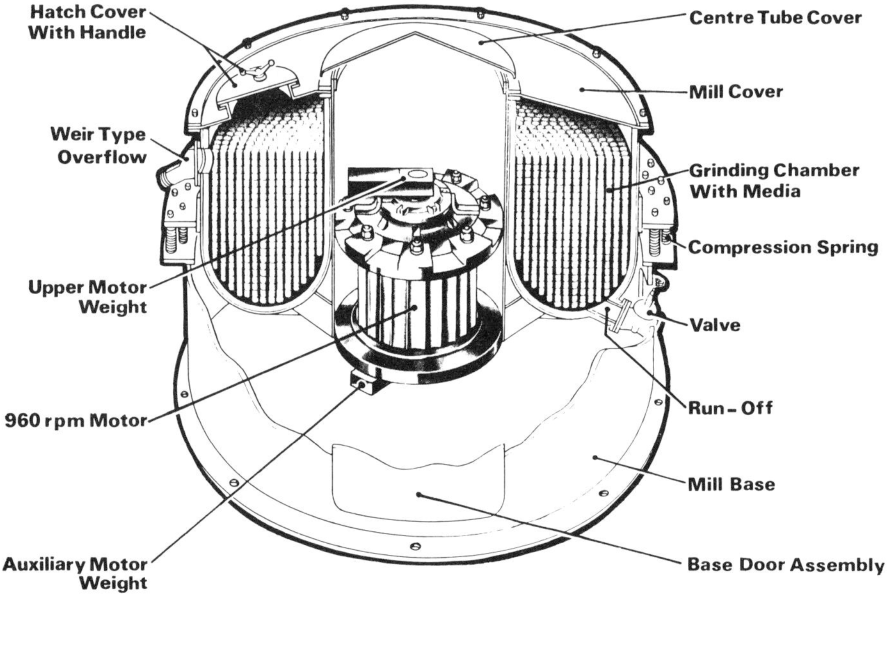

Hatch Cover With Handle
Centre Tube Cover
Mill Cover
Weir Type Overflow
Grinding Chamber With Media
Compression Spring
Upper Motor Weight
Valve
Run-Off
960 rpm Motor
Mill Base
Base Door Assembly
Auxiliary Motor Weight

the glaze to the desired degree of fineness. Unfortunately a ball mill takes several hours to grind most glazes unless each of the recipe ingredients is sufficiently fine (which is unusual). Even if each of the glaze ingredients is in very fine powder form, some milling is desirable to mix the batch homogeneously, so that the glaze stays more uniformly in suspension instead of settling out preferentially.

A revolutionary mill based upon the Vibro-Energy mill principle has, however, been developed. Known as the Op-po mill, this machine is now becoming popular for the grinding of small batches of material and for this purpose it is undoubtedly very much superior to conventional equipment. The Op-po mill will, for example, grind most ceramic materials, glazes, colours, etc. up to 80 times faster than will a ball mill, and the milling time for an average glaze is therefore reduced from a matter of hours to minutes.

This efficiency is obtained from a patented drive unit which transmits opposed reciprocating high-frequency vibrations to standard grinding jars which contain the grinding medium and the charge to be ground. The perfectly balanced action ensures long life from the machine which is equally effective for wet or dry milling.

Since feed material up to $\frac{3}{4}$ in. can be accepted and reduced to the desired fineness in a matter of a few minutes, the Op-po mill is ideal for the rapid grinding of small batches of glaze or other materials. The machine is, however, about seven times as expensive as a small ball mill of similar capacity.

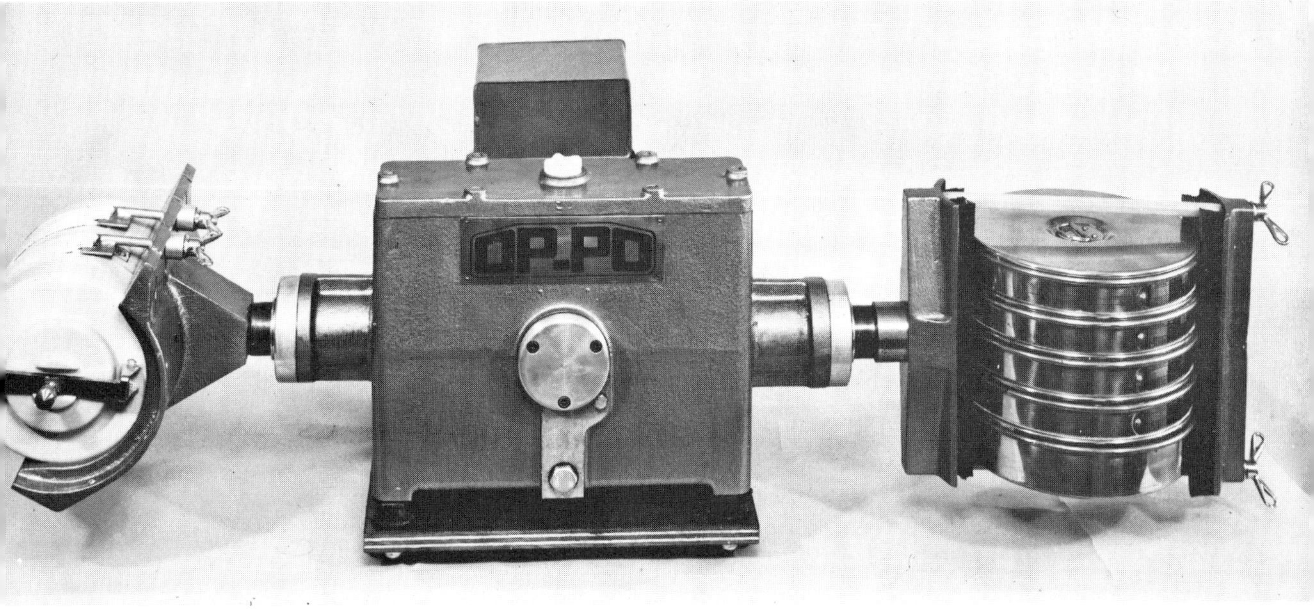
OP-PO

Fig. 38
Op-po mill
(By courtesy of Podmore & Sons Ltd)

14. Glaze preparation

Prepared glazes are usually purchased in dry powdered form and theoretically only require the addition of water to render them suitable for use. However, it is not uncommon for glaze batches to contain nodules of sintered material or, when mixed with water, undispersed lumps, and so it is necessary to sieve the glaze after mixing with water.

Certain types of speckled glazes may be produced by the introduction of coarsely ground colouring pigments, e.g. coarsely ground ilmenite or manganese dioxide, in which case passing such glazes through a fine sieve would result in the removal of the speckling agent. With this exception, however, it is best to lawn all glazes through a sieve of 60- or 80-mesh (preferably 80) after preparation of the slop glaze.

Sieving, incidentally, is a satisfactory way of mixing dry materials and if various glaze materials have to be mixed together this can be accomplished by sieving the dry glaze mixture two or three times through a sieve of about 20- or 40-mesh followed by storage. When the glaze is required for use it must, of course, be sieved again through 60- or 80-mesh after mixing with water. Schools do sometimes prepare bulk batches of dry mixed glazes in this way from which they take glaze as required, although it must be mentioned that sieving glazes in dry form would not be allowed in factories unless under exhaust draught conditions. This is due to the health hazard of siliceous or potentially toxic materials being liberated as dust into the air breathed by the operative.

Additions of colouring oxides or stains may be made at any stage but, with all colouring pigments, greater freedom from specking is obtained if the pigment is mixed with a little water and

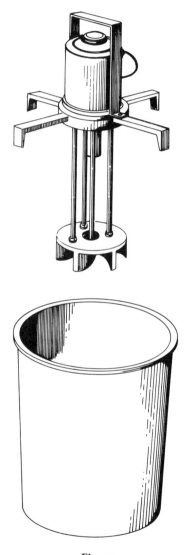

Fig. 39
Rapid mixer
Useful for the rapid and complete mixing of glazes and slips.

passed through a fine (200-mesh) sieve before adding to the glaze. Nevertheless, unless the glaze is thoroughly mixed, specking may still occur from undispersed particles and this is why the most even colour is obtained when the colouring pigment is actually ground with the glaze.

Gums and other glaze binders should be mixed with water to a paste or cream-like consistency and mixed into the glaze prior to the final sieving operation. Adding the powdered binder directly to the slop glaze results in the formation of small lumps which, unless one has the facilities of a rapid mixer, demand an excessive amount of mixing to break down.

A further important point is that a glaze slip which has been allowed to age for a little while generally suspends better and is easier to use than one put into use immediately after preparation. This is thought to be largely due to the fact that the glaze powder particles naturally tend to bunch together and time is needed for the water to penetrate fully into the pores between the particles, thus enabling them to be dispersed. The slop glaze should therefore be allowed to stand for several hours, after which any excess water can be decanted away, the glaze adjusted for thickness, thoroughly stirred, and sieved before being put into use.

GLAZE CONSISTENCY AND ADJUSTMENT

Uniformity of coverage is of major importance with glazes prepared for dipping. Consequently the fluidity of the glaze, i.e. the ratio of glaze to water, may be adjusted to make it more suitable to the size and design of the ware to be dipped. In general, however, the actual fluidity or consistency of the glaze is varied by the potter to match the porosity of the ware being glazed, very porous pottery demanding the use of a much more dilute glaze than is desirable with more vitreous pieces. Adjustment is best carried out by decanting away all the surplus water (so that the glaze is too thick) and after the glaze has been stirred and sieved, adding back the required amount of water to obtain the proper thickness which is dependent upon the ware porosity.

Some potters gauge the porosity of biscuit ware by putting it to the lip or tongue and noting the degree of suction which results; others judge purely by feel or visual appearance. Whatever method is preferred, once some idea of the degree of porosity has been determined, the glaze slip will have to be adjusted to suit the porosity. Again, the correct glaze slip viscosity can be gauged by experience—by dipping the hand into the glaze and noting the way in which the glaze adheres or runs off the fingers, or by observing the thickness by stirring, but it can also be determined by weighing, or by the use of a hydrometer.

The thicker the consistency of a glaze slip the heavier it is. It is therefore common in pottery factories for one pint of the prepared slop glaze to be weighed using a special conical measure which contains exactly one pint when full to the brim. Future batches of the same glaze can then be prepared to the same density as before by adjusting the glaze/water ratio to obtain the same pint weight.

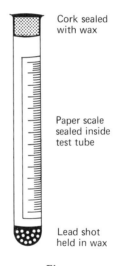

Cork sealed with wax

Paper scale sealed inside test tube

Lead shot held in wax

Fig. 40
A simple hydrometer

A simpler method, however, is to use a hydrometer. One can be made very easily by putting a few pieces of lead shot into a test tube into which has been fitted a piece of paper graduated with a numbered vertical scale (*see* Fig. 40). A cork is then tightly fitted and preferably sealed with wax so that it cannot be removed and water cannot enter. When placed into slop glaze, the hydrometer should ride in the glaze like a fishing float in water and the actual level of the glaze surface can be read off on the scale. If any future batches of that particular glaze have to be prepared to the same consistency then this can easily be done by adjustment of the glaze slip until the same reading is obtained on the hydrometer.

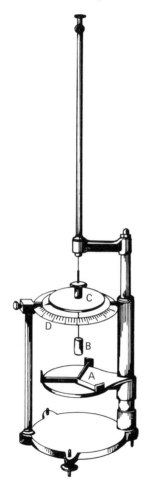

Fig. 41
Torsion viscometer

Used extensively in industry to measure the viscosity of clay and glaze slips. A container of slip is placed on to stand *A* so that the cylinder *B* is immersed. The flat disc *C* is rotated through 360° and clipped into position. When released the degree of overswing on scale *D* is read off as an indication of the viscosity.

(By courtesy of A. Gallenkamp & Co. Ltd)

An instrument widely used in industry for measuring viscosity is the torsion viscometer (*see* Fig. 41).

It is important to bear in mind that such methods can only assist in obtaining a similar viscosity from successive batches of the same glaze—or one of a similar density. A low-solubility glaze, for example, is heavier than a leadless glaze owing to its lead content and for the same reading on a hydrometer the low-solubility glaze will be less viscous, i.e. more dilute than the leadless one. Another way of looking at it is that a pint of low-solubility glaze will be heavier than a pint of leadless glaze having the same water content.

Finally, it is important to check the suitability of the glaze viscosity for the ware porosity by glazing a test piece and scratching the glaze film with a needle or with the finger nail to observe the thickness.

GLAZE BINDERS

Most glazes when dry have very little strength and suffer damage easily through such operations as handling during preparation for firing, this problem being particularly acute with the larger articles. Since most dry glaze surfaces are 'dusty' a further problem arises whenever one has to handle pots having differently coloured glazes, for it is easy to transfer traces of glaze from one pot to another via the fingers. In addition, those potters who prefer to decorate their pottery by painting directly on to the unfired glaze surface, as in the maiolica technique, often find that the glaze film is too loose to permit accurate brushwork.

For these reasons it may be desirable to introduce a binder into the glaze to bind or glue together the glaze particles, resulting in a much firmer glaze film. The amount of binder added is usually less than 1 per cent but may be as high as $2-2\frac{1}{2}$ per cent, when the glaze film will become quite brittle and provide a very good surface for painted decoration. The binder burns away during subsequent firing at about 300–400°C.

A major disadvantage of binders is their high rate of shrinkage, which may cause the glaze

Fig. 42
11-inch diameter bowl by Alan Caiger-Smith
Red earthenware with tin glaze and on-glaze painting.

film to crack during drying thus bringing a risk of crawling. A further problem with the use of organic binders such as the gums and starches, (but not with the S.C.M.C. types) is that, in time, and especially during warm weather, they decompose, releasing a smell which has to be experienced to be believed! For this reason a few drops of an antibacterial agent are sometimes also added to the glaze.

The commonly used binders are the following.

SODIUM CARBOXYMETHYLCELLULOSE

Commonly referred to as S.C.M.C., this is the best type of binder since it is at least as powerful as the others and has the advantage of being resistant to bacterial attack. Different grades are available, the popular ones being Courlose and Cellofas.

GUM ARABIC

A popular and inexpensive binder.

GUM TRAGACANTH

Similar to gum arabic but more expensive and more difficult to dissolve in water. Both gum arabic and gum tragacanth will dissolve much more easily in hot water than cold.

OTHERS

Starch, sugar, and seaweed extracts are commonly used.

The addition of binders to glazes considerably increases the glaze viscosity. However, this increased viscosity is accompanied by reduced absorption of water from the glaze slip due to the water-retentive properties of the binder. Thus one has a situation where dipped pieces tend to pick up less glaze owing to reduced water absorption but more glaze owing to the higher glaze slip viscosity and surface tension. This has the effect of reducing glaze pick-up on the very porous pieces but increasing glaze pick-up on the vitreous pieces. In addition to this the glaze coat will take longer to dry and this increases the risk of glaze 'runs' on the dipped pot unless care is taken.

If it is considered necessary to add a binder to a glaze, this addition should always be made to the fully ground glaze rather than into the grinding mill whilst the glaze is being ground since the increase in viscosity which results from the addition of binders would appreciably reduce the efficiency of the grinding action.

One other application of binders is in the production of special paint, made from a thick mixture of alumina or zircon powder, binder and water. This mixture can be used for separating a lid from its pot, i.e. on casseroles and coffee pots. The contact surfaces, of course, are kept clear of glaze and either the lid or the pot contact area is painted. The binder serves to hold the film really firm when dry but burns away during firing.

This preparation is also used by some potters for painting on to the base of pots (after the glaze has been removed) instead of placing the pots on to kiln batts lined with placing sand or coated with batt wash. It is, however, probably best to use batt wash on the kiln shelves, using the zircon paint as an additional precaution on large pots or on those which have a heavy coat of glaze.

THE USE OF ELECTROLYTES

When clay or glaze slips are prepared the theoretical state of suspension is for each individual particle to be suspended in the water, gradually dropping downwards until it settles out. Consequently, at any given time the slip is always denser at the bottom than at the top and if allowed to stand for only 15 minutes the difference due to the amount of settling may be very noticeable. In practice, however, complete dispersion of the individual particles is seldom achieved owing to the tendency of the particles to attract their neighbours, producing progressively larger agglomerates or 'flocks' which rapidly settle out under their own weight. Furthermore, since these flocks of particles cannot so easily pass each other as could the small individual particles, a greater quantity of water is needed to provide sufficient space for the agglomerates to pass each other and thus allow fluid flow.

It is, however, easily possible by the use of an electrolyte, either to thoroughly disperse the particles—the process known as deflocculation—

or to do the opposite, creating more flocks, which is referred to as flocculation. Electrolytes such as calcium chloride or magnesium sulphate are commonly used as flocculants, whilst sodium silicate or soda ash are used as deflocculants.

Deflocculation

When a few drops of an alkaline solution such as sodium silicate or sodium carbonate solution are added to a slop glaze, the glaze becomes more fluid. This happens because the alkaline solution contains free OH^- ions (hydroxyl ions), negatively charged, which attach themselves to the glaze particles, thus counteracting their mutual electrical attraction and causing the particles to repel each other, so that the flocks disintegrate, each particle becoming separately suspended. Each particle, in fact, becomes surrounded with a negatively charged water envelope, a few molecules in thickness, the complete unit of particle and water envelope being referred to as a micelle. Owing to the absence of agglomerates and the greater ability of the small particles to slip past each other, the deflocculated suspension is able to achieve the same degree of fluidity with a smaller water content. Thus by the addition of a deflocculant less water is needed to obtain the same degree of fluidity, i.e. the glaze slip is denser but equally fluid.

The amount of electrolyte added is rather critical. Too much electrolyte may cause the slip to flocculate instead of deflocculate. The amount added is normally in the region of 0·2 to 0·5 per cent by weight of the dry glaze, the deflocculant being added a little at a time until the glaze slip reaches the maximum fluidity which, ideally, should be determined by the use of a viscometer. The effect is particularly pronounced with clay slips (casting slip production) and consequently the addition of some clay to a glaze enables the glaze slip to be more strongly deflocculated.

Deflocculated slips often take much longer to settle out than normal ones but when they do settle they tend to set harder and thus more effort is needed to restore the suspension. The fact that deflocculated glaze slips set harder is due to the very tight packing achieved by the individual

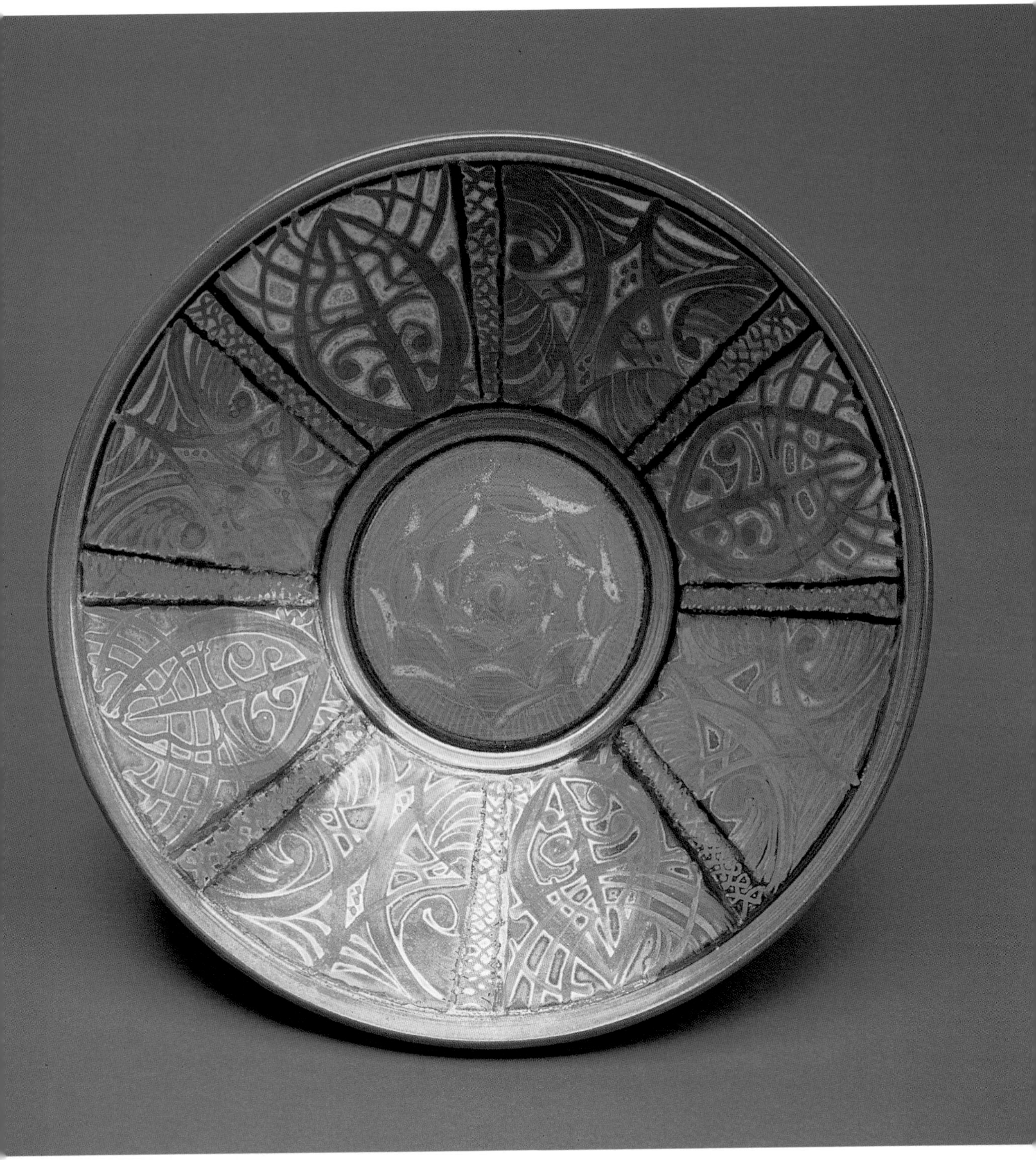

Shallow bowl by Nick Caiger-Smith, reduced silver lustre on tin glaze

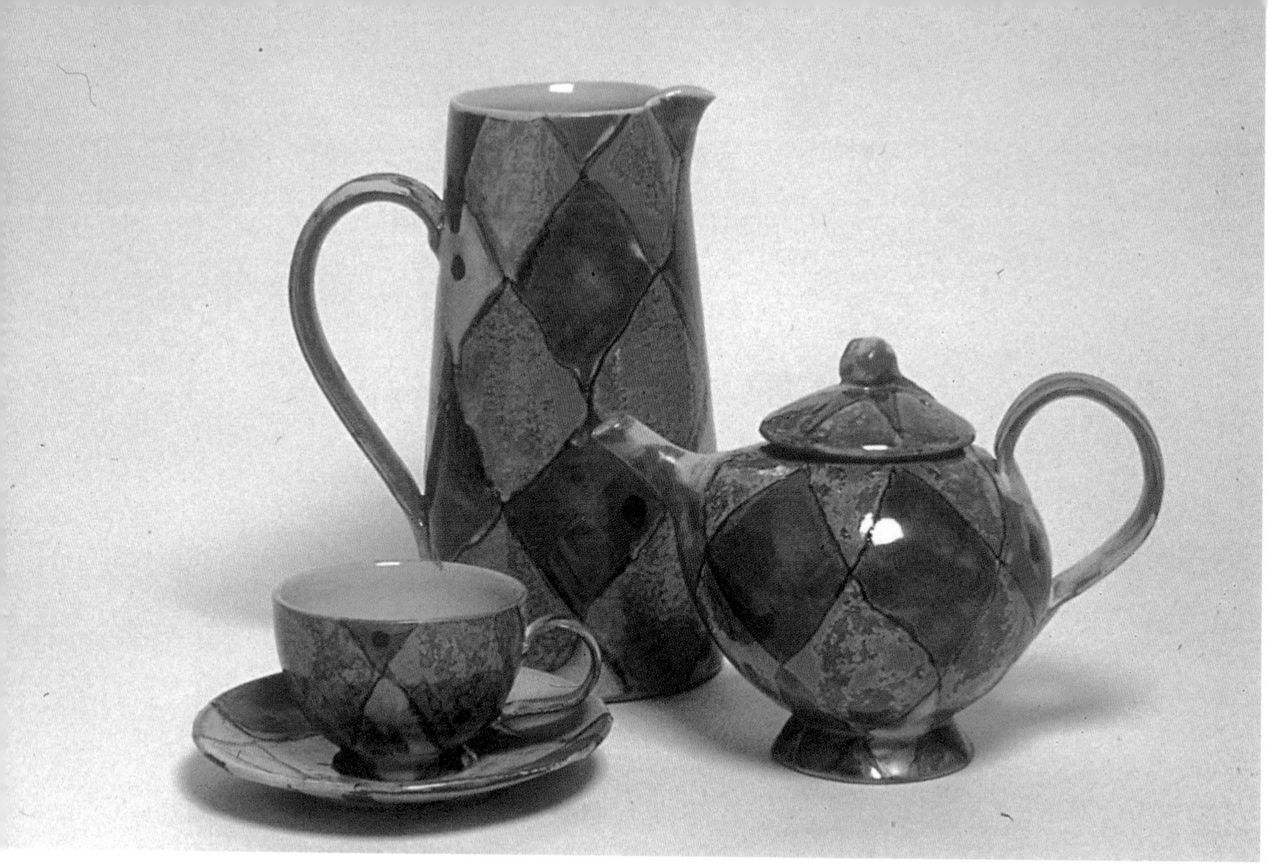

ABOVE

'Quilt' pattern reduced stoneware by Dartington Pottery
Features a deliberate mixture of matt and shiny glazes and a combination of thick glazes and very thin glazes. Design by Petra Tilley; glazes by Stephen Course.

BELOW

Gecko plate and jug by Louise Darby
Finely thrown and turned white stoneware pieces. Satin finish black and pink glazes inlaid into incised and carved Gecko design.

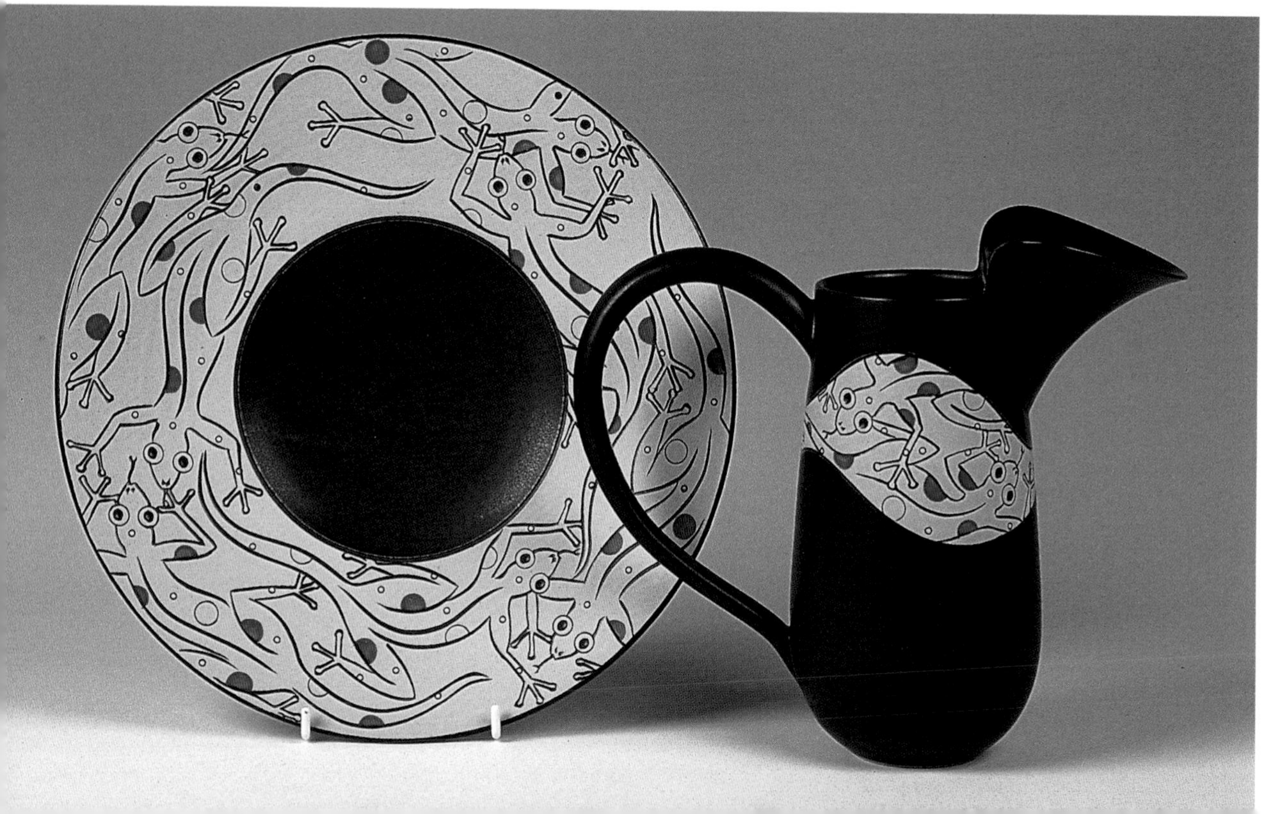

RIGHT

Thrown bottle by Margaret Frith, 1997

Various celadon glazes with wax motif and other poured and trailed glazes.

BELOW

Crystalline glazed porcelain vase by Lawrence Carter

The glaze was rapidly fired in an electric kiln to 1280° followed by rapid cooling to 1100°. The temperature was then held and then lowered in progressive stages to 1000° with a few hours soak at each stage to facilitate crystal growth resulting in spectacular crystalline inclusions in the glassy glaze matrix.

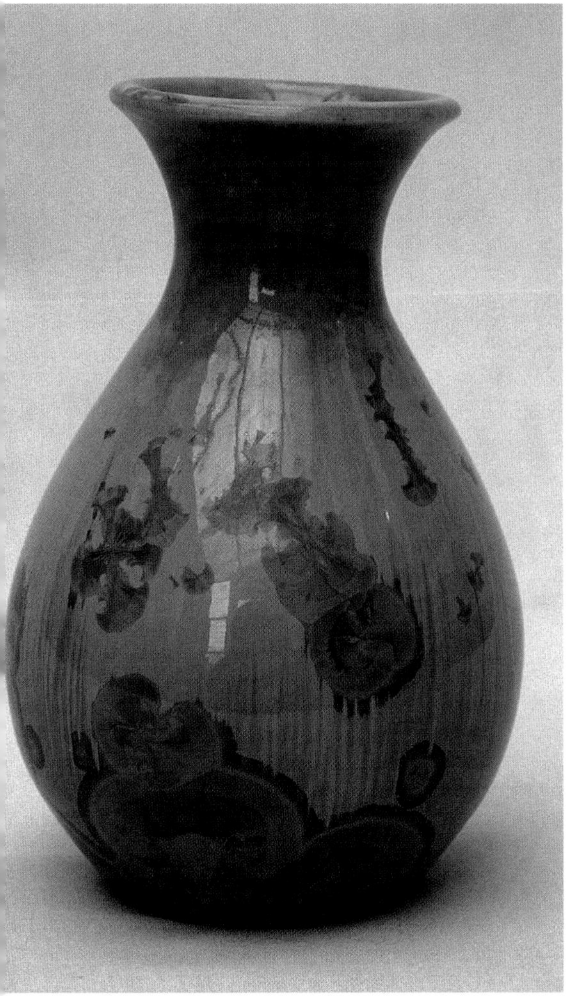

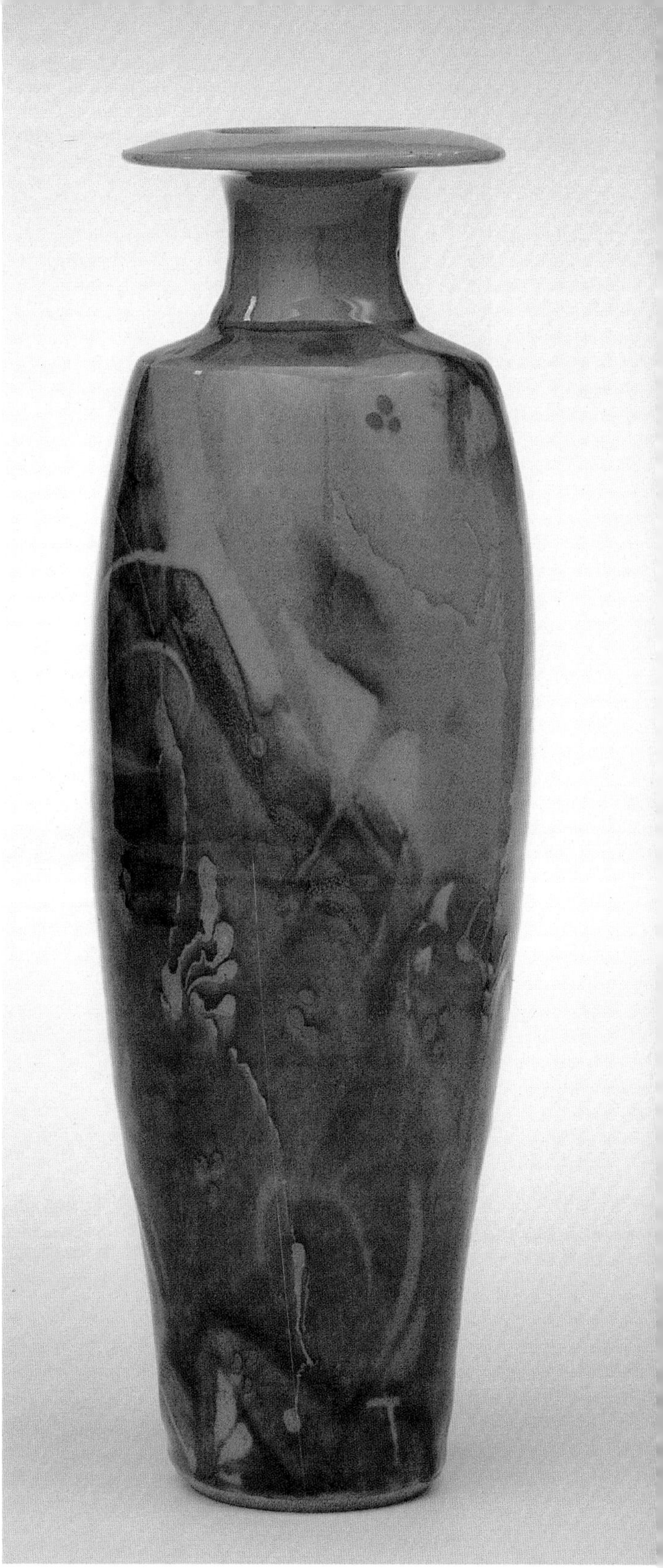

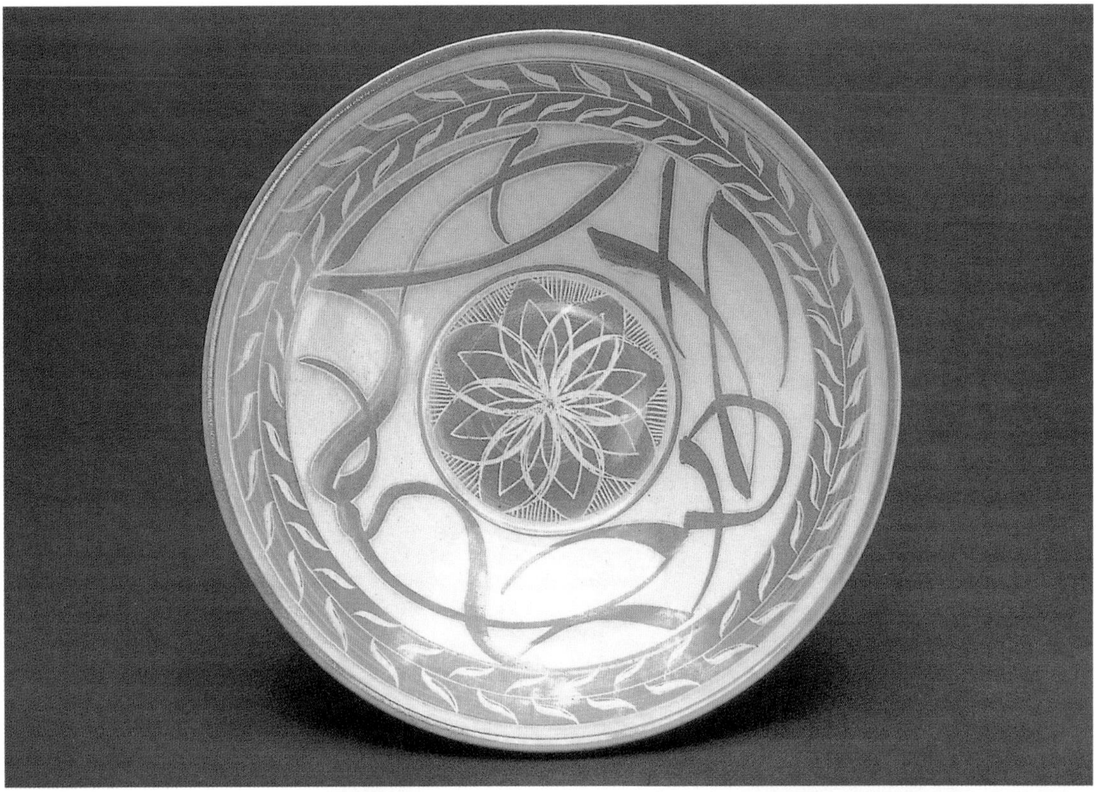

ABOVE
Shallow bowl by Nick Caiger-Smith, reduced silver lustre on tin glaze

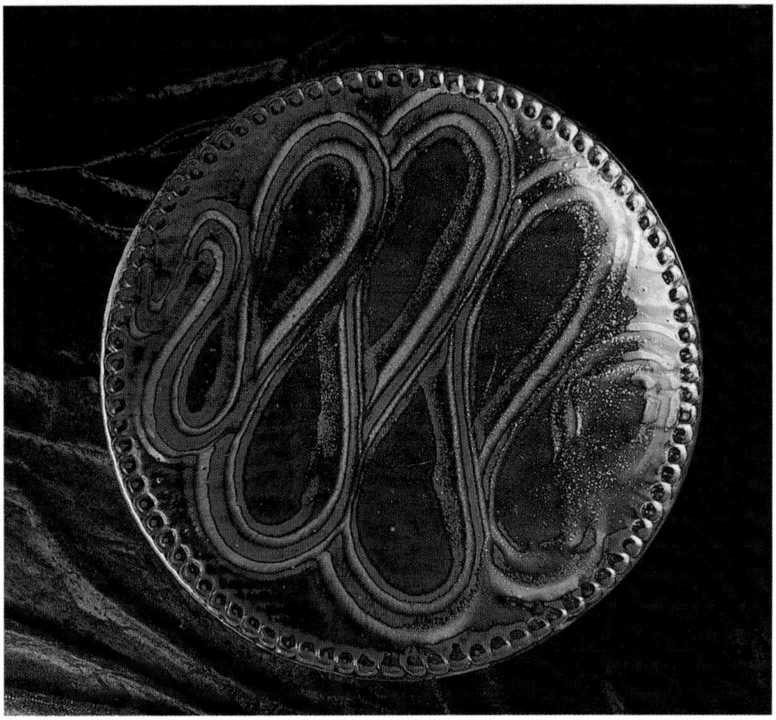

RIGHT
Slipware dish by Edward Hughes

particles settling together into a dense mass.

Deflocculation of glaze slips is very useful if glaze has to be applied by dipping to very vitreous pieces. By adjusting the glaze slip to give the highest pint weight and then deflocculating it, a very dense but fluid glaze can be obtained which provides an adequate coat when vitreous pieces are dipped into it. For porous pottery, flocculated slips are more useful.

Flocculation

Electrolytes such as calcium chloride or magnesium sulphate are very useful flocculants for addition to glazes. A flocculated slip is one in which a very large number of flocks or agglomerates are present. These flocks naturally tend to settle out fairly quickly but because of their larger, irregular size, when they settle they cannot pack so closely together to produce such a dense layer as can individual particles. Consequently the sediment can be easily redispersed into the glaze.

Because the water is not chemically bonded to the particles and the slip is therefore less water-retentive, porous pottery dipped into a flocculated glaze slip absorbs water much more quickly than it would from a deflocculated slip and as a result of this very fast absorption of water, glaze pick-up is greater. The actual glaze coat, however, is not so dense as a normal glaze coat, the coat being looser and more 'fluffy' because of the loose packing of the large flocks of glaze particles which have large pores between them. The glaze is also noticeably creamier and more pleasant to work with.

A flocculated glaze slip will therefore give a greater pick-up of glaze than will a normal glaze slip because of the increased speed at which the water can be removed from the glaze slip. The glaze slip tends to settle out more quickly but can more easily be reconstituted and is better to work with.

GLAZE SUSPENDERS

In previous pages I have discussed glaze binders and deflocculants which have a marked effect in slowing down the rate at which glaze suspensions settle out. The addition of clay to a glaze has a similar effect, this being due to the very small particle size of clays coupled with their comparatively low density. Consequently the presence of clay in a glaze slip is very useful in maintaining the glaze suspension. This is why 'raw' glazes, which usually contain an appreciable amount of clay, suspend better than, for example, glaze frits.

The clay which has the finest particle size is bentonite and this clay, therefore, has excellent suspending properties. Additions of up to 3 per cent to the dry weight of a glaze considerably assist the glaze to stay in suspension. More than 3 per cent may cause cracking of the unfired glaze layer due to the high drying shrinkage characteristic of all very plastic clays. The fired glaze colour may also be affected.

Very often a combination of a few drops of calcium chloride and 2–3 per cent of bentonite is added to a glaze. The calcium chloride, being a flocculant, makes the glaze settle more quickly and also, because of the larger flocks which are formed, makes the glaze more creamy and easier to work with. The bentonite counteracts the increased rate of settling, however, and so the combination of flocculant plus suspender results in a creamy glaze which is pleasant to use and works well yet does not settle too quickly.

COLLOIDAL PARTICLES

Particles which are so small that they cannot be seen with the most powerful optical microscope are commonly referred to as being of colloidal size. An indication of the very small size of colloidal particles is given by the fact that they cannot be filtered in the ordinary sense. Colloidal particles pass right through filter paper and also through fired clay filters. Filter paper will retain particles larger than 5 microns (0·005 mm) and fired clay filters will retain particles as small as 0·2 micron (0·0002 mm) but colloidal particles are usually in the size range of 0·1 micron to 0·001 micron and can only be filtered by using a membrane.

A substance in the colloidal state is often described as a colloidal 'solution' but this is incorrect since the properties of a solution are quite different from those of a colloidal suspension. The presence of colloidal particles in a liquid may be detected by passing a strong beam of light through the liquid in a dark room, the light being scattered by the surface of any colloidal particles, which are thus revealed as tiny specks of light. Substances in true solution never scatter light in this way.

Fig. 43
Stoneware bottles (oxidized) by Hans Coper

Although colloidal particles are appreciably larger than molecular size they are small enough to be pushed about by the impact of the rapidly moving molecules of the suspending liquid. If in fact the colloidal suspension is strongly illuminated and examined under a powerful microscope it will be seen that the particles occasionally move about the liquid with a rapid but irregular motion as the suspending molecules collide with them. This motion of the particles is known as the *Brownian movement* (after Robert Brown who first detected the phenomenon in 1827) and is characteristic of all colloidal particles in suspen-

sion. The action which causes this movement is the reason why colloidal particles remain in suspension indefinitely, since particles which are constantly in motion have no opportunity to settle.

Very finely divided materials such as ball clays and especially bentonite contain a large amount of colloidal particles and these tend to reduce the rate at which other, larger particles settle, since they act as a barrier through which the larger particles have to pass in order to settle out. For this reason addition of bentonite aids the suspension qualities of a slop glaze.

Another very characteristic feature of colloidal particles is the existence of an electrical charge on each particle. The charge may be negative or positive but in the case of clays (and most other materials) the charge is negative. Since each colloidal particle carries the same charge, the particles tend to repel each other, but by introducing ions having charges opposite to those on the colloidal particles it is possible to neutralize the charges which keep the particles apart. The particles then tend to coagulate into groups which settle out more rapidly because of their weight. This is the process of flocculation, mentioned previously, and is usually produced by addition of positive ions introduced by calcium salts such as calcium chloride.

For glazes containing constituents which tend to settle out of suspension much more quickly than the other ingredients, addition of bentonite plus calcium chloride to flocculate the suspension can be very useful. Although the glaze may settle more quickly it settles evenly, since the flocks which are formed imprison particles of all the glaze ingredients and any tendency to preferential settlement is therefore reduced.

The addition of Na^+ ions to a clay suspension initially has the effect of increasing the negative charge on the particles but with increasing addition of Na^+ ions the negative charge on the particles is decreased until it becomes neutralized. This is why clay slips can be markedly deflocculated with low alkali addition but become flocculated if a little too much is added.

15. Glaze application

Glazes may be applied to pottery in several ways. The methods of application can be classified as wet, powder, and gaseous.

Wet application methods include all those by which the suspension of the glaze materials, in water or other medium, is applied to the ware. Application by dipping, painting and pouring would therefore come into this class.

The powder process is now seldom used. It involves dusting the dry glaze on to slightly damp ware or ware which has been painted with a tacky medium, or rolling the damp piece in contact with dry powdered glaze.

Gaseous methods of application involve exposing the pottery to the action of gases formed from volatile glaze materials during the firing process. Common examples are salt-glazing and the practice of coating the inside of saggars etc. with a high-lead glaze, so that the volatile constituents driven off by the firing process maintain an atmosphere of glaze vapour around any high-lead-glazed articles contained in the saggar. This reduces dullness of the glaze by volatilization from the pottery articles and helps to preserve a good gloss.

It is perhaps also important to mention the Egyptian Paste technique, in which soluble glaze materials are actually mixed with the clay from which the pottery articles are made, with the result that during the drying process the soluble materials migrate to the surface of the pottery to form a glaze film. This practice is, however, rather unpredictable. Application by gaseous means is likewise very limited and the powder technique is restricted by the toxic nature of many glaze powders. By far the most common methods of glaze application are therefore the various wet techniques.

DIPPING

The dipping process is the most common way of applying glazes to ceramic objects. The porous biscuit or clay pots are simply dipped or immersed into a bucket or tub of glaze prepared to suitable consistency by mixing with water. Water from the glaze slip enters the porous article but leaves behind it, as a film on the pottery, the glaze particles which were suspended in the water and these produce the glaze coat. It will be appreciated that the longer a pot is immersed the thicker will be the glaze film picked up by the pot but this is only true as long as the pot is porous. Once the pottery becomes saturated with water, no more water can be absorbed and further contact of the pottery and glaze in the dipping tub may result in a softening of the deposited glaze film and an uneven coat.

Since there is a relationship between the thickness of the pottery and the thickness of the glaze coating deposited in a given time, a thin piece will absorb less water than a thick one and consequently the glaze film deposited on the pottery will be less. Consequently very thin, porous pots should be dipped in a glaze of a thicker consistency than is necessary for pots of a thicker cross-section. Pots which vary considerably in thickness, therefore, tend to show a variation in glaze pick-up from the same dipping action; the thicker areas generally having the thickest deposit of glaze. Similarly, variations in the porosity of the pottery will cause a variation in glaze thickness.

Success in dipping depends to a large degree upon experience and judgment. The ideal procedure is to immerse the pot quickly into the glaze, shake the pot under the glaze surface, withdraw, empty, and then shake the dipped pot vigorously to remove excess glaze. For various reasons this ideal often cannot be attained and the actual dipping technique is therefore often varied to suit the article being glazed. The industrial dipper bounces or 'bumps' large heavy pieces (such as cisterns and water closets) after dipping, on the edge of the dipping tub or on a springy plank, so as to obtain a more even distribution of the glaze coat. With plates too large to span in the hand, the industrial dipper makes use of a special hook or thumbstall so that the plate can be gripped firmly between the hook and the fingers of the same hand (*see* Fig. 45).

This involves partly immersing the inverted article followed by a sudden short upward movement which splashes glaze over the whole of the inner surface. The pot is then completely immersed to complete the dipping operation.

Immediately after a dipped piece is placed down, any areas from which glaze is missing owing to contact with the fingers can be 'touched-up' by gently touching the finger, wet with glaze, against the area concerned, so that glaze runs from the finger on to the pot.

Very soft and porous biscuit ware which has

Glaze surface
Quickly jerk upwards
to glaze the interior
Partly immerse
Immerse to the required
exterior level

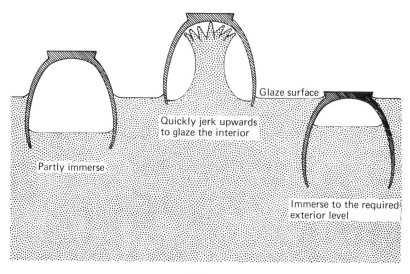

Fig. 44
Double-dipping technique

When coating 'hollow' ware such as vases—and especially those having narrow necks—it is often best to glaze the inside first and then to glaze the outside by a separate dipping action. As soon as the inside surface has been evenly coated, by rotating the pot, the glaze should be quickly emptied out and the pot shaken vigorously whilst inverted. This serves to remove any drops which would otherwise cling to the rim and to prevent an excessively thick accumulation of glaze in the base of the piece which would quite likely craze.

Open, hollow shapes, such as certain cups and small bowls, can usually be glazed using the double-dipping technique illustrated in Fig. 44.

been fired at a temperature well below the maturing temperature of the clay will be very absorbent and the consistency of the glaze should be more dilute than would be necessary with pots of lower porosity. With soft-fired biscuit ware, it is fairly easy to achieve a satisfactory glaze coating, free of runs, which remains firm after dipping. For this reason it is common for schools and craft potters to soft-fire all pottery, whether earthenware or stoneware, and to use a glaze of thin consistency, preferring ease of application to the somewhat poorer fired results which might result with earthenware. With extremely porous pieces, some potters quickly dip the pottery into water prior to dipping into glaze, so as to reduce

Fig. 45
Industrial dipping of flat ware
Note use of the metal hook on the dipper's thumb enabling him to span the piece easily.
(By courtesy of Josiah Wedgwood & Sons Ltd)

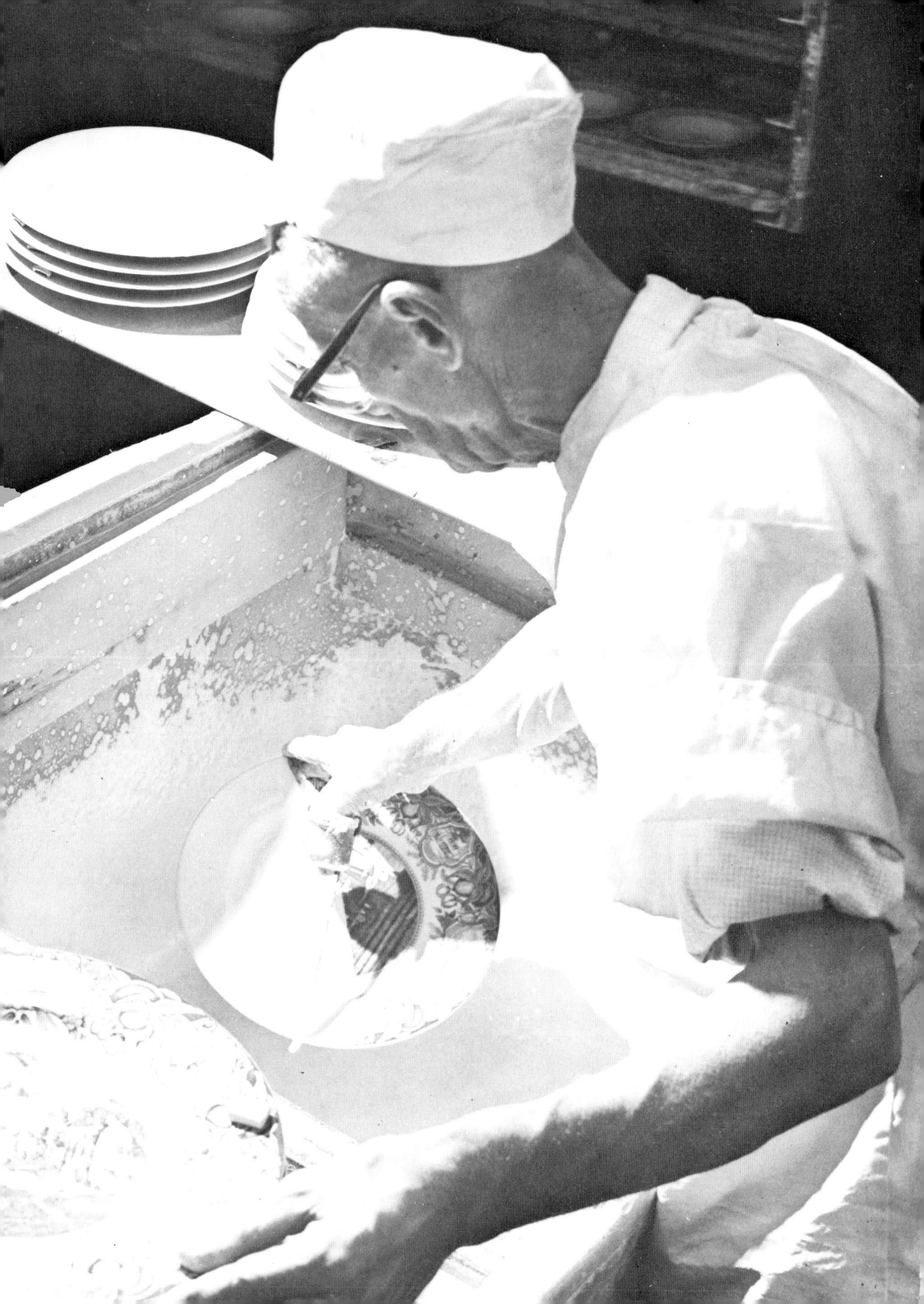

the porosity of the pot and thus the thickness of the glaze coat.

Dipping the more vitreous pieces demands greater care and expertise because the glaze film tends to run more easily. There is also a greater tendency for pin-holes to form, since the pores in the pottery do not so easily permit the displacement of the air they contain on account of their smaller diameters. With relatively vitreous pottery it is often necessary either to flocculate the glaze slip by the addition of magnesium sulphate (Epsom salt) or calcium chloride which has the effect of thickening it, or to use a glaze binder. Further information about the setting-up of glazes is given in Chapter 14. In general, however, a glaze prepared for dipping consists merely of the powdered glaze and water mixed together, adjusted for density, and sieved 80-mesh.

POURING

Where there is not enough glaze for dipping, or where the physical size of a pot precludes the possibility of dipping, it is often best to glaze the outside by pouring a cascade of glaze over it. If the piece is rapidly turned whilst the glaze is being poured it is possible to obtain an even coat. A good method is to invert a clean dustbin lid or similar receptacle on to a banding wheel or whirler, using plastic clay worked in between the receptacle and the whirler face to provide a firm and even seating. The pot to be glazed can then be inverted on to two strips of wood placed across the receptacle, taking care to see that the pot is reasonably concentric with the whirler. The whirler is set into rotation and the glaze poured on, using a jug large enough to ensure that the piece can be completely glazed from one pouring action. It is not necessary to rotate small pieces if these can be covered fairly easily by the poured glaze; it is often possible to hold a small piece in the hand whilst the glaze is poured over it.

SPRAYING

Frequent spraying of glazes demands the use of a spray booth fitted with a duct exhausting out of the building (in booths not fitted with ducts

Fig. 46
Spray gun

to atmosphere the fine glaze powder liberated into the air is breathed by the sprayer and such booths should not be used in schools), an air compressor and, of course, a spray gun (Fig. 46).

Spraying is a good way of glazing pottery objects. A satisfactory and uniform glaze coverage can easily be obtained with a little practice. One disadvantage is that an appreciable proportion of the glaze is lost as 'over-spray' although in industry, spray booths containing a recirculatory water cascade are sometimes used to catch much of the overspray, which then settles out in a sump and can be recovered. A good point, however, is that since one can make use of almost every drop of glaze, spraying demands the preparation of very little reserve glaze.

The basic principles controlling the consistency of glazes suitable for the spraying process are exactly the same as those for dipping. In general, the more porous pieces of pottery require glazes of thinner consistency. If the air pressure used with a thin glaze is too high, the coating may increase in thickness too rapidly and produce a characteristic rippling of the glaze surface often referred to as an 'orange peel' effect. This also occurs if the spray gun is too close to the piece being sprayed. The best way to obtain good results on pottery of low porosity, or vitreous pieces, is to use a thick, heavy glaze slip atomized by the least practical air pressure.

There are two basic methods of spraying known as 'wet spraying' and 'dry spraying'. The difference lies in the water content of the glaze slip and in the spray pattern which is often adjusted so as to give a greater concentration with the wet spraying technique than with the dry spraying technique (where the spray pattern is more scattered). The result is that glazes applied by wet spraying tend to form a wet film on the pottery surface whereas the dry spraying technique forms a very powdery deposit. The relative advantages and disadvantages of the two systems can be briefly summarized as follows.

1. Glazes for dry spraying are often flocculated and weigh around 36 oz per pint. Wet spray glazes often contain binders and are of lower pint weight.

2. Dry spraying demands greater experience to obtain satisfactory results.

3. It is a slower method of glaze application than wet spraying.

4. It gives excellent results on awkwardly shaped objects and is useful for filling angles with a heavy glaze without cracking.

5. Dry spraying demands a glaze which melts several cones below the final glaze-firing temperature, or a longer soaking period, otherwise the fired surface may be rough.

This is not necessary with glazes which are very fluid when at their maturing temperature since these heal any imperfections relatively easily.

6. Dry spraying gives a much dustier coat than does wet spraying which tends to give a firmer deposit.

Glaze binders are often added to spray glazes to promote greater adhesion in the dry state.

Fig. 47
Crystal glazed vase by Lawrence Carter

Spray guns operate by directing a stream of air across the open end of the nozzle containing the glaze slip. This atomizes the glaze slip which is being forced out of the nozzle and produces a spray. The shape of the spray, i.e. the spray pattern, can be altered by fitting different types of air caps to the spray gun. The normal pattern is a circular area.

The spray gun is usually adjusted so that when the trigger is depressed slightly, air only is released from the gun, the glaze not being ejected until the trigger is depressed still further. This enables the operator to blow any dust or dirt off the surface of the pot about to be sprayed. For large-scale work it is common for a separate glaze cylinder, which may contain several gallons of glaze, to be used; for smaller tasks one can use a spray gun fitted with a cup containing glaze fed by gravity.

PAINTING

Painting of glazes is not common but it can be

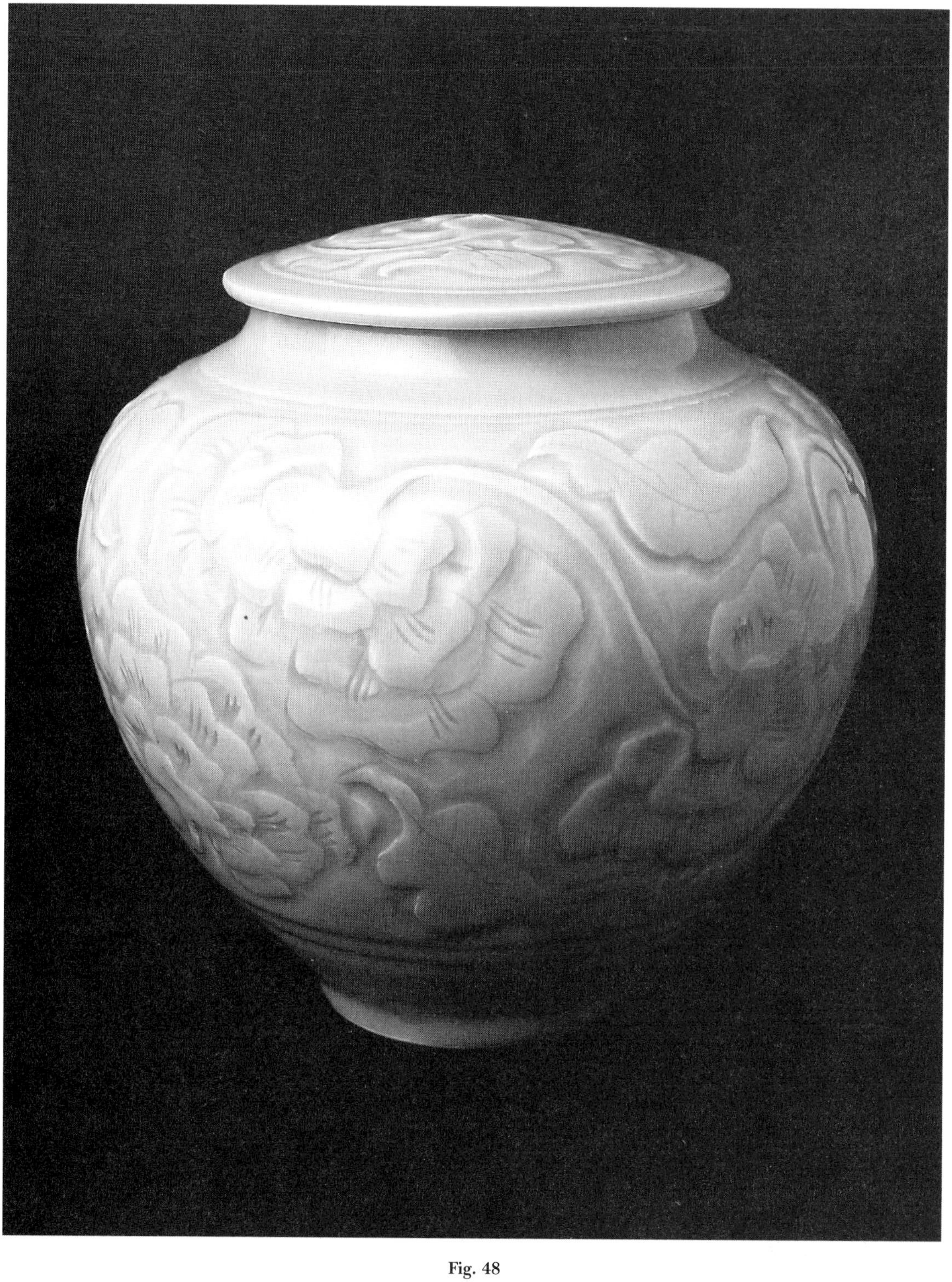

Fig. 48
Thrown ginger jar by Margaret Frith
Reduced porcelain 1280°C, carved decoration,
blue celadon glaze.

useful for applying glaze in areas not easily reached by the spraying process, or in instances where only a small selected area of a pot is to be glazed. A fully loaded soft brush must be used so as to prevent 'dragging' as the glaze is being applied. A binder or glycerine is mixed with the glaze, to promote a much smoother brushing action and produce a more uniform film. Nevertheless it is usually necessary to apply two or three coats to avoid the patchiness that results from a variation in glaze thickness.

THICKNESS OF THE GLAZE COAT

The optimum deposit of glaze differs from one glaze type to another. Decorative crystalline glazes, for example, need to be applied thickly if the most attractive appearance is to be obtained. On the other hand a thin glaze coating is desirable with glazes from which maximum craze resistance is required.

Stoneware and other high-temperature glazes are usually made exclusively from raw materials which will lose a relatively high percentage of their weight as volatiles during the firing process. Earthenware and low-temperature glazes usually contain a high proportion of frit which, of course, is prefired material and the material loss from these glazes during firing is very low. To compensate for the material lost, high-temperature glazes should therefore be applied a little more thickly than is necessary with earthenware, majolica, and other low-temperature glazes.

The range of glaze thickness in the unfired state will be found to vary from about 0·01 in. up to about 0·08 in. with an average of around 0·03 in. (i.e. about 1/32 in.). Naturally, the fired coat is always thinner than the unfired coat owing to the loss of volatiles and the consolidation which takes place during fusion. Glaze thickness may be determined by scratching the unfired glaze with a needle although, with experience, it becomes possible to judge the correct glaze thickness merely by observation.

GLAZE REMOVAL

Many pots will be set down flat on to the kiln shelves for firing, in which case the glaze on the base or foot ring of such pots must be removed. This may be done shortly after dipping, i.e. when the glaze film is still a little damp. The unwanted glaze is removed with a sponge or damp piece of felt—some potters use a specially constructed, felt-faced rubbing board or wheel head. If this cleaning operation is done properly it will suffice to prevent the pots from sticking, but if additional precautions are desired then the cleaned surfaces may be painted with a zircon paint (*see* page 86) or, preferably, the shelves painted with a batt wash made from equal parts of zircon and china clay, or from alumina hydrate. Alternatively, the area concerned can be painted with a wax resist which prevents glaze adhesion during the subsequent glazing process, the wax burning away during firing at about 300–400°C (570–750°F).

Wax resists

The traditional type of wax resist is one prepared by mixing candle-wax with about 25 per cent or so of paraffin and then melting the mixture in a suitable container. Many potters keep a special 'wax pot' for this purpose, often similar to a carpenter's glue-pot, i.e. a pot within a pot, the intermediate space containing water.

In this way the wax resist is not over-heated and, when melted satisfactorily (the point at which it begins to smoke) does not cool and solidify so quickly when the heating source is removed. This type of resist is excellent in providing a strongly resisting film of wax but one has to work very rapidly. A disadvantage is that a brush used for the painting of such resists is rendered useless for any other type of work. The brush must incidentally be kept free of moisture since water coming into contact with the molten wax results in an alarming spitting and fizzling.

Emulsion wax resists, i.e. liquid mixtures of oil, wax or resins with water, are naturally much simpler to use and are therefore becoming increasingly popular. The only problems are that one may have to wait for the water content of the emulsion to evaporate after application and that the emulsions generally do not give such a strongly resisting action as do the solid wax/paraffin mixtures.

16. Glaze firing

Firing is the climax of the potter's labour. The most carefully produced pieces may easily be ruined if the firing operation is not carried out correctly and although a discussion of how to fire a kiln is not strictly within the scope of a book about glazes there are a number of inter-related topics which are worthy of further consideration.

A previous section (page 6) discussed the different approach of the craft potter to his industrial counterpart in connexion with the firing processes—the industrial potter being motivated by considerations of obtaining an inert body during the glost firing, the craft potter regarding high biscuit porosity as of paramount importance. Consequently, with porous bodies the industrial potter usually biscuit fires to a higher temperature than the glost; the craft potter usually the reverse.

An important point with earthenware is that the pottery must at some stage in its production, be fired to the firing range of the clay (normally 1 100–1 150°C (2 010–2 100°F)) if satisfactory craze-resistance is to be obtained. It does not matter whether this range is reached during the biscuit or glost firing; the important point is that it must be reached at some point in the pottery process if the body is to develop its correct co-efficient of expansion. Otherwise stresses are created during cooling after glost firing which result in crazing of the glaze (see pages 106–9). The most common cause of crazing is in fact an insufficient degree of firing.

With the low biscuit/high glost technique, once the temperature of the glost firing exceeds that of the biscuit, the body itself begins to decompose still further and gases are given off which have to bubble through the glaze layer. This produces bubbles in the glaze which burst upon reaching the surface producing pinholes or small craters. In order to allow more time for these bubble craters to dissipate it is necessary to 'soak' the pottery, i.e. to hold the kiln at the glaze firing temperature for half an hour (or longer) so that the craters have an opportunity to heal themselves before the glaze becomes too viscous as it cools.

A reasonable firing speed for the glost firing is an average (over the whole firing) of 100°C (210°F) per hour, but the actual speed of firing is of much more importance during the biscuit firing than with the glost. It is common knowledge that the first 350°C (660°F) or so of a biscuit firing must be taken very slowly in order to avoid cracking or explosion due to water vapour driven off from the chemically combined water present in the clay crystal and that once this process is more or less complete the firing can be speeded up. If the subsequent speed of firing is too rapid, or the pots are much thicker than usual, then the heat of the firing may not have been given sufficient opportunity to penetrate into the ware. As a result the ware temperature may lag considerably behind the temperature of the kiln and the ware may be insufficiently fired. This is why it is more correct to speak in terms of 'heat work' rather than temperature—and why the apparent difference between the temperature at which a cone is supposed to collapse and the temperature at which it actually collapses (as indicated by pyrometer readings), varies with firing speed. Fast-fired biscuit will therefore be more porous than more slowly fired pieces.

After the biscuit ware has been glazed it should be allowed to dry out before being subjected to the glost firing operation. Even so, it is likely that

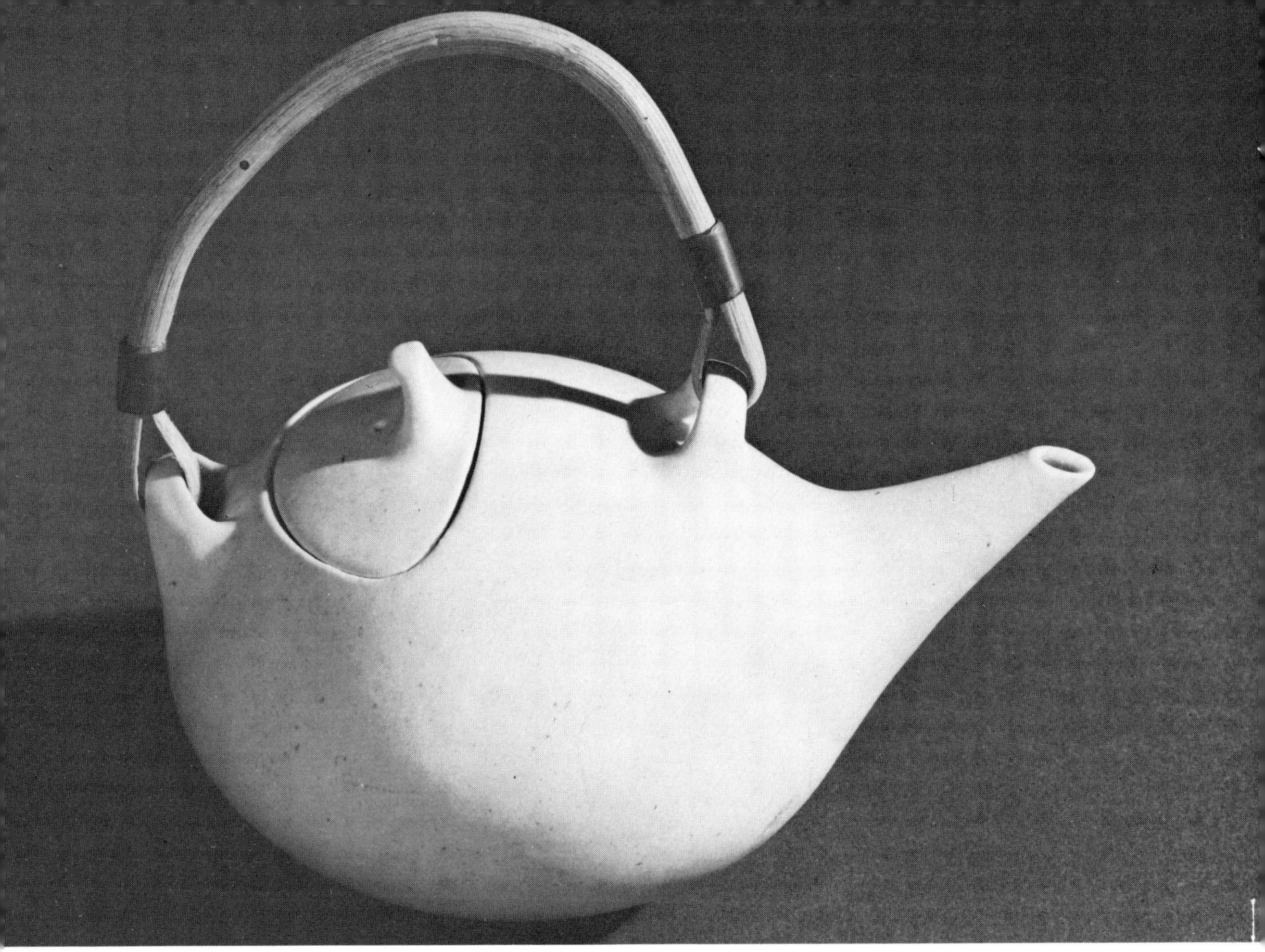

Fig. 49
Cast stoneware tea pot by Ruth Duckworth
Cane handle, matt white glaze.
(C.o.I.D. photograph)

Fig. 50
Stoneware bowl by Michael Casson
Dolomite glaze with inlay decoration. $12\frac{1}{2}$ inches diameter.
(By courtesy of the Craftsmen Potters Association of Great Britain)

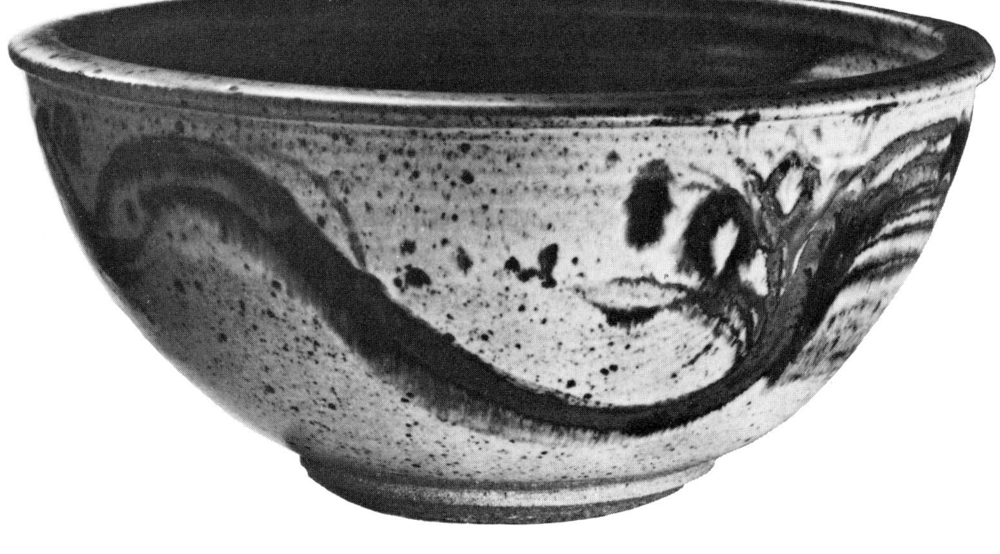

some water will be retained by the biscuit ware. If this is driven off too quickly the vigorously escaping steam may lift or rupture the glaze film causing subsequent crawling. It is therefore advisable to fire carefully for the first hour but apart from this initial stage the glaze can be fired up quite rapidly.

At red heat most glazes are in the sintering stage, resulting in the glaze film becoming quite hard and cracking rather like parched earth. As heating is continued and the glaze begins to flow, these cracks are filled in by the glaze, which becomes progressively more molten.

Fig. 51
9½-inch tall stoneware form by Robin Welch
Rubbed with copper oxide. Matt white glaze crawled for greater effect.
(By courtesy of the Craftsmen Potters Association of Great Britain)

During the fusion or melting process the glaze will bubble very appreciably, this activity being considerably increased by gases bubbling through from the body once the biscuit firing temperature has been exceeded. When the glost firing temperature is reached the kiln is adjusted to maintain this temperature, i.e. to 'soak' for half an hour or so, the bubbling then subsiding to produce a smooth, placid glass.

Most small pottery kilns, whether fired by gas, oil or electricity, tend to cool quickly after switching off. With certain types of rutile or zircon opacified glazes, the speed of cooling may be too rapid to allow the opacifying crystals to crystallize out of solution before the glaze becomes rigid, with the result that the glaze fires semi-opaque or transparent instead of opaque. Similarly, artistic or crystalline glazes may not be properly developed. In such cases it may be necessary to 'fire down'. This involves adjusting the kiln to a low or medium temperature setting to introduce some heat into it but not sufficient to prevent it from cooling. The object is to slow the cooling rate over the range from the glaze firing temperature down to about 950–850°C (1 740–1 560°F) for high-temperature glazes and 800–650°C (1 470–1 200°F) for earthenware and low-temperature glazes. Below this point the glazes are more or less rigid and their degree of crystallization is fixed.

The glaze is obviously most prone to crystallization while it is in its most fluid condition. Therefore the most influential part of the cooling cycle is the first 100–200°C (210–390°F) cooling below glaze firing temperature, the tendency of the glaze to crystallize being reduced with increasing viscosity as the glaze nears its liquidus point.

With glossy glazes, fairly rapid cooling is needed for optimum results. The longer the glaze is molten the greater the degree of crystallization and volatilization and therefore the duller the glaze surface. With glazes containing a high amount of borax used over red bodies which contain an appreciable amount of lime, slow cooling conditions may produce a purplish opalescent discoloration due to the formation of calcium borate crystals. As the glaze and body are pyroplastic at high temperature, strains produced by rapid cooling tend to be absorbed quite easily and some potters remove vent plugs or open cooling ports or dampers to reduce temperature quickly within the kiln. Such measures, however, are seldom necessary since the natural cooling speed of kilns is usually sufficiently rapid, but if cooling does have to be speeded, care must be taken since pyrometer readings cannot be trusted whilst the kiln is cooling. This is because the cold air entering the kiln will fall to the base whilst hot air in the top of the kiln continues to influence the thermocouple tip, which is almost always in the upper section of the kiln. Thus there is a marked temperature variation across the kiln which, if allowed to persist much below 750°C (1380°F) (i.e. dull red heat), may cause cracking of the pots or the kiln furniture.

REDUCTION

A reduction atmosphere is easily obtained by cutting back the primary or secondary air supply, or both, until the flames begin to burn yellow with a smoke haze. The damper is then partly closed back to put the kiln chamber under pressure. This will be indicated by flame at the spy hole and perhaps also at the damper.

The majority of stoneware or porcelain glazes developed for reduction firing give of their best under light to medium reduction conditions only. Heavy reduction is almost never required and may result in certain stoneware bodies becoming dark grey and crystalline so that they lose all their strength, such pots being broken easily with the fingers.

It is best to avoid reduction conditions with stoneware and porcelain until the temperature has risen above 1000°C (1830°F) so that most of the carbon in the clay has burned away. If too much carbon remains there will be a risk of bloating (*see* page 116). The degree of reduction can be increased towards the end of the firing if necessary. This will tend to reduce the rate of temperature increase and so will have the advantage of 'soaking' the glaze as well as creating the maximum required amount of reduction while the glaze is in its most molten state—and thus most susceptible to reduction conditions. Since kilns are not airtight they tend to reoxidize to a certain degree during cooling which may produce oxidized effects where the glaze is thin and on edges and handles. If a fully reduced effect is needed the burners can be put at a low position to fire down under reduction conditions with the damper slightly open.

Two low-temperature reduction techniques

are worthy of mention. If a low-melting-point leadless glaze (e.g. an alkaline frit such as Podmore P.2250) is stained with 3–5 per cent of copper oxide and fired (oxidizing) to its maturing range, then cooled and fired to 650°C (1200°F) with reduction for about 15–30 minutes while held at this temperature, a good copper red may be obtained.

Fig. 52
Thrown oval bottle by David Frith
Iron glazes with waxed motifs.

An alternative technique to produce a reduced copper red decoration is to prepare a mixture of 50 per cent of red clay and 50 per cent of copper carbonate which can then be applied as a paint or paste over, preferably, a fired white tin glaze and fired at 650°C (1200°F) with 15–30 minutes reduction. After firing, the red clay can be brushed away to reveal the reduced copper film which will have become incorporated into the glaze surface.

Fig. 53
Stoneware dish by Ray Finch

SOME IMPORTANT POINTS

Setting the ware in the kiln

This operation—commonly referred to as kiln
placing—must be done carefully with due consideration of the fact that with the low-biscuit/
high glost technique the pottery may warp if
not set down evenly. Further shrinkage of the
pots will occur once the biscuit firing temperature
has been exceeded and bowl shapes may shrink

down on to the feet of kiln props or other inert
objects such as cone stands.

To minimize the risk of specking, any loose
particles on the kiln roof and shelves should be
carefully brushed or vacuumed away. Batt wash
should be applied to new kiln furniture and any
specks of glaze on batts used in the previous firing
should be rubbed down and the area recovered
with batt wash. A good wash can be made from
a 50/50 mixture of zircon and china clay, or

alumina hydrate, mixed with water to a suitable consistency for painting.

When placing glazed ware into the kiln, hold the pieces firmly; trying to hold the pieces delicately with thumb and finger is much more likely to result in the glaze film becoming damaged—unless, of course, the pots are very small.

If any glaze is knocked away during the placing process then apply some more, either touched on with a finger or soft brush, followed by carefully rubbing level when dry. Be careful to avoid transferring glaze on the fingers from one pot to another of a different colour and be similarly careful to avoid transferring the wash on the shelves to the pots.

Cones and temperature control

Probably the best way to control a firing is by a combination of pyrometer and cones, the latter being used to determine the end-point of a firing and the pyrometer being especially useful to show kiln temperature and to indicate rate of temperature increase or decrease. Cones measure heat-work, which is a function of time and temperature, whereas pyrometers indicate actual temperature. Consequently the supposed temperature at which a cone squats is likely to be different from the actual temperature inside the kiln as indicated by a pyrometer, and an apparent difference of 40°C (100°F) or more between the temperature indicated by the pyrometer and that suggested by the squatting of a cone is not in any way unusual. The squatting temperature is obviously also affected by variation in firing cycle, slower cycles causing a slightly earlier collapse of the cone than faster ones.

There are basically two types of cone in use, the American 'Orton' cone and the British 'Staffordshire' cone (which has replaced 'Seger' cones). The so-called squatting temperatures of the Orton and Staffordshire cones are reasonably similar (*see* page 131) for the same cone number but whereas Staffordshire cones are designed to be stood upright, Orton cones are designed to be used in an inclined position (this is why British publications show cones mounted upright whereas American ones show them inclined at an angle). If either type of cone is mounted incorrectly a false reading is likely to result.

Cones are also affected by reduction atmospheres which, under severe conditions, may cause them to bloat or to form a refractory outer skin which can cause them to remain upright after the supposed collapsing temperature has been exceeded.

17. Development and testing

It would seem to be common sense to carry out experiments in very logical fashion, working one step at a time and observing the results from each step before moving further. Yet many people carry out experiments with careless abandon—often putting an unknown quantity or a careless mixture of materials into a glaze. Under such circumstances it is hardly surprising that difficulty is encountered in reproducing any particular effect.

In any series of tests it is important to know the basic properties of the constituent test materials so that one can work scientifically towards the desired result. This may involve separate tests of the individual materials before committing them to any mixture. Nevertheless one must allow for the fact that certain mixtures produce unexpected results: for example, a mixture of chromium and zinc will give brown instead of green, the presence of an appreciable amount of lime will bleach iron colours, etc.

If two or more colouring oxides or stains are to be added to a glaze it is important to bear in mind that the quantity of each to be added should be reduced if the resultant colour is not to be too dark. It must also be borne in mind that the colouring effects obtained by additions of colouring pigments to white glazes are quite different from those obtained from additions to transparent glazes and also that lead, leadless and alkaline glazes will usually each give a different colour response.

Furthermore, results on a flat tile may be quite different from those on a vertical surface and consequently, trials carried out on small pots (or sections) are of more value than those carried out on small test tiles.

It is also desirable that the particle size of materials used in tests be consistent from test to test, since the chemical activity of a material increases with smaller particle size; thus in any series of trials involving the production of small batches of glaze which are subsequently ground, the degree of grinding must be controlled.

DETERMINING THE QUANTITY

Naturally it is essential that one should know the precise amount of materials used in each test. Where additions of materials have to be made to a glaze in liquid form it is also important that the density of the slop glaze be exactly the same in each test. Alternatively, of course, one can calculate the dry weight of glaze present in the slop mixture by using Brogniart's formula (*see* page 130).

Very often one wishes to make an addition of a certain percentage of one material to another. If a particular recipe for example details that 5 per cent of a colouring pigment be added to a glaze, it is generally accepted that 100 parts of the dry glaze be taken (or its slop equivalent) and 5 parts of the required pigment be added. This, however, results in 105 parts of coloured glaze of which 5 parts is the pigment and thus the actual percentage pigment present is not 5 per cent but 4·76 per cent. Nevertheless it has become common practice amongst craft potters to work in this fashion for such recipes since it is more convenient to take 100 parts of the base glaze. The industrial ceramist, on the other hand, would tend to calculate the exact quantities so that the final glaze consisted of 95 per cent of the base glaze and 5 per cent of the colouring pigment. Naturally, if a glaze recipe indicates the percentage requirement of each constituent then this must be adhered to (the complete glaze then totalling 100 units).

A good set of scales is essential if tests are to be carried out accurately. In general, the beam type of scale will be found to be more accurate than the spring-balance type. If very small amounts of a material have to be weighed out and one has scales which are not sufficiently accurate then it may be best to weigh out the smallest accurate amount on the scales and then physically to divide the amount of powder with a knife to obtain the desired amount. Thus 25 g required on a scale accurate only to 100 g would demand that this quantity be quartered.

METHODS OF TESTING

Probably the most satisfactory way of carrying out a fired test of a glaze is to prepare trial pieces cut from a typical clay pot so that each piece includes a section of the side wall and base, and then to biscuit fire each piece. When used as glaze trials and stood upright in the kiln such trials have the advantage of showing the glazed effect on a vertical surface in addition to that on a horizontal plane. On each test it is also desirable to vary the thickness of glaze application, since the whole appearance of a glaze may depend upon the thickness of the coat.

In any series of tests devoted to comparing the fusion characteristics of different mixtures, or to developing a glaze to fuse at a certain temperature range, it is useful to prepare small 'fusion buttons', i.e. small mounds of each mixture placed on a test tile and fired to the required temperature range, the degree of fusibility of each button being indicated by its surface and radius of curvature.

KEEPING RECORDS

In a college once attended by the author there was a large framed notice which read 'Note books have good memories; so have scraps of paper—when you can find them!'

Use a book to record each test made, with notes about the firing treatment and observations about the fired result in addition to the recipe.

If each trial is given a reference number, painted on with underglaze colour or a mixture of oxide and glaze before firing, then the trials may be kept in a suitable reference number order and the composition of any trial quickly referred to in the record book when required.

The necessity to compile accurate records of all tests may seem tedious at the time but is often invaluable at a later date. Complete and accurate records take hardly more time to compile than incomplete or innacurate ones. If each test is numbered as suggested above, so that one can relate quickly from the fired sample to the record of its composition and treatment accurately detailed in the record book then such information, sooner or later, will prove invaluable.

LINE BLENDS (TWO-COMPONENT BLENDS)

Most blending procedures involve the mixing of two materials only, such mixtures sometimes being referred to as 'line blends'. Such blends often consist of a small amount of material—perhaps an oxide or stain—added to a much larger quantity of glaze.

If the quantity of the smaller constituent is to be varied it is often much easier to do this by dilution instead of by attempting to weigh out the precise amount of material required. For example, supposing one wished to investigate the range of colour tones obtained from 1 to 5 per cent of iron oxide added to a glaze then one could do this by using the following chart.

X (glaze plus 5% iron oxide)		100	80	60	40	20	—
Y (glaze only)		—	20	40	60	80	100
% iron oxide in mix	5	4	3	2	1	0	

In this chart X is the glaze mixed with 5 per cent of iron oxide and Y is the same base glaze but with no iron addition. By using Y to dilute X as indicated, one can weigh out comparatively large amounts and obtain a blend which avoids the difficulty of weighing out very small quantities of iron oxide. In the chart above, for example, it will be appreciated that a 50/50 mixture of *X* and *Y* will give a mixture containing approximately 2½ per cent iron oxide.

If, in the example above, *X* and *Y* were two different-coloured glazes then such a blending arrangement would demonstrate the effect of gradually decreasing one and increasing the other. A careful examination of the fired results often may indicate a combination which would produce an unusually attractive effect.

TRI-AXIAL BLENDS (THREE-COMPONENT BLENDS)

Many of the most attractive coloured glazes result from a mixture of three colouring pigments or glazes. Such three-component blends can best be charted by using a triangular chart as below.

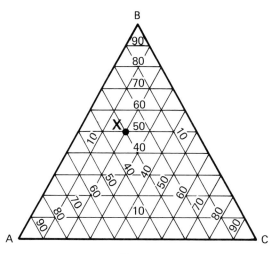

Fig. 54
Chart for three-component blends

With this type of chart the composition of any one point in the chart can be indicated by counting the number of lines distance between the point concerned and each corner of the chart. Since each of the three corners respectively represents 100 per cent of one of the three components, then a point seven lines away from the component in the corner diametrically opposite would represent 7/10th dilution, i.e. 30 per cent

content of that constituent. Thus the point marked X in the chart above consists of 30 per cent *A*, 50 per cent *B* and 20 per cent *C*.

This type of chart lends itself well to glaze formulations, since glaze constituents can be classified into the three groups of basic, amphoteric and acidic oxides. The chart can then be used to indicate the maturing range for each combination.

CHECKS TO ENSURE CONSISTENCY OF SUCCESSIVE GLAZE BATCHES

It is important for the studio potter as well as the industrial potter to check each new batch of prepared glaze, so as to ensure that the fired result will be identical to that of the previous batch.

The most important single factor is to keep a fired standard or 'master' which is truly representative of the desired effect from the standard glaze. This serves as a comparison when carrying out a visual inspection of the fired test glaze.

Where consistency of fired colour is of much importance it is desirable that the fired standard, and any check of a glaze batch to determine the precise colour, be on a tile or other flat surface because the apparent colour of a glazed article may vary slightly with a change in contour. It is also important to take into account the fact that the apparent colour will vary with a change in lighting conditions and that a difference in shade between the standard and the test piece may not be apparent in either dull or exceptionally bright light but will show up well under good lighting conditions. It is therefore desirable to carry out fired colour checks in a consistent light source which is bright and even. Good daylight but without bright sunlight would be ideal but since this cannot be relied upon, many concerns use an artificial light source utilizing 'daylight' fluorescent diffused lighting to illuminate a selected test area.

USUAL CHECKING PROCEDURE

For glazes where consistency of colour is not of paramount importance the best way to conduct a visual check is to prepare trial pieces having both vertical and horizontal planes as mentioned earlier. Although this test would be quite sufficient for the average craft potter it is often also useful to carry out a flow-trial comparison with the previous glaze batch since such trials best reveal any difference in viscosity of the molten glaze.

To carry out a flow trial, a weighed quantity of the previous glaze batch known to be satisfactory is placed on to an inclined plane alongside an identical quantity of the test glaze and fired in the kiln to the normal glost firing temperature. Identical glazes should flow down the plane to the same degree. For this type of trial it is usual to make use of a slip cast and fired testing block which has two recesses to house the glaze powder and a channel leading from each down which the glaze flows after firing (*see* Fig. 55).

A flow trial to indicate the molten viscosity and a fire trial to indicate the general appearance

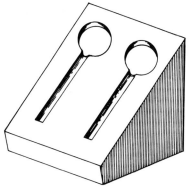

Fig. 55
Flow-trial block

would give a reliable indication of the nature of the fired glaze. The unfired nature of the glaze should have been determined at the milling stage by ensuring that the degree of grinding is similar to that of previous batches, a sieve analysis and some form of sedimentation check being used to determine the degree of grinding and rate of settling respectively.

18. Pottery faults and their remedy

Although this chapter is devoted to an examination of the various 'defects' which may appear in the glazed and fired article it must be realized that it is important to relate the phenomenon to the function of the ware or the intention of the potter.

Crazing, for example, may be deliberately produced in the fired glaze to enhance the beauty of a certain article and in this context could hardly be classified as a fault. Similarly, devitrification, blistering and several other so-called 'faults' may be deliberately promoted to advantage under certain circumstances. Faults such as cracking and dunting could hardly be other than faults, since they may result in the destruction of the piece. It is therefore apparent that much depends upon whether the phenomenon is intended or otherwise, and if the latter, whether it reduces the appeal or utility of the article.

CRAZING

Crazing takes the form of very fine cracks spread throughout the glaze but especially in those areas that are more thickly glazed than others. If the pottery body is porous the crazing permits moisture to enter into the pottery article, making it unhygienic.

The craze lines may be so fine that they are difficult to detect with the unaided eye—especially with coloured glazes. Vases containing water are sometimes found to have caused a moisture deposit on the surface on which they have been placed. This is usually caused by crazing of the glaze.

For pottery which is used purely decoratively rather than functionally, however, crazing can be regarded as a decoration and can give an attractive appearance if spread uniformly over the pottery. Such glazes are referred to as 'crackle' glazes and were discussed on page 68.

The fundamental cause of crazing is a difference in the degree of contraction of the body and of the glaze covering it. If the coefficient of expansion (and contraction) of the body and the glaze were exactly the same, crazing would theoretically never occur. However, when pottery is being used it is often heated and cooled, e.g. when being used for hot foods, or washed in hot water. Under these circumstances the first part of the pottery to be affected by this heat or cold will be the surface, the temperature difference then passing by conduction into the body until the pot becomes more or less uniform in temperature. In view of the time lag, however, the glaze begins to expand sooner than the body when being heated and begins to contract prior to the body when being cooled.

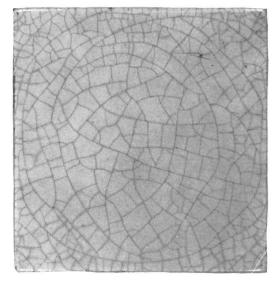

Fig. 56
Crazing

It has been shown earlier (page 12) that glasses and glazes can withstand far more compression than tension without cracking. This is to say that they can withstand being squeezed, without giving way, much more easily than they can withstand the same force trying to pull them apart. It therefore follows that suddenly chilling a hot pottery surface is much more likely to cause the glaze to crack than suddenly heating it. This characteristic of glasses and glazes of withstanding compressive forces more easily than tensile ones is used by ceramists to prevent crazing by deliberately attempting to put the glaze film into a state of compression. When pottery ware is then heated the glaze is compressed still further but the cooling operation, instead of forcing the glaze into tension, merely results in a reduction of the compressive forces present in the glaze.

The coefficient of expansion of the glaze should therefore be slightly less than the coefficient of expansion of the body to which it is applied. However, in view of the fact that the expansion coefficient of a clay depends considerably upon the degree of firing it receives, it would be best at this juncture to review the circumstances under which the silica content of a body controls its coefficient of expansion.

The role of silica

It has been mentioned earlier that silica occurs abundantly in volcanic rocks and consequently also in clays, the decomposition product of volcanic rocks, and in sandstone and flint. Consequently all pottery clays and bodies contain silica, either combined with the clay mineral, or introduced separately in the form of calcined and finely ground flint pebbles (*see* page 28) or ground silica sand.

Just as silica can be located in so many different materials so does the silica crystal itself occur in several different forms or modifications. When silica is heated some of it changes from one form to another, only to revert to the original form when it is subsequently cooled. Other modifications of silica change permanently to another form and this new form remains when the silica is cooled.

The most important crystal modifications of silica are as follows and each of these modifications can be considered to be present in the pottery body when fired

Alpha-quartz	$\rightleftharpoons$	Beta-quartz
Alpha-tridymite	$\rightleftharpoons$	Beta-tridymite
Alpha-cristobalite	$\rightleftharpoons$	Beta-cristobalite

Of these the alpha- and beta-quartz and the alpha- and beta-cristobalite modifications are of particular concern. Whenever these silica forms change from one modification to another under the influence of heat, an expansion takes place; similarly, when the silica is subsequently cooled and beta-quartz, for example, reverts to its original form of alpha-quartz, a contraction of the silica mass takes place.

Expansion in 100 millimetres
0
0·5
1·0
1·5
β Cristobalite
β Quartz
α Quartz
α Cristobalite
0 100 200 300 400 500 600 700 800 900 1000 1100 1200 1300
Temperature °C

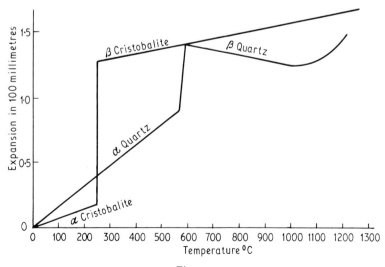

Fig. 57
Thermal expansion of silica minerals

Fig. 57 explains the unusual behaviour of silica in more detail. When silica is heated it gradually expands until a temperature of approximately 225°C (440°F) is reached when it suddenly expands very considerably as the alpha-cristobalite content is converted to beta-cristobalite, which of course has the same chemical composition (SiO_2) but a larger volume. As heating is continued another sudden expansion occurs at a temperature of approximately 570–575°C (1 060–1 070°F) when alpha-quartz changes to beta-quartz.

However, as heating continues, all other forms of silica begin to change into beta-cristobalite, this conversion progressing with increasing rapidity as the temperature is raised higher. If silica is heated above 1 200°C (2 190°F) for example, most of it is converted into beta-cristobalite. Thus the greater the heat treatment to which a pottery clay or body is subjected, the more cristobalite is developed. This is a very important phenomenon.

As silica is cooled it gradually contracts until a temperature of approximately 575–570°C (1 070–1 060°F) is reached, at which point the beta-quartz content reverts to its original alpha-form accompanied by a sudden contraction. As the silica is cooled still further, the point at which beta-cristobalite reverts to the alpha-form is reached at approximately 225°C (440°F). This beta- to alpha-cristobalite change causes a further and more severe volume contraction. These sudden expansions at certain temperatures when the silica is heated, and the sudden contractions at the same temperatures when it is cooled, occur every time the silica, or a body containing silica, is fired.

It will therefore be appreciated that the formation of cristobalite in the body is due to the body being fired to a comparatively high temperature and that this formation takes place slowly and results from the conversion of the various forms of silica present in the clay or body recipe. The greater the amount of cristobalite formed, the

Compression
A
B
C

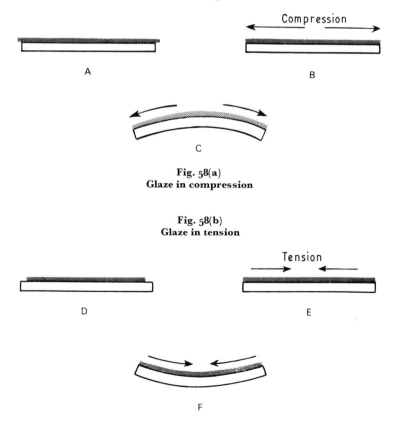

Fig. 58(a)
Glaze in compression

Fig. 58(b)
Glaze in tension

Tension
D
E
F

greater will be the coefficient of expansion (and contraction) of the body.

Effect of silica inversions on the glaze

When a glaze is applied to a pottery body and subsequently fired in the glost kiln, the body, with the glaze covering it, contracts once the kiln firing has finished and cooling begins. As the glaze is molten it absorbs any stresses which are created until it becomes more or less rigid at around 850-650°C (1 560-1 200°F). Below this point any stresses set up during cooling cannot be released by glaze flow but remain fixed and consequently, if the pottery body has been properly fired, the sudden contractions caused by the quartz and cristobalite inversions at 573°C (1 060°F) and 225°C (440°F) respectively, result in a compressive stress being applied to the glaze. This compression then remains in the glaze when the ware is taken from the kiln.

In the case of earthenware, the silica content of the body is controlled to be just sufficient to produce the correct amount of cristobalite when the pottery body is fired in the earthenware range, i.e. 1 100-1 150°C (2 010-2 100°F). It will be appreciated that if this temperature range is not reached at some point in the pottery process then sufficient cristobalite will not be developed and therefore the coefficient of expansion will not be as high as it should be. Insufficient heat treatment is, in fact, the most common cause of crazing.

If the explanation of the silica inversions sounds rather complex then Fig. 58 may be referred to as a summary. *A* shows a slab of biscuit ware of high coefficient of expansion on which has been placed a glaze having a lower coefficient of expansion (and contraction). By firing the two together and then cooling, we arrive at *B* where both the glaze and body occupy the same area but the glaze wants to spread itself out over a greater surface than that offered by the biscuit slab and is therefore in a state of compression. If the body were very thin or elastic this compression would relieve itself by the glaze forcing the body to bend (*C*). *D* illustrates a glaze having a higher coefficient of expansion (and contraction) than that of the body which, when fired with the glaze and then cooled, results in *E* where the

glaze is being stretched by the body in an attempt to cover it. This is the condition of tension in which crazing can occur so easily. The glaze tension tries to relieve itself by bending the body as in *F* which is the opposite of *C*.

It is obviously possible to affect crazing resistance by changing the composition or type of body. Generally speaking, the finer the particle size of the material, the more reactive it becomes. If the silica present in pottery bodies is not ground sufficiently finely, less cristobalite will tend to be formed. Incidentally, pure silica will not form cristobalite until a temperature of 1 450°C (2 640°F) has been reached, but in the presence of feldspar, stone, whiting, dolomite, talc, and also iron oxide, cristobalite may form at temperatures as low as 900-950°C (1 650-1 740°F). Talc tends to have a marked effect in this respect but it has to be imported and for this reason it is not often used in England.

Other factors

Silica can be added to a porous body to increase the expansion by forming more cristobalite and yet can be added to the glaze to decrease expansion. The reason is that in a glaze silica is dissolved by the fluxes to form silicates which have low expansion characteristics. Adding silica to either the glaze or the body or both can therefore help to overcome crazing.

Porous bodies will absorb moisture from the atmosphere through minute pores in the glaze causing the body to swell—the phenomenon known as moisture expansion. Generally speaking, the greater the porosity the greater the moisture expansion; a figure of 0·03 per cent increase in volume is common. Moisture expansion can result in a situation where the expansion of the body releases all the compression in the glaze. Continuing expansion then results in a tensile stress being developed in the glaze, causing crazing. This is the cause of the crazing seen on industrial tiles in bathrooms or kitchens after they have been in use for a considerable period of time.

PEELING

Peeling is the reverse of crazing and is caused by

the glaze having too much compression, owing to the coefficient of expansion of the glaze being very much lower than that of the body on which it is applied. Peeling appears as very fine cracks in the glaze, the edges of which tend to ride over one another, i.e. overlap. It tends to take place on the edges of pottery, such as the top rims of cups and mugs. The sharp edges of glaze can usually be detected with the finger and can easily be broken away.

Peeling is a comparatively uncommon fault and can generally be relieved by firing the biscuit or glost firing to a lower temperature so that less cristobalite is formed in the body during firing. Grinding the flint content of the body more coarsely would have a similar effect by reducing the conversion to cristobalite on account of the reduced activity of the larger particles.

Alternatively, the glaze can be adjusted by replacing some of the flux content with fluxes of higher expansion: for example, replacing some of the lead or borax frit by an alkaline frit, partly replacing whiting or dolomite by feldspar etc. Direct addition of an alkaline frit naturally would solve the problem of peeling but since such frits mature in the lower temperature range some addition of clay or silica would also be necessary if the firing range of earthenware or stoneware glazes was not to be reduced.

Peeling may be particularly prevalent on curves of sharp radius. If the top lip or handle of a cup is shaped too sharply then the risk of the glaze shelling away is much increased. In such areas the glaze normally tends to be very thin and this reduces the risk of peeling but if the glaze coat is of normal thickness on such areas then peeling is likely.

Sometimes the glaze flakes away from earthenware handles when a very low biscuit firing is carried out (to give good glaze pick-up) followed by a glost firing insufficient to develop the body. In this case, the shelling of the glaze is due to a combination of insufficient bond between the glaze and body, i.e. insufficient buffer layer, and a difference in coefficient of expansion caused by the low glost firing. The thickness of the glaze coat accentuates the problem. This fault is more related to crazing than peeling. Flaking may also be caused by insufficient bond due to the presence of a scum (usually soluble salts) on the biscuit surface.

SCUMMING

(a) **On the biscuit**

This is generally due to the presence of soluble salts in the body. As the pots dry after the making process, the water escaping from the body brings the soluble salts with it in solution, and as the water evaporates away the soluble salts precipitate out to form a scum on the surface of the pot—usually on rims and edges where drying is most rapid. This results either in the glaze running away from the scummed portion after dipping, or, more commonly in the glaze flaking away from this area after glost firing.

Soluble salts may be troublesome where water is taken from a static tank. If the water remains for a long period of time the amount of soluble salts in the tank water tends to increase, since the water evaporates and the soluble salts present become concentrated. In some areas the normal mains water supply contains such a high proportion of soluble salts that these can result in scumming on pottery. Certain natural earth materials such as the ochres may contain variable amounts of soluble salts and if these are incorporated in clay recipes in large amounts it is advisable to add barium carbonate ($2\frac{1}{2}$ per cent) to the body recipe. This converts the soluble salts to insoluble ones by double decomposition. Certain natural clays, especially the terra-cottas, may also contain troublesome quantities of soluble salts. Even the water used for throwing, or in any sponging operation afterwards, may contain sufficient soluble salts to cause scumming. A few drops of vinegar added to the water will usually prevent this.

(b) **On the glaze**

If the pottery is once-fired then the causes may be any of those mentioned above.

Scumming on the fired glaze of pottery produced by the standard two-fired method is, however, usually caused either by soluble salts present in the glaze—in which case 2 per cent of barium carbonate or a little vinegar should be added—or by a deposit produced during firing from products of combustion. Sulphur gases present in certain solid fuels or oil-fired kilns are notorious in this respect. Fly-ash in certain types of solid-fuel kilns may also be deposited on the glaze, causing a scum. This can easily be verified by enclosing one of the pots in the firing in a tightly sealed saggar so that combustion products cannot come into contact with the glazed surface. If scumming is caused by sulphur products then a coat of whiting applied to the inside walls of the muffle may help in absorbing the sulphur.

Scumming may sometimes be caused by excessive amounts of certain materials present in the glaze. The presence of more than 8 per cent of manganese in a glaze may cause the manganese to precipitate from glaze solution forming a dark brown or purplish scum.

CRAWLING

Crawling is characterized by bare areas of the ware from which the molten glaze has withdrawn. The edge of the glaze coat surrounding the unglazed area is usually thickened and smoothly rounded. In all cases crawling results from surface tension forces overcoming the adhesion or wetting tension, the severity of the crawling varying from an isolated, minute patch to 'beading' in which the glaze may form into small beads resembling drops of water on a waxed or greasy surface.

A number of factors can cause or influence the crawling of glazes but the most common cause is undoubtedly the presence on the biscuit or clay ware before dipping of oil, grease, or deposits of dust or similar material. This results in lack of adhesion at the glaze/body interface thus allowing the glaze to roll away during the firing operation. Another common cause is knocking or otherwise damaging the unfired glaze surface. This can break the bond between the biscuit and the glaze film, which results in a dislodged portion of glaze falling away from the pot when in the kiln, or this portion melting with the rest

of the glaze film and then being pulled away by surface tension.

Excessive shrinkage of the glaze after application may cause the glaze film to crack, producing crawling in the fired glaze. Siccatives or binders such as starch, Courlose, Kirkose, Cellofas, gum arabic, gum tragacanth, will all cause high shrinkage rates as also will excess additions of clays, especially the highly plastic ones such as bentonite. A thick coating of glaze can aggravate this.

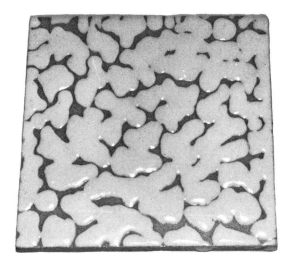

Fig. 59
Crawling

Over-grinding the glaze may produce excessive formation of colloidal material causing high shrinkage but, probably more important, it will produce a dusty glaze which has poor adhesion. Owing to its greater chemical activity the over-ground glaze may also dissolve excess amounts of silica and alumina from the body, causing the glaze to become abnormally viscous and therefore further increasing the risk of crawling.

Glazes which are relatively viscous when molten are always more prone to crawling than are very fluid glazes, the increased degree of flow of the latter tending to heal over any cracks or craters present in the glaze film. Opaque glazes, especially zircon opacified ones, are more viscous than transparent glazes and thus more liable to crawling.

Crawling sometimes arises over underglaze

decoration, particularly with cobalt blues, chrome greens and pinks. This has been attributed to their 'dryness' due to lack of sufficient flux, or to the presence of soluble salts so that the glaze cannot easily 'wet' the colour. The use of more flux or the addition of binder to the colouring pigment may help. Any relatively chemically inactive portion such as underglaze decoration or refractory grog particles may not be properly 'wetted' by the molten glaze thus promoting crawling. A glaze which might be ideal for porcelain, for example, may crawl on the rougher surface of stoneware and not flow so readily. In general however, most instances of crawling arising from a too viscous glaze layer may be corrected by addition of flux to the glaze.

Other possible causes of crawling are—

(*a*) Soluble salts in the body causing a deposit on the surface of the ware. Barium carbonate should be added to the body recipe.

(*b*) Soluble salts present in the water supply used when sponging the ware or when turning pots on the wheel. This can be cured by adding a little vinegar to the water.

(*c*) Glaze applied when the ware is not at the correct degree of dryness, especially with once-fired ware.

(*d*) Thick and thin sections of ware.

(*e*) Glaze constituents which dissociate vigorously and produce large volumes of gases causing pinholes and craters may produce crawling if present in large amounts. Colemanite is a notable offender and may result in patches of glaze being ejected from the pot. Part replacement by a calcium borate frit or slower firing may cure this.

(*f*) The presence of high proportions of glaze constituents which shrink appreciably at high temperatures, such as zinc oxide (unless calcined) and bone ash.

CUT GLAZES

This is another form of crawling and generally results from the glaze surface being scratched or otherwise marked after dipping. When the ware is fired, cut glazes show as a bare streak of biscuit showing through the glaze in the same position

as the damage caused to the unfired glaze film. Other possible causes include a thin smear of oil or grease, perspiring fingers, soluble salts etc.

DUNTING

This is the name given to a crack which generally passes completely through the pot, i.e. through both glaze and body, and is caused by thermal shock or stress. The line of fracture of a dunt is nearly always a gently curved one and has no sharp corners. It is usually possible by inspecting the edges of the crack to tell whether a dunt has

Fig. 60
Dunting

occurred when pottery is being heated in the kiln or whether it occurred during the cooling operation. If the dunt occurred when the pottery was being heated, the edges of the crack will have been rounded as the glaze subsequently melted during the firing operation. If the dunt occurred during the cooling operation then the edges will be sharp and the dunt may be difficult to see.

Dunts hardly ever occur during the biscuit fire process, being largely confined to the glost fire and particularly to the cooling cycle. They can be caused by having too much flint present in the body, the dunt then occurring usually at either the quartz or cristobalite inversions (*see* pages 107–9). The usual cause, however, is either trying to cool the kiln too quickly or trying to take pots out of the kiln before they are cool enough. As has been mentioned previously, the kiln can be cooled fairly quickly down to about 750°C (1380°F) without much risk of dunting but below this point cooling should be at a reasonably slow pace—especially over the silica inversion points. The kiln door can be opened in stages once the temperature drops below 200°C (390°F).

Pots which are fairly thick at the base and have a much thinner cross-section near the top may often dunt when the base of the pot is placed flat upon a kiln shelf during firing. This is because the base of the pot takes considerably longer to heat up (due to conduction by the kiln shelf) than does the top of the pot. During cooling, however, the heat retained by the kiln shelf keeps the pot base hotter than the top. The resulting stress between the top and the bottom of the pot may result in a dunt, especially if the firing cycle is rapid. Placing the pot on stilts, saddles, etc. so as to allow an air gap between the pot base and the kiln shelf usually overcomes this problem.

Some bodies are specially prepared to fire satisfactorily at earthenware temperatures of 1100–1150°C (2010–2100°F) but can also be fired at stoneware temperatures. The manufacturer sometimes adds cristobalite to these bodies to give satisfactory craze-resistance at the lower temperature. Unfortunately cristobalite formed at the higher temperatures by conversion of silica in the body can result in an excess of cristobalite and produce severe volume shrinkage at the beta-to-alpha cristobalite inversion, causing dunting. When bodies of this type are used for stoneware it is best to carry out the glost firing as rapidly as possible consistent with obtaining a satisfactory glazed surface.

A similar problem may arise with ware which has to be refired at the normal glost firing temperature. With each refiring more cristobalite may be formed, causing excess shrinkage at the cristobalite inversion. This is why the percentage of dunted ware is generally greater with refired pieces than with pieces drawn from the first glost

firing.

Other possible causes are—

(*a*) Ware made with curves of too sharp radius, particularly on rim or foot of bowls.

(*b*) Thick and thin sections of ware.

(*c*) Overfiring (causing excessive cristobalite conversions).

(*d*) Too much compression in the glaze. This is likely to cause dunting in cylindrical shapes.

(*e*) Stresses created during firing of complex or large shapes may result in dunting in one particular place. This may be avoided by changing the design or drilling a hole in the area of the clay article concerned.

(*f*) Dunts frequently occur at improperly sealed joints or cracks in the biscuit ware. Dunts consistently springing from casting holes may sometimes be prevented by filling in the holes during making or by making the holes larger.

PINHOLING

During glaze fusion, minute gas bubbles are formed from decomposition of the glaze and also of the body which it covers. These gas bubbles gradually increase in size as the melt becomes more fluid until they eventually float upwards through the glaze to the surface where they burst. The pinholes which are thus produced should be healed over by flow of the molten glaze but if the pinholing is excessive or is still being produced at the end of the firing operation then the smoothing out process may be insufficient and pinholes remain in the glaze. Such circumstances may arise if the clay ware is inadequately fired followed by a rapid glost firing to a much higher temperature. A slightly higher biscuit firing would cure the problem by burning away most of the volatile material present in the clay.

Generally speaking, the thicker the glaze coat the larger the bubbles which are formed and therefore the bigger the holes produced when the bubbles burst. Consequently, a thinner glaze application may cure pinholing, since not only are the bubbles smaller but their upward journey is shorter and they tend to be released more quickly from the glaze. On the other hand, a very thin deposit of glaze is very often badly pin-holed. This is due to lack of sufficient glaze to allow fluid flow to fill in the pinholes after the bubbles have burst.

Poor firing technique may prevent the pin-holes from healing over. It is best to soak the glost firing for a period of about $\frac{1}{2}$ hour or so at the maximum firing temperature as this allows the glaze more time to flow and thus fill any pinholes or craters formed in it. If pinholing still persists and this appears to be due to the glaze, use a longer soaking period and cool the glaze more slowly over the first 100°C after firing.

Pinholing is, however, more often a body defect than a glaze defect, especially if the pin-holes are isolated and comparatively large. Such large pinholes in the body are difficult for the glaze to fill and can arise in a number of ways. With cast pottery, pinholes can easily be caused by introducing air bubbles into the casting slip, usually by a too vigorous mixing. The industrial practice is to keep the prepared casting slip under slow agitation in a large tank or 'ark' during which time the air bubbles trapped in the slip slurry escape to the surface. Air bubbles can also be forced into incorrectly wedged or incorrectly pugged clay. Finishing the clay ware with a damp sponging operation will usually smooth out any craters present on the surface of the pot and lend itself to a smoother glaze surface. However, the use of excess water or very dirty water should be avoided for this can also lead to pinholing problems.

Other possible causes of pinholing are—

(*a*) Casting pottery in dirty or very old moulds. (Similarly the first cast or two in new moulds may give trouble.)

(*b*) The addition to the slip of too much dry scrap from previous casting operations.

(*c*) Underglaze colour applied too heavily causes pinholes over the painted area.

(*d*) If making your own clay by dry mix method be certain of obtaining a thorough mixing of the ingredients.

(*e*) Soluble salts in the body.

(*f*) Ware not dry before dipping—especially biscuit ware.

(*g*) Excessive agitation of the glaze, thus forcing air bubbles into it.

MATT GLAZES BECOME GLOSSY

True matt glazes are produced by the development of fine crystals formed in the glaze but a very rapid cooling can prevent these crystals from being developed in sufficient quantity to produce the matt finish before the glaze becomes rigid. The glaze may therefore appear glossy. Reasonably slow cooling conditions are essential for matt glaze development.

Glossy glazes may be changed to matt ones by the addition of materials which have the effect of raising the maturing temperature of the glaze with the result that the glaze is immature and matt when fired at the temperature normally used for the glossy glaze. Such underfired glazes, however, have a quality which is not so pleasant as that of the crystalline matts and, owing to the imperfect glass formation, such glazes are more prone to acid attack.

Overfiring the glaze is a very common cause of matt glazes firing to a glossy finish.

DEVITRIFICATION

Occasionally when pottery is taken from the glost kiln it is found that the transparent glaze has turned a little milky, particularly where the glaze is most thickly applied. This milkiness occasionally takes on a pinkish or purplish dis-coloration when the transparent glazes are used over red bodies.

This milkiness, referred to as devitrification, is generally caused by crystallization taking place in the glaze-forming calcium and zinc silicates or calcium borate. This crystallization takes place whilst the molten glaze is cooling over the first 100–200°C (210–390°F) below glaze firing temperature. Once the temperature of the kiln drops to below about 900°C (1650°F) for stone-ware or 750°C (1380°F) for earthenware the glaze is normally rigid and no further devitrifica-tion takes place. However, the longer the time taken to cool the kiln down to this temperature range, the greater the risk of devitrification occurring.

Calcium borate is formed by a reaction between calcium present in the body and borax present in the glaze. It therefore follows that those glazes low in borax will tend to form less calcium borate. Leadless glazes generally contain far more borax than low-solubility types and devitrification is consequently much more likely to occur. Changing from a leadless to a low-solubility glaze usually prevents devitrification. If the biscuit fire is carried out to a temperature at least as high as that of the subsequent glost fire, the biscuit ware will tend to become comparatively non-reactive during the glost fire and calcium cannot be leached out so easily. This decreases the likelihood of calcium borate formation.

An increase in the alumina content makes glazes more viscous at the same firing temperature and crystal formation is therefore hindered. Addition of a few percent of alumina or china clay will therefore make the glaze less prone to crystallization.

BLISTERING

Blistering is sometimes loosely termed boiling and in fact the glaze surface does often take the appearance of a boiled, viscous liquid. It may be considered to be a very severe form of pinholing but instead of a pinhole a pronounced crater is usually formed which may reveal the biscuit ware inside the crater.

By far the most common cause is severe over-firing, actually causing the molten glaze to boil. A similar effect is commonly produced by an excessively rapid firing while the glaze is becoming molten, and especially in the last 50°C (120°F) or so. If the firing has been very rapid, gases may still be produced quite vigorously, causing the molten glaze to froth.

Cobalt, iron, and especially zinc, manganese and nickel may each alter their state of oxidation during firing, releasing gases which may cause pinholing or blistering of the glaze over any decoration in which these oxides are excessively used.

Manganese dioxide is sometimes added in large quantities to an underslip or glaze which is then covered by another glaze of different colour, both glazes maturing in the same firing. The manganese dissociates upon heating as follows—

$$3MnO_2 \longrightarrow Mn_3O_4 + O_2$$

The liberated oxygen bursting through the upper glaze may then form large craters which heal over as firing progresses resulting in decorative 'rings' or colour splashes in the fired glaze. Coloured stains, being calcined or fritted mixtures of oxides, do not cause the same pinholing or blistering problems.

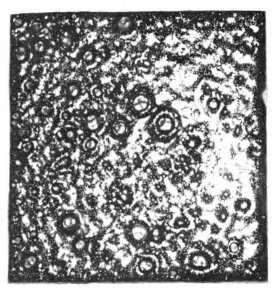

Fig. 61
Blistering

A combination of rapid firing and too much fat oil or underglaze medium used with underglaze colours may also produce excessive gas formation and cause blistering in the covering glaze.

SPIT-OUT

This fault appears occasionally on pottery after on-glaze enamels, transfers, or lustres have been applied to a fired glaze surface and fired at around 750°C (1380°F). The ware becomes covered with minute, broken blisters which soon fill with dirt.

Earthenware is particularly prone to this fault but porcelain, stoneware and other vitreous types of body are not subject to it unless the biscuit is porous owing to underfiring. This fact led to the theory that spit-out is caused by the presence of water vapour which has penetrated the glazed ware and become absorbed in the body. Upon subsequent heating, such as when on-glaze enamels are fired, it is thought that the water is turned to steam, and as the pressure builds up, it forces its way through the glaze layer as soon as this becomes sufficiently soft.

Refiring old glost earthenware (spit-out does not occur with new earthenware) prevents the fault from subsequently occurring. Reducing the firing temperature by 5–10°C (10–20°F) may stop an outbreak of spit-out by making the glaze more rigid and therefore preventing the steam bubbles from bursting their way through.

Some potters grind away the glaze from a small area of the back of a glost plate and cover this with a soft lead borosilicate flux, prior to the decorating fire. This acts as a vent in allowing the gases to escape from the biscuit ware through the ground area rather than elsewhere through the glaze. The low-melting-point flux then melts to seal the pinholes formed in it.

The fault does not occur with on-glaze enamels used on stoneware, porcelain or bone china, since either the biscuit is too vitreous to permit moisture retention or the glazes are too stiff to allow steam to pass through at the on-glaze enamel firing temperature of 750°C (1 380°F). Decorative glazes applied on to these bodies and fired in the region of 850–900°C (1 560–1 650°F) may, however, result in spit-out if the body is porous.

DROPPERS

These are round, discoloured spots or patches formed on the glaze surface by droplets of glaze falling from the roof of the kiln. Such droppers are usually brownish or a honey colour due to a combination of glaze with iron in the brickwork. In kilns constructed from white refractory insulation bricks the droppers may be clear, on account of the high purity of the bricks.

The problem is an important one in industry, where pottery is fired in continuously operated kilns, but not such a problem with craft potters since the firing is done intermittently and the interior kiln roof can be cleaned down as and when necessary, any potential droppers being chipped away. In the industry, tunnel kiln cars are often fitted with a shelf at the very top of the setting upon which no ware is placed, the batts serving merely to catch droppers falling from the roof. A coating of zircon wash over any brickwork which is becoming glazed is useful since the zircon is extremely refractory and combines with the glaze film to make it very viscous.

OVERFIRING AND UNDERFIRING

Overfiring is characterized by the glaze running, often forming a curtain of glaze around the base. Decoration both under and on the glaze may have blurred outlines and coloured glazes may alter colour—reds and pinks becoming brownish, and turquoise glazes becoming greener. Opaque glazes may become semi-opaque and matt glazes may become glossy. The glaze reacts more with the body and there is a consequent increase in specking and blotching (which may, incidentally, be very attractive). With more severe overfiring the glaze will become pinholed or blistered and lack shine due to volatilization of the ingredients.

Underfiring is characterized by a 'dead'-looking glaze, lacking shine and badly pinholed. In severe cases the glaze layer is cracked like dried mud. Very slight underfiring may merely produce slight dimpling and dullness.

BLOATING

Bloating takes the form of blisters or bulges visible on the fired surface of a pot. If the pot is cut in section across a bloat a void will usually be found. In the case of small bloats on the surface, if these are broken open with a hammer a void will be found which often contains a characteristic powdery deposit. Bloating often occurs with vitreous bodies but is relatively uncommon in porous bodies, such as earthenware.

The most common cause of bloating is over-firing the clay body. When this happens the flux content virtually begins to boil and bubble. Under these circumstances most potters would reduce the firing temperature on subsequent firings. In the case of stoneware this would mean reducing the glost firing temperature and since this may then make the glaze immature the

Fig. 62
Bloating

glaze would have to be softened. This can often be done with stoneware glazes by adding feldspar but since the alumina-to-silica ratio of feldspar is 1:6 and the proportion of alumina to silica in the base glaze is likely to be in the region of 1:6 to 1:10, a small addition of silica may also be needed to preserve the glaze balance.

Occasionally however it may be desirable to make the clay body more refractory so that it withstands the firing. This would normally be done by adding to the clay, materials such as grog or china clay. A refractory ball clay (most ball clays vitrify at stoneware temperatures) or fireclay could also be used. One must bear in mind, however, that whilst a clay of this type may be refractory in comparison to a stoneware clay body under oxidizing conditions, under reduction firing conditions the iron content of the ball

clay or fireclay can act as a vigorous flux, thus effectively reducing the vitrification point. At cone 9 some ball clays and fireclays which would be quite refractory under oxidizing conditions will bloat under reduction conditions.

Bloating can also be caused by the surface of the clay body being sealed off during firing before most of the gases created by decomposition of the clay body under heat have had time to escape. This is particularly true of clays which have a high carbon content. If the biscuit firing is not carried out at a high enough temperature then most of these volatiles will remain in the clay body until the temperature in the glost firing exceeds that of the biscuit when the volatiles are then released. If at this point the glaze surface has fluxed and healed over, then the gases created by decomposition of the carbon compounds may be imprisoned within the clay body with the result that the body swells, bloats or ruptures to allow the pressure to be released. When bloating is due to this particular cause the body is often very dark and there may be a black core present. This, incidentally, is often seen inside building bricks.

Under these circumstances the remedy is obviously to fire more slowly after the temperature to which the biscuit firing was taken has been exceeded, perhaps to increase the biscuit firing temperature (even a slight increase may burn away a large proportion of the volatiles) or to add materials to the clay body which will effectively open it up. Grog, silver sand or a calcined material, such as calcined china clay, would be useful for this purpose.

It is perhaps important to note also that some buff- or red-coloured grogs contain so much iron oxide that they cause localized fluxing under reduction firing conditions.

COLOUR VARIATION

If the fired colour of a glaze shows a variation in density of colour, this is almost always due to a variation in thickness of the coloured glaze. Where the application is thinner the colour of the body underneath tends to show through more prominently and if the body is whitish the more thinly glazed areas will be lighter in colour than the areas glazed more thickly.

Coloured glazes are best applied by the spraying process since one can obtain a more even glaze coat than is possible with other methods of glaze application. Application of coloured glaze by dipping can be done quite successfully but care is needed to avoid any glaze 'runs' (unless such runs are desired, as with certain ornamental wares) since these will result in a deep line or area of colour. It is often better to dip the pot twice with an intermediate drying-out period (do not, however, let the first coat go dry or the second coat may flake away). Similarly two or three coats of sprayed glaze will give a more consistent colour than one coat.

Any finger marks or areas from which glaze is missing may be touched up with glaze on the finger or by using a soft brush or glaze mop but, especially when the glaze is highly coloured, care must be taken to ensure that the touched-up area is subsequently rubbed smooth and level with the surrounding glaze. Use of dipping tongs or a thumb hook may be useful with certain shapes to avoid excessive finger marking.

Areas of pottery biscuit-fired near flames or elements may be scorched and relatively vitreous, whereas the remainder of the pot is of normal porosity, and the varying degree of absorption may cause colour variation due to a variation in glaze thickness. A similar problem arises with cast pottery owing to the 'casting flash'—a vitreous patch formed where the slip first touches the mould when poured in. Such casting spots are least troublesome if they are on the pottery base and the slip should therefore be introduced to fall on this area first, from the minimum pouring height.

In such cases where the pottery is of varying porosity or is vitreous or very thin it is often best to prepare the glaze for dipping to a high pint weight and deflocculated.

An unusual mottling or 'hammer finish' may occur with certain coloured glazes. If the glaze surface is inclined to the light it may be seen to be undulating, the high spots being more darkly coloured than the surrounding areas. This may be due to large bubbles forming during firing, the molten glaze bubbles bursting and the edges or perimeter of the bubbles not flowing back completely to fill the hollows. Slower firing may cure the problem, or the use of prepared stains instead of oxide colouring pigments—or calcining the oxides before use in the glaze.

CHANGE IN COLOUR

There are many and varied causes of a change in the fired colour of a glaze. If green colours turn brown this may be due to the combination of chromium oxide or a stain containing chromium with zinc in the glaze.

A pink tinge may result from the combination of chromium with tin oxide, and the use of certain black or green colours containing chrome as a decoration on or under tin-opacified glazes may result in a pink halo around the decorated area. Chromium colours often volatilize in the kiln and cause a pink tinge on nearby tin-glazed pottery.

Ironing is a fault which results in a copper-coloured streak on the surface of the glaze over a cobalt decoration. This is caused by insufficient fluxing of the cobalt stain, too thick a colour deposit, or too thin a glaze. Painting the area concerned with red lead or a low-melting glaze or frit, and then refiring, will usually correct this defect.

Red glazes produced from selenium often blacken owing to the formation of black lead selenide by the combination of lead vapour in the kiln with selenium in the glaze. Any trace of localized reduction arising from the presence of carbonaceous matter or minute splashes of other glazes (especially copper) will cause black specks in these glazes which are extremely sensitive.

If selenium glazes are applied too thinly or are overfired they tend to fire transparent or white. Slow firing may cause the same problem.

Gold lustre glazes may fire to a semi-matt black if underfired.

Many turquoise glazes become greener when overfired and bluer when underfired. Pink and orange glazes tend to become brown with overfiring.

Iron glazes are very susceptible to lime (which

bleaches them). Consequently, any increase in the calcium content of an iron glaze or in the body beneath may appreciably lighten the colour. Pink glazes on bodies containing talc may fade.

SPECKING

This is a tiresome fault which has various causes but which is almost always due to contamination of the glaze by some extraneous material. Very often this may arise in unexpected circumstances: for example, dirt has been drawn into kilns by recirculation fans and deposited on the ware inside the kiln, and small granules of ware or carborundum carried away by exhaust draught from ware grinding or polishing operations have been deposited on an exterior roof and from here the particles have occasionally been blown by the prevailing wind through open windows and on to ware for firing. Sometimes specking may result from rust blown through burners from the gas main. The use of a filter might prevent this and if possible a filter should also be used on the burner blower and on circulation fans. Any creation of dust around burners or fans may result in contaminants being drawn into the kiln. Contaminants falling on to glazed ware for firing will of course result in specking on the exposed surface only and this offers a means of diagnosis.

Other important factors are—

(*a*) Rust or dust from overhead pipes or ledges falling into prepared glaze or the presence in the glaze of particles of colouring pigment from previously dipped decorated pieces.

(*b*) Check that water supply used for glazes does not contain specking agents.

(*c*) Check that there are no large holes in lawn used for glazes. Try using a finer lawn.

(*d*) Leakage of insulating powder through cracks in the kiln roof.

(*e*) Specks falling from the top kiln shelf on to ware below. Brush shelves and place top shelf ware first.

(*f*) 'Spurting' of new saggars or kiln props.

(*g*) Silicon carbide (carborundum) is a notorious cause of specking. Use alumina or corundum grinding wheels instead of carbor-undum ones and, if silicon carbide is used as a local reducing agent, make sure that none leaks on to floors or is otherwise able to contaminate other glazes.

Specks tend to show up more where the glaze is thickest and when it is overfired. Specks in high-fired biscuit show up more than in low-fired biscuit and will therefore show through the glaze more. White glazed terra cotta may show marked and attractive mottling or specking when overfired.

WHITE SPOT

White spots in glazes may be caused by contamination in which case the particles, under magnification, are usually found to be irregular in shape as well as variable in size. If the spots are in, rather than on, the glaze and are reasonably consistent and smooth then there are two other possible causes—

(*a*) Combustion of impurities results in craters in the glaze. When the glaze flows back into these craters only the clear fraction of the glaze may flow, the colouring pigment remaining in position. Refiring or a slower firing or a longer soaking period may correct this fault, which often occurs with pink glazes. In addition to impurities, the addition of excess manganese, nickel, or certain other oxides (*see* 'Blistering') to a white glaze may cause excessive gas formation, resulting in craters and subsequent white spots.

(*b*) Very white spots in a white glaze are usually caused by incorrect or insufficient dispersion of the opacifier in the glaze. Stir more thoroughly and use Disperzon in preference to other types of zircon opacifier.

STARVED GLAZE

This is the name given to a glossy glaze which lacks shine. The usual cause is an insufficient application of glaze, or underfiring, although overfiring may produce a similar result owing to volatilization of some of the ingredients.

Irregular dullness, i.e. a dull patch, is also

referred to as 'sucked' ware. A glazed pot fired near to new and highly porous refractory bricks or props may show a dull patch due to absorption of glaze vapour by the refractory. The remedy is to coat the refractory with a bat wash to seal it or, in severe cases, to use a fusible wash. If a mixed glaze and biscuit firing is carried out, a biscuit pot in close proximity to a glazed one might similarly cause a dull patch on the glazed article.

SULPHURING

This appears as a dull scum or discoloration on the surface of the glaze. In slight cases it may be possible to rub this scum away with the fingers but usually it remains as a permanent effect. As the name implies, this fault is due to interaction with the glaze of sulphur gases present in the kiln atmosphere. Most pottery clays contain a little combined sulphur although generally not sufficient to cause any problems. An appreciable amount of sulphur may, however, be contained in certain fuels, especially certain oil fuels, and is released when the fuel is burned.

Sulphuring may be overcome by allowing a little more ventilation, thus causing the kiln to cool a little more quickly and reducing the length of time the pottery glaze is susceptible to attack by the sulphur gases. In extreme cases, however, it is necessary to change the fuel to a type containing less sulphur. If the kiln is of the muffle type, the muffle should be as tightly sealed as possible and the entry of combustion products will be minimized or prevented during firing if the atmosphere of the muffle is kept at a pressure higher than the muffle exterior around which the combustion products pass. A coat of whiting applied to the inside walls of the kiln is helpful in absorbing sulphur gases. Addition of 2 or 3 per cent of whiting to the glaze or body is also said to be useful. By reacting with sulphur in the body this reduces the amount released into the atmosphere.

DIMPLED SURFACE

With this defect the fired glaze is characterized by a 'hammered' surface, rather similar to the surface of an orange—hence the term 'orange peel' which is often used to describe it. A common cause is the use of excessive pressure when spraying, or holding the spray gun too close to the article being sprayed. The presence of large gas bubbles imprisoned beneath the glaze surface is another common cause. During cooling the bubbles shrink, the glaze surface immediately above then sags to fill the recess, and a depression results. A slower firing cycle or a longer soaking period often remedies the problem by allowing sufficient time for the bubbles to escape. Underfiring or overfiring can also be responsible for a dimpled surface.

19. Health and safety with glazes and ceramic materials

Whenever one considers any hazards associated with ceramic materials, it is very important to adopt a just sense of proportion. It is true that some ceramic materials can give rise to some hazard when they are handled or used, but it is necessary to quantify the degree of hazard to properly evaluate whether a significant risk arises with their use.

A mother, suspecting that her child had taken sleeping pills, gave him a drink of salt water to make him sick. This didn't work so she gave him another and then a third and fourth. Four days later the little boy died of salt poisoning. Salt – the material we use on our food – is a poison. However, it only becomes hazardous if it is ingested in unusually large amounts. And so it is with ceramic materials.

In other words, a poison by definition is 'too much of something'. Every material has a threshold limit above which there is considered to be some risk to health and below which long experience has shown there is no significant risk. Some materials have relatively low limits and some much higher or indeed, no practical limit. This degree of hazard should be considered when evaluating the consequences of a hazardous material being handled or liberated into the environment.

LABELLING OF HAZARDOUS MATERIALS

Labelling standards in various countries are similar in that potentially harmful materials are identified but the labelling system is often different. In the USA for example, suppliers submit formulas or products to an independent toxicological evaluation within the Art & Craft Materials Institute, Inc. which evaluates them in accordance with the American Society for Testing & Materials (ASTM) D-4236 Chronic Hazard Labelling Standard. Products which after such evaluation are certified to contain no materials in sufficient quantities to be toxic or injurious to humans or to cause acute or chronic health problems can carry either the AP Seal (Approved Products Non Toxic) or the CP Seal (Certified Product Non Toxic). Materials which are considered to be potentially harmful are given the HL Health Label (Caution Required) Seal which certifies that they have been properly labelled in a program of toxicological evaluation by a medical expert and conform to ASTM D-4236 or ASTM C-1023. In the case of HL Health Labelled products, the hazard (e.g. 'contains lead silicate frit') is identified and appropriate safety advice is also given on the label in a similar manner to the European labelling system for hazardous substances.

Under current European labelling legislation ('CHIP' Regulations)[1], all hazardous substances listed in the 'Approved List' (which is an official inventory of hazardous substances), must carry a label indicating the degree of hazard. Extremely hazardous materials are labelled 'Very Toxic', less hazardous materials are labelled 'Toxic' and below that in terms of toxicity come 'Harmful', 'Corrosive' and 'Irritant' classifications. However, a few hazardous materials do not appear in the Approved List. These are generally special preparations such as ground flint or quartz and also lead frits. With these substances the supplier is required to 'self classify' into one of the above label categories. Materials which are not considered hazardous do not carry any hazard label.

Very few of the ceramic materials encountered by craft potters or ceramicists and listed in suppliers catalogues are hazardous to a degree which demands Toxic labels. Several materials carry 'Harmful' labels. The great majority do not require hazard labels at all. In determining any hazard, one can therefore be guided by the label. However, it is important to bear in mind that most materials are to some extent harmful when taken into the body by mouth or by inhalation, the degree of harm depending on the toxicity of the material, its fineness, the amount taken in and the duration.

CERAMIC MATERIAL HAZARDS

The main hazards involved in using ceramic materials are:

Silicosis	A respiratory disease arising from the inhalation of silica dust over a period of time.
Poisoning	From the ingestion of inherently toxic materials.
Dermatitis	Arising from continual handling of wet clay, repeated contact with glaze suspensions, or contact with skin irritants such as turpentine.

The most important problem is silicosis arising from the inhalation of excess amounts of free silica over a period of time. At this point we need to ask some questions. Why do we need silica?... and what is respirable free silica?

Silica is the fundamental constituent of glazes and glasses and undoubtedly the most important ceramic material. We can't really make glazes without it. We also need it in clay bodies as a means of obtaining the desired thermal expansion to enable the glaze to fit the body. About 60% of the earth's crust consists of silica so it is an exceedingly common material which is present in all clays and rock materials from which many of our raw materials are derived. It occurs as veins of quartz in rocks and as secondary deposits of sandstone etc. Silica is, incidentally, very hard and during the timeless erosion of rocks and minerals it is the most resistant of the rock materials which is why we have sand on our beaches; the other rock materials having been washed away or dissolved. Sand is almost pure silica.

In the formation of igneous rocks from which our clays and other raw materials are developed, Mother Earth melted together most of the silica with other materials to produce silicates. Silica which is not combined in this way is the 'free' silica present as quartz. So we have 'combined' silica (as silicates) and 'free' silica. It is the free silica which can be hazardous when ground to a fine dust. Particles smaller than 5 microns – particles which are too small to be seen by the naked eye in normal lighting – can be carried in the air stream and pass the body's natural defences to eventually cause damage to the lungs. Coarser particles can be filtered out by the nose and mucous lining of the trachea. So we talk of 'respirable' free silica as the hazardous fraction.

Industry has adopted Occupational Exposure Standards, being that maximum concentration of dust to which workers may be exposed for 8 hours per day, 40 hours per week without effect. The OES for free crystalline quartz and flint is 0.1 mg/m.

GLAZE MATERIALS

From a hazard viewpoint, the materials used in ceramics can broadly be divided into two groups:

(*a*)   Naturally occurring materials which contain free silica and which are taken from the ground and processed. These include clay, feldspars, dolomite, limestone, quartz, flint, etc.

(*b*)   Chemical compounds and synthetic materials such as barium carbonate, nickel oxide, lead frits etc. which have to be handled with particular care due to their inherent toxicity.

Naturally occurring materials

These are invariably quite innocuous in their raw state but a few materials can give rise to health and safety problems when they are ground to fine particle sizes and the dust is inhaled.

Since silica is such a major constituent of the earth's crust, it is inevitable that materials extracted from the ground will contain silica in one form or another. All clays, for example, are hydrated alumino silicates generally containing 40 - 70% of silica, most of which is in combined form. China clays generally have less than 5% free silica, but ball clays, fireclays and red clays may contain up to 30%. If dry and finely powdered, the respirable fraction could be as high as 10% but invariably it is lower than this due to clumping together of fine particles into agglomerates which are not of respirable size. With china clays the respirable fraction is usually less than 0.5% which does not pose a significant problem.

In the case of ground materials such as feldspar, nepheline syenite, petalite, lepidolite, spodumene, dolomite, whiting, wollastonite, basalt, fluorspar, colemanite, magnesite etc., there is no significant hazard. They are regarded as 'nuisance dusts' rather than hazardous dusts. Cornish stone and granite can contain 1 – 5% of respirable free silica but this is not considered sufficient to warrant a 'Harmful' hazard label. This also applies to talc if it is of the usual platy structure and fibre-free. There is concern that some American talcs may contain some fibrous material and greater care would be needed with these.

With all the above materials there would not be any significant health risk arising from occasional slight contact with liberated dust. Thus the occasional mixing of a stoneware glaze from these materials should not pose any problem. If, however, it is done on any sort of bulk scale or if a significant amount of dust is being created during any process, then common sense demands that precautions or preventive action be taken. This could include mixing of materials in damp or slop form to avoid dust generation, or to wear a respirator.

There are however some materials which contain 90% free silica and these demand special care when handled in finely powdered form since they may contain 20 – 40% of respirable free silica depending on the degree of grinding. These materials are: quartz, usually made from ground sands or quartzite; flint made from calcined and ground flint pebbles, and cristobalite made from ground flint fired above 1100°C. To conform to the COSHH Regulations, quartz, flint and cristobalite each are assigned 'Harmful' hazard labels. There is no problem whatever in handling them in damp or wet form but if handling gives risk of airborne dust then this must be done under dust extraction apparatus, or outside in an area away from other people and/or an approved dust mask must be used. The aim must be to avoid the generation of airborne dust by appropriate standards of dust control and cleanliness.

Chemical compounds and synthetic materials

Here we have materials some of which may cause health risks because of their inherent toxicity. They include:

Antimony oxide	Barium carbonate
Copper carbonate	Cadmium compounds
Manganese dioxide	Lead bisilicate frit
	Vanadium pentoxide

All the above carry 'Harmful' hazard labels. In addition there are a few materials which are more hazardous and require 'Toxic' labels. These are:

Cobalt oxide	Lead oxide (red lead)
Nickel oxide	Lead carbonate
Chromium oxide	(white lead)
Lead sesquisilicate	Lead monosilicate

The reason for the inclusion of cobalt is because most cobalt oxides contain some nickel oxide and it is the latter which is dangerous (carcinogenic). The lead compounds are not allowed in glazes, having been replaced by lead bisilicate frit which is safer. Incidentally, ceramic fibres less than 6 microns diameter are now (1997) considered carcinogenic and thus labelled 'Toxic'.

In industry, the handling of the above materials for weighing out purposes etc. has to be done under adequate dust extraction conditions or factory approved respirators used. Also good standards of personal and departmental hygiene have to be maintained.

OTHER CONSIDERATIONS

Some of the above compounds are used in underglaze colours, ceramic glaze and body stains and especially in overglaze colours ('China paints'). Consequently, some of these may be 'Hazard' labelled and care must be taken when using them.

A few other materials need special mention. These include certain anti-bacteriological agents (biocides), some of which are very poisonous. The tiny amounts sometimes added to brush-on glazes etc. does not cause the glaze to become significantly more hazardous but care must be taken if handling the agent itself. Also, special regulations apply to the use and storage of hydrofluoric acid which is a very hazardous substance sometimes used for the etching of fired glaze or glass.

Materials such as sodium silicate and sodium carbonate (soda ash) used in the preparation of casting slips and in Egyptian paste are skin irritants. So, too, is alkaline frit if kept in slop storage since it is very slightly soluble and creates a caustic solution.

Glaze spray booths

If glaze is applied by spraying, it is important that this should be done in a spray booth and that this should either be exhausted to outside atmosphere or is of a design which catches the very fine overspray particles. Some spray booths merely have a coarse filter at the back which is incapable of catching the respirable size particles and such spray booths

must be connected to discharge to outside atmosphere. Alternatively one can have spray booths which have a pumped waterfall system to catch overspray and these are perhaps best of all since they have the added advantage of enabling some glaze to be reclaimed.

Kiln fumes

Fumes emanate from the kiln during the firing of clays, glazes and colours. These consist mainly of water vapour and carbon dioxide but they also include sulphur dioxide, fluorine, carbon monoxide and traces of other gases. Tests show that very close (a few centimetres or an inch) to the kiln, the noxious gas concentration may be above acceptable levels but these gases rapidly dissipate and room concentrations are not a problem given reasonable ventilation. With electric kilns this can be the opening of windows or the installation of a small powered fan mounted above and behind the kiln in an exterior wall or window , or a canopy and extraction duct with larger installations. Alternatively, Orton Vents or similar fan extraction systems can be mounted on the kiln. An extraction canopy and flue is essential with gas and oil fired kilns.

Kilns should be located in a separate, ventilated room away from the normal work area.

Floor cleaning

Whenever conditions permit, wet mopping of floors is recommended. Dry brushing should not be done because this liberates fine particles back into the air. Alternatively, vacuuming can be done using an approved cleaner with fine filters capable of collecting particles less than 5 microns (which pass through a normal domestic vacuum cleaner). The 'wet or dry' vacuum cleaners are very good if the correct filters are fitted.

RECOMMENDED HEALTH AND SAFETY PROCEDURES

The comments given previously allied to the following summary list of procedures should ensure safe working in all ceramic studios and departments.

* Well ventilated room
* Readily cleaned work surfaces and floors
* Ideally, drains available to facilitate floor cleaning by a wet method
* No eating, no drinking, no smoking in workroom
* Clean up spillages as they occur
* Close bags and containers after use
* Clean equipment and utensils by wet sponging
* Walls and windows: clean at least once per month
* Avoid airborne dust: prevent rather than control it
* Use wet processes not dry ones e.g. fettling/scraping dry pots should be avoided. Instead, sponge/trim/turn/carve when leatherhard
* If cannot totally control dust, wear protective clothing – plastic or rubber aprons minimum
* Wash hands at end of work session

It should be emphasised that ceramics is a safe craft. The hazards involved are no more dangerous than those in other crafts; they are merely different in nature. Provided the above precautions are followed there should not be any significant risk to health from ceramic materials or processes. It has become fashionable to knock ceramics and it needs to be restated that ceramics is a **safe craft.**

DISPOSAL OF MATERIALS

The disposal of hazardous materials into our environment is a subject that has demanded and received the careful attention of various authorities. There are regulations governing the amount and manner in which waste materials are allowed to be discharged and these are progressively becoming more stringent.

In general, ceramic materials do not pose any special problems from a disposal viewpoint since, in most cases, one is merely returning the material from whence it came. However, it is not being returned in the same dilution as the source or, in the case of some ceramic compounds and pigments, it has a certain inherent toxicity which demands that care be taken to minimise its deposition into our environment. We all have a duty to exercise such care. If you have surplus ceramic materials, it is therefore best to pass them onto another potter or ceramics department that perhaps can make use of them thus avoiding the further addition of harmful substances into our environment.

If you have to dispose of a product, you can often be guided by its label. Most ceramic materials do not require hazard labels and there is no problem in the relatively small amounts generated by craft users being treated in the same way as domestic waste. In the case of materials carrying a hazard label, these too can be disposed of on approved landfill sites in the small quantities normally used by craft potters. With larger quantities of these however, it is best to contact the local waste authority for disposal advice.

Clay slip constitutes by far the greatest volume of waste material from a pottery. Although clay slip is a non-hazardous material, effluent regulations apply when any materials are discharged to drains and ample water should be used to ensure proper dilution. In industry, large settling tanks are used to take out most of the suspended clay. In the case of slop glaze, some factories discharge into lagoons which, when full, are reclaimed or buried when solid.

Materials such as finely ground flint, quartz or cristobalite can be mixed with water to a paste or slurry and then put into a suitable container and disposed of as non-toxic waste on landfill sites. Some materials and contaminated packaging are better sent to an incineration plant.

1 Chemicals (Hazard Information and Packaging) Regulations 1993; amended by Chemicals (Hazard Information and Packaging for Supply) Regulations 1994 and subsequent amendments

20. Glaze recipes

A number of glaze recipes are given below which vary in maturing range from the low-temperature Raku type to glazes suitable for porcelain and stoneware. All are for oxidized firings except where reduction is indicated.

RAKU GLAZES

(850–900°C; 1560–1650°F)
Green (oxidized)/Red (reduced)

Alkaline frit	94
Bentonite	1
Copper oxide	5

This base of alkaline frit plus bentonite provides a good Raku glaze base for colouring by any oxide or stain.

Red-brown

Lead sesquisilicate	90
China clay	5
Red iron oxide synthetic	5

A warm red-brown glaze of the low-solubility type.

Taggs Yard turquoise

P.2250 alkaline frit	63.4
P.2245 borax frit	24
Tin oxide	4
Bentonite	4
Copper carbonate	4.6

Pale Yellow (s. reduced)

2275 Alkaline frit	80
2270 Calcium borate frit	9.5
China clay	5
Tin oxide	5
Chromium oxide	0.5

EARTHENWARE (900-1050°C) GLAZES

White base
(980–1040°C; 1800–1900°F)

Lead bisilicate	88
China clay	5
Tin oxide	7

High-shine transparent
(1050°C; 1922°F)

Lead bisilicate	55
2270 Calcium borate frit	30
China clay	15

Lime matt
(1020–1060°C; 1870–1940°F)

Lead bisilicate	60
Feldspar	24.4
Whiting	6.0
Alumina	5.8
Zinc oxide	3.8

Lithium alkaline blue
(1000–1050°C; 1830–1920°F)

Flint	54
Lithium carbonate	30
China clay	10.5
Copper carbonate	3.5
Bentonite	2

Translucent matt
(1000–1080°C; 1830–1980°F)

Lead bisilicate	67
Feldspar	9.3
Zinc oxide	19
Silica	4
Bentonite	0.7

ARTISTIC GLAZES

The artistic glazes detailed below produce their characteristic effects by crystallization from glaze solution; consequently, slow cooling conditions plus a sufficiently thick coat are essential for optimum development. Where lead sesquisilicate is given as a recipe ingredient, the use of a lead sesquisilicate containing a trace of titania is recommended, as the titania appreciably assists crystal development.

Mottled green *
(960–1060°C; 1760–1940°F)

Lead sesquisilicate	80
Zinc oxide	5
China clay	7.5
Ilmenite	5
Copper oxide	2.5

Rutile fleck
(960–1060°C; 1760–1940°F)

Lead sesquisilicate	88
Rutile	7
Ilmenite	1
China clay	4

Beige matt
(1000–1100°C; 1830–2010°F)

Lead sesquisilicate	53
Alumina (calcined)	11
Feldspar	18
Barium carbonate	10
Colemanite	3
Zinc oxide	1
Tin oxide	3
Manganese dioxide	1.5

Black matt *
(1000–1050°C; 1830–1920°F)

Lead sesquisilicate	45
Whiting	6
Feldspar	24
China clay	21
Cobalt oxide	2
Copper oxide	2
Red iron oxide	8

Transparent green crystal *
(980–1050°C; 1800–1920°F)

Lead sesquisilicate	77
Zinc oxide	5
China clay	7.5
Ilmenite	5
Copper oxide	2.5
Rutile (dark)	3

Flecked blue
(980–1050°C; 1800–1920°F)

Lead bisilicate	85
Rutile	7
Ilmenite	1
China clay	5
Cobalt oxide	2

* = not food safe

Fig. 63
by Derek Emms

EARTHENWARE GLAZES

(1020–1150°C; 1870–2100°F)
The zircon listed in some of these recipes is opacifier-grade zircon which is more finely ground than standard waterground zircon. It is sold under various trade names such as Disperzon, Superzon, Zircosil 5, Zircosil 1, Superpax, Ultrox etc.

Transparent leadless

Borax frit	90
China clay	10

White opaque
As above plus 12%
Zircon 7% tin oxide

Matt white
As above white opaque glaze plus 18% zinc oxide and 4% titanium dioxide

Transparent low solubility

Borax frit	65
Lead bisilicate	25
China clay	10

White opaque
As above plus 12% Zircon or 7% tin oxide
Matt white
As above white opaque glaze plus 18% zinc oxide and 4% titanium dioxide

Transparent low solubility

Lead bisilicate	80
China clay	20

White opaque
As above plus 12% Zircon or 8% tin oxide

Matt white
As above white opaque glaze plus 18% zinc oxide and 4% titanium dioxide

Vellum white

Lead bisilicate	50
Borax frit	20
Zircon (water-ground)	12
Titanium dioxide	2.5
Tin oxide	3
Zinc oxide	6
China clay	7

Shiny leadless

Cacium borate frit	48
Standard borax frit	42
China clay	10

Glossy brown

Lead bisilicate	70
Iron spangles	12
China clay	9
Tin oxide	4
Manganese dioxide	5

Black semi-matt slip glaze
(1050–1120°C; 1920–2050°F)

Red clay	46.3
Lead bisilicate or borax frit	46.3
Manganese dioxide	3.7
Cobalt oxide	3.7

Bright blue
(1060–1120°C; 1948–2048°F)

Lead bisilicate frit	70
Potash feldspar	14
Whiting	10
China clay	6
Cobalt oxide	1

Black matt slip glaze
(1050–1120°C; 1920–2050°F)

Red clay	85
Iron oxide	10
Manganese dioxide	3.3
Cobalt oxide	1.7

Warm grey
(1060–1150°C; 1940–2100°F)

Borax frit	72
China clay	8.5
Tin oxide	4.5
Dolomite	12
Manganese carboante	2.5
Cobalt carbonate	0.5

Transparent slip glaze
(1080–1140°C; 1980–2080°F)

Lead bisilicate	58
Clay	35
Whiting	6
Bentonite	1

STONEWARE AND PORCELAIN GLAZES

Where feldspar is listed as a recipe ingredient either soda or potash feldspar can be used but potash feldspar is generally preferable. All recipes are for oxidized firings except where reduction is indicated.

Transparent
(1220–1280°C; 2230–2340°F)

Feldspar	46
Whiting	19
Barium carbonate	2.5
Flint	23
China clay	15

Add 12–15% Zircon opacifier or 5–8% tin oxide to produce white opaque.

Semi-opaque vellum
(1250°C; 2280°F)

Feldspar	46
Talc	15
Colemanite	15
Dolomite	10
China clay	5
Flint	20
Disperzon	3

Green crystal glaze
(1250°C; 2280°F)
(based on the 4 : 3 : 2 : 1 formula)

Feldspar	40
Flint	30
Whiting	20
China clay	10
Nickel oxide	2
Copper oxide	3

Textured brown
(1260°C; 2300°F)

Cornish stone	40
China clay	20
Whiting	20
Iron oxide	8

Grey matt
(1260°C; 2300F; reduction)

Feldspar	51.5
Dolomite	17
Whiting	3
China clay	23.5
Manganese dioxide	5

Speckled matt
(1260°C; 2300°F; reduction)

Feldspar	40
Calcium borate frit	12
Dolomite	7
Talc	15
China clay	5
Flint	20
Ilmenite	1

Porcelain transparent
(1250°C; 2280°F)

Nepheline syenite	34
Whiting	18
Flint	30
China clay	16
Zinc oxide	2

Add 5% tin oxide to produce white opaque.

Treacle glaze
(1250°C; 2280°F)

Feldspar	45
Whiting	9
Zinc oxide	4
Magnesium carbonate	3
Barium carbonate	11
China clay	5
Flint	18
Iron oxide	5

Translucent semi-matt
(1230°C; 2250°F)

Feldspar	65
Dolomite	13
China clay	22

Ash glaze semi-matt
(1260°C; 2300°F)

Feldspar	40
Ash	40
Ball clay	20

Matt white 'sugar' glaze
(1200°C; 2190°F)

Feldspar	22
Whiting	14
Zinc oxide	6
China clay	18
Flint	26
Zircon opacifier	14

Albany glaze
(1240°C; 2260°F)
Dark treacle-brown similar to Albany slip. Attractive mottling may result when used as once-fire glaze.

Red clay (Etruria marl)	55
Standard borax frit	41
Iron oxide	4

Tenmoku
(1260°C; 2300°F)

Feldspar	43
Flint	19
China clay	15
Whiting	13
Iron oxide	10

Mottled black/brown
(1260°C; 2300°F)

Red clay	62
Standard borax frit	35
Iron oxide	3

Chun glaze
(1260°C; 2300°F)
Low-solubility glaze

Potclays 2205	10
Whiting	20
Quartz	30
Feldspar	40
Black iron oxide	1

Mottled black/brown
(1280°C; 2340°F)

Potash feldspar	49
Basalt	49
Bentonite	2

Rusty red fleck
(1280°C; 2340°F)

Feldspar	50
Dolomite	20
China clay	15
Bone ash	9.5
Ilmenite	5.2
Chromium oxide	0.3

Carter crystal glaze
(1280°C max)

2266 frit (Potclays)	45
Calcined zinc oxide	25
Flint	20
Titanium dioxide	8
Calcined china clay	0.5
Alumina	0.5
Bentonite	1.0

(Calcining of zinc oxide and china clay is done at 1000°C)

Additions of cobalt, manganese, nickel, rutile or other pigments are made to develop colour and emphasize crystals. Very fast firing is needed from 1000°-1280°C then crash cooling to 1100°C with a very long soak at this temperature. The glaze is then progressively cooled with soaking periods at 30°C intervals terminating in a final short soak at 1000°C. The kiln is then switched off to cool.

Textured matt white crystalline
(1280°C; 2340°F)

Potash feldspar	60
Dolomite	20
China clay	20

Fig. 64
by Derek Emms

Semi-matt lilac-red, flecked
(1280°C; 2340°F; reduction)

Potash feldspar	45
Whiting	25
China clay	24
Talc	5
Copper carbonate	0.6
Black iron oxide	0.6

Semi-matt blue
(1250°C; 2280°F)

Potash feldspar	50
Whiting	15
Cornish stone	18
China clay	12
Tin oxide	3
Cobalt oxide	1
Red iron oxide	1

Dappled green

Feldspar	50
Dolomite	20
China clay	15
Bone ash	9
Vanadium pentoxide	5
Copper oxide	1

Ministry of Education Administrative Memorandum No. 517 Restrictions on the use of certain types of glazes in the teaching of pottery

1. REGULATIONS

Regulations made by the Minister of Labour and National Service under the Factories Acts prohibit in factories manufacturing pottery the use of a glaze which is not a leadless glaze or a low-solubility glaze. In some schools and establishments of further education, however, raw lead glazes or glazes containing a high percentage of soluble lead are still used. After consultation with the Minister of Labour and National Service the Minister [of Education] reached the conclusion that, in the interests of the health of pupils and students, the use of glazes should be regulated. He accordingly asked all Authorities and Governors and Managers to see that the advice in the following paragraphs, which necessarily embodies certain technical terms, is carefully followed in all schools or establishments of further education for which they are responsible.

2. RAW LEAD GLAZES

The use of glazes containing over 5 per cent of soluble lead has been forbidden in the pottery industry for some years. The Minister considers that their use should be confined to advanced courses in ceramic design and technology in establishments of further education where, in the opinion of the Principal, these glazes must be used occasionally if the subject is to be properly taught. They should not be used at all in courses of the following kind—

(a) Pottery craft courses in schools;

(b) Non-vocational pottery craft courses in establishments of further education;

(c) Vocational courses for apprentices in the ceramic industry.

3. LOW-SOLUBILITY GLAZES

Low-solubility glazes (i.e. those containing not more than 5 per cent of soluble lead) are not open to the same objection as raw lead glazes; they may continue to be used in schools and establishments of further education of all kinds provided proper precautions are taken.

4. PRECAUTIONS

The following precautions should be observed where any process is carried out involving the use of raw lead glazes, low-solubility glazes or any form of lead compound in the preparation of frits, colours, etc.—

(a) Glazing should be done only in a room suitably equipped for the purpose.

(b) Since the danger of lead poisoning is greatest where lead or its compounds are inhaled, processes which are likely to give rise to these compounds in dust form in the air should not be allowed unless there is efficient exhaust ventilation or a suitable respirator is used. Where a spray is used there should be a separate booth with efficient exhaust fan. The Minister understands that these processes are normally confined to establishments of further education.

(c) Anyone who has carried out any of the processes should wash their hands and use a nail brush immediately afterwards.

(d) All benches and working surfaces should be washed down after use and splashes of glaze should be removed from floors or walls.

(e) Food should not be eaten in any room used for pottery making.

(f) Protective clothing (e.g. overalls or aprons) should be worn during all pottery classes and should be washed as necessary. An apron with bib of impervious material should be worn by anyone while actually engaged on glaze dipping and should be washed after use.

APPENDIX 2
Low-solubility glaze test

DEFINITION

'Low-solubility glaze' means a glaze which does not yield to dilute hydrochloric acid more than five per cent of its dry weight of a soluble lead compound calculated as lead monoxide when determined in the manner described below.

METHOD OF TESTING

A weighed quantity of the material which has been dried at 100°C and thoroughly mixed is to be continuously shaken for one hour, at the common temperature, with 1 000 times its weight of an aqueous solution of hydrochloric acid containing 0·25 per cent by weight of hydrogen chloride. This solution is thereafter to be allowed to stand for one hour and then filtered. The lead salt contained in the clear filtrate is then to be precipitated as lead sulphide and weighed as lead sulphate.

The Pottery (Health) Special Regulations, 1947, prohibit the use of glazes other than leadless and low-solubility glazes in factories.

APPENDIX 3
Acid-resistance testing

Several countries are now adopting a test for metal release based upon attacking the ware with a 4 per cent solution of acetic acid at room temperature for 24 hours. The metals to be controlled by the test do, however, vary from country to country except for lead which is included in all regulations.

The U.S.A. imposes a limit of 7 ppm of lead (Pb) and 0·5 ppm of cadmium (Cd). In Europe and Scandinavia the metal released is related to the actual surface area attacked by the acid and the results are expressed in milligrammes per square decimetre (mg/dm^2). The Finnish test, which is generally regarded as the most stringent one, permits a maximum of 0·6 mg/dm^2 of lead, zinc, cadmium and antimony taken together.

THE FINNISH TEST

The Finnish regulations are as follows—

'The use of an implement or utensil is prohibited if it contains arsenic soluble in foodstuffs. Lead, zinc, cadmium or antimony must not appear in the implement or utensil in such a degree or form that if the implement or utensil is kept for 24 hours at room temperature in an acetic acid solution of 4 per cent, more than 0·6 mg of these metals is segregated against each full square decimetre of the surface of the implement or utensil which comes into contact with the foodstuff. In normal use it must not give off colour on the foodstuff or dissolve in the above-mentioned acetic acid solution in such a degree that the colour of the acid changes.'

The regulations do not indicate the precise manner in which the test should be conducted but the method used by the British Ceramic Research Association is first to wash a test plate in a dilute detergent solution followed by rinsing with water and allowing to drain until dry. The plate is then filled to the rim with 4 per cent acetic acid and the whole protected with a plastic cover to prevent contamination and evaporation. After 24 hours at room temperature the solution is stirred and sampled for analysis.

APPENDIX 4
The borax bead method of testing metallic compounds

It is often useful to be able quickly to check or identify a metallic ceramic compound, the identity of which may be in some doubt. Under such circumstances the borax bead method of testing is extremely useful since it is very simple to carry out and an accurate result can be obtained in a very few minutes or less.

A short length of platinum wire is fitted at one end into a suitable holder so that the hot wire can be held in the hand and the other end of the wire is bent into a small loop. A wire about 6 cm long bent at one end into a loop 2–3 mm in diameter and inserted into a glass rod handle (by heating the glass) is quite adequate. The platinum wire loop is then dipped into borax powder and melted in a Bunsen burner flame which results in a glaze bead being formed around the loop when the wire is removed from the flame.

If the hot borax bead is touched to a trace of the powdered material to be tested and is then reheated in the oxidizing (flame tip) and reducing (the blue zone near the burner) sections of a Bunsen burner flame, a characteristic bead colour is obtained for each metallic substance. It is therefore a good test for differentiating between the metallic oxides.

All traces of a previous bead must be removed from the wire by melting and shaking away until the wire is clear before a new test is made.

Below are the colours obtained in some common bead tests.

The oxide and carbonate of the same metal will, of course, give a bead of the same colour but one can differentiate between the two by pouring some acid on to the powder. An oxide will remain relatively inert but a carbonate will effervesce, vigorously liberating gas bubbles.

	Oxidizing Flame		Reducing Flame	
	Hot	Cold	Hot	Cold
Antimony	yellow	colourless	yellow	colourless
Chromium	yellow	green	green	green
Cobalt	blue	blue	blue	blue
Copper	green	blue	colourless	brown
Iron	yellow	green	green	green
Manganese	violet-brown	violet	colourless	colourless
Molybdenum	yellow	colourless	brown	brown
Nickel	violet	brown	colourless-grey	colourless-grey
Titanium	colourless	colourless-white	yellow-grey	yellow
Tungsten	yellow	colourless	yellow	brown
Uranium	yellow	yellow-brown	green	green
Vanadium	yellow	green	brown	green

Brogniart's formula for dry matter content of a liquid

This is a very useful formula to calculate the amount of dry material present in a liquid. Provided that one pint or one litre of the suspension can be exactly taken and the specific gravity of the dry material is known (*see* below), then the dry content can easily be determined. The formula is as follows—

$$W = \frac{(p - 20) \times g}{g - 1}$$

W = dry content (in oz) of one pint;
p = Weight (in oz) of one pint of liquid;
g = specific gravity of dry material.

or
$$W = \frac{(p - 568) \times g}{g - 1}$$

W = dry content (in grammes) of 1 pint;
p = weight (in grammes) of 1 pint of liquid;
g = specific gravity of dry material.

or
$$W = \frac{(p - 1\,000) \times g}{g - 1}$$

W = dry content (in grammes) of 1 pint;
p = weight (in grammes) of 1 litre of liquid;
g = specific gravity of dry material.

Specific gravity. This is generally taken as 2·5 for all clays but with glazes the specific gravity varies within the following limits—

Stoneware, porcelain, and all leadless glazes	2·6
Low-solubility glazes	3·0–4·0
Lead bisilicate frit	4·57
Lead sesquisilicate frit	5·0

EXAMPLE OF CALCULATION

Suppose we need to know how much dry glaze is present in two gallons of leadless glaze slip, one pint of which weighs 28 oz.

$$W = \frac{(28 - 20) \times 2·6}{2·6 - 1} = \frac{8 \times 2·6}{1·6} = 13 \text{ oz}$$

One pint contains 13 oz of dry material and therefore contains $28 - 13 = 15$ oz water.

Two gallons contain 16×13 oz = 13 lb dry glaze and 15 lb water (i.e. 1·5 gallons since 1 gallon weighs 10 lb).

Temperature equivalents of cones

°C	°F	Staffordshire cone	Orton cone (standard)	°C	°F	Staffordshire cone	Orton cone (standard
600	1 112	022	022	635	1 175		020
614	1 137		021	650	1 202	021	
625	1 157	022A		670	1 238	020	

Appendix 6—*continued*   Appendix 6—*continued*

°C	°F	Staffordshire cone	Orton cone (standard)	°C	°F	Staffordshire cone	Orton cone (standard)
683	1 260		019	1 100	2 012	1	03
690	1 274	019		1 110	2 030	1A	
710	1 310	018		1 120	2 048	2	02
717	1 324		018	1 130	2 066	2A	
730	1 353	017		1 137	2 079		01
747	1 372		017	1 140	2 084	3	
750	1 382	016		1 150	2 102	3A	
790	1 454	015	016	1 154	2 109		1
805	1 481		015	1 160	2 120	4	2
815	1 499	014		1 170	2 138	4A	3
835	1 535	013		1 180	2 156	5	
838	1 540		014	1 186	2 167		4
852	1 566		013	1 190	2 174	5A	
855	1 571	012		1 196	2 185		5
880	1 616	011		1 200	2 192	6	
884	1 623		012	1 215	2 219	6A	
894	1 641		011	1 222	2 232		6
900	1 652	010	010	1 230	2 246	7	
920	1 688	09		1 240	2 264	7A	7
923	1 693		09	1 250	2 282	8	
940	1 724	08		1 260	2 300	8A	
950	1 742	08A		1 263	2 305		8
955	1 751		08	1 270	2 318	8B	
960	1 760	07		1 280	2 336	9	9
970	1 778	07A		1 290	2 354	9A	
980	1 796	06		1 300	2 372	10	
984	1 803		07	1 305	2 381		10
990	1 814	06A		1 310	2 390	10A	
1 000	1 832	05	06	1 315	2 399		11
1 010	1 850	05A		1 320	2 408	11	
1 020	1 868	04		1 326	2 419		12
1 030	1 886	04A		1 346	2 455		13
1 040	1 904	03		1 350	2 462	12	
1 046	1 915		05	1 366	2 491		14
1 050	1 922	03A		1 380	2 516	13	
1 060	1 940	02	04	1 410	2 570	14	
1 070	1 958	02A		1 431	2 608		15
1 080	1 976	02		1 435	2 615	15	
1 090	1 994	01A					

Note: The collapsing temperature is a function of time and temperature and it will vary, therefore, according to firing conditions.

The Fahrenheit figures are calculated from the Celsius values.

APPENDIX 7
Temperature conversion chart

°C	0	10	20	30	40	50	60	70	80	90
				DEGREES FAHRENHEIT						
0	32	50	68	86	104	122	140	158	176	194
100	212	230	248	266	284	302	320	338	356	374
200	392	410	428	446	464	482	500	518	536	554
300	572	590	608	626	644	662	680	698	716	734
400	752	770	788	806	824	842	860	878	896	914
500	932	950	968	986	1 004	1 022	1 040	1 058	1 076	1 094
600	1 112	1 130	1 148	1 166	1 184	1 202	1 220	1 238	1 256	1 274
700	1 292	1 310	1 328	1 346	1 364	1 382	1 400	1 418	1 436	1 454
800	1 472	1 490	1 508	1 526	1 544	1 562	1 580	1 598	1 616	1 634
900	1 652	1 670	1 688	1 706	1 724	1 742	1 760	1 778	1 796	1 814
1 000	1 832	1 850	1 868	1 886	1 904	1 922	1 940	1 958	1 976	1 994
1 100	2 012	2 030	2 048	2 066	2 084	2 102	2 120	2 138	2 156	2 174
1 200	2 192	2 210	2 228	2 246	2 264	2 282	2 300	2 318	2 336	2 354
1 300	2 372	2 390	2 408	2 426	2 444	2 462	2 480	2 498	2 516	2 534
1 400	2 552	2 570	2 588	2 606	2 624	2 642	2 660	2 678	2 696	2 714
1 500	2 732	2 750	2 768	2 786	2 804	2 822	2 840	2 858	2 876	2 894
1 600	2 912	2 930	2 948	2 966	2 984	3 002	3 020	3 038	3 056	3 074
1 700	3 092	3 110	3 128	3 146	3 164	3 182	3 200	3 218	3 236	3 254
1 800	3 272	3 290	3 308	3 326	3 344	3 362	3 380	3 398	3 416	3 434
1 900	3 452	3 470	3 488	3 506	3 524	3 542	3 560	3 578	3 596	3 614
2 000	3 632	3 650	3 668	3 686	3 704	3 722	3 740	3 758	3 776	3 794
2 100	3 812	3 830	3 848	3 866	3 884	3 902	3 920	3 938	3 956	3 974
2 200	3 992	4 010	4 028	4 046	4 064	4 082	4 100	4 118	4 136	4 154
2 300	4 172	4 190	4 208	4 226	4 244	4 262	4 280	4 298	4 316	4 334
2 400	4 352	4 370	4 388	4 406	4 424	4 442	4 460	4 478	4 496	4 514
2 500	4 532	4 550	4 568	4 586	4 604	4 622	4 640	4 658	4 676	4 694

°C	°F
1	1·8
2	3·6
3	5·4
4	7·2
5	9·0
6	10·8
7	12·6
8	14·4
9	16·2
10	18·0

APPENDIX 8
The common elements of ceramics and their oxides

Element	Symbol	Atomic weight	Oxide	Formula	Molecular weight	
Aluminium*	Al	27	Aluminium oxide	Al_2O_3	102	Alumina
Antimony	Sb	122	Antimony trioxide	Sb_2O_3	292	
Barium*	Ba	137	Barium oxide	BaO	153	
Boron*	B	11	Boric oxide	B_2O_3	70	
Cadmium	Cd	112	Cadmium oxide	CdO	128	
Calcium*	Ca	40	Calcium oxide	CaO	56	Lime
Carbon	C	12	Carbon dioxide	CO_2	44	
Chromium	Cr	52	Chromic oxide	Cr_2O_3	152	
Cobalt	Co	59	Cobaltic oxide	Co_2O_3	166	
Copper	Cu	64	Cupric oxide	CuO	80	
Hydrogen	H	1				
Iron	Fe	56	Ferric oxide	Fe_2O_3	160	
Lead*	Pb	207	Lead monoxide	PbO	223	Litharge
			Lead oxide	Pb_3O_4	686	Red lead
Lithium*	Li	7	Lithium oxide	Li_2O	30	Lithia
Magnesium*	Mg	24	Magnesium oxide	MgO	40	Magnesia
Manganese	Mn	55	Manganese dioxide	MnO_2	87	
Nickel	Ni	59	Nickel oxide	Ni_2O_3	165	
Nitrogen	N	14				
Oxygen	O	16				
Phosphorus	P	31	Phosphorus pentoxide	P_2O_5	142	
Potassium*	K	39	Potassium oxide	K_2O	94	Potash
Selenium	Se	79	Selenium dioxide	SeO_2	111	
Silicon*	Si	28	Silicon dioxide	SiO_2	60	Silica
Sodium*	Na	23	Sodium oxide	Na_2O	62	Soda
Strontium*	Sr	88	Strontium oxide	SrO	104	
Sulphur	S	32	Sulphur dioxide	SO_2	64	
Tin	Sn	119	Tin oxide	SnO_2	151	
Titanium	Ti	48	Titanium dioxide	TiO_2	80	Titania
Vanadium	V	51	Vanadium pentoxide	V_2O_5	182	
Zinc*	Zn	65	Zinc oxide	ZnO	81	
Zirconium	Zr	91	Zirconium oxide	ZrO_2	123	Zirconia

*These twelve elements are those very commonly found in glaze formulae.

APPENDIX 9

Glaze oxides and introductory raw materials

Oxide to be introduced	*Means of introduction*	*Solu-bility*	*Formula*	*Formula weight or molecular weight*
Na_2O Sodium oxide	Soda feldspar (albite)	Insol.	$Na_2O.Al_2O_3.6SiO_2$	524·3
	Cornish stone (mixed)	Insol.	$\left.\begin{array}{l}0{\cdot}417Na_2O\\0{\cdot}310K_2O\\0{\cdot}273CaO\end{array}\right\}1{\cdot}18Al_2O_3.8{\cdot}565SiO_2$	705·3
	Nepheline syenite	Insol.	$\left.\begin{array}{l}0{\cdot}764Na_2O\\0{\cdot}236K_2O\end{array}\right\}1{\cdot}11Al_2O_3.4{\cdot}88SiO_2$	474·5
	Alkaline frit	Insol.	Use manufacturer's data	
	Sodium carbonate	Sol.	Na_2CO_3	106
	Borax	Sol.	$Na_2O.2B_2O_3.10H_2O$	381·5
K_2O Potassium oxide	Potash feldspar (orthoclase)	Insol.	$K_2O.Al_2O_3.6SiO_2$	556·5
	Cornish stone	Insol.	As Na_2O above	
	Nepheline syenite	Insol.	As Na_2O above	
	Potassium carbonate	Sol.	K_2CO_3	138
	Potassium nitrate	Sol.	KNO_3	101
PbO Lead oxide	Lead monosilicate	Insol.	$PbO.SiO_2$	283·3
	Lead bisilicate	Insol.	$PbO.2SiO_2$	343·3
	Lead sesquisilicate	Insol.	$PbO.1{\cdot}5SiO_2$	313·4
	Galena	Insol.	PbS	239
	Litharge	Insol.	PbO	223·2
	Red lead	Insol.	Pb_3O_4	685·6
	White lead	Insol.	$2PbCO_3.Pb(OH)_2$	775·7

Appendix 9—*continued*

Oxide to be introduced	*Means of introduction*	*Solu-bility*	*Formula*	*Formula weight or molecular weight*
CaO calcium oxide	Whiting	Insol.	$CaCO_3$	100
	Calcium carbonate	Insol.	$CaCO_3$	100
	Dolomite	Insol.	$CaCO_3 . MgCO_3$	184·4
	Lime feldspar (anorthite)	Insol.	$CaO . Al_2O_3 . 2SiO_2$	278·1
	Colemanite (borocalcite)	Insol.	$2CaO . 3B_2O_3 . 5H_2O$	412
	Bone ash (calcium phosphate)	Insol.	$Ca_3(PO_4)_2$	310·2
MgO Magnesium oxide	Magnesium carbonate	Insol.	$MgCO_3$	84·3
	Magnesite (magnesium carbonate)	Insol.	$MgCO_3$	84·3
	Dolomite	Insol.	$CaCO_3 . MgCO_3$	184·4
	Talc (steatite, soapstone)	Insol.	$3MgO . 4SiO_2 . H_2O$	379·2
Li_2O Lithium oxide	Lithium carbonate	Insol.	Li_2CO_3	73·9
	Petalite	Insol.	$Li_2O . Al_2O_3 . 8SiO_2$	612
	Lepidolite	Insol.	$\left.\begin{matrix} 0{\cdot}503Li_2O \\ 0{\cdot}369K_2O \\ 0{\cdot}128Na_2O \end{matrix}\right\} 1{\cdot}04Al_2O_3 . 3{\cdot}76SiO_2$	387·6
SrO Strontium oxide	Strontium carbonate	Insol.	$SrCO_3$	147·6
ZnO Zinc oxide	Zinc oxide	Insol.	ZnO	81·4
BaO Barium oxide	Barium carbonate	Insol.	$BaCO_3$	197·4
Al_2O_3 (alumina)	China clay	Insol.	$Al_2O_3 . 2SiO_2 . 2H_2O$	258·1
	Alumina (calcined)	Insol.	Al_2O_3	101·9
	Alumina hydrate (aluminium hydroxide)	Insol.	$Al_2(OH)_6$	156

Appendix 9—*continued*

Oxide to be introduced	*Means of introduction*	*Solubility*	*Formula*	*Formula weight or molecular weight*
B_2O_3 Boric oxide	Borax	Sol.	$Na_2O \cdot 2B_2O_3 \cdot 10H_2O$	381·5
	Boric acid	Sol.	$B_2O_3 \cdot 3H_2O$	123·7
	Colemanite (borocalcite)	Insol.	$2CaO \cdot 3B_2O_3 \cdot 5H_2O$	412
	Calcium borate frit	Insol.	Various—use manufacturer's data	
	Borax frits	Insol.	Various—use manufacturer's data	
SiO_2 Silica	Flint	Insol.	SiO_2	60·1
	Silica (quartz)	Insol.	SiO_2	60·1
	China clay (kaolin)	Insol.	$Al_2O_3 \cdot 2SiO_2 \cdot 2H_2O$	258·1

APPENDIX 10
Table of chemical and physical constants

ABBREVIATIONS

AM	Amorphous	I	Cubic crystals
D	Decomposes	II	Tetragonal crystals
DELIQ	Deliquescent	III	Hexagonal crystals
H	Hardness on Mohs' scale	IIIa	Rhombohedral crystals
HYG	Hygroscopic	IV	Rhombic crystals
M	Melts	V	Monoclinic crystals
–	Loses	VI	Triclinic crystals
SUB	Sublimes		

EXAMPLE ON THE USE OF THE CONVERSION FACTORS

How much Na_2O, Al_2O_3 and SiO_2 is introduced by 600 lb of albite?

$$Na_2O \text{ introduced } = 600 \times 0.188 = 70.8 \text{ lb}$$
$$Al_2O_3 \text{ introduced } = 600 \times 0.194 = 116.4 \text{ lb}$$
$$SiO_2 \text{ introduced } = 600 \times 0.688 = 412.8 \text{ lb}$$

Material	Formula	Mol. wt.	Oxides entering fusion	Mol. wt. of oxides	Conversion factor	Melting point (°C)	S.G.	Colour and physical properties
Albite	(*See* Feldspar (soda))							
Alumina	Al_2O_3	101·9	Al_2O_3	101·9	1·0	2 050	3·75	AM. III
Alumina hydrate	$Al_2(OH)_6$	156	Al_2O_3	101·9	0·653	D 300	2·42	White. AM
Anorthite	(*See* Feldspar (lime))							
Antimony oxide	Sb_2O_3	291·5	Sb_2O_3	291·5	1·0	Red heat	5·2–5·67	White. IV
Barium carbonate	$BaCO_3$	197·4	BaO	153·4	0·777	D 900 M 1 360	4·27	White. IV
Barium oxide	BaO	153·4	BaO	153·4	1·0	1 923	4·7–5·5	III, I
Bone ash	(*See* Calcium phosphate)							
Boric acid	$B_2O_3 . 3H_2O$	123·7	B_2O_3	69·6	0·563	D 185	1·47	VI
Borax	$Na_2O . 2B_2O_3 . 10H_2O$	381·5	Na_2O B_2O_3	62·0 69·6	0·162 0·365	Red heat	1·694	Colourless. V
Boric oxide	B_2O_3	69·6	B_2O_3	69·6	1·0	577	1·75–1·8	
Borocalcite	(*See* Colemanite)							
Calcium borate	$Ca(BO_2)_2$	125·7	CaO B_2O_3	56·1 69·6	0·446 0·554	1 100	–	Colourless. IV
Calcium carbonate	$CaCO_3$	100·1	CaO	56·1	0·561	D 825	2·72–2·92	White

Appendix 10—*continued*

Material	*Formula*	*Mol. wt.*	*Oxides entering fusion*	*Mol. wt. of oxides*	*Conversion factor*	*Melting point (°C)*	*S.G.*	*Colour and physical properties*
Calcium chloride	$CaCl_2$	111·0	CaO	56·1	0·508	774		Colourless. I
Calcium fluoride	CaF_2	78·1	CaO	56·1	0·719	1 360	3·15–3·18	Colourless. I
Calcium oxide	CaO	56·1	CaO	56·1	1·0	2 570	3·13–3·4	I
Calcium phosphate	$Ca_3(PO_4)_2$	310·2	CaO P_2O_5	56·1 142·0	0·541 0·459	1 670	3·2	White. AM
Cerium oxide	CeO_2	172·1	CeO_2	172·1	1·0	1 950	6·74	IV or AM
China clay	$Al_2O_3 . 2SiO_2 . 2H_2O$	258·1	Al_2O_3 SiO_2	101·9 60·1	0·395 0·466	1 770	2·5	Colour varies. V
Chromium oxide	Cr_2O_3	152·0	Cr_2O_3	152·0	1·0	*c.* 2 060	5·04	Green. III
Cobalt chloride	$CoCl_2 . 6H_2O$	238	CoO	74·9	0·315	$-6H_2O$, 100	1·84	Red. V
Cobalt oxide (black) (cobalto-cobaltic oxide)	Co_3O_4	240·8	CoO	74·9	0·933	—	6·07	Black. I
Cobaltic oxide	Co_2O_3	165·9	CoO	74·9	0·903	—	4·8–5·6	Black-grey
Cobaltous oxide	CoO	74·9	CoO	74·9	1·0	2 860	5·68	Green-brown
Colemanite	$2CaO . 3B_2O_3 . 5H_2O$ (variable)	412	CaO B_2O_3	56·1 69·6	0·272 0·508	1 100	2·5	
Copper carbonate (basic)	$CuCO_3$ $Cu(OH)_2$	221·2	CuO	79·6	0·720	—	4·0	Dark green. V
Copper oxide (IC)	CuO	79·6	CuO	79·6	1·0	1 148	6·4	Black. I
Copper oxide (OUS)	Cu_2O	143·1	CuO	79·6	1·13	1 235	6·0	Red. I
Cornish stone (mixed)	$\left.\begin{matrix}0{\cdot}417\ Na_2O\\0{\cdot}310\ K_2O\\0{\cdot}273\ CaO\end{matrix}\right\}1{\cdot}18\ Al_2O_3 . 8{\cdot}565\ SiO_2$	705·3	Na_2O K_2O CaO Al_2O_3 SiO_2	62·0 94·2 56·1 101·9 60·1	0·088 0·134 0·080 0·142 0·085	*c.* 1 200	2·5	White
Cryolite	$3NaF . AlF_3$	210	Na_2O Al_2O_3	62·0 101·9	0·443 0·243	1 020	2·95	III. H 2·5
Dolomite	$CaCO_3 . MgCO_3$	184·4	CaO MgO	56·1 40·3	0·304 0·219	D	2·9	III. H 3·5–4·5
Feldspar (potash) (orthoclase)	$K_2O . Al_2O_3 . 6SiO_2$	556·5	K_2O Al_2O_3 SiO_2	94·2 101·9 60·1	0·169 0·183 0·648	*c.* 1 200	2·55	V. H 6
Feldspar (soda) (albite)	$Na_2O . Al_2O_3 . 6SiO_2$	524·3	Na_2O Al_2O_3 SiO_2	62·0 101·9 60·1	0·118 0·194 0·688	*c.* 1 200	2·61–2·64	Grey. VI. H 6–6·5
Feldspar (lime) (anorthite)	$CaO . Al_2O_3 . 2SiO_2$	278·1	CaO Al_2O_3 SiO_2	56·1 101·9 60·1	0·202 0·366 0·432	*c.* 1 550	2·7–2·763	Grey. VI. H 6–6·5
Ferric oxide	Fe_2O_3	159·7	Fe_2O_3	159·7	1·0	1 565	5·2–5·3	Red-black. III
Ferrous oxide	FeO	71·9	Fe_2O_3	159·7	1·111	1 420	4·96–5·4	Black
Ferroso-ferric oxide	Fe_3O_4	231·6	Fe_2O_3	159·7	1·035	1 538	5·0–5·4	Red-black. I
Flint	SiO_2	60·1	SiO_2	60·1	1·0	1 600–1 750	2·2–2·6	White (fired)
Fluorspar	CaF_2	78·1	CaO	56·1	0·718	1 360	2·97–3·25	I. H 4
Galena	PbS	239·3	PbO	223·2	0·918	1 114	7·4–7·6	Black, silvery. I
Gypsum	$CaSO_4 . 2H_2O$	172·2	CaO	56·1	0·326	1 360	2·3–2·4	H 1·5–2
Haematite	(*See* Ferric oxide)							

Appendices

Appendix 10—*continued*

Material	Formula	Mol. wt.	Oxides entering fusion	Mol. wt. of oxides	Conversion factor	Melting point (°C)	S.G.	Colour and physical properties
Heavy spar	$BaSO_4$	233·4	BaO	153·4	0·657	1 580	4·476	
Ilmenite	$FeO . TiO_2$	151·8	Fe_2O_3	159·7	1·042		4·44–4·90	Black-brown. III
			TiO_2	79·9	0·521			
Kaolin	(*See* China clay)							
Lead bisilicate	$PbO . 2SiO_2$	343·3	PbO	223·2	0·650	*c.* 815	4·5	Yellow-white
			SiO_2	60·1	0·350			
Lead monosilicate	$PbO . SiO_2$	283·3	PbO	223·2	0·788	*c.* 700		Yellow
			SiO_2	60·1	0·212			
Lead sesquisilicate	$PbO . 1·5 SiO_2$	313·4	PbO	223·2	0·713	*c.* 760		Yellow
			SiO_2	60·1	0·192			
Lead carbonate	$PbCO_3$	267·2	PbO	223·2	0·835	D	6·43	White. IV
Lead carbonate (white lead)	$2PbCO_3 . Pb(OH)_2$	775·7	PbO	223·2	0·863	D	6·46	White. AM
Lead oxide	PbO	223·2	PbO	223·2	1·0	880	8·74–9·5	Yellow. AM
Lead oxide (red lead)	Pb_3O_4	685·6	PbO	223·2	0·977	D 500	9·1	Red. AM
Lepidolite	0·503 Li_2O ⎫ 0·369 K_2O ⎬1·04 Al_2O_3 . 3·76 SiO_2 0·128 Na_2O ⎭	387·6	Li_2O	29·9	0·077	1 170	2·8–2·9	Grey-white. V
			K_2O	94·2	0·244			
			Na_2O	62·0	0·160			
			Al_2O_3	101·9	0·264			
			SiO_2	60·1	0·155			
Litharge	(*See* Lead oxide, PbO)							
Lime	(*See* Calcium oxide)							
Lithium carbonate	Li_2CO_3	73·9	Li_2O	29·9	0·405	618	2·11	White
Lithium oxide	Li_2O	29·9	Li_2O	29·9	1·0	Sub. 1 000	2·1	White
Magnesium carbonate	$MgCO_3$	84·3	MgO	40·3	0·478	D 350	3·04	White. III & IV
Magnesite	(*See* Magnesium carbonate)							
Magnesium oxide	MgO	40·3	MgO	40·3	1·0	2 800	3·22–3·654	A M.I
Magnetite	(*See* Ferroso-ferric oxide)							
Manganese carbonate	$MnCO_3$	114·9	MnO	70·9	0·615	D	3·6	Rose pink. IIIa
Manganous oxide	MnO	70·9	MnO	70·9	1·0	1 650	5·1	Green. I
Manganese dioxide	MnO_2	86·9	MnO	70·9	0·816	$-\frac{1}{2}O_2$, 1 080	4·7–5	Black. IV
Minium	(*See* Lead oxide, Pb_3O_4)							
Nepheline syenite	0·764 Na_2O ⎫ ⎬1·11 Al_2O_3 . 4·88 SiO_2 0·236 K_2O ⎭	474·5	Na_2O	62·0	0·131	1 140–1 200	2·55–2·65	White. III
			K_2O	94·2	0·199			
			Al_2O_3	101·9	0·215			
			SiO_2	60·1	0·127			
Nickel oxide (OUS)	NiO	74·7	NiO	74·7	1·0	—	6·6–6·8	Greenish black. I
Nickel oxide (IC)	Ni_2O_3	165·4	NiO	74·7	0·903	$-O_2$, 600	4·84	Black
Paris white	(*See* Calcium carbonate)							
Pearl ash	(*See* Potassium carbonate)							
Petalite	$Li_2O . Al_2O_3 . 8SiO_2$	612	Li_2O	29·9	0·049		2·39–2·46	White. V
			Al_2O_3	101·9	0·166	1 350		
			SiO_2	60·1	0·098			
Potassium carbonate	K_2CO_3	138·2	K_2O	94·2	0·682	896	2·3	DELIQ. V

Appendix 10—*continued*

Material	Formula	Mol. wt.	Oxides entering fusion	Mol. wt. of oxides	Conversion factor	Melting point (°C)	S.G.	Colour and physical properties
Potassium chromate	K_2CrO_4	194·2	K_2O Cr_2O_3	94·2 152·0	0·485 0·391	971	2·7	Yellow. IV
Potassium nitrate	KNO_3	101·1	K_2O	94·2	0·466	334, D 400	2·1	IV, IIIa
Potassium oxide	K_2O	94·2	K_2O	94·2	1·0	Red heat	2·32	Grey. Unstable
Rutile	(*See* Titanium dioxide)							
Silica (cristobalite)	SiO_2	60·1	SiO_2	60·1	1·0	1 713	2·32	I, II
Silica (quartz)	SiO_2	60·1	SiO_2	60·1	1·0	1 713	2·651	IIIa
Silica (tridymite)	SiO_2	60·1	SiO_2	60·1	1·0	1 670	2·26	IV
Sodium carbonate	$Na_2CO_3 . 10H_2O$	286·2	Na_2O	62·0	0·217	− 5H$_2$O, 34	1·45	V
Sodium carbonate	Na_2CO_3	106	Na_2O	62·0	0·585	852	2·5	White powder
Sodium chloride	NaCl	58·5	Na_2O	62·0	0·530	800	2·17	I
Sodium oxide	Na_2O	62·0	Na_2O	62·0	1·0	Red heat	2·27	Grey. DELIQ. Unstable
Sodium silicate	Na_2SiO_3	122·1	Na_2O SiO_2	62·0 60·1	0·508 0·492	1 088	2·4	V
Spodumene	$Li_2O . Al_2O_3 . 4SiO_2$	372·2	LiO_2 Al_2O_3 SiO_2	29·9 101·9 60·1	0·080 0·274 0·046	1 150		White. V
Stannic oxide	SnO_2	150·7	SnO_2	150·7	1·0	1 127	6·6-6·9	White. II
Stannous oxide	SnO	134·7	SnO_2	150·7	1·119	D 700-950	6·446	Black. II, I
Steatite	(*See* Talc)							
Strontium carbonate	$SrCO_3$	147·6	SrO	103·6	0·701	D 1 075	3·62	White. IV
Strontium oxide	SrO	103·6	SrO	103·6	1·0	2 430	4·7	White. I
Talc	$3MgO . 4SiO_2 . H_2O$	379·2	MgO SiO_2	40·3 60·1	0·106 0·159		2·6-2·8	White. V
Tin oxide	(*See* Stannic and Stannous oxides)							
Titanium oxide (anatase)	TiO_2	79·9	TiO_2	79·9	1·0	1 560	3·84	Brown. II
Titanium oxide (rutile)	TiO_2	79·9	TiO_2	79·9	1·0	1 640	4·26	Brown. II
Titanium oxide (precipitated)	TiO_2	79·9	TiO_2	79·9	1·0	1 600	4·0	White
Uranium oxide (OUS, IC)	U_3O_8	842·2	U_3O_8	842·2	1·0	—	7·2	Olive green
Vanadium Pentoxide	V_2O_5	181·9	V_2O_5	181·9	1·0	690	3·357	Yellow-red. IV
Witherite	(*See* Barium carbonate)							
Whiting	(*See* Calcium carbonate)							
Zinc carbonate	$ZnCO_3$	125·4	ZnO	81·4	0·649	− CO$_2$, 300	4·42-4·45	VI
Zinc oxide	ZnO	81·4	ZnO	81·4	1·0	> 1 800	5·6	White. AM
Zirconium oxide	ZrO_2	123·2	ZrO_2	123·2	1·0	2 700	5·49	V
Zirconium silicate (zircon)	$ZrSiO_4$	183·3	ZrO_2 SiO_2	123·2 60·1	0·672 0·328	2 550	4·56	Red-brown. II

Suppliers of craft ceramic materials

UK

Potclays Ltd.,
Brickkiln Lane, Etruria,
Stoke-on-Trent 7BP ST4
Tel 01782 219816

Potterycrafts Ltd.,
Campbell Road,
Stoke-on-Trent ST4 4ET
Tel 01782 645000

Bath Potters,
2 Dorset Close, Twerton, Bath,
Avon BA2 3RF
Tel 01225 337046

Cromartie Kilns Ltd.,
Park Hall Road, Longton,
Stoke on Trent ST3 5AY
Tel 01782 313947

Scarva Pty,
Unit 20, Scarva Road Industrial Estate,
Bambridge, Co. Down BT32 2QD
Tel 018206 69699

Macgregor & Moyer Ltd.,
27 Queensferry Street, Glasgow G5 0XJ
Tel 0141 429 4294

Ceramatech Ltd.,
Units 16 & 17, Frontier Works, 33 Queen
Street, London N17 8JA
Tel 0181 885 4492

Brick House Ceramic Supplies Ltd.,
The Barns, Sheepcote Farm
Sheepcote Lane, Silver End, Witham
Essex CM8 3PJ
Tel 01376 585665

Holmcroft Craft Supplies,
186 The Street, Capel, Surrey RH5 5EN
Tel 01306 711126

Medcol Ltd.,
Unit 17, Wood Browning Industrial Estate,
Bodmin, Cornwall
Tel 01208 72260

Clayman,
Morells Barn, Park Lane, Lagness,
Chichester, W. Sussex PO20 6LR
Tel 01243 265845

Jackie Topping
35 The Middlings, Sevenoaks
Kent TN13 2NW
Tel 01732 457011

Europe

Cerama A/S,
Hammerholmen 44 148, Avedore Holme,
DK-2650, Hvidovre, Denmark
Tel 004536 772222

Ceradel,
600 Route de Grasse, Quartier des Combes,
Mas Patfredal 06220 Vallauris, France

Kahlen Keramik,
Neuhausstr. 2-10, 5100 Aachen-Forst,
Germany
Tel 0049 241 9209211

Colpaert,
Groendreef 51, B-900, Gent/Gand, Belgium
Tel 00 32 9 2262826

Scan-Form,
Andebuvei-Arnadal,N-3170 Sem V/Tonsberg,
Norway
Tel 0047 33 33 9377

North America

American Art Clay Co. Inc,
4717 W. 16th Street, Indianapolis,
Indiana 46222, USA

Laguna Clay Company,
14400 Lomitas Avenue, City of Industry,
California CA 91746, USA
Tel 800 452 4862

Aardvark Clay & Supplies Inc.,
1400 E. Pomona Street, Santa Ana,
California CA 92705, USA

Hammill & Gillespie Inc.,
154 Livingston Avenue, P.O. Box 104,
Livingston NJ
07039-0104, USA

Kickwheel Pottery Supply Inc.,
6477 Peachtree Ind. Blvd.,
Atlanta, GA 30360, USA

Mile Hi Ceramics Inc.,
77 Lipan Street, Denver, CO 80223, USA

Ohio Ceramic Supply Inc.,
P.O. Box 630, Kent. OH 44240, USA

Orton Ceramic Foundation,
P.O Box 2760, Westerville OH 43086-2760,
USA

North Star Equipment Inc.,
P.O. Box 189, Cheney, WA 99004, USA

Olympic Kilns,
6301 Button Gwinnett Drive, Atlanta,
GA 30340, USA

Standard Ceramic Supply,
P.O. Box 4435, Pittsburgh, PA 15205-0435,
USA

Bennetts Pottery Supply,
431 Enterprise Street, Ocoee, Florida, 34761,
USA

Greenbarn Potters Supply Ltd.,
9548-192 Street, Surrey, British Columbia,
Canada V4N 3R9

Ceramics Canada,
7056-D Farrell Road, S.E., Calgary,
Alberta, Canada
Tel 403 255 1575

Plainsman Clay Ltd.,
P.O.Box 1266, Medicine Hat,
Alberta T1A 7M9, Canada

Spectrum Glazes,
40 Hanlan Road, Unit 33, Woodbridge,
Ontario L4L 3P6, Canada

Tucker's Pottery Supplies Inc.,
15 West Pearce Street, Unit 7,
Richmond Hill, Ontario L4B 1H6, Canada
Tel 800 304 6185

The Pottery Warehouse,
2071 S.Wellington Road, Nanaimo, British
Columbia, Canada V9R 5X9
Tel 250 716 9966

Pottery Supply House,
Box 192, Oakville, Ontario, Canada
Tel 905 827 1129

For a comprehensive list of suppliers in North
America, refer to *Potters Guide*, published by The
American Ceramic Society, PO Box 6136,
Westerville OH 43086-613, USA

Rest of the world

CCG Industries Ltd.,
33 Crowhurst Street, Newmarket, Auckland,
New Zealand

Gillian Bickell Potteries,
24 Staal Street, Kya Sands, Randburg,
Republic of South Africa

Walker Ceramics (Aust) P/L,
5 Lusher Road, Croyden,
Victoria, Australia
Tel 423 397 2914

Index